MILLER'S

collectables

MILLER'S

collectables

MADELEINE MARSH *GENERAL EDITOR*

2002/3
VOLUME XIV

MILLER'S COLLECTABLES PRICE GUIDE 2002/3

Created and designed by
Miller's
The Cellars, High Street
Tenterden, Kent, TN30 6BN
Tel: 01580 766411
Fax: 01580 766100

General Editor: Madeleine Marsh
Managing Editor: Valerie Lewis
Production Co-ordinator: Kari Reeves
Editorial Co-ordinator: Deborah Wanstall
Editorial Assistants: Kim Cook, Maureen Horner
Production Assistants: Gillian Charles, Clare Gillingham, Ethne Tragett
Advertising Executive: Jill Jackson
Advertising Co-ordinator & Administrator: Melinda Williams
Advertising Assistant: Jo Hill
Designer: Philip Hannath
Advertisement Designer: Simon Cook
Indexer: Hilary Bird
Jacket Design: Victoria Bevan
Production: Angela Couchman
Additional Photographers: Dennis O'Reilly, Robin Saker
North American Consultants: Marilynn and Sheila Brass

First published in Great Britain in 2002
by Miller's, a division of Mitchell Beazley,
imprint of Octopus Publishing Group Ltd,
2–4 Heron Quays, London E14 4JP

© 2002 Octopus Publishing Group Ltd

A CIP catalogue record for this book is
available from the British Library

ISBN 1-84000-543-2

Illustrations by CK Digital, Whitstable, Kent, England
Printed and bound by Rotolito Lombarda, Italy

Front cover illustrations:
Lucie Attwell's Story Book, published by Dean, c1930, 10 x 9in (25.5 x 23cm). **£50–55/$70–80 ⊞ MEM**
A Cornish Ware flour shaker, early mark, 5½in (14cm) high. **£45–50/$65–75 ⊞ TAC**
An orange straw cloche hat, 1920s, 8in (20.5cm) diam. **£50–55/$70–80 ⅄ CCO**

How To Use This Book

I t is our aim to make this guide easy to use. In order to find a particular item, turn to the contents list on page 7 to find the main heading, for example, Ceramics. Having located your area of interest, you will see that larger sections have been sub-divided by subject or maker. If you are looking for a particular factory, maker, or object, consult the index, which starts on page 454.

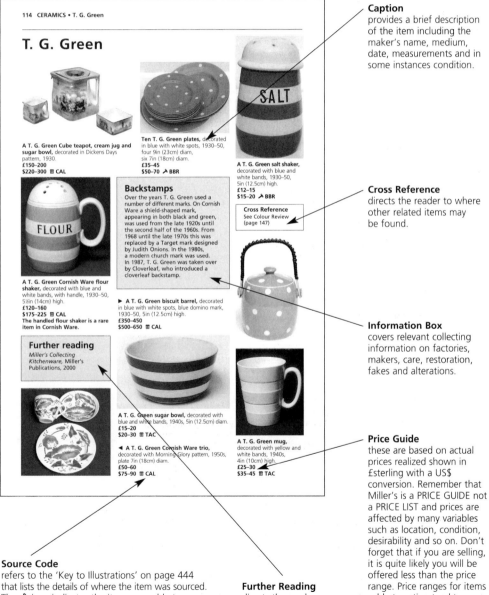

114 CERAMICS • T. G. Green

T. G. Green

A T. G. Green Cube teapot, cream jug and sugar bowl, decorated in Dickens Days pattern, 1930.
£150–200
$220–300 ⊞ CAL

Ten T. G. Green plates, decorated in blue with white spots, 1930–50, four 9in (23cm) diam, six 7in (18cm) diam.
£35–45
$50–70 ➚ BBR

A T. G. Green salt shaker, decorated with blue and white bands, 1930–50, 5in (12.5cm) high.
£12–15
$15–20 ➚ BBR

Cross Reference
See Colour Review
(page 147)

A T. G. Green Cornish Ware flour shaker, decorated with blue and white bands, with handle, 1930–50, 5½in (14cm) high.
£120–160
$175–225 ⊞ CAL
The handled flour shaker is a rare item in Cornish Ware.

Backstamps
Over the years T. G. Green used a number of different marks. On Cornish Ware a shield-shaped mark, appearing in both black and green, was used from the late 1920s until the second half of the 1960s. From 1968 until the late 1970s this was replaced by a Target mark designed by Judith Onions. In the 1980s, a modern church mark was used. In 1987, T. G. Green was taken over by Cloverleaf, who introduced a cloverleaf backstamp.

▶ A T. G. Green biscuit barrel, decorated in blue with white spots, blue domino mark, 1930–50, 5in (12.5cm) high.
£350–450
$500–650 ⊞ CAL

Further reading
Miller's Collecting Kitchenware, Miller's Publications, 2000

A T. G. Green sugar bowl, decorated with blue and white bands, 1940s, 5in (12.5cm) diam.
£15–20
$20–30 ⊞ TAC

◀ A T. G. Green Cornish Ware trio, decorated with Morning Glory pattern, 1950s, plate 7in (18cm) diam.
£50–60
$75–90 ⊞ CAL

A T. G. Green mug, decorated with yellow and white bands, 1940s, 4in (10cm) high.
£25–30
$35–45 ⊞ TAC

Caption
provides a brief description of the item including the maker's name, medium, date, measurements and in some instances condition.

Cross Reference
directs the reader to where other related items may be found.

Information Box
covers relevant collecting information on factories, makers, care, restoration, fakes and alterations.

Price Guide
these are based on actual prices realized shown in £sterling with a US$ conversion. Remember that Miller's is a PRICE GUIDE not a PRICE LIST and prices are affected by many variables such as location, condition, desirability and so on. Don't forget that if you are selling, it is quite likely you will be offered less than the price range. Price ranges for items sold at auction tend to include the buyer's premium and VAT if applicable.

Source Code
refers to the 'Key to Illustrations' on page 444 that lists the details of where the item was sourced. The ➚ icon indicates the item was sold at auction. The ⊞ icon indicates the item originated from a dealer.

Further Reading
directs the reader towards additional sources of information.

Acknowledgments

We would like to acknowledge the great assistance given by our consultants who are listed below. We would also like to extend our thanks to all the auction houses, their press offices, dealers and collectors who have assisted us in the production of this book.

ANTIQUE AMUSEMENT CO
Mill Lane, Swaffham
Bulbeck, Cambridge CB5 0NF
(Amusement & Slot Machines)

BEVERLEY/BETH
30 Church Street
Alfie's Antique Market
Marylebone
London NW8 8EP
(Ceramics)

ALAN BLAKEMAN
BBR Elsecar Heritage Centre
Wath Road, Elsecar, Barnsley
Yorks S74 8AF
(Advertising, Packaging, Bottles, Breweriana)

MARILYNN & SHEILA BRASS
PO Box 380503, Cambridge
USA MA 02238-0503
(Cookery)

JIM BULLOCK
Romsey Medal Centre
5 Bell Street, Romsey
Hants SO51 8GY
(Military Medals)

DR D. DOWSON
Old Tackle Box
PO Box 55, Cranbrook
Kent TN17 3ZU
(Fishing Tackle)

ANDREW HILTON
Special Auction Services
The Coach House, Midgham Park
Reading, Berks RG7 5UG
(Commemorative Ware)

DAVID HUXTABLE
S03/05 Alfies Antique Market
13–25 Church Street
London NW8 8DT
(Advertising Tins)

KEN LAWSON
Specialized Postcard Auctions
25 Gloucester Street
Cirencester GL7 2DJ
(Postcards)

PAUL MULVEY
Cloud Cuckooland
12 Fore Street
Mevagissey
Cornwall PL26 6UQ
(Photographs)

MARK OLIVER
Bonhams
101 New Bond Street
London W1Y 9LG
(Decorative Arts)

GAVIN PAYNE
The Old Granary
Battlebridge Antique Centre
Nr Wickford, Essex SS11 7RF
(Telephones)

MALCOLM PHILLIPS
Comic Book Postal Auctions
40–42 Osnaburgh Street
London NW1 3ND
(Comics)

ALVIN ROSS
Oxfordshire
(Puppets)

MAUREEN SILVERMAN
Planet Bazaar
149 Drummond Street
London NW1 2PB
(Sixties & Seventies)

DOMINIC WINTER
The Old School
Maxwell Street, Swindon
Wiltshire SN1 5DR
(Books)

Contents

How To Use This Book.....................5
Acknowledgments 6
Introduction 8

Advertising & Packaging 9
Aeronautica.................................17
Amusement & Slot Machines 20
Antiquities..................................23
Architectural Salvage...................25
Art Deco 28
Art Nouveau................................29
Arts & Crafts 30
Mabel Lucie Attwell.....................31
Autographs..................................34
Automobilia 38
Bathrooms...................................40
Bicycles.......................................43
Black History & Memorabilia 45
Books 49
Bottles...58
Boxes...60
Breweriana 62
Colour Review 65–80
Butlin's..81
Buttons 82
Cameras.......................................84
Ceramics......................................87
Colour Review 145–152
Christmas 153
Cigarette & Trade Cards 155
Comics & Annuals 159
Commemorative Ware 161
Corkscrews.................................167
Cosmetics & Hairdressing 170
Crime...174
Doctor Who...............................176
Dolls 178
Colour Review 185–200
Ephemera 201
Erotica.......................................202
Fans 203
Fifties 204
Film & TV 207
Games 209
Garden & Farm Collectables.......212
Glass..216
Guinness 228
Handbags & Luggage 230
Horse Brasses.............................232
Colour Review 233–248
Hot Water Bottles 249
Jewellery....................................251

Kitchenware 261
Lighting 272
Medals 276
Militaria & Emergency Services...280
Money Boxes 289
Newspapers & Magazines 290
Osbornes....................................292
Owls 293
Paper Money 295
Photography...............................297
Plastic 299
Politics 301
Postcards....................................307
Posters 309
Puppets......................................312
Colour Review 313–320
Radios, Gramophones & Tape Recorders ...321
Railwayana 326
Rock & Pop 329
Scent Bottles..............................338
Science & Technology.................339
Scripophily 343
Sewing 345
Shipping.....................................347
Silver & Metalware 350
Sixties & Seventies......................354
Smoking & Snuff Taking..............356
Sport 358
Stanhopes 368
Sunglasses & Lorgnettes 369
Teddy Bears & Soft Toys.............370
Telephones 372
Textiles & Costume 374
Tiles...384
Colour Review 385–400
Tools..401
Toys 403
Treen & Wood............................420
Valentines..................................421
Walking Sticks............................422
Wallpaper...................................423
Watches & Clocks.......................424
World War II...............................426
Writing.......................................427
Record Breakers.........................429

Baca Awards...............................430
Directory of Specialists 432
Directory of Collectors' Clubs......438
Directory of Markets & Centres...441
Key to Illustrations......................444
Index to Advertisers....................453
Index 454

Introduction

As we at Miller's know only too well, anything and everything can be collectable. New sections in this year's guide range from hot water bottles, to Tupperware, to wallpaper. As these examples show, an object doesn't have to be expensive in the first place to become collectable in the future. Many of the items in this book were designed to be discarded and some, for example pot lids and bottles, have literally been rescued from rubbish tips. But as the saying goes – where there's muck, there's brass – occasionally lots of it, as the lucky bottle digger who excavated a Victorian poison flask in the shape of a coffin discovered (see Record Breakers pp429). What makes such items desirable is their rarity. Disposable or ephemeral objects tend by their very nature to get thrown away, hence the value of those that escape the trashcan. Objects in this year's guide include a *Daily Mail* No. 1 from 1896, a pair of torn tickets for a Beatle's concert, football programmes, and the first ever Christmas card which made a record price of £22,350 ($32,400) when at auction.

As ever, this guide is full of surprises and where else would you find a pair of collectable wellies (see pp390). Interest in antique fashion has expanded considerably over the past couple of years, to the extent that some major stores now have vintage departments. Clothing illustrated here ranges from Victorian dresses to a pair of 1970s Nylon Y-fronts (see pp399). In addition to Costume and Textiles, there are also individual sections on Handbags, Cosmetic Accessories and Jewellery.

For those with more traditionally masculine tastes, we feature Automobilia, Aeronautica and Railwayana. For the first time, we devote a special section to crime and the macabre hobby of collecting memorabilia connected with famous criminals. Countering this, we also have collectables associated with the police, and in the wake of the events of 11 September 2001, we look at the history of firefighters, with a selection of objects commemorating their courage over the decades. Other new subjects this year include Black History and Memorabilia, and Politics, which includes a wide range of items both serious and satirical.

There are all sorts of reasons why objects become collectable. Nostalgia is a powerful spur. Many people will no doubt remember playing with the Barbies in our doll section, or the Dinky, Corgi and Matchbox cars illustrated in toys. Condition is all important when it comes to such objects, and price ranges reflect the difficulty of finding examples that have escaped the cheerfully destructive hands of children. If you grew up hiding behind the sofa to watch the Daleks on television, you will enjoy our section on *Doctor Who*, and how much people are prepared to spend to recapture their childhood TV memories is demonstrated by the thousands of pounds paid at auction for original props and puppets from series such as *Doctor Who* and *Thunderbirds*.

Our rock and pop section will take you back to your teenage years, whether you were a punk or a Beatles fan. Whilst in Radios and Gramophones you might even find the original machines on which you listened to your favourite music.

The objects in *Miller's Collectables Price Guide* reflect every aspect of human life. In our bathroom section we lift the lid on Victorian lavatories and the history of sanitation. In ceramics we look at Cornish Ware and how humble kitchen storage jars can be worth hundreds of pounds. We go out into the garden to find some valuable garden gnomes and we also look at the collectable owl. We celebrate the sweet childhood images of Mabel Lucie Attwell, and take a peek at the naughty world of Erotica. The earliest items shown in this book date from before Christ, whilst our Collectables of the Future page suggests which of today's purchases might well become the antiques of tomorrow.

The great joy of compiling, and hopefully reading this book is the infinite variety of objects there are to collect, and the fascinating stories behind them. If you have an interesting collection yourself or there are further subjects you would like to see covered by this guide, please let us know. Also if you would like to become a member of the Miller's Club do contact us. Club members are invited to nominate candidates for the BACAS – the British Antiques and Collectables Awards – which were started by Miller's to recognize excellence in the industry. We value your input and we look forward to receiving your suggestions. Thank you for your support and as ever happy hunting!

Advertising & Packaging

A Conrad W. Schmidt boxwood paper knife,
late 19thC, 12in (30.5cm) long.
£55–65
$80–95 ⊞ MLu

◀ **A Hudson's Soap dish,** enamelled, chipped, 1900–20, 14¼in (36cm) wide.
£400–450
$600–650 ⊁ BBR

A Lever's Toilet Soaps revolving display case, glass to four sides, the interior fitted with three graduated glass shelves, 1890–1900, 23¾in (60.5cm) high.
£1,300–1,500
$2,000–2,200 ⊁ BBR

A Lancashire Insurance Company pottery capital matchstriker, 1910, 3in (7.5cm) high.
£25–30
$35–45 ⊞ HUX

An Iceberg Cigarettes packet, in red and brown, 1910, 3½in (9cm) high.
£90–100
$130–150 ⊞ HUX

A Royle's Mantle, Costume and Family Mourning Warehouse wooden coat hanger, 1910–20, 16in (40.5cm) long.
£18–20
$20–30 ⊞ MRW

A Cherry Blossom shoe-shine stand, with red and black lettering and cherries, 1920–30, 12in (30.5cm) high.
£550–600
$800–900 ⊁ BBR

> Items in the Advertising & Packaging section have been arranged in date order within each sub-section.

An Ingram's Omega Whirling Spray, in brown and black, 1920, 11in (28cm) long, in original box.
£18–20
$20–30 ⊞ HUX

▶ **A Kiwi Boot Polish metal turntable display stand,** with red kiwi on top, and nine tins of Kiwi Boot Polish, 1920–30, 14½in (37cm) high.
£110–130
$160–190 ⊁ BBR

An Ovaltine pottery jug and mug, transfer-printed in brown, red and yellow, 1920, jug 8in (20.5cm) high.
£80–100
$115–145 ⊞ SMI

A Five Cents copper
display soda glass,
c1920, 5½in (14cm) high.
£150–170
$200–250 ⊞ MSB

A Fyffes bananas yellow cardboard
display, 1920s, 10in (25.5cm) high.
£50–55
$75–80 ⊞ HUX

A Cooperative Wholesale Society pistol-
shaped glass sweet container, with original
contents, c1920, 6in (15cm) long.
£35–60
$50–100 ⊞ MURR

▶ A Bovril pine box,
1920–30, 10in (25.5cm) wide.
£15–20
$20–30 ⊞ AL

A Perrier Water paper fold-up fan,
1920–30, 8¾in (22cm) long.
£12–14
$15–18 ⊞ HUX

An Aero chocolate bar shop
dummy, c1930, 4½in (11.5cm) long.
£12–15
$15–20 ⊞ HUX

A cardboard egg box for 24 eggs,
c1930, 12in (30.5cm) long.
£22–26
$30–35 ⊞ AL

A Chocolat Lanvin stand-up lithographed tin display, in red and
gold, c1930, 6½in (16.5cm) long.
£45–55
$60–80 ⊞ MSB

A papier-mâché sweet container,
modelled as a roasted turkey,
German, c1930, 7in (18cm) long.
£75–85
$110–125 ↗ MSB

A Mr Therm brass cap badge, designed by
Eric Fraser for Gas Light & Coke Co, 1930s,
2in (5cm) long.
£25–30
$35–45 ⊞ REN

A Strawberry tak-home
Sundae paper cone,
1935, 4½in (11.5cm) high.
£15–20
$20–30 ⊞ MSB

◀ A pair of shop display joints of ham,
1930s, 18in (45.5cm) long.
£50–60
$75–100 each ⊞ SMI

Cross Reference
See Colour Review
(page 65–66)

A Puritan Soles coloured rubberoid bust of a Puritan, with red and white raised lettering, 1930s–40s, 11in (28cm) high.
£170–200
$250–300 ⏵ BBR

A Zippo lighter tape measure, 1960s, 3in (7.5cm) long.
£15–20
$20–30 ⊞ COB

A Crawford's Biscuits metal ice-cream wafer maker, 1940s, 5in (12.5cm) high.
£35–40
$50–60 ⊞ HUX

An EKCO glass advertising tile, for use as a shop window decoration, 1955, 8in (20.5cm) square.
£25–30
$35–45 ⊞ GM

A Wrigley's Spearmint Chewing Gum dummy pack, 1960s, 3in (7.5cm) square.
£8–10
$10–15 ⊞ HUX

◀ A Pillsbury Dough boy rubber doll, American, 1971, 7in (18cm) high.
£12–15
$15–20 ⊞ MRW

◀ A Rapitan cardboard sun reflector, with silver surface, Canadian, 1960s, 26in (66cm) wide.
£10–12
$15–18 ⊞ RTT

▶ A Coca-Cola seat, in the shape of a Coke bottle top, 1950s, 14in (35.5cm) diam.
£30–35
$45–50 ⏵ SAF

A Durex illuminated plastic sign, c1955, 12in (30.5cm) long.
£30–35
$45–50 ⊞ HUX
The word condom has been in use since the early 18th century and is said to be named after Colonel Condom, a British Guards Officer who wanted to protect his troops from venereal disease. Condoms were made of everything from cloth to animal intestines until the introduction of vulcanized rubber in the mid-19th century. In 1932, the London Rubber Company launched Durex, the name derived from the sheath's most important features: Durability, Reliability and Excellence.

Advertisement & Showcards

A Marston, Thompson & Evershed advertisement, depicting a multi-coloured picture of the brewery buildings, 1890–1900, 35 x 45in (89 x 114.5cm), framed.
£600–700
$870–1,000 ↗ BBR

A Dicker's Dorset Sausages pressed cardboard advertising sign, early 20thC, 10½in (26.5cm) wide.
£20–24
$30–35 ⊞ RUSS

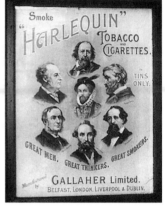

A Gallaher Limited tobacco and cigarette advertisement, depicting multi-coloured portraits of famous people, 1910–20, 28 x 22½in (71 x 57cm), framed.
£200–220
$300–320 ↗ BBR

An Edison Bell Needles showcard, holding various gramophone needle tins, 1920s, 12in (30.5cm) high.
£100–125
$140–180 ⊞ MURR

A Harris Bacon stand-up cardboard cut-out figure of a seated pig, in pink and brown, some surface marks, 1930s–40s, 29in (73.5cm) high.
£80–90
$115–130 ↗ BBR

A Whiteway's Cydrax cardboard display stand, 1930s, 12in (30.5cm) high.
£35–50
$50–75 ⊞ MURR

An Ovaltine cardboard cut-out advertising display, 1940s, 19in (48.5cm) high.
£45–55
$65–80 ↗ DW

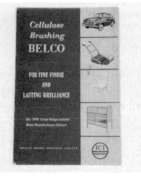

An ICI shop cardboard display advertisement, yellow and white lettering on a red ground, c1956, 12in (30.5cm) high.
£12–15
$18–20 ⊞ MRW

A Carnation Milk showcard, c1960, 12in (30.5cm) high.
£15–20
$20–30 ⊞ HOP

Enamel Signs

Enamel signs were a common form of street decoration from the 1880s (when manufacturing techniques were developed) until the 1950s, when they were generally replaced by paper posters and tin signs. Popular locations included not just shops, but trams, omnibuses and above all train stations.

The expansion of the railways not only allowed signs to be distributed around the country but also provided advertisers with a captive audience. W H Lever negotiated a special contract with the train companies and personally chose the sites for Lever products such as Sunlight Soap, particularly favouring the walls around the station booking office. Soap manufacturers were among the first to use enamel signs and other makers soon followed suit. By their very nature enamel signs were durable and, unlike today, advertising campaigns were long-running. Famous images such as Fry's Five Boys – 'Desperation – Pacification – Expectation – Acclamation – Realization, It's Fry's' – permeated the national consciousness, making this a desirable sign today.

Values of enamel signs depend on subject, age, and size. Smaller, domestically convenient sizes are popular, as are unusually shaped examples that depart from the traditional rectangle. Condition is an important factor although, since signs were hung outside for decades and often carelessly removed, in most instances some wear and tear is unavoidable.

A J. A. Nadeau cast-iron and tin watchmaker's trade sign, with traces of gilt, the tin dial painted front and reverse with Roman numerals in black on a cream ground, some wear, American, 19thC, 49¾in (126.5cm) high.
£950–1,150
$1,400–1,600 ⚡ SK(B)

A Brasso Metal Polish enamel advertising sign, black and white lettering on a green ground, chipped, 1900–20, 24in (61cm) high.
£230–250
$330–360 ⚡ BBR

▶ A Hudson's Soap enamel advertising sign, black and white lettering on a green ground with red borders, outer border retouched, 1900–20, 18in (45.5cm) wide.
£100–110
$145–160 ⚡ BBR

An R. White's Mineral Waters enamel advertising sign, blue and white, c1910, 24in (61cm) high.
£90–100
$130–150 ⊞ HUX

A We Deliver to All Parts Daily tin-on-board advertising sign, 1920s, 13in (33cm) wide.
£75–85
$110–125 ⊞ HOP

A Rowntree's Chocolates enamel advertising sign, white lettering on a dark blue ground, with a black and white picture of Rowntrees No. 3 Factory York, coloured coat-of-arms to either side, minor chips and rust, 1910–20, 30in (76cm) wide.
£800–850
$1,200–1,300 ✗ BBR

A Fry's Chocolate enamel advertising sign, depicting five boys, white lettering on a blue ground, surface damage, chips and rust spots to outer edge, 1920–30, 18in (45.5cm) wide.
£60–70
$90–100 ✗ BBR

A Fry's enamel advertising sign, depicting a schoolboy looking into a sweetshop window, minor chips and rust spots, 1910–20, 14in (35.5cm) high.
£850–900
$1,200–1,300 ✗ BBR

An Arthur Davy's Yorkshire Polony enamel advertising sign, white and yellow lettering on a blue ground, with red polony links, some surface damage and chips to edge, 1920–30, 24in (61cm) wide.
£180–200
$250–300 ✗ BBR

A Milkmaid Sweetened Condensed Milk enamel advertising sign, black lettering on a red ground, 1930s, 12in (30.5cm) square.
£75–100
$100–150 ⊞ MURR

Miller's is a price GUIDE not a price LIST

◄ **An Orange Maid enamel advertising sign,** double-sided to stand outside a shop, yellow and white lettering on a blue and red ground, 1940–50, in a wooden frame.
£25–30
$35–45 ✗ BBR

An Oxo Cube enamel double-sided advertising sign, the reverse inscribed 'Oxo Makes All Meat Dishes', red and cream on a blue ground, slight rusting, 1930–40, 13½in (34.5cm) square.
£60–70
$90–100 ✗ BBR

► **A Ruston Power tin advertising sign,** red lettering on a white border with yellow, green and black centre, 1950s, 30in (76cm) diam.
£50–70
$75–100 ⊞ JUN

A Swan Vestas enamel advertising sign, white lettering on a black ground, c1950, 15in (38cm) high.
£40–50
$60–80 ⊞ CRN

Tins

A Huntley & Palmer's biscuit tin, decorated with golfing and polo scenes in green, blue and yellow, c1890, 7in (18cm) diam.
£270–300
$400–450 ⊞ HUX

A Colman's Mustard tin, decorated with a scene from Queen Victoria's Diamond Jubilee, 1897, 8in (20.5cm) wide.
£150–170
$220–250 ⊞ TMa

▶ **A Huntley & Palmer's biscuit tin,** modelled as a set of books, brown, cream, red and green, c1901, 3½in (9cm) wide.
£100–120
$145–175 ↗ DN

A Fry's 'Tourist' Chocolate tin, decorated with a mountain scene, c1910, 4¾in (12cm) wide.
£200–225
$300–330 ⊞ HUX

A Smith's Schooner Navy Cut tobacco tin, black lettering on a gold ground, 1880–90, 6in (15cm) wide.
£150–200
$200–300 ⊞ MURR

A B. Muratti, Sons & Co Kaiser Wilhelm Gold Tipped Cigarettes tin, decorated with Kaiser Wilhelm in black, gold, red and yellow, 1905, 4¼in (11cm) wide.
£225–250
$320–360 ⊞ HUX

A McVitie & Price biscuit tin, decorated with the Pied Piper of Hamelin in green, blue, yellow and red, 1890s, 10in (25.5cm) wide.
£150–200
$220–300 ⊞ MURR

A Rowntree's sweet tin, modelled as a rugby ball, c1900, 2in (5cm) long.
£90–100
$130–150 ⊞ MRW

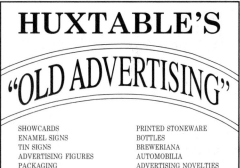

A Clarnico tin, modelled as a golf club, 1910–20, 5¾in (14.5cm) long.
£170–190
$250–275 ↗ BBR

A Pascall tin, modelled as a rifle, 1910–20, 6in (15cm) long.
£180–200
$250–300 ↗ BBR

A Maison Lyons eight-sided sweet tin, decorated with a party scene in blue, yellow, red and green, c1920, 6in (15cm) wide.
£35–50
$50–75 ⊞ MURR

A Fullers Earth Cream tin, decorated in pink, green, red and cream, 1920s, 2in (5cm) diam.
£7–10
$10–15 ⊞ YR

An Abonne cigar tin, decorated with six raised cigars, c1925, 4½in (11.5cm) square.
£30–35
$45–50 ⊞ HUX

A Bulwark Cut Plug Tobacco tin, decorated with a nautical scene in blue and white, 1920s, 7in (18cm) wide.
£15–20
$20–30 ⊞ COB

A Cadbury's Milk Tray Chocolates tin, decorated in brown, green and yellow, 1950s, 7in (18cm) wide.
£10–12
$15–20 ⊞ RTT

A Sharp's Super Kreem Toffee tin, decorated with Sir Kreemy Nut feeding a macaw in blue, black, yellow and green on an orange ground, 1930, 9in (23cm) high.
£85–95
$125–145 ⊞ TMa
Sharp's introduced their Macaw trademark c1915, along with the slogan 'Sharp's Toffee Speaks For Itself'. Five years later they added the figure of Sir Kreemy Nut.

A World Cup Willie's Football tin, modelled as a football, inscribed 'Lovell's Newport Mon' with black lettering on orange, on a green circular base, 1966, 5½in (14cm) high.
£60–70
$90–100 ↗ BBR

▶ A Cadbury's Smash tin, 1984, 5in (12.5cm) high.
£10–12
$15–20 ⊞ YR
1980s tins featuring Martians are more valuable than 1970s examples.

Aeronautica

A Britannic Aeroplane wooden advertising plaque, 1910, 13in (33cm) wide.
£60–65
$90–100 ⊞ COB

An RFC brass badge, 1915, 1½in (4cm) diam.
£30–35
$45–50 ⊞ COB

A bust of Louis Bleriot, by Leo Roussel, commemorating the first flight across the English Channel in July 1909, 8in (20.5cm) high.
£400–450
$580–650 ⊞ AU

A tapestry, depicting the Spirit of St Louis and Lindbergh, with other pilots, American, 1928, 59in (150cm) wide.
£350–375
$500–575 ⊞ AU

A vesta case, commemorating Eastbourne Jubilee Aviation Rally and Garden Party, June 1933, 2½in (6.5cm) wide.
£250–300
$350–450 ⊞ AU

An airman's emergency kite, 1930s, 21in (53.5cm) long.
£75–85
$100–125 ⊞ COB

A Swiss Lever Superior Aeroplane Timekeeper watch, base metal, 1920, 2in (5cm) diam.
£40–50
$60–80 ⊞ COB

A wooden model aircraft, 1938, 29in (73.5cm) wide.
£130–150
$190–220 ⊞ COB

A United Airlines passenger brochure, with map and pictures, 1949, 9 x 12in (23 x 30.5cm).
£20–25
$30–40 ⊞ J&S

A model of a DC3 aeroplane, mounted on a metal sphere, on a black base, 1940s, 14in (35.5cm) high.
£250–300
$350–450 ⊞ COB

▶ A London Airport badge, 1960s, 1in (2.5cm) diam.
£5–8
$8–12 ⊞ COB

A BOAC pottery tankard, c1960, 5in (12.5cm) high.
£15–20
$20–30 ⊞ HUX

Balloons & Airships

It was a bag filled with hot-air that enabled man to fly. This was discovered by French inventors Joseph and Etienne Montgolfier who, on 5 June 1873, launched the first unmanned balloon flight. Three months later they sent up a larger balloon at Versailles containing the world's first air passengers: a rooster, a duck, and a sheep. The earliest manned balloon flights took place later that year. One pioneer landed in a French village only to be attacked with pitchforks by inhabitants, terrified at the appearance of this unnatural flying monster.

Airships (also known as dirigibles) evolved from the balloon. The first successful airship was created by Henry Giffard of France in 1852. Numerous refinements took place in France and Germany in the second half of the 19th century, with the introduction of an internal combustion engine (1872), the electric motor (1883) and the rigid airship (1897). Ferdinand Graf von Zeppelin of Germany produced rigid airships from c1900 which were used to bomb Paris and London during WWI. Developments continued in the interwar years, but after a succession of disasters culminating with the destruction of the Hindenburg in 1937, the airship was virtually abandoned as a viable means of air travel. Its precursor, however, the hot-air balloon, still remains in flight, with famous balloonists including Richard Branson. Memorabilia relating to both these early forms of air transport is very collectable, and rarities attract strong prices.

A pearlware plate, depicting Graham's balloon flight from White Conduit House, printed in red, c1828, 9½in (24cm) diam.
£400–450
$580–650 ⊞ AU

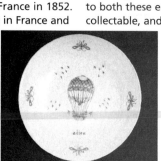

A hand-painted balloon plate, inscribed 'adieu' (farewell), in red, green and blue, French, c1840, 9in (23cm) diam.
£450–500
$650–720 ⊞ AU

▶ A black and white photographic postcard, depicting a hot-air balloon, French, 1906, 5½in (14cm) long.
£23–25
$30–35 ⊞ WI

A swivelling watch fob, with a hot-air balloon scene engraved on stone, c1900, 2in (5cm) long.
£60–70
$90–100 ⊞ MRW

◀ A Balloon Post postcard, 'Life-Boat Saturday', slight corner creasing, 1903.
£1,000–1,200
$1,500–1,750 ↗ VS
Although dated 29 August 1903, this balloon was not flown until 5 September as it had an accident just as it was taking off from Manchester. It was therefore flown from Alexandra Palace on 5 September with much of the mail being dropped at various areas in London. This card has a clear Enfield cachet, '1.15pm 8th September 1903', being sent to Manchester with receiving cachet '9.45pm' on the same day.

A Royal Doulton Hudson Fulton celebration plate, depicting different modes of air travel, 1909, 10in (25.5cm) diam.
£300–350
$450–500 ⊞ AU

A colour illustration postcard, depicting a hot-air balloon scene, German, 1909, 5½in (14cm) high.
£23–25
$30–35 ⊞ WI

A Carlton ware model of an airship, crested, 1914–18, 4¾in (12cm) long.
£50–60
$75–90 ⊞ RUSS

A brass airship searchlight, by Pittsburgh Electrical Specialities Co, American, late 1920s, 7½in (19cm) long.
£175–200
$250–300 ⊞ AU

▶ **A blue and white ceramic plate,** commemorating the first Atlantic crossing by a hot-air balloon and gondola, 1958, 10in (25.5cm) diam.
£65–75
$95–110 ➹ RCo

A brass airship ashtray, c1910, 8in (20.5cm) long.
£120–130
$175–200 ⊞ COB

Five Ogden's cigarette cards, depicting different hot-air balloons, from a set of 50, 1912.
£250–275
$350–400 ⊞ WI

A bronze commemorative plaque, for a balloon event, German, 1928, 3½in (9cm) long.
£350–400
$500–600 ⊞ AU

A Royal Doulton jug, depicting a pre-WWI aviation scene including an airship, 1910–12, 6½in (16.5cm) high.
£750–850
$1,100–1,250 ⊞ AU

A model airship, 1916, 38in (96.5cm) long.
£400–450
$580–650 ⊞ COB

Six photographs of an R101 airship leaving its mooring, 1931, 3¼in (8.5cm) long.
£25–30
$35–45 ⊞ J&S

A Poole plate, decorated with an airship design, 1980s, 6in (15cm) diam.
£18–20
$20–30 ⊞ DCA

Amusement & Slot Machines

An Automatic Amusement Co spinning dial fortune teller, The Gypsy, first patented c1889, 24in (61cm) high.
£750–850
$1,100–1,250 ⊞ HAK

A Mechanical Trading Co grip test machine, London, c1895, 18in (45.5cm) high.
£3,000–4,000
$4,500–5,800 ⊞ HAK

A Société Générale D'automatique electric pig, Paris, c1898, 32in (81.5cm) high.
£7,000–8,000
$10,200–11,500 ⊞ HAK

Insurance values

Always insure your valuable collectables for the cost of replacing them with similar items, regardless of the original price paid. Both dealers and auctioneers can provide a valuation service for a fee.

▶ **An Automatic Sports Co machine,** with football game, London, c1896, 32in (81.5cm) high excluding stand.
£4,000–4,500
$5,800–6,500 ⊞ HAK

A British American Novelty Co fortune card dispenser, The Automatic Astrologer, London, c1910, 30in (76cm) high.
£550–600
$800–900 ⊞ HAK

A Hooper Automatic Co electric shock machine, London, c1918, 22in (60cm) high.
£450–550
$650–800 ⊞ HAK

A bubble gum machine, Belgian, 1910–20, 15in (38cm) high.
£200–250
$300–350 ⊞ RUL

A wax-headed Cleveland fortune teller, 'Grandmothers Predictions', the remainder in USA, 1915, 87in (221cm) high.
£3,000–4,000
$4,500–5,800 ⊞ CAm

► **A Max Jentsch & Meerz slot machine,** The Charlie Chaplin, Leipzig, German, c1918, 26in (66cm) high.
£750–850
$1,000–1,300 ⊞ HAK

► **A Little Fivewin slot machine,** 1920s, 27in (68.5cm) high.
£500–550
$720–800 ⊞ JUN

▶ **A Tivoli one-armed bandit,** with keys, 1960s, 29in (73.5cm) high.
£40–50
$60–80 ➤ SAF

A wall-mounted Bajazzo clown ball catching game, German, 1926, 29in (73.5cm) high.
£350–400
$500–600 ⊞ CAm

An Allwyn ball bearing game, with keys, French, 1930s, 22½in (57cm) high.
£300–350
$450–500 ➤ SAF

A Jennings Club Chief amusement machine, 1940, 30in (76cm) high.
£700–800
$1,000–1,200 ⊞ JUN

◀ **A set of three Bryan's Magic machines,** Magic String Cutter, Magic Spirals and Disappearing Disc, c1940, 23in (58.5cm) high.
£200–300
$300–450 each ⊞ CAm

A Mini-Match wall-mounted slot machine, with keys, 1980s, 25½in (65cm) high.
£25–30
$35–45 ➤ SAF

Antiquities

◀ **A Mycenaean one-piece violin-bow style bronze brooch,** complete with pin, spring and catchplate, green patina, 13thC BC, 3¾in (9.5cm) long.
£85–95
$125–140 ⊞ ANG

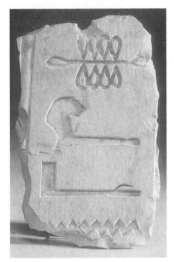

An Egyptian limestone fragment, with blue-filled hieroglyphs, part of an inscription suggesting the words 'palace' and 'governor of', Middle Kingdom, 21st–18thC BC, 9¼in (23.5cm) high.
£700–800
$1,000–1,150 ↗ Bon

A Mycenaean pottery jug, with simple painted decoration, 13th–11thC BC, 5½in (14cm) high.
£200–220
$300–330 ⊞ HEL

A Mediterranean alabaster vase, with decorated rim, 8th–6thC BC, 3in (7.5cm) diam.
£230–270
$330–390 ⊞ HEL

◀ **A group of Egyptian glazed faïence amulets,** late Dynastic Period, 8th–4thC BC, ½in (1cm) long.
£20–30
$30–45 each ⊞ HEL

An Egyptian carved steatite amulet, modelled as a cat, late Dynastic Period, 8th–4thC BC, ½in (1cm) high.
£70–80
$100–115 ⊞ HEL

An Etruscan terracotta votive head of a female, hair dressed beneath a diadem, traces of pink slip on the lips, 4thC BC, 9in (23cm) high.
£500–600
$720–870 ↗ Bon

A **Campanian terracotta askos,** modelled as a dove with folded wings, the body with white slip, the beak-shaped spout with traces of red slip, with perforated filler hole and black strap handle, 7¾in (19.5cm) long.
£800–1,200
$1,150–1,750 ↗ P
Ex-Bomford Collection.

A **fragment from a Samian ware red glass bowl,** with moulded decoration, 1stC, 4in (10cm) square.
£45–50
$65–75 ⊞ HEL
This fragment was found in London in the 1940s.

A **Roman aubergine glass jug,** with outfolded rim, tall cylindrical neck, rounded shoulder tapering to narrow base and rectangular handle, 1stC, 4¼in (11cm) high.
£1,000–1,100
$1,500–1,600 ↗ Bon

▶ A **Roman pottery jug,** with trefoil lip and single handle, 2nd–4thC, 3½in (9cm) high.
£50–60
$75–90 ⊞ Sama
This ancient Roman vessel was found in the Holy Land.

A **Roman marble cinerary urn,** the top of architectural outline, the base deeply carved in relief with ram's head, birds and festoons with anthemion motif to the sides, and carved inscription to Mepidus, 1st–2ndC, 11in (28cm) high.
£4,300–4,500
$6,250–6,500 ↗ CMS

A medieval silver ring brooch, with wide outwardly curving rim complete with pin engraved with owner's initials BN, 14th–15thC, 1¼in (3cm) diam.
£35–40
$50–60 ⊞ ANG
This rare item was found in Lincolnshire.

A **Roman bone lidded pyxis,** the exterior carved with two figures, one of a plump old woman, naked, holding a staff and carrying a round container, the second figure of Eros, naked, carrying two containers, dark brown patina and repaired crack across middle, 3rdC, 2¼in (5.5cm) high.
£850–950
$1,250–1,380 ↗ Bon

A **medieval silver-gilt annular brooch,** with hand-tooled flower devices with twisted loop, complete with pin and most gilding, 1¾in (4.5cm) diam.
£340–380
$490–570 ↗ Gle

A **Tudor knife,** found in London, c1600, 7in (18cm) long.
£30–35
$45–50 ⊞ BSA

▶ A **silver fork,** with ivory handle, the silver ferrule with two prongs, recovered from the River Thames, c1680, 5½in (14cm) long.
£90–100
$130–145 ⊞ ANG

Architectural Salvage

A carved oak corbel, c1660,
11in (28cm) high.
£1,800–2,000
$2,600–3,000 ⊞ SEA

A granite pillar,
17thC, 83in
(211cm) high.
£850–950
$1,250–1,350
⊞ RECL

**A Portland stone
balustrade,** from a
set of 32, 18thC,
32in (81.5cm) high.
£150–180
$220–260 ⊞ OLA

An oak door, with
original frame, c1799,
75in (190.5cm) high.
£750–1,000
$1,100–1,500 ⊞ OLA

**A selection of Victorian
terracotta crown chimney pots,**
some with brown saltglaze finish,
c1890, largest 54in (137cm) high.
£70–120
$100–170 each ⊞ HOP

**A mid-Victorian ham stone
Dorset/Devon window surround,**
39in (99cm) high.
£225–250
$320–360 ⊞ OLA

**A selection of galvanized dolly
tubs,** c1930, largest 26in (66cm) high.
£15–20
$20–30 ⊞ HOP

▶ **A pair of brass wall
plaques depicting the
lion and the unicorn,**
one inscribed 'George V
AD1910–1936', the other
'King George's Field',
1936, 11in (28cm) high.
£360–400
$500–600 ⊞ OLA

A copper-domed chimney vent,
with revolving blade centre section,
plaque inscribed 'Ewart
& Son Ltd Ventilation Engineers
346–350 Euston Road London
NW', c1900.
£130–150
$190–220 ⚒ RTo

Door Stops & Boot Scrapers

A Regency cast-iron boot scraper,
16in (40.5cm) wide.
£120–180
$160–260 ⊞ OLA

A Victorian cast-iron boot scraper,
14in (35.5cm) wide.
£75–85
$110–125 ⊞ HCJ

A brass cupid door stop,
1850, 17in (43cm) high.
£260–290
$380–440 ⊞ GBr

◄ **A cast-iron boot scraper,** with pierced, arched ends and a rectangular tray base, ex-Pitchford Hall, 19thC, 14in (35.5cm) long.
£70–80
$100–120
↗ WBH

► **A painted cast-iron door stop,** modelled as a stork with its beak in a jar, from Aesop's Fables, 19thC, 11½in (29cm) high.
£950–1,050
$1,400–1,500 ↗ S
This door stop was always used by the actor Sir Ralph Richardson to keep his dressing room door ajar, hence its high value.

A rampant lion cast-iron door stop, 1860, 15in (38cm) high.
£165–185
$240–270 ⊞ GBr

Heating

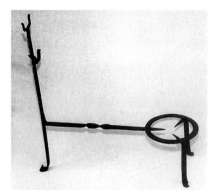

A wrought-iron adjustable pot stand, French, c1750, 23in (58.5cm) long.
£225–250
$320–360 ⊞ SEA

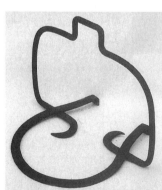

A wrought-iron warming stand, 18thC, 13in (33cm) long.
£35–40
$50–60 ⊞ HCJ

A pair of wrought-iron fire dogs, French, 18thC, 22in (56cm) high.
£440–480
$650–700 ⊞ SEA

A Regency cast-iron hobbed register grate, 37in (94cm) high.
£500–600
$720–870 ⊞ WRe

A painted wooden fire surround, the pilasters with pendant harebells, early 19thC, 76in (193cm) wide.
£190–220
$275–325 ✗ WBH

A Coalbrookdale cast-iron fire basket, c1840, 36in (91.5cm) wide.
£2,000–2,400
$3,000–3,500 ⊞ ASH

A brass coal scuttle, in the shape of a helmet, with embossed flower and foliate panels, foliate loop handle with turned ebony grip, on a spreading foot, 19thC, 22in (56cm) high, with matching shovel.
£450–500
$650–720 ✗ AH

A Victorian cast-iron and tiled forward grate, 38in (96.5cm) high.
£450–500
$650–720 ⊞ WRe

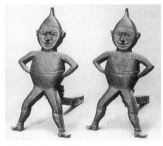

A pair of cast-iron figural andirons, modelled as brownies with green glass eyes, illegible foundry mark, losses to log rests, American, late 19thC, 15½in (39.5cm) high.
£650–750
$950–1,100 ✗ SK(B)

A cast-iron tiled combination grate, c1900, 48in (122cm) high.
£500–550
$720–800 ⊞ WRe

◀ **A Petrolux paraffin stove,** early 20thC, 27in (68.5cm) high.
£70–80
$100–120 ✗ SWO

▶ **An Ideal Standard cast-iron radiator,** on four column feet, restored, 1920–50, 21in (53.5cm) long.
£220–250
$320–360 ⊞ OLA

A pine and brass coal box, c1920, 18in (45.5cm) long.
£70–80
$100–120 ⊞ OLA

Art Deco

An Art Deco walnut sideboard,
with Bakelite and chrome handles,
60in (152.5cm) wide.
£425–475
$620–690 ⊞ HSt

**An Art Deco set of three chrome wall
lights,** 14in (35.5cm) high.
£300–500
$440–720 ⊞ ASA

A Katzhütte bust, Austrian,
1930s, 8in (20.5cm) high.
£350–400
$500–600 ⊞ MD

◄ **An Art Deco Vitascope
electric mantel clock,** with
automated ship movement,
in a light green Bakelite
case, 12¾in (32.5cm) high.
£340–380
$500–600 🔨 AG

► **An Art Deco
enamelled glass scent
bottle,** 5in (12.5cm) high.
£65–75
$95–115 ⊞ TWAC

**A ceramic stylized
model of a kangaroo,**
by Mougin Frères,
Nancy, French, 1920s–30s,
15in (38cm) high.
£150–175
$220–250 ⊞ ZOOM

◄ **An Art Deco-style
lady's platinum-cased
cocktail watch,** set with
82 diamonds, 1930s.
£550–600
$800–900 🔨 WilP

An Art Deco silver and enamel pin, with a central
cartouche depicting St Christopher, ½in (1cm) wide.
£75–85
$110–120 ⊞ DRJ

Art Nouveau

A brass aide-memoire, c1900, 2½in (5cm) high.
£20–30
$30–50 ⊞ VB

A copper jardinière, in the shape of a cauldron, on three swept supports terminating in spade-shaped motifs, with two handles, unmarked, 1885, 12¾in (32.5cm) diam.
£160–180
$230–260 ⚒ P(B)

▶ **A table lamp,** with shell shade, on a Tiffany-style anodized base, American, c1900, 17¾in (45cm) high.
£400–440
$580–650 ⚒ WilP

A gold and mother-of-pearl pendant brooch, c1900, 1½in (4cm) wide.
£350–450
$500–650 ⊞ ASA

A Montjoye enamelled glass vase, by Legras, French, c1900, 11in (28cm) high.
£380–450
$575–650 ⊞ OND

▶ **An Art Nouveau carved mahogany photograph frame,** 13in (33cm) high.
£85–95
$125–145 ⊞ AMR

A copper vase, attributed to WMF, the hammered body with stylized plant forms, with applied geometric brass handles, on a spreading foot, base marked with running ostrich within a lozenge, 1905, 11¾in (30cm) high.
£230–250
$330–360 ⚒ P(B)

A sterling silver and _plique-a-jour_ enamel pendant, the shaped plaque decorated with blue-grey _plique-a-jour_ enamel in a trellis and floral vine design, with cabochon green and pink stones and a rose-cut diamond, 1910, 2¾in (7cm) long.
£600–700
$850–1,000 ⚒ SK

◀ **A Hancock & Sons Morrisware vase,** designed by George Cartlidge, decorated with red flowers and blue and purple foliage on a mottled green ground, green printed factory mark, green painted signature, after 1918, 6¼in (16cm) high.
£1,000–1,200
$1,500–1,750 ⚒ S(S)

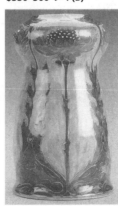

A silver and enamel brooch, with yellow metal inlay, maker's mark 'A.J.S', Birmingham 1912, 2in (5cm) wide.
£100–120
$145–175 ⚒ DD

Arts & Crafts

A copper blind convex mirror, embossed with butterflies and birds, with butterfly wing and mother-of-pearl detail, late 19thC, 16in (40.5cm) diam.
£530–580
$750–850 ⚲ **GAK**

A silver beaker, by James Dixon & Sons, with punchwork decoration, on three ball feet, Sheffield 1888, 3¼in (8.5cm) high, 5.25oz.
£260–300
$360–440 ⚲ **F&C**

An oak cabinet, by Goodall Lamb & Heighway, with overhanging cornice above a panel door and metalware hinges, the lower section fitted with three short drawers and three open shelves, on a block base, c1890, 78in (198cm) high.
£550–650
$800–950 ⚲ **P(B)**

Miller's is a price GUIDE not a price LIST

▶ **An oak and copper plant stand,** with stylized floral embossed panels, on four square legs, c1900, 27½in (70cm) high.
£180–220
$220–320 ⚲ **P(B)**

A brass coal scuttle, with repoussé decoration, 1895, 16in (40.5cm) long.
£100–120
$145–175 ⚲ **SWO**

A copper charger, c1890, 17in (43cm) diam.
£350–450
$500–650 ⊞ **ASA**

An Art Nouveau brass wall clock, the square brass dial with embossed Roman numerals and Celtic banding, with brass weights and pendulum, Scottish, 10¾in (27.5cm) square.
£200–250
$300–350 ⚲ **TRM**

◀ **An Art Nouveau oak wall cabinet,** the cupboard door with pottery plaque inset depicting dancing figures, recess and side shelves with carved motifs, Dutch, 27in (68.5cm) wide.
£375–425
$550–620 ⚲ **TRM**

A silver necklace, set with two black cabochon moonstones and four blister pearls within a pierced and foliate border, late 19thC/early 20thC, 19in (48cm) long.
£425–495
$620–720 ⚲ **S(S)**

Mabel Lucie Attwell

At the turn of the century, children's illustration was one of the few artistic areas where women could compete on an equal footing with men, and none were more successful than Mabel Lucie Attwell (1879–1964). The ninth child of a London butcher, Attwell put herself through art school by selling drawings for one guinea a piece. She began illustrating children's books and postcards in the 1900s and, together with her husband, artist Harry Earnshaw, she also worked in advertising. Attwell's greatest fame, however, came after WWI, partly inspired by necessity when in 1916 Harold, who had joined the Artists' Rifles, had his right arm blown off, which left her financially responsible for their family of three children. She fulfilled the task admirably.

In the inter-war years Mabel Lucie Attwell became a household name. Her famous bun-cheeked infants, the antithesis of her own long, strong-boned face and said to be inspired by her daughter Peggy (b1909), appeared on everything from biscuit tins to bathroom plaques and advertised every conceivable product from toothpaste to the London Underground. Attwell characters were turned into dolls and games. Shelley china was decorated with the 'Boo-Boos' (a series of roly-poly fairies), and the young princesses Elizabeth and Margaret both ate from Attwell nursery ware. There were endless books and annuals; countless postcards and greetings cards (in 1941 alone postcard sales topped two million).

Although her professional career never faltered, Attwell's personal life was marked by tragedy. One son died from pneumonia aged 20, the other never fully recovered from a serious car crash. Her husband became increasingly ill from his war wounds and died in 1937. Her drawings, however, never lost their cheerful charm. Attwell merchandise is still being produced today, there is an active collectors' club and demand for vintage material (the earlier the better) continues to rise.

Mabel Lucie Attwell, three *Boo-Boos* books, with green, brown and red jackets, 1920–22, 5 x 6in (12.5 x 15cm).
£90–110
$130–160 ⊞ MEM

◄ **Mabel Lucie Attwell,** *Little So Shy* cut-out book, by Valentines & Sons, 1910, 11in (28cm) high.
£150–160
$220–240 ⊞ MEM

J. M. Barrie, *Peter Pan & Wendy,* illustrated by Mabel Lucie Attwell, published by Hodder & Stoughton, 12 mounted colour plates, in original yellow cloth binding, 1924, 9 x 7in (23 x 18cm).
£110–130
$160–190 ⊞ BIB

A Mabel Lucie Attwell nursery plate, decorated in yellow, green and red on a pale blue ground, 1930s–40s, 9in (23cm) diam.
£80–100
$115–145 ⊞ I&M

A Mabel Lucie Attwell cut-out calendar, by Valentines & Sons, with the figure of a golfer in shades of brown, on a wooden base, 1930s, 9in (23cm) wide.
£175–185
$250–270 ⊞ MEM

A Shelley Mabel Lucie Attwell nursery plate, decorated in yellow, green, black and red on a white ground, c1930; 7in (18cm) diam.
£130–150
$190–220 ⊞ BD

A Mabel Lucie Attwell warming dish with lid, decorated in yellow and green, c1930, 8in (20.5cm) diam.
£200–225
$300–330 ⊞ MEM

A Shelley Mabel Lucie Attwell nursery mug, decorated in blue, pink and green, 1930s, 4in (10cm) high.
£175–195
$255–285 ⊞ BD

Two porcelain Mabel Lucie Attwell toothbrush holders, decorated in yellow, brown, red and blue, German, c1934, 4in (10cm) high.
£90–120
$130–150 each ⊞ MEM

A Mabel Lucie Attwell Nestol advertising puzzle, 1934, 9 x 7in (23 x 18cm), in original box.
£180–200
$250–300 ⊞ MEM

A pack of Mabel Lucie Attwell Dorma white bed sheets, unopened, 1930s, 20in (51cm) long.
£80–90
$115–130 ⊞ MEM

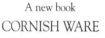

Two Mabel Lucie Attwell Bijou Mottoes, by Valentines & Sons, decorated in pink, blue yellow and green, 1930–40, 3 x 5in (7.5 x 12.5cm), framed.
£15–20
$20–30 each ⊞ MEM

▶ **A Mabel Lucie Attwell kitchen jotter,** decorated in yellow, blue and red, c1950, 12 x 6in (30.5 x 15cm).
£15–17
$20–25 ⊞ CRN

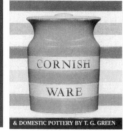

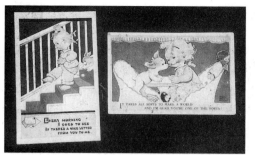

Two Mabel Lucie Attwell postcards, 1950s.
£5–10
$10–15 ⊞ MEM

▶ A Mabel Lucie
Attwell Peek
Frean's biscuit
tin, c1960, 8in
(20.5cm) diam.
£20–30
$30–50 ⊞ MEM

A Mabel Lucie Attwell
cut-out calendar, by
Valentines & Sons, Dundee,
1953, 10in (25.5cm) high.
£35–45
$50–70 ⊞ MEM

An Old Hall stainless
steel children's plate,
in original blue box with
Mabel Lucie Attwell design,
c1960, 8in (20.5cm) diam.
£25–35
$30–50 ⊞ MEM

▶ A Mabel
Lucie Attwell
Kinnerton's
Easter chocolate
box, 1992,
9in (23cm) wide.
£20–25
$30–35 ⊞ MEM

Lucie Attwell's Story for
a Poppet, published by
Dean, 1961, 8 x 5in
(20.5 x 12.5cm).
£16–18
$20–25 ⊞ J&J

A set of eight Mabel
Lucie Attwell Huntley
& Palmer's biscuit tins,
1960s, 5in (12.5cm) diam.
£120–140
$170–200 ⊞ MEM

A Mabel Lucie Attwell
Memories of Yesterday
porcelain jam pot, in
green and brown, c1992,
3½in (9cm) high.
£35–45
$50–70 ⊞ MEM

Three Mabel Lucie
Attwell Memories of
Yesterday lapel badges,
one inscribed 'Memories UK
Mabel Lucie Attwell Club',
c1990, 3in (7.5cm) high.
£5–8
$10–15 each ⊞ MEM

Autographs

Buzz Aldrin, a signed colour photograph, half-length, wearing a white spacesuit, an image of the moon in the background, c1969, 10 x 8in (25.5 x 20.5cm).
£200–220
$290–320 ⚒ VS

Fred Astaire, a signed photograph, 1940s, 10 x 8in (25.5 x 20.5cm).
£300–340
$450–500 ⊞ SDP

Cross Reference
See Rock & Pop
(page 329)

Lauren Bacall, an autograph and photograph, mounted, 1970s, 10 x 8in (25.5 x 20.5cm).
£50–60
$75–90 ⊞ SDP

The Beatles, signatures of all four Beatles on a piece of brown paper, adhesive marks not affecting signatures, 1964.
£1,000–1,100
$1,500–1,600 ⚒ DW
A note of provenance states that the signatures were obtained by W. F. Charlton, Director of British Airways Helicopters, during the filming of *A Hard Day's Night*. '...they had use of Mr Charlton's office, he met them on a daily basis and came to the conclusion that they were a really nice group of young men.'

Enid Blyton, an autograph letter expressing satisfaction that her books were on the reading list in school, 1959, 3½ x 5½in (9 x 14cm).
£300–330
$450–480 ⊞ IQ

Napoleon, a letter written by Mounier and a photograph, both signed by Napoleon, mounted, 1813, 9 x 7in (23 x 18cm).
£900–1,000
$1,300–1,500 ⊞ IQ

Sir Adrian Boult, a postcard showing Boult, half-length, in old age studying a score, 1939, 6 x 4in (15 x 10cm).
£55–65
$80–95 ⚒ DW

Leslie Caron, a signed photograph, mounted, 1950s, 10 x 8in (25.5 x 20.5cm).
£35–38
$50–60 ⊞ SDP

Charlie Chaplin, a signed photograph, 1930s, 7 x 5in (18 x 12.5cm).
£450–500
$650–720 ⊞ SDP

José Collins, a signed silver print by Dorothy Wilding, Royal Photographer, also signed by Wilding, 1932, 20 x 13in (51 x 33cm).
£180–200
$250–300 ⊞ BoC

Arthur Conan Doyle, a signed sepia postcard, c1910.
£650–750
$950–1,100 ⚡ VS

Harry H. Corbett, a signed and inscribed photograph, three-quarter length, late 1950s–early 1960s, 10 x 8in (25.5 x 20.3cm).
£100–120
$145–175 ⚡ VS

◀ Charles Darwin, a signed attendance register for the Philosophical Club of the Royal Society, with the signatures of John Tyndall, Lyell, Richard Patridge, Muller and 15 others, with pencil minutes of the meeting and observations of procedure and scientific matters discussed, dated 22nd November 1855, 2°.
£850–950
$1,250–1,350 ⚡ DW

Aleister Crowley, a signed note, 'in haste – O.K. will expect you at Mr Chase', with photograph, mounted, 14 x 17in (35.5 x 43cm).
£315–350
$450–500 ⊞ IQ
English writer and black magician, Aleister Crowley (1875–1967), first became interested in the occult at Cambridge. He went on to form his own order, the Silver Star, and settled for several years in Sicily with a group of disciples. Rumours of drugs, orgies and sacrifice abounded leading to his expulsion from Italy. Many of those associated with him died tragically. Crowley gained the reputation of 'the wickedest man alive' and, even after his death, memorabilia connected with the 'great beast', as he liked to be called, is still sought after.

Walt Disney, a small signed card, London, 1935.
£700–800
$1,000–1,150 ⚡ VS

Cross Reference
See Politics
(page 301)

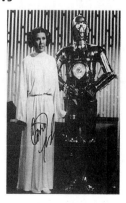

▶ Carrie Fisher, a signed colour photograph, full-length, wearing a *Star Wars* costume, 1970s, 10 x 8in (25.5 x 20.5cm).
£35–40
$50–60 ⚡ VS

Edward, Duke of Windsor and Wallis, Duchess of Windsor, a signed printed leaflet with details of the landing arrangements issued by the Cunard Line for the voyage of RMS *Queen Elizabeth* from New York, 18th April 1956, also signed by Ginger Rogers, minor staining.
£240–280
$350–400 ⚡ VS

Isadora Duncan, a signed photograph, and unsigned photograph, mounted, 1919, largest 9 x 5in (23 x 12.5cm).
£675–750
$975–1,100 ⊞ SDP

◀ Margot Fonteyn, a photograph and signed letter, 1955, 6 x 8in (15 x 20.5cm).
£65–75
$95–115 ⊞ SDP

George Formby a signed photograph, 1936, 11 x 8½in (28 x 21.5cm).
£100–110
$145–160 ⚲ VS

Jimi Hendrix and the Walker Brothers, a signed official tour programme, also signed by Scott Walker and Englebert Humperdinck, 7th April 1967, 10½ x 8in (26.5 x 20.5cm).
£1,400–1,600
$2,000–2,300 ⚲ Bon

Adolf Hitler, a publicity postcard by Hoffman, signed in ink, c1937, 6 x 4in (15 x 10cm).
£1,800–2,000
$2,600–2,900 ⊞ IQ

Clark Gable, a signed copy of *The Stars and Stripes,* 'Daily newspaper of US Armed Forces in the European Theater of Operations', 28th July 1943.
£130–150
$190–220 ⚲ DW
Obtained in person by a lady who worked for the American Red Cross during WWII and who 'bumped into' Gable whilst on duty. Autographs of Gable as a member of the US armed forces in WWII are rare. Unlike many of his peers, Gable had a distinguished military career.

▶ **Matt Groening,** a signed and inscribed colour still from *The Simpsons*, depicting the family, with additional ink sketch of Bart Simpson drawn to image, 19th June 1999, 8 x 10in (20.5 x 25.5cm).
£190–210
$275–300 ⚲ VS

Sid James, a signed photograph, 1960s, 5 x 3in (12.5 x 7.5cm).
£135–150
$200–220 ⊞ SDP

▶ **Vivien Leigh,** a signed photograph, dressed in costume, slight surface creasing, 1940s–50s, 6½ x 5in (16.5 x 12.5cm).
£220–250
$320–360 ⚲ VS

King George III, a signed military commission appointing Philip Perry an adjutant in the 21st Regiment of Dragoon (or Royal Forresters) commanded by John Manners, Marquess of Granby, countersigned by William Pitt The Elder, given at the Court at Saville House, with embossed paper seal affixed, folds, 27th October 1760.
£330–350
$480–500 ⚲ VS

◀ **Jacqueline Kennedy,** a signed envelope and card expressing gratitude for expressions of sympathy following the assassination, stamped, 1964, 6 x 3in (15 x 7.5cm).
£90–100
$130–150 ⊞ IQ

Arthur Lowe, a signed postcard, wearing *Dad's Army* costume, 1970s.
£120–140
$175–200 ⚲ VS

Manchester United, 11 team autographs on a single autograph album leaf, including W. Robertson, T. Jones, E. Hine, J. Griffith, S. Bamford, and Billy McKay, 1st December 1934.
£80–100
$115–145 ⚒ DW

Alan Alexander Milne, a signed copy of *If I May*, inscribed on the front free endpaper 'For Irene Rooke – the adorable Marion – in admiration and gratitude from A. A. Milne.', original quarter cloth binding, rubbed, worn and faded, inner front hinge cracked, New York, 1921.
£50–60
$75–90 ⚒ WW

Ayrton Senna, a signed colour photograph, 1990s, 9½ x 7in (24 x 18cm).
£850–950
$1,250–1,400 ⚒ DW

Items in the Autographs section have been arranged in alphabetical order.

Field Marshal Lord Roberts, a sepia portrait, signed as Commander in Chief in India, 1880s.
£85–95
$125–140 ⚒ DW

James Stewart, an original pen and ink cartoon of Harvey on white artist's card, signed, 1980s.
£240–260
$350–380 ⚒ DW
Harvey was one of Stewart's most successful, if somewhat curious, films. It centred on an eccentric (played by Stewart) who could see and converse with a giant rabbit named Harvey, much to the consternation of the rest of the cast who could see nothing. Stewart took pride in producing these cartoon sketches and they are much sought after today.

Cross Reference
See Crime (page 174)

▶ **George Bernard Shaw,** signed card to Mrs Lyth, Postmistress at Ayot St Lawrence, asking for three pounds' worth of three-halfpenny stamps, 23rd July 1938.
£160–180
$230–260 ⚒ VS

Leon Trotsky, a document from the Russian civil war, signed in blue pencil, 1918, 6in (15cm) square.
£720–800
$1,000–1,250 ⊞ IQ

Automobilia

A Rolls-Royce chauffeur's silver and enamel cap badge, in original box, c1913, 2½in (6.5cm) high.
£275–350
$400–500 ⊞ MURR

▶ A cast-iron hand-operated Surrey petrol pump, maker's plate reads 'Model CH 1 Consumer Pump. Serial No CH1/ 8431 Pat No 306358/28/ Manufactured By Avery Hardoll Ltd Oakcroft Road Chessington Surrey', 1920s, 70in (178cm) high.
£120–140
$175–200 ⚒ BBR

▶ A Packard Luxurious Motoring advertising pamphlet, c1920, 6 x 11in (15 x 28cm).
£12–15
$15–20 ⊞ HO

A glass posy vase, with brass fitting, from a luxury car, 1920s, 7in (18cm) high.
£35–40
$50–60 ⊞ HO

A Brooklands badge, gold lettering on light and dark blue, dated 1935, 1½in (4cm) square.
£30–35
$45–50 ⊞ COB

A motorcycle helmet shop display card, black lettering on white and orange, 1940s–50s, 10in (25.5cm) high.
£10–12
$15–18 ⊞ MRW

A Seddon Diesel lorry badge, c1950.
£45–55
$60–80 ⊞ HOP
The Seddon sign was designed by B. H. Seddon, daughter of the founder.

▶ A collection of vehicle excise licences, 1950s, 3½in (9cm) diam.
£5–8
$10–15 each
⊞ COB

Four key rings, 1960s,
largest 2½in (6.5cm) long.
£5–15
$8–20 each ⊞ HUX

An aluminium Hackney Carriage sign,
1950s–60s, 11in (28cm) wide.
£14–15
$18–20 ⊞ BiR

A quart oil bottle, 1950,
14in (35.5cm) high.
£3–5
$5–10 ⊞ BLM

A painted, pressed aluminium motorcycle trade plate,
GR stamp, issued in Gloucester, July 1923, 7in (18cm) wide.
£45–50
$65–75 ⊞ MW

◀ **An MC250 Grand Prix
silver cup,** with Coca-Cola
badge, French, 1951,
10in (25.5cm) high.
£250–350
$350–500 ⊞ COB

Number plates

Motor vehicle registration plates were first
introduced in Paris in 1893, spreading to the
rest of France by 1901. According to the UK
press, British drivers were generally opposed
to this measure considering that the number
plate made the private motor car look like 'a
common cab prowling for hire'. But with 5,000
vehicles now in use, Parliament was determined
to exert control. The Motor Car Act, passed on
1st January 1904, stipulated both the licensing
of drivers and the registration of vehicles. The
first registration number 'A1' was granted to
Earl Russell, the Under Secretary for Air, who
had queued all night to secure it. In 1959, this
plate was sold for charity for £2,500 – an early
example of the collectable appeal of an
interesting number plate.

An aluminium motorcycle front number plate,
issued in London, March 1960–62, 10in (25.5cm) wide.
£1–2
$3–5 ⊞ MW

Bathrooms

The Victorian period saw the building of new sewer systems, the passing of numerous acts to improve water supplies and sanitation, and a revolution in personal hygiene. The first public lavatory was opened in London in 1851, instigated by Sir Henry Cole, organizer of the Great Exhibition. Bathrooms became increasingly common in middle and upper class homes, and were filled with the latest fixtures and fittings.

In the 1880s, Thomas Crapper perfected the standard flushing toilet cistern and developed the U-bend, which prevented sewer fumes and rats from entering the house. In 1884 Jennings exhibited what was said to be the first pedestal lavatory and the same company was also responsible for introducing the oval 'picture frame' lavatory seat. Since lavatory bowls were no longer encased in wooden surrounds they became increasingly decorative, often painted with flowers both inside and out.

Other well-known manufacturers included Twyford, Brahmah, Shanks and Royal Doulton. Crapper was not the only lavatory pioneer whose name was to become immortalized in the English language. Edward Johns won an award for his WC at the 1876 Philadelphia Exhibition, hence the American colloquialism 'john'.

A walnut-framed bidet, with inset French faïence blue and white liner, floral-painted, on turned supports and stretchers, early 19thC, 23½in (59.5cm) wide.
£1,300–1,500
$2,000–2,200 ➤ RBB

A Victorian mahogany and lead-lined toilet cistern, 22in (56cm) wide.
£550–600
$800–870 ⊞ WRe

A porcelain water fountain, with floral decoration, French, c1889, 36in (91.5cm) high.
£1,000–1,200
$1,500–1,750 ⊞ OLA

A Victorian ceramic lavatory bowl, by Stock Sons & Taylor, Birmingham, Rd No. 19753, 16½in (42cm) high.
£80–100
$115–145 ➤ SWO

A pair of Victorian globe bath taps, refurbished, 5in (12.5cm) high.
£160–180
$230–260 ⊞ OLA

▶ **A pair of Victorian nickel-plated roll-top bath collars,** 4in (10cm) long.
£70–90
$100–130 ⊞ WRe

A pair of Shanks & Co polished brass long throw-plunger bath taps, 1¼in thread, fully reconditioned, 1895.
£300–350
$450–500 ⊞ WRe

A Staffordshire Royal washdown pedestal lavatory bowl, blue and white transfer-printed, decorated with flowers and foliage, late 19thC, 15½in (39.5cm) high.
£330–360
$480–520 ⚒ E

▶ **A waterfall lavatory,** with church seat and flushing cistern, bowl c1890, seat 1920, 96in (244cm) high.
£1,800–2,000
$2,600–3,000 ⊞ C&R

A Morrison Ingham & Co Triton patent embossed lavatory bowl, with enclosed trap, c1895, 16in (40.5cm) high.
£900–1,100
$1,300–1,600 ⊞ WRe

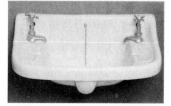

An Edwardian cloakroom basin, with nickel-plated taps, fully reconditioned, 22in (56cm) wide.
£500–550
$720–800 ⊞ WRe

A white Excelsior washdown pedestal lavatory bowl, with S-trap, 1898, 16in (40.5cm) high.
£450–500
$650–700 ⊞ OLA

A Doulton & Co mahogany lavatory seat, c1897.
£225–250
$325–375 ⊞ WRe

▶ **A collection of enamelled iron soap dishes,** in pastel colours, French, c1900, largest 5½in (14cm) long.
£12–15
$15–20 each ⊞ HOP

A blue and white Excelsior washdown pedestal lavatory bowl, with S-trap, 1898, 16in (40.5cm) high.
£900–1,000
$1,300–1,500 ⊞ OLA

A pair of Victorian polished brass roll-top bath taps with collars, fully reconditioned, 1890s, 6in (15cm) high.
£290–330
$425–475 ⊞ WRe

A pair of nickel-plated basin taps, with ½in thread, fully reconditioned, c1890, 5in (12.5cm) high.
£180–200
$250–300 ⊞ WRe

An enamel soap, sponge and toothbrush holder, blue with a white liner, early 20thC, 7in (18cm) high.
£25–30
$35–45 ⊞ B&R

An Edwardian Bathena cloakroom basin and nickel-plated taps, reconditioned, 25in (63.5cm) wide.
£450–500
$650–720 ⊞ WRe

A pair of Art Deco bath taps, refurbished and re-nickeled, 6in (15cm) high.
£200–220
$280–320 ⊞ OLA

A Thomas Crapper & Co Sanitary Specialities mounted advertisement, c1905, 16 x 12in (40.5 x 30.5cm).
£18–20
$25–30 ⊞ J&S

An Edwardian pair of Shanks & Co nickel-plated lever taps, fully reconditioned, 6in (15cm) high.
£270–300
$400–440 ⊞ WRe

An Art Deco-style nickel-plated bath spray mixer, ¾in thread, fully reconditioned, 1930s.
£450–500
$650–720 ⊞ WRe

◀ **A Royal Doulton p-trap lavatory,** with nickel-plated flush pipe clip, 1930, 16in (40.5cm) high.
£400–450
$580–650 ⊞ WRe

A Twyfords high level lidded china cistern, c1910, 20in (51cm) wide.
£400–450
$580–650 ⊞ WRe

An Art Deco nickel-plated bath mixer set, ¾in thread, fully reconditioned, 1930s, 7in (18cm) wide.
£380–420
$550–650 ⊞ WRe

A brass and cast-iron heated towel rail, with fluted radiator, fully reconditioned, c1935, 37in (94cm) high.
£500–550
$700–800 ⊞ WRe

A set of wall-mounted taps and soap tray, French, 1940s, 9in (23cm) wide.
£250–300
$350–450 ⊞ OLA

Bicycles

A Stevengraph, entitled 'The Last Lap', woven in silk, printed label to verso, woven in Ventnor, manufactured in Coventry and London, dampstained, c1870, 2 x 6in (5 x 15cm), with original mount.
£200–220
$300–330 ➤ DW

An Alldays & Onions bicycle anvil, for repairing chains, c1880.
£55–65
$80–100 ⊞ BAJ

A 'La Percutante' shaft-drive gentleman's bicycle, with black-painted frame, re-nickeled driving mechanism, 36-spoke wooden rims with aluminium linings, Christy saddle, wooden handlebars with cork grips, French, late 1890s, 28in (71cm) tyres fitted, 22½in (57cm) frame.
£900–1,000
$1,300–1,500 ➤ Bon

▶ **A Humber enamel sign,** in the shape of the Humber transfer with the running man trademark, white lettering on a black ground, marked 'Willing & Co Ltd London', late 1890s, 23½in (59.5cm) high.
£150–200
$220–300 ➤ P(Ba)

A Penny Farthing, with oval backbone, fluted front and rear forks, hollow rims, radial spokes, cranked down bars, U-section replaced, saddle cover, handles and pedals cut down from original, some rusting and repairs, early 1880s, rear wheel 16in (40.5cm) diam.
£800–900
$1,150–1,300 ➤ P(Ba)

A Victorian brass and silver-plated four-turn cyclist's buglet, by J. Higham, Manchester, stamped, 7½in (19cm) wide.
£500–550
$700–800 ➤ Bon

A silver-plated cycling prize, modelled as a rider wearing fashionable period cycling attire preparing to mount a penny farthing, on a wooden plinth, c1880, 7in (18cm) long.
£600–650
$870–950 ⊞ TML

A stein, decorated with a cycling scene, German, 1895–1900, 6in (15cm) high.
£200–230
$300–330 ⊞ AU

A League of American Wheelmen stein, the base with lithophane, inscribed 'Indianapolis 1898', 6in (15cm) high.
£550–650
$800–1,000 ⊞ AU

A Quadrant open-framed tricycle, with central chainwheel, 1in-pitch chain-driving fixed differential with contracting band brake, the whole on hangers from the frame, non-extended raised bars with plunger-type brake lever operating rear brake, double plate fork crown, c1899, 22in (56cm) frame .
£500–600
$720–870 P(Ba)

An Ever Ready battery wooden bicycle lamp, deep version with fluted reflector and magnifying lens, trade label to case interior, original varnished wood finish, weathered, early 20thC, 4½in (12cm) high.
£60–70
$90–100 P(Ba)

A silver-plated pewter WMF inkwell, probably presented as a trophy, c1905, 10in (25.5cm) wide.
£800–850
$1,150–1,250 AU

▶ **An Excelsior bicycle,** American, c1910.
£550–600
$800–900 YEST

A Bradbury Cycles advertising postcard.
£40–45
$60–70 VS

▶ **A Thanet light touring bicycle,** frame design built using silver solder, c1949.
£700–800
$1,000–1,150 AVT

An Eagle drop-front tandem, American, 1900–05.
£1,000–1,250
$1,500–1,800 AU

An Alldays & Onions child's bicycle, with photographs of original owner (not shown), 1914, 40in (101.5cm) long.
£400–450
$580–650 BAJ

A Cyclops human-powered vehicle, by Burrows Engineering, Norwich, with alloy rimmed front driver/steerer, 84-tooth chain ring, 12-tooth sprocket, 26in chrome-titanium rear rim, 1986, 52in (132cm) wheelbase.
£750–800
$1,100–1,200 P(Ba)
The Cyclops is shrouded in an aerodynamic fibreglass housing and gained its name from the fact that this casing had no window. The rider viewed the road using fibre optic technology connected to a pair of goggles requiring only a minute single aperture in the housing's nose.

A Mobo Tot Cycle, 1950s.
£70–80
$100–120 JUN

Black History & Memorabilia

This section is devoted to Black history and memorabilia. It begins with material commemorating the history of slavery and moves on to reflect on the vast amount of black memorabilia mass-produced from the late 19th century and into the 20th.

Manufactured for a predominantly white audience, the images on the objects portrayed are often stereotypical, derogatory and racist. Blacks are generally represented as servants, piccaninnies, savages or entertainers. The golly, which first appeared in *The Adventures of Two Dutch Dolls* (1895) by Florence K. and Bertha Upton, and was adopted by Robertson's jam and marmalade company in 1914, became a favourite nursery and advertising character. It is not just the images that can seem shocking, but the language, 'Darkie' toothbrushes, the 'Nigga' motorcycle repair

outfit, even the word Golliwogg itself. It was only in the 1950s/60s with the development of the Civil Rights movement and growing social and political awareness that attitudes, and as such the portrayals of Blacks on everyday domestic objects (and vocabulary), began to change.

However offensive some of these objects might seem today, they are a part of our culture and a physical representation of how Blacks were considered and portrayed by whites at a certain period in history. It is a measure of how times have changed that not only has much of this imagery become unacceptable (Robertson's have now abandoned their famous golly), but that these artefacts, made by and for a white audience, are now sought-after by black collectors (particularly in the USA).

A white metal anti-slavery ticket, 'Wilberforce For Ever', the reverse with 'Humanity Is The Cause Of The People', pierced for suspension, 1807, 1½in (4cm) diam.
£220–250
$320–360 ⊞ TML
British politician William Wilberforce (1759–1833) was a prominent figure in the abolition of the slave trade. Converted to evangelical Christianity, he promoted anti-slavery legislation in the House of Commons achieving his first success on 25 March 1807 with the passing of the bill to abolish the slave trade in the British West Indies. This did not, however, free those enslaved before the bill became law. Wilberforce continued to campaign for the Black cause. Thanks in part to his efforts, the Slavery Abolition Act he had promoted throughout his political life was eventually passed in 1833, one month after his death.

A manuscript proposal of the Royal African Company, responding to the House of Commons' request 'for ye better settling of trade to Africa and securing of same to this Kingdom and ye Plantations', c1709, 2°.
£900–1,100
$1,300–1,600 ⋏ DW
An important document in the history of the slave trade which accelerated considerably at this time and through the reigns of the first three Georges, leading to the establishment of the British Empire in Africa and the British Colonies in America.

A manuscript letter book, compiled by M. J. Simper, a high-status resident of Antigua, possibly a plantation owner, with detailed discussion of day-to-day conditions including sugar and rum production, trade with Britain and America, and negro slave conditions and clothing and provisions requirements, modern cloth boards, 1823–24, 4°.
£1,000–1,200
$1,500–1,700 ⋏ DW

LOCATE THE SOURCE

The source of each illustration in Miller's can be found by checking the code letters below each caption with the Key to Illustrations, pages 444–452.

A porcellaneous mug, printed with a slavery scene entitled 'Liberty Given to the Slaves', faded, c1835, 2¼in (5.5cm) high.
£80–90
$115–130 ➶ SAS

A London Anti-Slavery Convention white metal medal, by J. Davis, 1840, 2in (5cm) diam.
£220–250
$320–360 ⊞ TML

The Dandy Slave, from the *Illustrated London News,* 1861, 8 x 5½in (20.5 x 14cm).
£35–45
$50–70 ⊞ CWO

A pair of bronze figures of Moroccan boys, made in Vienna, c1890, 6in (15cm) long.
£400–450
$580–650 ➶ TWr

A pack of Golly playing cards, illustrated by and © Florence Upton for Thomas de la Rue & Co, c1900, 4 x 2¾in (10 x 7cm).
£50–55
$75–85 ⊞ HUX

Florence K. and Bertha Upton, *The Adventures of two Dutch Dolls,* first editions, original pictorial boards with cloth spines, c1895, 4°.
£170–200
$250–300 ➶ WW

A Simon & Halbig black bisque-headed doll, No. 1009, with fixed brown glass eyes, open mouth with red painted lips and nostrils and upper teeth, feathered eyebrows, dark brown wig, fully jointed composition body, wearing a pink velvet dress, underclothes, socks and leather shoes, bonnet decorated with gold coins, German, chipped, c1900, 27in (68.5cm) high.
£1,200–1,400
$1,750–2,000 ➶ Bon

A group photograph of an integrated school class, c1908.
£30–34
$45–50 ⊞ VP

> **Cross Reference**
> See Colour Review (page 71)

◄ **A photograph of a Black boy dancing Le Cake-Walk,** Paris, France, c1905.
£28–32
$40–45 ⊞ VP

A child's plate, illustrated by and © Florence Upton, 1908–18, 10in (25.5cm) diam.
£100–150
$145–225 ⊞ MURR

A Spin & Old Maid card game, by Thomas de la Rue, 1910–20, 3½ x 2in (9 x 5cm).
£35–45
$50–70 ⊞ MURR

A Christmas Greeting postcard, c1910, 5½ x 3½in (14 x 9cm).
£30–35
$40–50 ⊞ CWO

A postcard 'I'se Pining For You in Dis Pair', c1910, 5½ x 3½in (14 x 9cm).
£30–35
$40–50 ⊞ CWO

◀ **Three gramophone needle tins,** with decorated lids, c1920, largest 2in (5cm) wide.
£40–80
$65–115 ⊞ HUX

A Robertson's Golly Golden Shred Recipes book, c1928, 8 x 5in (20.5 x 12.5cm).
£25–35
$40–50 ⊞ MURR

An All-Blacks Pure Mint sweet tin, c1930, 5in (12.5cm) high.
£140–180
$200–250 ⊞ HUX

A Diase tin, 'Le meilleure essence pour le moteur humain', French, c1930, 4½in (11.5cm) high.
£30–35
$40–50 ⊞ HUX

A Negri Vert Brillant De Chrome tin, c1930, 4in (10cm) high.
£22–26
$30–35 ⊞ HUX

◀ **A 'Nigga' Motor Cycle Repair Outfit,** c1930, 4in (10cm) wide.
£40–45
$60–70 ⊞ HUX

▶ **Four 'Darkie' De Luxe tooth-brushes,** c1930, 6¼in (16cm) long.
£10–12
$15–20 each ⊞ HUX

A collection of Norah Wellings dolls, with brown velour doll in striped trousers, various smaller dolls, two dressed as Islanders in grass skirts, with a plush cat with green glass eyes, 1930s, largest 19¼in (49cm) high.
£550–650
$800–1,000 ⚲ DN

An autographed photograph of Lena Horne, by W. T. Gray, the first black woman vocalist to be featured with a white band, American, c1940.
£45–55
$65–80 ⊞ VP

A Rhum Georgetta enamel thermometer, 1940s, 11½in (29cm) high.
£32–35
$45–50 ⊞ HUX

A Combex rubberized doll, 1940–50, 6in (15cm) high.
£30–35
$45–50 ⊞ RUSS

A postcard, 'I can spare you this little lump of coal–keep it dark!', 1948, 5½ x 3½in (14 x 9cm)
£25–28
$35–45 ⊞ CWO

A pair of Murano glass novelty candlesticks, 1940–50, 24in (61cm) high.
£275–325
$400–480 ⚲ Bon(C)

A WWII photograph of a black sailor, c1944.
£30–35
$45–50 ⊞ VP

A Zulu Lulu plastic cocktails sticks card, 1950s, 9 x 11in (23 x 28cm).
£40–45
$60–70 ⊞ SpM

A Merrythought cloth Golly, with painted button eyes and red felt mouth, c1960, 17in (43cm) high.
£100–120
$145–175 ⚲ Bon

▶ **A Banania key ring,** c1965, 1½in (4cm) long.
£3–4
$4–8 ⊞ HUX

A Training School for Communists group photograph, including Martin Luther King and Miles Horton, Belmont Massachusetts, c1960.
£25–30
$35–40 ⊞ VP

Books

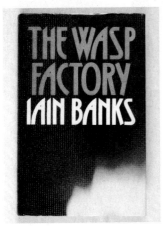

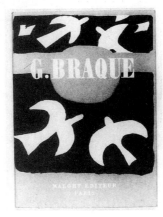

Benjamin Britten, *Tribute to Benjamin Britten on his Fiftieth Birthday*, first limited edition, signed by Benjamin Britten, published by Faber & Faber, 1966, 9 x 6in (23 x 15cm).
£85–95
$125–145 ⊞ SDP

Iain Banks, *The Wasp Factory*, first edition, 1984, 8¾ x 5¾in (22 x 14.5cm).
£120–140
$170–200 ⊞ BIB

Georges Braque, *Cahier de Georges Braque 1917–1947*, edited by Maeght Editeur, Paris, with dust jacket, c1947, 4°.
£50–60
$70–90 ↗ DW

▶ **Elizabeth Barrett Browning,** *Mrs. Browning*, poetical works, published by Nimmo Hay & Mitchell, Edinburgh, c1880, 8 x 5in (20.5 x 12.5cm).
£12–18
$15–20 ⊞ AnS

John Buchan, *Mr Standfast*, first edition, published by Hodder & Stoughton, 1919, 7½ x 5in (19 x 12.5cm).
£65–75
$95–115 ⊞ BAY

Agatha Christie, *Murder is Easy*, first edition, original dust jacket, loss to spine, 1939.
£800–1,000
$1,150–1,500 ↗ DW

◀ **Jean Cocteau,** *Le Secret Professionnel Suivi Des Monologues De l'Oiseleur*, first illustrated edition, published by Au Sans Pareil, Paris, 1925, 4°.
£900–1,100
$1,300–1,600 ↗ S

DAVID ALDOUS-COOK
for
REFERENCE BOOKS
on
ANTIQUES & COLLECTABLES
PO Box 413
Sutton, Surrey,
SM3 8SZ
Telephone/Fax
020-8642-4842

Lindsey Davis, *The Silver Pigs, A Novel,* signed presentation copy of author's first book, published by Sidgwick & Jackson, 1989, 9½ x 6½in (24 x 16.5cm).
£650–700
$900–1,000 ⊞ BIB
Copies of Lindsey Davis's first novel are scarce, hence the value of this signed presentation copy.

I. E. A. Dolby, *The Journal of the Household Brigade,* published by W. Clowes & Sons, 1879, 10 x 8in (25.5 x 20.5cm).
£40–45
$60–70 ⊞ BAY

Colin Dexter, *The Dead of Jericho,* first edition, published by Macmillan, 1981, 8 x 5¼in (20.5 x 13.5cm).
£410–460
$600–650 ⊞ BIB

Charles Dickens, *David Copperfield,* illustrated by H. K. Browne, first edition, published by Bradbury & Evans, 1850, 9 x 6in (23 x 15cm).
£450–500
$650–720 ⊞ BAY

◄ **Arthur Conan Doyle,** *The Vital Message,* author's presentation copy, inscribed 'To Lady Glenconnor with kind remembrance from a co-worker Arthur Conan Doyle', with four black and white plates, published by Hodder & Stoughton, 1919, 8°.
£320–360
$470–520 ↗ DW

► **Arthur Conan Doyle,** *The Firm of Girdlestone,* first edition, published by Chatto & Windus, 1890, 8 x 6in (20.5 x 15cm).
£100–125
$145–175 ⊞ BAY

Sebastian Faulks, *A Trick of the Light,* first edition, published by The Bodley Head, 1984, 8¾ x 5¾in (22 x 14.5cm).
£450–500
$650–750 ⊞ BIB

Ian Fleming, *Dr No,* first edition, 1958, 8 x 5½in (20.5 x 14cm).
£450–500
$650–720 ⊞ BIB

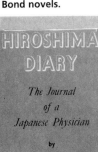

◀ **Ian Fleming,** *Goldfinger*, first edition, dust jacket designed by Richard Chopping, published by Jonathan Cape, worn, stained, 1959, 8°.
£4,400–4,800
$6,500–7,000 ⚐ **DW**
Author's signed presentation copy inscribed to the front endpaper 'To Lionel, something more to read! From Ian'. This copy was given to his friend and employer Lionel Berry Viscount Kemsley, owner of Kemsley Newspapers, which included *The Sunday Times,* **for which Fleming worked as Foreign Manager. The position particularly suited him as he was allowed prolonged periods of absence in order to write his Bond novels.**

Sue Grafton, *O is for Outlaw, The New Kinsey Millhone Mystery*, first edition, published by Macmillan, 1999, 9½ x 6½in (24 x 16.5cm).
£170–190
$250–280 ⊞ **BIB**

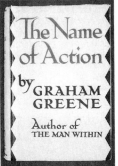

◀ **Michihiko Hachiya,** *Hiroshima Diary, The Journal of a Japanese Physician*, published by Gollancz, 1955, 8¾ x 5¾in (22 x 14.5cm).
£20–25
$30–40 ⊞ **BIB**

Graham Greene, *The Name of Action*, first edition, published by Heinemann, dust jacket slightly worn, 1930, 8°.
£1,900–2,100
$2,700–3,000 ⚐ **DW**

Graham Greene, *Stamboul Train*, first edition, published by Heinemann, dust jacket worn, 1932, 8°.
£400–450
$580–650 ⚐ **DW**

Cross Reference
See Colour Review
(page 72–74)

Nick Hornby, *Fever Pitch, A Fan's Life*, first edition, 1992, 8¾ x 5¾in (22 x 14.5cm).
£250–275
$350–400 ⊞ **BIB**

Ernest Hemingway, *A Farewell to Arms*, first English edition, published by Jonathan Cape, rebound in leather by Bayntun, 1929, 7½ x 5in (19 x 12.5cm).
£320–360
$470–570 ⊞ **BAY**

Georges Hugnet, *Pablo Picasso,* with six etchings by Pablo Picasso, first edition, one of 200 copies, binding signed by Pierre Lucien Martin, 1961, original wrappers, 1941, 12°.
£700–800
$1,000–1,150 🪶 S
Picasso produced six illuminations in wash which surround the four parts of the poem. The images were then reworked by him in etching and printed. He drew three female cubist heads for the work and a large female figure, the interior of which contained Hugnet's surrealist text.

Jerome K. Jerome, *My Life and Times,* first edition, author's presentation copy inscribed 'To Carl Hentschel from his affectionate friend Jerome K. Jerome, 16.9.26', with cigarette card portrait of author, 1926, 8°.
£230–260
$330–380 🪶 DW
Carl Hentschel was the original model for Harris, one of the *Three Men in a Boat.*

Edward Lear, *Journals of a Landscape Painter in Southern Calabria,* first edition, with 20 tinted litho plates and two maps, in later cloth gilt binding, 1852, 8°.
£400–500
$580–720 🪶 DW

▶ **Rev F. O. Morris,** *A History of British Birds,* second edition, in six volumes, with 355 hand-coloured engraved plates, 1870, 8°.
£5,000–5,500
$7,250–8,000 🪶 DW

Henry Mayhew, *London Labour and the London Poor; a Cyclopaedia of the Condition and Earnings of Those That Will Work, Those That Cannot Work, and Those That Will Not Work,* published by Griffin, Bohn & Co, in four volumes, with wood engravings, 1861–62, 8°.
£750–800
$1,100–1,200 🪶 DW

A. A. Milne, *The Red House Mystery,* first edition, signed by the author, dust jacket, 1922, 8°.
£2,200–2,400
$3,200–3,500 🪶 BBA
This is Milne's first piece of detective fiction, written for his father, to whom it is dedicated.

Patrick O'Brian, *The Thirteen Gun Salute,* first edition, published by Collins, 1989, 9 x 5½in (23 x 14cm).
£140–180
$200–250 🪶 AHa

William Morris, *The Defence of Guenevere and other poems by William Morris,* illustrated by Jessie M. King, black and white plates, Kelmscott Press, 1904, 8°.
£300–350
$450–500 🪶 DW

◀ **Iain Pears,** *The Raphael Affair,* published by Gollancz, 1990, 8 x 5½in (20.5 x 14cm).
£250–300
$360–440 ⊞ BIB

▶ **Ellis Peters,** *Saint Peter's Fair, The Fourth Chronicle of Brother Cadfael,* first edition, 1981, 8 x 5in (20.5 x 12.5cm).
£250–300
$360–440 ⊞ BIB

Pigot & Co, *British Atlas,* part three only, 18 hand-coloured engraved maps, c1830s, oblong 2°.
£420–450
$620–650 ➹ DW

Terry Pratchett, *The Colour of Magic,* first edition, signed by Colin Smythe, boxed, 1983, 8 x 6in (20.5 x 15cm).
£6,000–6,500
$8,700–9,400 ⊞ BIB

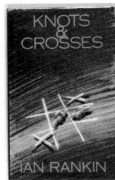

Ian Rankin, *Knots & Crosses,* first edition, signed, 1987, 8¾ x 5¾in (22 x 14.5cm).
£1,250–1,500
$1,800–2,200 ⊞ BIB

Herbert Read, *Unit One, The Modern Movement in English Architecture, Painting and Sculpture,* first edition, dust jacket, 1934, large 8°.
£120–150
$175–225 ➹ DW

Further reading

Miller's Antiques Price Guide,
Miller's Publications, 2002

▶ **Henry M. Stanley,** *In Darkest Africa,* third edition, two volumes, published by Samson Low, 1890, 9 x 6in (23 x 15cm).
£350–400
$500–600 ⊞ BAY

William Shakespeare, *Twelfth Night or What You Will,* illustrated by W. Heath Robinson, published by Hodder & Stoughton, 1908, 10 x 8in (25.5 x 20.5cm).
£125–150
$180–220 ⊞ BAY

P. F. Warner (ed), *British Sports and Sportsmen, Cricket and Football,* limited edition, No. 572 of 1,000, with plates and illustrations, c1933, 14½ x 10½in (37 x 26.5cm).
£100–150
$145–225 ➹ RTo

◀ **Ellen Terry,** *The Story of My Life,* first edition, signed by author, published by Hutchinson, 1912, 8 x 6in (20.5 x 15cm).
£40–50
$60–80 ⊞ SDP

Children's Books

Richard Adams, *Watership Down*, first edition, author's signature inserted, with folding map, Published by Rex Collings, dust jacket, 1972, 8°.
£1,500–1,800
$2,200–2,600 🔨 BBA

Aesop's Fables, illustrated by Arthur Rackham, first edition, published by William Heinemann, with 13 colour plates, 1912, 8 x 6in (20.5 x 15cm).
£130–160
$200–230 ⊞ BAY

Aesop's Fables, illustrated in colour by Edward Detmold, first trade edition, published by Hodder & Stoughton, 1915, 11 x 9in (28 x 23cm), with box.
£325–375
$460–560 ⊞ BAY

Hans Anderson, *Fairy Tales and Legends*, illustrated by Rex Whistler, first edition, published by Cobden Sanderson, 1935, 8 x 6in (20.5 x 15cm).
£40–50
$60–80 ⊞ BAY

◀ **Enid Blyton,** *A Prize for Mary Mouse*, published by The Brockhampton Press, 1950s, 3 x 6in (7.5 x 15cm).
£10–12
$15–20 ⊞ OCB

Cicely Mary Barker, *The Lord of the Rushie River*, published by Blackie & Son, c1940, 6 x 4in (15 x 10cm).
£40–45
$60–70 ⊞ J&J

◀ **Enid Blyton,** *Noddy's Own Nursery Rhymes*, first edition, 1958, 10 x 9in (25.5 x 23cm).
£85–95
$125–145 ⊞ BIB

Insurance values

Always insure your valuable collectables for the cost of replacing them with similar items, regardless of the original price paid. Both dealers and auctioneers can provide a valuation service for a fee.

◀ **Harmsen van der Beek,** a full page illustration from *Noddy Meets Father Christmas*, by Enid Blyton, 1953–54, 6½ x 4¾in (16.5 x 12cm).
£3,000–3,300
$4,400–4,800 ⊞ BRG
Noddy was created in 1949 by Enid Blyton who described the character in words and Harmsen van der Beek who visualized him. Noddy was instantly successful and 24 books were published. Beek died in 1953 and Enid Blyton in 1968 but new books, records and videos are still being published worldwide every year. Other artists have illustrated Noddy since Beek, but all follow his original visualization. With sales in excess of 200 million books worldwide in 20 languages, Noddy books are still on the Top Ten list in countries as diverse as Australia and Japan. Noddy translates into Oui Oui (France), Doddi (Iceland) and Hilitos (Spain). The current value of Noddy merchandising is in excess of £35 million (US$50 million) annually and there is considerable interest in period Noddy material.

A Bookano stories pop-up book, 1930s, worn, 8 x 7in (20.5 x 18cm).
£20–30
$30–50 ⊞ A&J

Walt Disney's Version of Pinocchio, published by Collins, 1940, 11 x 9in (28 x 23cm).
£60–70
$90–100 ⊞ SDP

Rev Charles Lutwidge Dodgson (Lewis Carroll), *The Hunting of the Snark,* illustrated by Henry Holiday, first edition, published by Macmillan, 1876, slim 8°.
£550–600
$800–900 ⚒ DW

◀ **Kenneth Grahame,** *The Wind in the Willows,* illustrated by Arthur Rackham, first trade edition, published by The Heritage Press, 1940, 10 x 7in (25.5 x 18cm).
£350–400
$500–600 ⊞ BIB

▶ **Joan Hickson,** original artwork for *Postman Pat,* comprising a double page spread of eleven paintings, 1970s, 15 x 11in (38 x 28cm).
£300–345
$450–500 ⊞ BRG

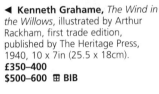

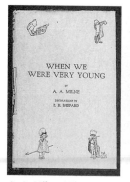

A. A. Milne, *When We Were Very Young*, illustrated by E. H. Shepard, first edition, published by Methuen & Co, 1924, 8°.
£4,400–4,800
$6,500–7,000 ⚒ BBA
With this book is a dust jacket for the second edition.

◀ **A. A. Milne**, *The House at Pooh Corner*, illustrated by E. H. Shepard, first edition, published by Methuen & Co, 1928, 8 x 5in (20.5 x 12.5cm).
£500–550
$720–800 ⊞ BIB

A. A. Milne, *The Pooh Calendar*, designed by A. E. Taylor, illustrated by E. H. Shepard, published by Methuen & Co, 1930, 4°, and *The Christopher Robin Calendar*, 1929.
£700–800
$1,000–1,200 ⚒ BBA

A. A. Milne, *Winnie-the-Pooh* and *The House at Pooh Corner*, Russian text by Boris Zakhoder, illustrated by B. Diodorov and G. Kalinovskiy, dust jacket, New York 1967, 8°.
£225–275
$320–400 ⚒ BBA
The dust jacket reads 'Winnie-the-Pooh has become a Russian bear. His name has been changed to Vinni-Pukh, and he converses in the Russian language as if he had spent his entire life on the banks of the Volga.'

Frank Richards, *Lord Billy Bunter*, first edition, published by Cassell, 1956, 7 x 5in (18 x 12.5cm).
£40–50
$60–80 ⊞ BIB

◀ **Jonathan Swift**, *Gulliver's Travels*, illustrated by Arthur Rackham, first edition, published by Dent, 1909, 9 x 7in (23 x 18cm).
£130–150
$200–220 ⊞ BAY

Louis Wain, *Daddy Cat*, published by Blackie & Son, 1914, slim 8°.
£350–400
$500–600 ⚒ DW

Cookbooks

Grandma's Old Fashioned Molasses Recipes, published by Boston Molasses Co, 1930, 7¼ x 5¼in (18.5 x 13.5cm).
£7–10
$10–15 ⊞ MSB

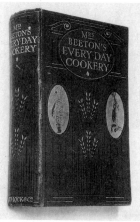

Proven Recipes Showing the uses of the Three Great Products from Corn, published by the Corn Products Refining Co, c1925, 6½ x 5½in (16.5 x 14cm).
£12–15
$15–20 ⊞ MSB

◀ **Mrs Beeton's Every-Day Cookery,** published by Ward Lock & Co, 1909, 8 x 6in (20.5 x 15cm).
£30–35
$40–50 ⊞ SMI

Hannah Glasse, *The Art of Cookery made Plain and Easy,* fifth edition, Dublin, 1791, 7 x 4½in (18 x 11.5cm).
£400–450
$580–650 ⊞ OPB

Janet McKenzie Hill, *The Up-To-Date Waitress,* 1923, 7½ x 5¼in (19 x 13.5cm).
£16–18
$20–30 🪓 MSB

William Kitchiner, *The Cook's Oracle,* first American edition, published by Munroe & Francis, 1822, 7¼ x 4¾in (18.5 x 12cm).
£450–520
$650–750 🪓 OPB
Ex-Peter Stern Collection.

Marjorie Kinnan Rawlings, *Cross Creek Cookery,* 1942, 8½ x 5¾in (21.5 x 14.5cm).
£60–70
$90–100 ⊞ MSB

> **Miller's is a price GUIDE not a price LIST**

New American Book of Cookery, and Housekeeper's Assistant, published by B. Skinner, 1853.
£150–180
$220–260 ⊞ OPB

Louis Eustache Ude, *The French Cook,* seventh edition, published by John Ebers, 1822, 9 x 6in (23 x 15cm).
£100–125
$145–175 ⊞ BAY

J. H. Walsh, *The English Cookery Book: uniting a good style with economy, and adapted to all persons in every clime; containing many unpublished receipts in daily use by private families,* published by G. Routledge & Co, 1859, 6½ x 3¾in (16.5 x 9.5cm).
£85–95
$125–145 ⊞ SEE

Hugo Zieman and Mrs. F. L. Gillette, *White House Cook Book,* 1911, 9¾ x 7in (25 x 18cm).
£20–25
$30–40 ⊞ MSB

Prayer Books & Bibles

The Book of Common Prayer, 1851, 6 x 4in (15 x 10cm).
£40–50
$60–80 ⊞ DHA

A late Victorian Bible, leather with tooled brass bandings, 9in (23cm) high.
£40–45
$60–80 ⊞ HO

An eastern European Bible, with celluloid pictorial cover, 1947, 5 x 3in (12.5 x 7.5cm).
£18–22
$25–35 ⊞ DP

Bottles

A Bellarmine stoneware mid-brown salt-glazed jug, with bearded mask on neck, minor chips to lip and base, 1660–70, 8½in (21.5cm) high.
£280–320
$400–450 ➤ BBR

▶ **A salt-glazed flask,** modelled as a book, 1840, 4in (10cm) high.
£320–360
$450–500 ⊞ JHo

◀ **A dark olive-green glass wine bottle,** with applied string rim, sloping neck and kick-up with base pontil, chip to rim, 1690–1700, 6in (15cm) wide.
£300–350
$450–500 ➤ BBR

A mallet-shaped opaque glass bottle, with applied string rim, c1740, 8in (20.5cm) high.
£200–240
$300–350 ⊞ CAL
Early bottles were initially sealed with oiled hemp, then with a loose-fitting cork tied on to the ridged band around the neck, known as the string rim. As such, bottles were stored standing until the late 17th century when, with the development of the corkscrew, tight-fitting corks were introduced and bottles could be stored on their sides.

Cross Reference
See Colour Review
(page 75)

▶ **An olive-amber glass Handysides bottle,** with applied lip above a short neck, the body embossed 'Handyside's Consumption Cure', 1890–1900, 10¾in (27.5cm) high.
£750–850
$1,100–1,250 ➤ BBR
This is the only recorded example of a Handyside's cure bottle in this olive-amber colour, hence its high value.

A salt-glazed flask, engraved Osland, Crown & Cannon, St John Str, Clerkenwell, the body with a moulded figure of Jim Crow, London, c1836, 10in (25.5cm) high.
£450–500
$650–720 ⊞ JHo
The character of Jim Crow was created by actor Thomas Dartmouth Rice, who became very popular in the 1830s with a song-and-dance routine called 'Jump Jim Crow', which was performed at the Surrey Theatre in 1836.

An R. H. Quine's ice-blue glass bottle, wedge shaped, with flat base, embossed 'poison' to both sides of shoulder, '4oz' to base, patent 1893, 5¾in (14.5cm) long.
£375–425
$550–620 ⚒ BBR

▶ **A cobalt-blue poison bottle,** modelled as a submarine, embossed 'Poison' across the body, with registered number to base, restored, 1900–20, 3in (7.5cm) wide.
£60–70
$90–100 ⚒ BBR

Five cobalt-blue glass poison bottles, c1900, largest 5in (12.5cm) high.
£6–7
$9–12 each ⊞ QW

◀ **A stoneware ginger beer bottle,** with wired stopper, black transfer-printed 'Ginger Beer P. Sullivan Beaconsfield', around a portrait of Cecil J. Rhodes in a foliate wreath, with entwined initials to reverse, 1900–20, 11in (28cm) high.
£120–140
$170–200 ⚒ BBR

A Boots stoneware ginger beer bottle, c1900, 7in (18cm) high.
£20–25
$30–35 ⊞ QW

A Walker's Universal Mixture clear glass hexagonal bottle, for veterinary medicine, 1920s, 7in (18cm) high.
£5–6
$8–10 ⊞ BoC

A commemorative Coronation Ale bottle, with stopper and seal, embossed 'Reading', with original label dated 'June 22 A.D. 1911', 8¼in (21cm) high.
£35–40
$50–60 ⊞ HUX

Boxes

A walnut snuff box, the central medallion depicting Frederick the Great mounted on a horse, dated 1749, 3½in (9cm) diam.
£150–175
$225–255 ⊞ MB

A burr walnut snuff box, c1800, 3½in (9cm) wide.
£130–150
$200–220 ⊞ MB

A table snuff box, with pentagon design in ebony, mahogany and tulipwood, ivory centre, c1820, 3½in (9cm) diam.
£100–120
$145–175 ⊞ MB

A engine-turned yew snuff box, c1810, 3¼in (8.5cm) diam.
£100–120
$145–175 ⊞ MB

A William IV rosewood vanity box, inlaid with mother-of-pearl, c1830, 12in (30.5cm) wide.
£500–600
$720–870 ⊞ MB

► **A brass-bound mahogany box,** with brass military-style handles and original Bramah lock, mid-19thC, 11in (28cm) wide.
£270–300
$400–440 ⊞ OTT

A burr-elm veneered campaign tea caddy, c1840, 4in (10cm) wide.
£200–220
$290–320 ⊞ MRW

A lady's Victorian burr-walnut travelling box, the vanity compartment complete with mirror to underside of lid, cut-glass bottles and jars, with silver-plated top, lift-out tray, above a drawer with writing slope, 12¼in (31cm) wide.
£650–700
$900–1,000 ↗ TRM

An oak-veneered tea caddy, with hinged lid, c1860, 7in (18cm) long.
£180–200
$260–290 ⊞ MRW

A Tunbridge ware stamp box, c1860, 2in (5cm) square.
£60–70
$90–100 ⊞ MB

A tin gloves box, c1870, 12in (30.5cm) long.
£40–45
$60–70 ⊞ TMa

► A Tartan ware
box, c1880,
2in (5cm) high.
£35–40
$50–60 ⊞ VBo

A Mauchline ware
sycamore beaker box,
with a printed illustration
of North Parade,
Eastbourne, containing a
medicine beaker, 1880,
3in (7.5cm) high.
£60–70
$90–100 ⊞ MB

A tin box, with looped
carrying handle and
strap closure, c1880,
11in (28cm) high.
£15–20
$20–30 ⊞ AL

► A tin deed
box, with
leather strap
fastening,
c1880, 16in
(40.5cm) wide.
£15–20
$20–30 ⊞ AL

◄ A Tunbridge
ware stamp
box, with
George V stamp
on lid, c1930,
1½in (4cm) high.
£65–75
$95–115 ⊞ VB

Breweriana

A silver claret label,
London, c1820,
2in (5cm) wide.
£145–165
$200–240 ⊞ CAL

An S-shaped silver decanter label, by
George Unite, 1846,
1½in (4cm) high.
£115–135
$165–195 ⊞ CAL

Five Wedgwood ceramic bin labels, Cowslip, Madeira,
Moselle and Rum stamped verso 'Wedgwood', and
No. 10 stamped verso 'Charles Farrow, London', 19thC,
5½in (14cm) wide.
£400–450
$580–650 ⚒ P(B)

A cast-iron cork press, modelled as a crocodile, late
19thC, 11½in (29cm) long.
£200–250
$300–350 ⚒ P(B)

A Dunville's Whisky enamelled pub tray,
with blue lettering on a
white ground, late 19thC,
12in (30.5cm) diam.
£80–100
$115–145 ⊞ CAL

A Brontë Yorkshire Liqueurs miniature flagon,
of French brandy and
honey, the paper label with
a shoulder portrait of
one of the Brontë sisters,
1900–30, 3in (7.5cm) high.
£20–30
$30–45 ⊞ ES

**Miller's is a price GUIDE
not a price LIST**

**A Buchanan's Black & White Whisky
advertisement figure,** modelled as
a pair of Scottish terriers, together
with a letter from James Buchanan
& Co, early 20thC, 11in (28cm) high.
£200–240
$290–350 ⚒ P(B)
**The accompanying letter confirms
that these figures were distributed
throughout the world, and the
last price paid for them, in 1939,
was 3s 9d.**

**A Royal Doulton Wm. Younger
& Co advertising ashtray,** white
with black lettering, 1920s,
6in (15cm) high.
£35–50
$50–75 ⊞ MURR

**A Johnnie Walker advertising
jug,** red and black lettering on a
white body, 1920s, 6in (15cm) high.
£40–50
$60–80 ⚒ BBR

An Old Taylor Bourbon Whiskey rubberoid advertising figure of a jockey, with yellow shirt, blue waistcoat and white jodhpurs, 1920–30, 14¾in (37.5cm) high.
£120–140
$170–200 ➤ BBR

A Sandeman ceramic advertising figure, wearing a black cloak and hat, holding a red glass, on an oblong plinth, 1930–40, 15¼in (38.5cm) high.
£55–65
$80–100 ➤ BBR

A William Lawson's Scotch Whisky rubberoid advertising figure of a bare-fisted fighter, Bob Fitzsimmon, on a plaster-filled plinth, 1920–30, 13½in (34.5cm) high.
£320–350
$450–500 ➤ BBR

A Teacher's Scotch Whisky rubberoid advertising figure of a schoolmaster, holding a diploma, 1920–40, 14½in (37cm) high.
£200–250
$300–350 ➤ BBR

▶ **An Old Grans Special Scotch Whisky advertising water jug,** c1930, 8in (20.5cm) high.
£65–95
$95–145
⊞ MURR

◀ **A Buchanan's Black & White Scotch Whisky advertising water jug,** c1930, 7in (18cm) high.
£85–130
$120–190
⊞ MURR

▶ **A Canadian Club Whisky wood and composite advertising figure,** modelled as an ice hockey player, 1940–50, 10in (25.5cm) high.
£150–200
$220–280
⊞ MURR

A Ricard Anisette ceramic water jug, light brown with blue interior, 1950s, 6½in (16.5cm) high.
£18–20
$25–30 ⊞ HUX

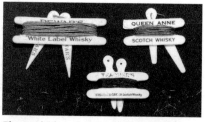

Three whisky advertising measurers, Dewar's White Label, Queen Anne Scotch Whisky, and Teacher's Highland Cream, c1950, 2in (5cm) wide.
£12–14
$17–20 ⊞ HUX

An articulated wooden bottle stopper, modelled as the head and neck of a clown, painted in red, white, black and green, c1950, 4in (10cm) high.
£18–22
$25–30 ⊞ CAL

A Clinch & Co shop display advertisement, 1950s–60s, 11 x 8in (28 x 20.5cm).
£18–20
$25–30 ⊞ MRW

A Pernod advertising water jug, c1960, 11in (28cm) high.
£10–12
$15–20 ⊞ HUX

A Noilly Prat Vermouth carafe, c1960, 7in (18cm) high.
£10–12
$15–18 ⊞ HUX

A Gaymer's Cyder plastic back-bar figure, of a town crier, wearing a magenta, red, black and white costume, c1960, 6¼in (16cm) high.
£20–25
$30–35 ⊞ HUX

> **Cross Reference**
> See Colour Review (page 76)

◀ **A bottle of 'The Macallan 25 year old Anniversary Malt' whisky,** distilled 1962, bottled 1987, with wooden crate.
£120–140
$170–200 ⚒ P(B)

A Watney's Ale Jubilee advertising figure, modelled as a porcelain dray horse in the shafts of a wooden wagon bearing three barrels, produced for the Queen's Silver Jubilee, 1977, 15in (38cm) long.
£40–45
$60–65 ⊞ Mo

A Royal Doulton Greene King Lambeth plaque, of a king wearing pale green and ermine robes, with gold orb, sceptre and crown, on a purple carpet, 1960–70, 23in (58.5cm) high.
£130–150
$190–220 ⚒ BBR

A Beswick Worthington E back-bar figure, modelled as two rugby players, 1970s, 10in (25.5cm) high.
£130–175
$200–250 ⊞ MURR

Colour Review

A Lefèvre-Utile Petit-Beurre biscuit tin, modelled as a tram, France, c1898, 11½in (29cm) long.
£800–900
$1,200–1,300 ⊞ HUX

A Fry's Chocolate miniature bagatelle game tin, c1900, 3½in (9cm) long.
£200–225
$300–330 ⊞ TMa

A C.W.S. custard powder shop counter advertising string box, c1900, 9in (23cm) high.
£180–200
$250–300 ⊞ SMI

A Sanatogen tin advertising sign, depicting Grecian figures, surface scratches and rust spotting, 1910–20, 22in (56cm) high.
£25–30
$35–45 ⚒ BBR

A Prince Albert Crimp Cut pipe and cigarette tobacco tin, 1907, 4½in (11.5cm) high.
£35–40
$50–60 ⊞ BRT

A Stolckwerk Chocolate machine, made in Germany for the French market, c1900, 6½in (16.5cm) high.
£100–120
$150–175 ⊞ HUX

▶ **A Pegrams Tartan ware tea tin,** early 20thC, 7in (18cm) long.
£25–30
$35–45 ⊞ MRW

A Marcella circular tin, 'All Ranks Smoke Marcella Cigars', some surface rusting, 1910–20, 6½in (16.5cm) high.
£18–22
$25–30 ⚒ BBR

A White Star Line Aerial Grey cigarette tin, with original paper lining/ wrapping, 1917–20, 6in (15cm) high.
£500–850
$700–1,250 ⊞ MURR

A Dennis's Pig Powders advertising tin, 1920s, 19in (48.5cm) long.
£150–175
$225–275 ⊞ JUN

A papier-mâché pig shop display, 1920s, 17in (43cm) high.
£200–250
$300–350 ⊞ SMI

A Nestor Fausta Luxe cigarette tin, 1920s, 4¼in (11cm) long.
£200–225
$300–325 ⊞ HUX

A Paysandu Ox Tongues advertising mirror, c1920, 19in (48.5cm) high.
£225–250
$325–350 ⊞ SMI

An Elmas cigarette tin, 1920s, 3½in (9cm) long.
£90–100
$130–150 ⊞ HUX

A Ruberoid Roofing enamel advertising sign, 1920, 36in (91.5cm) high.
£100–125
$140–180 ⊞ TMa

A Lyons Assorted Toffees tin, in the shape of a book, the front with a supermarine Rolls-Royce S6, details of the aeroplane to the base, 1930s, 6½in (16.5cm) high.
£140–160
$200–230 ⋏ BBR

A Camp Coffee with Chicory box, complete with unopened contents, c1940, 9in (23cm) high.
£40–50
$60–75 ⊞ MRW

A Huntley & Palmer's tin, in the shape of a Worcester vase, 1924, 10in (25.5cm) high.
£145–165
$200–250 ⊞ TMa

A Bird's Post Toasties Corn Flakes box, 1950s, 8in (20.5cm) high.
£25–30
$35–45 ⊞ YR

A Caley Double Fruit dummy chocolate bar, 1950s, 5in (12.5cm) long.
£9–10
$10–15 ⊞ HUX

◀ A Practo D.D.T. cardboard pump action container, 1950s, 6in (15cm) high.
£5–7
$8–10 ⊞ YR

▶ A Pepsodent toothpaste cardboard advertising shop display card, 1950s, 12in (30.5cm) high.
£18–20
$25–30 ⊞ MRW

A Remington Super-Sixty advertising shop display card, 1960s, 12in (30.5cm) high.
£12–15
$15–20 ⊞ MRW

A set of six French porcelain plates, depicting different ballooning events, each signed 'R. Soulier', with hand-painted title, c1840, 9in (23cm) diam.
£2,500–3,000
$3,500–4,500 ⊞ AU

'Les Dirigibles en Manoeuvre', a hand-coloured lithograph on paper, after Gamy, depicting the German military dirigibles by Parceval and Gross on manoeuvres in Cologne, printed by Mobileau, Paris, copyright 1909, 35½in (90cm) long, unframed.
£115–135
$170–200 ↗ BKS

▶ **A Bougie Du Siècle box,** decorated with a hot air balloon, 11in (28cm) high.
£9–10
$12–15 ⊞ HUX

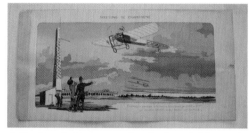

A Meeting de Champagne hand-coloured lithograph on paper, after Gamy, depicting Olieslaeger flying his Bleriot monoplane, printed by Mabileau, Paris, copyright 1910, 35½in (90cm) high, unframed.
£200–225
$300–330 ↗ BKS

A Sadler aeroplane china teapot, 1920s, 8in (20.5cm) long.
£425–465
$600–680 ⊞ JUN

▶ **A Clarnico Air Race Assortment card box,** 1920s, 10in (25.5cm) long.
£30–45
$45–65 ⊞ MURR

A gramophone needles tin, depicting an airship above sky scrapers, c1930, 2in (5cm) long.
£100–120
$145–175 ⊞ HUX

A Poole plate, depicting an airship, 1930s, 6in (15cm) diam.
£15–20
$20–30 ⊞ DCA

◀ **A bronze plaque,** commemorating a ballooning event in Germany, 1929, 4in (10cm) long.
£350–400
$500–600 ⊞ AU

An Arts and Crafts oak writing bureau, by G. Laird, Glasgow, the stained-glass double door bookcase over an open shelf, fall-front and single drawer with further open shelves below.
£300–400
$450–600 WilP

An Arts and Crafts copper kettle and stand, 14½in (37cm) high.
£250–350
$350–500 ASA

A Byzantine glass, designed by Carl George von Reichenbach for Poschmeyer, Oberwieslau, Munich, 1906, 6in (15cm) high.
£1,400–1,700
$2,000–2,500 ALiN

◄ A Charles Horner silver and enamel brooch, c1900, 2in (5cm) diam.
£180–250
$250–350 ASA

An Art Nouveau silver pendant, enamelled in shades of green, blue and pink, c1910.
£110–130
$160–190 G(B)

An Art Nouveau copper box, with embossed initials, 10in (25.5cm) long.
£115–130
$160–190 CAL

A Minton Secessionist charger, with tube-lined decoration of waterlilies, printed factory mark to base 'No 7', slight damage to rim, 1910, 15in (38cm) diam.
£800–850
$1,150–1,250 P(B)

Two French celluloid reticules, decorated with diamante and silk tassels, 1920s, 15in (38cm) long.
£150–200
$220–290 GAD

► A Fielding's Jam 42 jam pot, in the shape of a caravan, 1930s, 6in (15cm) long.
£100–175
$145–255 MURR

A Goldscheider ceramic wall mask, in the form of a lady's head, 1930s, 10in (25.5cm) high.
£500–550
$720–800 BD

A Lea Stein blue laminated plastic brooch, in the form of a lady's head, 1930–40, 2½in (6.5cm) high.
£40–45
$60–65 HT

A Mabel Lucie Attwell Swan Pen shop advertisement, 1925, 15in (38cm) high.
£180–200
$260–300 ⊞ MEM

A Mabel Lucie Attwell motto soap set, by the British Legion, 1920–30, 6in (15cm) long.
£45–50
$65–75 ⊞ MEM

A Mabel Lucie Attwell biscuit tin, c1935, 8in (20.5cm) high.
£225–250
$325–375 ⊞ HUX

A Shelley Mabel Lucie Attwell three-piece tea service, comprising toadstool teapot and cover, sugar bowl and elf milk jug, decorated in polychrome enamels, printed marks to base, 1930s, elf 6in (15cm) high.
£650–750
$950–1,150 ⋔ Pott

A Shelley Mabel Lucie Attwell Flying pattern sugar basin, 1930, 7½in (19cm) diam.
£350–400
$500–600 ⊞ BD

The Lucie Attwell Kiddy's Cutlery, spoon and pusher, c1940, in original box, 5in (12.5cm) long.
£35–45
$50–65 ⊞ MEM

A Mabel Lucie Attwell Diddums celluloid doll, 1930s, 13in (33cm) high.
£180–200
$260–290 ⊞ MEM

The Lucie Attwell Hanky House, cardboard with pull-down front revealing seven handkerchiefs and picture, marked at side, late 1930s, 6in (15cm) long.
£145–165
$200–250 ⊞ MEM

◄ **A Mabel Lucie Attwell cut-out plywood string holder,** 1930s, 6¾in (17cm) high.
£85–95
$125–140 ⊞ MEM

► *Lucie Attwell's Super Book of Fun No 3,* Dean first edition, 1969, 10 x 8in (25.5 x 20.5cm).
£50–55
$75–80 ⊞ BIB

A 15ct gold suspension medal, for the Thomas Reid Five-mile Championship, St Helen's Bicycle Club, 24th May 1882.
£570–630
$800–950 ⊞ **AU**

A Calcott Bros display poster, full-colour lithograph mounted on a W. H. Smith advertising distribution department canvas stretcher, some damage, 1890s, 30 x 50in (76 x 127cm).
£250–300
$350–450 ⚒ **P(Ba)**

A German glass stein, with metal mounts, painted with a cycling scene, 1895–1900, 10in (25.5cm) high.
£525–575
$750–850 ⊞ **AU**

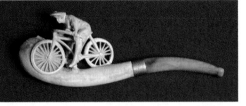

A French carved cheroot holder, surmounted by a figure of a lady cyclist, c1900, 6in (15cm) long.
£500–600
$720–870 ⊞ **AU**

A German china figure of a lady cyclist with billowing dress, the underside depicting a saucy image of her rear view, c1900, 7in (18cm) wide.
£400–450
$580–650 ⊞ **AU**

A Swift pacing bicycle, with wooden rims and leather saddle, 1910.
£750–850
$1,100–1,250 ⊞ **JUN**

A Coventry Eagle Bicycles framed card advertising sign, c1910, 32in (81.5cm) high.
£550–650
$800–950 ⊞ **JUN**

A Royal Doulton stein, depicting male and female cyclists, 1914–18, 6½in (16.5cm) high.
£580–650
$850–950 ⊞ **AU**

A Raleigh advertising card, framed, 1920s, 22 x 30in (56 x 76cm).
£300–350
$450–500 ⊞ **JUN**

A Raleigh Chopper Mark II bicycle, 1974–75.
£400–450
$580–650 ⊞ **TBoy**

A Venetian blackamoor torchère stand, 19thC, 40in (101.5cm) high.
£1,700–2,000
$2,500–3,000 ⚹ S
Ex-Ralph Richardson.

▶ **A Negronoir Café Exquis advertising sign,** c1930, 14in (35.5cm) high.
£70–75
$100–110 ⊞ HUX

A Sphinx pin, modelled as a blackamoor, 1960s, 4in (10cm) high.
£40–45
$60–65 ⊞ CRIS

A Simon & Halbig bisque-head mulatto doll, with weighted brown glass eyes, open mouth with upper teeth, dimpled chin, on a fully-jointed composition body, incised '12, S&H 1039, DEP', Germany, c1910, 25in (63.5cm) high.
£1,200–1,400
$1,750–2,000 ⚹ Bon

▶ **A Negronoir Café Exquis**

An 'I's got an idea' greetings card, c1950, 5in (12.5cm) high.
£6–7
$9–10 ⊞ CWO

▶ **A Robertson's Golden Shred plaster illuminated display figure,** 1963, 28in (71cm) high.
£850–900
$1,250–1,300 ⚹ BBR

A Lyons' Tea money box, Germany, 1925, 6in (15cm) high.
£270–300
$400–440 ⊞ HUX

A Mr Golly soft toy, by Deans Rag Book Co, 1950s, 13in (33cm) high.
£60–70
$90–100 ⊞ TAC

A Banania Tapioca tin, 1925, 7in (18cm) high.
£20–25
$30–35 ⊞ HUX

A theatre programme, for *The Black and White Minstrel Show*, 1962, 8¾in (22cm) high.
£3–4
$4–6 ⊞ HUX

A Bakelite, wood and metal card or envelope holder, modelled as Josephine Baker, 1910–30, 8in (20.5cm) high.
£130–135
$190–200 ⊞ LBe

Louis de Bernières, *The Troublesome Offspring of Cardinal Guzman,* first edition, published by Secker & Warburg, 1992, 9½ x 6½in (24 x 16.5cm).
£175–195
$250–280 ⊞ BIB

R. D. Blackmore, *Lorna Doone,* Dulverton edition, fourth edition, original decorated cloth, published by Sampson Low Marston & Co, 1920, 9 x 7in (23 x 18cm).
£40–50
$60–75 ⊞ BAY

James M. Cain, *The Postman Always Rings Twice,* first edition, original orange cloth blocked and lettered in blue, original dust jacket, published by Alfred A. Knopf, New York, 1934, 8°.
£1,400–1,500
$2,000–2,200 ↗ DW

Charles Dickens, *A Christmas Carol,* illustrated by A. C. Michael, original cloth elaborately gilt-blocked, published by Hodder & Stoughton, 1911, 10 x 8in (25.5 x 20.5cm).
£190–220
$275–325 ⊞ BAY

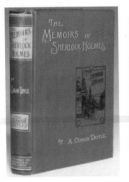

Sir Arthur Conan Doyle, *The Memoirs of Sherlock Holmes,* first edition, illustrated by Sidney Paget, original dark blue cloth, blocked and titled in black and gilt, published by George Newnes, c1894, 8°.
£3,300–3,500
$4,800–5,000 ↗ S

Ian Fleming, *Thunderball,* author's inscription on front endpaper, published by Jonathan Cape, 1961, 7¾ x 5¼in (19.5 x 13.5cm).
£4,300–4,600
$6,250–6,650 ↗ WW

Graham Greene, *It's a Battlefield,* first edition, original cloth, dust jacket designed by Youngman Carter, published by Heinemann, 1934, 8°.
£1,100–1,300
$1,600–2,000 ↗ DW
This was the first issue to show the price of 7/6 on the front flap of the dust jacket.

Shere Hite, *The Hite Report on Love, Passion and Emotional Violence,* signed by the author, published by Optima, 1987, 9½ x 6in (24 x 15cm).
£20–25
$30–35 ⊞ BIB

Sir Walter Scott, *Lady of the Lake,* with tartan cover, 19thC, 3½ x 2¼in (9 x 5.5cm).
£40–45
$60–65 ⊞ Fai

Minette Walters, *The Sculptress,* first edition, signed by the author, published by Macmillan, 1993, 8¾ x 5¾in (22 x 14.5cm).
£50–60
$75–90 ⊞ BIB

► **Oscar Wilde,** *The Picture of Dorian Gray,* first edition, illustrated by Henry Keen, original cloth decorated and titled in gilt, published by John Lane, The Bodley Head, 1925, 10 x 7in (25.5 x 18cm).
£110–120
$160–175 ⊞ BAY

Cradock, *Josephine Goes Travelling*, illustrated by Honor Appleton, undated, 10 x 8in (25.5 x 20.5cm).
£15–20
$20–30 ⊞ OCB

Cicely Mary Barker, *Flower Fairies of the Wayside*, published by Blackie & Son, 1940s, 6 x 4in (15 x 10cm).
£40–45
$60–65 ⊞ J&J

Birn Bros, *Popeye the Pirate*, first edition, illustrated, c1939, 10 x 8in (25.5 x 20.5cm).
£60–70
$90–100 ⊞ BIB

Elinor M. Brent-Dyer, *Ruey Richardson – Chaletian*, first edition, published by Chambers, 1960, 7 x 5in (18 x 13cm).
£65–75
$95–110 ⊞ OCB

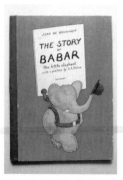

Jean de Brunhoff, *The Story of Babar the little elephant*, first UK edition, preface by A. A. Milne, published by Methuen, 1934, 14 x 10in (35.5 x 25.5cm).
£130–150
$190–220 ⊞ BIB

The Animals' Trip to Sea, first edition, coloured pictorial boards, published by Ernest Nister, c1895, 10 x 12in (25.5 x 30.5cm).
£130–145
$190–210 ⊞ BIB

Selma G. Lanes, *The Art of Maurice Sendak*, first edition, published by Abram, 1993, 11 x 12in (28 x 30.5cm).
£35–40
$50–60 ⊞ BIB

◄ **J. K. Rowling,** *Harry Potter and the Philosopher's Stone*, first edition, first issue, published by Bloomsbury, 1997, 8°.
£8,000–10,000
$11,500–14,500 ⚘ WW
Only 300 copies of this edition, bound in this way, were ever issued. They were destined for school libraries and clean copies are therefore hard to find. A further 200 proof copies were issued in white paper wrappers. Uncorrected proof copies, with slight cover variation, were also issued and are more common, and therefore less valuable, than this hardback first edition.

Robert Tyndall, an original watercolour illustration, entitled Noddy and the Bunkey, 1960, 6½ x 5in (16.5 x 12.5cm).
£1,250–1,450
$1,800–2,000 ⊞ BRG

► **Andy Pandy and Teddy Drink,** an original watercolour illustration, 1970s, 5in (12.5cm) square.
£200–225
$300–330 ⊞ BRG

An Old Tom flask,
Chesterfield, 1840,
10in (25.5cm) high.
£275–325
$400–470 ⊞ JHo

A green Hamilton bottle, embossed 'The Scarborough
Brewery Company Ltd' around 'Crystalis Waters', dolphin and
fountain trademark to centre, 1880–1900, 7in (18cm) high.
£400–450
$580–650 ⚒ BBR

A ginger beer bottle,
embossed 'The Brewery,
Henley-on-Thames',
c1900, 7in (18cm) high.
£30–35
$45–55 ⊞ QW

A blue poison bottle,
c1900, 1880–1910,
7in (18cm) high.
£10–12
$15–20 ⊞ QW

A blue poison bottle,
with remains of original
paper label, 1880–1910,
4in (10cm) high.
£6–7
$8–12 ⊞ QW

A blue bottle, embossed
'Handysides Consumption
Cure', 1890–1910,
7½in (19cm) high.
£450–500
$650–720 ⚒ BBR

▶ **A blue wasp-waist
poison bottle,** embossed
'Stephensons Patent
No. 6324', 1890–1900,
7½in (19cm) high.
£1,200–1,400
$1,700–2,000 ⚒ BBR

A green Codd bottle,
embossed 'Crocketts Ltd
Worcester', 1900–20,
8in (20.5cm) high.
£4–5
$7–10 ⊞ QW

◀ **A green Codd bottle,**
embossed 'Davies & Co,
Burton Salmon' with
salmon pictorial trademark
to front, the rear embossed
'E. Breffit & Co Ld, Makers
Castleford', 1890–1900,
7½in (19cm) high.
£170–200
$250–300 ⚒ BBR

A Shamrock Whiskey pub mirror, produced for Kirker Greer & Co, Belfast, c1900, 36 x 28in (91.5 x 71cm).
£700–800
$1,000–1,200 ⊞ HON

◀ A multicoloured framed advertisement for Hall's Wine, The Bloom of Perfect Health, slight surface marks, 1890–1900, 29 x 23in (73.5 x 58.5cm).
£450–550
$650–800 ⋟ BBR

A pair of Margrave Brothers whisky dispensers, advertising Pearl Irish Whisky and Excelsior Scottish Whisky, with etched, gilded and painted decoration and cut-glass conical covers, c1890, 21in (53cm) high with covers.
£1,750–2,100
$2,500–3,000 ⋟ P(B)

▶ An articulated wooden bottle stopper, carved and painted as a man, early 20thC, 6in (15cm) high.
£35–40
$50–60 ⊞ CAL

A Claymore whisky pottery advertising figure, made for Greenlees, 1900–20, 15½in (39.5cm) high.
£1,400–1,500
$2,000–2,200 ⋟ BBR

◀ A German pottery stein, showing firefighters at work, inscribed 'Gott sur Ehr dem nächsten zur Wehr', c1908, 16in (40.5cm) high.
£1,000–1,250
$1,500–1,800 ⊞ AU
The value of this item lies in its firefighting content.

◀ A Bénédictine paper advertising fan, France, c1910, 9in (23cm) wide.
£40–45
$60–65 ⊞ HUX

A Long John whisky advertising figure, made of composite material, 1930s, 10in (25.5cm) high.
£150–200
$220–280 ⊞ MURR

A Gitanes water jug, 1950s, 7½in (19cm) high.
£40–45
$60–65 ⊞ HUX

A Beswick Babycham advertising figure, c1955, 5in (12.5cm) high.
£45–55
$65–80 ⊞ HUX

A porcelain button, painted with a butterfly, late 18thC, 1½in (4cm) diam.
£180–210
$250–300 ⊞ TB

A steel button, with cut-steel and glass 'jewels', c1890, 1¼in (3cm) diam.
£25–35
$35–50 ⊞ EV

▶ **A selection of metal buttons,** hand-painted and transfer-painted, some with glass 'jewelled' centre, 1890–1930s, largest 1in (2.5cm) diam.
£2–12
$3–17 each ⊞ EV

▶ **A set of six pressed wood buttons,** hand-painted with metal shanks, c1930, 1¼in (3cm) diam.
£25–30
$35–45 ⊞ EV

Three plastic Disney character buttons, Mickey Mouse, Pluto and Donald Duck, c1940, ¾in (2cm) high.
£3–6
$5–8 each ⊞ TB

▶ **A set of five pink plastic buttons,** decorated with black poodles, 1950s, ½in (1cm) diam.
£4–5
$6–7 ⊞ LBe

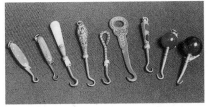

A selection of Victorian glove button-hooks, the largest 2in (5cm) long.
£5–40
$8–60 each ⊞ VB

A set of six Satsuma buttons, c1870, 1½in (4cm) diam, in original case.
£430–460
$600–660 ⊞ JBB

An ivory button, painted with a finely-detailed miniature of a bird in a river landscape, under bevelled glass, set in a silver mount, mid-19thC, 1in (2.5cm) wide.
£210–275
$300–400 ⊞ TB

A Liberty & Co silver and enamel button, hallmarked L. & Co, Cymric, 1900–10, 1in (2.5cm) diam.
£100–120
$145–175 ⊞ TB

An Ault art pottery wryneck vase, designed by Dr Christopher Dresser, c1880, 10in (25.5cm) high.
£600–650
$850–950 ⊞ HUN

A Bargeware or Measham Ware teapot, the domed lid topped with a traditional small teapot, inscribed and dated 1914, 12in (30.5cm) high.
£300–400
$450–580 ⊞ JBL

◄ **A Bassano Scottish bagpiper,** Italy, 1950s, 11in (28cm) high.
£200–250
$300–350 ⊞ LBe

A Beswick model of Winnie the Pooh, designed by Albert Hallam, issued 1968–90, 2½in (6.5cm) high.
£45–50
$65–75 ⋗ BBR

A Don Pottery blue and white plate, 1820–34, 8in (20.5cm) diam.
£140–160
$200–250 ⊞ CAL

A Staffordshire blue and white meat platter, decorated with Wild Rose pattern, 19thC, 15in (38cm) wide.
£85–95
$125–145 ⊞ MCC

A Bonzo water jug, German, c1930, 6½in (16.5cm) high.
£175–200
$250–300 ⊞ HUX

► **A Burmantofts faïence jardinière-on-stand,** impressed marks, Nos. 2053/4, c1890, 40¼in (102cm) high.
£900–1,000
$1,300–1,500 ⋗ AH

A Bovey Tracey Devon ware Toby jug, c1950, 10in (25.5cm) high.
£300–360
$450–500 ⊞ DHA

A Bo'ness glazed and hand-painted bowl, with fluted rim, 1830–40, 9½in (24cm) diam.
£40–50
$60–80 ⊞ JEB

► **A Charles Brannam Liberty stoneware vase,** with three wrythen handles, the interior with a brown glaze, impressed marks, c1900, 11¾in (30cm) high.
£200–225
$300–330 ⋗ BLH

A Burleigh Ware coffee cup and saucer, decorated with Sunray pattern, 1930s, cup 2½in (6.5cm) high.
£40–50
$60–80 ⊞ BUR

A Burleigh Ware Budgie jug, 1930s, 8in (20.5cm) high.
£300–350
$450–500 ⊞ BD

A Carlton Ware charger, decorated with Blue Oak pattern, 1930s, 13in (33cm) diam.
£230–260
$330–380 ⊞ StC

◄ **A Carlton Ware canister,** marked 'Made in England' 1930s, 6in (15cm) high.
£85–95
$125–145 ⊞ LBe

► **A Carlton Ware Rouge Royale dish,** hand-painted in Wild Duck pattern, 1950s, 7in (18cm) wide.
£140–160
$200–240 ⊞ HO

A Derek Clarke studio pottery vase, with blue crystaline effect decoration, 1990s, 5½in (14cm) high.
£350–375
$500–550 ⊞ PGA

A Clarice Cliff Conical sugar shaker, decorated with Nasturtium pattern, c1930, 6in (15cm) high.
£500–600
$720–870 ⊞ BD

A Clarice Cliff Athens jug, decorated with Mondrian pattern, 1930s, 7½in (19cm) high.
£1,300–1,500
$1,900–2,200 ⊞ BD

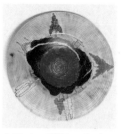

A Clarice Cliff Inspiration charger, decorated with Caprice pattern, c1930, 18in (45.5cm) diam.
£3,700–4,000
$5,500–5,800 ⊞ BD

A pair of Clarice Cliff plates, decorated with Fragrance pattern, rim chips, 1930s, 9in (23cm) diam.
£120–150
$175–225 🔨 G(B)

A Clarice Cliff Conical sugar shaker, decorated with Orange Erin pattern, c1930, 6in (15cm) high.
£2,750–3,000
$4,000–4,500 ⊞ BD

A Clarice Cliff Bon Jour shape sugar shaker, decorated with Blue Crocus pattern, c1930, 5in (12.5cm) high.
£800–900
$1,150–1,300 ⊞ BD

◄ **A Clarice Cliff coffee cup and saucer,** decorated with Gayday pattern, c1930, cup 2½in (6.5cm) high.
£170–200
$250–300 ⊞ BD

A Clarice Cliff Wilkinson's bowl, decorated with Crocus pattern, printed mark, 1930s, 3½in (9cm) diam.
£110–130
$160–190 🔨 G(B)

A Crown Devon musical jug, decorated with Daisy Daisy pattern, 1920s, 8in (20.5cm) high.
£300–325
$440–480 ⊞ AU

▶ **A Susie Cooper Paris shape jug,** decorated with Nursery pattern, 1930s, 4in (10cm) high.
£450–500
$650–720 ⊞ BD

Butlin's

Sir William Heygate Edmund Colborne ('Billy') Butlin (1900–80) opened the first Butlin's at Skegness in 1936. Holiday camps had existed in Britain for 30 years, but it was Butlin who turned them into a mass attraction. 'All the jollity and comradeship of a camping holiday plus all the amenities of the first-class hotel' boasted the first advertisements, which promised cosy Elizabethan chalets, sport, concert parties and four good meals a day for £2 5s a week – 'a week's holiday for a week's pay'. More sites soon opened, and after WWII (when they were rented to the armed forces), Butlin's holiday camps boomed. Entertainment was provided by the famous Redcoats whose cry of 'Wakey Wakey' became a national catchphrase. Because of licensing laws, all campers had to wear a badge.

New patterns were introduced each season, different designs were produced for every camp, for specific events and clubs, and for all categories of staff. All in all, thousands of badges were manufactured which are collectable today, along with other Butlin's memorabilia.

A Butlin's jigsaw, red and blue on a yellow ground, 1960s, 9½ x 12in (24 x 30.5cm), in original box.
£12–15
$16–20 ⊞ HUX

A Butlin's Xmas 1962 glass mug, with red lettering, 3in (7.5cm) high.
£5–6
$7–9 ⊞ HUX

A Butlin's soft-centre sweets tin, 1960s, 5½in (14cm) high.
£8–9
$10–12 ⊞ HUX

► A Butlin's Holiday Worlds ashtray, 1960s, 5½in square.
£4–6
$6–9 ⚒ FLD

A Butlin's Skegness badge, in red, blue and yellow, 1965, 1in (2.5cm) high.
£3–5
$4–7 ⊞ HUX

A Butlin's advertising mirror, 1960s, 3 x 2½in (7.5 x 6.5cm).
£3–5
$4–7 ⊞ HUX

◄ A Butlin's Beaver Club badge, in red, white and blue, 1960s, 2in (5cm) diam.
£2–4
$3–4 ⊞ HUX

Buttons

Eleven Victorian silver lustre glass buttons, with four- and two-hole metal shanks, largest 1in (2.5cm) diam.
£6–9
$10–15 each ⊞ EV
These silver glass buttons are often confused with cut-steel buttons. If unsure when buying, use a magnet.

A glazed ceramic button, with transfer-printed design of a mythological head wearing a helmet depicting a bird, set in a darkened brass border, mid-19thC, 1¼in (3cm) diam.
£60–100
$85–150 ⊞ TB

Nine pearl buttons, one hand-painted, c1850–1960, largest 2in (5cm) high.
£6–8
$8–12 each ⊞ EV

Two gilded copper and silver-plated sporting buttons, depicting boars within a belt, French, 19thC, 1in (2.5cm) diam.
£25–35
$40–50 ⊞ TB

A set of four Victorian black glass buttons, with four-hole metal shanks, 1in (5cm) diam.
£24–30
$35–45 ⊞ EV
These black glass buttons, popular in the Victorian period and used for mourning wear, are sometimes mistaken for jet. The fossilized wood, however, was very rarely used for buttons, as it was too fragile and prone to chipping. Black glass such as this is also referred to as French jet.

A Victorian brass button, depicting St George and the Dragon, c1860, 1½in (4cm) diam.
£10–15
$15–20 ⊞ EV

▶ **A brass and wood button,** the stamped brass moon and falling star applied to a wood background, French, 1880–90, 1¼in (3cm) diam.
£30–35
$45–50 ⊞ TB

A set of six dyed horn buttons, 19thC, ½in (1cm) diam.
£3–5
$5–8 ⊞ EV

A set of six .925 silver butterfly buttons, French, c1880, in red leather case.
£110–120
$160–175 ⊞ JBB

A set of nine buttons, bearing the lithographed portraits of famous French ladies, mounted under celluloid, marked Paris, c1890, ½in (1cm) diam, in a shaped box.
£110–130
$160–190 ⊞ JBB

A stamped brass button,
depicting the arrival of Lohengrin, 1890–1900, 1½in (4cm) diam.
£10–15
$15–20 ⊞ TB

A set of five Ruskin glazed earthenware buttons, c1880, ½in (1cm) diam.
£40–50
$60–75 ⊞ SLL

Ten pearl-backed buttons, Austrian, c1890–1920, largest ½in (1cm) diam.
£2–3
$3–5 each ⊞ EV

◄ **An Art Nouveau silver button,** in the form of a female head with flowing hair, hallmarked, c1901, 1½in (4cm) diam.
£40–50
$60–75 ⊞ TB

A set of six tin-backed brass buttons, each depicting an open car, 1920–30, 2in (5cm) diam.
£25–40
$35–60 ⊞ JBB

A set of six ivory buttons, modelled as prowling lions, Tanzanian, 1920–30, 1in (2.5cm) long.
£10–12
$15–18 each ⊞ JBB

A set of six Art Deco plastic buttons and a matching buckle, in red, grey and silver, the buttons with self-shanks, centre fastening, 1in (2.5cm) diam.
£40–45
$60–65 ⊞ EV

A set of six Art Deco buttons, in deep pink celluloid with silvery metal overlay, ½in (1cm) diam.
£18–24
$25–35 ⊞ EV

A Bimini glass and metal button, 1940–50, 2in (5cm) diam.
£10–12
$15–18 ⊞ JBB

Cameras

A mahogany and brass magic lantern, professionally converted to electrical operation, complete with chimney and slide carrier, c1895, 19¾in (50cm) long.
£250–300
$360–440 ⊞ APC

An Otto Berning & Co Dusseldorf Robot Star 25 camera, with spring motor, capable of 25 exposures, 1969, 4¼in (11cm) wide.
£150–175
$220–255 ⊞ HEG

A Coronet Midget Bakelite novelty camera, in red, c1935, 2½in (6.5cm) high, in black stud-fastening case.
£60–80
$90–115 ⊞ HEG
This novelty camera was made in five different colours, and prices vary according to colour.
Black £50–60 ($75–90).
Brown and red £60–80 ($90–115).
Green £100–130 ($145–190).
Blue £120–180 ($175–260).

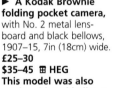

◀ **An Expo pocket watch camera,** in silver-coloured base metal, the winding knob forming the lens cap, 1905–35, 2¼in (5.5cm) diam.
£120–140
$175–200 ⊞ HEG

▶ **A Kodak Brownie folding pocket camera,** with No. 2 metal lens-board and black bellows, 1907–15, 7in (18cm) wide.
£25–30
$35–45 ⊞ HEG
This model was also made with red bellows, valued at £30–35 ($45–50).

A Hasselblad 500C camera, 1985, 8in (20.5cm) long.
£850–950
$1,250–1,400 ⊞ VCL

An Eastman Kodak Jiffy Kodak V.P. camera, made in the US, 1930, 6in (15cm) wide, in original cardboard box.
£40–50
$60–75 ⊞ HUX

Three Kodak Brownie box cameras, a Six-20 Model D, a Flash II and a Flash IV, 1950s, 4in (10cm) high.
£5–10
$8–15 each ⊞ VCL

A Kodak Signet 35 compact 35mm camera, with Ektor lens and Synchro 300 shutter, 1951–58, 4in (10cm) wide.
£70–80
$100–115 ⊞ HEG

An Ernst Leitz Leica M3 camera, chrome-finished, with Elmar f1.8 5cm lens, c1955, 5¾in (14.5cm) wide.
£500–700
$720–1,000 ⊞ VCL

A Kodak 930 Kodamatic Instant Camera, 1975, 6½in (16.5cm) wide, in original box.
£8–10
$12–15 ⊞ VCL

A Jaeger le Coultre Compass camera, with stereoscopic head, complete with accessories, Swiss, c1938, 3in (7.5cm) high.
£1,000–1,200
$1,500–1,750 ⬈ RBB

◀ **A Minolta 16 sub-miniature 16mm cassette-loading camera,** silver, 1957–60, 3in (7.5cm) wide.
£25–35
$35–50 ⊞ HEG
Minolta produced this camera in six different colours: black, chrome, blue, green, red and gold. Prices vary according to colour from £25–90 ($35–130).

A Paillard Bolex H16 16mm cine camera, with triple lens turret, Switar lenses, filters, instructions, and original receipts, 9¾in (25cm) high, in original carrying case.
£250–300
$350–450 ⊞ APC

▶ **A Polaroid SX-70 folding Land camera,** with auto-focus, c1970, 7in (18cm) wide.
£30–40
$45–60 ⊞ VCL

A Carl Zeiss Jena Rolleicord Art Deco-style camera, Germany, c1934, 8½in (21.5cm) high.
£150–200
$225–280 ⊞ VCL

A Carl Zeiss Jena Rolleiflex camera, with Tessar f3.5 75mm lens, for 120 roll film, 1932–38, 8in (20.5cm) high.
£70–80
$100–115 ⊞ HEG

A Carl Zeiss Jena Rolleiflex SLX camera, with Planar lens, c1980, 5½in (14cm) high.
£220–250
$320–360 ⊞ VCL

▶ **A Sanderson hand-and-stand camera,** with polished wood interior and leather exterior, c1900–20, 6½in (16.5cm).
£180–200
$260–300 ⊞ HEG

A Tessina 16mm sub-miniature camera, Swiss, c1960, 2½in (6.5cm) wide.
£300–400
$440–580 ⊞ VCL

A Universal Camera Corporation Univex AF Deluxe Folding Camera, with bellows, for 00 film, in green cast metal, 1935–39, 4in (10cm) high, in original box.
£30–35
$45–50 ⊞ HEG
This model was produced in various colours.

A Carl Zeiss Jena Rolleiflex SL66 camera, single lens reflex, c1975, 7in (18cm) long.
£500–600
$720–850 ⊞ VCL

A W. Watson & Sons quarter-plate field camera outfit, in mahogany and brass, with Waterhouse stops and photographic plates, camera and lens marked, c1895, in manufacturer's original leather case.
£250–350
$375–500 ⊞ APC

▶ **A Zorki 2C Leica copy camera,** with green body, Russian, 1955–60, 5½in (14cm) wide, in original leather case.
£80–100
$115–145 ⊞ HEG
This example is green, but the Zorki 2C was also made in black, valued at £40–60 ($60–80) and grey, valued at £80–100 ($115–145).

A Carl Zeiss Jena Rolleiflex Sl35E camera, with Planar f1.8/80 lens, c1980, 6in (15cm) wide.
£125–150
$180–220 ⊞ VCL

A Tasco binocular camera, 110 film cassette, c1975, 5in (12.5cm) deep.
£40–45
$60–65 ⊞ VCL

A Zeiss Super Iconta C camera, with 105mm f3.5 Tessar lens, 120 roll film, 1950–55, 6in (15cm) wide.
£160–180
$230–260 ⊞ HEG

Ceramics
Animals

A porcelain model of a sitting dog, 1830–40, 2in (5cm) high.
£90–110
$130–160 ⊞ SER

▶ A pottery model of a tiger cub, Russian, c1930–40, 4in (10cm) high.
£40–50
$60–80 ⊞ MRW

◀ A pottery model of birds on a trough, by Jerome Massier, French, c1880, 6in (15cm) wide.
£140–160
$200–230 ⊞ MLL

A model of two bears, on a grassy base, indistinct signature, Russian, dated 1911, 11in (28cm) high.
£300–375
$450–550 ➶ Pott

◀ A Fürstenburg porcelain model of two kittens, black and white with green eyes, 1950–60, 5in (12.5cm) high.
£90–100
$130–150 ⊞ WAC

A Royal Crown Derby Imari cat paperweight, in yellow, red and blue, c1985, 5in (12.5cm) high.
£70–80
$100–120 ➶ Pott

A Winstanley pottery model of a cat, hand-painted in Tiger pattern No. 4, c1998, 10in (25.5cm) high.
£30–40
$40–60 ⊞ RIA

Bargeware

Bargeware, also known as Meashamware, is the name given to treacly-brown glazed earthenware, decorated with applied pieces of clay. These were moulded into various shapes including flowers, grapes, pheasants and even lizards and newts, and crudely painted in pinks, blues and greens.

Said to be used by the people who worked the barges along the inland waterways (hence its name), bargeware was a popular gift, often brought back from a journey. Typical shapes include large teapots (often with a smaller teapot on the lid), jugs, mugs and bowls. Many pieces have a cartouche applied to the side impressed with printer's block letters.

Inscriptions can include a date and the name of the recipient (if the piece was a specific commission), or more generalized phrases such as 'A Present to a Friend' or 'Home Sweet Home' if it was bought off the shelf.

Bargeware was manufactured from the mid-19th century by small potteries in the Burton-on-Trent area, the Midlands and the Cotswolds. Although very few pieces are marked, known makers include William Mason who began making bargeware in the 1880s at Church Gresley, Derbyshire. In 1901, the went into partnership with Mr Cash and as Mason, Cash & Co, the firm continued to produce the pottery until c1939.

A bargeware double-spouted teapot, with small cherub between the spouts, cartouche inscribed 'a present from', decorated in pink and green, c1875, 8in (20.5cm) high.
£550–650
$800–950 ⊞ JBL

A bargeware sugar bowl, elaborately decorated with flowers and foliage in red, blue and green, c1880, 6in (15cm) diam.
£180–230
$260–330 ⊞ JBL

A bargeware teapot, probably from Church Gresley, with teapot knop to domed cover, decorated with coloured sprigs of flowers and birds, cartouche impressed 'A H Simpson Esqr. Royal Artillery 1882', 15in (38cm) high.
£450–550
$650–800 ⚒ DN

A bargeware teapot-on-stand, decorated with pink and blue flowers with green foliage, cartouche inscribed 'Mr A Johnson Bath 1882', 11in (28cm) high.
£300–350
$450–500 ⊞ JBL

A bargeware money box, with traditional applied decoration in blue and pink, cartouche inscribed 'Put A Penny In', slot at front for coins, c1900, 5in (12.5cm) high.
£200–250
$300–350 ⊞ JBL

A bargeware teapot, with applied mounts, cartouche inscribed 'God Bless Our Home', late 19thC, 12½in (32cm) high.
£120–140
$170–200 ⚒ G(B)

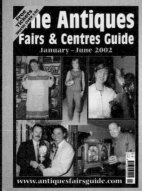

Beswick

A Beswick model of a Dalmatian, Arnoldene, No. 961, 1941–93, 5¾in (14.5cm) long.
£50–60
$75–100 ✎ MED

A Beswick model of a cockerel, No. 2059, 20thC, 10in (25.5cm) high.
£570–620
$800–900 ✎ GAK

Condition

The condition is absolutely vital when assessing the value of a collectable. Damaged pieces on the whole appreciate much less than perfect examples. However a rare desirable piece may command a high price even when damaged.

◀ A Beswick model of a brown Scottish terrier, No. HN965, 1928–46, 3¾in (9.5cm) high.
£300–400
$450–550 ✎ BBR

A Beswick model of Little Pig Robinson, designed by Arthur Gredington, wearing a blue striped dress and carrying a brown basket with yellow cauliflowers, 1948–74, 3¾in (9.5cm) high.
£80–100
$115–145 ✎ BBR

A set of three Beswick wall-hanging seagulls, No. 658, designed by Mr. Watkin, decorated in white, black and yellow gloss, printed mark, 1938–67, largest 12in (30.5cm) long.
£140–160
$200–230 ✎ BBR

◀ A Beswick model of a white bull terrier, No. 970, designed by Arthur Gredington, printed mark, 1942–75, 5½in (14cm) high.
£60–80
$90–110 ✎ BBR

A Beswick model of a Shire horse, No. 818, decorated in rocking horse grey, 1952, 8in (20.5cm) long.
£350–400
$500–600 ⊞ PAC

A Beswick model of a white fantail pigeon, on a green base, No. 1614, 1959–69, 6in (15cm) wide.
£450–550
$650–800 ✎ Pott

◀ A Beswick model of a sitting fox, No. 2348, decorated in brown, white and black, 1970–83, 12¼in (31cm) high.
£170–200
$250–300 ✎ MED

Blue & White

A blue and white platter, decorated with Pagoda pattern, 18thC, 21in (53.5cm) long.
£110–130
$160–190 ⊞ MCC

A blue and white leaf-shaped pickle dish, with stalk handle, decorated with Willow pattern, 18thC, 6in (15cm) long.
£120–140
$170–200 ↗ DA

A blue and white pearlware tankard, decorated with buildings, trees and a stream, early 19thC, restored, 7in (18cm) high.
£320–350
$450–500 ↗ GAK

◀ **A blue and white plate,** decorated with a castle pattern, c1820, 9in (23cm) diam.
£160–190
$230–270 ⊞ SCO

▶ **A Staffordshire blue and white half-pint mug,** 19thC, 4in (10cm) high.
£30–40
$40–60 ⊞ MCC

A Samuel Barker & Son Swinton blue and white meat dish with well, No. 20, decorated with Willow pattern, blue griffin and shield mark to base, damaged, c1850, 21in (53.5cm) long.
£100–120
$145–175 ⚒ LF

A Booths blue and white supper set, comprising a central oval dish and six shaped dishes, decorated with Real Old Willow pattern, with treen tray, 19thC, 16½in (42cm) diam.
£150–180
$220–260 ⚒ GAK

An early Victorian blue and white toothbrush holder, 7in (18cm) high.
£35–38
$50–55 ⊞ CAL

A blue and white platter, with moulded juice channels and reservoir, decorated in Gothic Ruins pattern, with foliate printed border and shaped rim, printed mark for Charles Meigh to base, 19thC, 21in (53.5cm) long.
£200–250
$300–350 ⚒ Mit

A blue and white plate, decorated with Willow pattern, 19thC, 10in (25.5cm) diam.
£12–15
$15–20 ⊞ MCC

A blue and white milk jug, c1920, 10in (25.5cm) high.
£225–250
$320–360 ⊞ SMI

A blue and white spongeware pottery bowl, 1890, 5¼in (13.5cm) diam.
£30–35
$40–50 ⊞ OD

> **Cross Reference**
> See Colour Review (page 78)

▶ **A Copeland Spode blue and white plate,** Blue Italian pattern, Spode mark, 20thC, 9in (23cm) diam.
£10–15
$15–25 ⊞ OD

◀ A Dedham Pottery blue and white moulded plate, decorated with Turkey pattern, with crackle glaze, American, 1896–1943, 8½in (21.5cm) diam.
£110–125
$160–180 ⚒ JMW

A Copeland Spode blue and white quail egg set with cruet, Blue Italian pattern, 1930s, 2½in (6.5cm) long.
£75–100
$115–145 ⊞ BEV

Burleigh Ware

A Burleigh Ware milk jug, decorated with Sunray pattern, c1930, 4in (10cm) high.
£25–40
$40–60 ⊞ BUR

A Burleigh Ware Dickens Series character jug, Pickwick, 1940s, 4in (10cm) high.
£50–65
$70–90 ⊞ BUR

A Burleigh Ware hors d'oeuvres dish, decorated with Meadowland pattern in orange and green, c1930, 8in (20.5cm) diam.
£25–30
$40–50 ⊞ HO

A Burleigh Ware set of six egg cups and stand, decorated with Golden Days pattern in yellow, green and red, c1930, egg cup 2in (5cm) high.
£80–100
$115–145 ⊞ BUR

A set of Burleigh Ware bird jugs, Kingfisher, Blue Tit, Budgerigar, Bullfinch and Wren, decorated in naturalistic colours, 1955, 4in (10cm) high.
£200–250
$300–350 each ⊞ ERC

◄ **A Burleigh Ware character jug,** of Rt. Hon. J. C. Smuts, hand-coloured in brown, red, yellow and green, 1941, 5in (12.5cm) high.
£440–480
$650–700 ↗ Pott

Burmantofts

◄ **A Burmantofts faïence stick stand,** No. 1860, moulded with a band of stylized leaves on a fluted ground, decorated in light to dark green, impressed marks, c.1900, 24in (61cm) high.
£275–325
$400–470 ↗ AH

LOCATE THE SOURCE

The source of each illustration in Miller's can be found by checking the code letters below each caption with the Key to Illustrations, pages 444–452.

A Burmantofts faïence vase, decorated in blue, green, turquoise and yellow, 1890–1910, 9in (23cm) high.
£300–400
$440–580 ⊞ ASA

A Burmantofts faïence frog group, No. 1995, modelled as two frogs cuddling on a mushroom, decorated with a green glaze, glass eyes, impressed marks to base, c1900, 5in (12.5cm) high.
£380–420
$560–620 ↗ Pott

Carlton Ware

A Carlton Ware teapot, decorated with Early Blush pattern, c1880–1900, 5in (12.5cm) high.
£270–300
$400–450 ⊞ BEV

A Carlton Ware pedestal bowl, decorated with Floribunda pattern, c1929, 5in (12.5cm) wide.
£430–470
$620–700 ⊞ MI

A Carlton Ware jug, decorated with Butterfly and Dahlia pattern, c1930, 5in (12.5cm) high.
£500–600
$720–870 ⊞ BD

Two Carlton Ware chocolate beakers with lids, decorated in red, yellow, cream and green, c1930, 5in (12.5cm) high.
£100–125
$145–175 ⊞ BD

A late Victorian Carlton Ware biscuit barrel, No. 246831, transfer-printed in flow-blue trailing flowers and gilt, the cover with knop finial, 5in (12.5cm) high.
£150–180
$200–250 ⚒ DA

A pair of Carlton Ware candlesticks, c1930, 4in (10cm) high.
£200–225
$300–330 ⊞ BEV

A pair of Carlton Ware candlesticks, decorated in blue and white, c1930, 4in (10cm) high.
£250–270
$350–400 ⊞ BEV

A Carlton Ware cameo box, decorated with Moonlight pattern, c1920, 6in (15cm) long.
£300–350
$450–500 ⊞ BEV

A Carlton Ware vase, decorated with Chinoiserie pattern, c1930, 8in (20.5cm) high.
£130–150
$200–220 ⊞ BD

A Carlton Ware Tulip sugar shaker, 1930–32, 6¼in (16cm) high.
£75–85
$115–125 ⊞ StC

◀ **A Carlton Ware tube-lined bowl,** decorated with Trees and Fields pattern, 1930s, 9in (23cm) wide.
£550–600
$800–900 ⊞ BEV

A Carlton Ware vase, decorated with Lacecap Hydrangea pattern, 1930s, 6¼in (16cm) high.
£750–850
$1,000–1,200 ⊞ StC

A Carlton Ware jug, decorated with High Oak pattern, 1930s, 5¼in (13.5cm) high.
£80–100
$115–145 ⊞ StC

A Carlton Ware basket, moulded with Foxglove pattern, late 1930s, 6½in (16.5cm) wide.
£100–120
$145–175 ⊞ StC

A Carlton Ware butter dish, decorated with Wild Rose pattern, 1948, 5in (12.5cm) wide.
£25–30
$35–45 ⊞ StC

A Carlton Ware tray, decorated with Blackberry pattern, 1937, 10in (25.5cm) wide.
£75–85
$115–125 ⊞ StC

A Carlton Ware breakfast set, moulded with Apple Blossom pattern, c1940.
£650–800
$950–1,200 ⊞ AOT
This green Apple Blossom piece is one of the most sought-after Carlton Ware breakfast sets from the moulded floral range.

A Carlton Ware Walking Ware teapot, with white glaze and yellow shoes, 1978, 9in (23cm) high.
£150–170
$200–250 ⊞ BEV
Walking Ware was developed by husband and wife team Roger Michell and Danka Napiorkowska, and manufactured by Carlton from 1973.

▶ **A Carlton Ware Hovis teapot,** 1970s, 6¼in (16cm) high.
£60–70
$90–100 ⊞ StC

A Carlton Ware Rouge Royale vase, hand-painted with Wild Duck pattern, 1950s, 6in (15cm) high.
£240–280
$350–400 ⊞ HO

Chintz Ware

A Barker Bros sugar shaker, with all-over multi-coloured floral pattern, c1930, 8in (20.5cm) high.
£80–100
$115–145 ⊞ BD

A Royal Winton dish, decorated with Hazel pattern, c1930, 7in (18cm) long.
£100–120
$145–175 ⊞ BD

Checking chintz

Hazel, with its distinctive black ground, is one of the most popular of all Royal Winton chintz patterns. For maximum value, patterns should be crisp and clean. With all chintz ware check pieces carefully for scratches, fading or restoration.

A Royal Winton butter dish, decorated with the Kinver pattern, c1930, 6in (15cm) long.
£100–120
$145–175 ⊞ BD

A Barker Bros biscuit barrel, with all-over multi-coloured floral pattern, c1930, 6in (15cm) high.
£80–100
$115–145 ⊞ BD

A Royal Winton bowl, decorated with Hazel pattern, c1930, 8in (20.5cm) square.
£225–250
$320–360 ⊞ BEV

A Royal Winton muffin dish, decorated with all-over multi-coloured floral pattern, with blue rim, c1936, 6½in (16.5cm) diam.
£110–130
$160–190 ⊞ AOT

▶ **A Royal Winton covered cheese dish,** decorated with all-over multi-coloured floral pattern, base marked 'AUS. RD 29775', dated 1952, 6½in (16.5cm) wide.
£100–120
$145–175 ⊞ FL

A James Kent bowl, 1930s, 6½in (16.5cm) diam.
£30–40
$50–60 ⊞ DBo

A Royal Winton vase, decorated with Cheadle pattern, c1930, 6in (15cm) high.
£180–200
$250–300 ⊞ BEV

A Royal Winton Marguerite teapot, decorated with all-over multi-coloured floral pattern, c1940, 8in (20.5cm) long.
£240–270
$350–400 ⊞ AOT

Clarice Cliff

A Clarice Cliff coffee can and saucer, decorated with Mondrian pattern, c1930, cup 2in (5cm) diam.
£700–800
$1,000–1,150 ⊞ BD

A Clarice Cliff Conical cup and saucer, decorated with Crocus pattern, c1930, cup 2½in (6.5cm) high.
£200–250
$300–350 ⊞ BD

Three Clarice Cliff side plates, decorated with Crocus pattern, c1930, 7in (18cm) diam.
£40–50
$60–80 ⋏ G(L)

A Clarice Cliff Conical tea cup and saucer, decorated with Red Sunrise pattern, c1930, cup 2½in (6.5cm) high.
£450–500
$650–720 ⊞ BD

A Clarice Cliff Circus plate, decorated by Dame Laura Knight, c1930, 8in (20.5cm) diam.
£800–900
$1,150–1,300 ⊞ BD

A Clarice Cliff Bon Jour shape jam pot, decorated with Honolulu pattern, c1930, 4in (10cm) wide.
£550–650
$800–950 ⊞ BD

A Clarice Cliff Pixie nursery mug, c1930, 4in (10cm) high.
£225–275
$320–400 ⊞ JEZ

A Clarice Cliff Bizarre Dover jardinière, decorated with triangular and diamond motifs in shades of brown, purple and blue with green outlines, 1930s, 6½in (16.5cm) high.
£400–500
$580–720 ⋏ GH

A Clarice Cliff bowl, decorated with Cabbage Flower pattern, 1930s, 6½in (16.5cm) diam.
£160–190
$225–275 ⋏ G(L)

◄ A Clarice Cliff plate, decorated with Orange Roof Cottage pattern, printed mark, 1930s, 8in (20.5cm) diam.
£320–360
$450–500 ⋏ GAK

► A Clarice Cliff Bizarre ribbed ovoid vase, decorated with Viscaria pattern, printed marks, 1930s, 4½in (11.5cm) high.
£200–250
$300–350 ⋏ WW

Susie Cooper

A Susie Cooper trio, decorated with pink Patricia Rose pattern, c1930, plate 7in (18cm) diam.
£100–125
$145–175 ⊞ BD

A Susie Cooper consommé dish and stand, decorated in green and red on a white ground, 1930s, stand 7in (18cm) diam.
£40–50
$60–80 ⊞ BD

A Susie Cooper Kestrel teapot, decorated with green Patricia Rose pattern, c1930, 7½in (19cm) high.
£120–150
$175–225 ⊞ BD

A Susie Cooper Quadrapets cereal bowl, 1930s, 5½in (14cm) diam.
£120–150
$175–225 ⊞ BD

A Susie Cooper box and cover, decorated with Pomeranian pattern, 1930s, 4in (10cm) wide.
£900–1,000
$1,300–1,500 ⊞ BD

A Susie Cooper studio pottery vase, decorated with incised squirrels on a butterscotch glaze, signed, c1930, 11½in (29cm) high.
£300–330
$450–480 ⊞ RUSK

Copeland

A pair of Copeland square section vases, decorated with flowers and foliage in blue and gilt, 'WMP' monograms, seal marks containing 'C', 1878–83, 8½in (21.5cm) high.
£220–250
$320–360 ⚒ WW

A Copeland stoneware jug, decorated with rugby players in white relief on a brown ground, beneath a band of floral decoration, 1895, 2in (5cm) high.
£300–350
$450–500 ⚒ ANA

◄ **A Copeland Spode sucrier,** decorated with Cabbage Leaf pattern, c1860, 6in (15cm) wide.
£240–280
$350–400 ⊞ JP

Crown Devon

A Crown Devon Daisy Bell musical cigarette box, decorated in red, green and blue, 1920s, 8in (20.5cm) long.
£500–550
$700–800 ⊞ AU

A Crown Devon doorstop, modelled as a dog, decorated in brown, black and white, 1930s, 10in (25.5cm) long.
£80–100
$115–145 ⊞ BD

▶ A Crown Devon Pixie four-piece cruet set, c1940, 3½in (9cm) high.
£120–140
$175–225 ⊞ AOT

A Crown Devon model of a greyhound, painted in natural tones of beige, brown and black, on a black octagonal base, c1930, 6in (15cm) high.
£100–120
$145–175 ⋏ Pott

A Crown Devon vase, decorated with two pheasants and butterflies among flowers against a ruby lustre ground, gold printed mark, 1930s, 11½in (29cm) high.
£370–400
$500–600 ⋏ S(S)

A Crown Derby Auld Lang Syne musical jug, c1940, 6in (15cm) high.
£120–140
$175–225 ⊞ AOT

Crown Ducal

Cross Reference
See Rhead (page 132)

◀ A Crown Ducal vase, No. 121, decorated with running yellow, orange and blue glaze over a brown base, 1920s mark, 8¾in (22cm) high.
£40–50
$60–80 ⊞ DEC

A Crown Ducal flower holder, modelled as a tree trunk, decorated with yellow, blue, red and black running glaze, with holes for eight blooms, 1920s, 3½in (9cm) high.
£20–25
$30–40 ⊞ DEC

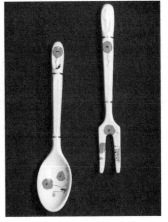

A pair of Crown Ducal salad servers, decorated with Poppy pattern, c1930, 9in (23cm) long.
£65–75
$95–115 ⊞ BD

Cups, Saucers & Mugs

A *Diana* Cargo tea bowl and saucer, decorated with Diving Birds pattern, c1817, saucer 5½in (14cm) diam.
£270–300
$400–440 ⊞ RBA
These items were rescued from the vessel *Diana* which foundered c1817.

Cross Reference
See Colour Review (page 148)

An alphabet mug, printed *en grisaille* with interior scenes, inscribed 'C C Cook Cat Clock, early 19thC, 5in (12.5cm) high.
£100–120
$145–175 ⋌ GAK

A Shelley mug, hand-painted with Harmony pattern, c1930, 4in (10cm) high.
£70–75
$100–110 ⊞ BEV

A Gaudy Welsh mug, No. 1104, decorated with Grape pattern, 1829–90, 2¾in (7cm) high.
£75–95
$110–140 ⊞ CoHA

A Gaudy Welsh frog mug, decorated with Wagon Wheel pattern, with serpent handle, the interior with a yellow and black frog, 19thC, 5in (12.5cm) high.
£300–330
$450–500 ⋌ TMA

A Shelley trio, in Mode shape, 1931, cup 3in (7.5cm) high.
£225–25
$320–360 ⊞ BEV

A Minton trio, 1912–50, plate 8in (20.5cm) diam.
£30–35
$40–50 ⊞ CAL

A Derbyshire salt-glazed mug, decorated with a hunting scene, 1840, 5½in (14cm) high.
£160–180
$230–260 ⊞ OD

A Shelley trio, in Queen Anne shape, decorated with Black Leafy Tree pattern, 1927–29, cup 3½in (9cm) high.
£140–160
$200–250 ⊞ BEV

A Tarot tea reading cup and saucer, 1930s, saucer 4in (10cm) diam.
£40–45
$60–70 ⊞ LBe

A Pink Panther mug, 1981, 5in (12.5cm) high.
£60–70
$90–100 ⊞ TAC

Denby

A blue Denby Art Pottery vase, with early hand-painted Danesby Ware mark, mid-1920s, 4½in (11.5cm) high.
£55–65
$80–90 ⊞ KES

▶ **A Denby Byngo,** with mottled blue/brown trial glaze, late 1930s, 3½in (9cm) high.
£100–130
$140–190 ⊞ KES

A Denby mushroom vase, with cream glaze, c1938, 6in (15cm) diam.
£35–45
$50–70 ⊞ KES

A green Denby squirrel bowl, with Gretna glaze, c1938, 12½in (32cm) diam.
£200–225
$300–330 ⊞ KES

A brown Denby Utility teapot, produced for H.M. Forces, late 1940s, 3½ pint size.
£25–30
$35–45 ⊞ KES

A Glyn Colledge plate, decorated in green, brown, blue and red, believed to be a Denby blank, c1948, 9in (23cm) diam.
£40–50
$60–80 ⊞ DSG

A Denby Greenwheat dinner service, comprising eight dinner plates, six salad plates, six soup bowls, six cereal bowls, four serving dishes, a coffee pot and 11 other matching items, 1950s.
£150–180
$220–260 ↗ CAu
Greenwheat, designed by Albert Colledge in 1956, was one of the Denby's most successful lines.

Doulton

This year's Doulton section includes a selection of prototype figures from the Royal Doulton archives, sold through Phillips. Two hundred and sixty-three lots were offered, with an estimated value of some £250,000 ($360,000). The sale, however, totalled £423,570 ($615,000), proving the pulling power of these comparatively recent (post WWII) but genuinely unique items. Prototype figures are among the most desirable Royal Doulton products, including both one-off designs that never actually went into manufacture, as well as the original models that inspired the

mass-produced versions. Modern limited edition pieces are far more accessible. In some cases pieces have escalated in value, 'But what goes up does go down,' warns Philips expert Mark Oliver, 'and today's market is perhaps more cautious and more realistic than in recent years.' Oliver offers the following cautionary advice, 'If possible, don't buy from a large volume limited edition and allow a three to five year period before anticipating an appreciation in price. And finally buy because you like the object, not just as an investment.'

A Doulton stoneware commemorative jug, inscribed 'Emin Pasha Relief Expedition 1887–1890', chip to foot, 7½in (19cm) high.
£130–150
$200–220 ↗ SWO

A Doulton Lambeth stoneware teapot, c1890, 3½in (9cm) high.
£100–120
$145–175 ⊞ DSG

A Royal Doulton model of a bulldog, draped with a Union flag, No. 645658, green printed mark, early 20thC, 6in (15cm) high.
£180–200
$250–300 ↗ CDC

A Doulton Lambeth vase, by Emily E. Stormer, decorated with incised styled acanthus leaves, c1890, 6½in (16.5cm) high.
£250–300
$350–450 ↗ G(B)

A Royal Doulton stoneware jardinière, by Hannah Barlow, decorated in shades of brown and green, c1905, 10in (25.5cm) high.
£1,800–2,000
$2,600–2,900 ⊞ JE

A pair of Royal Doulton Chine Ware baluster vases, the rough lace ground decorated with floral sprays and gilding, the neck and foot in deep blue glaze, circle, lion and crown and Doulton Slater patent marks, 1902–39, 10¾in (27.5cm) high.
£140–180
$200–250 ↗ MED

◀ **A Royal Doulton Pear's Soap dish,** with deep blue glaze, butterfly-wing detail, 1914–18, 6in (15cm) wide.
£100–120
$145–175 ⊞ MURR

A Doulton model of Ann Hathaway's cottage, with matt glaze, Royal Doulton circle mark, lion and crown, 7¼in (18.5cm) long.
£600–700
$870–1,000 ⚒ BBR

A Doulton Dickens ware vase, decorated in red, green and black, c1930, 6in (15cm) high.
£170–200
$250–300 ⊞ BD

A Doulton Farmer John character jug, designed by Charles Noke, decorated in shades of brown with a white collar, circle mark, lion and crown, 1938–60, 3¼in (8.5cm) high.
£40–50
$60–80 ⚒ BBR

A Royal Doulton prototype group of a middle-aged couple seated in deck chairs, decorated in yellow, blue and green, marked, 1970, 6½in (16.5cm) high.
£6,000–6,500
$8,700–9,400 ⚒ P

A Royal Doulton prototype figure of a seated woman, Reading the Tea Leaves, wearing a yellow dress, marked, 1960s, 5½in (14cm) high.
£3,300–3,600
$4,700–5,000 ⚒ P

A Royal Doulton Punch and Judy Man character jug, No. D6596, 1964–69, 2½in (6.5cm) high.
£200–225
$300–330 ⊞ ML

▶ **A Royal Doulton prototype figure of King of the Castle,** wearing an orange jumper and blue trousers, marked, 1970s, 6in (15cm) high.
£3,500–3,800
$5,000–5,500 ⚒ P

◀ **A Royal Doulton model of a West Highland terrier,** a version of No. HN1048, in black basalt, marked, 1970s, 9in (23cm) long.
£1,200–1,400
$1,750–2,000 ⚒ P

▶ **A Royal Doulton proto-type figure of Patience,** wearing a turquoise dress with a green shawl, marked, 1970s, 6¾in (17cm) high.
£3,000–3,250
$4,400–4,700 🪧 P

A Doulton figure of Statue of Liberty Bunnykins, No. DB198, decorated in red, blue, cream and green, 1970–80, 3in (7.5cm) high, boxed.
£60–70
$90–100 🪧 Pott

A Royal Doulton proto-type figure of Indian Warrior, decorated in brown, yellow and orange, marked, 1970s, 9in (23cm) high.
£3,500–4,000
$5,000–6,000 🪧 P

◀ **A Royal Doulton figure of Morris Dancer Bunnykins,** No. DB204, marked, 1970–80, 4½in (11.5cm) high, with box.
£25–28
$35–40 🪧 BBR

A Royal Doulton model of Snowman Savings Book, marked, 5¼in (13.5cm) high.
£70–80
$100–120 🪧 BBR

A Doulton figure of Jockey Bunnykins, No. DB169, decorated in yellow, cream and green, No. 174 of a limited edition of 2,000, 1970–80, 3in (7.5cm) high, boxed with certificate.
£130–150
$200–220 🪧 Pott

A Royal Doulton figure of Widdicombe Fair, marked, 1980s, 8¼in (21cm) high.
£3,000–3,400
$4,500–5,000 🪧 P

◀ **A Royal Doulton figure of Welcome Home,** No. HN3299, No. 3,398 of a limited edition of 9,500, 1991, 8½in (21.5cm) high.
£120–140
$175–200 🪧 Pott

Earthenware, Stoneware & Country Pottery

A stoneware character jug, the buff-coloured head decorated with treacle glaze features and tricorn hat, c1840, 11in (28cm) high.
£450–550
$650–800 ⊞ JBL

An agate body top hat and lid with hen and chicks, 1881, 6¼in (16cm) high.
£160–180
$230–260 ⊞ IW

An Ellgreave Pottery jug, 1940, 2¾in (7cm) high.
£10–15
$15–20 ⊞ OD

A slipware cradle, 1880, 8¼in (21cm) long.
£400–500
$580–720 ⊞ IW

A Buckley pottery flower pot, 1890, 6in (15cm) high.
£75–85
$115–125 ⊞ IW

A Savoie pottery jug with lid, 1900, 5in (12.5cm) high.
£40–50
$60–80 ⊞ MLL

A Savoie pottery jug, brown with cream spots, 1880, 4in (10cm) high.
£34–38
$50–60 ⊞ MLL

A Donyatt pottery jar, for Rogers Pottery, pre-1900, 5¼in (13.5cm) high.
£200–240
$300–350 ⊞ IW

A Claypits Ewenny jug, 1930s, 4½in (11.5cm) high.
£40–45
$60–70 ⊞ IW

Egg Cups

A Wedgwood jasper ware egg cup, c1790, 2½in (6.5cm) high.
£550–600
$800–880 ⊞ AMH

A cane ware egg cup, possibly Spode, c1810, 1¾in (4.5cm) high.
£140–150
$200–220 ⊞ AMH

A Spode egg cup, decorated with Girl at the Well pattern, c1820, 2½in (6.5cm) high.
£190–200
$275–300 ⊞ AMH

A Sèvres-style egg cup, probably Minton, c1840, 2½in (6.5cm) high.
£500–550
$700–800 ⊞ AMH

A Copeland & Garrett egg cup, with gilt decoration, 1833–38, 2½in (6.5cm) high.
£140–150
$200–220 ⊞ AMH

A Minton egg cup, No. A2641, decorated in red, blue, green and gilt, c1855, 2¼in (5.5cm) high.
£200–220
$300–330 ⊞ AMH

A Davenport blue and white egg cup, No. 3731, c1870, 2½in (6.5cm) high.
£90–100
$130–150 ⊞ AMH

A Staffordshire egg cup, decorated in green, pink and gold, c1870, 2¼in (5.5cm) high.
£65–70
$90–100 ⊞ AMH

◀ **Four egg cups,** modelled as a cockerel, an elephant, a cat and a cat chasing a mouse, decorated in black, orange, red and green, 1920s, largest 2¾in (7cm) high.
£20–30
$30–50 each ⊞ CoCo

> Items in the Ceramics section have been arranged in date order within each sub-section.

▶ **Two egg cups,** modelled as a rabbit and a hare, decorated in red, yellow, blue and green, 1920s–30s, largest 3in (7.5cm) high.
£25–35
$30–50 each ⊞ CoCo

An egg cup, modelled as the Three Little Piggies, decorated in blue, yellow, red and green, 1920–30, 2½in (6.5cm) high.
£25–30
$35–45 ⊞ CoCo

Fairings

Two fairings, depicting a dentist and patient,
l. entitled 'A long pull and a strong pull', decorated in blue, green and pink, restored, c1870, 2¾in (7cm) high.
£220–260
$320–380 ⚹ SAS
r. entitled 'Out by Jingo', decorated in orange, pink and green, restored, c1870, 2¼in (5.5cm) high.
£400–480
$580–700 ⚹ SAS

A fairing, entitled 'To Let', decorated in black and white, c1870, 2¼in (5.5cm) high.
£340–380
$500–575 ⚹ SAS

A fairing, entitled 'Lor three legs, I'll charge 2d', decorated in red and blue, c1870, 2¼in (5.5cm) high.
£280–330
$410–475 ⚹ SAS

▶ **A matchholder fairing,** modelled as a girl beside a wheelbarrow, decorated in orange, pink and green, c1870, 2¼in (5.5cm) high.
£40–50
$60–75 ⚹ SAS

A fairing, entitled 'Cancan', decorated in green, red and blue, c1870, 2¼in (5.5cm) high.
£360–400
$500–580 ⚹ SAS

A matchstriker fairing, modelled as two dogs at the village pump, decorated in brown and white, c1870, 2¼in (5.5cm) high.
£40–50
$60–75 ⚹ SAS

A fairing, entitled 'Five o'clock Tea', decorated in brown, black and white, some damage to ears, c1870, 2¼in (5.5cm) high.
£75–90
$110–130 ⚹ SAS

▶ **A fairing,** entitled 'A Safe Messenger', decorated in brown and green, c1870, 2¼in (5.5cm) high.
£120–140
$175–200 ⚹ SAS

A fairing, entitled 'Looking Down Upon His Luck', decorated in pink, green and blue, c1870, 2¼in (5.5cm) high.
£120–140
$175–200 ⚹ SAS

Figures

A brown Victorian miniature ceramic bust, 4in (10cm) high.
£55–65
$80–95 ⊞ HO

A Goldscheider figure, 'Stockings', by Thomasch, decorated in pink, blue and green, 1930, 18in (45.5cm) high.
£2,750–3,000
$4,000–4,400 ⊞ BD

A Goldscheider figure, of a young man in classical dress, matt glazed in dark hues and gilt, rectangular lozenge to rear inscribed 'Goldscheider Wien', some rubbing and minor restoration, c1885–1918, 19in (48cm) high.
£135–165
$195–240 ⚒ MED

A Hummel figure, No. 42, Good Shepherd, TMK 3, decorated in red and brown, 1957–64, 6½in (16.5cm) high.
£115–135
$175–225 ⊞ ATH

◀ **A Compton Pottery angel group,** decorated in red, brown and blue, 1900–10, 6½in (16.5cm) high.
£150–190
$220–275 ⊞ DSG

A porcelain half-figure doll of a child, decorated in pink, blue and brown, 1920–30, 4in (10cm) high.
£30–35
$45–50 ⊞ HO

A Hummel figure, No. 165, Mother's Darling, decorated in blue and brown, with original paper label, TMK 3, 1957–64, 5½in (14cm) high.
£120–150
$175–215 ⊞ ATH

A Royal Dux figure of Elly Strobach, with brown hair, holding a blue cloth, 1930–40, 9½in (24cm) high.
£200–230
$290–330 ⊞ KA

A Goebels figure, Soldier Boy, wearing an orange jacket and green trousers, dated 1957, 6in (15cm) high.
£60–70
$90–100 ⚒ Pott

◀ **A Kevin Francis figure of Marilyn Monroe,** colourway 2, pink on a green base, No. 926 of 1,000 limited edition boxed with certificate, 1990, 9in (23cm) high.
£90–100
$130–145 ⚒ Pott

Goss & Crested China

An Alexandra model of St Paul's Cathedral, with City of London crest, 1906–37, 5½in (14cm) high.
£35–40
$50–60 ⊞ G&CC

An Arcadian model of a folding camera, with Arundel crest, 1903–33, 2½in (6.5cm) high.
£40–45
$60–65 ⊞ G&CC

An Arcadian model of a despatch rider, with Wendover crest, 1903–33, 4¾in (12cm) long.
£95–110
$140–160 ⊞ G&CC

▶ **An Arcadian model of a charabanc,** with Winchester College crest, 1903–33, 5½in (14cm) long.
£45–55
$65–80 ⊞ G&CC

An Arcadian jug, modelled as a Welsh woman, decorated in red and black, 1900–25, 2¾in (7cm) high.
£32–36
$48–55 ⊞ CCC

An Arcadian model of a black cat as a telephone operator, with Weymouth and Melcombe Regis crest, 1900–25, 2½in (6.5cm) high.
£110–125
$160–180 ⊞ CCC

An Arcadian model of an inverted horseshoe, with white heather and horseshoe decoration, with blue, red and yellow ribbon, inscribed 'Lucky White Heather from Preston Paignton', 1915–20, 4in (10cm) high.
£30–40
$45–60 ⊞ ES

A Carlton Ware bust of John Bull, with Hastings crest, 1902–30, 4in (10cm) high.
£25–30
$35–45 ⊞ G&CC

A Carlton Ware dish, with crest, 1906–27, 3in (7.5cm) diam.
£18–22
$27–33 ⊞ AnS

A Goss model of the Warwick font at Monmouth, white glazed, with four crests, c1900, 2in (5cm) high.
£100–125
$145–180 ⊞ CCC

A Coronet ware model of a schoolboy on a scooter, with Cockenzie crest, 1910–24, 3¾in (9.5cm) high.
£25–30
$35–45 ⊞ G&CC

A model of a ferris wheel, with Rhyl crest and inscribed 'Yr Hafandec Ar Finy Don', 1950s, 3½in (9cm) high.
£14–16
$20–25 ⊞ CRN

◄ **A Goss model of a Welsh bronze caudron,** with Llandudno crest, 1900–25, 3in (7.5cm) high.
£34–38
$50–55 ⊞ CCC

A Goss parian ware bust of Sir Moses Montefiore, modelled wearing a hat, first period, 1882–90, 5½in (13cm) high.
£225–245
$325–355 ⊞ G&CC

A Goss parian ware bust of King Edward VII, with black-printed goshawk mark, inscribed 'Copyright, Pub. as Act direct (See 54 Geo III, C.56), W. H. Goss, Stoke-on-Trent, 7 May 1901', c1901, 3½in (9cm) high.
£180–220
$260–320 ↗ DN

► **A Goss model of a Carmarthen coracle,** with Welsh crest, 1900–25, 5½in (13.5cm) long.
£80–90
$115–130 ⊞ CCC

A Goss model of the St Albans ancient cooking pot, with badge and motto of the Northumberland Fusiliers, 1885–1929, 2¼in (5.5cm) high.
£90–110
$130–160 ⊞ MGC

A Goss model of Lloyd George's early home in Criccieth, c1900–25, 4in (10cm) wide.
£140–160
$200–230 ⊞ CCC

A Goss model of the Rayleigh cooking pot, with badge and motto of the Royal Engineers, 1885–1929, 2in (5cm) diam.
£45–55
$65–80 ⊞ MGC

A Goss twin-lobed dish, with a view of the Empire Exhibition, Glasgow, 1938, 6in (16cm) diam.
£38–42
$57–63 ⊞ MGC

A Goss model of a giant lobster trap, with Dartmouth crest, 1890–1920, 3¼in (8.5cm) high.
£35–40
$50–60 ⊞ G&CC

A Goss model of a Welsh leek, with Carnarvon crest, 1900–25, 3½in (9cm) high.
£35–40
$50–60 ⊞ CCC

▶ **A Goss model of the Bournemouth Pilgrim Bottle,** with Kirkwall crest, 1890–1928, 3½in (9cm) high.
£22–25
$33–35 ⊞ G&CC

Items in the Goss & Crested China section have been arranged in alphabetical order by factory.

A Goss model of Twickenham Pope's Pipe, with Maidstone crest, 1890–1920, 4¾in (12cm) long.
£38–45
$55–65 ⊞ G&CC

A Grafton model of the Royston Crow, with Watford crest, 1900–33, 2½in (6.5cm) high.
£50–60
$75–90 ⊞ G&CC

A Grafton model of a mouse, with blue glass eyes and Hastings crest, 1900–33, 3½in (9cm) high.
£20–25
$30–35 ⊞ G&CC

A Grafton model of a comical cat, seated, wearing a yellow bow, with Castleton crest, 1900–25, 6in (15cm) high.
£65–75
$95–110 ⊞ CCC

A Swan model of a cat with arched back and raised tail, with Finchley crest on one side, and 'My word if you're not off' on the other, 1900–25, 3¼in (8cm) high.
£30–36
$45–55 ⊞ CCC

A Willow Art model of a black cat on a pouffé, with Bath crest, 1905–30, 3½in (9cm) high.
£30–35
$45–50 ⊞ G&CC

A Willow Art model of the Monnow Bridge, Monmouth, with Monmouth crest, 1900–25, 3¾in (9.5cm) high.
£55–65
$80–95 ⊞ CCC

▶ **A Wil-Wat model of the Leaking Boot statue at Cleethorpes,** the boot joined to the hand by string, with Cleethorpes crest, 1900–33, 6¼in (16.cm) high.
£90–100
$130–145 ⊞ G&CC

Gouda

A Gouda flat dish, in Hariet design, painted by G. Hey in black, orange, green and blue, 1922, 12½in (32cm) diam.
£225–275
$325–400 ⊞ OO

Four Gouda bonbon dishes, by Nabloes, decorated in cream orange, blue and brown, 1931, 2½in (6.5cm) diam.
£18–22
$27–33 each ⊞ OO

A Gouda Zuid-Holland Rhodian vase, hand-painted in orange, blue and green, 1924, 8in (20.5cm) high.
£350–400
$500–580 ⊞ MI

T. G. Green

Thomas Goodwin Green bought a pottery in Church Gresley, Derbyshire in 1864. The company specialized in utilitarian earthenware and affordable kitchenware and by the time of Green's death in 1905 it was a large concern. Under the management of his sons, the factory was modernized and produced an astonishing variety of ceramics including tableware. Their most famous line of all, introduced c1926, was a range of blue and white striped kitchen china: Cornish Ware.

According to legend, the name for this Derbyshire product was suggested by a south of England salesman, who claimed that the colours reminded him of 'the blue of the Cornish skies and the white crests of the waves'. True or not, there was certainly no doubt about Cornish Ware's success. In 1928 it received the Certificate of the Institute of Hygiene, the first of several awards. The clean and modern design appealed to a new generation of housewives,

many of whom were learning to do without the assistance of a full-time cook and, because they were spending more time in the kitchen, wanted objects that were attractive as well as functional. Cornish Ware became an instant classic.

T. G. Green experimented with other colours – Sunlit Yellow, Cornish Gold (a buff colour), red and black (both rare and very sought after today). However, blue and white remained the perennial favourite. A huge range of items was produced, ranging from plates and bowls to more unusual pieces, such as egg separators and rolling pins, which were not a success at the time since the striped design marked the pastry. Today however, these rarities are highly collectable. If shape is one indicator of value, another is simply a few printed letters. Cornish Ware became known for its named storage jars, and the more unusual inscriptions (Lux, Soap Flakes, Macaroni) can now command high sums.

◀ A T. G. Green **Ivanhoe vase,** decorated in green and red, 1890–1910, 6in (15cm) high:
£180–200
$250–300 ⊞ CAL

▶ A T. G. Green **blue and white jug,** 1900–10, 7in (18cm) high.
£125–150
$180–220 ⊞ CAL

A T. G. Green **mug,** hand-painted in yellow, green and red, with green-glazed interior, c1925, 5in (12.5cm) high.
£25–30
$35–45 ⊞ CAL

A T. G. Green **yellow and white globe teapot,** green shield mark, 1930–60, 5in (12.5cm) high.
£225–250
$320–360 ⊞ GeN

◀ A T. G. Green Cornish Ware **blue egg cup,** 1930–50, 4in (10cm) high.
£80–100
$115–145 ⊞ CAL

A T. G. Green **Streamline plate,** with green bands, 1930, 7in (18cm) diam.
£2–3
$5–8 ⊞ CAL

A T. G. Green cruet set, on a clover leaf base, decorated in blue with white spots, blue domino mark to base, 1930–50, base 5¾in (14.5cm) long.
£140–160
$200–230 ⚒ BBR

A T. G. Green Cube teapot, cream jug and sugar bowl, decorated in Dickens Days pattern, 1930.
£150–200
$220–300 ⊞ CAL

A T. G. Green biscuit barrel, decorated in blue with white spots, blue domino mark, 1930–50, 5in (12.5cm) high.
£350–450
$500–650 ⊞ CAL

Backstamps

Over the years T. G. Green used a number of different marks. On Cornish Ware a shield-shaped mark, appearing in both black and green, was used from the late 1920s until the second half of the 1960s. From 1968 until the late 1970s this was replaced by a Target mark designed by Judith Onions. In the 1980s, a modern church mark was used. In 1987, T. G. Green was taken over by Cloverleaf, who introduced a cloverleaf backstamp.

Ten T. G. Green plates, decorated in blue with white spots, 1930–50, four 9in (23cm) diam, six 7in (18cm) diam.
£35–45
$50–70 ⚒ BBR

▶ **A T. G. Green salt shaker,** with screw lid, decorated with blue and white bands, green shield mark to base, 1930–50, 5in (12.5cm) high.
£12–15
$15–20 ⚒ BBR

◀ **A T. G. Green sugar bowl,** decorated with blue and white bands, 1940s, 5in (12.5cm) diam.
£15–20
$20–30 ⊞ TAC

A T. G. Green Cornish Ware flour shaker, decorated with blue and white bands, with handle, 1930–50, 5½in (14cm) high.
£120–160
$175–225 ⊞ CAL
The handled flour shaker is a rare item in Cornish Ware.

▶ **A T. G. Green Cornish Ware trio,** decorated with Morning Glory pattern, 1950s, plate 7in (18cm) diam.
£50–60
$75–90 ⊞ CAL

A T. G. Green mug, decorated with yellow and white bands, 1940s, 4in (10cm) high.
£25–30
$35–45 ⊞ TAC

A T. G. Green Tally Ho teapot, decorated in blue and white, 1950s, 4½in (11.5cm) high.
£115–125
$160–180 ⊞ CAL
This pattern was made briefly in the 1950s for the Canadian market.

▶ A T. G. Green Cornish Ware pepper shaker, decorated with black and white bands, 1960, 5½in (14cm) high.
£100–120
$145–175 ⊞ CAL
Black Cornish Ware is very rare – it was only produced experimentally, not commercially.

A T. G. Green Cornish Ware egg separator, 1950s, 4in (10cm) high.
£95–110
$140–160 ⊞ CAL

◀ A T. G. Green coffee set, with four cups, designed by Judith Onions, decorated in Sark honey and black, 1968, coffee pot 8½in (21.5cm) high.
£70–80
$100–120 ⊞ CAL

A T. G. Green Cornish Ware Melior cafetière, decorated with blue and white bands, 1950, 6in (15cm) high.
£180–220
$260–320 ⊞ CAL

A T. G. Green Channel Isles cruet set, designed by Judith Onions, decorated in Jersey Green with a white glaze, 1968, 10in (25.5cm) long.
£30–40
$40–60 ⊞ CAL

A T. G. Green cup, decorated with blue and white bands, Judith Onions mark to base, 1970s, 2½in (6.5cm) high
£10–11
$15–18 ⊞ TAC

A T. G. Green measuring jug, decorated with blue and white bands, Judith Onions mark to base, 1970s, 5in (12.5cm) high.
£30–35
$40–60 ⊞ TAC

◀ A Barley Sugar storage jar, decorated with blue and white bands, Hygiene seal still attached, black shield mark to base, 1920–60, 5½in (14cm) high.
£300–350
$450–500 ⊞ GeN

A Coffee storage jar, decorated with blue and white bands, 1930–50, 4½in (11.5cm) high.
£75–85
$115–125 ⊞ TAC

A T. G. Green Cornish Ware biscuit barrel, decorated with blue and white bands, with wicker handle, 1930–50, 5in (12.5cm) high.
£400–450
$580–650 ⊞ CAL

A Cherries storage jar, decorated with blue and white bands, black shield mark to base, 1920–60, 3½in (9cm) high.
£90–120
$130–170 ⊞ GeN

A Flour storage jar, decorated with blue and white bands, 1920–60, 6in (15cm) high.
£70–80
$100–120 ⊞ TAC

A T. G. Green tea jar, decorated with blue and white bands, T. G. Green Church Gresley mark to base, 1980s, 6in (15cm) high.
£60–70
$90–100 ⊞ TAC
This mark replaced the Judith Onions Target mark in the 1980s.

A Cloves storage jar, decorated with blue and white bands, no lid, black shield mark to base, 1920–60, 3¾in (9.5cm) high.
£120–140
$170–200 ⋌ BBR

A Lux storage jar, decorated with blue and white bands, lid missing, black shield mark to base, 1930–50, 5½in (14cm) high.
£500–550
$700–800 ⋌ BBR
This jar is particularly rare.

A Parsley storage jar, decorated with blue and white bands, black shield mark to base, 1920–60, 3½in (9cm) high.
£100–110
$145–165 ⊞ GeN

Jugs

A Booths Lowestoft Border milk jug, decorated in red, green, pink and blue, c1906, 4½in (11.5cm) high.
£55–65
$80–100 ⊞ CoCo

A Bretby jug, decorated in turquoise and pink, c1935, 12in (30.5cm) high.
£60–80
$95–115 ⊞ DSG

A Brownfield & Son semi-glazed jug, decorated with Mistletoe pattern in brown and white, 1881 mark, 8in (20.5cm) high.
£50–55
$70–80 ⊞ TAC

► **A Hollinshead & Kirkham pottery jug,** decorated with Autumn pattern, 1933–42, 6in (15cm) high.
£70–80
$100–110 ⊞ HO

An Empire ware jug, decorated with yellow ochre and brown glaze, marked, 1933, 7¼in (18.5cm) high.
£40–45
$60–70 ⊞ OD

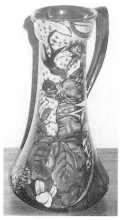

A Thomas Forrester & Son Phoenix ware jug, decorated with shades of blue, green and purple, 8½in (21.5cm) high.
£170–190
$250–275 ⊞ AOT

A Minton Pugin-style parian jug, with orange, green and gilt enamel decoration, c1850, 9in (23cm) high.
£220–250
$320–360 ⊞ JAK

A Royal Barum ware North Devon pottery washbowl and jug, designed by C. H. Brannam, decorated in green and blue, c1950, jug 7in (18cm) high.
£235–255
$330–360 ⊞ CRN

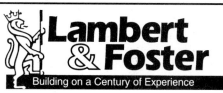

Lustre Ware

Lustre is a decorative technique which gives a metallic, sometimes iridescent appearance to the surface of a ceramic (generally pottery) vessel. Various metals were used including silver, copper and gold. When fired on a brown ground, gold particles produced a range of yellows. On a white, cream or buff surface, however, gold created the pink and purple lustres found on 19th-century Staffordshire and Sunderland pottery.

A Sunderland creamware lustre jug, depicting the Iron Bridge near Sunderland built by R. Burdon, decorated in red, green, pink and blue, c1830, 8in (20.5cm) high.
£580–640
$850–950 ⊞ RdV

A pink lustre bowl, with floral cartouches in green, blue and yellow, c1840, 6in (15cm) diam.
£25–30
$35–45 ⊞ JACK

A Sunderland lustre plaque, with pink and gilt surround, inscribed with a verse, impressed 'Dixon & Co', c1840, 7 x 8in (18 x 20.5cm).
£150–175
$225–255 ⊞ IS

A silver lustre coffee pot, c1840, 11in (28cm) high.
£100–150
$145–225 ⊞ TWr

A Sunderland copper lustre jug, with pink lustre rim, decorated with flowers in yellow, blue and green, c1840, 4in (10cm) high.
£45–55
$60–80 ⊞ SER

A Newcastle lustre plaque, attributed to C. T. Maling, with pink and gilt surround, 1855, 7 x 8in (18 x 20.5cm).
£260–290
$380–420 ⊞ IS

A Sunderland lustre plaque, attributed to Anthony Scott, Moore & Co, Southwick Union Pottery, depicting a frigate in full sail, with pink and gilt surround, 1860–70, 8 x 9in (20.5 x 23cm).
£160–190
$225–275 ⊞ IS

A Pilkington's Royal Lancastrian lustre vase, shape No. 2769, decorated by Gladys Rodgers with leaves and cherries on a red ground, mark '8', 1914–23, 4¾in (12cm) diam.
£130–150
$200–220 ✎ WW

A Ruskin purple lustre vase, with impressed marks, c1922, 3½in (9cm) high.
£180–220
$260–320 ✎ WW

Majolica

A Minton majolica teapot, modelled as a Chinese man clutching a mask with a spout mouth, his plaited hair forming the handle, impressed marks, 19thC, 8in (20.5cm) wide.
£350–450
$500–650 ⏷ GAK

A Delphine Massier majolica duck, decorated in deep blue, deep brown, russet and yellow, c1880, 5in (12.5cm) wide.
£350–400
$500–600 ⊞ MLL

A majolica jug, modelled as a corn on the cob in yellow and green, 19thC, 9½in (24cm) high.
£75–95
$110–140 ⏷ WBH

A majolica duck, painted in brown, green, yellow and white, Portuguese, c1900, 9in (23cm) wide.
£150–175
$220–255 ⊞ MLL

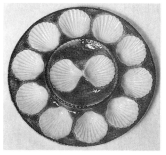

A majolica oyster-server, in green and white, possibly French, c1900, 13in (33cm) diam.
£200–225
$290–325 ⊞ MLL

A George Jones majolica plate, Rhapsody pattern, in yellow, purple and green, printed and impressed marks for February 1923, 10in (25.5cm) diam.
£50–60
$75–90 ⊞ ES

Maling

A Maling lustre bowl, decorated with trees, flowers and geese in greens, white and orange on a deep blue ground, gilded, on three feet, with flower frog, c1929, 9in (23cm) diam.
£340–400
$490–580 ⊞ AOT

A Maling lustre miniature bowl, in pink, blue, yellow and green, 1920s, 3¼in (8.5cm) diam.
£40–50
$60–75 ⊞ DSG

▶ **A Maling gilded lustre inkwell and lid,** in brown, green, red and yellow, c1930, 5in (12.5cm) high.
£90–120
$130–175 ⏷ SWO

A Maling breakfast cup and saucer, in blue and white, c1929, cup 4in (10cm) high.
£55–80
$80–115 ⊞ AOT

A **Maling vase,** decorated with Japanese Lantern pattern in orange, green, cream and purple on a mottled blue ground, c1930, 7in (18cm) high.
£180–260
$260–380 ⊞ AOT

▶ A **Maling matt lustre bowl,** decorated with gilded dragons on a deep blue ground, c1930, 9½in (24cm) diam.
£160–220
$230–320 ⊞ AOT

A **Maling jug,** decorated with Delphinium pattern in cerise, mauve, yellow and green on a blue ground, c1930, 7in (18cm) high.
£200–240
$290–350 ⊞ AOT

A **Maling lustre dish,** decorated with pink, blue and yellow flowers and a central pattern in pink, 1935, 11in (28cm) wide.
£35–40
$50–60 ⊞ JACK

A **Maling embossed lustre plate,** decorated with Daffodil pattern in white, yellow and green on a blue ground, c1936, 11¼in (28.5cm) diam.
£260–280
$380–400 ⊞ AOT

Mason's Ironstone

A **Mason's dessert dish,** decorated with Japan pattern, 11in (28cm) wide.
£350–380
$500–570 ⟋ P

A **pair of Mason's bottle vases and covers,** pattern No. 9985, printed marks, 1850–90, 9in (23cm) high.
£60–100
$90–145 ⟋ WW

A **Mason's gilded dessert dish,** decorated with red flowers on a deep blue and white ground, 1830–35, 11in (28cm) wide.
£320–360
$450–500 ⊞ JP

▶ A **Mason's lustre ginger jar,** decorated with Fruit Basket pattern in green, red and ochre on a cream ground, 1935–39, 8in (20.5cm) high.
£145–165
$200–250 ⊞ TAC

An **ironstone two-handled baluster vase,** probably Mason's, decorated with exotic creatures and stylized foliage in ochre and gilt on a blue-black ground, the interior iron-red with gilt floral border, 1840–60, 22½in (57cm) high.
£400–500
$580–720 ⟋ RFA

Meakin

James Meakin founded his pottery in Hanley, Staffordshire, in 1851. His two sons, James and George, took over the family business which became known as J. & G. Meakin. A third son, Alfred, established his own factory in Tunstall, Staffordshire, in 1874. The majority of items shown here are from the Alfred Meakin pottery, which produced domestic tableware both for the home market and for export.

Some of the company's most interesting patterns were produced in the 1950s. Cashing in on the post-war interest in foreign travel

Alfred Meakin produced plates illustrated with colourful and romanticized foreign scenes from across the world – Paris, Venice and cities in the USA were particularly popular locations.

During the same period, J. & G. Meakin launched their Studio Ware range – streamlined monochrome designs, inspired by the hugely successful American Modern tableware produced by American designer Russell Wright from the late 1930s. Still very affordable, post-war works by both these factories are beginning to attract collectors.

An Alfred Meakin Royal Marigold trio, 1930s, plate 6in (15cm) diam.
£14–16
$20–25 ⊞ BoC

A set of six late Victorian Alfred Meakin plates, decorated with Selwyn pattern in blue and white with gilding, 9in (23cm) diam.
£16–18
$20–30 ⊞ BoC

An Alfred Meakin *Bleu de Roi* tureen with lid, 1930s, 10in (25.5cm) diam.
£14–16
$20-25 ⊞ BoC

A J. & G. Meakin Sunshine jug, decorated with hand-painted orange flowers and green leaves, 1930s, 7in (18cm) high.
£40–50
$60–75 ⊞ MCC

Six Alfred Meakin fruit bowls, decorated with blue cornflowers, 1950s, 6½in (16.5cm) diam.
£18–22
$30–35 ⊞ BoC

An Alfred Meakin Cactus trio, decorated in red, blue, green and yellow, 1950s, plate 7in (18cm) diam.
£15–20
$20–30 ⊞ FLD

▶ An Alfred Meakin Oklahoma plate, decorated with cowboy and girl in a 'Surrey with a fringe on the top' in pastel colours, 1950s, 10in (25.5cm) diam.
£10–12
$15–18 ⊞ HSt

An Alfred Meakin cup, decorated with a port scene in vibrant colours, 1950s, 4in (10cm) diam.
£1–2
$2–3 ⊞ FLD

An Alfred Meakin plate, decorated with a street vendor in vibrant colours, 1950s, 10in (25.5cm) diam.
£3–4
$5–6 ⊞ FLD

A J. & G. Meakin Studio Ware jug, decorated in coffee colour, 1950s, 7in (18cm) high.
£9–11
$13–16 ⊞ TAC

◄ **An Alfred Meakin cup and saucer,** decorated in apple green with chequered saucer, 1950–60, saucer 5¾in (14.5cm) diam.
£3–4
$5–6 ⊞ FLD

► **A set of six J. & G. Meakin Wishing Well plates,** decorated in grey and pale pink, early 1960s, 7in (18cm) diam.
£12–15
$18–22 ⊞ HSt

An Alfred Meakin Bill and Ben plate, decorated with flowerpots and plants in red, green and yellow, 1950s, 9½in (24cm) diam.
£10–12
$15–18 ⊞ HSt

Midwinter

A Midwinter Stylecraft coffee cup and saucer, decorated with Hawaii pattern in red, blue and yellow, early 1950s, saucer 5in (12.5cm) diam.
£4–5
$6–8 ⊞ FLD

A Midwinter Stylecraft teapot, decorated with Homeware Red pattern designed by Jessie Tait, c1953, 5in (12.5cm) high.
£40–45
$60–65 ⊞ HSt

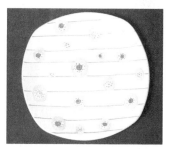

A Midwinter plate, decorated with Festival pattern, c1955, 6¼in (16cm) diam.
£15–18
$20–25 ⊞ FLD

◄ **A Midwinter plate,** designed by Terence Conran, decorated with Plant Life design in red and green, c1956, 6in (15cm) diam.
£70–80
$100–115 ⊞ REN
Interest in Midwinter continues to grow, particularly the 1950s designs by Terence Conran, and prices have escalated.

A Midwinter umbrella cake stand, decorated with Red Domino pattern, 1950s, 8¼in (21cm) diam.
£30–35
$45–50 ⊞ FLD

A Midwinter Stylecraft dinner and tea service, designed by Terence Conran, decorated with Nature Study pattern printed in black with skeletal leaves, 85 pieces, printed marks, 1955–60, gravy boat 8½in (21.5cm) wide.
£900–1,000
$1,300–1,500 ⚚ S(S)

A Midwinter teapot, decorated in Spanish Garden pattern, designed by Jessie Tait, c1966, 5½in (14cm) high.
£20–25
$30–35 ⚚ AND

A Midwinter coffee pot, decorated with Sienna design, in orange and olive green, 1960s, 9in (23cm) high.
£15–20
$20–30 ⊞ FLD

Moorcroft

A Moorcroft Macintyre Aurelian Ware vase, decorated with red and blue stylized poppies and gilt foliate panels, marked 'M428/64' and '314901', c1900, 9¾in (25cm) high.
£600–750
$870–1,000 ↗ Mit

A pair of Moorcroft Macintyre cups, with blue and green floral decoration on a pale green ground, c1908, 2½in (6.5cm) high.
£150–170
$220–250 ↗ SWO

▶ **A Moorcroft Plum Wisteria vase,** decorated with red, yellow and purple fruit, green foliage and Art Deco bands on a blue ground, c1930, 8in (20cm) high.
£800–1,000
$1,150–1,500 ⊞ BD

A Moorcroft black-glazed dished plate, with two kiln points, marked 'Moorcroft Burslem' and '788', 1914–18, 8¾in (22cm) diam.
£70–85
$100–125 ↗ MED

A Moorcroft vase, decorated with African Lily flambé pattern in red, yellow and green on a pastel blue/green ground, 1950, 5in (12.5cm) high.
£400–450
$580–650 ⊞ GAA

A Walter Moorcroft vase, decorated with pink flowers and brown leaves on a deep blue ground, signed 'W. Moorcroft', c1920, 4in (10cm) high.
£160–180
$230–260 ⊞ MRW

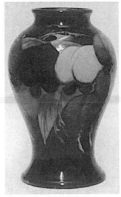

A Moorcroft vase, decorated with Wisteria pattern in yellow and purple on a blue ground, marked on base, late 1940s, 6½in (16.5cm) high.
£350–400
$500–580 ↗ Pott

A Moorcroft candlestick, decorated with Anemone pattern in red, purple and green on a yellow ground, 1950s, 3½in (9cm) high.
£140–170
$200–250 ⊞ DSG

Noritake

A Noritake comport, decorated with woodland cottages beside a lake, with gilt and blue border, on an EPNS pedestal, c1920, 9in (23cm) diam.
£100–120
$145–175 ✦ Pott

A Noritake oval dish, decorated with fruit and flowers and a pale green border with gilt bands, blue Komaru mark, c1920, 10½in (26.5cm) wide.
£80–90
$115–130 ⊞ DgC

A Noritake lustre condiment set, decorated with a tropical scene on a peach ground, green Komaru mark, c1920, mustard pot 1½in (4cm) high.
£50–55
$75–80 ⊞ DgC

◀ **A Noritake oval wall plaque,** moulded with a dead duck and acorns, in naturalistic colours, printed mark, 20thC, 18in (45.5cm) wide.
£250–300
$360–440 ✦ GAK

A Noritake three-lobed dish, pale blue with black and gilt decoration and centre handle, green Komaru mark, c1920, 8in (20.5cm) wide.
£70–80
$100–115 ⊞ DgC

A Noritake condiment set, with cruet and preserve pots decorated with red and gilt motifs on a matching tray, green Komaru mark, c1920, jam pot 4in (10cm) high.
£80–90
$115–130 ⊞ DgC

A Noritake bowl, decorated in blue with red and white flowers and green and yellow leaves, pierced rim, c1920, 7in (18cm) wide.
£30–40
$45–60 ⊞ DgC

A Noritake part tea set, decorated with blue and yellow flowers and a pale blue border, blue Komaru mark, cup 3in (7.5cm) high, c1915.
£140–160
$200–230 ⊞ DgC

A Noritake shallow bowl, decorated with stylized flowers in blue and gilt on a cream ground, c1920, 6in (15cm) diam.
£110–130
$160–190 ✦ Pott

A Noritake trio, decorated with Howo Bird pattern in blue and white, blue Komaru mark, c1920, cup 4in (10cm) high.
£30–35
$45–65 ⊞ DgC

A Noritake condiment set, with gilt decoration on red bands, c1925, 7in (18cm) wide.
£80–90
$115–130 ⊞ JACK

Pen Delfins

Pen Delfin was started in a garden shed on Coronation Day 1953 by freelance artist Jean Walmsley Heap and Jeannie Todd, both colleagues at Burnley Building Society. Their original intention was to produce clay models as Christmas gifts for friends. Since their shed was over-looked by Pendle, the legendary Lancashire Witch Hill, they called their little figures Pen Delfins, the second part of the name inspired by the 'elfin' quality of their creations. Early products included witches, pixies and elves and the mid-fifties saw the introduction of the popular Rabbit family, which helped to transform Pen Delfin from a part-time hobby into a full-time business.

The company continued to expand, moving to larger premises and exporting figures across the world. Today it attracts a large and enthusiastic collectors' club. In the 1950s you could have purchased a hand-crafted Pen Delfin figure for as little as 7s (35p). Today, rarities and early models can sell for hundreds of pounds.

◀ **A pair of Pen Delfin Rabbit bookends,** dressed in blue and pink, minor damage, 1958–65, 8in (20.5cm) high.
£650–700
$1,000–1,200 ⚲ Pott

▶ **A Pen Delfin model,** Shiner, dressed in pink dungarees, 1960–67, 4in (10cm) high.
£350–400
$500–600 ⊞ AHJ

A Pen Delfin model of a **pixie girl,** Bod, dressed in orange, minor damage, 1965–67, 5in (12.5cm) high.
£220–250
$300–350 ⚲ Pott

▶ **A Pen Delfin wall plaque,** modelled as a flying Pendle witch, finished in pewter, 1980, 7in (18cm) high.
£400–450
$580–650
⚲ Pott

A Pen Delfin Model of the Year, Woody, dressed in turquoise trousers, 1997, 4¼in (11cm) high.
£60–70
$90–100 ⊞ AHJ

Plates & Dishes

A child's plate, black transfer-printed with cottage scene, 1820, 6½in (16.5cm) diam.
£45–50
$65–75 ⊞ OD

A James Green dish, with pink flowersprays on a white ground, blue and gilt border, c1873, 9in (23cm) diam.
£30–35
$45–50 ⊞ CAL

▶ A Coalport Kingsware plate, decorated in black with a Japanese design, 1900, 9in (23cm) diam.
£40–60
$60–90 ⊞ ES

A green-glazed plate, with realistic-looking Huntley & Palmer's biscuits, impressed marks to base 'RD 305509', 10¼in (26cm) wide.
£180–200
$250–300 ⚒ BBR

A child's plate, decorated with a girl with a basket, a cat and a dog, moulded floral border, c1830, 5in (12.5cm) diam.
£60–70
$90–100 ⊞ IW

An asparagus cradle, cream ground with moulded decoration in green and brown, c1880, 10 x 14in (25.5 x 35.5cm).
£225–245
$320–350 ⊞ MLL

▶ A Brent Leigh dish, with moulded decoration of leaves and flowers, c1935, 13in (33cm) wide.
£18–20
$20–30 ⊞ JACK

A nursery plate, the centre with inscription, the border moulded and enamelled with animals and flowers in shades of green and brown, c1835, 6¼in (16cm) wide.
£70–85
$100–130 ⚒ SAS

A Bo'ness wall plate, with floral decoration in autumn colours, c1880, 10¼in ((26cm) diam.
£40–45
$60–65 ⊞ JEB

An Old Bill dish, transfer-printed in brown with an illustration of Old Bill, the WWI solider created by artist Bruce Bairnsfather, 1917, 7in (18cm) wide.
£50–55
$75–80 ⊞ LeB

Poole Pottery

A Poole Pottery twin-handled vase, designed by Truda Carter, Yo pattern, painted by Gwen Haskins, c1950, 7in (18cm) high.
£300–340
$450–500 ⊞ MI

A Carter, Stabler & Adams pottery vase, inscribed 'EP', c1930, 10in (25.5cm) high.
£1,600–1,800
$2,300–2,600 ⊞ BD

A Poole Pottery vase, designed by Truda Adams, decorated with tulips by Pat Summers, impressed and painted marks, c1930, 9½in (24cm) high.
£625–700
$950–1,000 ⊞ RUSK

A Poole Pottery vase, designed by Truda Adams, decorated with harebells, impressed marks, c1930, 7in (18cm) high.
£240–270
$350–400 ⊞ RUSK

◀ **A Poole Pottery plate,** from designs by Tony Morris, with studio backstamp, 1963, 10in (25.5cm) diam.
£280–320
$400–450 ⊞ HarC

A Poole Pottery Aegean vase, decorated in shades of brown, 1970–75, 9in (23cm) high.
£70–80
£100–120 ⊞ DSG

A Poole Pottery vase, impressed factory marks, c1960, 5½in (14cm) high.
£130–150
$200–220 ⚒ SWO

▶ **A Poole Pottery Olympus bowl,** brown earthenware, 1977, 8in (20.5cm) diam.
£40–50
$60–75 ⊞ DSG

Three Poole Pottery Delphis vases, decorated in shades of red and yellow, 1970s, 4in (10cm) high.
£15–20
$20–30 each ⊞ HarC

Pot Lids & Prattware

Pot lids are the covers of the small domestic earthenware containers used to hold a wide range of 19th-century cosmetic and comestible products. As well as typographical pieces – advertising contents and manufacturer – pictorial pot lids were also produced. Felix Pratt (1813–94) was one of the pioneers of colour-transfer printing. From the late 1840s, F. & R. Pratt of Stoke-on-Trent produced thousands of decorative pot lids, the majority designed by resident artist Jesse Austin. Some of the earliest lids, decorated with ursine pictures, were for bear's grease: a Victorian pomade for the hair produced from Russian bears. Other popular subjects include contemporary celebrities (Duke of Wellington, Prince Albert), commemorative scenes (Crimean War, Great Exhibition) and

reproductions of paintings and landscapes. F. & R. Pratt remained in production until 1920, when the business was purchased by Cauldon Potteries Ltd, who reissued several Prattware pot lids on a creamier, more porcellaneous base. Other major pot lid producers include Ridgway and Co and T. J. & J. Mayer, active from 1843, and whose designs were again reissued in the 20th century.

While pictorial pot lids are sought after for their images, advertising pot lids can also be very collectable. Toothpaste lids have been commanding high prices in the current market, as this section shows. The majority of lids illustrated have no base, which generally makes little difference to their value. American buyers of advertising lids however like, if possible, to have the complete pot.

◀ **A pot lid**, by F. & R. Pratt, No. 19, depicting a bear, a lion and a cockerel, c1855, 3in (7.5cm) diam.
£70–90
$100–130 ⊞ JBL
This pot commemorates the Crimean War, with the English lion subduing the Russian bear.

A pot lid, 'Polar Bears', by F. & R. Pratt, No. 18, polychrome-decorated, c1850, 3in (7.5cm) diam.
£200–270
$300–400 ⊞ JBL

A pot lid, 'Strasburg', by T. J. & J. Mayer, No. 331, polychrome-decorated, coloured border and base, c1850, 4¾in (12cm) diam.
£180–200
$260–300 ➤ BBR

A pot lid, 'Shakespeare's Birthplace', No. 227, with a leaf and scroll border, c1860, 5in (12.5cm) high.
£130–170
$200–220 ⊞ JBL

▶ **A pot lid, 'The Enthusiast',** by F. & R. Pratt, No. 245, c1860, 4in (10cm) diam.
£75–85
$100–125 ⊞ SER

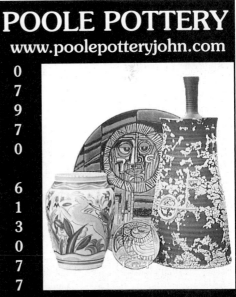

A pot lid, 'The Late Prince Consort', by F. & R. Pratt, No. 153, c1862, 4in (10cm) diam.
£75–110
$100–160 ⊞ JBL
This portrait lid was made to commemorate the death of Albert, Queen Victoria's husband.

A pot lid, 'A Pretty Kettle of Fish', by F. & R. Pratt, No. 48, polychrome-decorated, c1875, 4in (10c) diam.
£50–80
$75–115 ⊞ JBL

A pot lid, 'Uncle Toby Courting the Widow Wadman', by F. & R. Pratt, No. 328, polychrome-decorated, c1880, 4in (10cm) diam.
£45–65
$65–100 ⊞ GRI
This scene comes from Laurence Sterne's novel *Tristram Shandy*. It is an engraving after a painting by C. R. Leslie.

A paste jar, 'Mending the Nets', by F. & R. Pratt, No. 70, 19thC, 4in (10cm) high.
£70–100
$100–150 ⊞ JBL

A pot and lid, by F. & R. Pratt, No. 62, polychrome illustration on lid, c1890, 3in (7.5cm) wide.
£110–120
$160–175 ⊞ GRI

A pot lid, 'Marbrero Toothpaste', 1890–1900, 3½in (9cm) wide.
£240–260
$350–380 ⚒ BBR
The picture of a toothbrush makes this lid desirable.

A pot lid, 'American Dentrifice', blue transfer-printed, 3½in (9cm) diam.
£200–220
$300–320 ⚒ BBR

LOCATE THE SOURCE
The source of each illustration in Miller's can be found by checking the code letters below each caption with the Key to Illustrations, pages 444–452.

A pot lid, 'Valentine's Cherry Blossom Tooth Paste, with coloured overglaze transfer of a Chinese lady, 2¾in (7cm) square, with original base.
£320–350
$450–500 ⚒ BBR

A pot lid and base, 'Rose Paste', black transfer-printed lettering on pink background, with gold band, damaged, 3½in (9cm) diam.
£120–140
$175–200 ⚒ BBR

Quimper

A Quimper faïence basket, modelled as two swans with outstetched necks forming the handle, decorated in brown, blue and yellow, c1920, 9in (23cm) high.
£160-175
$230–250 ⊞ MLL

A Quimper solitaire set, decorated with a man and a woman in blue and orange, c1920, platter 9in (23cm) wide.
£425–465
$620–680 ⊞ MLL

▶ **A Quimper cup and saucer,** Broderie design, 1925–30, saucer 9½in (24cm) wide.
£40–45
$60–65 ⊞ SER

A Quimper pin dish, Butterfly/Bagpipe shape, c1920, 7in (18cm) wide.
£75–95
$100–150 ⊞ MURR

◀ **A pair of Quimper plates,** Corbeille design, decorated in red, green and blue, c1930, 9in (23cm) diam.
£110–125
$160–180 ⊞ MLL

A Quimper plate, decorated with a man in blue, orange and green, with yellow border, c1922, 7¼in (18.5cm) diam.
£35–40
$50–60 ⊞ SER

▶ **A Quimper fish dish,** Petit Breton design, c1930, 10½in (26.5cm) wide.
£40–45
$60–65 ⊞ SER

A pair of Quimper vases, polychrome-decorated, c1930, 9in (23cm) high.
£180–200
$260–300 ⊞ MLL

A Quimper jug, decorated in shades of brown and green, c1930, 4in (10cm) high.
£65–75
$95–110 ⊞ SER

A pair of Quimper clogs, decorated with orange brown and green, 20thC, 4in (10cm) long.
£15–20
$20–30 ⊞ SER

Radford

A Radford trio, decorated with swags of flowers and foliage on a cream ground, 1924, plate 7in (18cm) diam.
£12–14
$15–20 ⊞ DBo

A Radford milk jug, decorated with blue and pink flowers on a cream ground, c1930, 3in (7.5cm) high.
£45–50
$65–75 ⊞ BEV

A Radford Egyptian ware vase, decorated with yellow, green and blue geometric shapes on a beige ground, c1930, 10in (25.5cm) high.
£160–175
$230–250 ⊞ BEV

A Radford model of a hummingbird, in blue, yellow and brown, c1935, 6in (15cm) high.
£135–150
$200–220 ⊞ BEV

A Radford vase, decorated with red flowers on a cream ground, c1930, 3in (7.5cm) high.
£8–10
$10–15 ⊞ WAC

▶ **A Radford vase,** decorated in yellow, pink, blue and green, c1940, 9in (23cm) high.
£135–150
$195–220 ⊞ BEV

Charlotte Rhead

Two Bursley Ware dishes, designed by Charlotte Rhead, both decorated with stylized spring flower design on a beige mottled ground within a green border, both signed, 1930s, largest 12in (30.5cm) wide.
£170–210
$250–300 ⚒ GAK

A Crown Ducal vase, designed by Charlotte Rhead, stepped Art Deco shape, decorated in orange, buff, green and black on a cream ground, c1932, 6in (25.5cm) high.
£220–260
$320–380 ⊞ AOT

◀ **A Crown Ducal vase,** designed by Charlotte Rhead, No. 132, decorated with orange, yellow, black and gold on a light orange ground, printed and inscribed marks, 1930s, 10¼in (26cm) high.
£260–300
$380–450 ⚒ Mit

A Crown Ducal jug, designed by Charlotte Rhead, decorated with red and purple flowers on a sponged orange ground, 1930s, 7⅞in (20cm) high.
£230–260
$330–380 ⚲ WW

A Crown Ducal wall plaque, designed by Charlotte Rhead, decorated with blue and purple flowers on a light-coloured ground with blue rim, printed marks, inscribed with monogram, 1930s, 12½in (32cm) diam.
£210–250
$300–350 ⚲ Mit

A Bursley Ware cream jug and sugar basin, designed by Charlotte Rhead, No. TL37, decorated with Daisy pattern in blue, orange and green on a cream ground, 1940s, sugar bowl 2in (5cm) high.
£150–180
$220–260 ⊞ BDA

Rosenthal

A Rosenthal porcelain dish, designed by Raymond Peynet, depicting two musicians in pastel colours on a cream ground, c1950–60, 6in (15cm) wide.
£80–100
$115–150 ⊞ RDG

A Rosenthal porcelain dish, designed by Raymond Peynet, decorated in brown and black, depicting a couple on a carousel, c1950–60, 4½in (11.5cm) wide.
£40–50
$60–75 ⊞ RDG

A Rosenthal porcelain vase, decorated with a man and a cockerel on a horse, 1960s, 12in (30.5cm) high.
£150–200
$220–300 ⊞ BRU

Royal Copenhagen

◄ **A Royal Copenhagen model of a fisherwoman,** with a blue shawl, c1948, 9in (23cm) high.
£500–580
$720–850 ⊞ PSA

► **A Royal Copenhagen faïence vase,** decorated in blue and purple on a white ground, 1950s, 11½in ((29cm) high.
£130–150
$200–220 ⊞ ORI

A Royal Copenhagen model of two squirrels, in brown on a white base, c1957, 12in (30.5cm) high.
£450–500
$650–720 ⊞ PSA

◀ **A Royal Copenhagen vase,** decorated with a white and blue flower on a white ground, 1960s, 7½in (19cm) high.
£50–60
$75–90 ⊞ MARK

> **Miller's is a price GUIDE not a price LIST**

A Royal Copenhagen model, 'Potatoes Woman', in blue, brown and white, c1960, 10½in (26.5cm) high.
£250–300
$350–450 ⊞ PSA

▶ **A Royal Copenhagen group,** depicting two lovers, restored, printed mark and No. 1132, 18½in (47cm) high.
£500–550
$720–800 ⚒ GAK

Royal Winton

A Royal Winton plate, depicting Anne Hathaway's cottage in naturalistic colours, c1930, 9in (23cm) diam.
£70–80
$100–115 ⊞ BEV

A Royal Winton teapot, decorated in Margaret Rose pattern in pink and green on a yellow ground, c1930, 5in (12.5cm) high.
£160–180
$230–260 ⊞ BEV

A Royal Winton lustre vase, decorated with Oriental design in colours on a dark blue ground, with red interior, 1930s, 9in (23cm) high.
£225–250
$320–360 ⊞ BEV

Ruskin

◀ **A pair of Ruskin Pottery orange lustre candlesticks,** c1915, 7in (18cm) high.
£250–275
$360–400 ⊞ GAA

▶ **A Ruskin Pottery bottle vase,** decorated with green mottled glaze, impressed mark 'Ruskin 1930', 1930, 6¼in (16cm) high.
£100–125
$150–180 ⚒ MED

A Ruskin Pottery gourd shape vase, decorated in pale yellow crystalline glaze, c1920, 8in (20.5cm) high.
£280–325
$400–470 ⊞ RUSK

Shelley

A Shelley cat, black, with 'Good Luck' inscribed on side, 1910–15, 5in (12.5cm) high.
£80–100
$115–145 ⊞ BEV

A Shelley Queen Anne trio, decorated with Anemone pattern in blue and yellow, c1930, plate 6in (15cm) diam.
£100–125
$145–180 ⊞ BD

A Shelley bowl, printed black marks within a cartouche, 1900–30, 5in (12.5cm) diam.
£15–20
$20–30 ⊞ ES

A Shelley Harmony dish, with three compartments, hand-painted in turquoise and grey, 1930s, 10in (25.5cm) wide.
£80–90
$115–130 ⊞ BEV

◄ **A Shelley chamberstick,** decorated in grey, orange, turquoise and green, c1930, 6in (15cm) diam.
£70–80
$100–115 ⊞ BEV

A Shelley dish, decorated with a rural scene in pastel colours, 1930s, 4½in (11.5cm) diam.
£24–28
$35–40 ⊞ WAC

A Shelley Harmony vase, decorated in turquoise, blue and mauve, c1930, 8½in (21.5cm) high.
£110–120
$150–175 ⊞ BEV

◄ **A Shelley Blue Rock egg cup,** decorated with blue and mauve blossoms, tiny blossom inside, blue rim, manufacturer's stamp in green, 'Blue Rock 13691' in blue on base, 1952, 2¼in (5.5cm) high.
£25–30
$35–45 ⊞ FL

Shorter

A Shorter & Son planter, shape No. 169 L/S, decorated in mottled brown and cream glaze, early 1930s, 7½in (19cm) wide.
£40–45
$60–65 ⊞ DEC

A Shorter & Son two-handled vase, designed by Mabel Leigh, with mottled green and silver matt glaze, maker's printed mark and Mabel Leigh mark to base, early 1930s, 7in (18cm) wide.
£40–45
$60–65 ⊞ DEC

◄ **A Shorter & Son chamberstick,** decorated in mottled blue, green and brown matt glaze, 1930s, 5¾in (14.5cm) wide.
£30–35
$45–50 ⊞ DEC

A Shorter & Son Thisbe vase, design attributed to Clarice Cliff, in dripping green glaze, damaged, early script stamp, early 1930s, 6½in (16cm) high.
£20–25
$30–35 ⊞ DEC

A Shorter & Son Mendosa shallow earthenware bowl, with sgraffito panels of scrolling flowers and leaves on a turquoise ground, 1930s, 10¼in (26cm) diam.
£90–100
$130–145 ✗ CAu

A Shorter & Son character jug, designed by Colin Shorter, modelled as a guardsman, decorated in black, red and yellow, 1940s, 6½in (16.5cm) high.
£75–85
$110–125 ⊞ BEV

A Shorter & Son Festival vase, with matt white glaze, slight scratching to glaze, 1950s, 11in (28cm) wide.
£24–28
$35–42 ⊞ DEC

Staffordshire

A Staffordshire pastille burner, modelled as a house in naturalistic colours, c1850, 4in (10cm) high.
£140–150
$200–220 ⊞ SER

A Staffordshire Prattware figure of Bacchus, decorated in pink, brown and green glaze, 1780–1800, 5in (12.5cm) high.
£150–170
$220–250 ⊞ SER

A Staffordshire figure of a child, with red, blue and yellow robe and matching scarf, possibly by Enoch Wood, restored, 1820–30, 4½in (11.5cm) high.
£150–170
$220–250 ⊞ SER

A Staffordshire figure of a clergyman, preaching from a pulpit, with a verger at a reading desk below, wearing black robes, c1835, 10in (25.5cm) high.
£450–500
$650–720 ⊞ ML

▶ **A Staffordshire figure of a man,** with a turquoise frock coat and grey trousers, carrying a black hat, 1840–50, 7in (18cm) high.
£100–130
$145–190 ⊞ ML

▶ **A pair of Staffordshire dogs,** in brown and white, c1850, 7½in (19cm) high.
£450–500
$650–720 ⊞ TUN

A Staffordshire spill vase, modelled as a pair of foresters wearing turquoise jackets, c1850, 13in (33cm) high.
£350–400
$500–580 ⊞ ML

▶ **A Staffordshire biblical group,** depicting Rebecca at the well with Abraham, in pink, yellow, red and brown, c1855, 13in (33cm) high.
£150–200
$220–290 ⊞ TUN

A Staffordshire watch-holder group, the man in a blue coat with a musical instrument, the woman carrying an animal, the central pillar decorated with strawberries and leaves, 1855, 12½in (32cm) high.
£125–150
$180–220 ⊞ **TUN**

A Staffordshire spill vase, entitled 'Good Companions', depicting a brown horse and black and white cow drinking from a fountain, beneath a tree with birds, c1855, 10in (25.5cm) high.
£150–180
$220–250 ⊞ **TUN**

A Staffordshire figure of a sailor, in a pale blue shirt, red scarf and yellow hat, c1855, 12in (30.5cm) high.
£250–300
$360–440 ⊞ **TUN**

A Staffordshire Parr figure, depicting Hamlet wearing a black plumed hat, black cape trimmed in red, with red trousers and white hose, and holding a skull, c1860, 11in (28cm) high.
£350–400
£500–580 ⊞ **TUN**

◀ **A pair of Staffordshire models of cats,** with painted faces and blue collar bows, c1870, 8in (20.5cm) high.
£350–400
$500–600 ⊞ **ML**

A Staffordshire figure, entitled 'The Wounded Soldier', in blue, red, pink and yellow, c1855, 10in (25.5cm) high.
£350–400
$500–580 ⊞ **TUN**

▶ **A Staffordshire Parr figure,** depicting Garibaldi in a red shirt, 1863, 12½in (32cm) high.
£600–650
$900–1,000 ⊞ **TUN**

LOCATE THE SOURCE

The source of each illustration in Miller's can be found by checking the code letters below each caption with the Key to Illustrations, pages 444–452.

A Staffordshire figure of a lady, wearing a green jacket and pink skirt, c1860, 4½in (11.5cm) high.
£30–35
$45–50 ⊞ **IW**

A Staffordshire group, entitled 'Auld Lang Syne', one man with a yellow tam-o-shanter, one with a red rug over his legs, and one in a red, white and green kilt and sash, c1855, 9in (23cm) high.
£250–300
$360–450 ⊞ **TUN**

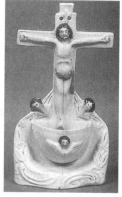

A Staffordshire stoop, depicting Christ crucified, with three angels, c1880, 8in (20.5cm) high.
£125–150
$180–220 ⊞ **SER**

Studio Pottery

A Michael Cardew Winchcombe stoneware teapot, decorated in brown with yellow slip, c1930, 5in (12.5cm) high.
£450–500
$650–725 ↗ RBB

► **An Isle of Wight basket pot,** cream and green mottled earthenware with woven cane handle, c1940, 7in (18cm) diam.
£30–40
$45–60 ⊞ DSG

A slipware charger, in the style of Thomas Toft, decorated with the Royal arms, motto and inscription within a hatched border, slight restoration, 20thC, 17¾in (45cm) diam.
£90–100
$130–150 ↗ Bon
Although the maker of this particular charger is unknown, slipware examples of this type were potted by Bernard Leach at St Ives. Leach was interested in reviving traditional art forms that were being undermined by industry and was particularly inspired by the 17th-century slipware of Thomas Toft.

A Derek Clarkson pottery bottle vase, yellow with crystalline decoration in shades of blue, c1990, 8¼in (21cm) high.
£250–300
$360–450 ⊞ PGA

A Leach pottery Standard Ware bowl, with 'Z' design, impressed seal mark, c1960, 9in (23cm) diam.
£90–100
$130–150 ⊞ RUSK

A Yelland Pottery cup and saucer, by Michael Leach, with green glaze, 1960, saucer 5¾in (14.5cm) diam.
£15–20
$20–30 ⊞ IW

A Holmegaard cast stoneware vase, designed by Arne Bang, model No. 6, with brown and grey glaze, marked AB, c1937, 5in (12.5cm) high.
£275–300
$400–450 ↗ TREA

A Bernard Leach stoneware pot and cover, probably made in Kyoto, the unglazed cover painted in blue and green with a well-head within concentric circles, the base with foliate motifs, cracks to cover, the base marked 'BL' in black enamel, c1934, 3½in (9cm) diam.
£350–400
$500–600 ↗ Bon

A Katherine Pleydell-Bouverie stoneware vase, decorated with sgraffito overlapping arch motif within Greek key border, impressed 'KBP' within a rectangle and 'Cole' within a triangle, 1925–28, 5in (12.5cm) high.
£350–400
$500–580 ↗ CAu

SylvaC

A SylvaC spring onion pot, decorated in green, cream and brown, No. 5042, 1930s, 5in (12.5cm) high.
£30–35
$45–50 ⊞ TAC

A SylvaC posy bowl, the border with three rabbits and leaves, in green and brown, No. 1312, 1930s, 9in (23cm) diam.
£45–55
$65–80 ⊞ TAC

A SylvaC duck, with white body and yellow beak and feet, No. 1499, 1930s, 4½in (11.5cm) high.
£40–45
$60–65 ↗ BBR

A SylvaC Scottish terrier, with beige body and brown nose and collar, No. 1209, 1950s, 11in (28cm) high.
£70–80
$100–115 ↗ BBR

A green SylvaC dog, 1950s, 4in (10cm) high.
£40–50
$60–75 ⊞ TAC

Three SylvaC comic rabbits, in graduated sizes, 1950s, largest 8in (20.5cm) high.
£30–50
$45–75 each ⊞ TAC

A SylvaC dog and basket, decorated in yellow and brown, No. 1996, 1950s, 5in (12.5cm) wide.
£30–35
$45–50 ⊞ TAC

A beige SylvaC long-eared dog, 1950s, 7in (18cm) high.
£40–45
$60–65 ⊞ TAC

A brown SylvaC chipmunk, 1960s, 7in (18cm) high.
£25–30
$35–45 ⊞ TAC

▶ **A SylvaC spaniel,** lying down, with a brown head and brown patches on body, 1950s, 3½in (9cm) long.
£30–35
$45–50 ↗ BBR

Troika

A Troika charger, painted and incised dark blue and red, on a blue ground, impressed Trident mark, 1963–65, 10in (25.5cm) diam.
£250–300
$360–450 ⊞ TRO

A Troika ashtray, green with ochre dots, 1960s, 5in (12.5cm) square.
£50–70
$75–100 ⊞ MURR

A Troika River Thames plaque, signed 'Troika St Ives', with painted Trident mark, 1963–65, 10½in (26.5cm) high.
£650–750
$1,000–1,100 ⊞ TRO

► **A Troika ceramic drum,** by Ann Lewis, decorated with red circles and blue bands, 1967–70, 6½in (16.5cm) diam.
£275–325
$400–470
⊞ TRO

A Troika slab vase, probably by Benny Sirota, with oxide decoration, marked 'Troika St Ives BS', 1963–65, 7½in (19cm) high.
£200–250
$300–360 ⊞ TRO

A Troika cylinder vase, by Honor Curtis, decorated in beige and dark blue, signed 'Troika St Ives Cornwall HC', late 1960s, 6½in (16.5cm) high.
£170–190
$250–275 ⊞ TRO

> **Cross Reference**
> See Sixties & Seventies (page 354)

◄ **A Troika cylinder vase,** deep blue with light brown circles and bands on a brown and grey ground, signed 'Troika Cornwall AB', late 1970s, 14in (35.5cm) high.
£300–360
$450–520 ⊞ TRO

Wade

A Wadeheath Flaxman Pluto, decorated in yellow and black, 1937–38, 6½in (16.5cm) long.
£200–250
$300–360 ✎ Pott

Four Wade Disney Hat Box series animals, including Bambi, Lady and Scamp, 1950s–60s, largest 2½in (6.5cm) high.
£10–20
$15–30 each ⊞ PC

Two Wade gingerbread figures, an adult and two children, 1995, adult 4¼in (11cm) high.
£20–30
$30–45 each ⊞ PC

Four Wade animals, Bactrian Camel, Grizzly Cub, Grizzly Bear and Llama, in beige and white, 1950s, largest 2in (5cm) high.
£15–30
$20–45 each ⊞ PC

A Wadeheath panda, decorated in black and white enamels, 1950s, 7in (18cm) high.
£350–400
$500–600 ✎ Pott

◄ **Two Wade figures,** Yogi Bear and Mr Jinks, Yogi with red scarf, Mr Jinks with blue bow tie, 1962–63, largest 2½in (6.5cm) high.
£65–75
$100–110 ✎ BBR

A Wade Thomas the Tank Engine money box, decorated in blue, red, yellow and black, 1986, 6½in (16.5cm) long.
£100–120
$150–175 ✎ Pott

► **Three Wade Mr Men and Little Miss Figures,** Little Miss Giggles, Mr Happy and Mr Bump, for Robell Media Promotions, late 20thC, 3¾in (9.5cm) high.
£35–40
$50–60 ✎ BBR

A Wade Blow Up polar bear, 1962–63, 6in (15cm) high.
£80–100
$120–150 ✎ Pott

A Wade spaniel, brown, limited edition No. 0104 of 1,000, September 1994, 3¼in (8.5cm) high.
£15–20
$20–30 ✎ BBR

Wedgwood

A Wedgwood lustre ware fluted bowl, decorated with four gilt dragons on a mottled lustre ground, slight crazing, pattern No. Z4831, printed mark, c1920, 7¼in (18.5cm) high.
£170–200
$250–300 ↗ WW

A Wedgwood Drabware custard cup, modelled as a beige artichoke, with gilt outlines, c1790, 3½in (9cm) high.
£350–400
£500–600 ⊞ US

A pair of Wedgwood black basalt baluster vases, applied on either side with masks, with panel of dancing figures, integral socle, impressed marks, late 19thC, 8½in (21.5cm) high.
£100–120
$150–175 ↗ GAK

◄ **A Wedgwood grey vase,** designed by Keith Murray, c1930, 8in (20.5cm) high.
£800–850
$1,200–1,250
⊞ BD

A Wedgwood black basalt bowl, designed by Keith Murray, 1930s–40s, 9in (23cm) diam.
£400–480
$600–700 ⊞ BEV

A Wedgwood vase, designed by Keith Murray, cream with horizontal ribbing, 1930s–40s, 6in (15cm) diam.
£300–350
$450–500 ⊞ BEV

► **A Wedgwood plate,** designed by Eric Ravilious with Garden pattern, 1950s, 7½in (19cm) diam.
£135–150
$200–225 ⊞ REN

Three Wedgwood pattern Russell Hobbs electrically-heated pots, a coffee percolator and milk warmer decorated in Glen Mist pattern, and a coffee percolator in Poppy pattern, 1970s, percolators 10in (25.5cm) high.
£8–10
$10–15 each ⊞ AND

Wemyss

A Wemyss plate, painted with sweet peas in cerise, purple and green, blue rim, c1900, 5in (12.5cm) diam.
£150–200
$220–300 ⊞ RdeR

A Wemyss preserve pot, painted with hive and bees in brown, yellow, green and black, blue rim, c1900, 5in (12.5cm) high.
£270–300
$400–450 ⊞ RdeR

◄ **A Wemyss porridge bowl,** decorated with a black cockerel, inscribed in red 'Save yer braith tae cuil yer parritch', the rim with white leaves on a deep blue ground, c1920, 7in (18cm) diam.
£300–350
$450–500 ⊞ RdeR

A Wemyss spiral-moulded jardinière, painted with roses in pink and green, green rim, slight damage, c1900, 8¾in (22cm) diam.
£90–110
$130–160 ✗ WW

A Wemyss pig, by Plichta, painted in pink and green with flowering clover, late 1930s, 12in (30.5cm) wide.
£500–700
$750–1,000 ⊞ RdeR

Worcester

A Worcester figure of a girl, with shoulder-length hair and flowing garments, painted in natural colours, impressed mark, c1862, 11¼in (28.5cm) high.
£330–360
$470–500 ✗ HYD

A Royal Worcester wall vase, modelled as an orchid in green and white with gilt highlights, printed mark in green, 1892, 7¾in (20cm) high.
£100–150
$150–220 ✗ L&E

A Royal Worcester figure, entitled 'The Loafer', by James Hadley, c1925, 5in (12.5cm) high.
£240–270
$350–400 ⊞ GRI

A Royal Worcester figure, entitled 'Friday's Child', depicting a boy in green trousers with red belt and sandals feeding a kitten from a red-rimmed bowl, 1950s, 7in (18cm) high.
£150–180
$220–260 ⊞ WAC

Genuine Carlton Ware
The Carlton Ware Collectors Club
Telephone 020 8318 9580

Colour Review

◀ **A Royal Doulton pottery vase,** by Frank Butler, incised with Art Nouveau-style flowers and trailing foliage, c1908, 13¾in (35cm) high.
£500–550
$700–800 ⚏ AH

A Denby mug, by Glyn Colledge, 1948–55, 6in (15cm) high.
£45–60
$65–95 ⊞ DSG

A Doulton Lambeth faïence pilgrim flask, by Mary Butterton, assisted by Alice Campbell, No. L325, printed circular factory marks, painted artist's monograms, 1890s, 14¼in (36cm) high.
£700–800
$1,200–1,500 ⚏ S(NY)
Ex-Harriman Judd Collection.

▶ **A pair of Royal Doulton Tutankhamen vases,** 1923–29, 11in (28cm) high.
£1,300–1500
$1,900–2,200 ⊞ I&M

◀ **A Royal Doulton baseball player prototype character jug,** by David Briggs, No. D6624, printed factory mark, minor damage, 1970, 8½in (21.5cm) high.
£6,500–7,500
$9,500–11,000 ⚏ P

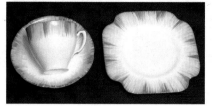

◄ **A Goldscheider double dancing group,** c1930, 15in (38cm) high.
£2,750–3,000
$4,000–4,500 ⊞ BD

A Grafton china trio, 1930, plate 6in (15cm) square.
£10–12
$15–20 ⊞ CAL

A pair of Gray's Pottery coffee cans and saucers, designed by Susie Cooper, in bold geometric design, factory mark 8071, saucer 4½in (11.5cm) diam.
£250–275
$360–400 ⚲ RFA

A T. G. Green Mocha ware jug, 1910, 6¼in (16cm) high.
£100–120
$145–175 ⊞ WCa

◄ **A T. G. Green Pharos design biscuit barrel,** design No. 753176, registered 1930, 7in (18cm) high.
£450–500
$650–720 ⊞ CAL

► **A T. G. Green Streamline biscuit barrel,** 1930, 8in (20cm) high.
£180–200
$260–290 ⊞ CAL

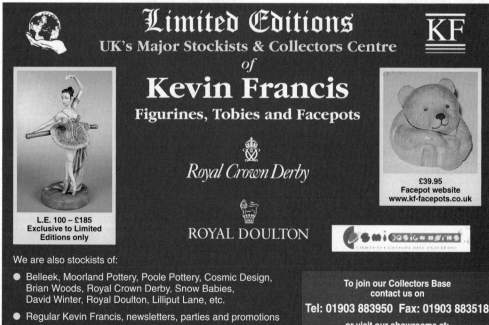

A T. G. Green Cornish Ware jar, 1930s, 7in (18cm) high.
£60–65
$90–100 ⊞ CAL

A T. G. Green Cornish Ware sugar shaker, 1950, 7in (18cm) high.
£750–1,000
$1,100–1,500 ⊞ CAL
This rare red and white design was produced as a prototype only.

▶ **A Hancock's Cremorne vase,** c1930, 13in (33cm) high.
£270–300
$400–450 ⊞ BEV

A T. G. Green Flair TV dinner plate, in the Patio shape, 1956, 9in (23cm) wide.
£25–30
$35–45 ⊞ CAL

A Hummel Meditation figure, No. 13/0, TMK2, Bee trademark, 1950s, 6in (15cm) high.
£160–180
$230–260 ⊞ ATH

A T. G. Green Cornish Ware marmalade pot, 1966, 4in (10cm) high.
£40–50
$60–75 ⊞ CAL
This is from the range designed by Judith Onions.

◀ **A James Kent Apple Blossom chintz teapot,** c1930, 7in (18cm) high.
£175–200
$250–280 ⊞ BD

A Longchamps majolica cachepot, 1890, 9in (23cm) high.
£330–350
$470–500 ⊞ MLL

A Bernard Leach Standard ware dish with handle, St Ives Pottery, c1954, 6½in (16.5cm) wide.
£20–25
$30–35 ⊞ GRo

A Maling hand-painted lustre plate, 1930s, 11in (28cm) diam.
£170–200
$250–280 ⊞ TAC

◀ **A Midwinter Red Domino coffee cup and saucer,** 1950s, saucer 4¾in (12cm) diam.
£18–22
$25–35 ⚒ FLD

▶ **A Moorcroft Pomegranate vase,** c1930, 12in (30.5cm) high.
£1,600–1,800
$2,300–2,600 ⊞ BD

A Mosaic tin-glazed earthenware model of a cat, with inset glass eyes, marked, early 20thC, 9½in (24cm) high.
£550–650
$800–950 ➶ TEN

▶ **A Prattware polychrome pot lid,** inscribed around rim 'I consent she replied if you promise that no jealous rival shall laugh me to scorn', 19thC, 4in (10cm) diam.
£70–100
$100–145 ⊞ JBL

A *Nanking* Cargo Pagoda River tea bowl, c1850, 3in (7.5cm) diam.
£120–140
$175–200 ⊞ RBA

▶ **A model of a cat,** Portuguese, 20thC, 10in (25.5cm) high.
£25–28
$35–45 ⊞ WAC

A Noritake dressing table set, blue Komaru mark, c1920, tray 18in (45.5cm) wide.
£150–170
$220–250 ⊞ DgC

A Pearson's vase, c1945, 8½in (20.5cm) high.
£40–60
$60–90 ⊞ DSG

A Quimper plate, 1930, 8½in (21.5cm) diam.
£80–90
$115–130 ⊞ MLL

A Radford jug, in unusual square shape, c1940, 11in (28cm) high.
£135–150
$195–220 ⊞ BEV

A Rookwood Arts & Crafts vase, signed 'William Henschel', 1910, 5in (12.5cm) high.
£750–825
$1,100–1,200 ⬈ TREA

A Royal Copenhagen faïence vase, designed by Nils Thorssen, 1950s, 11½in (29cm) high.
£130–150
$190–220 ⊞ ORI

A Royal Winton chintz milk jug, decorated with Majestic pattern, 1930s, 3in (7.5cm) high.
£90–100
$130–145 ⊞ BEV

▶ **A Shelley vase,** c1930, 7in (18cm) high.
£55–60
$80–90 ⊞ BEV

A Royal Winton Rosebud coffee pot, 1930s, 8in (20.5cm) high.
£85–95
$125–140 ⊞ BD

A Shelley jug, decorated with Maytime pattern, 1930s, 4in (10cm) high.
£75–85
$100–125 ⊞ DBo

◀ **A Shelley vase,** decorated with Tulip pattern, 1930, 10in (25.5cm) high.
£225–250
$325–350 ⊞ BEV

A Shelley cup and saucer, in Vogue design, 1930, 3in (7.5cm) high.
£160–180
$230–260 ⊞ BEV

A Shelley Baby's Plate, decorated with a Red Riding Hood scene, 1940–60, 8in (20.5cm) diam.
£70–90
$100–130 ✦ G(L)

A Staffordshire group depicting the death of Nelson, c1850, 9in (23cm) high.
£250–300
$350–450 ⊞ ML

◀ **A Staffordshire spill vase,** modelled as a doe with young fawn, c1855, 12in (30.5cm) high.
£200–250
$300–350 ⊞ TUN

▶ **A Staffordshire jug,** modelled as a monkey playing a viola, c1870, 12in (30.5cm) high.
£450–500
$650–720 ⊞ ML

◀ A SylvaC rabbit, No. 1065, 1950s, 6in (15cm) high.
£55–65
$80–95 ⊞ TAC

A Troika storage jar, by Alison Brigden, decorated with Snakeskin pattern, signed 'Troika Cornwall AB', late 1970s, 8½in (21.5cm) high.
£170–190
$250–275 ⊞ TRO

A Sally Tuffin Double Dove plate, designed for Dennis China Works, 1996, 10in (25.5cm) diam.
£100–120
$145–175 ⊞ NP

A Royal Worcester figure, 'Saturday's Child', depicting a child knitting watched by a cat, 1951, 6in (15cm) high.
£220–240
$320–350 ⊞ WAC

A Wemyss preserve pot, painted with plums, c1900, 5in (12.5cm) high.
£180–200
$260–290 ⊞ RdeR

▶ A Winstanley hand-painted tabby cat, c1998, 12in (30.5cm) high.
£55–65
$80–95 ⊞ RIA

Christmas

Decorated Christmas trees were first recorded on the Continent in the 17th century. Queen Charlotte, German-born wife of George III, is credited with introducing the Christmas tree to the UK. On Christmas day, 1800, she held a party for the children of Windsor, the centrepiece of which was a yew tree decorated with sweetmeats, toys and candles. Christmas trees remained a Royal institution and it was Prince Albert who helped turn them into a national one. Not only did he present trees to schools and army barracks, but in 1848 he allowed the *Illustrated London News* to produce a full page engraving of his and Victoria's family Christmas tree. Suddenly everybody wanted one.

America did not take up the custom until c1855, but it was the USA which brought modern technology to Chrismas decorations. Thomas Edison was the first to decorate a tree with electric light bulbs in 1882, and the first commercial Christmas or fairy lights were produced by the Edison General Electric Co, New Jersey, in December 1901. Christmas crackers were pioneered in the 1840s by British confectioner Tom Smith, who decided that his sweets would sell better if contained in brightly coloured exploding packages.

The first Christmas card was commissioned in 1843 by Sir Henry Cole, instigator of the Great Exhibition. He asked artist J. C. Horsley to design a card that he could send to friends, rather than writing to them all in person. The idea took off, manufacturers began to produce Christmas cards and in 1880 the General Post Office first introduced the slogan 'Post Early for Christmas'.

A moveable Christmas card, c1880, 5 x 3in (12.5 x 7.5cm).
£75–85
$110–125 ⊞ SDP

A cut-out moveable Christmas card, c1880, 5 x 3in (12.5 x 7.5cm).
£100–110
$150–150 ⊞ SDP

Cross Reference
See Colour Review (page 185)

▶ **A Victorian Longton earthenware Christmas plate,** decorated with a robin singing, inscribed 'A Happy Christmas to You', 14½in (37cm) diam.
£130–150
$190–220
↗ G(L)

A Christmas pudding wrapper, 'Ye Olde English Plum Pudding', New Zealand, 1900, 4 x 14in (10 x 35.5cm).
£3–4
$5–10 ⊞ HUX

◀ **A bisque-headed Father Christmas doll,** by Simon & Halbig, with brown wig and kid-leather beard on a five-piece composition body, with painted boots and original red and white Santa costume and holding a Christmas tree, German, c1900, 8in (20.5cm) high.
£300–400
$450–580 ↗ Bon

▶ **A Christmas cake decoration,** modelled as a snowbaby, c1910–20, 3½in (9cm) high.
£75–85
$110–125 ⊞ MURR

A white-glazed pudding basin, black transfer-printed with 'Gunstone's Christmas Puddings, Made by Wm Gunstone & Sons Ltd. Sheffield', c1880–90, 3½in (9cm) high.
£70–80
$100–115 ⚲ BBR

A Harvino Toffee tin, decorated in colour with Father Christmas and children, c1920, 6in (15cm) wide.
£40–50
$60–75 ⊞ MURR

A box of Caley standard crackers, c1930, 11in (28cm) square.
£40–50
$60–75 ⊞ MRW

Prices

The price ranges quoted in this book reflect the average price a purchaser might expect to pay for a similar item from a similar source. The price will vary according to the condition, rarity, size, popularity, provenance, colour and restoration of the item, and this must be taken into account when assessing values. Don't forget that if you are selling it is quite likely that you will be offered less than the price range.

A lead figure of Santa Claus, by Hills, 1950s, 2½in (6.5cm) high.
£50–60
$75–90 ⊞ RUSS

A Christmas pudding, with card inscribed 'With best wishes for Christmas and the New Year from The Queen and The Duke of Edinburgh, Christmas 1962', in original box, 7½in (19cm) square.
£40–45
$60–65 ⊞ HUX

A Trifari Christmas wreath pin, gold-coloured with green, blue and red paste stones, 1950s, 2in (5cm) wide.
£50–60
$75–90 ⊞ CRIS

A Spinx Christmas tree pin, with clear and red paste stones, 1960s, 2¼in (5.5cm) high.
£40–45
$60–65 ⊞ CRIS

A Father Christmas Toby jug, commissioned by Ed Pascoe, limited edition, 1989, 6in (15cm) high.
£225–275
$320–400 ⊞ DCA

A Trifari Christmas tree pin, gold-coloured with clear, red, blue and green paste stones, 1950s, 2¼in (5.5cm) high.
£65–75
$100–110 ⊞ CRIS

▶ **A silver-plated Christmas spoon,** by ARS Edition using Hummel designs, with enamel finial depicting an angel praying beside the baby Jesus, the bowl inscribed, 1983, 5in (12.5cm) long, in original box.
£20–35
$30–50 ⊞ ATH

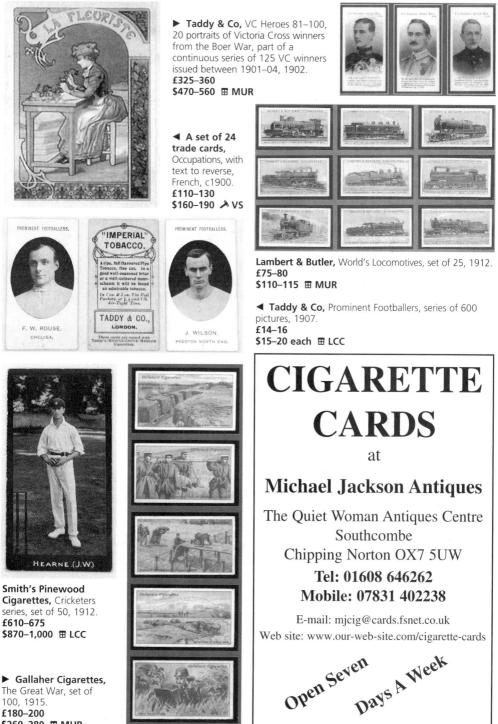

Cigarette & Trade Cards

▶ **Taddy & Co,** VC Heroes 81–100, 20 portraits of Victoria Cross winners from the Boer War, part of a continuous series of 125 VC winners issued between 1901–04, 1902.
£325–360
$470–560 ⊞ MUR

◀ **A set of 24 trade cards,** Occupations, with text to reverse, French, c1900.
£110–130
$160–190 ⤳ VS

Lambert & Butler, World's Locomotives, set of 25, 1912.
£75–80
$110–115 ⊞ MUR

◀ **Taddy & Co,** Prominent Footballers, series of 600 pictures, 1907.
£14–16
$15–20 each ⊞ LCC

F. W. ROUSE. CHELSEA.

"IMPERIAL" TOBACCO.

A ripe, full flavoured Pipe Tobacco, fine cut. In a good well-seasoned briar or a well-coloured meerschaum it will be found an admirable tobacco. In 1 oz. & 2 oz. Tin Foil Packets, or 1 & 1 lb. Air-Tight Tins.

TADDY & CO., LONDON.

These cards are issued with Taddy's 'MYRTLE GROVE MEDIUM' Cigarettes.

J. WILSON. PRESTON NORTH END.

HEARNE.(J.W)

Smith's Pinewood Cigarettes, Cricketers series, set of 50, 1912.
£610–675
$870–1,000 ⊞ LCC

▶ **Gallaher Cigarettes,** The Great War, set of 100, 1915.
£180–200
$260–280 ⊞ MUR

Typhoo Tea, Ancient Annual Customs, 25 cards, 1922.
£35–40
$50–60 ⊞ MAr

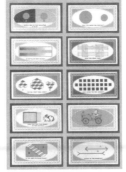

Godfrey Phillips, Optical Illusions, set of 25 cards, 1925.
£45–50
$65–75 ⊞ MUR

W. D. & H. O. Wills, British Butterflies, 50 cards, 1927.
£45–50
$65–75 ⊞ MAr

W. D. & H. O. Wills, Radio Celebrities, cigarette cards in album, 1930.
£9–10
$12–15 ⊞ LCC

John Player & Sons, Tennis, cigarette cards in album, 1930s.
£9–10
$12–15 ⊞ LCC

W. D. & H. O. Wills, Military Aircraft, five uncut sheets comprising complete set of 50 cards, compiled late 1930s, date stamped 24 March 1966.
£80–120
$115–175 ⋏ VS

◀ **W. D. & H. O. Wills,** Safety First, cigarette cards in album, produced in conjunction with the government, 1934.
£9–10
$12–15 ⊞ LCC

John Player & Sons, Derby and Grand National Winners, set of 50 cards, 1933.
£70–80
$100–115 ⊞ MUR

▶ **John Player & Sons,** Motor Cars, set of 50 cards, 1935.
£50–60
$75–90 ⊞ MAr

Liebig trade cards, Symbols of Power, 1971.
£50–70
$75–100 ⊞ MAr

John Player & Sons,
Golf, complete set of
25, 1939.
£80–100
$115–150 ⚒ VS

**Philadelphia Chewing
Gum Corporation,** War
Bulletin, 88 cards depicting
events from WWII, 1965.
£95–110
$150–160 ⊞ MUR

Brooke Bond, Magic World of Disney, set of 25
cards, 1989.
£5–6
$7–10 ⊞ LCC

◀ **John Player & Sons,** History of Motor Racing, set of
30 cards from Tom Thumb cigars, 1986.
£25–30
$35–45 ⊞ LCC

Brooke Bond, The Secret Diary of Kevin Tipps, set of 50
American-size cards from PG Tips tea, 1995.
£7–9
$10–15 ⊞ LCC

Brooke Bond, International
Footballers, set of 20 cards
from PG Tips tea, 1998.
£3–5
$5–7 ⊞ LCC

Topps Bubblegum, X Files,
set of 72 cards, 1997.
£8–10
$12–15 ⊞ LCC

Comics & Annuals

Action Comics, New Year cover, 1945.
£40–50
$60–75 ⚹ CBP

The Beano Book,
No. 1, 1940.
£2,800–3,000
$4,000–4,500 ⚹ CBP

Miller's is a price GUIDE not a price LIST

Fantastic Four 1 comic,
1961.
£350–400
$500–580 ⚹ CBP

Adventure comic,
Nos. 27–52,
March–September, 1922.
£230–250
$330–380 ⚹ CBP

The Dandy comic,
48 issues between 1,155
and 1,205, 1964.
£190–220
$275–320 ⚹ CBP

Funny Wonder comics,
1893–1942.
£2–12
$5–15 each ⊞ DPO

▶ **The Beano Comic,**
No. 13, 1938.
£500–550
$720–800 ⚹ CBP

The Beano Comic,
No. 5, 1938.
£600–700
$870–1,000 ⚹ CBP

▶ **Champion The Wonder Horse** annual,
1958, 9 x 11in (23 x 28cm).
£4–6
$5–8 ⊞ YR

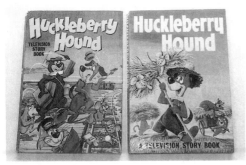

Two *Huckleberry Hound Television Story Book*
annuals, 1961, 9 x 11in (23 x 28cm).
£5–7
$6–10 ⊞ YR

The Magic Comic,
No. 1, 1939.
£1,200–1,500
$1,750–2,200 ↗ CBP

Mickey Mouse Weekly
comic, No. 1, 1936.
£250–280
$360–400 ↗ CBP

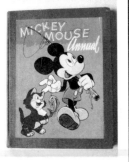

Mickey Mouse Annual,
1948, 8 x 10in
(20.5 x 25.5cm).
£45–50
$65–75 ⊞ SDP

Nipper's Magazine, 1921.
£2–3
$5–8 ⊞ J&S

Rover & Wizard, 1 July–20 December, 1967.
£100–110
$150–160 ↗ CBP

▶ *Superman* comic, No. 44, 1947.
£140–160
$200–230 ↗ CBP

New Triumph comics, Nos. 771–792, 1939.
£1,800–2,000
$2,500–3,000 ↗ CBP

LOCATE THE SOURCE

The source of each illustration
in Miller's can be found by
checking the code letters
below each caption with the
Key to Illustrations, pages
444–452.

More Adventures of Rupert Bear,
1937, 4°.
£550–600
$800–870 ↗ DW

◀ *Amazing Spider-Man* comic,
No. 20 issued with the cover of
No. 21, January 1965.
£450–500
$650–720 ↗ CBP

Commemorative Ware
Exhibitions

A polychrome pot lid, entitled 'The Grand International Building of 1851' and inscribed 'For the Exhibition of Art and Industry of all Nations', c1851, 5in (12.5cm) diam.
£90–120
$130–175 ⊞ JBL

A light-green moulded pint glass, commemorating the Festival of Britain, 1951, 5in (12.5cm) high.
£38–45
$55–65 ⊞ MURR

> **Cross Reference**
> See Politics (page 301)

Two glasses, commemorating the Festival of Britain, with red, white and blue emblems, 1951, largest 3in (7.5cm) high.
£3–6
$4–8 each ⊞ HUX

An ivory comb, inscribed 'GREAT EXHIBITION OF 1862/THE EAST FRONT VIEW', decorated with a view of the exhibition building, 1862, 3¼in (8.5cm) long.
£50–60
$75–90 ⊞ TML

A 7in record, commemorating the Festival of Britain, 'Make your own recording in music', by Pavilion, green and white, 1951.
£65–75
$95–110 ⊞ MURR

A Festival of Britain postcard, 1951.
£12–15
$15–20 ⊞ REN

> **LOCATE THE SOURCE**
> The source of each illustration in Miller's can be found by checking the code letters below each caption with the Key to Illustrations, pages 444–452.

▶ **A Festival of Britain watermark on paper,** 1951, 7 x 5in (18 x 12.5cm).
£12–15
$15–20 ⊞ REN

A wooden box, commemorating the Festival of Britain, made of wood from the old London Bridge, 1951, 7in (18cm) wide.
£50–60
$75–90 ⊞ MURR

A red plastic fold-away beaker, commemorating the Festival of Britain, 1951, 2in (5cm) high.
£30–35
$45–50 ⊞ MURR

Military

A brass box, containing 14 paper discs inscribed with the names and dates of the Duke of Wellington's Continental victories, the reverse inscribed with the legend in 11 lines within a wreath, 1815, discs 1¾in (4.5cm) diam.
£150–175
$220–255 ⊞ TML

A Staffordshire pot lid, with portrait of the Duke of Wellington and date 'Sept 14th 1852', with malachite border and gold line decoration, the base similarly decorated, restored, 1852, 4¾in (12cm) diam.
£300–360
$440–520 ⚒ SAS

A pink lustre jug, commemorating the Crimean War, printed in black and enamelled in red and blue, the reverse with the Sailor's Return, rim chip, 1856, 4¼in (11cm) high.
£80–100
$115–145 ⚒ SAS

A commemorative plate, with a portrait of Lord Baden Powell, 1914–18, 8in (20.5cm) diam.
£40–45
$60–65 ⊞ RCo

◄ **A Copeland tyg,** commemorating the Boer War, decorated in red, pink, yellow and green, c1900, 7in (18cm) high.
£1,000–1,200
£1,500–1,750 ⊞ RdV

A ceramic jug, in the form of President Wilson, wearing a grey jacket and red and white striped trousers, inscribed 'Welcome Uncle Sam', enamel flaking, c1917, 10½in (26.5cm) high.
£220–260
$320–380 ⚒ SAS

A ceramic jug, in the form of Marshall Joffre, wearing a dark blue jacket and red trousers, inscribed 'Ce que J'Offre', c1917, 10¼in (26cm) high.
£350–420
$500–600 ⚒ SAS

A ceramic jug, in the form of Marshall Foch, wearing a light blue jacket and trousers with brown boots, enamel flaking, c1917, 11¾in (30cm) high.
£100–120
$145–175 ⚒ SAS

A ceramic jug, in the form of Sir John French, wearing a green jacket and trousers with brown boots, inscribed 'French pour les Français', c1917, 9¾in (25cm) high.
£250–300
$350–450 ⚒ SAS

A ceramic jug, in the form of Admiral Beatty, wearing a dark blue jacket and trousers, inscribed 'Dread nought', c1917, 9¾in (25cm) high.
£250–300
$350–450 ✗ SAS

A ceramic jug, in the form of Lord Kitchener, wearing a dark blue jacket and trousers, inscribed 'Bitter for the Kaiser', c1917 10¼in (26cm) high.
£350–420
$500–600 ✗ SAS

A ceramic jug, depicting the Allies, George V, the Czar of Russia, King Albert of Belgium and President Poincaré, 1914–18, 8in (20.5cm) high.
£65–75
$95–110 ⊞ RCo

A T. G. Green commemorative mug, inscribed 'To Commemorate Peace The Great European War', 1919, 4in (10cm) high.
£70–80
$100–120 ⊞ CAL

Items in the Commemorative Ware section have been arranged in date order within each sub-section.

Royalty

A pressed boxwood plaque, probably by Westwood, inscribed 'HRH George Prince of Wales Installed Regent of the British Dominions 5 Feb. 1811', 3¼in (8.5cm) diam.
£130–150
$200–220 ⊞ TML

A blue and white ceramic plate, inscribed 'Her Majesty Caroline Queen of England', with impressed border, 1820, 5¾in (14.5cm) diam.
£450–550
$650–800 ✗ SAS

◄ **A Coronation mug,** printed in black with portraits of King William IV and Queen Adelaide, rim restored, 1831, 3½in (9cm) high.
£250–300
$350–450 ✗ SAS

▶ **A Swansea pottery plate,** commemorating Queen Victoria's Coronation, printed in purple with named and dated portrait, impressed mark, 1838, 6¼in (16cm) diam.
£280–330
$400–480 ✗ SAS

A brown stoneware spirit flask, impressed 'William IVths Reform Cordial', c1832, 7½in (19cm) high.
£210–250
$300–360 ✗ SAS

A copy of *The Court Journal: Gazette of the Fashionable World*, celebrating Queen Victoria's 18th birthday, 1837, 11 x 9in (28 x 23cm).
£15–20
$20–30 ⊞ J&S

A Swansea pottery mug, commemorating Queen Victoria's Coronation, printed in purple with portraits centred by a crown, name and dates inscribed, 1838, 3¼in (8.5cm) high.
£600–700
$870–1,000 ⚒ SAS

A Copeland pottery comport, Albert in Memoriam, for the Art Union of London, printed in black, brown and green with central inscribed portrait and three cartouches depicting his achievements, within a border inscribed with an extract from his 1848 speech, gilt rim, printed marks, 1861, 16¼in (41.5cm) diam.
£1,700–2,000
$2,500–3,000 ⚒ SAS

Two ceramic figures, commemorating the wedding of Prince Edward and Princess Alexandra, French, 1863, 15in (38cm) high.
£1,700–2,000
$2,500–3,000 ⊞ BRT

A pottery mug, commemorating the wedding of George and Mary, 6th July 1893, 3½in (9cm) high.
£150–180
$220–260 ⊞ BRT

> **LOCATE THE SOURCE**
> The source of each illustration in Miller's can be found by checking the code letters below each caption with the Key to Illustrations, pages 444–452.

A W. H. Goss pin dish, commemorating Queen Victoria's Diamond Jubilee, with crinkle edge, 1897, 3½in (9cm) diam.
£50–75
$75–115 ⊞ MURR

A Doulton Lambert brown stoneware jug, commemorating Queen Victoria's Diamond Jubilee, moulded with young and old portrait ovals, inscribed in white, unmarked, 1897, 7¼in (18.5cm) high.
£25–30
$35–45 ⚒ SAS

A programme of the Royal Procession to St Paul's Cathedral, and thanksgiving service, celebrating Queen Victoria's Diamond Jubilee, 22nd June 1897, 9 x 6in (23 x 15cm).
£25–30
$35–40 ⊞ J&S

A Queen's Day programme,
1897, 14 x 5in (35.5 x 12.5cm).
£18–20
$20–30 ⊞ J&S

A chocolate tin, commemorating
the Coronation of King Edward VII
and Queen Alexandra, decorated in
pink, green and yellow on a blue
ground, June 1902, 5in (12.5cm) wide.
£20–35
$30–50 ⊞ MURR

A Crown Ducal tyg, designed by
Charlotte Rhead, commemorating
Edward VIII's Coronation, decorated
in blue, orange and gilt, 1937,
7in (18cm) high.
£280–330
$400–480 ⚒ SAS

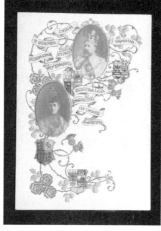

**An Edward VII and Alexandra Royal
menu,** embossed and appliquéd,
1902, 7 x 4½in (18 x 11.5cm).
£20–25
$30–35 ⊞ J&S

**Two Royal Doulton porcelain
mugs,** commemorating the
Coronation of King Edward VII and
Queen Alexandra, 1902, largest
3¼in (8.5cm) high.
£60–85
$100–120 each ⊞ GWR

A T. G. Green beaker, commemorating King George and Queen
Mary's Silver Jubilee, 1936,
5in (12.5cm) high.
£30–40
$40–60 ⊞ CAL

A silk, commemorating the
Coronation of King Edward VII and
Queen Alexandra, 1902, 14 x 8in
(35.5 x 20.5cm).
£300–350
$450–500 ⊞ AEL

A Rowntree & Co chocolate tin,
commemorating the Coronation
Fête, Crystal Palace, with full
contents, 1911, 5½in (14cm) long.
£100–120
$145–175 ⊞ RUSS

**A copy of *The Illustrated London
News,*** Record of the Lying-in-State
and Funeral of his Late Majesty
King George V, 1936, 14 x 10in
(35.5 x 25.5cm).
£10–12
$15–18 ⊞ J&S

A terracotta jug, by Longpark of Torquay, commemorating Edward VIII's Coronation, the rim and foot coloured mauve, painted with floral sprays, incised inscription, 1937, 6in (15cm) high.
£150–180
$220–260 ⚒ SAS

An Aynsley plate, No. 6743, commemorating Queen Elizabeth II's Coronation, the central portrait within a gilt floral border, gilt rim, 1953, 8in (20.5cm) diam.
£55–65
$80–100 ⊞ MGC

A T. G. Green Mocha Ware mug, commemorating the marriage of Prince Charles and Lady Diana Spencer, decorated in blue, orange and black on a yellow ground, limited edition, 1981, 4½in (11.5cm) high.
£50–70
$70–100 ⊞ CAL

A mug, commemorating Edward VIII's Coronation, 1937, 5in (12.5cm) high.
£30–35
$45–50 ⊞ AnS

An Oxo tin, commemorating Queen Elizabeth II's Coronation, 1953, 4in (10cm) wide.
£4–5
$5–8 ⊞ ES

A Royal Worcester urn and cover, commemorating the marriage of Prince Charles and Lady Diana Spencer, with twin Prince of Wales feather handles, decorated in colours with coats-of-arms and inscription, banded in puce and gilt, 1981, 8¼in (21cm) high.
£170–200
$250–300 ⚒ SAS

A copy of *The Illustrated London News,* Special Number, featuring the Death of King George VI, 1952, 14 x 10in (35.5 x 25.5cm).
£10–12
$15–18 ⊞ J&S

A Charbonnel & Walker chocolate box, commemorating the engagement of Prince Charles and Lady Diana Spencer, 1981, 4in (10cm) diam.
£3–5
$5–8 ⊞ RTT

A Royal wedding programme, commemorating the marriage of Prince Andrew and Sarah Ferguson, 1986, 11 x 9in (28 x 23cm).
£10–15
$15–20 ⊞ COB

Corkscrews

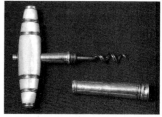

A silver pocket corkscrew, with double scroll swivel handle, white metal sheath, restored, re-threaded shaft, silver seal marked 'HC', early 18thC, 3in (7.5cm) long.
£450–500
$650–700 ✗ P(B)

A silver pocket corkscrew, with banded mother-of-pearl handle, the plain tapering sheath with base marked 'SP' for Samuel Pemberton, and 'ME', late 18th/early 19thC, 3in (7.5cm) long.
£300–350
$450–500 ✗ P(B)

A folding pocket corkscrew and hoof pick, 19thC, 3in (7.5cm) long.
£30–40
$40–60 ⊞ JOL

A Henshall-style corkscrew, c1850, 5in (12.5cm) long.
£75–85
$115–125 ⊞ CAL
In 1795, Rev Samuel Henshall patented a design for a corkscrew with a button or disc that prevented the screw or 'worm' from entering too far into the cork. The brush at the end of the handle was used for cleaning the neck of the bottle and for removing traces of sealing wax.

A Farrow & Jackson-type brass butterfly wing-nut corkscrew, marked 'Wilson & Co' to both wings, 19thC, 5½in (14cm) long.
£160–190
$225–275 ✗ P(B)

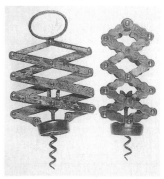

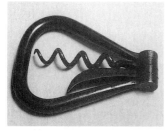

A four-pillar 'King's Screw' corkscrew, with nickel body and side-winder handle, the turned bone handle with brush and hanging ring, 19thC, 9in (23cm) long.
£650–750
$900–1,100 ✗ P(B)

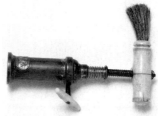

A wide rack 'King's Screw' corkscrew, with turned bone handle with brush and side-winder handle, the bronze barrel with tablet marked 'Dowler Patents, Ne Plus Ultra', replacement brush, 19thC, 7in (18cm) long.
£360–400
$500–600 ✗ P(B)

l. A Wiers concertina corkscrew, by James Heeley & Sons, Birmingham, with traces of gilt/bronze finish, patented 1884, 5¼in (13.5cm) long.
£45–50
$65–75
r. A Wiers double concertina corkscrew, by James Heeley & Sons, Birmingham, marked 'Double No. 4283', patented 1884, 4¼in (11cm) long.
£600–650
$850–950 ⊞ CS
The double concertina corkscrew is very rare, hence its value.

◄ **An engine-turned silver roundlet corkscrew,** with initials, London 1879, 3in (7.5cm) long.
£440–480
$650–700 ⊞ CAL

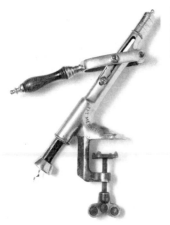

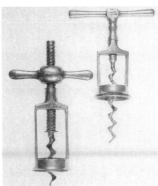

A Chambers bar corkscrew, named 'The Merritt', marked 'Chambers Patent', replacement worm, patented 1888, 17in (43cm) long.
£170–200
$250–300 ✗ P(B)

l. A steel corkscrew, named 'The Challenge, c1880, 5½in (14cm) long.
£25–30
$35–45 ⊞ CS
r. A steel corkscrew, named 'The Surprise', registered by George Willets in 1884, 5in (12.5cm) long.
£12–15
$15–20 ⊞ CS

A Heeley's patent double lever corkscrew, named 'The Empire', marked 'J. heeley & Sons patent', lacks nickel-bronze plating, action loose, 1890, 6in (15cm) long.
£900–1,000
$1,300–1,500 ✗ P(B)

A 'Hercules' corkscrew, with a Dorset wine merchant's advertisement, German, 1890, 7in (18cm) long.
£60–70
$90–100 ⊞ CAL

A brass 'Waiter's Friend' folding corkscrew and bottle opener, with Italian advertisement, German, c1890, 4in (10cm) long.
£90–110
$130–160 ⊞ CAL

A Berkeley registered straight pull corkscrew, with nickel-capped rosewood handle and banded rosewood shank with flat button, top of band marked 'Rd 202169', 1896, 5½in (14cm) long.
£160–190
$225–275 ✗ P(B)

A continuous action corkscrew, named 'Monopol', German, c1900, 5½in (14cm) long, with original cardboard box.
£20–25
$30–40 ⊞ CS

A Thomason corkscrew, with ringed bronze barrel, tablet marked 'Brookes & Son, Sheffield', replacement wooden handle, late 19thC, 6in (15cm) long.
£140–170
$200–250 ✗ P(B)

► **An Art Nouveau bronze straight pull corkscrew,** the crescent-shaped handle decorated with a grapevine, marked 'Miault', French, 6in (15cm) long.
£200–240
$300–350 ✗ P(B)

A bell cap wire cutter corkscrew, the wooden handle with a beer advertisement, American, c1900, 5½in (14cm) long.
£40–45
$60–65 ⊞ CAL

A William & Son medicine spoon and corkscrew, American, c1900, 3½in (9cm) long.
£85–95
$125–145 ⊞ CAL

A silver combination corkscrew and cigar cutter, by William Frederick Wright, engraved with leaves, hallmarked London 1903, 5½in (14cm) long.
£260–300
$380–440 ⚒ P(B)

▶ **A steel champagne tap,** with pull ring, early 20thC, 7in (18cm) long.
£90–100
$125–145 ⊞ JOL

A spring cage bell cork-screw, by Gotlieb Geibler Hallenberg, DRGM No. 596751, with wooden handle, German, c1920, 7in (18cm) long.
£20–25
$30–35 ⊞ BSA

An Edwardian brass bar corkscrew, named 'The Swift', with ebony handle, 16in (40.5cm) long.
£120–140
$170–200 ⊞ JOL

A silver penknife with corkscrew, hallmarked Sheffield 1911, 2in (5cm) long.
£50–60
$75–100 ⊞ JOL

A silver-plated corkscrew, modelled as a Highland terrier, 1930, 4in (10cm) long.
£50–60
$70–90 ⊞ BEV

A bronze figure corkscrew and bottle opener, Scandinavian, mid-20thC, 6in (15cm) high.
£75–85
$115–125 ⊞ CAL

A corkscrew, with wooden handle and wire breaker, c1920, 6in (15cm) long.
£24–28
$35–45 ⊞ CAL

▶ **A brass corkscrew and bottle opener,** modelled as Andy Cap and Flo, 1950s, 5in (12.5cm) high.
£40–50
$60–80 ⊞ JOL

Cosmetics & Hairdressing

In the Victorian period cosmetics were not greatly used. Generally speaking, ladies restricted themselves to soap and water and cold cream, which was supplied in similar ceramic pots to those containing potted meats and anchovy paste. A dusting of powder, a smear of lip salve and possibly a little bit of rouge were all permissible, as long as they were applied with restraint and in private. Not until after WWI did it become commonplace for ladies to flaunt both made-up faces and make-up containers in public.

The 1920s saw the birth of the compact which, with its compartments for powder, rouge, lipstick, and even cigarettes, reflected a new age of female liberation. The 1920s and '30s were a golden age in terms of design, with styles ranging from simple circular powder compacts to multi-sectioned vanity cases in a wide range of patterns.

Production of compacts (and cosmetics) ceased during the war, but with peace came a renewed desire for luxury and femininity and the compact industry flourished. As the '50s progressed, however, new technology not only brought new cosmetics (such as cream as opposed to loose powder) but also plastic disposable packaging. With the development of throwaway containers and changing fashions in the 1960s, the personal powder compact fell from popularity. Today vintage examples are sought after and there are collectors' societies both in the United Kingdom and America.

Two early Victorian wig powderers, the largest 10½in (26.5cm) long.
£15–20
$20–30 each ⊞ VB
Powdering wigs became fashionable in the early 18th century to conceal faded or discoloured hair. The wig was first greased with pomade and then dusted with ground starch or wheat flour, scented with essential oils and sometimes coloured. In 1795, however, the government introduced a powder tax of one guinea a year, and wigs eventually went out of fashion for all but liveried servants.

A Guerlain ointment pot, in white glaze with blue transfer lettering, base chips, French, 1900–20, 2¼in (5.5cm) high.
£40–50
$60–75 ⋟ BBR

A W. S. Park & Son Cold Cream pot, Australian, 1900–20, 2¾in (7cm) diam.
£125–150
$180–220 ⋟ BBR

A manicure set, with yellow Bakelite handles, in a yellow and black Bakelite holder set with rhinestones, original yellow tassel, 1920, 3in (7.5cm) long.
£250–280
$360–400 ⊞ LaF

> **Cross Reference**
> See Pot Lids (page 129)

◀ **A Lip Salve pot,** with flower and leaf transfer-decoration, slight damage, 1920–30, 2in (5cm) diam.
£35–40
$50–60 ⋟ BBR

A hairdresser's brass washbasin, on a turned wooden stand, c1920, 41in (104cm) high.
£350–400
$500–600 ⊞ MLL

A silver miniature brush set, comprising mirror, brush, comb and clothes brush, Birmingham 1922, brush 5in (12.5cm) long, in original box.
£150–175
$220–260 ⊞ GLa

A Ferd Mülhens 4711 talcum powder tin, decorated in turquoise and gold, German, c1925, 5in (12.5cm) high.
£15–20
$20–30 ⊞ HUX

A silver and enamel six-piece dressing table set, for Mappin & Webb, Birmingham 1930, in original box 14¼in (37cm) wide.
£245–285
$350–400 ⊞ GLa

A Yardley Old English Lavender talcum powder tin, c1930, 5in (12.5cm) high.
£12–15
$18–22 ⊞ HUX

A Cuticura talcum powder tin, 1930s, 5in (12.5cm) high.
£12–14
$18–20 ⊞ HUX

A bottle of Saturday Night Lotion, 1930s, 5in (12.5cm) high.
£12–14
$18–20 ⊞ HUX

A Bourjois Evening in Paris talcum powder tin, 1950s, 4½in (11.5cm) high.
£13–15
$20–22 ⊞ HUX

A wash and travel bag, decorated with hotel labels in pink, black and gold, with original contents, unused, American, 1950s, 9in (23cm) wide.
£40–45
$60–65 ⊞ HSt

A Boots Drug Co Solidified Tonair Brilliantine tin, 1950s, 3½in (9cm) wide.
£10–12
$15–18 ⊞ HUX
While the Victorians used bear's grease to slick down and moisturize their hair, the 20thC saw the development of non-animal based products such as brilliantine, made from vegetable and mineral oils.

A Coty Talc for Men tin, c1960, 5in (12.5cm) high.
£7–8
$10–12 ⊞ HUX

Compacts

A celluloid compact, in *faux* marble, the lid surmounted by a deep pink rose, 1920s, 1½in (4cm) high.
£100–125
$150–180 ⊞ LBe

Two powder tins, unbranded, one blue with wet weather silhouettes, one green with children's silhouettes, c1920, 2½in (6.5cm) diam.
£18–20
$27–30 each ⊞ TMa

▶ **A gilt compact,** with original rouge and swans-down puff, original cord and tassel, c1930, 3in (7.5cm) diam.
£130–150
$190–220 ⊞ LaF

A brass dressing table compact, on three legs, 1940s, 2½in (6.5cm) diam.
£175–195
$250–280 ⊞ LBe

A locket compact, with silhouette motif, American, 1940s, 1½in (4cm) diam.
£65–75
$100–110 ⊞ LBe

A brass compact with chain, with a theatrical mask in pink enamel, 1940s, 3in (7.5cm) high.
£150–175
$225–255 ⊞ LBe

An Evans carry-all, in gold, a compartment for cosmetics to one side, the other side for coins, cigarettes and lighter, American, c1950, 3in (7.5cm) square.
£100–120
$145–175 ⊞ LaF

A silver and enamel compact, inscribed 'With love from Maurice, 16.1.44', 1944, 2½in (6.5cm) square.
£120–180
$175–260 ⊞ ASA

A Deva Dassy bracelet compact, in gold coloured metal and jade green plastic, 1940s, 2½in (6.5cm) wide.
£265–300
$380–440 ⊞ LBe

A silver powder compact, made for Fiat's 50th anniversary, decorated with red, blue, green and white cars, 1940s, 3in (7.5cm) diam.
£345–385
$500–570 ⊞ SSM

A basket-shaped compact, by Kigu, decorated in gold basketweave, the lid with jewelled flower motif, two stones missing, c1950, 2in (5cm) diam.
£90–100
$125–145 ⊞ LaF

A Yardley's English Lavender powder compact, decorated with a rustic scene in shades of brown, yellow and blue, 1950s, 3in (7.5cm) diam.
£20–25
$30–40 ⊞ LBe

A Stratton gilt compact, the lid set with diamantes, c1960, 3in (7.5cm) diam.
£35–40
$50–60 ⊞ SBL

Shaving

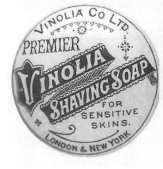

A Rasoir Star tin, razor and blades, the tin decorated in orange and cream on a green ground, French, c1920, 2½in (6.5cm) wide.
£30–35
$45–50 ⊞ HUX

The Dime safety razor, with original tin, 1920s, 3in (7.5cm) high.
£32–35
$45–50 ⊞ HUX

A tin of Vinolia shaving soap, with brown transfer decoration, 1930–40, 3¼in (8.5cm) diam.
£18–20
$25–30 ⋗ BBR

◄ **A moustache cup and saucer,** with green, pink and white floral decoration and gilt rim, probably German, 1930, cup 3in (7.5cm) high.
£120–140
$170–200
⊞ MLa

► **Hai Karate Body Talc and After Shave Lotion,** c1970, largest 6in (15cm) high.
£8–10
$10–15 ⊞ HUX

A tin of Thibaud Gibbs & Co shaving soap, with gold lettering on a black ground, 1925–35, 3½in (9cm) high.
£12–15
$15–20 ⊞ HUX

A Pears Jif shaving stick, in a tin decorated with blue and cream stripes, 1925–35, 3½in (9cm) high.
£12–14
$15–20 ⊞ HUX

Crime

Fascination with real-life crime is no new phenomenon. In the 19th century, the Staffordshire potters made a killing themselves from producing models of famous highwaymen and murderers; in our own age interest is reflected in the plethora of crime-related TV programmes, films, books, articles etc.

This section looks at memorabilia associated with celebrated criminals. Whilst many might find the idea of buying Charles Manson's signature ghoulish to say the least, collectors of the genre claim that there is little difference between watching a documentary or reading a biography of a killer and buying an autographed letter by the same person. Whatever one's personal moral convictions, however, there is no denying that these objects have a market value and that, with the passage of time, even the most horrific killer can somehow be transformed into an interesting and collectable historical figure.

Two Staffordshire figures of Tom King and Dick Turpin, decorated in black, yellow, red and green, c1850, 8in (20.5cm) high.
£450–500
$650–720 ⊞ TUN

A Staffordshire model of Potash Farm, rented by the murderer James Rush, decorated in blue, yellow red and green on a cream ground, c1860, 9in (23cm) high.
£345–385
$500–550 ⊞ TUN
James Rush was hanged in 1849 for shooting dead Isaac Jermy and his son, and wounding his wife and servant. Rush had mortgaged his home, Potash Farm, to Jermy for £5,000 but then forged a document which gave him complete ownership of the farm.

The Impartial Protestant Mercury, Friday, March 10th to Tuesday, March 14th 1684, covering the executions of the three murderers of Thomas Thynn, 11 x 7in (28 x 18cm).
£60–80
$95–115 ⊞ HaR

Le Petit Journal, the back cover depicting an electrocution scene in America, French, 1899, 18 x 12in (45.5 x 30.5cm).
£35–40
$50–60 ⊞ IQ

Henry Mayhew and John Binny, The Criminal Prisons of London and Scenes of Prison Life, first edition, with wood engravings, original blind-stamped cloth gilt, new endpapers, 1862, 8°.
£200–220
$300–330 ⋏ DW

► Ethel Le Neve, Her Life Story with the True Account of Their Flight and Her Friendship for Dr. Crippen, c1910, 7 x 5in (18 x 12.5cm).
£50–60
$70–90 ⊞ IQ

A Post Office 'Wanted' poster of Bonnie and Clyde, by US Department of Justice, Washington DC, 1934, 8in (20.5cm) square, framed.
£450–500
$650–720 ⊞ IQ

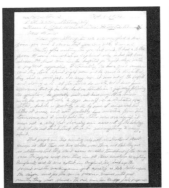

John R. H. Christie, an envelope forged to his sister-in-law, two days after he murdered his wife, 1952, 4 x 7in (10 x 18cm).
£1,000–1,200
$1,500–1,800 ⊞ IQ

Ethel Christie, a hand-written letter from 10 Rillington Place mentioning her concern at the death of a woman and baby living in the top flat, 1949, 9 x 7in (23 x 18cm).
£1,800–2,000
$2,600–2,900 ⊞ IQ

Robert Stroud, the Birdman of Alcatraz, an autograph letter with two signatures, written to a family member from Alcatraz, 1954, 10 x 8in (25.5 x 20.5cm).
£600–650
$870–950 ⊞ IQ

Charles Manson, the 1960s' murderer, a two-sided letter on Manson's personal stationery, 1970s, 10 x 8in (25.5 x 20.5cm).
£250–275
$350–400 ⊞ IQ

Docteur Marcel Petiot, famous French murderer and one of the last people to be guillotined, a prescription on his headed notepaper, 1939, 7 x 5in (18 x 12.5cm).
£550–600
$800–870 ⊞ IQ

Patty Hearst, an FBI 'Wanted' poster, c1974, 15 x 10in (38 x 25.5cm).
£180–200
$250–300 ⊞ IQ

Piers Paul Read, *The Train Robbers, Their Story*, signed by Buster Edwards, Bruce Reynolds, Tommy Wisbey, Roger Cordrey, Jimmy White, Charles Wilson and Jimmy Hussey, paperback, published by Coronet, 1979, 7 x 4½in (18 x 11.5cm).
£225–255
$320–360 ⊞ IQ

Reg & Ron Kray, Our Story, with Fred Dinenage, 1988, 10 x 6in (25.5 x 15cm).
£130–150
$200–220 ⊞ IQ

The Killer Autograph, a *Daily Mail* illustration of John Lennon signing his last autograph to Mark Chapman, 1990, 18 x 12in (45.5 x 30.5cm).
£30–40
$40–60 ⊞ IQ

▶ **A plastic electric chair,** battery-operated, gives a shock, 1995, 7½in (19cm) high.
£40–50
$60–80 ⊞ IQ
This is sold in America as a tourist souvenir item.

Doctor Who

Doctor Who was first aired on 23 November 1963. The BBC had commissioned an educational programme in which the Doctor's travels were meant to provide information on science and history. 'No cheap-jack bug-eyed monsters', warned the head of drama. Thankfully, producer Verity Lambert ignored these instructions. The second story saw the introduction of the Daleks (devised by Terry Nation), and a TV legend was born. Until the final story in December 1989, generations of children hid behind the sofa on Saturdays to watch the adventures of the time-travelling doctor, his glamorous assistants and his monstrous opponents. From William Hartnell in the first episode to Sylvester McCoy in the last, seven different Doctors took control of the Tardis. Tom Baker is often regarded as the definitive Time Lord. 'Exterminate! Exterminate!', became a national catchphrase and the word Dalek entered the Oxford English Dictionary. TV merchandising was still in its infancy in the early sixties. The first item produced was *The Dalek Book* in June 1964, toys and games were introduced by Christmas the following year, and since then, production of Doctor Who merchandise has never stopped. During the 1980s the show gained a large fan base in the USA, and thanks to video and TV repeats the programme continues to attract new viewers and collectors.

A photograph and autograph of William Hartnell, the first Doctor Who, 1960s, 10 x 8in (25.5 x 20.5cm).
£200–225
$300–325 ⊞ WHO

A set of 50 *Doctor Who and the Daleks* cigarette cards, mint, 1965.
£110–125
$160–180 ⊞ WHO

▶ *The Dalek Pocketbook and Space-Travellers' Guide,* published by Panther Books, 1965, 7 x 5in (18 x 12.5cm).
£40–50
$60–75 ⊞ WHO

Miller's is a price GUIDE not a price LIST

An original *Doctor Who* Ice Warrior costume, worn by Bernard Bresslaw in the 1965 series *The Ice Warriors*, with green-painted fibreglass body, mounted on a wood and metal armature, on a wheeled rectangular plinth painted to resemble ice, the interior bearing the signature of Debbie Watling, who played the Doctor's assistant Victoria during Patrick Troughton's period as Dr Who, and signed on the shoulder by Nicola Bryant who played the Doctor's assistant, Peri, during Colin Baker's period as the Doctor, c1965, 75in (190.5cm) high.
£800–1,000
$1,150–1,500 ⚲ RFA

◀ **An original *Doctor Who* Dalek,** wood, canvas, metal and plastic, the domed top with orange lights, the structure painted in blue, silver and grey, mounted on casters with articulated plunger, ray gun and sensor, the interior signed in green felt-tip pen 'John Pertwee, the Doctor', 1973, 75in (190.5cm) high.
£4,500–5,000
$6,500–7,250 ⚲ RFA
The Daleks were created by Terry Nation in the Doctor's second adventure, *The Red Planet*. They were designed by Raymond Cusick and remain to this day one of the most popular monsters in television history, with the name appearing in the Oxford English Dictionary. This Dalek is one of five built for the 1973 stage show the *Ultimate Adventure*, with John Pertwee as the Doctor.

A *Doctor Who* flyer and signed photograph of Trevor Martin, who played Doctor Who in the play *The Seven Keys to Doomsday* at the Adelphi Theatre in 1974, mounted and framed, frame 14 x 16in (35.5 x 40.5cm).
£300–350
$450–500 ⊞ WHO

A BBC Talking Dalek, by Palitoy, red and black plastic, 1975, 6in (15cm) high, in original box.
£100–125
$150–180 ⊞ WHO

A *Doctor Who* giant robot, by Denys Fisher, 1976, 10in (25.5cm) high, in original box.
£90–100
$130–150 ⊞ WHO

◀ **Two *Doctor Who* magazines,** with original fold-out posters, 1975 and 1976, 11 x 8in (28 x 20.5cm).
£20–25
$30–35 each ⊞ WHO

Cross Reference
See Colour Review (page 192)

A *Doctor Who* head-piece, warn by Martin Clunes in *Snake Dance*, 1983, 14in (35.5cm) high.
£550–600
$800–1,000 ⊞ WHO

A *Doctor Who* Tetrap gun, a wood and fibreglass prop used in *Time in the Rani*, 1987, 20in (51cm) long.
£550–600
$800–870 ⊞ WHO

A *Doctor Who* Dalek, manufactured by This Planet Earth, black, silver and blue, with detachable claw, with plaque inscribed 'This Planet Earth Limited', 'The Dalek from *Remembrance Of The Dalek*, taken from the original BBC mouldings, Serial No. 15497A', and signed in black marker 'I Clarke', late 1980s, 67in (170cm) high.
£2,000–2,500
$2,900–3,600 ↗ Bon(C)
This was made from the original mould for a 1988 television Dalek and modified to look like a Dalek from the 1966 film *Dalek Invasion Earth, 2150 AD*.

A page of original artwork for *Doctor Who* magazine, originally in black and white, with later colouring for *Voyager* book, 1985, 12½ x 9½in (32 x 24cm).
£300–350
$450–500 ⊞ BRG

A part set of *Doctor Who* pewter chess pieces, by Danbury Mint, 38 pieces including 7 different kings, part of a larger boxed set, 1992, 3in (7.5cm) high.
£20–25
$30–35 each piece ⊞ WHO

Dolls

A china pincushion doll, c1930s, 4in (10cm) high.
£85–120
$125–175 ⊞ MURR

A cut-out male doll, with 62 pieces of clothes and accessories, contained in 12 folded paper pockets, doll and costumes all hand-coloured aquatint, the sections bound but now lacking boards, early 19thC, doll 8¼in (21cm) high.
£230–260
$330–380 ⊞ F&C

A wax-over-composition doll, with blonde curly wig, weighted brown glass eyes, cloth body with wax over lower arms and legs, wearing original blue silk dress with lace, blue bonnet, stockings and leather marked shoes, slight damage, c1870, 22in (60cm) high.
£350–400
$500–580 ⌕ Bon(C)

A wooden peg-top doll, wearing Welsh traditional dress, 19thC, 7in (18cm) high excluding hat.
£150–180
$220–260 ⌕ G(L)

A Chad Valley Mabel Lucie Attwell Bambino doll, with black curly hair, brown velvet body and wearing orange felt dungarees, c1932, 16in (40.5)cm high.
£350–450
$500–650 ⊞ MEM

A Lenci felt-headed doll, with painted facial features, wearing an embroidered hat and costume, wooden clogs, with paper label 'No. 82-B', 1930s, 9½in (24cm) high.
£150–200
$220–300 ⊞ ES

▶ **A Mattel talking Beany doll,** with yellow hair, wearing a red jumper and turquoise cord dungarees, 1967, 11in (28cm) high.
£40–45
$60–65 ⊞ HarC

Bisque

A bisque-headed needlecase doll, wearing a cream and red dress, 19thC, 7½in (19cm) high.
£60–70
$90–100 ⊞ PSA

▶ **A Madame Barrois bisque-headed fashion doll,** with mohair wig, fixed blue glass eyes, leather body with bisque lower arms, wearing a brown dress and red leather boots, body incorrect, French, c1880, 16in (40.5cm) high.
£700–800
$1,000–1,200 ⋏ Bon

A DEP bisque-headed doll, mould 289, with blonde wig, weighted brown glass eyes and pierced ears, on a fully-jointed wooden body, wearing a cream dress and cape with lace bonnet and leather shoes, German, c1905, 15in (38cm) high.
£200–250
$300–360 ⋏ Bon

◀ **An Alt, Beck & Gottschalk bisque shoulder-headed doll,** with long blonde hair, fixed blue glass eyes, cloth body with bisque lower arms and composition lower legs, wearing original white knitted clothes, German, c1900, 12in (30.5cm) high.
£200–250
$300–360 ⋏ Bon(C)

Cross Reference
See Colour Review
(page 189)

A Kestner 192 bisque-headed doll, with mohair wig, weighted blue glass eyes and pierced ears, on a five-piece composition body with fixed wrists and painted socks and shoes, wearing a white dress, German, c1905, 10½in (26.5cm) high.
£700–800
$1,000–1,200 ⋏ Bon

An Armand Marseille bisque-headed doll, with brown wig and blue sleep eyes, on a five-piece baby body, wearing contemporary white clothes, some damage, French, early 20thC, 21in (53.5cm) high.
£140–180
$200–260 ⋏ G(L)

◀ **An S.F.B.J. bisque-headed doll,** with brown wig and eyes, on a jointed composition body, wearing original brown velvet coat and hat and cream dress, socks and shoes, French, early 20thC, 21in (53.5cm) high.
£400–450
$580–650 ⊞ BaN

A Heubach Koppelsdorf bisque-headed doll, mould 321, with short blonde wig and weighted blue eyes, on a composition baby body, wearing a white dress and pink knitted jacket and bonnet, German, c1910, 15in (38cm) high.
£130–150
$190–220 ⚒ Bon(C)

A Shoenau & Hoffmeister bisque-headed doll, with long brown wig and blue eyes, on a jointed composition body, wearing a cream dress and cap, together with a fabric covered trunk containing a collection of clothes for a small doll, impressed '4½' and '1901', German, 22¾in (58cm) high.
£300–350
$450–500 ⚒ DN

▶ **A DEP bisque-headed doll,** with brown mohair wig, weighted blue glass eyes and pierced ears, on a fully-jointed composition body, wearing original pink frilled organza dress and matching bonnet, German, c1910, 25in (63.5cm) high.
£450–550
$650–800 ⚒ Bon(C)

A Simon & Halbig bisque-headed Oriental doll, mould 1129, with black mohair wig, slanted and weighted brown glass eyes and pierced ears, on a fully jointed composition body, wearing a pink jacket and trousers, German, c1910, 13½in (34.5cm) high.
£350–450
$500–650 ⚒ Bon(C)

Items in the Dolls section have been arranged in date order within each sub-section.

▶ **An S.F.B.J. bisque-headed doll,** with brown wig and blue sleep eyes, on a jointed composition body, wearing original pink silk and lace-trimmed dress, the head impressed '301', French, early 20thC, 18¼in (46cm) high, in original cardboard box marked 'Mon Amour de Poupée'.
£230–270
$330–400 ⚒ DN

A Rose O'Neill bisque Kewpie doll, with moulded top-knot and painted eyes, jointed at shoulders, with star-fish hands, incised 'Germany', c1910, 7in (18cm) high.
£250–300
$360–440 ⚒ Bon

An Armand Marseille bisque-headed doll, mould 290, with brown wig and blue sleep eyes, on a jointed composition body, wearing a blue checked shirt, French, early 20thC, 24in (61cm) high.
£150–180
$220–260 ⚒ G(L)

Plastic

This section, devoted to plastic dolls, includes a selection of Barbie products. Created by Mattel in 1959, Barbie has been through innumerable permutations and has acquired legions of friends and an extensive family. The examples shown below all come from what is known as the Vintage Era (1959–72). Collectors often subdivide this into two major categories: the Ponytail Era (1959–66) and the Mod Era (1967–72). In addition to Barbie herself, characters shown include boyfriend Ken; friends Jamie, Stacey and Midge; Midge's boyfriend Alan, and Barbie's cousin Francie. Mattel created a whole range of celebrity friends for their best-selling doll, including Truly Scrumptious, from the 1968 film *Chitty Chitty Bang Bang*.

Mattel was also among the first companies to produce Afro-American dolls in the 1960s, such as Brad (friend of Alan) and Julia. Julia was based on a popular US TV character played by Diahann Carroll, and the actress herself voiced the talking doll.

As these examples show, prices for Vintage Barbie material (both dolls and outfits) can be extremely high, but whilst age and rarity are always important, values are also critically affected by condition.

▶ **A Miss Rosebud plastic doll,** with blonde wig, wearing original peach knitted dress, blue cape and shoes, c1960, 7½in (19cm) high.
£35–40
$50–60 ⊞ PAR

A British National Doll Co hard plastic toddler doll, wearing original white and blue dress and white shoes, 1950, 13in (33cm) high.
£30–40
$45–60 ⊞ A&J

A Polyflex plastic doll, with a brown wig, wearing a blue and white spotted dress, French, c1950, 16in (40.5cm) high.
£60–70
$70–100 ⊞ T&D

> Miller's is a price GUIDE not a price LIST

▶ **A Rosebud plastic doll,** with blonde wig and blue eyes, wearing a pink knitted jumper, red trousers and white plastic shoes, c1960, 11in (29cm) high.
£40–45
$60–65 ⊞ PAR

A Pedigree plastic black doll, wearing a white dress, red jacket and white plastic shoes, c1960, 20in (51cm) high.
£70–80
$100–115 ⊞ PAR

A plastic bride doll, with plastic moulded hair, wearing a white net-covered wedding gown trimmed with rosebuds, and white net veil on a band of rosebuds, 1960s, 8½in (21.5cm) high.
£10–15
$15–20 ⊞ GRa

A Palitoy plastic doll, wearing a short yellow dress and white plastic shoes, c1960, in original box, 11 x 7in (28 x 18cm).
£140–165
$200–240 ⊞ T&D

A Mattel Freckles Midge doll, with auburn wig and blue eyes, wearing the 'Country Club Dance' outfit of white dress with gold-striped bodice and trim, long white gloves and white shoes, American, c1962, 11½in (29cm) high.
£450–500
$650–720 ⊞ T&D

A Mattel Ken doll, wearing the 'Play Ball' outfit of red cap, grey shirt and trousers with red stripe trim, red socks, baseball glove and carrying a bat, American, c1962, 12in (30.5cm) high.
£135–165
$200–240 ⊞ T&D

A Mattel Alan doll, wearing the 'Dream Boat' outfit of hat with red band, grey patterned shirt, olive green jacket and brown trousers, American, c1962, 12in (30.5cm) high.
£130–150
$200–225 ⊞ T&D

◀ **A Mattel 'long-haired American girl' Barbie doll,** wearing the 'Saturday Matinée' outfit of fur-trimmed tweed suit and matching hat, brown gloves and peep-toe shoes, American, c1966, 11½in (29cm) high.
£1,200–1,400
$1,750–2,000 ⊞ T&D
This model of 'American girl' doll is valued at £700–800 ($1,000–1,150) without the outfit. The outfit, available separately, is valued at £500–600 ($720–870).

A Mattel Midge doll, straight-leg version, wearing a lime green crop-top and red shorts, American, c1963, 12in (30.5cm) high, in original box.
£240–270
$350–400 ⊞ T&D
This doll has never been removed from its original box.

A Mattel Barbie doll, with blonde ponytail and white lips, wearing a red swimsuit, American, c1965, 12in (30.5cm) high, in original box.
£540–600
$800–870 ⊞ T&D

◀ **A Mattel Francie doll,** straight-leg version, wearing a red on white polka dot crop-top and matching reverse polka dot shorts, American, c1966, 12in (30.5cm) high, in original box.
£350–400
$500–580 ⊞ T&D

A Mattel Stacey 'Twist and Turn' doll, wearing a multicoloured print top, American, c1967, 12in (30.5cm) high, in original box.
£600–700
$870–1,000 ⊞ T&D
This doll has never been removed from its original box.

A Mattel Truly Scrumptious doll, from the film *Chitty Chitty Bang Bang*, in a pink dress with lace overlay, American, c1968, in original box 15 x 6in (38 x 15cm).
£450–500
$650–720 ⊞ T&D
This doll has never been removed from its original box.

A Mattel Talking Stacey doll, in a pink, green and blue beach outfit, American, c1968, in original box, 13 x 4½in (33 x 11.5cm).
£380–425
$560–620 ⊞ T&D
This doll has never been removed from its original box.

A Mattel Walking Jamie doll, wearing 'Pepsi' outfit of red and white shirt with matching headband, white trousers and eye-shield, American, c1968, 11½in (29cm) high.
£250–285
$360–420 ⊞ T&D

Dolls' Houses & Dolls' House Furniture

Ten pewter dolls' house plates, with moulded pewter food including fish, fruit, bread and a blancmange, German, late 18thC, largest 2½in (6.5cm) diam.
£380–430
$560–620 ⚒ Bon(C)

A tinplate dolls' house mirror-on-stand, painted in wood-grain effect, the wing mirror on scroll supports, probably by Evans & Cartwright, 1810–50, 4½in (11.4cm) high.
£280–330
$420–480 ⚒ Bon

A late Victorian dolls' house, designed as a pair of semi-detached houses, with double opening front, cream exterior walls with green details, four rooms, decorated and with carpet and curtains, some restoration required, 24 x 15in (61 x 38cm).
£320–360
$470–540 ⚒ WAL

▶ **A dolls' house porcelain coffee set and tray,** decorated with green, yellow and blue roses, French, c1890, tray 3in (7.5cm) wide, together with a Coalport trinket and glass ware.
£100–120
$145–175 ⚒ Bon

A dolls' house fire screen, with lithophane picture of a young girl with a dog, in an ornate gilt frame with candle holder to back, late 19thC, 4¾in (12cm) high.
£750–850
$1,100–1,250 ⚒ Bon

A pair of Simon & Halbig dolls' house dolls, each with weighted blue glass eyes and five-piece composition bodies, the girl with long blonde mohair wig, wearing a cream cotton dress with lace collar, the boy with curly brown wig, wearing red knitted shorts, jumper and bobble hat, German, c1910, 4¾in (12cm) high.
£450–500
$650–720 ⚒ Bon

▶ **A John Mitchell Victorian-style doll's house,** painted in pale green with white woodwork, with three rooms, complete with furniture and furnishings, 1970s, 12in (30.5cm) wide.
£170–220
$250–320 ⚒ WAL

A dolls' house pram, with cream and gold scroll decoration, with yellow silk seats and silk hood, 1890s, 3¼in (8.5cm) long.
£550–650
$800–950 ⚒ Bon

A painted wooden dolls' house, with cream exterior, glazed windows with etched top panels, four rooms and wooden staircase, side opening giving access to rear bathroom, with fittings, furniture and furnishings, 1920s, 39½in (100.5cm) wide.
£900–1,200
$1,300–1,750 ⚒ Bon(C)

▶ **A Moritz Gottschalk dolls' house,** with lithographed brick paper exterior and green tiled roof, with original wallpaper and flooring, containing fittings and furniture, German, c1900, 30in (76cm) wide.
£1,200–1,500
$1,750–2,200
⚒ Bon(C)

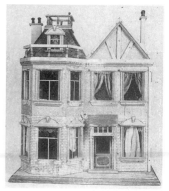

A dolls' school house, 'Boston House, Miss Pinkerton's Academy', with Victorian-style double opening front giving access to classroom, library, dormitory, dining room, gymnasium, cloakroom and bathroom, with all furniture and fittings, 1933, the front 25 x 37in (63.5 x 94cm).
£230–260
$330–380 ⚒ WAL
This was made by the girls of Eastbourne High School.

A Silber Fleming dolls' house, with brick-effect papered front, orange sides and green front door, four rooms, each with papered walls, fireplace, rugs and curtains, some refurbishment needed, c1890, 21in (53.5cm) wide.
£260–300
$380–440 WAL

Miller's is a price GUIDE not a price LIST

A Duncan Mirylees Victorian-style dolls' shop, 'The Antique Shop', made from a Camp Coffee packing case with brick-effect paper over, square bay shop window with display, two rooms and staircase, c1978, 15in (38cm) wide.
£160–200
$230–300 ⚒ WAL

Colour Review

► **A Rowntree's Christmas tin,** modelled as a house with Father Christmas outside, c1930, 4½in (11.5cm) wide.
£100–120
$145–175 ⊞ HUX

◄ **A set of five Hovells Christmas firework crackers,** 1940s, in original box, 9in (23cm) square.
£45–50
$65–75 ⊞ MRW

A moveable cut-out Christmas card, c1880, 4in (10cm) high.
£65–75
$95–110 ⊞ SDP

A chromolithograph cut-out of Father Christmas, c1880, 9in (23cm) high.
£40–45
$60–65 ⊞ SDP

A Christmas pudding in a tin, unopened, with original key, 1960s, 6in (15cm) high.
£18–20
$26–30 ⊞ HUX

An original Christmas advertisement for Chesterfield cigarettes, 1950, 13½in (34.5cm) high.
£5–6
$8–10 ↗ SAF

A SylvaC holly vase, c1950, 6in (15cm) high.
£20–25
$30–35 ⊞ TAC

A Weiss Christmas tree pin, set with crystals, 1950s, 3in (7.5cm) high.
£150–175
$220–255 ⊞ CRIS

A set of six decorated glass Christmas bauble decorations, 1940–50, in original box, 7 x 5in (18 x 12.5cm).
£8–10
$12–15 ⊞ HO

A set of 12 Pifco Christmas tree fairy lights, 1950s, in original box, 12 x 4in (30.5 x 10cm).
£23–27
$33–40 ⊞ FLD

A Father Christmas character jug, limited edition, 1998, 6in (15cm) high.
£110–135
$160–195 ⊞ DCA

▶ *The Beano Book*, 1951,
11 x 8in (28 x 20.5cm).
£85–95
$125–140 ⊞ OCB

The Picture Show Annual,
1929, 11 x 9in (28 x 23cm).
£60–70
$90–100 ⊞ SDP

*The Dandy Monster
Comic,* second edition,
1940, 11 x 8½in
(28 x 21.5cm).
£650–700
$950–1,000 ↗ CBP

The Dr Who Annual,
first edition, 1965,
11 x 8in (28 x 20.5cm).
£35–40
$50–60 ⊞ WHO

A watercolour of
Rupert the Bear,
by John Harrald,
5¾in (14.5cm) square.
£85–95
$120–140 ⊞ BRG

◀ A *Rupert* annual,
with unused magic
painting pages, 1967,
11 x 8½in (28 x 21.5cm).
£80–90
$115–130 ↗ CBP

A *Star Trek Annual 1977,*
11½ x 8¾in (29 x 22cm).
£4–5
$6–8 ⊞ CMF

A creamware plate, decorated in Holland, commemorating William V of Holland, c1790, 10in (25.5cm) diam.
£270–300
$390–440 ⊞ JHo

A Bristol blue glass rolling pin, printed in yellow and enamelled in colour, commemorating the Crimean War, 1856, 16¼in (41cm) long.
£90–110
$130–160 ↗ SAS

▶ **A Rowntree chocolate tin,** with contents, commemorating the Coronation of Edward VII, c1902, 2 x 5in (5 x 12.5cm).
£35–40
$50–50 ⊞ MRW

The Official Programme of the Coronation Review, produced for the Coronation of George V, 1911, 10 x 7in (25.5 x 18cm).
£20–25
$30–35 ⊞ J&S

A badge commemorating the New York World's Fair, 1939, 2in (5cm) wide.
£25–30
$35–45 ⊞ REN

A Festival of Britain powder compact, c1951, 3¼in (8.5cm) diam.
£40–45
$60–65 ⊞ HUX

A Wedgwood mug, commemorating the Coronation of Queen Elizabeth II, designed by Eric Ravilious, 1953, 4in (10cm) high.
£225–250
$325–360 ⊞ REN

A loving cup, by J. & J. May, commemorating the birth of Prince William, painted with views of Highgrove House with a perambulator, decorated in gilt, the underside inscribed and numbered 31 of 50, 1982, 4¼in (11cm) high.
£900–1,100
$1,300–1,600 ↗ SAS

A set of 50 Queen Elizabeth II Coronation cigarette cards, by P. Allman, 1953.
£35–40
$50–60 ⊞ LCC

◀ **A signed presentation photo-graph of Diana, Princess of Wales,** commemorating her visit to Zimbabwe, 1993, 8 x 10in (20.5 x 25.5cm).
£2,400–2,500
$3,500–3,600 ⊞ AEL

A Yardley's Old English Lavender ceramic shop-counter display, by Dresden, modelled as a woman and two children selling lavender, c1910, 12in (30.5cm) high.
£400–450
$580–650 ⊞ HUX

▶ **A glass dressing-table pot,** the hinged lid hand-painted with Bonzo carrying a red rose, 1920s, 4in (10cm) diam.
£150–175
$225–255 ⊞ MURR

A ceramic powder bowl, by Sitzendorf, 1920, 4in (10cm) high.
£140–150
$200–220 ⊞ BAO

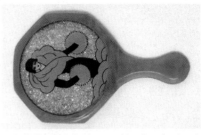

A Bakelite hand mirror, with a hand-painted figure of a lady on a glitter background, 1920s, 4in (10cm) high.
£130–150
$190–220 ⊞ LBe

An Art Deco compact, lacquered in red and gold, 1920s, 3½ x 2in (9 x 5cm).
£40–60
$60–90 ⊞ ASA

A silver and blue enamel six-piece brush set, 1930–32, in original box, 7 x 13½in (18 x 34.5cm).
£275–325
$400–550 ⊞ GLa

A Bakelite compact, by LSM, inset with a picture of an autumnal landscape, c1938, 3in (7.5cm) square.
£60–70
$90–100 ⊞ LaF

An enamel and mother-of-pearl compact, modelled in the shape of a camera, 1930s, 4in (10cm) wide.
£60–70
$90–100 ⊞ SBL

A Maydew Solidified Brilliantine tin, 1940s, 3½in (9cm) wide.
£12–14
$18–20 ⊞ HUX

A handbag set of compact, cigarette case and lighter, in mother-of-pearl, decorated with hand-painted poodles, 1950s, compact 3in (7.5cm) wide.
£225–250
$325–360 ⊞ LBe

A plastic swivel mirror, the cover designed as the face of a cat, 1970s, 3½in (9cm) wide.
£40–45
$60–65 ⊞ LBe

A woodentop peg doll, with jointed legs, in floral print long dress, German, doll 19thC, dress 20thC, 11¾in (30cm) high.
£60–70
$90–100 ⚒ G(L)

A Simon & Halbig bisque-headed doll, with weighted blue glass eyes, open mouth and upper teeth, long mohair wig, on a fully-jointed composition body, wearing striped dress, underclothes and leather boots, c1910, 25½in (65cm) high.
£900–1,100
$1,300–1,600 ⚒ Bon

A Jumeau bisque-headed doll, for S.F.B.J., with sleep eyes and long wig, on a composition and wooden jointed body, French, 1915–20, 29in (74cm) high.
£1,100–1,250
$1,600–1,800 ⊞ DOL

A Limoges bisque-headed doll, with fixed blue eyes, open mouth, teeth and wig, on a jointed composition body, wearing bonnet, dress and shoes, French, 1920s, 19in (48cm) high.
£90–110
$130–160 ⚒ G(L)

A Tudor-style suburban detached dolls' house, with fixed front bay window and opening front door, with four rooms, complete with electric lighting and period furniture and fittings, with access by removeable rear panel, late 1920s, 16½in (42cm) high.
£275–325
$400–470 ⚒ WAL

A Tri-ang Ultra Modern Series Art Deco-style detached dolls' house, with integral garage, glass windows, balconies and removeable sun room, with three fitted fireplaces, decorated rooms and curtains, on simulated crazy paving base, No. 53, 1930s, 40in (101.5cm) wide.
£650–750
$950–1,100 ⚒ WAL

A Bisque button-hole Kewpie doll, in fisherman's creel, slight damage, 1920s, 2in (5cm) high.
£55–65
$80–90 ⊞ DOL

Three sailor dolls, with hatbands for Queen Mary, Mauretania and Viking III, 1960s, 9in (23cm) high.
£15–45
$20–65 each ⊞ COB

▶ **A B. N. D. plastic doll,** original, c1960, 9in (23cm) high.
£40–45
$60–100 ⊞ PAR

◀ **A plastic doll,** with sleep eyes, wearing a knitted dress with a doll in the pocket, 1950s, 12in (30.5cm) high.
£20–25
$30–35 ⊞ GRa

A Victorian scrap book, containing a number of Louis Wain cats, 17 x 13in (43 x 33cm).
£270–300
$390–440 ⊞ MRW

A block of six Victorian chromo-lithograph cut-out scraps of angels, c1880, 10in (25.5cm) wide.
£35–40
$50–60 ⊞ SDP

A paper fan, with eye slits, advertising cream products, 1920s, 8½in (21.5cm) wide.
£120–150
$175–220 ⊞ LBe

A pack of calling cards, bound with original red ribbon, 1930s, 2 x 3½in (5 x 9cm).
£30–35
$45–50 ⊞ LBe

A set of 50 Wills' Association Footballers cigarette cards, including Stanley Matthews, 1935.
£60–65
$90–95 ⊞ LCC

A theatre programme, for the Hippodrome theatre, Coventry, 1948, 9 x 5in (23 x 13cm).
£1–2
$2–3 ⊞ MRW

A set of 25 Taddy's Royalty Series No. 25 cigarette cards, including Princess Victoria, the Duke of Cambridge and Princess Louise, Duchess of Fife, 1904.
£400–430
$580–625 ⊞ LCC

A set of 90 Star Trek Topps Bubblegum cards, American, 1997.
£9–10
$13–15 ⊞ LCC

A set of 50 Wills' Speed Series cigarette cards, including the Bristolian Express, Coronation Express, Coronation Scot Express and Princess Elizabeth, 1938.
£15–18
$20–27 ⊞ LCC

A set of 50 A&BC Gum *Outer Limits* cards, based on the TV series, 1966.
£140–160
$200–230 ⊞ MUR

A vinyl stool, on wooden legs, late 1950s, 17in (43cm) high.
£34–45
$50–65 ⊞ ZOOM

A Formica cocktail table, 1950s, 24in (61cm) high.
£55–65
$80–95 ⊞ FLD

A glazed ceramic vase, hand-decorated, West German, c1950, 28¼in (72cm) high.
£20–25
$30–35 ⊞ V&S

▶ **Four** *Practical Wireless* **magazines,** 1950s.
£0.50–1
$1–1.50 ⊞ GM

A Piero Fornasetti newspaper rack, 1950s, 16in (40.5cm) wide.
£250–280
$360–410 ⊞ ZOOM

A Jens Quistgaard enamel Koben ware water pitcher, in Dansk design, late 1950s, 10in (25.5cm) high.
£70–80
$100–115 ⊞ ORI

A ceramic dish, Austrian, mid-1950s, 10in (25.5cm) diam.
£15–20
$20–30 ⊞ HSt

A Verner Panton cone chair, in covered fabric, 1958.
£650–700
$950–1,000 ⊞ ZOOM

A Herbert Krenchel enamel salad bowl, in Krenit design, 1955, 10in (25.5cm) diam.
£60–70
$90–100 ⊞ ORI

An ornamental vase, modelled as a fish, 1950s, 4in (10cm) high.
£20–25
$30–35 ⊞ LBe

A pair of Vari-vue novelty plastic sunglasses, featuring a pin-up girl, late 1950s.
£38–42
$55–65 ⊞ SpM

**A Shirley Temple glass cereal
bowl,** 1940s, 6½in (16.5cm) diam.
£18–20
$27–30 ⊞ HUX

A Clark Gable Lyon's toffee tin,
1940s, 6½in (16.5cm) high.
£18–20
$27–30 ⊞ HUX

**An original studio model of
Stingray,** in wood and plastic,
made by Reg Hill, Associate
Producer of the TV series, the
prototype for other studio models,
1963, 22in (56cm) long.
£9,000–10,000
$13,000–14,500 ↗ FO
Ex-Philip Rae collection.

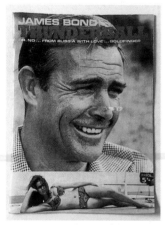

A James Bond magazine, c1966,
13in (33cm) high.
£5–8
$8–10 ⊞ CTO

**A ceramic model of the Pink
Panther,** UAC marked on base,
1980s, 8in (20.5cm) high.
£60–70
$90–100 ⊞ TAC

**A *Nightmare Before Christmas*
plastic figure,** of Mayor Loose,
1993, 7in (18cm) high.
£45–55
$65–80 ⊞ TB

**A knife used by Leonardo
DiCaprio,** in the film *The Beach,*
mounted with descriptive plaque,
colour still of DiCaprio from the
film and Fox Archives certificate of
authenticity, framed and glazed, with
holster attached to back of frame,
2000, frame 20in (51cm) square.
£600–700
$875–1,000 ↗ FO

Three fibreglass Jack O'Lanterns,
used as dressing on the set of
Sleepy Hollow, 1999, largest
12in (30.5cm) high.
£300–350
$440–500 ↗ FO

▶ **A Spanish poster for Dr Who
and the Daleks,** 1986, 40 x 32in
(101.5 x 81.5cm).
£180–200
$260–290 ⊞ WHO

A mahogany solitaire board, with coloured spiral marbles, 19thC, 14in (35.5cm) diam.
£800–900
$1,150–1,300 ✗ G(B)

A hand-made glass marble, with basket-weave incisions, c1880, 1in (2.5cm) diam.
£25–30
$35–45 ⊞ MRW

A pack of Royal National Patriotic playing cards, c1900, 3½ x 2in (9 x 5cm).
£120–150
$175–220 ⊞ MURR

A ball bearing puzzle, of a mounted soldier, German, c1910, 2½in (5cm) diam.
£10–12
$15–18 ⊞ HUX

▶ **A Humpty Dumpty game,** by Parker Brothers, USA, 1920s, in original box, 7 x 13in (18 x 33cm).
£50–55
$75–80 ⊞ J&J

A Radio Questionaire game, by the Durable Toy and Novelty Corp, USA, 1928, in original box, 9in (23cm) square.
£18–20
$27–30 ⊞ J&J

A Chad Valley Stumpy Joe quoits game, complete, c1930, in original box, 8in (20.5cm) high.
£18–20
$27–30 ⊞ J&J

A Superman Speed Game, by Milton Bradley Co, USA, complete with four painted wooden pieces, wooden die and oval board, early 1940s, in original box, 16 x 9in (60.5 x 23cm).
£700–750
$1,000–1,100 ✗ CBP

An Enid Blyton stencil and painting set, c1950, in original box, 13in (33cm) wide.
£18–22
$27–32 ⊞ J&J

An 'Art Studies' pack of playing cards, plastic coated, featuring pin-up girls, American, 1950s, in original box, 3½in (9cm) high.
£32–36
$48–55 ⊞ SpM

A War of the Daleks board game, by Denys Fisher, 1975, in original box, 18in (45.5cm) wide.
£100–125
$145–180 ⊞ WHO

A Victorian cranberry glass bell, c1860, 9in (23cm) high.
£135–150
$195–220 ⊞ AOY

A facet-cut cranberry/ ruby glass decanter, c1880, 11in (28cm) high.
£200–230
$300–330 ⊞ GRI

A late Victorian opaline glass biscuit barrel, with plated mounts, swing handle and applied butter-fly and floral beadwork, 10in (25.5cm) high.
£70–80
$100–115 ✗ DD

A Victorian cranberry glass baluster jug, with frilled rim, clear handle and jewelled decorations, 10½in (26.5cm) high.
£100–120
$145–175 ✗ WBH

An Art Nouveau glass vase, 7in (18cm) high.
£170–190
$250–275 ⊞ BEV

A gilt-metal inkstand, with cranberry glass trays and clear bottles, c1880, 8in (20.5cm) wide.
£150–165
$220–240 ⊞ GRI

A pair of Jack-in-the-Pulpit cranberry glass vases, c1900, 13in (33cm) high.
£380–425
$570–625 ⊞ AOY

A Carnival glass bowl, by Imperial Glass Co, with open rose pattern inside and panelled rose outside, American, c1910, 9in (23cm) diam.
£175–195
$250–280 ⊞ CAL

◀ **A Fenton Carnival glass vase,** in diamond and rib pattern, 1910, 10in (25.5cm) high.
£110–130
$160–190 ⊞ CAL

An amethyst glass specimen vase, with gilt and enamel decoration, c1910, 6in (15cm) high.
£55–60
$80–90 ⊞ GRI

An Art Deco-style jug, moulded, 1907–40, 7in (18cm) high.
£18–22
$27–33 ⊞ TWAC

◄ **A cut-glass scent bottle,** with amethyst colouring, c1920, 5in (12.5cm) high.
£125–140
$180–200 ⊞ GRI

A Bohemian cut-glass goblet, overlaid with painted flowers and enamel, c1920, 5in (12.5cm) high.
£45–55
$65–80 ⊞ BRU

▶ **A George Davidson cloud glass vase,** c1922–39, 7in (18cm) high.
£80–90
$115–130 ⊞ BEV

◄ **A George Davidson glass candlestick,** in rare orange colour, 1922–39, 2in (5cm) high.
£60–70
$90–100 ⊞ BEV

A George Davidson cloud glass vase, 1922–39, 9in (23cm) high.
£70–80
$100–115 ⊞ BEV

A Venetian glass millefiori figure, 1930s, 9in (23cm) high.
£190–220
$275–320 ⊞ BRU

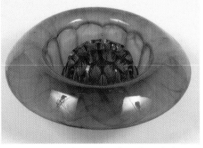

A George Davidson glass bowl, with down-turned rim and matching flower block, c1930, 12in (30.5cm) diam.
£130–150
$190–220 ⊞ BEV

▶ **A Monart jade glass bowl,** the rim flecked with mica, 1924–61, 6in (15cm) diam.
£45–55
$65–80 ⊞ TCG

A pair of glass candlesticks, Czechoslovakian, c1930,
3in (7.5cm) high.
£15–18
$20–27 ⊞ CAL

A Jobling jade glass deep bowl, with fir
cone pattern, c1932, 9in (23cm) diam.
£60–65
$90–95 ⊞ CAL

◀ **A James Powell & Sons,
Whitefriars glass lamp base,**
designed by Barnaby Powell, in
amber threaded on amber, 1930s,
10in (25.5cm) high.
£200–250
$290–360 ⊞ RUSK

A decanter and six glasses, the
decanter modelled as a lady in a
crinoline dress, 1930s, decanter
8¼in (21cm) high.
£150–175
$220–255 ⊞ LBe

A Murano glass vase, by Barovier, Italy,
1930s, 6in (15cm) high.
£270–300
$400–440 ⊞ BRU

A Vasart glass bowl, flecked with metallic
particles, 1950s, 5in (12.5cm) high.
£70–80
$100–115 ⊞ MCC

A Murano glass vase,
designed by F. Poli for
Seguso, Italy, c1950,
13in (33cm) high.
£280–320
$420–470 ⊞ BRU

A glass cream jug, designed by Eric
Hoelund for Boda, Sweden, 1950s,
4½in (11.5cm) high.
£70–80
$100–115 ⊞ MCC

A Murano glass bowl, Italian, late 1950s,
27in (68.5cm) wide.
£225–275
$325–400 ⊞ ZOOM

A Holmegaard glass vase, designed by Per Lutken, Denmark, 1950–60, 10in (25.5cm) high.
£110–130
$160–190 ⊞ ORI

A silver and glass cocktail shaker, with silver lid and banding, 1950s, 9in (23cm) high.
£25–30
$35–45 ⊞ SCM

A Murano cased glass vase, 1950s, 2in (5cm) high.
£25–35
$35–50 ⊞ MCC

A Holmegaard glass Gulvase vase, designed by Otto Breuer, Denmark, 1960s, 10in (25.5cm) high.
£35–40
$50–60 ⊞ ORI

◄ **A coloured glass vase,** Italian, 1960s, 10in (25.5cm) high.
£50–60
$75–90 ⊞ HSt

► **A Holmegaard cased glass Gulvase vase,** designed by Otto Breuer, Denmark, 1960s, 12in (30.5cm) high.
£120–140
$175–200 ⊞ ORI

A Holmegaard fried egg ashtray, designed by Per Lutken, Denmark, 1950–60, 7in (18cm) diam.
£40–50
$60–75 ⊞ ORI

◄ **An Orrefors cased glass Rosebud vase,** designed by Erika Lagerbielke, blue and amethyst cased in clear glass, 1999, 6in (15cm) high.
£120–160
$175–230 ⊞ HaG

A James Powell & Sons, Whitefriars glass Bubbles vase, designed by Geoffrey Baxter, c1960, 8in (20.5cm) high.
£110–135
$160–190 ⊞ BRU

A glass dump, with swirls within the glass, c1860, 3in (7.5cm) high.
£160–200
$230–290 ⊞ JBL

▶ **A St Louis pinwheel paperweight,** 1971, 3in (7.5cm) diam.
£300–350
$450–550 ⊞ DLP

A cat paperweight, transfer-printed, 1930s, 4½in (11.5cm) diam.
£100–125
$145–175 ⊞ LBe

◀ **A St Louis paperweight,** Marguerite, 1991, 2¼in (5.5cm) diam.
£90–110
$130–160 ⊞ SWB

▶ **A Caithness paperweight,** Everest, No. 279 of a limited edition of 750, 1993, 4in (10cm) diam.
£50–60
$70–90 ⊞ SWB

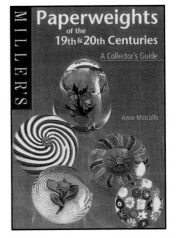

◄ **A beaded bag,** with tortoiseshell mount and chain, 1900, 8in (20.5cm) long.
£75–85
$110–120 ⊞ **Ech**

A glass-beaded bag, with silver gate top, c1890, 7in (18cm) high.
£280–320
$400–470 ⊞ **LaF**

A chinoiserie-embroidered silk bag, the ivory clasp with raised figure, 1900–10, 6¾in (17cm) long.
£400–450
$580–650 ⊞ **CRIS**

A beaded purse, with enamel top and chain handle, 1920–30, 6½in (16.5cm) long.
£350–400
$500–600 ⊞ **CRIS**

A crocodile clutch bag, in the shape of a liner with funnels, with chrome fittings, 1930s, 10½in (26.5cm) wide.
£225–250
$320–360 ⊞ **LBe**

An embroidered calico handbag, with a Bakelite top, 1930s, 10in (25.5cm) long.
£190–220
$275–325 ⊞ **LBe**

A plastic and Perspex bag, decorated with a poodle, 1950s, 15in (38cm) long.
£230–260
$330–380 ⊞ **SpM**

► **A frog-shaped wicker bag,** 1950s, 14in (35.5cm) long.
£400–450
$600–650 ⊞ **CRIS**

A plastic cool box, covered in postcard print vinyl, 1960s, 17in (43cm) long.
£28–32
$40–50 ⊞ **HSt**

► **A Harmony leather bag,** with plastic handles, c1970, 9in (23cm) square.
£45–50
$65–75 ⊞ **SBL**

A Pucci handbag, 1960s, 8½in (21.5cm) long.
£350–400
$500–600 ⊞ **SBT**

Ephemera

The last will and testament of James Green, with the seal of Edward Cook, Chancellor of the County of Gloucester, embossed with the Royal coat-of-arms, dated 9 September 1811, 9½ x 11½in (23 x 29cm).
£30–35
$45–50 ⊞ ES

A Victorian cut-out chromolithograph scrap of a Punch and Judy show, c1880, 7 x 5in (18 x 13cm).
£50–55
$75–80 ⊞ SDP

A Victorian cut-out chromolithograph scrap, 'Pigs at School', c1880, 7 x 11in (18 x 28cm).
£60–65
$90–95 ⊞ SDP
Compiling scrap albums was a popular Victorian hobby. In addition to pictures taken from newspapers, magazines and other miscellaneous ephemera, manufacturers also produced sheets of glossy, brightly-coloured chromolithographic scraps specifically designed to be cut out and stuck into books and greeting cards, and on to screens etc. Major printers included Louis Prang in the USA, Raphael Tuck in the UK, and Zoecke & Mittmeyer and Mamelok & Soehne in Germany.

A strip of Victorian cut-out chromolithograph scraps, 'The Three Little Kittens', c1880, 5 x 18in (12.5 x 45.5cm).
£50–55
$75–80 ⊞ SDP

A copy of the Freedom of the City of London, awarded by the Goldsmiths' Company, 1919, in original red wallet, 3 x 4in (7.5 x 10cm).
£20–25
$30–35 ⊞ WAB

A Barclays Bank cheque book, in original plastic cover, 1960s, 8½in (21.5cm) wide.
£4–6
$6–9 ⊞ Mo

Erotica

▶ **A WWII pin-up girl tin silhouette,** on a wooden stand, c1940, 6in (15cm) high.
£30–35
$45–50 ⊞ SpM

A Time for Bed Vaudoscope drop-card viewer, with one-penny slot, 1904, 69in (175.5cm) high.
£800–850
$1,150–1,250
⊞ JUN

A Tabarin Theatre programme, illustrating show girls, French, 1939, 9in (23cm) square.
£15–20
$20–30 ⊞J&S

Miller's is a price GUIDE not a price LIST

Four erotic match books, late 1940s, 2½in (6.5cm) high.
£8–10
$12–15 ⊞ SpM

An erotic handkerchief, featuring a dog looking up a woman's skirt, 1940–50, 11in (28cm) square.
£85–95
$125–140 ⊞ LBe

An erotic glass tumbler, the exterior painted with a bride, the reverse undressed, 1950s, 5½in (14cm) high.
£10–15
$15–20 ⊞ SpM

An Esquire calendar, with decorated envelope, 1953, 11 x 9in (29 x 23cm).
£135–150
$200–220 ⊞ SpM

***Men Only* magazine,** featuring a Marilyn Monroe pin-up inside, 1956, 7 x 5in (18 x 12.5cm).
£8–12
$12–18 ⊞ RTT

An International Exotic Glamourwear catalogue, 1970s, 11 x 8in (28 x 18cm).
£15–20
$20–30 ⊞ PLB

A pin-up poster, after Jean d'Ylen, c1950, 18¾ x 12¼in (47.5 x 31cm).
£110–130
$160–190 ⚲ VSP

Fans

A fan, the silk leaf painted with the surrender of a fort, the reserves decorated with ribbon-work, spangles and sequins, the ivory sticks painted with gilt and the arms of Spain, the guardsticks carved and gilded with drums and helmets, French, c1775, framed, 24in (61cm) wide.
£1,500–1,800
$2,150–2,600 ⊞ LDC

▶ A *carnet de bal* **fan,** ivory with silver mount and attached pencil, c1840–50, 4¼in (11cm) wide.
£85–95
$125–140 ⊞ VB
This type of fan was used at balls so that a lady could inscribe the names of her dance partners on the different leaves. Ivory provided a perfect wipe-clean surface.

A fan, the silk leaf painted with mythological characters with ivory-painted faces, gold sequins, net spyholes and embroidered flowers, silvered tortoiseshell sticks, Italian, c1800, 8in (20.5cm) wide.
£230–270
$330–390 ⊞ LDC

An ivory brisé fan, decorated in cream and brown, c1820–30, 7in (18cm) wide.
£130–150
$200–220 ⊞ VB

A Chinese brisé fan, each side painted with figures with applied painted ivory heads and fabric clothes, the lacquer sticks gilded with Chinese figures, late 19thC, 9¾in (25cm) wide, in a fitted lacquer case.
£50–70
$75–100 ↗ RTo

A late Victorian black lace fan, painted with flowers and leaves, 14in (35.5cm) wide.
£40–50
$60–75 ⊞ VB

A paper fan, decorated in the style of Kate Greenaway, late 19thC, 11in (28cm) wide.
£60–70
$90–100 ↗ SWO

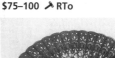

A pierced celluloid fan, painted with pink and white flowers, 1910, 5in (12.5cm) wide.
£14–18
$20–30 ⊞ VB

An Edwardian pierced fretwork fan, hand painted with yellow, blue and white flowers, 13½in (34.5cm) wide.
£35–40
$50–60 ⊞ VB

A bamboo, paper and celluloid fan, decorated with a peacock, 1920, 8½in (21.5cm) wide.
£14–18
$20–30 ⊞ VB

An advertising paper fan, decorated with a red lady, red sticks, 1920s, 8in (20.5cm) wide.
£30–35
$45–50 ⊞ VB

Fifties

A Dansk Koben ware enamel pan, by Jens Quistgaard, Danish, 1950s–60s, 10in (25.5cm) diam.
£70–80
$100–115 ⊞ ORI

A Dansk teak Viking bowl, by Jens Quistgaard, marked, Danish, 1950s–60s, 24in (61cm) wide.
£300–350
$450–500 ⊞ ORI

A Dansk teak two-handled fruit bowl, by Jens Quistgaard, marked, Danish, 1950s–60s, 10in (25.5cm) diam.
£120–140
$175–200 ⊞ ORI

A Dansk teak tray, by Jens Quistgaard, marked, Danish, 1950s–60s, 24in (61cm) wide.
£80–90
$115–130 ⊞ ORI

A Dansk mark.

Teak

Teak was a favourite material for furniture and domestic items in the 1950s and 1960s, particularly in Scandinavia. Native to India, Burma and Thailand, and noted for its extreme durability, teak became readily available after the war in Indo-China, when forests were felled to make roads for military transport. In 1954, Danish designer Jens Quistgaard and American entrepreneur Ted Nierenberg founded Dansk International Designs to market Scandinavian designs in the USA. 'From peasant craft to a sophisticated line . . . Dansk wooden pieces are up to the minute in design, practical and exquisitely crafted', noted one contemporary writer. Very fashionable in the 1950s, Dansk products are highly collectable today, and Quistgaard's VIII-8 ice bucket is now regarded as an icon of post-war domestic design.

A Dansk teak ice bucket, by Jens Quistgaard, with plastic liner, Danish, 1950s–60s, 16in (40.5cm) high.
£125–150
$180–220 ⊞ ORI

A set of four aluminium storage canisters, with black lids, for flour, sugar, coffee and tea, American, 1950s, the largest 8in (20.5cm) high.
£18–20
$25–30 ⊞ FLD

Cross Reference

See Colour Review (page 191)

► **A vinyl record folder,** decorated with musical instruments, 1950s, 8in (20.5cm) high.
£18–20
$27–30 ⊞ HSt

Furniture

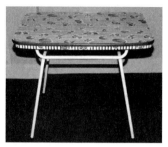

A Formica-topped table, with metal legs, decorated with fruit, 1950s, 36in (91.5cm) wide.
£65–75
$100–110 ⊞ HSt

A George Nelson oval soft-edge dining table, by Herman Miller, No. 5259, the putty-coloured plastic top with white rubber trim to edge, on satin chrome crossed legs, American, 1950s, 78in (198cm) wide.
£350–400
$500–600 ↗ TREA

A Kandya plywood stacking chair, designed by Carl Jacobs, 1950.
£160–180
$230–260 ⊞ ORI

A kidney-bean table, on three legs, 1950s, 16in (40.5cm) wide.
£14–16
$20–25 ⊞ FLD

A conical wicker chair, on metal supports, 1950s.
£35–40
$50–60 ⊞ FLD

A wire chair, by Harry Bertoia, 1950s.
£150–200
$220–290 ⊞ ZOOM

▶ **A child's vinyl-covered chair,** with blue seat, 1950s.
£50–60
$75–90 ⊞ FLD

A Fritz Hansen Ant three-legged chair, designed by Arne Jacobsen, model No. 3100, 1952.
£200–220
$300–330 ⊞ ORI

▶ **A Formica-topped cocktail table,** the black surface with party design, 1950s, 19in (48.5cm) high.
£20–25
$30–35 ⊞ FLD

◀ **A white moulded chair,** by Eero Saarinen, 1957.
£500–600
$720–870 ⊞ ZOOM

A diner chrome bar stool, with vinyl seat, 1950s, 24in (61cm) high.
£60–70
$90–100 ⊞ TRA

Pottery & Porcelain

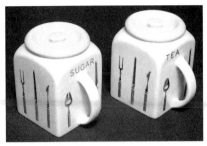

A pair of Bristol Longline storage jars, with yellow lids, decorated with cutlery, c1950, 6in (15cm) high.
£34–38
$50–55 each ⊞ **B&R**

A Paragon Festival of Britain bone china mug, decorated in white and gilt on a turquoise ground, 1951, 4in (10cm) high.
£250–300
$360–440 ⊞ **BRT**

A pair of black and white textured vases, with flower decoration in red, yellow and blue, Italian, 1950s, 7in (18cm) high.
£30–35
$45–50 ⊞ **V&S**

A black fish ashtray, with green fins and tail, orange mouth and coloured spots, foreign, 1950s, 3in (7.5cm) high.
£20–25
$30–35 ⊞ **LBe**

A Crown Clarence Autumn 15-piece coffee set, made for the C. W. S. and the Pioneer Society, 1950s, coffee pot 9¾in (25cm) high.
£100–120
$150–175 ⊞ **ES**

A black vase, hand painted with white stripes and red, orange, blue and green squares, Austrian, 1950s, 4in (10cm) high.
£18–20
$27–30 ⊞ **HSt**

► **A Beswick vase,** the shape designed by Arthur Hallam, the zebra stripe pattern created by Jim Hayward, 1950s, 8in (20.5cm) high.
£45–50
$65–75 ⊞ **BEV**

A pottery string holder, modelled as a cat's head, black with blue bow, 1950s, 6in (15cm) wide.
£40–45
$60–65 ⊞ **LBe**

◄ **A glazed ashtray,** hand-painted in black, white and turquoise on a red ground, Italian, 1950s, 5in (12.5cm) wide.
£15–18
$20–27 ⊞ **V&S**

A Rye Pottery vinegar bottle, in white, with black stripes, 1955, 4¼in (11cm) high.
£30–40
$45–60 ⊞ **DSG**

Film & TV

A Shirley Temple glass water jug, 1940s, 4½in (11.4cm) high.
£18–20
$27–30 ⊞ HUX

A grey woollen cardigan worn by Marlon Brando in *The Godfather,* with original label for Western Costume Co, Hollywood, with 'Marlon Brando # 1' typed in, and two colour pictures from the film showing Brando wearing a similar cardigan, slight damage, 1972.
£1,800–2,000
$2,600–3,000 ➤ FO

A spacecraft/spacesuit joystick from *2001: A Space Odyssey,* Bakelite and metal, 1959, 10in (25.5cm) long.
£350–400
$500–600 ➤ FO
This unused joystick was one of a batch manufactured in 1959 and supplied for the 1968 film *2001: A Space Odyssey* and for Gerry Anderson's *UFO,* for spacecraft interiors and spacesuit chest-packs.

A fibreglass Kryat dragon-bone from *Star Wars,* part of the Kryat dragon skeleton, mounted with photograph and plaque, framed and glazed, 1977, 13 x 18in (33 x 45.5cm).
£800–1,000
$1,150–1,500 ➤ FO
This item was accompanied by a description by the original owner, detailing how he came across the 'bones' in the Tunisian desert.

◀ **A** *Blade Runner* **crew jacket,** in black bomber style, with Blade Runner embroidered on the back in red and white, 1982.
£750–850
$1,100–1,250 ➤ FO

ABC Film Review **magazine,** with Sean Connery on the cover, July 1965, 9 x 7in (23 x 18cm).
£4–6
$6–9 ⊞ CTO

A *Some Like it Hot* **metal thermometer,** showing Marilyn Monroe in a classic pose from the film, 1960s, 12½in (32cm) high, in original packaging.
£90–100
$130–145 ➤ VS

◀ **Three promotional items for** *Clockwork Orange,* a press booklet, a set of front-of-house stills, and an advertisement folder, c1971, booklet 11 x 9in (28 x 23cm).
£225–250
$325–360 ⊞ CTO

Cross Reference
See Autographs (page 34)
See Doctor Who (page 176)
See Toys (page 403)

A Nostromo Perspex and plastic airlock from *Alien,* made by Bill Pearson, with sliding outer door and fully detailed interior, and original miniature body used in filming the ejection sequence, 1979, 12in (30.5cm) wide.
£1,000–1,200
$1,500–1,750 ➤ FO

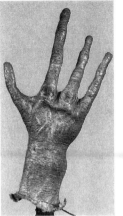

A moulded latex prototype *E.T.* hand, with internal metal rods for manipulation, with lighting apparatus including titanium bulb and power pack for forefinger, and four original four-fold publicity posters for the Spielberg film.
£650–750
$950–1,100 FO

Items in the Film & TV section have been arranged in date order within each sub-section.

◄ **A model of Roger Moore as James Bond in *A View to a Kill*,** with fibreglass head and body, latex hands, and etched aluminium Rolex watch, used in filming the Golden Gate Bridge sequence, in a display case with plaque and invitation to film premiere, and an additional film still of the model in use, 1985, case 36in (91.5cm) high.
£8,000–10,000
$11,500–14,500 FO

Six Prop casino chips from *Licence to Kill*, each marked 'Casino de Isthmus City', mounted with a still featuring Timothy Dalton as Bond at the casino, framed and glazed, 1989, 10 x 12in (25.5 x 20.5cm).
£240–280
$350–410 FO

A blue cotton polo shirt worn by Tom Cruise in *Rain Man*, by Carroll & Co, Beverly Hills, with original label reading 'Tom Cruise "Charlie" Sc #64 thru 78 No Coat same pants from Sc #61', with colour still of Tom Cruise and Dustin Hoffman, signed by both, framed and glazed, 1988, photo 16 x 13in (40.5 x 33cm).
£1,000–1,200
$1,500–1,750 FO

A star pendant worn by Christina Ricci in *Sleepy Hollow*, mounted with a still of Ricci wearing the pendant, together with a descriptive plaque, framed and glazed, 1999, 27½ x 18in (80 x 45.5cm).
£450–500
$650–720 FO

A 007 *Tomorrow Never Dies* calculator, 1997, 4in (10cm) wide.
£30–35
$45–50 GRa

A model gateway to Hallowe'en Town from *The Nightmare before Christmas*, foam and wood, with working light, 1993, 31in (78.5cm) high.
£1,500–2,000
$2,200–3,200 FO

◄ **A Thai Police form from *The Beach*,** signed on screen by Leonardo DiCaprio as Richard Fischer, mounted with certificate of authenticity from Fox Archives, together with descriptive plaque, framed and glazed, 2000, 16 x 19½in (40.5 x 49.5cm).
£420–470
$600–680 FO

Games

Three miniature bone dice, 1850–70, 4mm square.
£10–15
$15–20 ⊞ MRW

Two rosewood and bone whist markers, c1910, 1½in (4cm) diam.
£50–55
$75–80 ⊞ HO

A Victorian leather dice shaker, 4½in (11.5cm) high.
£12–15
$18–20 ⊞ HO

◀ **A handmade glass marble,** with basket-weave incisions, c1880, 1in (2.5cm) diam.
£25–30
$35–45 ⊞ MRW

A Staunton ebony and boxwood weighted chess set, by The British Chess Company, with original box and label, c1900, king 4¼in (11cm) high.
£650–800
$1,000–1,150 ⊞ TMi
Howard Staunton (1810–74) was regarded as perhaps the world's leading chess player in the 1840s. In 1851 he organized the first modern international chess tournament, and the chess pieces that he designed in 1849 were adopted as the standard model, preferred over all other types for use in serious tournaments and matches. In the best quality sets, ebony was used for the black pieces and boxwood for the white. In cheaper sets, all pieces were made from boxwood and coloured accordingly.

◀ **A Ping Pong or Gossima table game,** by J. Jaques & Son and Hamley Bros, c1900, in original box, 9 x 32in (23 x 81.5cm).
£90–100
$130–145 ⊞ J&J

> **Cross Reference**
> See Colour Review (page 193)

A pack of Goodall's Bystander Fragments playing cards, Fragments from France, by Capt Bruce Bairnsfather, featuring his 'Old Bill' character, 1917–19, 3½ x 2in (9 x 5cm).
£45–60
$65–90 ⊞ MURR

A pack of Schneider Trophy playing cards, by Waddingtons, featuring Flying Boat Supermarine S6, c1929, 2 x 3½in (5 x 9cm).
£25–35
$35–50 ⊞ MURR

An Old Maid card game, by Chad Valley, 1920, 4in (10cm) square.
£18–20
$27–30 ⊞ J&J

A Puzzle Drive with Anchor Stone puzzles, 1920s, 3¾in (9.5cm) square.
£20–25
$30–35 ⊞ HUX

A Dover Patrol or Naval Tactics game, by H. P. Gibson & Sons, instructions missing, 1930s, 8 x 15in (20.5 x 38cm).
£25–30
$35–45 ⊞ J&J

A Bounce-O table basket ball game, by Sa-Vu, c1930, in original box, 6 x 7in (15 x 18cm).
£20–25
$30–35 ⊞ J&J

A Jack of All Trades card game, by Kum-Bak of London, 1930s, 4 x 3in (10 x 7.5cm).
£15–18
$20–25 ⊞ J&J

An Air Raid Puzzle game, 1940s, 4 x 5in (10 x 12.5cm).
£25–30
$35–45 ⊞ HUX

A Game of Commando board game, by Chad Valley, c1940, 9 x 14in (23 x 35.5cm).
£15–20
$20–30 ⊞ J&J

A Race to Toy Town game, by Chad Valley, 1950s, 7 x 12in (18 x 30.5cm).
£18–20
$25–30 ⊞ J&J

A Shredded Wheat circular ball bearing puzzle game, illustrated with Rin Tin Tin and Rusty, 1950s, 1¼in (3cm) diam.
£22–24
$32–36 ⊞ HUX

A Motorist puzzle game, 1950s, 4 x 5in (10 x 12.5cm).
£15–18
$20–25 ⊞ HUX

The Army Game board game, by Bell, based on the Granada TV comedy show, 1959, 14in (35.5cm) square.
£15–20
$20–30 ⊞ J&J

A Bugs Bunny Tiddley Winks game, by Berwick, 1963, 8 x 11in (20.5 x 28cm).
£8–10
$12–15 ⊞ J&J

> **Cross Reference**
> See Toys (page 403)

A Waddington's Succession game, some damage, 1976, 4½ x 6in (11.5 x 15cm).
£2–3
$3–5 ⊞ CMF

◀ **A Mastermind logic game,** by Vic-Toy, with Design Centre logo, 1972, 12½ x 5in (32 x 12.5cm).
£8–10
$12–15 ⊞ HUX

Jigsaws

A Boyhood of Raleigh wooden jigsaw puzzle, by Zig Zag Puzzles, 1910, 5 x 7in (12.5 x 18cm).
£30–35
$45–50 ⊞ J&J

A Heart of London jigsaw puzzle, by Chichester Jig-Saw Map Puzzles, 1930s, 6 x 8in (15 x 20.5cm)
£10–15
$15–20 ⊞ COB

A Last of the Mohicans jigsaw puzzle, by Waddington's, 1930s, 11 x 9in (28 x 23cm).
£12–15
$18–20 ⊞ J&J

▶ **An Imperial Empire Flying Boat wooden puzzle,** by Victory, c1930, 16in (40.5cm) wide.
£180–220
$260–320 ⚲ P(WM)

A Royal Navy 3-D Battleship wooden jigsaw puzzle, 1930s, 14 x 12in (35.5 x 30.5cm).
£10–20
$15–30 ⊞ COB

◀ **A Joyful Mystery birthday card jigsaw puzzle,** 1950s, in original envelope, 4 x 5in (10 x 12.5cm).
£12–15
$18–20 ⊞ J&J

Garden & Farm Collectables

A limestone garden roller, with wrought-iron handle, early 19thC, 30in (76cm) wide.
£235–265
$330–380 ⊞ DOR

A wooden cart wheel, with original paint, c1850, 54in (137cm) diam.
£125–150
$180–220 ⊞ HOP

A pair of Shaker woven splint basket oxen muzzles, American, mid-19thC, 14in (35.5cm) diam.
£2,000–2,400
$3,000–3,500 ⚒ SK(B)

A watering can, c1900, 13in (33cm) long.
£18–25
$30–35 ⊞ HOP

A selection of steel and iron spades, with elm handles, 1900s, largest 43in (109cm) long.
£20–40
$30–60 each ⊞ HOP

Two Victorian elm potato dibbers, with metal ends, original green paint, largest 38in (96.5cm) long.
£40–45
$60–70 each ⊞ HOP

A Citadol brass garden syringe, c1910, 25in (63.5cm) long.
£20–25
$30–40 ⊞ GaB

An iron and wood drain spade, c1920, 80in (203cm) long.
£10–15
$15–20 ⊞ AL

▶ **A brass garden sprayer,** c1920, 18in (45.5cm) high.
£70–80
$100–120 ⊞ AL

A copper garden sprayer, with wooden handle, c1920, 30in (76cm) high.
£80–100
$115–145 ⊞ AL

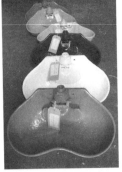

A selection of painted cast-iron cattle drinkers, c1920, 14in (35.5cm) wide.
£15–20
$20–30 each ⊞ HOP

A berry trug, 1920s,
37in (94cm) high.
£60–70
$90–100 ⊞ SMI

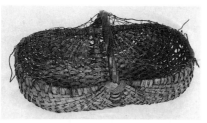

A snail basket, French, c1920,
23in (58.5cm) wide.
£45–50
$65–75 ⊞ AL

Two wooden trugs, c1930,
largest 20in (51cm) wide.
£30–35
$45–55 each ⊞ AL

A walnut basket, French, c1930,
18in (45.5cm) wide.
£25–30
$35–45 ⊞ AL

A collection of Popular Gardening,
1946–49.
£2–3
$5–6 each ⊞ HOP

◄ Two tinplate garden bird scarers, modelled as cats
with marble eyes, c1930, largest 13in (33cm) long.
£20–25
$30–35 each ⊞ HO

Items in the Garden
& Farm Collectables
section have been
arranged in date
order within each
sub-section.

The Gardeners'
Chronicle, July 24, 1948.
£2–3
$5–6 ⊞ HOP

Two crescent-shaped
flowerbed edgers, with
original green paint, c1950,
largest 48in (122cm) long.
£8–15
$15–20 each ⊞ HOP

Garden Furniture

A Coalbrookdale cast-iron Gothic pattern garden seat, the back and supports pierced with tracery and foliage, with oak slatted seat, c1900, 49in (124.5cm) wide.
£575–625
$850–900 ⚒ RTo

A pair of Blackberry pattern aluminium bench ends, c1960, 32in (81.5cm) high.
£60–75
$90–110 ⊞ HOP

A metal-framed garden chair, with wooden slats, worn, c1920.
£22–27
$30–40 ⊞ AL

Sculpture & Ornaments

Garden gnomes were initially an aristocratic fashion, decorating the grounds of country mansions. The two gnomes shown here date from the 18th century. In the mid-19th century, Sir Charles Isham created a celebrated rockery at Lamport Hall, Nottinghamshire, designed as a miniature mountain landscape complete with crystal caves, gem-stone mines and miniature trees and peopled with terracotta gnomes imported from Germany. Sir Frank Crisp (1843–1919) built another famous gnome grotto at Friar Park, Oxfordshire and by the early 1900s advertisements for model gnomes were appearing in *Connoisseur* magazine.

A stone stoup, 17thC, 7in (18cm) high.
£425–475
$620–700 ⊞ SEA

A European limestone garden gnome, late 18thC, 24in (61cm) high.
£1,000–1,200
$1,500–1,800 ⊞ OLA

◄ **Four reconstituted stone pineapple finials,** on square bases, c1950, 12in (30.5cm) high.
£35–40
$50–60 each ⊞ HOP

A European limestone garden gnome, 18thC, 27in (68.5cm) high.
£1,000–1,200
$1,500–1,800 ⊞ OLA

A selection of stone troughs,
19thC, largest 18in (45.5cm) long.
£75–100
$115–145 each ⊞ HOP

A selection of plaster garden ornaments, including ducks, frogs and owls, c1950, largest 7in (18cm) high.
£8–10
$10–15 each ⊞ HOP

A Continental terracotta gnome,
c1920, 30in (76cm) high.
£1,000–1,200
$1,500–1,800 ⊞ OLA

▶ **A motorized wooden windmill,**
with sails, c1960, 72in (183cm) high.
£200–250
$300–350 ⊞ HOP
This windmill was built for a nursery garden bulb promotion.

A pair of composition stone rabbits, c1950, 7in (18cm) high.
£180–200
$250–300 ⊞ OLA

Traps

A cast-iron man trap, 18thC, 70in (178cm) long.
£625–675
$900–1,000 ⊞ HCJ

A cast-iron gin trap, 19thC, 11in (28cm) long.
£8–18
$10–20 ⊞ HCJ

A wooden box trap, 18thC,
28in (71cm) wide.
£100–110
$140–160 ⊞ HCJ

▶ **An oak and elm mousetrap,**
19thC, 12in (30.5cm) wide.
£55–75
$80–110 ⊞ HOP

Glass

A clear glass dish, cut with bands of flutes, prisms and diamonds, c1810, 10½in (26.5cm) long.
£230–280
$330–400 ⊞ Som

A yellow vaseline glass star dish, c1920, 4in (10cm) square.
£45–50
$65–75 ⊞ BEV

A pair of red opaque glass vases, by Michael Powolny, Austrian, c1920, 7in (18cm) high.
£110–130
$160–190 ⊞ BRU

A Sowerby black glass compote, with detachable stand, 1876, 8in (20.5cm) diam.
£120–140
$170–200 ⊞ CAL

◀ **Three green-striped glass vases,** with flower-petal rims, in a silver-plated mount, c1900, 13in (33cm) wide.
£250–300
$360–440 ⊞ CB

A pair of Art Nouveau glass vases, by Stuart & Sons, with brown-coloured swirls, Stourbridge, c1905, 8½in (21.5cm) high.
£225–245
$320–360 ⊞ RUSK

A green glass Jack-in-the-Pulpit vase, c1900, 16in (40.5cm) high.
£400–450
$600–650 ⊞ SHa

Three glass penny licks, c1920, 3in (7.5cm) high.
£20–25
$30–40 ⊞ HO
Penny licks were the precursor of ice-cream cones. The street vendor would fill the glass with a penny's worth of ice-cream. Once it was consumed, the glass was returned (although not necessarily washed) for the next customer. Penny licks were banned from many British towns in the 1920s for spreading diseases. Wafer cones, arguably invented for the St Louis World Fair, USA, in 1904, provided a far more hygienic alternative.

◀ **A James Powell & Sons, Whitefriars wave ribbed glass bowl,** in Sanctuary blue, designed by William Butler, c1920, 10in (25.5cm) diam.
£300–350
$450–500 ⊞ RUSK

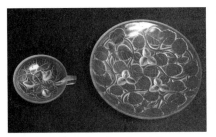

A pressed clear glass bowl with four dishes, signed 'André Delatte', French, c1928, bowl 9in (23cm) diam.
£120–150
$175–225 ⊞ CAL

A Monart glass bowl, decorated with lemon, amber, turquoise and gold aventurine, c1930, 9½in (24cm) diam.
£150–180
$220–260 ⊞ RUSK

A Stombelt pale blue glass vase, etched mark 'Stromberg-Shyttan', c1930, 8in (20.5cm) high.
£75–85
$115–125 ⊞ RUSK

A Lalique blue-stained and opalescent Coupe Muguet glass bowl, signed, 1930–31, 9½in (24cm) diam.
£900–1,100
$1,300–1,600 ⊞ RUSK

A Gray-Stan flattened globular-shaped vase, decorated with apricot marble swirls, engraved mark 'Gray-Stan', c1930, 6½in (16.5cm) high.
£230–260
$330–390 ⊞ RUSK

A Murano white and gold glass bowl, by Barovier, Italian, 1930s, 11in (28cm) diam.
£150–180
$220–260 ⊞ BRU

A Venetian glass millefiori figure, 1930s, 9in (23cm) high.
£190–220
$275–325 ⊞ BRU

A Jobling jade glass bowl, with flower block, on a black glass stand, c1934, 5in (12.5cm) wide.
£45–55
$60–80 ⊞ CAL

A Steuben clear glass bowl American, 1950s, 7in (18cm) wide.
£25–30
$35–40 ⊞ MCC

▶ **A Nuutajarvi Notsjo vase,** designed by Gunnel Nyman, free-blown clear crystal with spike-mould controlled bubbles, marked, 1947–58, 12¾in (32.5cm) high.
£125–145
$180–220 ⊞ RUSK

A Royal Brierley cut-glass jug, commemorating the Coronation of Queen Elizabeth, c1953, 12in (30.5cm) high.
£125–145
$180–220 ⊞ RUSK

A Stella Polaris Orrefors clear glass vase, Swedish, 1950s, 7in (18cm) high.
£140–160
$200–250 ⊞ BRU

A Murano red-cased glass vase, with original label, 1950s, 9½in (24cm) high.
£25–30
$35–40 ⊞ MCC

A Val St Lambert blue and clear glass vase, 1950s, 10in (25.5cm) high.
£250–275
$350–400 ⊞ MCC

An Orrefors Kraka-style blue glass vase, by Sven Palmqvist, 1950s, 7in (18cm) high.
£400–500
$650–720 ⊞ MCC

▶ **A Stromberg pink-and-yellow cased glass ashtray,** 1950s, 5in (12.5cm) wide.
£25–30
$35–45 ⊞ MCC

An Orrefors glass plate, designed by Sven Palmqvist, blown yellow and steel-blue crystal with controlled bubbles, marked 'Orrefors Kraka Nr.486 Sven Palmqvist', c1955, 2in (5cm) high.
£225–275
$330–400 ⋰ TREA

A glass bird, designed by Oiva Toikka Nuutajarvi, Finnish, 1950s, 8in (20.5cm) wide.
£300–400
$440–580 ⊞ MCC

A Kosta amethyst-coloured glass bowl, by Elis Berg, Swedish, 1950s, 8½in (21.5cm) high.
£90–100
$125–145 ⊞ MCC

◀ **A white opaque glass vase,** by Tapio Wirkkala, Finish, c1950, 6in (15cm) high.
£68–75
$100–110 ⊞ BRU

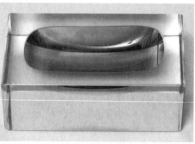

▶ **A Holmegaard freeform clear glass bowl,** by Per Lutken, signed, 1950s–60s, 8in (20.5cm) wide.
£50–60
$70–90 ⊞ ORI

A Holmegaard glass candlestick,
by Per Lutken, 1950s–60s,
4in (10cm) high.
£45–50
$65–75 ⊞ ORI

Per Lutken

Danish designer Per Lutken (1916–98)
is regarded as one of Scandinavia's
leading 20th-century glassmakers.
From 1942, he was chief designer at the
Kastrup and Holmegaard Glassworks,
where during the '40s and '50s he
created fluid, organic shapes in a subtle
range of colours. Lutken produced
domestic tableware as well as art
glass. In the 1960s he pioneered the
development of strong and practical
pedestal drinking glasses and during
the '70s he experimented with streaked
and textured studio ware. Today his
works attract many collectors.

**A Holmegaard beak
glass vase,** by Per
Lutken, 1950s–60s,
10in (25.5cm) high.
£60–70
$90–100 ⊞ ORI

An Elme black glass vase, by
Edvin Oiles, Swedish, early 1960s,
8in (20.5cm) high.
£75–85
$115–125 ⊞ MCC

Cross Reference
See Colour Review (page 194)

A pair of glass figures, by
G. Toffolo, Murano, decorated in
red, black and gold, signed, Italian,
c1960, 16in (40.5cm) high.
£350–400
$500–600 ⊞ BRU

▶ **A Mdina blue and yellow
glass bowl,** Maltese, 1960s,
6in (15cm) diam.
£18–22
$20–30 ⊞ HSt

**A Holmegaard Herveze glass heart
vase,** by Per Lutken, signed, designed
1950s, 1961, 5¾in (14.5cm) high.
£100–120
$145–175 ⊞ ORI

A green and clear glass fish, possibly
Murano, Italian, 1960s, 5in (12.5cm) high.
£50–60
$70–90 ⊞ REN

▶ **A Strömberg glass ice bucket,** Swedish,
with sterling silver mount by Aage Dragsted,
Danish, 1960s, 9½in (24cm) wide.
£50–60
$75–90 ⊞ DID

A blue glass vase,
by Lucciano Gaspari,
Murano, Italian, c1960,
13in (33cm) high.
£145–160
$200–230 ⊞ BRU

A Venini black-and-white glass VVV vase, one of seven designs by Gianni Versace for Venini, with random red and yellow squares, Italian, 1999, 10in (25.5cm) high.
£700–780
$1,000–1,200 ⊞ HaG

A Holmegaard amber glass Gulvase, by Otto Breuer, Danish, 1960s, 12in (30.5cm) high.
£50–60
$75–90 ⊞ ORI

A James Powell & Sons, Whitefriars, smoky-grey glass bark vase, by Geoffrey Baxter, 1960s, 8in (20.5cm) high.
£40–45
$60–70 ⊞ MCC

A Holmegaard set of smoky-grey glass vases, by Per Lutken, 1970s, 12in (30.5cm) high.
£100–120
$145–175 ⊞ MCC

A hand-made Maiori glass bowl, by Bebe Facente, Memphis, American, c1986, 13in (33cm) diam.
£500–550
$720–800 ⊞ FMa

A Capo Nord flat glass vase, by Seguso Viro, Murano, the black-and-white spiral of canes encased in blue, aquamarine and clear glass, Italian, 1999, 10in (25.5cm) high.
£650–700
$900–1,000 ⊞ HaG

A Baccarat lead crystal vase, by Nicholas Triboulot, French, designed 1996, 9½in (24cm) high.
£680–750
$1,000–1,100 ⊞ HaG

Carnival Glass

A Carnival glass bowl, orange with a marigold pattern, c1900, 8in (20.5cm) diam.
£25–30
$35–45 ⊞ SER

A Carnival glass fruit bowl, decorated with roses pattern, c1920, 9in (23cm) diam.
£45–50
$70–80 ⊞ ML

A Carnival glass spatula-footed plate, by Northwood Glass Co, Ohio, decorated with grape and cable pattern to the centre, American, c1910, 9in (23cm) diam.
£110–130
$150–200 ⊞ CAL

Cranberry Glass

A cranberry glass jug, with clear glass reeded looped handle, foot, 19thC, 8in (20.5cm) high.
£140–160
$200–230 ✗ GAK

A cranberry glass two-branch candelabrum, with wrythen stem and spreading circular foot, 19thC, 4½in (11.5cm) high.
£180–200
$250–300 ✗ GAK

▶ A Victorian part-cranberry glass vase, 12in (30.5cm) high.
£200–225
$300–330 ⊞ AOY

A Victorian cranberry and clear glass posy vase, formed as a hanging basket, 9½in (24cm) high.
£150–170
$220–250 ✗ DD

A cranberry glass bell, with folded-over foot and original handle, 1890, 10in (25.5cm) high.
£120–140
$170–200 ⊞ GRI

A Stourbridge cranberry glass cream jug and sugar bowl, the rims decorated with white threaded and clear crystal applied decoration, on frilled feet, c1895, bowl 5in (12.5cm) diam.
£260–300
$380–440 ⊞ GRI

A single coronet cut top cranberry glass lustre, c1900, 8in (20.5cm) high.
£300–320
$440–480 ⊞ GRI

A cranberry glass sugar or preserve bowl, with applied crystal frilled decoration, c1910, 5in (12.5cm) diam.
£80–100
$115–145 ⊞ GRI

A cranberry glass decanter, with clear glass stopper and reeded handle, c1900, 11in (28cm) high.
£190–220
$275–325 ⊞ GRI

A cross-cut cranberry and clear glass decanter, probably Stourbridge, c1930, 12in (30.5cm) high.
£150–170
$220–250 ⊞ GRI

A cranberry glass powder bowl, with clear glass rustic knop and frilled feet, 1910, 5in (12.5cm) diam.
£110–120
$160–180 ⊞ GRI

Davidson & Chippendale Glass

George Davidson (1822–91) founded the Teams Flint Glass Works in Gateshead near Newcastle in 1866. Initially the firm made chimney lamps, but soon moved on to producing tableware. After his father's death, Thomas Davidson (1860–1937) took control and introduced many new designs. He pioneered the glass flower block (registered 1910) and in the 1920s developed a new line of cloud glass. 'The latest addition is a unique purple cloud or alabaster effect,' reported the *Pottery Gazette and Glass Trades Review* in October 1923. 'This new treatment is offered in bowls with. . .flower blocks to match.' Cloud glass, made by trailing dark glass into lighter glass, was a popular line and came in various colours. In 1933 Davidson began to manufacture Chippendale glass – a range of pressed glass with broad facets. The design was first registered in the USA in 1907 and was produced under licence from Charles Pratt's National Glass Company. Initially it was imported to the UK, but Davidson bought the rights and the moulds and manufactured the glass until WWII.

A pair of George Davidson tazza clear glass compotes, 1885, 8in (20.5cm) diam.
£65–75
$90–110 ⊞ CAL

◄ **A George Davidson green cloud glass vase,** c1922–39, 7½in (19cm) high.
£70–80
$100–120
⊞ BEV

► **A George Davidson amber cloud glass vase,** c1922–39, 5½in (14cm) high.
£35–40
$50–60 ⊞ BEV

A George Davidson topaz glass fan vase, c1922–39, 5in (12.5cm) high.
£70–80
$100–120 ⊞ BEV

► **A Chippendale clear glass preserve pot,** 1907–40, 3in (7.5cm) high.
£9–11
$12–15 ⊞ TWAC

Two George Davidson green glass frogs/flower blocks, c1930, largest 7in (18cm) wide.
£36–40
$50–60 ⊞ BEV

A Chippendale green glass candlestick, 1907–40, 7½in (19cm) high.
£9–11
$12–15 ⊞ TWAC

A Chippendale clear
glass oil flask and
stopper, 1907–40,
8½in (21.5cm) high.
£10–12
$15–18 ⊞ TWAC

▶ A Chippendale clear glass mayonnaise
bowl, 1907–40, 5in (12.5cm) diam.
£6–8
$7–10 ⊞ TWAC

A Chippendale clear glass celery tray,
1907–40, 11in (28cm) wide.
£10–12
$15–18 ⊞ TWAC

**Miller's is a price GUIDE not
a price LIST**

▶ A Chippendale clear glass sugar bowl,
1907–40, 4¾in (12cm) high.
£6–8
$7–10 ⊞ TWAC

Decanters

◀ An oak tantalus, with three
square cut-glass decanters, 19thC,
13in (33cm) wide.
£350–400
$500–600 ⊞ MCC

A claret decanter, with fluted clear
glass body and silver-plated mounts,
c1910, 11in (28cm) high.
£350–400
$500–580 ⊞ DAD

◀ A clear Iittala Glass decanter,
by Tapio Wirkkala, Finnish, 1970s,
11in (28cm) high.
£90–110
$130–160 ⊞ MCC

A yellow glass decanter and six
shot glasses, by Moser, c1930,
decanter 10in (25.5cm) high.
£300–350
$450–500 ⊞ JEZ

Condition

The condition is absolutely
vital when assessing the
value of a collectable.
Damaged pieces on the
whole appreciate much less
than perfect examples.
However, a rare desirable
piece may command a high
price even when damaged.

Drinking Glasses

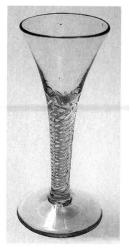

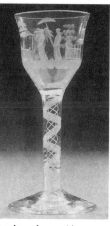

A cut-glass tumbler, with moulded base, c1810, 6in (15cm) high.
£50–60
$70–90 ⊞ JHa

A wine glass, with drawn trumpet bowl, multi-spiral air-twist stem, on a conical foot, c1750, 6½in (16.5cm) high.
£200–250
$300–350 ⊞ JHa

A wine glass, with ogee bowl engraved with two figures in a chinoiserie landscape, on a double series opaque twist stem with a conical foot, c1770, 5½in (14cm) high.
£340–400
$500–600 ⚒ S(S)

A liqueur glass, the ovoid bowl with swag engraving, c1780, 3¾in (9.5cm) high.
£35–40
$50–60 ⊞ TWAC

▶ **A diamond-cut port glass,** c1810, 3½in (9cm) high.
£20–30
$30–50 ⊞ JHa

A slice-cut Champagne flute, c1830, 6¼in (16cm) high.
£35–40
$50–60 ⊞ JHa

A thistle-cut sherry glass, c1820, 5in (12.5cm) high.
£20–25
$30–35 ⊞ JHa

◀ **A gram or gin glass,** with ball knop stem, c1840, 4in (10cm) high.
£25–35
$30–50 ⊞ JHa

▶ **A Continental port glass,** with engraved and moulded bowl, c1840, 4½in (11.5cm) high.
£25–30
$35–40 ⊞ JHa

A blaze- and feather-cut Champagne glass, c1820, 5in (12.5cm) high.
£30–40
$45–60 ⊞ JHa

A liqueur glass, with panel cut bowl and flattened knop, c1840, 3¼in (8.5cm) high.
£18–22
$25–35 ⊞ TWAC

A set of six James Powell & Sons, Whitefriars flint wine glasses, c1880, 4½in (11.5cm) high.
£145–165
$200–250 ⊞ RUSK

A Thomas Webb dimpled beer glass, c1900, 5½in (14cm) high.
£18–22
$25–35 ⊞ JHa

A press-moulded rummer, c1850, 6in (15cm) high.
£24–28
$35–40 ⊞ TWAC

A James Powell & Sons, Whitefriars sherry glass, with wrythen bowl and twisted stem, c1880, 4in (10cm) high.
£20–25
$30–40 ⊞ JHa

◄ **A pair of slice-cut pub rummers** c1900, 6in (15cm) high.
£65–75
$90–110 ⊞ RUSK

A turquoise wine glass, probably James Powell & Sons, Whitefriars, c1860, 5in (12.5cm) high.
£30–35
$40–50 ⊞ JHa

▶ **A pressed moulded beer tankard,** by Henry Greener, c1890, 4¼in (11cm) high.
£20–25
$30–35 ⊞ JHa

Items in the Glass section have been arranged in date order within each sub-section.

A Holmegaard neck-glass, Danish, 1970s, 4½in (11.5cm) high, boxed.
£20–25
$30–35 ⊞ PLB

A Champagne glass, the bowl engraved with Greek key and star pattern, c1870, 5in (12.5cm) high.
£15–20
$20–30 ⊞ JHa

A pair of Champagne tumblers, engraved with butterflies, c1910, 4in (10cm) high.
£63–70
$90–100 ⊞ JHa

Dumps & Paperweights

Dumps were made from waste glass, that would otherwise be dumped, hence their name. They were often produced by apprentices at bottle glassworks that produced green glass. Centres of manufacture include Sunderland, Stourbridge and Waterford. Depending on size, dumps can be used as either paperweights or doorstops. They are decorated with air bubbles, tears and sometimes contain sulphide images of figures or portrait medallions.

A green glass dump, the centre with cream and red bubbles, c1860, 5in (12.5cm) high.
£160–200
$230–300 ⊞ JBL

A Victorian green glass dump, with internal floral decoration, 5in (12.5cm) high.
£110–130
$150–200 ⊞ OCAC

A green glass dump, filled with effervescing bubbles, late 19thC, 3½in (9cm) high.
£130–160
$200–230 ⊞ JBL

A green glass dump, enclosing a sulphide portrait of Sir William Gladstone, late 19thC, 5in (12.5cm) high.
£130–150
$200–220 ⊞ RWA

A green glass dump, enclosing a sulphide figure of a child and parasol, late 19thC, 4in (10cm) high.
£170–190
$250–275 ⊞ RWA

◀ **A pair of pedestal paperweights,** one enclosing a motif of crossed machine guns below a coronet, the other inscribed 'Cambridgeshire Regiment', early 20thC, 3½in (9cm) high.
£230–250
$330–360 ✎ GAK

A Lalique amethyst-tinted glass paperweight, decorated with St Christopher, impressed mark, French, c1930, 4½in (11.5cm) high.
£600–700
$870–1,000 ⊞ RUSK

A Sabino glass paperweight, enclosing a nude figure, 1930s, 4½in (11.5cm) diam.
£200–250
$300–350 ⊞ JEZ

A Bohemian glass paperweight, enclosing a portrait, c1920, 4in (10cm) high.
£55–65
$80–100 ⊞ SWB

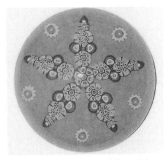

A Paul Ysart paperweight, with multicoloured millefiori floral decoration, signed, 1950–60, 3in (7.5cm) diam.
£480–530
$700–750 ⊞ SWB

A Baccarat paperweight, with multicoloured close-pack millefiori, c1970, 3in (7.5cm) diam.
£300–400
$440–580 ⊞ DLP

◀ **A Baccarat paperweight,** with a blue butterfly, limited edition, No. 33 of 125, 1978, 3in (7.5cm) diam.
£350–390
$500–580 ⊞ SWB

▶ **A St Louis paperweight,** green, cream and red, 1986, 2½in (6.5cm) diam.
£570–620
$850–900 ⊞ MLa

A Whitefriars blue-and-clear glass millefiori paperweight, limited edition, No. 28 of 487, 1975, 3½in (9cm) diam.
£450–500
$650–720 ⊞ SWB

A Chris Buzzini Bouquet paperweight, yellow, red, green and purple, limited edition, No. 23 of 25, American, 1991, 3in (7.5cm) diam.
£600–650
$870–970 ⊞ SWB

A Caithness Double Salamander paperweight, red, green and cream, limited edition, No. 17 of 25, 1993, 3in (7.5cm) diam.
£350–400
$500–600 ⊞ SWB

A Correia paperweight, decorated with black cats on a red ground, American, 1999, 3in (7.5cm) diam.
£85–95
$125–145 ⊞ SWB

A Ferro & Lazzarini Murano paperweight, red and cream, Italian, 2000, 3in (7.5cm) high.
£28–33
$35–45 ⊞ SWB

Guinness

A Guinness advertising mirror, with gold and black lettering on green background, 1920s–30s, 53½ x 38½in (136 x 99cm), in a wooden frame.
£2,200–2,500
$3,200–3,600 ⚒ BBR

Have a glass of Guinness when you're Tired

A Guinness gnome, with red hat and blue coat, sitting on a wooden stool, 1950s, 5in (12.5cm) high.
£230–260
$330–380 ⚒ BBR

A Guinness razor, 1935, 4in (10cm) long.
£60–70
$90–100 ⊞ HUX

GUINNESS goes so well with Cheese

A Guinness Celluloid advertising sign, depicting red Cheshire and English farmhouse cheeses with a pint of Guinness, 1950s–60s, 10 x 18in (25.5 x 45.5cm).
£150–175
$220–250 ⊞ MURR

◀ **A Guinness laminated card stand-up advertisement,** depicting golfers searching for a golf ball on a pebble beach, multicoloured, 1950s–60s, 10¼ x 7¼in (26 x 18.5cm).
£750–850
$1,000–1,250 ⚒ BBR

A Huntley & Palmer's Guinness biscuit tin, 1950s–60s, 10in (25.5cm) wide.
£140–150
$200–220 ⊞ MURR

▶ **A Guinness barometer,** the wooden frame inscribed 'Lovely Day for a Guinness', slight damage, 1950s, 8¼in (21cm) diam.
£40–50
$60–75 ⚒ DN

A set of Guinness Canasta playing cards, with rules and score sheet, made by Waddington's, 1951, 7 x 5in (18 x 12.5cm), in original box.
£40–50
$60–75 ⊞ MURR

A Guinness metal crate omnibus, red with yellow, white and black colouring, slight rusting, 1950s–60s, 18in (45.5cm) long.
£130–150
$190–220 ⚒ BBR

A Carlton Ware Guinness advertising model, shaped as a tortoise with a pint of Guinness on its back, painted in naturalistic colours, on a cream base inscribed 'My Goodness – My Guinness' in red lettering, red-printed maker's mark and impressed reference number, 1960–70, 3½in (9cm) high.
£75–90
$100–130 ⚒ DN

A Guinness silver-plated pocket watch, the face decorated with a smiling face glass of Guinness, a nodding toucan and 'Guinness Time' in red lettering, 1950s–60s.
£420–480
$580–700 ⚲ BBR

A Guinness tin tray, in naturalistic colours, inscribed 'Toucans in their nest agree, Guinness is good for you, Open some today and see, What one or Toucan do', 1950s, 12in (30.5cm) diam.
£60–75
$90–110 ⊞ MURR

A Guinness mains-operated illuminated clock, with Perspex face and chrome top, green and red lettering to face, 1950s–60s, 16in (40.5cm) high.
£300–350
$450–500 ⚲ BBR

A Guinness enamel badge, in the shape of a penguin and a glass of Guinness, embossed 'Draught Guinness' and 'Guinness is Good for You', 1950s–60s, 1½in (4cm) high.
£40–50
$60–75 ⚲ BBR

A pair of Guinness enamel cufflinks, 1950s–60s.
£40–45
$60–65 ⚲ BBR

◄ **A Guinness extra stout bottle,** to celebrate the company's bicentenary, 1759–1959, 1959, 9in (23cm) high.
£25–30
$35–45 ⊞ HUX

A Guinness stand-up advertisment, plastic-covered tin, red, black and cream, 'Guinness is Good For You, Enjoy it with Meals When Tired, Before Retiring', 6¼ x 9¼in (16 x 23.5cm).
£150–175
$220–255 ⚲ BBR

▶ **A Carlton Ware Guinness advertising simulated stoneware bottle,** with wire-bound cork stopper, 'Guinness Extra Stout' red seal label, inscribed 'Guinness is Good For You', around base, black-printed maker's mark and impressed reference number, 1960–70, 7in (17.5cm) high.
£20–25
$30–35 ⚲ DN

A Carlton Ware Guinness tea set, by James Blackmore, comprising teapot, jug, sugar bowl, black and white with gold harp and lettering, 1960, teapot 5¾in (14.5cm) high.
£500–550
$720–800 ⚲ BBR

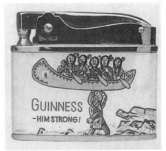

A Guinness cigarette lighter, with a coloured image of a Native American chief holding a canoe full of braves above his head, inscribed 'Guinness – Him Strong!' to one side and 'Good Health from Ireland' to the other, 1950s–60s, 1¾in (4.5cm) high, in original box.
£90–110
$130–160 ⚲ BBR

Handbags & Luggage

A late Victorian wooden chest, with domed top and lift-out tray, 37in (94cm) wide.
£250–300
$350–450 ⊞ **TPC**

◀ A beaded bag, with silver and gold-coloured beads and brass clasp, 1920, 6in (15cm) high.
£65–75
$90–110 ⊞ **Ech**

A beaded bag, with plastic tortoiseshell-effect clasp, 1900, 9in (23cm) high.
£75–85
$100–125 ⊞ **Ech**

A metal-beaded purse, with moonstone decoration, French, 1920–30, 8in (20.5cm) long.
£225–250
$320–360 ⊞ **CRIS**

A hessian steamer trunk, with wooden bands, leather corners, brass locks and reproduction labels, c1930, 36in (91.5cm) wide.
£85–95
$125–150 ⊞ **HO**

A chrome-framed snakeskin handbag, with integral purse, c1930, 11in (28cm) wide.
£45–50
$65–75 ⊞ **SBL**

A Biene & Davis embroidered chenille bag, with red, peach and lilac flowers and green foliage, with original purse, American, c1930, 8in (20.5cm) wide.
£100–120
$150–175 ⊞ **LaF**

A leather hat box, silk-lined, made for Harrods, c1930, 16in (40.5cm) wide.
£150–175
$220–250 ⊞ **HO**

A black crepe evening bag, with Austrian crystal decoration, c1940, 4in (10cm) wide.
£90–100
$130–150 ⊞ **LaF**

A wicker bag, with blue and black appliquéd butterflies and Lucite handle and frame, American, c1950, 11½in (29cm) wide.
£70–80
$100–115 ⊞ **SBL**

A plastic laminated bag, with Lucite handle, decorated with a picture of a Japanese lady wearing a red kimono, American, 1950s, 9½in (24cm) high.
£100–120
$150–175 ⊞ LBe

A black patent vinyl weekend bag, c1950s, 10in (25.5cm) high.
£45–50
$65–75 ⊞ LaF

A box handbag, by Pucci, multi-coloured, 1960s, 7in (18cm) high.
£350–400
$500–580 ⊞ SBT

▶ **A gilt-frame black silk evening bag,** decorated with gilt appliqué, c1970, 7in (18cm) wide.
£50–60
$75–100 ⊞ SBL

A Perspex handbag, white marble effect, mid-1950s, 8in (20.5cm) wide.
£160–180
$230–260 ⊞ HSt

A gilt chainmail bag, by Whiting & Davis, American, 1950s, 6in (15cm) wide.
£120–140
$175–200 ⊞ SBT

A leather suitcase, with chrome locks, 1960s, 22in (56cm) wide.
£55–65
$80–100 ⊞ HO

A Perspex and rhinestone handbag, by Midas of Miami, American, 1950s, 9in (23cm) wide.
£220–240
$320–350 ⊞ SpM

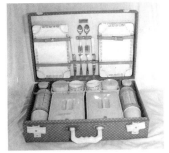

A picnic hamper, by Brexton, blue case with white fittings, 1950s, 30in (76cm) wide.
£120–140
$175–200 ⊞ PPH

LOCATE THE SOURCE

The source of each illustration in Miller's can be found by checking the code letters below each caption with the Key to Illustrations, pages 444–452.

A plastic vanity case, by Antler, grey snakeskin effect with red lining, fitted, c1970, 12in (30.5)cm wide.
£50–60
$75–100 ⊞ SBL

Horse Brasses

A **Victorian camel brass,** with owner's penknife and seal, 5in (12.5cm) wide.
£40–50
$60–75 ⊞ PJo

A **brass swinger,** single crescent, c1890, 3½in (9cm) diam.
£20–25
$30–35 ⊞ HBr

A **miller's horse brass,** c1920, 5in (12.5cm) high.
£5–10
$10–15 ⊞ PJo

▶ A **commemorative horse brass,** for King George V's Silver Jubilee, 1935, 3½in (9cm) diam.
£30–35
$45–50 ⊞ HBr

A **commemorative cast-brass shield,** for Queen Victoria's Golden Jubilee, 1887, 4in (10cm) high.
£100–120
$150–175 ⊞ HBr

A **commemorative cast-brass horse brass,** for Queen Victoria's Diamond Jubilee, 1897, 4in (10cm) high.
£110–125
$160–180 ⊞ HBr

A **Victorian horse brass,** 4in (10cm) diam.
£20–25
$30–450 ⊞ PJo

A **John Edgington advertising brass,** c1900, 4in (10cm) high.
£30–35
$45–50 ⊞ PJo

A **horse brass,** commemorating Ealing Victory Horse Parade, 1946, 5in (12.5cm) high.
£30–40
$45–60 ⊞ PJo

Colour Review

A coral and gold carved brooch, c1860, 2½in (6.5cm) wide.
£230–275
$330–400 ⊞ Ma

Seven Victorian bug brooches, coloured glass with brass settings, 1½in (4cm) wide.
£10–20
$15–30 each ⊞ VB

An Art Nouveau pendant, with blue topaz and pearls set in 9ct gold, c1890–1910, 1½in (4cm) long.
£260–290
$380–450 ⊞ AMC

A paste clip, with square-cut stones, 1930s, 6in (15cm) wide.
£50–60
$75–100 ⊞ SBL

A tin enamelled brooch, modelled as a bunch of forget-me-nots, c1910, 2in (5cm) wide.
£40–45
$60–65 ⊞ LBe

▶ **A pair of Art Deco cuff-links,** enamel on chrome, 1920s–30s, ½in (1cm) diam.
£75–95
$100–150 ⊞ SpM

A Chinese imitation jade necklace, original stringing, 1930s, 14in (35.5cm) long.
£8–10
$10–15 ⊞ STP

A plastic-covered wire posy brooch, 1939–45, 2in (5cm) long.
£25–30
$35–50 ⊞ REN

A crystal necklace, Czechoslovakian, c1930, 20in (51cm) long.
£45–50
$65–75 ⊞ LaF

A Weiss flower pin, 1950s, 4¼in (11cm) long.
£65–75
$95–110 ⊞ CRIS

▶ **A cherub chatelaine pin,** by Joseff of Hollywood, with faux pearls and rubies, 1940s–50s, 6in (15cm) long.
£400–450
$580–650 ⊞ CRIS

A Schiaparelli brooch and earrings set, modelled as fruit, 1950s, brooch 2in (5cm) long.
£225–250
$320–360 ⊞ CRIS

A Trifari pearl and enamel brooch and earrings set, modelled as pea pods, 1950s, brooch 2¾in (7cm) long.
£175–195
$250–280 ⊞ CRIS

A Trifari butterfly pin, 1950s, 1½in (4cm) wide.
£25–30
$35–45 ⊞ CRIS

A pair of rhinestone earrings, 1960s, 2in (5cm) long.
£30–35
$45–50 ⊞ LBe

► **A Stanley Hagler bangle,** 1960s–70s, 3in (7.5cm) wide.
£400–450
$580–650 ⊞ CRIS

► **A knot necklace,** with paste stones, French, 1960s, 14in (35.5cm) long.
£170–200
$250–300 ⊞ CRIS

A Venetian glass necklace, 1950s, 18in (45.5cm) long.
£100–125
$150–180 ⊞ LBe

A enamelled terracotta necklace, Danish, 1960s, 15in (38cm) long.
£130–150
$190–220 ⊞ LBe

► **A enamel and paste brooch,** by Hattie Carnegie, American, c1970, 3in (7.5cm) long.
£70–80
$100–115 ⊞ SBL

A enamel and paste bracelet, by Kenneth Jay Lane, American, c1970, 3½in (9cm) wide.
£40–50
$60–75 ⊞ SBL

A beaded necklace, by Miriam Haskell, 1970s, 15in (38cm) long.
£80–90
$115–130 ⊞ SBL

A banded storage tub with lid, with original paint, Scandinavian, dated 1850, 11in (28cm) high.
£160–180
$230–260 ⊞ NEW

A copper kettle, c1890, 9½in (24cm) high.
£110–125
$160–180 ⊞ AL

▶ **Two wooden bread boards,** c1920, 6in (15cm) diam.
£35–40
$50–60 each ⊞ SMI

A set of three Tupperware storage containers, 1970s, largest 9in (23cm) diam.
£20–25
$30–35 ⊞ Mo

▶ **A copper iced pudding mould,** c1860, 4in (10cm) high.
£380–420
$560–620 ⊞ MSB

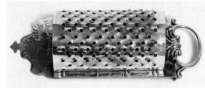

A brass cheese grater, Dutch, c1870, 12in (30.5cm) long.
£180–200
$260–300 ⊞ SMI

A copper game pie mould, c1880, 8in (20.5cm) wide.
£180–200
$260–300 ⊞ SMI

A set of five enamel storage jars, by B. B. Torsiene, French, 1920s–30s, largest 7in (18cm) high.
£80–100
$115–150 ⊞ AL

▶ **A set of Prestige Sky-Line kitchen utensils,** 1960s, in orignal box, 20 x 15in (51 x 38cm).
£35–40
$50–60 ⊞ HSt

A Kendrick brass and cast-iron coffee grinder, c1900, 5in (12.5cm) high.
£90–100
$130–150 ⊞ SMI

A flour tin, with original paint, c1920, 9in (23cm) high.
£90–100
$130–150 ⊞ SMI

A brass trawler mast-head light, c1880, 14in (35.5cm) high.
£260–300
$380–450 ⊞ AOY

An advertisement for Clark's Night Lights and Lamps, 1880s, modern frame.
£70–80
$100–115 ⚒ BBR

A Doulton Cricklite fairy light, with glass shade, marked 'S Clarke Patent Trade Mark Fairy', slight restoration, early 20thC, 8¼in (21cm) high.
£550–600
$800–870 ⚒ BBR

A Brocks fairy light, embossed 'Brocks Illumination Lamp made in Belgium', minor damage, early 20thC.
£100–120
$150–175 ⚒ BBR

▶ **A hand-painted chamberstick,** 1930s, 4½in (11.5cm) diam.
£16–18
$20–30 ⊞ TAC

A Cauldon chamberstick, 1930s, 8in (20.5cm) high.
£100–120
$150–175 ⊞ BEV

A set of Mazda Cinderella Disneylights, c1940s, in original display box, 12 x 7in (30.5 x 18cm).
£55–60
$80–90 ⊞ MRW

A plastic and teak rocket lamp, rewired, c1960, 47in (119.5cm) high.
£60–70
$90–100 ⊞ KA

A Plastacrush lamp, with Perspex base, 1960s–70s, 14in (35.5cm) high.
£25–30
$35–45 ⊞ FLD

A hanging lamp, by Louis Poulsen & Co, Danish, 1970s, with original box, 9in (23cm) high.
£45–65
$65–95 ⊞ PLB

A tin and chrome desk lamp, 1950s, 15in (38cm) high.
£150–200
$220–300 ⊞ ZOOM

▶ **A plastic Pink Panther lamp,** Italian, 1980s, 18in (45.5cm) high.
£50–60
$75–90 ⊞ TAC

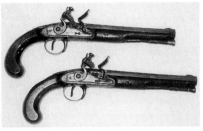

A pair of duelling pistols, breeches inscribed 'Jover & Son, London', lockplates engraved with trophies and scrolls, walnut fullstocks and brass-tipped ramrods, rebrowned barrels, c1785, barrels 9in (23cm) long, in a fitted oak case.
£3,500–4,000
$5,000–6,000 ⊞ WSA

An officer's full dress embroidered sabretache, of the South Nottinghamshire Yeomanry Cavalry, with gilt lace border, c1860, 14in (35.5cm) high.
£700–800
$1,000–1,200 ⚒ WAL

A Royal Flying Corps fret-cut wooden picture frame, c1914–18, 15 x 11in (38 x 28cm).
£225–250
$320–360 ⊞ AOY

An embroidered silk regimental postcard, of the South Lancashire Prince of Wales's Volunteers, c1916, 3½ x 5½in (9 x 14cm).
£35–40
$50–90 ⊞ GAA

◄ **A WWII book of matches,** Canadian, 2in (5cm) high.
£1–2
$2–3 ⊞ HUX

A WWII poster, 'Careless Talk Costs Lives', by Fougasse, 1940, 13 x 9in (33 x 23cm).
£225–250
$320–360 ⊞ REN

An RAF sector wall clock, with chain and fusee movement by Elliott Bros, repainted dial, numbered and dated 1943, 19in (48cm) diam.
£550–600
$700–800 ⚒ ONS

A WWII money box, the label inscribed 'Pennies Make Pounds', 3in (7.5cm) high.
£25–30
$35–45 ⊞ HUX

A WAAF recruitment poster, designed by Foss, 1949, 14½ x 9¾in (37 x 25cm).
£70–85
$100–125 ⚒ ONS

An RAF bandsman's hat, fur-covered, mid- to late-20thC, 8in (20.5cm) high.
£150–180
$220–260 ⊞ UCO

A model of an American Civil War Confederate standard bearer, by Michael Roberts & Co, in resin and white metal, hand-painted, 1997, 39½in (100cm) high.
£140–160
$200–230 ⊞ BONA

◄ **An Apulian owl skyphos,** decorated on both sides with Athena's owl between two palm fronds, Greek South Italian, restored, c4thC BC, 3in (8cm) high.
£750–850
$1,100–1,250 ⊞ CrF

► **A Rye Pottery owl jug,** damaged, c1840s, 6in (15cm) high.
£55–65
$80–95 ⊞ DCA

An owl double-sided night light, in ruby satin glass on a clear glass base, early 20thC, 4½in (11.5cm) high.
£350–440
$500–600 ➹ BBR

A Bretby model of an owl, on a rustic base, c1920, 12in (30.5cm) high.
£170–210
$250–300 ➹ G(L)

A cold-painted bronze model of an owl, by Franz Bergman, early 20thC, 6in (15cm) high.
£430–480
$625–700 ➹ TYL

A Royal Doulton flambé veined model of an owl, c1930, 11in (28cm) high.
£280–320
$400–450 ➹ G(L)

A ceramic owl lamp, 1930s, 6½in (16.5cm) high.
£200–250
$300–350 ⊞ LBe

A Zsolnay model of an owl, 1930s, 13in (33cm) high.
£700–800
$1,000–1,200 ⊞ KA

◄ **A Trifari owl pin,** 1950s, 2¼in (5.5cm) high.
£25–30
$35–45 ⊞ CRIS

A Trifari owl pin, decorated with paste stones, 1950s, 2½in (6.5cm) high.
£100–125
$150–180 ⊞ CRIS

◄ **A cane handbag,** with a felt owl under vinyl and Lucite handles, American, 1950s, 12in (30.5cm) wide.
£55–60
$80–90 ⊞ LaF

◄ **A Schuco mohair owl,** c1959, 2½in (6.5cm) high.
£75–90
$110–130 ➹ TED

PLASTIC • COLOUR REVIEW   239

A phenolic cruet set, 1930s,
4in (10cm) long.
£160–190
$230–280 ⊞ BEV

**A Bakelite Michelin Man money
box,** late 1930s, 6in (15cm) high.
£160–190
$230–275 ⊞ BEV

▶ **A urea formaldehyde bowl,** by
Beatl, 1940s, 8in (20.5cm) diam.
£120–150
$175–220 ⊞ GAD

**An Edbar International Corp VP
Twin plastic novelty camera,** made
for Woolworths, takes 127mm roll
film, c1938, 3in (7.5cm) wide.
£30–35
$45–50 ⊞ HEG
**These cameras came in various
colours, of which blue is the
rarest. The most common colour,
black, is valued at £5–10 ($8–15).**

A phenolic box, c1930s,
3in (7.5cm) diam.
£80–90
$120–130 ⊞ BEV

**A Perspex pen stand and card
stand,** American, 1950s,
3in (7.5cm) wide.
£20–25
$30–50 pair ⊞ LBe

A pair of plastic sunglasses, with batwing-style
frames, Italian, c1950.
£30–35
$45–50 ⊞ SBL

▶ **Three plastic
Tupperware
containers,**
with ribbed lids,
1960s, 5in
(12.5cm) diam.
£6–8
$9–12 each
⊞ Mo

Two plastic necklaces, with faceted beads,
c1960, 20in (51cm) long.
£15–20
$20–30 each ⊞ SBL

A plastic juice set, with six tumblers,
two stirrers and a jug, French, 1970,
10¼in (26cm) high, in original box.
£55–65
$80–100 ⊞ PLB

**An ABS plastic umbrella
stand,** Dedalo design
by Emma Gismondi
Schweinberger for Artemide
of Milan, Italian, 1970s,
14in (35.5cm) high.
£80–90
$120–140 ⊞ PLB

A pottery mug, commemorating the 1845 Corn Law repeal, enamelled with flowers and a sheaf of corn, star crack to base, c1846, 4in (10cm) high.
£130–150
$200–225 ↗ SAS

A commemorative plate, by Wallis Gimson, with a portrait of Benjamin Disraeli and a verse, c1881, 11in (28cm) wide.
£135–165
$200–240 ⊞ POL

A commemorative plate, by Wallis Gimson, with a portrait of the Marquis of Salisbury, c1887, 11in (28cm) wide.
£30–40
$45–60 ↗ SAS

A commemorative plaque, by Burgess & Leigh, with a portrait of Gladstone, 1898, 14¼in (36cm) diam.
£85–100
$125–150 ↗ SAS

A commemorative plate, by Meakin, with reversible portraits of Balfour and Asquith, inscribed 'Rule Britannia' and 'Britannia Rues', hairline crack, c1906, 4in (10cm) diam.
£45–55
$65–80 ↗ SAS

A commemorative Carnival glass bottle, embossed with President Dwight Eisenhower, first edition, c1969, 8in (20.5cm) high.
£60–70
$90–100 ⊞ CAL

◄ **A biscuit tin,** the lid with an illustration of Sir Winston Churchill, c1955, 10 x 8¼in (25.5 x 21cm).
£15–20
$20–30 ⊞ HUX

A car-bumper sticker, produced by Massachusetts Democrats, unused, signed by John F. Kennedy, American, c1960, 6in (15cm) wide.
£1,350–1,500
$2,000–2,200 ⊞ IQ

► **A collection of presidential campaign metal badges,** American, 20thC, largest 1½in (4cm) diam.
£40–50
$60–75 ⊞ IE

A biscuit tin, featuring Presidents of the USA with John F. Kennedy in the centre, American, 1961, 8½ x 9½in (21.5 x 24cm).
£25–30
$35–45 ⊞ HUX

A ceramic character jug, modelled as the *Spitting Image* character of Neil Kinnock, limited edition, No. 169 of 650, 1980s, 5in (12.5cm) high.
£30–50
$45–75 ➶ Pott

An Aynsley plate, with a portrait of Margaret Thatcher against a background of the Houses of Parliament, 1987, 10½in (26.5cm) diam.
£20–25
$30–35 ⊞ HUX

A Royal Doulton bust of Margaret Thatcher, printed factory mark, signed 'M. Woodhouse', c1982, 4¾in (12cm) high.
£400–480
$600–700 ➶ P

A pottery character jug, by Kevin Francis, depicting Mikhail Gorbachov, limited edition, No. 438 of 1,000, 9½in (23.5cm) high.
£40–50
$60–75 ➶ SAS

Harold Wilson, by Ben Pimlott, a political biography, published by HarperCollins, 1993, 8 x 5¼in (20.5 x 13.5cm).
£13–15
$20–25 ⊞ POL

A photograph of Sir Winston Churchill, signed by his grandson and granddaughter, 1990s, 30 x 23in (76 x 58.5cm).
£175–195
$250–280 ⊞ POL

A concrete garden gnome, modelled as Tony Blair, entitled 'The Urban Gardener', 2001, 16in (40.5cm) high.
£50–60
$75–90 ⊞ POL

▶ **A political cartoon,** by Martin Rowson, entitled 'Mad Cow', 1999, 9 x 11in (23 x 28cm).
£225–250
$320–360 ⊞ POL

A political badge, featuring Peter Mandelson, inscribed 'Bring Back Mandy', 2001, 1½in (4cm) diam.
£1–2
$2–3 ⊞ POL

◀ **An electoral campaign poster,** on behalf of the Labour Party, featuring William Hague as Margaret Thatcher, 2001, 7½ x 15½in (19 x 37cm).
£1–2
$2–3 ⊞ POL

A lithographic poster, 'Théâtre National de L'Opéra Carnaval 1892', by Jules Chéret, printed by Chaix, Paris, 47¼ x 33¾in (120 x 85.5cm).
£1,000–1,200
$1,500–1,800 ➶ S

Miller's is a price GUIDE
not a price LIST

A poster, 'P&O Cruises', by Greig, printed by Lamson Agency, c1930, 39¾ x 24¾in (101 x 63cm).
£750–800
$1,000–1,200 ➶ Bea(E)

A Compagnies de l'Ouest & de Brighton poster, 'Paris a Londres l'Angleterre & l'Ecosse', by G. Fraipont, detailing routes between Paris and London, 1894, 40 x 25in (101.5 x 63.5cm), glazed and framed.
£200–300
$300–450 ➶ P(WM)

◄ **A lithographic poster,** 'Philips', by Hans Oertle, printed by Emrik & Binger, Haarlem, c1924, 60 x 40in (152.5 x 101.5cm).
£1,150–1,250
$1,600–1,800 ⊞ VSP

A lithographic poster, 'Invest in the Victory Liberty Loan', by L. A. Shafer, printed by The W. F. Powers Co, New York, American, c1917, 29¼ x 39½in (74.5 x 100.5cm).
£330–370
$470–550 ⊞ VSP

◄ **A poster,** 'Miss England III Réalise La Plus Grand Vitesse sur l'Eau', advertising Castrol, mounted on linen, 1929, 30¾ x 23¾in (78 x 60.5cm).
£200–240
$300–350 ➶ ONS

◄ **A poster,** 'Shell', by A. Stewart-Hill, featuring Mousehole, Cornwall, c1934, 25 x 40in (63.5 x 101.5cm).
£2,700–3,000
$4,000–4,500 ⊞ REN

A poster, 'Redcar – It's Quicker by Rail', by Leonard Cusden, for LNER, printed by Jarrold & Sons, c1935, 39¾ x 50¾in (101 x 129cm).
£800–900
$1,200–1,300 ➶ Bea(E)

◄ **A poster,** 'Cruises Around Africa', by O. Anton, for German African Lines, 1936, 46 x 24in (117 x 61cm).
£550–600
$700–850 ⊞ REN

NORTH WALES
for HOLIDAYS

NEW YORK
EXPOSITION UNIVERSELLE
1939
Cᵉ Gᵉ TRANSATLANTIQUE

A poster, 'New York Exposition Universelle 1939', by A. M. Cassandre, for Cie Gle Transatlantique, printed by Alliance Graphique L. Danel, Paris, 39½ x 24½in (100.5 x 61.5cm).
£4,750–5,250
$7,000–7,500 ⊞ **VSP**

TEAMWORK WINS
UNITED STATES MARITIME COMMISSION

An American poster, 'Teamwork Wins', by C. P. Benton, for United States Maritime Commission, c1943, 40¼ x 30in (102 x 76cm).
£200–240
$300–350 ⚲ **ONS**

◀ **A poster,** 'North Wales for Holidays – Dolbadarn Castle, Llanberis', by John Mace, for London, Midland and Scottish Railway, c1936, 39 x 24¾in (99 x 63cm).
£550–600
$800–900 ⚲ **Bea(E)**
Dolbadarn Castle was built by Llewelyn the Great before 1230 and is now in the Snowdonia National Park.

SOUTHPORT
FOR A HOLIDAY IN WINTERTIME
FROM THE PAINTING BY FORTUNINO MATANIA R.I.
GUIDE FREE FROM INFORMATION BUREAU, SOUTHPORT

A poster, 'Southport – for a Holiday in Wintertime', by Fortunino Matania, for London, Midland and Scottish Railway, printed by Waterlow & Sons, c1936, 39¾ x 50¾in (101 x 126cm).
£4,600–5,000
$6,500–7,300 ⚲ **Bea(E)**

FISHGUARD-ROSSLARE
shortest sea route to and from SOUTHERN IRELAND
LUXURIOUSLY APPOINTED EXPRESS
STEAMERS TRAIN SERVICES
FACILITIES FOR CONVEYANCE OF MOTOR CARS
FURTHER INFORMATION FROM STATIONS OFFICES AND AGENCIES

A poster, 'Fishguard–Rosslare', by Arthur G. Mills, published by RWER, printed by Waterlow & Sons, c1950, 40¼ x 26in (102 x 66cm).
£600–700
$870–1,000 ⚲ **ONS**

▶ **A poster,** 'Wills's Cut Golden Bar', by Abram Games, c1950, 10 x 8in (25.5 x 20.5cm).
£270–300
$400–450 ⊞ **REN**

THE DUTCH
FIGHT ON
TO VICTORY

A WWII poster, 'The Dutch Fight on to Victory', 1942, 32 x 23¾in (81.5 x 60cm).
£420–470
$600–700 ⊞ **VSP**

THE ROYAL AIR FORCE
COVERS
THE WORLD
VOLUNTEER FOR
REGULAR SERVICE

A poster, 'The Royal Air Force covers the World, Volunteer for Regular Service', 1950, 40¼ x 24½in (102 x 62cm).
£60–70
$90–100 ⚲ **ONS**

WILLS'S
CUT GOLDEN BAR

FLY AER LINGUS

A poster, 'Fly Aer Lingus', by Bainbridge, c1950, 40¼ x 25½in (102 x 65cm).
£90–100
$130–150 ⚲ **ONS**

A poster, by John Minton, for London Transport, 1951, 40 x 25in (101.5 x 63.5cm).
£3,600–4,000
$5,000–6,000 ⊞ **REN**

A Universal film poster, 'Twilight for the Gods', 1958, 25 x 40in (63.5 x 101.5cm), with six colour lobby cards.
£25–30
$35–45 ↗ DN

A United Artists film poster, 'Thunderbird 6', 1960s, 30 x 40in (76 x 101.5cm).
£150–180
$220–260 ⊞ SDP

A United Artists film poster, 'Goldfinger', Belgium, 1964, 20 x 22in (51 x 56cm).
£225–250
$330–360 ⊞ SDP

A British Lion film poster, 'Girl on a Motorcycle', 1968, 30 x 40in (76 x 101.5cm).
£260–300
$380–440 ⊞ SDP

A Darien House children's poster, by John Sposato, 1969, 37 x 24½in (94 x 62cm).
£55–60
$80–90 ⊞ VSP

◄ **A Rank Organisation poster,** 'Carry On Girls', 1973, 40 x 30in (101.5 x 76cm).
£30–35
$40–50 ⊞ SDP

A Peter Max poster, 'Pan Am 747', October 1969, 42¼ x 28in (107.5 x 71cm).
£150–180
$220–260 ↗ ONS

► **A double feature poster,** 'Carquake' and 'The Giant Spider Invasion', c1977, 30 x 40in (76 x 101.5cm).
£40–50
$60–80 ⊞ Dri

A Bally poster, by Bernard Villemot, 1989, 60 x 40in (152.5 x 101.5cm).
£270–300
$400–450 ⊞ VSP

◄ Five cylinders for phonographs, 1900–10, 5in (12.5cm) high.
£5–10
$10–15 ⊞ GM

An HMV Model 2 wind-up gramophone, 1920, 27in (68.5cm) high.
£800–900
$1,200–1,300 ⚒ CBGR

A Pye Model P Classic radio, in a walnut cabinet with sunrise design, 1933, 18in (45.5cm) high.
£100–150
$145–225 ⊞ GM

An HMV 101 portable gramophone, 1928, 16in (40.5cm) long.
£130–160
$200–230 ⚒ CBGR

A Burgoyne Midget 5 portable wireless, with 5 valves, moving iron speaker, later case clips, 1930, 11in (28cm) wide.
£80–100
$115–145 ⊞ GM

► An Emor globe mains radio, three wavebands, globe turns for tuning, c1948, 43in (109cm) high.
£300–400
$450–550 ⊞ OTA

An Ekco Model AD36 Bakelite 'sad face' radio, designed by Wells Coates, limited production, case cracked, 1934, 16in (40.5cm) high.
£5,000–6,000
$7,250–8,750 ⊞ OTA

A French Ocean Cadre radio, with illuminated compartments at each end, 1955, 23in (58.5cm) wide.
£150–200
$220–300 ⊞ GM

An EMI Model TR52 professional tape recorder, 1962, 13in (33cm) wide.
£70–100
$100–150 ⊞ GM
This portable stereo recorder was widely used by the BBC and other broadcasting companies.

A Kolster Brander model RB10 Gavotte radio, long and medium wave, in a plastic cabinet, 1960, 12in (30.5cm) wide.
£30–35
$40–50 ⊞ GM

A Philips battery record player, 1960s, 16in (40.5cm) wide.
£65–75
$95–115 ⊞ PPH

A set of six plastic Beatles clothes tags, used in Apple's stores, 1960s, 2½in (6.5cm) wide.
£45–50
$65–80 ⚘ SAF

A bar of ABBA soap,
1970s, 4in (10cm) long.
£10–12
$15–20 ⚘ SAF

▶ **A Yellow Submarine thermos flask,** American, 1968, 6½in (16.5cm) high.
£155–185
$225–275 ⚘ SAF

The Beatles Scrap Book, by Walt Howarth, unused, 1966, 12 x 10in (30.5 x 25.5cm).
£35–40
$50–60 ⚘ CBP

A Beatles hair spray can, 1960s, 8in (20.5cm) high.
£20–25
$30–35 ⚘ SAF

A Beatles Cellophane tape display card, with 12 reels of tape, 1960s, 11in (28cm) high.
£125–150
$180–220 ⚘ SAF

A set of four Royal Doulton porcelain character jugs, depicting the Beatles, marked, 1984, 6in (15cm) high.
£500–600
$720–870 ⚘ FO

A Ray Charles LP record, by ABC Paramount, Dutch, 1961.
£15–20
$20–30 ⊞ TOT

A Jimi Hendrix electric toy guitar and amplifier, 1968, guitar 29in (73.5cm) long.
£150–180
$220–260 ⚘ SAF

▶ **A Jimi Hendrix stars and stripes stage shirt,** labelled 'Head Ease Los Angeles', with photographs of Jimi Hendrix wearing the shirt on stage at Temple Stadium, Philadelphia, 16th May 1970.
£16,000–18,000
$23,000–26,000 ⚘ Bon

A Jimmy Cliff single record, 'Wonderful World Beautiful People', by Island Records, Belgium, 1970.
£10–12
$15–20 ⊞ TOT

From Jimi Hendrix to Jimmy Somerville... whatever you're into, it's on eBay!

Buy

Sell

Music Memorabilia
Concert Programmes
Electric Guitars
Sheet Music
Rare Vinyl
Posters
Grand Pianos
Music Videos
Classic CDs
Signed Photos
Vintage Violins
Concert Tickets

You can buy and sell practically anything on eBay.

◀ **A singles record case,** featuring Donny and Marie Osmond on both sides, 1970, 8in (20.5cm) high.
£16–19
$20–30 ⚲ **SAF**

A Mick Jagger Sticky Fingers promotional standee, 1971, 69in (175.5cm) high.
£650–700
$900–1,000 ⚲ **FO**

A set of six Monkee pin badges, with original card advertisement, 1967, 3¼in (8.5cm) diam.
£18–20
$20–30 ⚲ **SAF**

Three Pink Floyd concert tickets, from the 1994 World Tour, 7in (18cm) wide.
£18–20
$20–30 ⚲ **SAF**

Two Elvis Presley film posters, '*Frankie and Johnny*', by United Artists, Sweden, 1966, and '*A Plein Tube Volle Gas*' (Speedway), by MGM, Belgium, 1968, largest 40 x 27in (101.5 x 68.5cm).
£100–120
$145–175 ⚲ **FO**

An embroidered jacket, designed by Granny Takes a Trip, worn by Gram Parsons and later given to Keith Richard, c1970.
£11,000–12,000
$16,000–17,500 ⚲ **FO**

A Sex Pistols Rock and Roll Swindle promotional standee, given to HMV shops, 1978, 33in (84cm) wide.
£225–250
$320–360 ⊞ **IQ**

A Tyrannosaurus Rex LP record, by EMI Records, mono, 1968.
£35–40
$50–60 ⊞ **TOT**

The Wind in the Willows LP record, with Debbie Harry, by EMI Records, mono, 1968.
£15–20
$20–30 ⊞ **TOT**

A Seeburg 148 Trash Can jukebox, playing 78rpm records, 1948, 60in (152.5cm) high.
£3,200–3,500
$4,500–5,000 ⊞ **KA**

Hot Water Bottles

As we at Miller's know, anything can be collectable and hot water bottles are no exception. The majority of examples shown dates from the early part of the 20th century. In the era before central heating, hot water bottles came in every style. There were miniature muff warmers for the hands, larger bottles for the feet and novelty designs to decorate as well as heat the bed. Bottles were produced by many major potteries such as Denby, Doulton, and Old Fulham Pottery.

Many hot water bottles cost pennies when they were made, today rare examples can fetch three-figure sums. Values depend on shape (novelty designs are the most collectable), decoration (look out for interesting transfers) and condition. Examples are often excavated by bottle collectors and can become damaged. A bottle will be worth more if it retains its original stopper and other features, such as labels or the leather handle on the Gladstone bag bottle shown below.

A Bourne Denby miniature muff warmer, c1910–20, 5½in (13.5cm) wide.
£225–275
$320–390 ⊞ MURR

A Handy muff warmer, transfer-printed in black on an off-white glaze, 1910–20, 4¾in (12cm) high.
£270–320
$400–450 ⋏ BBR

A Maws radium muff warmer, c1910–20, 6½in (13.5cm) wide.
£100–120
$145–175 ⊞ MURR

A Bourne Gladstone bag foot warmer, decorated with a blue glaze with brown top and stopper, with leather carrying handle, 1910–20, 9¾in (25cm) wide.
£400–450
$580–650 ⋏ BBR

A Denby Stoneware 'The Bungalow' foot warmer, transfer-printed in blue on an off-white glaze, 1910–20, 10½in (26.5cm) high.
£90–110
$130–160 ⋏ BBR

A bed warmer, with carrying handle, the front decorated with a cat and mouse in relief, the base printed 'Velray, Made in England', 1910–20, 7in (18cm) high.
£370–420
$550–620 ⋏ BBR

A fish foot warmer, with stopper, decorated with a bright yellow glaze, 1910–20, 14in (35.5cm) long.
£430–480
$620–700 ⋏ BBR

Condition

The condition is absolutely vital when assessing the value of a collectable. Damaged pieces on the whole appreciate much less than perfect examples. However a rare desirable piece may command a high price even when damaged.

A Bourne Denby Little Folks Foot warmer, transfer-printed in blue on an off-white glaze, restored, 1910–20, 6½in (16.5cm) high.
£100–120
$145–175 ⚒ **BBR**

A clock foot warmer, the face with raised numerals, decorated with a brown and tan glaze, with chain carrying handle, original paper label to side, 1910–20, 6¾in (17cm) high.
£320–360
$450–500 ⚒ **BBR**

An Old Fulham Pottery Adaptable hot water bottle, transfer-printed in black on an off-white glaze, 1910–20, 8½in (21.5cm) high.
£12–16
$15–20 ⚒ **BBR**

A Winton & Grimwades Mecca foot warmer, transfer-printed in green on a white glaze, 1910–20, 11in (28cm) high.
£180–220
$260–320 ⚒ **BBR**

A Nolon foot warmer, transfer-printed in black on an off-white glaze, 1910–20, 9¾in (25cm) high.
£5–10
$10–15 ⚒ **BBR**

A pair of chrome shoe warmers, c1930, 10in (25.5cm) long.
£55–65
$80–100 ⊞ **HO**

A King Sol hot water bottle, transfer-printed in black on an off-white glaze, 1910–20, 8in (20.5cm) high.
£70–90
$100–130 ⚒ **BBR**

A Doultons Reliable foot warmer, transfer-printed in brown on a white glaze, 1910–20, 8¾in (22cm) high.
£10–15
$15–20 ⚒ **BBR**

A Lawleys foot warmer, transfer-printed in black on an off-white glaze, with brown top, 1921, 10¼in (26cm) high.
£5–10
$10–15 ⚒ **BBR**

A rubber hot water bottle, modelled as a clown, by Roger Hargreaves, 1970, 12in (30.5cm) high.
£10–12
$15–18 ⊞ **HarC**

Jewellery
Bracelets

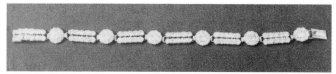

A Victorian silver and paste bracelet, 5in (12.5cm) long.
£100–120
$145–175 ⊞ Ma

◀ **An Art Deco chrome and red Bakelite bracelet,** Germany, 1930s, 8in (20.5cm) long.
£60–70
$90–100 ⊞ LaF

A vulcanite bangle, 1875, 1¾in (4.5cm) wide.
£40–45
$60–70 ⊞ AM

▶ **A Schiaparelli grey rhinestone bracelet,** 1950s, 7½in (19cm) long.
£450–500
$650–720 ⊞ CRIS

A Kramer blue stone bracelet, American, c1960, 1½in (4cm) wide.
£90–100
$130–150 ⊞ SBL

▶ **A Joachim rock crystal and hand-beaten silver bracelet,** Finnish, c1970, 2½in (6.5cm) wide.
£200–250
$300–350 ⊞ DID

◀ **A Chanel bracelet,** set with *faux* rubies, diamonds and pearls, 1980s, 2½in (6.5cm) wide.
£450–500
$650–720 ⊞ SBT

Brooches

◀ A Tunbridge ware brooch, 1830, 1½in (4cm) long.
£24–28
$35–45 ⊞ VBo

An 18ct gold commemorative brooch, set with black onyx and pearls, inscribed 'In memory of', the reverse with a locket, 1850, 2½in (6.5cm) wide.
£320–400
$450–550 ⊞ Ma

An 18ct gold 'target' brooch, the centre set with amethyst and gold balls, the reverse with a locket, c1860, 1¼in (3cm) diam.
£450–500
$650–720 ⊞ AMC

A hair brooch, set in a gold mount designed as a knot, the reverse with a locket, c1880, 1½in (4cm) wide.
£175–195
$250–300 ⊞ AMC

A Victorian Scottish silver buckle brooch, set with semi-precious stones, 2in (5cm) diam.
£120–140
$170–200 🔨 WBH

◀ **An Edwardian silver paste star brooch,** 1½in (4cm) high.
£60–100
$100–150 ⊞ Ma

A Scottish silver and agate brooch, the centre set with amber glass, c1890, 1in (2.5cm) diam.
£30–40
$40–60 ⊞ BWA

Three silver name brooches, Maggie, Agnes and Clara in gold inlay, 1900–20, 1½in (4cm) wide.
£40–50
$60–80 each ⊞ EXC

Cross Reference
See Colour Review (page 233–234)

A paste and glass brooch, 1920s, 1¼in (3cm) wide.
£5–6
$7–10 ⊞ STP

▶ **An Art Deco marcasite 'fruit salad' baguette pin,** set with red, blue and green stones, French, 1920s, 3½in (9cm) long.
£450–500
$650–720 ⊞ CRIS

A diamanté brooch, modelled as a car with a lady alighting, 1920, 3in (7.5cm) wide.
£245–285
$350–400 ⊞ SSM

An Art Deco gold metal and red glass brooch, modelled as flowers and buds, Czechoslovakian, c1930, 3in (7.5cm) wide.
£45–50
$65–75 ⊞ LaF

A winged Sphinx brooch, set with white, red, green and blue paste stones, 1940s, 2½in (6.5cm) wide.
£135–150
$200–220 ⊞ LBe

A brown enamel on sterling silver abstract brooch, designed by Henning Koppel for Georg Jensen, c1947, 1¼in (3cm) wide.
£600–700
$870–1,000 ⊞ DID

A Trifari blue Jelly Belly swordfish, set with white paste stones, 1940s, 3in (7.5cm) wide.
£360–450
$500–650 ⊞ CRIS

A Trifari gold-coloured leopard brooch, with *faux* ruby eyes, 1950s, 2in (5cm) wide.
£75–85
$115–125 ⊞ FMa

Two Trifari gold- and silver-coloured fruit pins, modelled as apples, 1950s, 1in (2.5cm) high.
£18–20
$25–30 ⊞ CRIS

A Coro silver tone and crystal floral **brooch,** American, c1950, 4in (10cm) high.
£35–40
$50–60 ⊞ LaF

A Sybil Dunlop silver and gold **brooch,** the centre set with a citrine, c1964, 2in (5cm) diam.
£600–700
$870–1,000 ⊞ DID

◀ A gold-coloured diamanté **brooch,** 1950s–60s, 2in (5cm) wide.
£4–5
$6–8 ⊞ STP

A Christian Dior diamanté **brooch,** modelled as the head of a circus horse, set with *faux* pearls, 1966, 4in (10cm) high.
£275–300
$400–440 ⊞ LBe

Cameos

Cameos became extremely popular from the beginning of the 19th century. 'A fashionable lady wears cameos at her girdle, cameos in her necklace, cameos on each of her bracelets, a cameo on her tiara,' noted the *Journal des Dames* in 1805. During the Victorian period, cameos were produced for every level of the market. They ranged from finely-carved precious stones to more affordable examples made from shell or lava stone (produced in Italy from the lava of Mount Vesuvius). Whatever the medium, however, classical subjects were a favourite theme.

A pair of gilt-metal-mounted **cameo bracelets,** each classical portrait within an acanthus frame on an eight-bar bracelet, one converted to a brooch, c1840, 2¼in (5.5cm) high.
£700–750
$1,000–1,100 ⋋ Bea(E)

▶ A silver-mounted cameo **brooch,** carved with a she-wolf suckling Romulus and Remus, with rope-twist border, c1900, 2¼in (5.5cm) high.
£300–350
$450–500 ⊞ AMC

◀ A conch shell cameo **brooch,** carved with a neoclassical lady's head and shoulders, 19thC, 2in (5cm) high.
£60–70
$90–100 ⋋ WilP

A gold-mounted cameo **brooch,** carved with a Roman soldier, c1900, 1¼in (3cm) high.
£200–225
$300–330 ⊞ AMC

Earrings

A pair of Christian Dior entremblant crystal earrings, by Mitchell Mayer, Austrian, 1951–54, 1in (2.5cm) high.
£160–190
$230–280 ⊞ LaF

◀ **A pair of diamanté drop earrings,** Austrian, c1950, 3in (7.5cm) long.
£7–8
$10–12 ⊞ STP

A pair of Miriam Haskell earrings, modelled as gold-coloured flowers with silver-coloured balls, 1940s, 1¼in (3cm) diam.
£225–250
$320–360 ⊞ SBT

▶ **A pair of yellow-painted metal and coloured glass earrings,** Austrian, 1960, 1in (2.5cm) high.
£5–6
$8–10 ⊞ STP

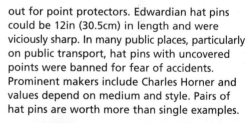

A pair of Butler & Wilson diamanté earrings, c1970, 4½in (11.5cm) long.
£130–150
$200–220 ⊞ SBL

Hat Pins

Hat pins were an essential part of a lady's wardrobe from the late 19th century until WWI. The crinolined skirts and close-fitting bonnets of the Victorian period were replaced by slim-line dresses and large picture hats, supported by piled-up hair and secured with a pair of hat pins. Pins came in many different designs and materials and numerous patents were taken out for point protectors. Edwardian hat pins could be 12in (30.5cm) in length and were viciously sharp. In many public places, particularly on public transport, hat pins with uncovered points were banned for fear of accidents. Prominent makers include Charles Horner and values depend on medium and style. Pairs of hat pins are worth more than single examples.

A pair of jet and cameo hat pins, c1875, 4in (10cm) long.
£165–185
$250–280 ⊞ AM

A silver bicycle hat pin, Birmingham 1898, 10in (25.5cm) long.
£175–195
$250–280 ⊞ SSM

A Charles Horner silver hat pin, set with a red semi-precious stone, 1910, 10in (25.5cm) long.
£60–65
$90–100 ⊞ VB

Two Norene gold-coloured hat pins, 1911, 10in (25.5cm) long.
£30–40
$40–60 each ⊞ VB

Jet

A pair of Whitby jet drop earrings, with swing bob, c1860, 3in (7.5cm) long.
£115–125
$170–180 ⊞ EMP

▶ **A Whitby jet locket,** with deep carving to both sides, c1860, 1½in (4cm) high.
£100–115
$145–165 ⊞ EMP

A horn brooch, decorated with acorns and oak leaves, c1860, 1½in (4cm) high.
£15–20
$20–30 ⊞ EMP

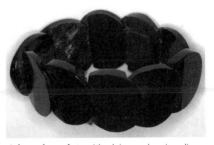

A horn bracelet, with plain overlapping discs, c1860, 1¼in (3cm) wide.
£20–25
$30–35 ⊞ EMP

▶ **A pair of French jet earrings,** c1860, 2in (5cm) long.
£225–250
$320–360 ⊞ AM

A Whitby jet carved knot brooch, c1860, 3in (7.5cm) wide.
£135–150
$200–220 ⊞ EMP

A Whitby jet faceted bar bracelet, on elastic, c1870, 1½in (4cm) wide.
£50–60
$80–90 ⊞ EMP

Different types of Jet

Whitby Jet, made from fossilized wood, has been used for jewellery since ancient times but it was not until the mid-19th century that it became highly fashionable. It is hand-carved, lightweight and warm to the touch. As the industry flourished, various man-made alternatives were developed, which are described below.

- **Vulcanite** is a compound of rubber and sulphur invented by Goodyear (tyres) in 1846. It is moulded and tends to have a brownish tinge, sometimes even khaki coloured, due to exposure to light.
- **French jet** is a black glass with a heavy, cold feel. The beads are generally shiny and black in appearance but some display a dull crêpe or satinized finish that is very attractive to the eye.
- **Vauxhall glass** is a black glass mounted on metal with a surprising lightness in design and weight, but cold to the touch as would be expected.
- **Bog oak jet** is a fossilized wood that has been compressed in Irish peat bogs and has a dull finish. Lightweight and warm to the touch, it is not as finely carved as Whitby jet.
- **Bois Durci** is a 19th-century compound of compressed wood powder painted black, sometimes with paste decoration.
- **Horn,** used by prehistoric man for essentials, survived to the Victorian age when fashion dyed it black. It can be distinguished by observing compacted hair showing through minor cracks on the backs of objects. It is dull in appearance.

A pair of brass two-arm wall sconces, c1910, 10in (25.5cm) high.
£140–160
$200–230 ⊞ JW

A desk lamp, with shell-shaped brass shade, flexible arm and black cast-iron base, 1920s, 13in (33cm) high.
£90–110
$130–160 ⊞ LIB

An Art Deco spelter table lamp, with marble-effect fan-shaped glass shade supported by a nude figure of a woman, 15in (38cm) high.
£300–350
$450–500 ⚒ SWO

► An Art Deco bronze lamp, modelled as a Chinese pheasant, painted in naturalistic colours, c1925, 22in (56cm).
£225–245
$320–350 ⊞ KA

LOCATE THE SOURCE
The source of each illustration in Miller's can be found by checking the code letters below each caption with the Key to Illustrations, pages 444–452.

► A Bakelite desk lamp, 1930s, 12in (30.5cm) high.
£125–145
$180–200 ⊞ ZOOM

A hanging lamp, with brass gallery, chain and ceiling rose and pink-frosted glass shade, 1920s, 15in (38cm) long
£130–150
$200–220 ⊞ LIB

An Art Deco chrome table lamp, with dancing nude support, 19in (48cm) high.
£90–100
$130–150 ⊞ ZOOM

A Lorraine glass lamp, designed by Pierre Davesn, with cream fabric shade, 1929–33, 13in (33cm) high.
£115–130
$160–180 ⊞ KA

A ceramic lamp, modelled as a dog in shades of brown, with glass eyes, 1930s, 7½in (19cm) high.
£165–185
$250–270 ⊞ LBe

◄ A chandelier, by Gino Sarfatti for Arteluce, Italian, 1953, 26in (66cm) high.
£400–500
$580–720 ⊞ MARK
The Italian designer Gino Sarfatti (1912–85) trained as an aeronautical engineer and founded Arteluce in 1939. Sarfatti won major awards for his lamp designs in the 1950s and his company made an important contribution to the development of post-war lighting in Italy.

An extendable desk lamp, by Ferdinand Solère, with chrome shade and stem, French, 1950s, 23in (58.5cm) high.
£125–150
$180–220 ⊞ ZOOM

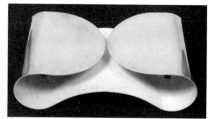

A pair of chrome wall lights, by Castiglioni for Flos, Italian, 1960s, 15in (38cm) wide.
£300–350
$450–500 ⊞ ZOOM

◀ **A Perspex and glass Plastacrush Dream lamp,** 1970s, 19½in (49.5cm) high.
£35–45
$50–65 ⊞ FLD

Candlesticks

A brass chamberstick, with snuffer and wick trimmer, c1800, 5in (12.5cm) high.
£425–475
$620–700 ⊞ SEA

▶ **A tin candle mould,** c1900, 10½in (26.5cm) high.
£100–125
$145–180 ⊞ B&R

▶ **An adjustable cast-iron candlestick,** French, early 19thC, 8in (20.5cm) high.
£80–90
$115–130 ⊞ B&R

A pair of brass piano sconces, c1910, 9½in (24cm) wide.
£130–150
$190–220 ⊞ MURR

A pair of copper-mounted wooden candlesticks, by A. E. Jones, c1900, 8½in (21cm) high.
£325–375
$470–550 ⊞ SHA

A pair of Benson brass tripod candlesticks, with trefid toes and six-point copper leaf drip pans, unmarked, 1902, 7in (18cm) high.
£650–750
$950–1,100 ⊞ HUN

◀ **A pair of brass candlesticks,** modelled as Felix the Cat, c1920, 8in (20.5cm) high.
£200–250
$300–360 ⊞ MURR

Lanterns

► **A miner's brass and polished steel lamp,** made by The Protector Lamp & Lighting Co for the Ministry of Power, c1890–1900, 10in (25.5cm) high.
£90–100
$130–150 ⊞ MRW

A pottery lantern, with reeded loop handle, the body pierced with small holes, probably Iranian, 11th–12thC, 9in (23cm) high.
£165–185
$240–270 ⊞ CrF

A lady's brass extending reading lantern, Dutch, c1770, 7in (18cm) high.
£600–675
$870–1,000 ⊞ SEA

A bull's eye lamp, 1920s, 4in (10cm) high.
£30–35
$45–50 ⊞ GAC

► **A Lucas self-generating brass carbide lamp,** 1910, 10in (25.5cm) wide.
£500–600
$720–870
⊞ JUN

► **A pair of brass and copper mast-head lights,** c1930s, 19in (48.5cm) high.
£550–600
$800–870 ⊞ AOY

Nightlights & Fairylights

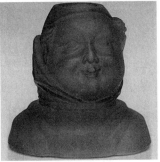

A glass nightlight, the monk's head in green satin glass on a clear satin glass base, 19thC, 4¼in (11cm) high.
£375–425
$550–620 ⚒ BBR

A Pearline fairylight, the blue shade on a matching petalled Pearline No. 24 base, registered number 176239, 1891, 4¼in (11cm) high.
£30–40
$45–60 ⚒ BBR

An amethyst glass nightlight, in the form of Edward VII, with ground top, registered number 298585, damaged, 1897, 4¼in (11cm) high.
£30–40
$45–60 ⚒ BBR

Medals
Commemorative

A silver medal, awarded by the Royal Humane Society to John Dymond for restoring the health of Sarah Binder, with contemporary suspension loop, 1777, 2¾in (7cm) diam.
£400–500
$580–720 ✒ DNW

> **Cross Reference**
> See Crime
> (page 174–175)

A white metal medal, commemorating the price riot at Covent Garden Opera House, 1809, 1¾in (45mm) diam.
£40–50
$60–75 ⊞ TML
The riots started with the opening of the New Covent Garden Theatre by J. P. Kemble, who increased prices of admission. This lasted about three months until the old prices were restored.

A white metal medal, by T. Wyon, commemorating the Battle of the Nile, 1798.
£100–125
$145–180 ⊞ TML

An engraved cartwheel penny, depicting Henry Fauntleroy, inscribed 'Fauntleroy, the Robber of Widows and Orphans, Executed at Newgate' and 'Such be the Fate of all Insolvent Bilking Bankers and Agents', the reverse a cartwheel penny, 1824, 1½in (36mm) diam.
£225–250
$320–360 ⊞ TML
Banker Henry Fauntleroy (1785–1824) was found guilty of forging signatures over a ten year period, and according to the contemporary press, misappropriated trust funds worth c£25,000 ($36,250) much of which he spent on gambling and mistresses. Though Fauntleroy pleaded his innocence, he was sentenced to execution and a crowd of 100,000 people were reported to have attended his hanging at Newgate. These engraved pennies were produced as souvenirs.

A bronze medal, by T. Wyon, commemorating Joseph Hanson, the industrial reformer, with a head of Hanson and the inscription 'The Weaver's Friend, Strangeways Manchester 1810', the reverse with loom, spinning wheel and printing machine within a wreath, 1810, 1¾in (42mm) diam.
£40–50
$60–75 ⊞ TML
Hanson was imprisoned and fined for acts on behalf of the Luddites. About forty thousand subscribers each contributed one penny to a fund set up to help him.

A silver medal, commemorating the great flood, depicting a swollen river and broken bridge, the reverse inscribed 'Presented by the Central Committee for the Flood Fund to Hugh Wright, Findhorn as an Honorary Reward for the Courage and Humanity shewn at the Great Flood, August 4th 1829', with claw and double loop suspension, 1829, 1¼in (3cm) diam.
£300–350
$450–500 ✒ DNW

A Society for the Protection of Life from Fire silver medal, depicting an eye within a sunburst with a banner inscribed 'Vigilo', the reverse inscribed 'To Edd. P.C. A65, who at the risk of his own life saved from Death by Fire a person at Marylebone St., May 14th 1840'.
£800–900
$1,200–1,300 ⚲ DNW

Cross Reference
See Militaria & Emergency Services (page 280–288)

A Brighton and Hove Motor Club medal, for the Brighton Bees Trial, 1933, 1in (25mm) diam, in original box.
£75–85
$110–125 ⊞ BiR

◀ **A prize silver medal,** awarded by the Worcestershire Bull Terrier Club, inscribed on reverse 'to commemorate win of Sporting Parson Cup by Mr Thompson's Dauntless Duchess at Worcester Ch. Show, 21.8.24', 1924, 1¾in (45mcm) diam.
£75–85
$110–125 ⊞ TML

Two May Day badges, one brass, 1934, the other aluminium, German, 1936, 1½in (38mm) diam.
£30–35
$45–50 each ⊞ AnS

▶ **A silvered-bronze medal,** by J. Fray, commemorating the visit of Joseph Chamberlain to South Africa, with a bust of Chamberlain, the reverse with an inscription, 1903, 2in (50mm) diam.
£65–75
$95–110 ⊞ TML

A silver-gilt and enamel Masonic medal, with past Masters' Jewel, presented to Professor Mohammed Fadel al Jamali, a former Premier of Iraq, presented by the Dar es Salam Lodge, Baghdad, the reverse with engraving, with riband and suspender, 1940–41.
£420–500
$580–720 ⚲ Gle

Two medals, awarded to Ronnie O'Hara for rescuing a dog at Middlesbrough docks, one the PDSA Gallantry Cross, gilt-metal and white enamel, the other the RSPCA Life Saving Medal, silver, both cased, together with their named presentation certificates, several newspaper cuttings and the recipient's National Registration Identity Card, 1949.
£600–700
$850–1,000 ⚲ DNW

Military

A Military General Service Medal, awarded to J. Hall, 38th Foot, with six bars for Busaco, Badajoz, Salamanca, Vittoria, St Sebastian, Nive, minor repair, 1793–1814.
£700–800
$1,000–1,200 ⚒ Gle

An army medal, awarded to 4815 Pte M. Geoghegan of the King's Own Scottish Borderers, with two bars inscribed 'Cape Colony' and 'Paardeberg', for the Queen's Campaign South Africa, 1900.
£135–150
$200–220 ⊞ RMC

A pair of Queen's South Africa medals, with four bars for Cape Colony, Tugela Heights, Relief of Ladysmith and Transvaal, and King's South Africa with two bars for South Africa 1901 and 1902, re-named to 9258 PO J. Hay, HMS *Powerful*.
£100–120
$150–175 ⚒ PFK
Only three members of the crew of this ship were present at the relief of Ladysmith.

A Queen's South Africa medal, with three bars for Transvaal, Orange Free State and Cape Colony, awarded to J. Donnelly, Royal Fusiliers, 1899–1902.
£100–120
$150–175 ⚒ PFK

A Royal Navy Medal, awarded to M18354 ERAI W. J. R. Vosper of HMS *Pembroke* for long service and good conduct, 1914–18.
£45–50
$65–75 ⊞ RMC

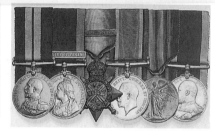

Three Royal Marines medals, the Star, the War Medal and the Victory Medal, awarded to 14843 Pte. S. A. Carpenter of Royal Marine Light Infantry, who survived the sinking of HMS *Louvain* in 1918, 1914–18.
£110–125
$160–180 ⊞ RMC

A group of six WWI medals, Distinguished Service, British War and Victory, Royal Navy Long Service and Good Conduct, awarded to Gunner H. C. E. Callaway, Royal Marines Artillery, 1914–18.
£1,100–1,300
$1,600–1,900 ⚒ Gle

A group of five WWII medals, Distinguished Flying, 1939–45 Star, Air Crew Europe Star, Defence Medal, War Medal, awarded to Sgt A. Massey, Royal Air Force, 1939–45.
£850–950
$1,250–1,400 ⚒ Gle

A group of four WWII medals, 1939–45 Star, Atlantic Star Bar, War medal, French Medal of Honour, awarded to G. Billett, mounted as worn, 1939–45.
£120–135
$175–200 ⊞ RMC

A group of five WWII medals, the India General Service, General Service, Long Service, Good Conduct, Defence and War and British Empire, awarded to Warrant Officer Albert Kirman, with Warrant dated November 1962, his certificate of service and copies of photographs.
£300–340
$450–500 ⚒ HOLL

Militaria & Emergency Services

A teak military chest, with two short and three long drawers and recessed brass handles, 19thC, 35¾in (91cm) wide.
£1,000–1,200
$1,500–1,750 ↗ WilP

► **A WWI Trench Art miniature coal scuttle,** made from a shell case, 1914–18, 6in (15cm) wide.
£40–50
$60–75 ⊞ AnS

► **An iron-bound water barrel,** with two wooden plugs and iron carrying handle, as used by soldiers, 19thC, 10in (25.5cm) wide.
£160–180
$230–260
⊞ ASB

► **A Mississippi 41st Army bandsman's mace,** silver-mounted, marked London, c1950s, 56in (142cm) long.
£1,200–1,500
$1,750–2,150
⊞ Q&C

Badges, Plates & Uniforms

A Victorian 2nd East Riding of Yorkshire Royal Garrison of Artillery Volunteers officer's sable bearskin, together with an Edwardian home-pattern service helmet in blue cloth and case, formerly the property of Capt H. Hall.
£1,300–1,400
$1,900–2,000 ⊞ Q&C

Items in the Militaria & Emergency Services section have been arranged in date order within each sub-section.

A Victorian Queensland Scottish Regiment other ranks' white metal helmet plate, Australian, mid- to late 19thC.
£160–200
$230–300 ↗ WAL

A Victorian Middlesex Regiment officer's helmet, 1880, 11in (28cm) high.
£350–450
$500–650 ⊞ CYA

◄ **A 3rd (Prince of Wales) Dragoon Guards NCO's silver arm badge,** hollow construction, some wear, 1887.
£160–200
$230–300 ↗ WAL

A 95th Saskatchewan Rifles officer's silver-plated pouch belt badge, by J. R. Gaunt, Montreal, pre-1914.
£220–250
$320–360 ⚹ WAL

A manufacturer's pattern for a 2nd Battalion The Lincolnshire Regiment pouch belt badge, with WW1 battle honours on a silver-plated backplate, possibly by Ludlows.
£330–360
$470–520 ⚹ WAL

An 11th (Lonsdale) Battalion The Border Regiment other ranks' brass cap badge, 1914–18.
£110–130
$160–190 ⚹ WAL

A Life Guards officer's uniform, all named or initialled to R. L. Loyd, Lt 16th Lancers 1914, Capt 1st Life Guards 1919, c1925.
£600–700
$870–1,000 ⚹ WAL

An Egyptian Port Said pith helmet, 1939–45.
£75–85
$110–125 ⊞ UCO

A German military tropical helmet, 1939–45.
£175–195
$255–275 ⊞ UCO

A German despatch rider's helmet, 1937.
£250–280
$360–400 ⊞ UCO

▶ A black ostrich-feather bonnet of the Black Watch Regiment, with red cockade, 1945–95.
£250–300
$360–440 ⊞ UCO

A bearskin of the Welsh Guards, of bamboo basket construction, with white and green cockade, 1950–60.
£250–300
$360–440 ⊞ UCO

Four Home Service helmets, with regional badges, 1960s.
£175–225
$255–325 each ⊞ Q&C

Edged Weapons

A broad-bladed hand-and-a-half sword, with wooden leather-covered grip, c1450–1500, blade 29½in (75cm) long.
£3,200–3,500
$4,500–5,000 ⊞ GV

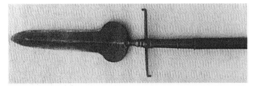

An American officer's spontoon head, stamped with maker's name 'Marsh', from the period of the American War of Independence, c1775–80, 10in (25.5cm) long.
£500–560
$725–825 ⊞ ASB

A Royal Horse Guards basket-hilt sword, engraved with crown, 'GR', and 'Harvey', with original fishskin grip, slight damage, dated 1759, blade 38in (96.5cm) long.
£2,000–2,400
$3,000–3,500 ⊞ WSA

An Irish officer's single-edged sword, retailed by J. Reed of Dublin, with gilt-brass hilt, original black leather scabbard with gilt-brass mounts, early 19thC, blade 32in (81.5cm) long.
£1,100–1,250
$1,600–1,800 ⊞ ASB
This sword is typical of those carried by infantry officers in Wellington's army.

A Victorian 2nd Cinque Ports Artillery Volunteers officer's 1821 pattern sword, the blade by Ravenscroft of London, in original steel scabbard c1875.
£300–350
$450–500 ⚔ WAL

A Victorian 1857 pattern cavalry trooper's sword and scabbard, the three-bar hilt with compressed leather grips, blade 35½in (90cm) long.
£250–275
$360–400 ⊞ GV

A Victorian Royal Horse Guards officer's 1874 pattern sword, in original brass-mounted scabbard with leather cover, blade 38½in (98cm) long.
£600–700
$870–1,000 ⚔ WAL

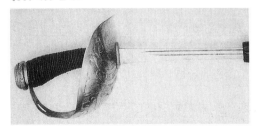

◀ **A 2nd Dragoon Guards 1912 pattern officer's sword,** the blade etched with crowned GVR, Royal arms, regimental badge, 'BAYS' and owner's initial 'F M W-S, c1918, blade 34in (86.5cm).
£650–750
$950–1,100 ⚔ WAL

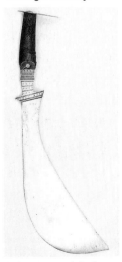

A Coorg sword Ayda-Katti, with partly chequered horn grip, the single-edged blade stamped 'G F Watson Indian Staff Corps 1896', Malabar, blade 17in (43cm) long.
£270–300
$400–450 ⚔ WAL

Firearms

A gunsmith's brass ladle, with turned wooden handle and stem, c1750, 28in (71cm) long.
£220–250
$320–360 ⊞ SEA
This item was used in the making of lead musket balls.

A flintlock Sea Service pistol, with walnut fullstock, regulation brass furniture, the 12in (30.5cm) barrel with ordnance marks and sold out of service mark, 1806.
£1,100–1,200
$1,600–1,750 ⊞ WSA

A brass-mounted powder horn, the brass top with inverted swivel adjustable charger, spring broken, c1810, 11in (28cm) long.
£150–180
$220–260 ⚹ WD

An 80-bore air gun, by Goodwin & Co, London, with walnut butt, the barrel with ram-rod rib beneath, engraved with trophies of flags and maker's name, iron ball reservoir beneath, early 19thC, 47½in (121cm) long.
£500–600
$720–870 ⚹ WAL

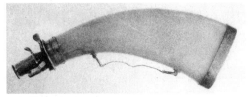

A flintlock blunderbuss, with walnut stock and brass barrel, trigger guard and butt cap, engraved lock inscribed 'Carter', early 19thC, 30in (76cm) long.
£550–650
$800–950 ⚹ CDC

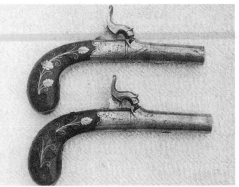

A pistol flask, from a pair of French pistols, with measure cap, c1840, 5in (12.5cm) long.
£350–400
$500–600 ⊞ ARB

A pair of turn-off barrel boxlock percussion pistols, signed 'C. Adams & Son, London', the walnut grips inlaid with nickel silver wire and leaves, one replacement hammer, c1825, 2¾in (7cm) barrels.
£550–600
$800–900 ⊞ ASB

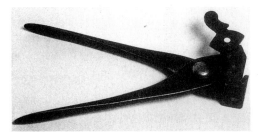

A .120 pocket revolver mould, 1850s, 7in (18cm) long.
£85–95
$125–140 ⊞ SPA

A percussion pistol, by Bentley of London, with powder flask and accessories, concealed in a leather-bound book, 1850–60, 8 x 5in (20.5 x 12.5cm).
£300–350
$450–500 ⊞ HEG

Firefighting

This year *Miller's Collectables Price Guide* includes a new section devoted to the history of firefighting.

The terrorist destruction of the World Trade Centre in New York brought both the role and the courage of firefighters to world attention. The objects illustrated below commemorate the story of brave men and tragic events, beginning in the 18th century and ending with an American fireman's helmet from the 1940s.

Many come from an American sale of fire-fighting memorabilia, held shortly after the attack on 11 September 2001. 'The perspectives and priorities of all Americans and the vast

majority of the world changed that day', noted a special introduction in the catalogue.

The objects fetched high prices, perhaps reflecting not only their rarity but also the embattled mood of the moment. 'The preservation and appreciation of historic fire-fighting artefacts is a worthy reminder of just how important our nation's fire-fighters, rescue workers and police are to us and how eternally grateful we are to them', concluded the catalogue. A portion of the proceeds of the sale was devoted to the Uniformed Fire-fighter's Association Widows' and Children's Fund in New York City.

A City of Boston Fire Department certificate, presented to Thomas D. Quincy, signed by Mayor James Armstrong, American, 1836, 16½in (42cm) high.
£200–230
$300–330 SK(B)

A fireman's black wool parade top hat, inscribed in gilt 'Friendship Fire Co 5 Inst. March 4th 1848', with owner's initial 'H.J.' on top, red brim liner, American, 6½in (16.5cm) high.
£2,100–2,500
$3,000–3,600 SK(B)

A Baltimore Equitable Society cast-iron firemark, painted red, green and black on a black ground, American, mid-19thC, 9½in (24cm) wide.
£950–1,000
$1,380–1500 SK(B)

A half-plate Daguerro-type of three members of The Union No. 2 Fire Company, in parade dress, with original mount, in later frame, American, c1850, 9 x 6in (23 x 15cm).
£6,300–7,000
$9,000–10,000 SK(B)
The men's helmets depict their rank – one star, two star, and clerk.

A red-painted leather fire bucket and cotton salvage bag, the bag labelled 'Daniel Sheaffer 1853', American, bucket 12½in (32cm) high.
£620–700
$900–1,000 SK(B)

A membership certificate of the Philadelphia Association for the Relief of Disabled Firemen, incorporating a coloured print by J. R. Smith, signed by the Association's President, Vice President and Secretary, framed and glazed, dated 1861, American, 19½in (49.5cm) square.
£630–700
$920–1,000 SK(B)

◀ **A leather-covered brass steamer composition nozzle,** stamped 'Button & Blake, Waterford N.Y. Patented June 7, Jan 10 1853 1860', American, 38in (96.5cm) long.
£700–800
$1,000–1,100 SK(B)

LOCATE THE SOURCE
The source of each illustration in Miller's can be found by checking the code letters below each caption with the Key to Illustrations, pages 444–452.

A photograph of the members of the Insurance Protective Department, Boston, Mass, framed and glazed, American, 1873, 18 x 22in (45.5 x 56cm).
£140–160
$200–230 ✗ SK(B)

A fireman's brass parade helmet, by Merryweather, with brass-edged visor, chin-strap and ear rosettes, c1880, 10in (25.5cm) high.
£650–700
$950–1,100 ⊞ UCO

A pair of late Victorian leather fire buckets, with painted cream shields, red crosses and swords, on a black ground, dated 1886, 12in (30.5cm) high.
£550–650
$800–950 ✗ RTo

A membership certificate of the Veteran Volunteer Firemen's Association of Baltimore, for Alexander Ramsey, with coloured chromolithograph of fire tender, signed by the President and Secretary, American, 1885, 10½ x 13¾in (26.5 x 35cm) high.
£250–300
$360–440 ✗ SK(B)

A German fireman's steel and brass helmet, late 19thC.
£120–160
$175–230 ⊞ ET

A Plainfield Fire Department certificate, declaring that 'Dan'l Hogan, Jr. has served as a Fireman', illustrated with firemen, cherubs and scrollwork, American, 1888, 17 x 22½in (43 x 56cm).
£210–250
$300–360 ✗ SK(B)

▶ **An oak tool box of the Latrobe Fire Dept. No. 5,** by Seagrave, with metal latch, American, 19thC, 24in (61cm) wide.
£350–400
$500–580 ✗ SK(B)

A shield-shaped souvenir booklet, for the Veteran Fireman's Association of New York excursion to Troy, Watertown and Buffalo, August 19–25, 1890, with six pages in Celluloid covers, American, 5¼ x 4in (13.5 x 10cm).
£140–160
$200–230 ✗ SK(B)

A photograph of the Barnicoat Fire Association, the men in dress uniform with soft hats and helmets, some damage, American, 1890, 17 x 21¾in (43 x 55.5cm).
£160–180
$230–260 ✗ SK(B)

▶ **A chief engineer's lantern,** by White Mfg. Co, the engraved bevelled glass front lens inscribed 'Chief Engineer' and 'A' surrounded by a wreath, patented 'Feb & Aug 1874, Bridgeport, Conn.', late 19thC, 13in (33cm) high.
£1,100–1,200
$1,600–1,750
✗ SK(B)

A scratch-built wooden model of a front-wheel drive ladder wagon, with six ground and two side ladders, American, c1900, 26in (66cm) long.
£140–160
$200–230 ✗ SK(B)

A Latvian fireman's helmet, with brass plate and trim, early 1900s.
£125–145
$180–220 ⊞ UCO

An Empire Apparatus fire extinguisher, inscribed with patent date 3 September 1898, American, 21in (53.5cm) high.
£230–260
$330–380 ✗ SK(B)

A Vulcan cast-iron and brass high-pressure Baltimore Apparatus Hydrant, by the Ross Valve Mfg. Co, with five 2½in steamer cups, American, c1900, 20in (53.5cm) high.
£550–650
$800–950 ✗ SK(B)

A Czechoslovakian fireman's leather-coated metal helmet, with a brass plate, early 1900s.
£160–180
$230–260 ⊞ UCO

A Veteran Firemen's Association aluminium presentation shield, inscribed 'VFA Testimonial to Veteran Firemen's Association Hartford, Conn. Oct. 1st 2nd 1900, from Veteran Firemen's Association Poughkeepsie, N.Y.', in original stained wood display frame, American, 20½in (52cm) high.
£1,450–1,650
$2,100–2,400 ✗ SK(B)

An Amoskeag Xtra Size 1 steam fire engine, by the American Locomotive Works, New Hampshire, with double crane-neck frame, American, 1905, 297in (754.5cm) long.
£15,500–16,500
$22,500–24,000 ✗ SK(B)
Built in 1905 for the Lynn, Massachusetts fire brigade, this engine was originally horse-drawn, was motorized at some point and then returned to being horse-drawn.

◀ **A Tientsin Volunteer Fire Brigade Long Service Medal,** with silver Maltese cross, the reverse inscribed 'Tientsin 1902 to 1907 presented by the British Municipal Councils for Long Service to W. A. Forbes', with four silver ribbon bars for 8, 11, 14 and 16 years, and top suspension brooch inscribed 'T.V.F.B 1902–1918', marked Birmingham 1909, c1918.
£470–520
$670–750 ✗ DNW

A Society for the Protection of Life from Fire silver medal, 5th type (from 1902), depicting a man rescuing a woman with two children, on a red ribbon, c1916.
£420–460
$600–660 ✗ DNW
This medal was awarded to Dr. D. R. Thomas, of Taffs Well, for rescuing three people from a fire caused by an exploding lamp, on 13 March 1916 at Radyr, near Cardiff.

A German fireman's metal helmet, with brass trim, Stuttgart, 1928.
£125–145
$180–210 ⊞ UCO

A model of the Friendship 1774 Hand Pumper, by Colark Ship Model Builders of Philadelphia, with red cast-iron handles and wheels, aluminium air chamber, brass pistons and rubber hoses, American, 1930s, 15½in (39.5cm) long.
£700–800
$1,000–1,150 ✗ SK(B)

A Haley fireman's black leather helmet, with gold lettering on a red ground, American, 1940s.
£150–175
$220–255 ⊞ UCO

Police

A pottery nursery plate commemorating Sir Robert Peel, printed in green within a moulded border enamelled in green, blue and yellow, 19thC, 6½in (16.5cm) diameter.
£50–60
$75–90 ✗ SAS
In 1829, Home Secretary Sir Robert Peel established the Metropolitan Police in London, hence the slang terms 'Peeler' and 'Bobby' for policemen.

A Georgian wooden tipstaff, by Hugh Laughton of Keighley, with brass tips, dated 1812, 18¼in (46.5cm) long.
£400–450
$580–650 ⊞ CCB

A police truncheon, 1830, 15in (38cm) long.
£175–200
$250–300 ⊞ MB

◄ **A German policeman's helmet,** with white metal plate, mid-20thC.
£125–145
$180–210 ⊞ UCO

A Metropolitan policeman's helmet, blue serge cloth over cork base, 1953–60.
£85–95
$125–140 ⊞ UCO

A collection of 42 police helmet badges, from British borough and county forces, mid-20thC, largest 4in (10cm) high.
£15–25
$20–35 each ⊞ Q&C

Money Boxes

A Tartan ware money box, with a transfer print of Glasgow University, 19thC, 3in (7.5cm) high.
£75–85
$115–125 ⊞ Fai

A Midland Bank Limited metal money box, 1930s, 3¼in (8.5cm) diam.
£12–15
$17–20 ⊞ HUX

A ceramic guitarist money box, inscribed 'One For The Record', 1960s, 7in (18cm) high.
£20–25
$30–35 ↗ SAF

A cast-iron 'city bank' money box, slight damage, c1900, 4in (10cm) high.
£25–35
$30–50 ⊞ HAL

A Queen Elizabeth II Coronation metal money box, c1953, 3in (7.5cm) high.
£15–20
$20–30 ⊞ FST

A TSB plastic rocket money box, red and white, 1960s, 11in (28cm) high.
£12–15
$17–20 ⊞ HUX

A tin post-box money box, decorated in red, black, and cream, c1916–20, 7in (18cm) high.
£45–65
$65–95 ⊞ MURR

▶ A steel partitioned money box, painted red, 1960, 8in (20.5cm) long.
£10–12
$15–18 ⊞ Mo

A Bakelite cat money box, with gold eyes, Japanese, 1930s, 4in (10cm) high.
£85–95
$125–145 ⊞ LBe

Miller's is a price GUIDE not a price LIST

Newspapers & Magazines

The London Gazette,
dated 31 August to
4 September 1682,
11 x 7in (28 x 18cm).
£40–50
$60–75 ⊞ HaR

The New Observator,
dated Saturday 10 January
1691, 11 x 8in (28 x 20.5cm).
£65–80
$95–115 ⊞ HaR

The Norwich Gazette,
dated 17 to 24 February
1728, with early engravings,
10 x 9in (25.5 x 23cm).
£100–150
$145–225 ⊞ HaR

**Bonner and Middleton
Bristol Journal,** dated
Saturday 1 July 1781,
21 x 13in (53.5 x 33cm).
£30–40
$45–60 ⊞ J&S

The Courier, featuring
articles about Wellington
and Robert Peel, 1813,
19 x 13in (48.5 x 33cm).
£20–25
$30–35 ⊞ J&S

The Times, dated 20 July
1863, bound, 23½ x 17¾in
(59.5 x 45cm).
£10–20
$15–25 ⊞ HaR

The Citizen, No. 1,
marked 'Specimen', 1876,
16 x 12in (40.5 x 30.5cm).
£60–65
$95–100 ⊞ J&S

▶ **Isle of Wight
Advertiser,** dated
Saturday 12 May
1888, 26 x 18in
(66 x 45.5cm).
£15–20
$20–30 ⊞ MRW

Army and Navy Gazette,
dated Saturday 25 May
1888, 15 x 11in (38 x 28cm).
£15–20
$20–30 ⊞ MRW

◀ **Daily Mail,** No. 1,
1896, 24 x 17in
(61 x 43cm).
£25–30
$35–45 ⊞ J&S

Condition

The condition is
absolutely vital
when assessing
the value of a
collectable. Damaged
pieces on the whole
appreciate much
less than perfect
examples. However
a rare desirable
piece may command
a high price even
when damaged.

Black & White Budget,
dated February 1900,
reporting on the Boer War,
11 x 8in (28 x 20.5cm).
£8–10
$10–15 ⊞ J&S

The Graphic, dated
Saturday 13 November
1880, the front cover
depicting scenes of
agitation in Ireland,
16 x 12in (40.5 x 30.5cm).
£6–8
$8–10 ⊞ HaR

The Play, the front cover
depicting Forbes Robertson
as Hamlet, 1913, 12 x 9in
(30.5 x 23cm).
£5–6
$7–8 ⊞ J&S

**Le Petit Echo de la
Mode,** French, 1930,
14 x 11in (35.5 x 28cm).
£5–6
$7–10 ⊞ J&S

**Marine Engineer
Officers' Magazine,**
dated May/June 1930,
9 x 6in (23 x 15cm).
£35–40
$50–60 ⊞ J&S

**News Of The World
promotional miniature
newspaper,** 1933,
5½ x 4in (14 x 10cm).
£18–22
$25–35 ⊞ RUSS

Bristol Evening Post,
No. 1, 1932, 16 x 12in
(40.5 x 30.5cm).
£45–50
$65–75 ⊞ J&S

Woman and Home,
dated June 1940, 12 x 9in
(30.5 x 23cm).
£2–3
$3–5 ⊞ MRW

LOCATE THE SOURCE

The source of each illustration in Miller's can be
found by checking the code letters below each
caption with the Key to Illustrations, pages
444–452.

Woman's Day, dated
Friday 13 June 1959,
13 x 10in (33 x 25.5cm).
£3–4
$5–6 ⚒ FLD

News Chronicle, dated
Thursday 10 July 1947,
reporting on the
engagement of Princess
Elizabeth and Lieutenant
Philip Mountbatten,
23 x 17in (58.5 x 43cm).
£2–4
$3–6 ⊞ HaR

Two copies of Ideal Home, 1949–50, 12 x 9in
(30.5 x 23cm).
£2–3
$3–5 each ⊞ MRW

Osbornes

An Osborne plaque, entitled 'Dover Castle', green, brown and cream, 1917, 3in (7.5cm) wide.
£20–30
$30–45 ⊞ **Rac**

An Osborne plaque, entitled 'Bath Abbey', brown and orange, 1918, 3in (7.5cm) wide.
£20–30
$30–45 ⊞ **Rac**

An Osborne plaque, entitled 'Western Towers, Westminster Abbey', brown and cream, 1923, 3¼in (8.5cm) wide.
£18–22
$30–40 ⊞ **JMC**

An Osborne plaque, entitled 'Burns' Cottage Interior', brown, cream and blue, 1920s, 4½in (11.5cm) wide.
£25–30
$35–45 ⊞ **JMC**

An Osborne plaque, entitled 'Temple Bar in Dr Johnson's Time', brown, cream and blue, 1920s, 8in (20.5cm) wide.
£55–60
$80–90 ⊞ **JMC**

An Osborne plaque, entitled 'The Old Folks at Home', 1930s, 9¼in (23.5cm) wide.
£25–30
$35–45 ⊞ **JMC**

An Osborne plaque, entitled 'RMS Queen Mary', cream, black, red and blue, c1936, 7in (18cm) wide.
£25–35
$30–50 ⊞ **MURR**

An Osborne plaque, entitled 'Coventry, City of Three Spires', 1940, 5in (12.5cm) wide.
£20–25
$30–35 ⊞ **JMC**

◀ **An Osborne plaque,** entitled 'Going to Market', brown, green, grey and cream, 1940s, 3¾ x 5¼in (9.5 x 13.5cm).
£25–30
$35–45 ⊞ **JMC**

Two Osborne figures of Mr Micawber and David Copperfield, from a set of eight Dickens characters, 1940s, largest 5in (12.5cm) high.
£55–65
$80–100 each ⊞ **JMC**

Owls

Throughout history, the owl has been both feared and venerated. In Ancient Greece, the owl was the symbol of Athena and is found on the back of coins bearing her image and other decorative objects such as ceramics. As well as being goddess of war, Athena was also goddess of wisdom, hence the persistent idea of the 'wise old owl' and the association of the bird with education.

The owl – which belongs to the order of birds called strigiformes – is carniverous, nocturnal and unlike other birds of prey has an almost noiseless flight. Its hearing and vision are acute. Possibly for these reasons the Romans called the owl 'strix' (plural: striges, hence strigiformes), the same word as used for a witch. Owls are traditionally connected with sorcery and Halloween. In some cultures they signify bad luck, in others, good.

Famous owls in literature include *The Owl and the Pussycat* (Edward Lear) and Owl in A. A. Milne's *Winnie the Pooh*. Hedwig, the owl in J. K. Rowling's *Harry Potter* stories, has stimulated a new range of soft toys and other merchandise and carries on the tradition of owls being associated with witchcraft, wizardry and seats of learning.

◀ **A red figure skyphos,** the sides decorated with an owl flanked by laurel leaves, Italian, 4thC BC, 3½in (9cm) diam.
£450–550
$650–800 ⚔ P

A hand-coloured lithograph of a tawny or wood owl, by John & Elizabeth Gould, printed by Charles Hullmandel, in a maple veneered frame, 1832–37, 20 x 13¾in (51 x 35cm).
£360–420
$500–600 ⚔ Bon

A Victorian silver novelty owl pepper pot, the pull-off lid pierced and set with two glass eyes, the body engraved with feathers, maker's mark of Edward Charles Brown, London 1873, 3in (7.5cm) high.
£420–480
$620–700 ⚔ Bon

◀ **A pair of Continental green-glazed pottery owl spill vases,** 10in (25.5cm) high.
£400–450
$600–650 ⊞ KA

A Victorian ceramic owl oil lamp, with green glass shade, 30in (76cm) high.
£450–500
$650–720 ⊞ BSa

A Victorian nursery oil lamp, with six-line Kosmos burner, the ceramic base decorated with owls among foliage, 24in (61cm) high.
£275–325
$400–480 ⊞ BSa

◀ **An Arts and Crafts hand-beaten copper wall-hanging clock,** set with a lapis lazuli-style stone, the original pendulum with hand-hammered owl decoration, 'Improve time in time while time lasts for sometimes no time when times past' in relief, late 19thC, 17in (43cm) high.
£1,800–2,200
$2,600–3,200 ⚔ TF

Edward Lear, *Nonsense Songs,* illustrated by L. Leslie Brooke, first edition, published by F. Warne & Co, the front cover depicting Owl from *The Owl and the Pussycat,* c1900, 9 x 7in (23 x 18cm).
£80–90
$115–135 ⊞ BIB

A terracotta owl, Italian, 1910–20, 24in (61cm) high.
£450–500
$650–720 ⊞ KA

A pottery figure of an owl, perched upon three books, painted in naturalistic colours, 1930s, 23in (58.5cm) high.
£400–450
$580–650 ⚒ HYD

A pair of ceramic owls, decorated in brown and cream, inscribed 'ENS voltstadt', German, 1930s–40s, 10in (25.5cm) high.
£250–300
$360–440 ⊞ KA

Two wooden owl inkwells, with red-painted ears, beaks and feet and glass bead eyes, with ceramic liners, German, 1930s–50s, 4in (10cm) high.
£35–40
$50–60 each ⊞ RUSS

A Steiff mohair owl hand puppet, brown and cream with green glass bead eyes, 1950–60.
£20–25
$30–40 ⊞ DMG

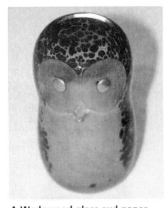

A Wedgwood glass owl paper-weight, decorated in brown, with gold eyes, 1970, 3in (7.5cm) high.
£20–25
$30–40 ⊞ DMG

A wooden owl clock, German, 20thC, 10in (25.5cm) high.
£70–80
$100–120 ⊞ DCA

A set of five Poole Pottery plates, by John Gould, decorated with owls in green, brown and cream, 1980s, 6in (15cm) diam.
£10–12
$15–17 each ⊞ DCA

Paper Money

An Alton Bank one pound note, 'payable at Alton or through Messrs. Austen, Maunde, Tilson, Bankers, London', October 1815.
£270–300
$400–440 ≯ P
The Austen in this partnership was the brother of Jane Austen.

A Bank of England one pound note, signed by Jacob Perkins, with vignette of Britannia seated with Scotia, Hibernia and cherubs flanked by portraits of George IV, c1819.
£200–250
$300–350 ≯ P

A Bank of England five pound note, c1820, 8in (20.5cm) wide.
£120–150
$175–225 ≯ P

A 10 shilling Treasury note, signed by John Bradbury, August 1914.
£300–350
$450–500 ≯ P

A United Kingdom of Great Britain and Ireland ten shilling note, with Dardanelles overprint, 1915, 5¼in (13.5cm) wide.
£475–525
$700–750 ≯ P

A Deutsch-Ostafrikanische Bank 200 rupien note, German East African, 1915.
£275–300
$400–440 ≯ P

A one pound Treasury note, signed by John Bradbury, part of first issue, the reverse with light pencil graffiti, August 1914.
£475–525
$700–750 ≯ P
The declaration of WWI on 4 August 1914 nearly caused a financial crisis. Gold full and half sovereigns were instantly withdrawn and replaced by paper money – one pound notes in black and ten shilling notes in red. These emergency notes were nicknamed 'Bradburys' after the signature of John Bradbury, Secretary to the Treasury, which appeared on the bottom. They are also known as Treasury notes.

LOCATE THE SOURCE
The source of each illustration in Miller's can be found by checking the code letters below each caption with the Key to Illustrations, pages 444–452.

A United Kingdom of Great Britain and Ireland 10 shilling Treasury note, signed by John Bradbury, 1918.
£725–775
$1,000–1,200 ✄ P

A United Kington of Great Britain and Ireland 10 shilling Treasury note, signed by Warren Fisher, 2nd issue, 1922, 5½in (14cm) wide.
£60–70
$90–100 ⊞ ML

A United Kingdom of Great Britain and Ireland one pound note, signed by John Bradbury, 1923, 6in (15cm) wide.
£27–30
$35–45 ⊞ ML

A Bank of England 50 pound note, dated 20 May 1932.
£625–675
$900–1,000 ✄ P

A Banca D'Italia 1000 lire note, Italian East African, 1938.
£250–300
$360–440 ✄ P

A Bank of England emergency issue blue one pound note, 1940, 6in (15cm) wide.
£12–14
$15–18 ⊞ ML
In 1940, the colour of one pound notes was changed from green to blue, and 10 shilling notes went from brown to mauve. Wartime banknotes were produced by offset lithography rather than recess printing and only in 1948 were the original pre-war colours restored.

A Bank of England mauve 10 pound note, signed by K. O. Peppiat, 1940–48.
£30–35
$40–50 ⊞ ML

A Commercial Bank of Scotland blue five pound note, signed by J. M. Erskine, dated 5 January 1943, 8in (20.5cm) wide.
£70–80
$100–120 ⊞ ML

A Bank of England white five pound note, signed by P. S. Beale, dated 17 September 1949, 8½in (21.5cm) wide.
£80–90
$115–135 ⊞ ML

A Bank of England green one pound note, signed by P. S. Beale, 1950, 6in (15cm) wide.
£20–25
$30–40 ⊞ ML

A Provincial Bank of Ireland 20 pound note, dated 20 November 1944.
£125–140
$180–200 ⊞ WP

A Clydesdale & North of Scotland Bank 100 pound note, signed by J. J. Campbell, part of a 5,000 print run for this date, dated 2 May 1951.
£420–470
$600–700 ✄ P

A Bank of England blue five pound note, signed by L. K. O'Brien, 1957, 6in (15cm) wide.
£12–15
$15–20 ⊞ ML

A Central Bank of Ireland orange 10 shilling note, 1968.
£14–16
$18–22 ⊞ WP

Photography

A *carte de visite*, depicting a coach and horses, c1870, 3 x 4in (7.5 x 10cm).
£14–16
$18–22 ⊞ J&S

A *carte de visite*, depicting tram transportation in Bristol, c1895, 3 x 4in (7.5 x 10cm).
£16–18
$22–28 ⊞ J&S

A photograph of two Native American infants, signed 'Elliott', copyrighted in 1898, 7 x 5in (18 x 12.5cm), in an Arts & Crafts oak frame.
£350–420
$500–600 ↗ TREA

▶ A WWI military wedding photograph, 1915, 4½ x 6½in (11.5 x 16.5cm).
£8–10
$12–15 ⊞ J&S

An album of photographs of Queen Victoria, with an original photograph of Queen Victoria laying the foundation stone to Mar Lodge, a hitherto unknown photograph of Queen Victoria and a large quantity of original photographs of Victorian Royalty and nobility, some signed, 1880–1920.
£850–950
$1,250–1,400 ↗ DW
These images provide hitherto unknown snapshots of Queen Victoria and her family as well as many leading Victorian courtiers and a record of a way of life long gone. This album was once in the possession of Lord 'Lucky' Lucan, who is still officially at large and sought for the murder of his children's nanny.

Three photographic portraits, mounted on card, c1900, 6 x 4in (15 x 10cm).
£0.50–1
$1–3 each ↗ DW

A photograph album, with 71 black and white photographs of high-ranking Victorians and four hitherto unknown photographs of Mrs Alice Keppel, 1889–92.
£500–600
$720–870 ↗ DW
Alice Keppel was Edward VII's most celebrated mistress. Ironically, she was also Camilla Parker-Bowles grandmother.

A photograph album, with 24 photographs showing Queen Alexandra and other members of the Royal family relaxing, including the future Edward VIII and George VI, image size approx 3 x 3in (7.5 x 7.5cm), in original Kodak album, small 4°.
£400–500
£580–720 ↗ DW
Queen Alexandra, a keen photographer, published a volume entitled 'Photographs from my Camera' in association with *The Daily Telegraph*, in order to raise money for charity in 1908 (copies of this book can be found in many second-hand bookshops). This album contains hitherto unknown images, including the Queen seated outside at a tea table, with a cigarette in her left hand.

A Victorian leather-bound photograph album, the pages with floral decoration and central cut-out, 12 x 9in (30.5 x 23cm).
£130–150
$190–220 ⊞ TAC

A Mauchlin ware sycamore photograph album, decorated with floral design and verse, c1880, 4 x 3in (10 x 7.5cm).
£50–60
£75–90 ⊞ MB

An onyx photograph album, with hardstone and gilt-metal decoration, late 19thC, 12 x 8in (30.5 x 20.5cm), with original fitted case.
£450–500
$650–720 ⋟ Mit

Miller's is a price GUIDE not a price LIST

A tooled-leather photograph album, with illustrations of historical scenes, c1880, 12 x 9½in (30.5 x 24cm).
£75–85
$110–125 ⊞ HEG

A Victorian velvet photograph frame, 8 x 7in (20.5 x 18cm).
£20–30
$30–45 ⊞ CAL

A Victorian red velvet double photograph frame, with gilt-metal corner decoration, 7 x 4½in (18 x 11.5cm).
£40–50
$60–75 ⊞ CAL

A silver photograph frame, the arched surmount with ribbon and reed borders, Chester 1908, 10¼ x 7½in (26 x 19cm).
£300–350
$450–500 ⋟ RTo

A silver photograph frame, Chester 1903, 6in (15cm) diam.
£280–320
$400–450 ⊞ HCA

A carved wood hanging photograph frame, with gilt decoration, 1920s, 12 x 9in (30.5 x 23cm).
£60–70
$90–100 ⊞ AMR

Plastic

This section on plastic includes a collection of Tupperware. This light and unbreakable polythene kitchenware was invented by American plastics chemist Earl S. Tupper (1908–83). After wartime restrictions were over, he launched his new product on to the market in 1946. He was particularly proud of the patented airtight seal, (inspired by the lids of paint cans) which was designed to keep the contents fresh for longer than in other containers.

Consumers, however, didn't know how to open these lids and Tupperware sold poorly in the shops until 1948 when the company introduced home demonstrations. One of their earliest demonstrators, a lady called Brownie Wise, came up with the idea of the Tupperware party and a marketing legend was born. These

now celebrated get-togethers were an instant success. For the company they offered direct access to the housewife. For women they provided not just home shopping and affordable plastics, but a social occasion and a job opportunity that they could combine with family life.

Beginning in the USA, Tupperware parties came to Britain in 1960 and today they still take place across the world. The Tupperware Corporation is now a $1.1 billion multinational company trading in over 100 countries. While new products include such esoteric creations as the Kimchi keeper and the Kimono keeper, there are collectors who focus on vintage products – the humble cereal containers and pudding bowls that made Tupperware a household name.

A Bakelite cheroot or cigarette holder, in the form of a hockey player's leg, c1890, 4in (10cm) high.
£65–75
$95–110 ⊞ WAB

▶ **A Bakelite Tiemaster,** 1930s–40s, 5in (12.5cm) high.
£18–22
$30–35 ⚲ MED

A Bakelite vesta case, 1915, 2¼in (5.5cm) wide.
£14–16
$18–22 ⊞ VB

A Bakelite coffee grinder, Italian, 1930s, 6in (15cm) high.
£70–80
$100–115 ⊞ GAD

Cross Reference
See Colour Review (page 239)

A Bakelite pipe rack, 1940s, 5¼in (13cm) high.
£15–20
$20–30 ⊞ DHAR

A Bakelite ashtray, featuring a drunken man leaning against a lampost, with inscription 'Oh What a Beautiful Evenin'!!', 1940s, 5in (12.5cm) high.
£20–25
$30–45 ⊞ HarC

A Bakelite tobacco jar, with decorative leaf borders, c1940, 5in (12.5cm) high.
£15–20
$20–30 ⊞ DHAR

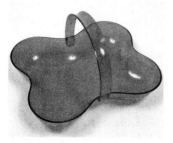

An orange Perspex basket, 1950s, 12in (30.5cm) wide.
£12–15
$17–20 ⊞ HSt

A pink Bakelite perpetual calendar, with floral decoration and inscription 'A Present from Weston-Super-Mare', 1950s, 5in (12.5cm) high.
£20–25
$30–35 ⊞ DHAR

A Tupperware white plastic cereal container, with flip top, c1960, 9in (23cm) high.
£10–12
$15–18 ⊞ Mo
This was one of the first to be produced in the UK.

A Tupperware Wonderlier green plastic pudding bowl, with white lid for steaming, 1960, 7½in (19cm) diam.
£10–12
$15–18 ⊞ Mo

Two Tupperware clear plastic containers, one for bran the other flour, with lids and scoops, 1960, largest 7in (18cm) high.
£12–15
$18–20 each ⊞ Mo

A Tupperware brown plastic spice container, with clear lid, 1960, 3in (7.5cm) high.
£8–10
$12–15 ⊞ Mo

A set of six Tupperware plastic beakers, various colours, 1960, 6in (15cm) high.
£30–35
$45–50 ⊞ Mo

▶ A set of six Tupperware clear plastic sundae vases, 1960s, 6in (12.5cm) high.
£20–25
$30–35 ⊞ Mo

Two ribbed Tupperware orange plastic containers, with flower motifs, 1962, largest 8in (20.5cm) diam.
£20–25
$30–35 ⊞ Mo
Very few of these containers were produced with a floral motif.

A Tupperware green plastic container, with a clear lid, 1960s, 3in (7.5cm) high.
£3–5
$5–7 ⊞ Mo

A Tupperware green plastic colander, with clear lid, 1960s, 8in (20.5cm) diam.
£8–10
$12–15 ⊞ Mo

Politics

Politics and politicians have inspired a wealth of decorative arts and commemorative material over the centuries. This section opens with an admission ticket to the trial of Warren Hastings, a famous political scandal in the 18th century, and closes with a Conservative mousemat from the 2001 British election campaign. 'Political memorabilia has been described as the small change of history,' says Andrew Hilton, from Special Auction Services, a saleroom that specializes in commemoratives. 'In many instances, the objects are not great works of art in themselves. A potter would turn something out quickly and cheaply to commemorate a current event. It didn't have to be a thing of beauty, it was there to make its point. And today, what attracts people to these items is that sense of holding history in your hands.'

Popular subjects include major political happenings such as the Reform Act of 1832 and great political figures. According to Hilton, the top five collectable British Prime Ministers are (in no particular ranking order) Wellington, Gladstone, Disraeli, Churchill and Margaret Thatcher. Items connected with less successful politicians can also be sought after because of their rarity value – so perhaps William Hague will one day prove desirable in the auction room! Objects illustrated range from the serious to the satirical. Again from more recent times, Hilton recommends material inspired by the *Spitting Image* TV show (such as the Margaret Thatcher teapot), as being among the most significant political commemoratives of the 1980s. This section also includes commemoratives relating to American and other foreign politicians.

An engraved admission ticket for the trial of Warren Hastings, admitting the bearer to the 23rd day of the trials, with a small piece torn from the top left-hand corner, which was a method of cancellation indicating entry to the trial, c1738, 8°.
£130–160
$190–220 ↗ DW
Warren Hastings, 1732–1818, a former Governor General of India, was impeached for financial irregularities by Parliament and put on trial, which was held sporadically over seven years between 1788 and 1795, thus making it one of the longest trials in British legal history.

A bronze medal commemorating the death of Charles James Fox, the reverse with an inscription 'Born Jany 13 1749, Died Sept 13 1806, Revered for Talent Fortitude & Patriotism', 1806, 1½in (4cm) diam.
£40–50
$60–75 ⊞ TML

A pottery plate commemorating Lord John Russell, printed in black with a portrait, 1832, 4in (10cm) diam.
£120–140
$175–200 ↗ SAS

A white stoneware jug, applied with a moulded cartouche of a deer and trees beneath the inscription 'Burdett & Liberty', with blue neck and handle, c1810, 4½in (11.5cm) high.
£200–240
$300–350 ↗ SAS

▶ **A three-volume set of books,** by Adam Smith, Edinburgh, an inquiry into the nature and causes of the Wealth of Nations, contemporary calf binding, 1819, 8½ x 5in (21.5 x 12.5cm).
£500–600
$720–870 ⊞ BAY

A London Pitt Club silver-gilt medal, by James Tassie, with a cameo glass bust of William Pitt, the reverse with inscription 'Henry Morgan Godwin Esqre', c1815, 1¾in (4.5cm) high.
£150–175
$220–255 ⊞ TML

◀ **A salt-glazed stoneware Reform flask,** modelled as Lord John Russell holding a scroll impressed 'The True Spirit of Reform', with 'Lord John Russell' impressed below, 'Preece, 72 High Holborn impressed to rear, c1832, 7in (18cm) high.
£300–350
$450–500 ⚒ BBR
Produced during the passing of the Reform Bill in 1832, Reform flasks were decorated with moulded portraits of the champions of parliamentary reform including Lord John Russell and Lord Brougham.

A Minton bisque figure of the Duke of Wellington, c1846, 11in (28cm) high.
£500–550
$720–800 ⊞ JAK

A salt-glazed stoneware Reform flask, modelled as Lord Brougham holding a scroll impressed 'The True Spirit of Reform', with 'Brougham Reform Cordial' impressed below, marked Doulton & Watts, c1832, 7in (18cm) high.
£190–230
$275–330 ⚒ BBR

▶ **A ceramic jug commemorating the Duke of Wellington,** black transfer-printed on a white body, 1850s, 5in (12.5cm) high.
£100–115
$145–170 ⚒ RCo

◀ **A Parian bust of Lord Palmerston,** on a named socle base, 1864, 10¾in (27.5cm) high.
£160–190
$230–275 ⚒ SAS

A ceramic jug commemorating the Duke of Wellington, decorated with a hand-coloured print, with silver lustre decoration to top, slight damage, 1850s, 6in (15cm) high.
£125–150
$180–220 ⚒ RCo
If undamaged this price range would be **£425–475 ($620–700).**

A Staffordshire pottery figure of Lord Palmerston, 1860, 3½in (9cm) high.
£90–110
$130–150 ⚒ RCo

▶ **A Parian bust of Richard Cobden,** by Adams & Co, published by John Stark, the reverse with impressed marks, lacking socle base, c1865, 13in (33cm) high.
£85–100
$125–150 ⚒ SAS

◀ **A Staffordshire pottery figure of Garibaldi,** with orange shirt, holding a rolled banner 'Liberte', 19thC, 13in (33cm) high.
£120–150
$175–220 ⚒ L&E

A pottery tankard commemorating Earl Russell and Lord Derby, black transfer-printed with named portraits, with decoration to handle and interior, c1865, 5¼in (13cm) high.
£260–300
$380–440 ↗ SAS

A Parian bust of John Bright, by Adams & Co, by John Stark, the reverse with impressed marks, lacking socle base, c1868, 14in (35.5cm) high.
£90–110
$130–160 ↗ SAS

A plate commemorating the Marquis of Salisbury, black transfer-printed, bordered by dog roses, c1880, 11in (28cm) wide.
£150–165
$220–250 ⊞ POL

A *carte de visite* depicting Abraham Lincoln, c1880, 4 x 3in (10 x 7.5cm).
£6–10
$8–15 ⊞ J&S

A plate commemorating William Gladstone, black transfer-printed with his commercial and political achievements bordered by roses, c1886, 11in (28cm) wide.
£85–95
$125–150 ⊞ POL

A loving cup commemorating Benjamin Disraeli, transfer-printed in black with a portrait, late 1880s, 5in (12.5cm) high.
£165–185
$250–270 ↗ RCo

A cast-iron bust of Randolph Churchill, bronze-finished, c1886, 5½in (14cm) high.
£90–110
$130–160 ↗ RCo

A bronze medal commemorating William Gladstone, the reverse with a 59-line inscription listing the Members of the House for the year, 1894, 3¾in (9.5cm) diam.
£130–150
$190–220 ⊞ TML

A base metal and enamel William Gladstone memorial badge, with a photographic portrait of Gladstone within an enamel heart, mounted on original printed card with inscription 'In Memoriam, W. E. Gladstone, Christian, Patriot, Statesman', 1898, 24 x 28¾in (61 x 73cm).
£55–65
$80–100 ⊞ TML

A National Union of Women's Suffrage Society leaflet, entitled 'White Slave Traffic', printed both sides, slightly creased, c1900, 8½ x 5½in (21.5 x 14cm).
£260–320
$380–450 ⚒ VS

A pottery jug commem- orating Beville Stanier, elected Member of Parliament for Shropshire, 1908, 6½in (16.5cm) high.
£75–85
$110–125 ⊞ POL

A political cartoon, 'The Man at the Wheel', taken from *Punch* magazine, c1929, 11 x 9in (28 x 23cm).
£14–16
$18–22 ⊞ POL

An Ashtead Pottery cream-glazed caricature jug of Stanley Baldwin, impressed to base 'The Right Hon Stanley Baldwin M.P', No. 509 of a limited edition of 1,000, 1924–37, 7¾in (19.5cm) high.
£120–150
$175–220 ⚒ BBR

▶ **Winston Churchill's autograph,** signed in black fountain pen, on an album page, 1931, 3¼ x 4in (8 x 10cm).
£800–1,000
$1,200–1,500 ⚒ Bon(C)

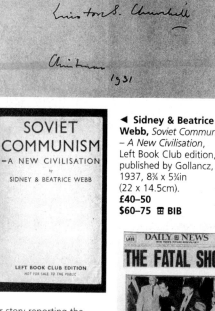

Charles de Gaulle, a signed letter written in French to Miss Eardley-Wilmot thanking her for her letter of encouragement and offering her services to the Free French, 1940.
£400–450
$580–650 ⚒ VS

SOVIET COMMUNISM
–A NEW CIVILISATION
by
SIDNEY & BEATRICE WEBB

LEFT BOOK CLUB EDITION
NOT FOR SALE TO THE PUBLIC

◀ **Sidney & Beatrice Webb,** *Soviet Communism – A New Civilisation,* Left Book Club edition, published by Gollancz, 1937, 8¾ x 5¾in (22 x 14.5cm).
£40–50
$60–75 ⊞ BIB

William Beveridge, *Full Employment in a Free Society,* published by Allen & Unwin, 1944, 8¾ x 6in (22 x 15cm).
£30–35
$45–50 ⊞ BIB
In 1942, economist **William Beveridge (1879–1963) produced his Report on Social Insurance and Allied Services (the Beveridge Report), which led to the creation of the Welfare State. Although the Labour Government implemented many of his suggestions, Beveridge himself was a member of the Liberal Party.**

▶ **The Daily News,** front cover story reporting the assassination of Lee Harvey Oswald by Jack Ruby, together with a cheque signed by Ruby dated 17 July 1956, 14 x 7in (35.5 x 18cm) .
£375–425
$560–620 ⊞ IQ
Two days after his arrest on suspicion of shooting President John F. Kennedy, Lee Harvey Oswald (1939–63) was shot down by local Dallas strip-club owner Jack Ruby in full view of TV cameras. Ruby was sentenced to death but died of cancer in 1967 while appealing for a retrial. Uncertainty and conspiracy theories continue to surround the Kennedy assassination.

The Daily Telegraph, reporting the assassination of President John F. Kennedy, 23 November 1963, 24 x 17in (61 x 43cm).
£8–10
$10–15 ⊞ IQ

A papier mâché bust of President John F. Kennedy, 1963, 6in (15cm) high.
£20–25
$30–35 ⊞ HUX

The Evening News & Star, reporting the assassination of President John F. Kennedy, 23 November 1963, 23 x 17in (58.5 x 43cm).
£8–10
$12–15 ⊞ IQ

Margaret Thatcher, a signed black and white photograph, 1970s, 10 x 8in (25.5 x 20.5cm).
£150–175
$220–250 ⊞ POL

A political poster, 'Proletarians of all Nations get United', 1973, 24 x 45¾in (61 x 115.5cm).
£70–80
$100–115 ⋏ VSP

▶ **A set of ten cardboard drinks mats,** with cartoons of Harold Wilson, 1960s–70s, 3½in (9cm) square.
£10–12
$15–18 ⋏ RCo

A ceramic plate, commemorating Edward Heath's term as Prime Minister, designed by A. Kitson Towler, 1975, 10in (25.5cm) diam.
£75–85
$110–125 ⊞ POL

A Labour Party pottery mug, black transfer-printed with portraits of Harold Wilson and Jim Callaghan, 1976, 4½in (11.5cm) high.
£30–40
$45–60 ⊞ POL

A 1979 General Election Mug, with photographic portraits of the Conservative, Labour and Liberal Party candidates, 1979, 3½in (9cm) high.
£28–32
$45–50 ⋏ RCo

▶ **A white pottery *Spitting Image* Mrs Thatcher teapot,** by Luck and Flaw, slight damage, 1981, 8¼in (21cm) high.
£90–120
$130–175 ⋏ SAS

Condition

The condition is absolutely vital when assessing the value of a collectable. Damaged pieces on the whole appreciate much less than perfect examples. However a rare desirable piece may command a high price even when damaged.

Margaret Thatcher, *The Downing Street Years,* limited edition, 1993, 10 x 6¾in (25.5 x 17cm).
£35–40
$50–60 ⊞ POL

A Royal Crown Derby dish, commemorating Margaret Thatcher, with a cobalt blue border and gilt inscription, 1990, 4½in (11.5cm) diam.
£30–40
$45–60 ↗ SAS

A ceramic plate, commemorating the 50th anniversary of the East Midlands Labour Party, by the Edwardian Fine China Co, No. 1 of a limited edition of 250, 1992, 11in (28cm) diam.
£30–40
$45–6 ↗ RCo

A video of the 1997 General Election, produced by the BBC, 1997.
£14–16
$18–22 ⊞ POL

A Toby jug, modelled as John Major, 1990s, 9in (23cm) high.
£125–145
$180–200 ⊞ POL

A Conservative Party video, 'No! No! No! Margaret Thatcher's Last Year in the House of Commons', presented by Lord Tebbit, 1994.
£10–13
$15–18 ⊞ POL

▶ **A Blair and Hague salt and pepper set,** by Ventnor Ceramics, Blair in a grey suit and red tie, Hague in a blue suit and blue tie, 2001, 5in (12.5cm) high.
£25–30
$35–45 ⊞ POL

A Labour Party campaign poster, 'The Repossessed', 2001, 12 x 17in (30.5 x 43cm).
£0.50–1
$1–3 ⊞ POL

A Bill Clinton Meanie Toy, 'Bull Clinton', dressed in Stars and Stripes shorts, white shirt and red tie, American, c1998, 8in (20.5cm) high.
£12–15
$18–20 ⊞ TBoy

▶ **A Conservative Party mouse mat,** 'Four years of Labour and he still hasn't delivered', red lettering on a black and white ground, 2001, 8 x 10in (20.5 x 25.5cm).
£4–5
$5–7 ⊞ POL

Postcards

A topographical postcard, depicting black and white vignettes of Mumbles linked by garlands of flowers, 1890.
£4–5
$5–7 ⊞ JMC
At this period, one side of the postcard had to be left free for the stamp, name and address. The picture and message had to share the other side.

A topographical postcard, depicting coloured vignettes of Windsor, 1897.
£15–20
$20–30 ⊞ JMC

► **A postcard,** depicting Shakespeare's House, Stratford-on-Avon in brown, green and cream, 1901.
£15–20
$20–30 ⊞ JMC

◄ **A Boer War postcard,** depicting an equestrian portrait of Colonel Baden-Powell, c1900.
£12–15
$17–20 ⊞ JMC

A London & South-Western Railway postcard, depicting St Paul's Cathedral in muted colours, published by Pictorial Post-Card Syndicate, 1900.
£35–40
$50–60 ⊞ JMC

A set of seven Raphael Kirchner postcards, *Les Péchés Capitaux.*
£120–150
$175–225 ⋏ VS

A bas-relief postcard of HRH Princess of Wales, with jewelled effect, 1900–10.
£10–15
$15–20 ⊞ ES

◄ **A photographic postcard,** depicting the Old Post Office, Lee, published by Twiss Bros, Ilfracombe, 1908.
£15–20
$20–30 ⊞ JMC

An RMS advertising postcard, with vignette in gold, blue, red and green, published by David MacBrayne, 1908.
£10–15
$15–20 ⊞ JMC

A postcard, depicting The University and Kelvingrove Park, in brown, red, green and blue, published by H. Cassiers, c1910.
£6–8
$10–15 ⊞ JMC

A comic postcard, depicting a banknote, c1910.
£8–10
$10–15 ⊞ WP

A comic postcard, red, blue and brown on a white ground, c1940.
£3–4
$5–6 ⊞ WP

A WWI Royal Flying Corps coloured silk embroidered postcard, c1916.
£25–30
$35–45 ⊞ GAA

A WWI Royal Engineers coloured silk embroidered postcard, 1915–18.
£12–15
$17–20 ⊞ GAA

A postcard, 'Just found a pebble on the beach at Perranporth', Wildt & Kray Series No. 2438, 1930–40.
£1–2
$3–5 ⊞ ES

A postcard, 'Mr Bruins is surprised', G. G. Series No. 310, 1930–40.
£1–2
$3–5 ⊞ ES

A Boy Scouts perfumed card, in aid of charity funds, 1916.
£15–20
$20–30 ⊞ MURR

Cross Reference
See Mabel Lucie Attwell (page 31–33)

▶ **Three Mabel Lucie Attwell postcards,** 1930s.
£5–10
$10–15 each
⊞ MEM

Posters

A London Brighton and South Coast Railway poster, by Charles Pears, printed in blue, white and red, 1924, 39½ x 60¼in (100 x 153cm).
£400–480
$600–700 ONS

A XXVII Internationaal Eucharistisch Congres poster, by Jan Th. Toorop, printed in red, gold and blue by N. V. J. Smulders & Co, Dutch, 1924, 13 x 8¼in (33 x 21cm).
£200–230
$300–330 VSP

A London, Midland & Scottish Railway poster, by Norman Wilkinson, printed in blue, green, white and grey by John Harn, c1925, 39½ x 25¼in (100.5 x 64cm).
£600–650
$850–950 Bea(E)

> **Cross Reference**
> See Colour Review
> (page 242–244)

A coloured lithographic Clear Light newspaper poster, printed by Karl Koch, German, c1930, 36¾ x 25½in (93.5 x 65cm).
£160–200
$230–300 VSP

A Castrol Golden Arrow World Land Speed Record poster, by Jean Pilod, printed in yellow, red, black and blue, French, 1929, 31½ x 23¾in (80 x 60.5cm).
£350–400
$500–600 BKS

◀ **An American Overseas Airlines poster,** by Lewitt Him, printed in blue, yellow, pink and white, 1940s, 40 x 25in (101.5 x 63.5cm).
£700–800
$1,000–1,200 REN

An Olivetti Lettera 22 poster, by Raymond Savignac, printed in red and purple on a green ground by Alfieri e Lacrois, Milan, Italian, c1950, 27¾ x 39¼in (70.5 x 99.5cm).
£350–430
$500–600 VSP

A GPO poster, '4d minimum foreign rate', by Tom Elkasley, 1950, 27 x 36in (68.5 x 91.5cm).
£1,300–1,500
$2,000–2,200 REN

A United Nations Fight For Freedom poster, printed in blue, white, red and yellow, c1943, 40½ x 28¼in (103 x 72cm).
£15–20
$20–30 ONS

◀ **A Triumph TR4 showroom advertising poster,** dated December 1962, 29½ x 39½in (75 x 100.5cm).
£230–270
$330–400
⚘ BKS

Miller's is a price GUIDE not a price LIST

A Philips Television poster, by A. M. Cassandre, printed in red, blue, black and brown by Smeets Weert, Dutch, 1951, 16¾ x 12½in (42.5 x 32cm).
£420–500
$600–700 ⚘ VSP

A Vermouth Linherr poster, by Athur Zegler, printed in cream, green, blue and red, by W. U. B. Innsbruck, c1955, 46½ x 32¼in (118 x 82cm).
£160–200
$230–300 ⚘ VSP

▶ **An Amerikansk Pop-konst poster,** by Roy Lichtenstein, Swedish, 1967, 39 x 28in (99 x 71cm).
£200–300
$300–450 ⊞ CJP

Film Posters

▶ **A Universal film poster,** *Man of a Thousand Faces,* 1957, 30 x 40in (76 x 101.5cm).
£100–120
$145–175 ⚘ DN

◀ **A Rank film poster,** *Carry on Henry,* 1960s, 40 x 27in (101.5 x 68.5cm).
£55–65
$80–100 ⊞ SDP

A Goya Films poster, *La Caravana de la Ilusion,* by Enzo Nistri, printed in blue, purple, red and yellow, by Graficas Valencia, c1955, 39½ x 27½in (100 x 70cm).
£80–100
$115–145 ⚘ VSP

A 20th Century-Fox film poster, *Bus Stop,* American, 1956, 41 x 27in (104 x 68.5cm).
£200–250
$300–350 ⚘ Bon(C)

▶ **A Mirsch Company film poster,** *The Great Escape,* American, 1963, 41 x 27in (104 x 68.5cm).
£350–390
$500–580 ⊞ SDP

A 20th Century-Fox film poster, *Batman,* 1966, 30 x 40in (76 x 101.5cm).
£600–700
$800–1,000 ⚘ Bon(C)

A United Artists film poster, *Bons Baisers de Russie,* French, 1963, 60 x 40in (152.5 x 101.5cm).
£500–600
$720–870 ⚘ FO

A 20th Century-Fox film poster, *Two For The Road*, 1966, 30 x 40in (76 x 101.5cm).
£80–100
$115–145 ⊞ SEY

A British Lion film poster, *The Man Who Fell To Earth*, printed in blue, red and white on a black ground, 1977, 30 x 40in (76 x 101.5cm).
£80–100
$115–145 ⊞ CTO

A United Artists film poster, *Never Say Never Again*, printed in red on a black and white ground, 1983, 30 x 40in (76 x 101.5cm).
£250–300
$360–440 ⋩ FO

Tretchikoff Prints

Vladimir Tretchikoff has been described as the most genuinely popular artist of the 20th century. Born in Siberia in 1913, he lived in China and Singapore before settling in South Africa in 1946. The self-taught painter became famous in the post-war period not for his original canvases but for reproductions, which appeared in department stores around the world. Typical subjects include exotic ladies, bathed in a distinctive luminous glow. Art

critics scoffed and serious accounts of period painting ignored him, but these affordable prints sold in their thousands, making Tretchikoff a fortune.

Hugely popular in the 1950s, in later years works by the artist were considered the epitome of bad taste. Today fashion has turned full circle. Tretchikoff is now seen as an icon of kitsch and his works are once again sought after.

A Water and Glass, Weeping Rose print, by Tretchikoff, the cream rose on a blue and green ground, 1948, 22 x 21in (56 x 53.5cm).
£15–18
$20–25 ⋩ FLD

An Orchid on the Stairs print, by Tretchikoff, printed in white, pink, blue and green, 1948, 22 x 21in (56 x 53.5cm).
£20–25
$30–35 ⋩ FLD

A Chinese Girl print, by Tretchikoff, printed in yellow, red, black and blue, 1950s, 25 x 21in (63.5 x 53.5cm).
£35–45
$50–60 ⋩ FLD

A Balinese Girl print, by Tretchikoff, printed in green, yellow, pink and blue, 1950s, 24 x 19in (61 x 48.5cm).
£40–45
$60–70 ⋩ HSt

▶ **A Zulu Girl print,** by Tretchikoff, printed in blue, brown, red, black and gold, 1955, 24 x 30in (61 x 76cm), framed.
£75–95
$110–140 ⊞ PLB

◀ **A Miss Wong print,** by Tretchikoff, printed in green, gold, pink and black, 1950s, 25 x 21in (63.5 x 53.5cm).
£35–45
$50–70 ⋩ FLD

Puppets

A Pelham donkey string puppet, with carrot, early 1950s, 8in (20.5cm) high, in original box.
£90–110
$130–160 ⊞ J&J

A Pelham sailor string puppet, 1950s, 12in (30.5cm) high.
£42–48
$60–70 ⊞ J&J

Two Pelham Walt Disney Character string puppets, with carved head, hands and feet, Jiminy Cricket wearing black tails, grey trousers and brown felt hat, and carrying a carved umbrella, and Pinocchio wearing black waistcoat, red shorts, shirt with bowtie and yellow felt hat, 1950s, 8in (20.5cm) high, in original boxes with blue printed labels.
£270–300
$400–440 ↗ Bon(C)

◀ **A Pelham wooden string puppet,** Bengo, 1960s, 6in (15cm) high, in original yellow box.
£10–15
$15–20 ⊞ ARo

A Pelham schoolmaster string puppet, 1960s, 14in (35.5cm) high.
£25–35
$30–50 ⊞ ARo

A Womble string puppet, Great Uncle Bulgaria, wearing a blue, red and yellow tartan hat, poncho and slippers, 1970s, 9in (23cm) high, in original window box.
£20–25
$30–35 ⊞ ARo

▶ **A Pelham golly string puppet,** 1980s, 9in (23cm) high.
£35–45
$50–70 ⊞ ARo

Colour Review

An abalone thimble case, c1800, 2in (5cm) high.
£75–85
$100–125 ⊞ DHA

Three Victorian lacemaker's bobbins, bone with glass spangles, engraved, largest 4in (10cm) long.
£15–25
$20–35 each ⊞ WAB

A cast-iron novelty sewing machine, by Steinfeldt Blasberg, German, 1868, 8in (20.5cm) high.
£8,500–9,000
$12,300–13,000 ⊞ WSM

A Victorian embroidered card needle book, 2in (5cm) wide.
£35–45
$50–65 ⊞ VB

◀ **Two pin-cushions,** one set in a fir cone, 1880–1920, tomato 1½in (4cm) diam.
£15–30
$20–45 each ⊞ VB

A Victorian glass thimble holder, modelled as a shoe, 2¼in (5.5cm) long.
£55–65
$80–95 ⊞ VB

A Victorian Tunbridge ware pincushion, 2in (5cm) diam.
£45–50
$65–75 ⊞ VBo

A Bakelite sewing box, decorated with a cat, 1920s, 3in (7.5cm) wide.
£165–185
$240–270 ⊞ LBe

Three pincushion dolls, c1920, 2in (5cm) high.
£10–30
$15–45 each ⊞ VB

◀ **A WWII pamphlet,** *Make Do and Mend,* prepared for the Board of Trade by the Ministry of Information, 8½ x 5½in (21.5 x 14cm).
£2–3
$3–5 ⊞ HUX

A brass sextant, by W. F. Sannon, London, 1840, 10 x 12in (25.5 x 30.5cm), in original mahogany case.
£650–700
$950–1,100 ⊞ BoC

A White Star Line postcard, from RMS *Oceanic*, 1903.
£15–20
$20–30 ⊞ JMC

A tin box, decorated with an illustration of HMS *Dreadnought*, 1906, 6in (15cm) square.
£75–90
$100–130 ⊞ COB

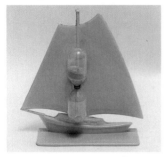

A plastic egg timer, modelled as a yacht, 1930s, 5in (12.5cm) high.
£60–70
$90–100 ⊞ REG

A Cunard Christmas annual, 1931, 6 x 4in (15 x 10cm).
£15–20
$20–30 ⊞ COB

A White Star Line Cruising Programme, 1934, 6 x 4in (15 x 10cm).
£15–20
$20–30 ⊞ COB

A Cunard White Star advertising brochure, for RMS *Queen Mary*, late 1930s, 10 x 12in (25.5 x 30.5cm).
£90–100
$130–150 ⊞ MRW

A Blue Star Line badge, 1950s, 1½in (4cm) diam.
£10–15
$15–20 ⊞ COB

A biscuit tin, decorated with an illustration of *Pride of the Clyde*, 1960s, 9in (23cm) wide.
£20–35
$30–50 ⊞ COB

A set of playing cards, featuring the *Stirling Castle*, 1960s, 2½ x 4in (6.5 x 10cm).
£5–10
$10–15 ⊞ COB

Paris Match magazine, Special France edition, 1961, 15 x 10in (38 x 25.5cm).
£30–35
$45–50 ⊞ COB

A Seguso cased glass vase, c1960, 5in (12.5cm) high.
£80–100
$115–150 ⊞ RUSK

A Mary Quant Perspex daisy ring, 1960s, 1¾in (4.5cm) wide, in original box.
£35–45
$50–65 ⊞ LBe

A powder compact, c1960s, 3in (7.5cm) diam.
£10–12
$15–20 ⊞ HUX

A James Powell & Sons, Whitefriars vase, designed by Geoffrey Baxter, c1967, 11in (28cm) high.
£125–145
$180–200 ⊞ RUSK

▶ **A Track Records poster,** The Who, 'I Can See for Miles', by Hapshash and the Coloured Coat, silkscreen-printed, some damage, 1967, 30 x 19¾in (76 x 50cm).
£140–150
$200–220 ⚒ Bon(C)

A glass bead tie, on a metal chain, 1960s, 12in (30.5cm) long.
£50–60
$75–90 ⊞ SBL

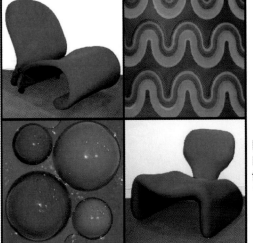

A Walking Jamie doll, in original outfit, c1968, 1½in (29cm) high.
£175–195
$250–280 ⊞ T&D

A piece of Trend Decor wallpaper, 1960s, 21in (53.5cm) wide.
£35–40
$50–60 per roll ⊞ TWI

A Live Action Barbie doll, in original outfit, with single record, c1968, doll 11½in (29cm) high.
£165–185
$240–270 ⊞ T&D

A fibreglass garden chair, in the shape of an egg, by Peter Ghyczy, 1960s, 33in (84cm) high.
£1,000–1,200
$1,500–1,750 ⊞ HSt

A set of eight chairs and a table, table by Anna Castelli Ferriera, chairs by Bodo, German, 1960s.
£2,500–2,800
$3,600–4,000 ⊞ ZOOM

An Ironstone Pottery plate, decorated with Beefeater pattern, 1960s–70s, 11in (28cm) wide.
£25–30
$35–45 ⊞ FLD

◄ **A plastic drinks trolley,** French, 1970s, 24in 61cm) wide.
£165–185
$250–270 ⊞ HSt

A biker's badge, 1970s, 1in (2.5cm) high.
£12–15
$15–20 ⊞ REN

A piece of Nairn wallpaper, 1970, 21in (53.5cm) wide.
£18–20
$20–30 per roll ⊞ TWI

A James Powell & Sons, Whitefriars strap vase, designed by Geoffrey Baxter, c1970, 7in (18cm) high.
£90–100
$130–150 ⊞ RUSK

A carved meerschaum and amber pipe, the bowl modelled as Sarah Bernhardt, c1900, 4in (10cm) long.
£400–450
$580–650 ⊞ SHA

An amber and cloisonné cigarette holder, .84 standard silver, workmaster's mark possibly of N. N. Zverev, Moscow, 1908–17, 4in (10cm) long.
£160–200
$230–280 ✦ RFA

A tobacco advertising fan, 1920, 8in (20.5cm) wide.
£100–120
$150–175 ⊞ SSM

A match striker, inscribed 'Send your telegrams via Eastern Minton', 1925, 5½in (14cm) high.
£135–150
$200–220 ⊞ HUX

A WWI cigar case, decorated with a portrait of an officer, German, 5 x 4in (12.5 x 10cm).
£60–70
$90–100 ⊞ AnS

A Swan Vestas display matchbox, complete with match, 1930–40, 15 x 25½in (38 x 65cm).
£70–80
$100–115 ✦ BBR

A cardboard advertising sign for Alba Cigarettes, c1930, 44¼ x 28¾in (112.5 x 73cm).
£185–195
$270–280 ✦ VSP

A pink faux shagreen cigarette box, 1930s, 6in (15cm) wide.
£15–20
$20–30 ⊞ LBe

A chrome table lighter, c1940–50, 4in (10cm) wide.
£20–25
$30–35 ⊞ RTT

A Rhodian Cigarettes advertising display stand, 1950s, 12in (30.5cm) high.
£30–35
$45–50 ⊞ HUX

A Maryland Stella advertising sign, by Hebert Leupin, printed by Druck Hug Söhne AG, Zurich, 1956, 50½ x 35½in (128 x 90cm).
£135–145
$190–200 ✦ VSP

Sportsman's Guide to the Shooting and Hunting Grounds of the United States and Canada, first edition, 1888, 7½ x 4¾in (19 x 12cm).
£100–130
$150–200 ⊞ OPB

A shield-shaped Swansea Town trade card, by J. Baines, Bradford, 1897, 5in (12.5cm) high.
£50–55
$70–80 ⚒ KNI

A ceramic figure of a Glasgow Celtic footballer, holding a football, handmade and painted, 19thC, 14in (35.5cm) high.
£1,000–1,200
$1,500–1,800 ⚒ P(NW)

◀ **Three Olympic Games official programmes,** for 1908, 1920 and 1928, largest 9 x 5in (23 x 12.5cm).
£450–500
$650–720 ⚒ P(NW)

A Scottish International cap, awarded to P. McWilliam for the football match against England, 1910, 9in (23cm) wide.
£370–420
$550–620 ⚒ P(NW)

A Northern Football League gold medal, presented to P. McWilliam, NUFC, 1903–04, 2in (5cm) high, in original case.
£260–300
$380–440 ⚒ P(NW)

A 15ct gold FA Cup winner's medal, awarded to P. McWilliam, engraved 'English Cup won by NUFCP McWilliam', 1910, 2in (5cm) high, in original case.
£5,000–6,000
$7,250–8,750 ⚒ P(NW)
Newcastle United defeated Barnsley 2–0 in a replay after the first match was tied 1–1. The replay took place five days later at Goodison Park in front of 69,000 spectators.

◀ **Charles Crombie,** *Rules of Golf,* containing 24 prints, c1918, oblong 4°, with accompanying letter.
£1,300–1,500
$2,000–2,250 ⚒ S

A leather and steel *kendo* mask, c1910, 16in (40.5cm) high.
£85–95
$125–145 ⊞ SA

A Mecca Cigarettes baseball card, Johnny Evers of the Chicago Nationals, 1911.
£100–110
$145–165 ⊞ HALL

A Press Steward badge, for the 1933 FA Cup Final, Everton v Manchester City, 3in (7.5cm) high.
£220–250
$320–360 ↗ P(NW)

A golfing playing card holder, for two packs of cards, 1940s, 5in (12.5cm) high.
£60–70
$90–100 ⊞ BEV

A set of croquet balls, in a pine box, c1920, 16in (40.5cm) long.
£55–65
$80–100 ⊞ SA

Two mahogany and brass Nottingham reels, with star-backed Slater catches, c1920, largest 3½in (9cm) diam.
£35–65
$50–100 each ⊞ SA

A stuffed and mounted Chub, by Cooper, in a bowfronted case, inscription reads 'Avon Chub, 4lbs 8oz, Caught by S. De'Courcy, Royalty Water, Christchurch 14th Nov: 1948', case 26in (66cm) wide.
£1,000–1,200
$1,500–1,800 ⊞ SA

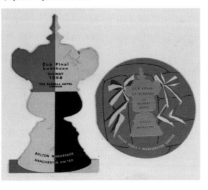

A set of Roehampton composition croquet balls, c1920, 8in (20.5cm) wide, in original box.
£55–65
$80–100 ⊞ SA

A Press Steward badge, for the 1934 FA Cup Final, Manchester City v Portsmouth, 1½in (4cm) diam.
£130–150
$200–220 ↗ P(NW)

An Amateur Cup football programme, Pegasus v Harwich & Parkeston, 1953, 9 x 6in (23 x 15cm).
£8–10
$10–15 ⊞ MRW

◀ **Two autographed luncheon menus,** for the 1957 and 1958 FA Cup Finals, Aston Villa v Manchester United and Bolton Wanderers v Manchester United, largest 10in (25.5cm) high.
£620–720
$900–1,000 ↗ P(NW)

An All England Women's Hockey Association programme, England v Belgium, 1953, 9 x 5in (23 x 12.5cm).
£8–10
$10–15 ⊞ MRW

An FA Steward's badge, for the 1963 centenary year, 2in (5cm) long.
£45–55
$60–80 ⚹ P(NW)

A signed photograph of Jean Alesi, mid-1990s, 6 x 4in (15 x 10cm).
£45–50
$65–75 ⊞ SSL

A boxing glove, signed by Jake La Motta, with a signed photographic print, 1950s, 12in (30.5cm) long.
£160–190
$225–275 ⚹ P(NW)

A Superintendent lapel badge, for the 1966 World Cup, Wembley, 1½in (4cm) square.
£220–250
$320–360 ⚹ P(NW)

▶ **A cricket bat,** signed by Sir Richard Hadlee, with details of his career record, 1987.
£300–400
$450–550 ⊞ SMW

◀ **A signed photograph of Ryan Giggs,** 1990s, 11½ x 15½in (29 x 39.5cm).
£100–110
$140–160 ⚹ SWO

An Avon plastic aftershave bottle, modelled as a golf ball, 1960s, 3in (7.5cm) high.
£20–25
$30–40 ⊞ LBe

A Heuer Trackmaster mechanical stopwatch, c1970.
£60–80
$90–120 ⊞ HARP

A Vodafone Manchester United replica shirt, signed, c2000.
£325–350
$470–500 ⊞ SSL

Three signed photographs of David Beckham, mounted and framed, c2000, 15 x 25in (38 x 63.5cm).
£200–220
$300–320 ⊞ SSL

Radios, Gramophones & Tape Recorders

▶ **Three early wireless valves,** 1922–25, 5in (12.5cm) high.
£15–25
$20–35 each ⊞ GM

A Gecophone crystal radio set, with headphones, 1923, 9in (23cm) wide.
£100–120
$150–175 ⊞ OTA
The term radio 'ham' comes from the word 'amateur'. Many enthusiasts put together their own crystal sets which, equipped with a single pair of headphones, could be listened to by only one person at a time. Britain's first sustained, regular broadcasting service was started by the Marconi station in February 1922, and consisted of only one half-hour programme every Tuesday evening. But November that year saw the launch of the British Broadcasting Service (two short news bulletins and a weather report made up the first day's programming) and soon radio became central to people's lives and living rooms.

A Cosmos Metro-Vick Radiophone, with five original valves, in original oak cabinet with retailer's plate for 'Walker & Hutton, Mechanical and Electrical Engineers, Scarboro', 1924, 17in (43cm) wide.
£900–1,100
$1,300–1,600 ⊞ OTA
When new, this Radiophone cost over £30 ($45), the equivalent of about three months' salary for an office worker in 1924.

Three Igranic coils, labelled 'What are the wild waves saying?', 1920s, 3½in (9cm) wide.
£4–5
$6–8 ⊞ GM
These coils were plug-in units used to determine the frequency range of a wireless.

A Philips 830C Bakelite and Arbolite radio, in a simulated walnut cabinet, 1932, 19in (48.5cm) high.
£400–450
$580–650 ⊞ GM

◀ **A Rolls-Caydon Rondo five-valve battery-operated portable wireless,** with moveable tuning figures within the central aperture of the main tuning knob, in a wood and cardboard cabinet, 1929, 15in (38cm) wide.
£80–100
$115–145 ⊞ GM

A Murphy B4 radio, designed by E. J. Power, in a walnut cabinet, 1932, 17in (43cm) high.
£100–120
$145–175 ⊞ OTA

An Ekco AC86 black and chrome Bakelite radio, designed by Serge Chermayeff, 1935–36, 22in (56cm) wide.
£300–350
$450–500 ⊞ OTA

▶ **A Philco 'People's Set' Model 444 radio,** 1936, 16in (40.5cm) high.
£250–300
$360–440 ⊞ OTA

A CWS Defiant Model MSH 948 radio, with motor-driven tuning and switchable tone filters, 1938, 31in (78.5cm) wide.
£180–220
$260–320 ⊞ OTA
In the 1930s, signatories of the Radio Wholesale Trading Agreement refused to supply Co-operative stores with receivers, because they saw the Co-op dividend as unfair price cutting. The Co-operative Wholesale Society defiantly organized the manufacture of its own brand of receivers, hence the name of this radio.

A Pye Model S radio, with rising sun fret motif in front of speaker, 1933, 19in (48.5cm) high.
£120–150
$175–220 ⊞ OTA
In 1929 Pye & Co adopted the classic rising sun motif on their wooden radio cabinets, inspired by a design the sales manager had seen on a colleague's cigarette case. It remained in use until 1948, when a new version of the radio was released without the usual clouds among its fretwork sun rays. The new image resembled the flag of Japan, Britain's war-time enemy. There was a public outcry and the wireless was rapidly withdrawn.

A Philco car radio, with tuner and amplifier/power pack as separate units, unrestored, 1937, 6in (15cm) wide.
£75–100
$110–145 ⊞ GM

A Colonial New World Globe Bakelite radio, American, 1934, 17in (43cm) high.
£800–900
$1,150–1,300 ⊞ GAD

A Murphy A30C console radio, designed by R. D. Russell, with 12-inch speaker mounted in acoustically treated cabinet, unrestored, 1936, 35in (89cm) high.
£80–100
$115–145 ⊞ GM

A Silvertone Bullet sprayed Bakelite radio, with push-button controls, American, 1938, 12in (30.5cm) wide.
£900–1,000
$1,300–1,500 ⊞ GAD

A Radio Acoustics Products three-valve superhet radio, in a walnut-veneered cabinet, unrestored, 1947, 21in (53.5cm) wide.
£80–100
$115–145 ⊞ GM

A GEC BC4750 three wave-band radio, with push-button wave-change, in a solid mahogany cabinet, c1947, 22in (56cm) wide.
£130–150
$190–220 ⊞ OTA

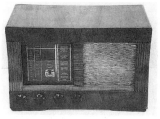

An Etronic RA640 AC mains radio, in wooden cabinet, c1948, 19in (48.5cm) wide.
£20–30
$30–45 ⊞ OTA

A Murphy 146 Baffleboard radio receiver, long and medium waves, with separate amplifier, unrestored, 1948, 33in (84cm) high.
£80–100
$115–145 ⊞ GM

An Ardente Type 309 hearing-aid booster amplifier, in dark green Bakelite cabinet, unrestored, 1950, 12in (30.5cm) wide.
£35–50
$50–75 ⊞ GM

A Bush DAC 90A AC/DC brown Bakelite radio, with two wavebands, 1950–51, 12in (30.5cm) wide.
£120–140
$175–200 ⊞ CORD
This model was also available in ivory and green Bakelite, rare.

A KB Toaster Model FB10 cream Bakelite radio, two wavebands, AC only, 1951, 10in (25.5cm) wide.
£150–180
$220–260 ⊞ CORD
This model was also available in red and green Bakelite.

A Rambler portable radio, in a carrying case, 1950s, 9in (23cm) wide.
£5–8
$8–12 ⋏ SAF

Miller's is a price GUIDE not a price LIST

◄ A Philips 353A Bakelite radio, with three wavebands including VHF, 1957, 16in (40.5cm) wide.
£70–80
$100–115 ⊞ CORD

A Bush DAC70C Bakelite and chrome table radio, with long and medium wave, unrestored, 1959, 13in (33cm) wide.
£30–40
$45–60 ⊞ GM

A Roberts RT7 transistor portable radio, with push-button wave-change and concentric volume and tone controls, cased in simulated leather finish, c1960, 11in (28cm) wide.
£40–50
$60–75 ⊞ GM

▶ **A Heathkit transistor radio,** in a brown leather case, 1970, 8in (20.5cm) high.
£15–20
$20–30 ↗ SAF

A Silvertone Model 1209 Medalist pocket transistor radio, with seven transistors, in an ice-blue and chrome-finish case, American, 1961, 7in (18cm) wide.
£25–35
$35–50 ⊞ OVE

A Sony Model TR 650 pocket transistor radio, with six transistors, in a black and silver-coloured finish, Japanese, 1963, 4in (10cm) high.
£35–55
$50–80 ⊞ OVE

A Heathkit Mohican portable communication receiver, by Daystrom, originally supplied either in kit form or ready-assembled, 1965, 12in (30.5cm) wide.
£45–60
$65–90 ⊞ GM

A Roberts RM33 mains transistor table radio, in a wooden cabinet, 1980, 12in (30.5cm) wide.
£20–30
$30–45 ⊞ GM
Many of these tiny but practical radios are still in use.

A Columbia two-minute cylinder graphophone, in a wooden case, 1906, 22in (56cm) high.
£375–425
$560–620 ⊞ CBGR

An HMV Model 1 hornless gramophone, in oak, c1920, 15in (38cm) wide.
£100–130
$145–190 ⊞ CBGR

◀ **A Peter Pan box camera-style miniature portable gramophone,** 1920s, 6in (15cm) high.
£160–180
$230–260 ⊞ CBGR

An HMV Model VI gramophone, with painted steel flower horn, c1912, 32in (81.5cm) wide.
£825–925
$1,200–1,350 ⊞ CBGR

A Columbia brown leatherette and chrome wind-up gramophone, 1920s, 17in (43cm) wide.
£30–40
$45–60 ➶ SAF

An Amplion oak flower-horn speaker, with nickel-plated base, c1924, 20in (51cm) high.
£180–200
$260–290 ⊞ OTA

◀ **An IM Pointmaster needle sharpener,** in original packaging, 1930s, 6in (15cm) wide.
£10–15
$15–20 ⊞ CBGR

▶ **A turntable speed tester,** paper, labelled for W. E. Salisbury of Marlborough, c1950, 5in (12.5cm) diam.
£1–2
$2–3 ⊞ CBGR

An HMV fibre-needle cutter, in original packaging, 1930s, 5in (12.5cm) wide.
£35–50
$50–75 ⊞ MURR

A Dansette record player, in red and cream case, in working order, 1960s, 15in (38cm) wide.
£20–25
$30–35 ➶ SAF

A Kudelski Nagra III tape deck, Swiss, 1968, 12in (30.5cm) wide.
£220–250
$320–360 ⊞ GM
This model became a world standard, and was used by many broadcasting companies.

A National portable record player and radio, with speakers integral to case lid, late 1960s, 13in (33cm) wide.
£50–60
$75–90 ⊞ PPH

Railwayana

A tin and brass railway lamp, in working order, 19thC, 15in (38cm) high.
£325–375
$470–560 ⊞ SEA

Miller's is a price GUIDE not a price LIST

A photograph of the London Transport Southern Region Royal Train locomotive, framed, c1910, 13 x 14in (33 x 35.5cm).
£55–65
$80–95 ⊞ HO

A presentation silver spanner, marking the opening of the Jagersfontein Railway, South African, marked 'Fine silver', maker's mark 'A.F&Co', 9¼in (23.5cm) long.
£120–140
$175–200 ✎ P(B)
The shaft of this spanner is inscribed on one side 'Jagersfontein' and 'Jany 31. 1905' on the other. The closed end is inscribed on one side 'Facsimilie of the Excelsior Diamond weight 971 carats found in the Jagersfontein Mine' and 'Presented to His Excellency Sir R.H.J. Goold Adam K.C.M.G.C.B. Lieut Governor O.P.C. on opening Railway Jagersfontein'.

◄ A brass locomotive shield, face polished, German, 19½in (49.5cm) high.
£1,700–1,900
$2,500–2,750 ✎ SRA
This was fitted to one of the few Orenstein & Koppel 2–8–0Ts exported to Africa between 1905 and 1907.

An LBSCR brass nameplate, 'St Catherine's Point', 1906, 57in (145cm) wide.
£13,500–16,000
$19,500–23,500 ✎ SRA
This plate was carried by the Class H1 4–4–2 LBSCR 40, built by Kitson as Works No. 4354 in February 1906. It was finally withdrawn in January 1944, the nameplates being fortunate to survive during the wartime scrap drive.

◄ A Southern Railway poster of Canterbury, in brown with red roofs and bright green trees, 1920s, 40 x 50in (101.5 x 127cm).
£2,700–3,000
$4,000–4,500
⊞ REN

► An L&SWR cast-iron sign, white with red lettering and border, 1923, 16in (40.5cm) high.
£55–65
$80–95 ✎ RAR

A CK&P cast-iron bridgeplate, painted in white with black lettering, 1864–1923, 12in (30.5cm) wide.
£320–360
$460–520 ⋗ SRA

A pair of mahogany signal box block instruments, one an SWR East Putney box Sykes lock and block from Mount Pleasant, the other a No. 4 Treadle lock and block to 'B' instrument, both with single circular enamel dials, c1920s, 13½in (34.5cm) high.
£130–160
$190–230 ⋗ P(C)

A GWR inner signal lamp, c1930, 11in (28cm) high.
£40–45
$60–65 ⊞ FST

A railway nameplate and works-plate, for Bristol, the worksplate for Peckett & Sons, 1923, nameplate 28in (71cm) wide.
£2,000–2,200
$3,000–3,200 ⋗ SRA
This set of plates was carried by a Peckett Type R2 0–4–0ST with outside cylinders that left the Works in October 1923. In December 1963 it went to the Brooklyn Engineering Company at Chandler's Ford, presumably for scrap.

A BR(M) guard's whistle and railway ashtray, the whistle with chain, the ashtray with 'Southampton Dock Centenary 1838–1938 Southern Railways' engraved around central company seal.
£25–30
$35–45 ⋗ P(C)

An LMS cast-brass nameplate crest, 'Royal Scot', 1927, 11in (28cm) diam.
£12,000–13,000
$17,500–18,850 ⋗ SRA
This plate was carried by the class 6P 4–6–0 LMS 6132 locomotive 'King's Regiment Liverpool'. Built at the North British Locomotive's Hyde Park Works as Works No. 23627 in September 1927, it was withdrawn in February 1964 to be cut up by the West of Scotland Shipbreaking Company of Troon in April 1965.

◄ **Two railway service brass badges,** one for LNER, one for LMS, 1930s, 1½in (4cm) wide.
£12–15
$18–22 each ⊞ COB

An LNER B1 cast brass nameplate, 'Springbok', 1942, face restored, 43in (109cm) wide.
£16,500–18,000
$24,000–26,000 ⋗ SRA
This plate was for the first of the class 4–6–0 loco-motives, LNER 8301, built at Darlington in December 1942. It was withdrawn from Colwick on 5 March 1962.

An LNER cast brass nameplate, 'Steady Aim', with three of its original six bolts, face restored, 1946, 58in (147.5cm) wide.
£19,000–21,000
$27,500–30,500 ↗ SRA
This plate, named for the horse that won the 1946 Oaks, was carried by the LNER Class A2/3 4–6–2 Pacific, LNER 512, built at Doncaster in 1946 as Works No. 2003, and was initially in service at Gateshead. It was withdrawn on 19 June 1965.

A Great Northern Railway of Ireland Class U engraved brass nameplate, 'Louth', 1948, 15in (38cm) wide.
£3,000–3,500
$4,400–5,000 ↗ SRA
This plate was carried by the Great Northern Railway of Ireland Class U 5ft 3in gauge 4–4–0 No. 202, built by Beyer Peacock as Works No. 7245 in January 1948. It became UTA No. 67 in 1958 and was withdrawn in May 1965.

A railway ticket-stamping machine, by Waterlow & Sons, London, 1950, 10in (25.5cm) high.
£85–95
$125–140 ⊞ FST

BRITAIN'S FIRST ALL-ELECTRIC MAIN LINE

A Vic Welch BR colour poster, publicizing the electrification of the Manchester–Sheffield line, c1955, 39¾ x 49½in (101 x 126cm).
£300–350
$440–500 ↗ Bea(E)
Vic Welch worked in the BR (LMR) design department.

▶ An LMS Tyer's signal box, two-needle absolute with F-type block, complete with bell-plunger and rotary commutator, side meshes and Tyer's transfer, in wooden housing, late 1940s, 18in (45.5cm) high.
£220–250
$320–360 ↗ SRA

A BR enamel station sign, 'Trent Station', red with white lettering, 1960s, 160in (406.5cm) wide.
£300–350
$440–500 ⊞ TRA

▶ A BR alloy works plate, grey letters on a blue ground, face restored, 1965, 8½in (21.5cm) wide.
£50–80
$75–115 ⊞ SOL

BRITISH RAILWAYS
DONCASTER
1965
ELECTRICAL EQUIPMENT BY ASSOCIATED ELECTRICAL INDUSTRIES & THE ENGLISH ELECTRIC CO.LTD.

BALHAM

◀ A London Underground red, white and blue enamel station sign, 'Balham', 1970s, 28in (71cm) wide.
£55–65
$80–95 ⊞ COB

Rock & Pop

A charcoal sketch of George Harrison, by Stuart Sutcliffe, the 'fifth Beatle', c1959, 14½ x 11¼in (37 x 28.5cm).
£1,300–1,500
$1,900–2,150 ⊞ IQ

Stuart Sutcliffe, a hand-written letter from Hamburg, on six sides, with original envelope, c1960.
£800–900
$1,150–1,300 ↗ FO
This extremely candid letter, written over several days and addressed to 'Dear Susan', an ex-girlfriend, tellingly expresses Sutcliffe's artistic frustrations.

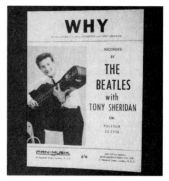

A Beatles song sheet, for 'Why', written by Bill Crompton and Tony Sheridan, published by Pan-Musik of Denmark Street, London, 1960s, 10 x 8in (25.5 x 20.5cm).
£20–25
$30–35 ↗ SAF

◄ **George Harrison,** a black and white photograph signed 'George Harrison x x', and inscribed on the reverse, in a different hand 'George Harrison, Maclatts [sic] lane, Woolton, 25', c1963, 5½ x 3½in (14 x 9cm).
£200–240
$300–350 ↗ FO
Mackets Lane was George Harrison's home address.

Two torn Beatles tickets, for a concert at Birkenhead, 10 February 1962.
£600–700
$870–1,000 ↗ FO

▶ **The Beatles,** a black and white photograph taken during a recording of their performance in the *Morecambe and Wise Show*, on Monday 2nd December 1963, 72 x 36in (183 x 91.5cm).
£160–200
$230–300 ↗ FO

Miller's is a price GUIDE not a price LIST

A black and white Beatles beach hat, American, 1964, 12in (30.5cm) wide.
£30–40
$45–60 ✗ SAF

A Beatles yellow plastic wallet, by Standard Plastic Products, with sepia images of the Beatles, American, 1964, 4½in (11cm) wide.
£60–70
$90–100 ✗ SAF

A copy of 'The Beatles Christmas Album' LP, issued for the US market, 1963.
£80–100
$115–145 ✗ SAF

A Beatles concert programme, for Brighton Hippodrome, Sunday 12 July 1964, with notes by original owner on the performance and the audience, 10 x 8in (25.5 x 20.5cm).
£150–180
$220–260 ✗ FO

◄ **A Beatles white three-ring binder,** with sepia images of the Beatles and facsimile signatures, American, 1964, 11¾in (30cm) high.
£50–60
$75–90 ✗ SAF

► **A Beatles pottery bowl,** by Washington Pottery, with images of the Beatles and facsimile signatures, American, 1964, 6in (15cm) diam.
£20–25
$30–35 ⊞ BTC

A set of four Beatles plastic dolls, with twisting heads, 1960, 4in (10cm) high.
£10–15
$15–20 ✗ SAF

► **A Beatles Burrite mug and plastic cup,** American, 1960s, mug 6in (15cm) high.
£10–15
$15–20 ✗ SAF

A Beatles calendar, by Beat Publications, complete, one page loose, 1964, 11 x 9in (28 x 23cm).
£30–40
$45–60 ✷ SAF

Two Beatles tickets, for Another Beatles Christmas Show, one ticket over-stamped 'Guest', Thursday 7th January 1965, 2½in (6.5cm) square.
£120–140
$175–200 ✷ FO

A set of four Beatles badges, 1965, 1¼in (3cm) diam.
£8–12
$12–18 ✷ SAF

A shop display stand-up cardboard cut-out of Paul McCartney, with a Rome concert poster, 1989, 33in (84cm) high.
£10–15
$15–20 ✷ SAF

▶ A signed concert programme for Paul McCartney's Liverpool Oratorio, 1990.
£100–120
$145–175 ▦ BTC

A Beatles cream record-carrying case, with individual and group images and facsimile signatures, Dutch, 1960s, 8½in (21.5cm) high.
£80–100
$115–145 ✷ SAF

Items in the Rock & Pop section have been arranged in alphabetical order.

▶ A Beatles Help! film poster, some damage, 1965, 30 x 40in (76 x 101.5cm).
£120–140
$175–200 ✷ CBP

A Beatles blue vinyl brunch bag, American, 1965, 8in (20.5cm) high.
£320–380
$470–570 ✷ SAF
It is unusual to find this item in such good condition.

A Beatles Yellow Submarine film poster, Le Sous-marin Jaune, with images of the Beatles and other characters from the film, Belgian, 1968, 21 x 13in (53.5 x 33cm).
£100–120
$145–175 ✷ Bon(C)

A 'Blues Fell This Morning' LP, released by Philips, including rare recordings of Southern blues singers, 1960.
£50–60
$75–90 ⊞ TOT

Buyers' tips

When purchasing vintage records, condition is crucial to value. Always buy the best you can afford.

If a single has lost its original centre (often taken out for jukebox play), its value can be halved. With EPs and LPs, sleeves are crucial to value and, like the record itself, should be in good condition. With singles (with the exception of a rare label or picture sleeve) it is less important. Original singles sleeves can be bought for £0.50p–5 ($0.75–8), and companies also produce reissued sleeves.

While with less successful bands there is likely to be little difference in value between a demo and a first-issue record, with big name artists the demo, or promotional record, is likely to be worth more.

There are many different factors that make a record collectable. Learn as much as you can before buying and do not collect what is in vogue. It is cheaper to buy when an artist is not currently fashionable.

A copy of the 'Catch A Wave' 10in LP double album, including tracks by Blondie, Motorhead and Ultravox, very good condition, 1978.
£15–20
$20–30 ⊞ TOT

A 'Kings of the Blues' 10in LP, issued by RCA as Volume 3 in their 'Backgrounds of Jazz' series, excellent condition, American, 1961.
£40–45
$60–65 ⊞ TOT

A Marc Bolan vinyl picture disc collection, featuring interviews in America, 1972, 7 x 4in (18 x 10cm).
£20–25
$30–35 ⚒ SAF

A Grateful Dead white metal buckle, modelled as a skull, in box signed by Jerry Garcia, 1988, buckle 3in (7.5cm) high.
£180–220
$260–320 ⚒ FO

The Corrs, a signed colour photograph, signed first names only, c2000, 10 x 8in (25.5 x 20.5cm).
£120–140
$175–200 ⚒ VS

An Embrace promotional CD, 'Drawn from Memory', in moulded gilt tin, 2000, 5in (12.5cm) diam.
£12–15
$18–20 ⊞ TOT

Cross Reference
See Colour Review (page 246)

A copy of the first Jimi Hendrix single, 'Hey Joe!', signed by Noel Redding, inscribed 'Best Wishes to Tony', issued by Polydor, 1966.
£80–100
$115–145 🔨 Bon

Jimi Hendrix's lucky silver dollar, dated 1889, 1½in (4cm) diam.
£1,600–1,900
$2,300–2,750 🔨 Bon
In 1966, Jimi Hendrix was stranded without any money when he missed the bus to a gig. Thereafter, he always carried a silver dollar, usually in his shoe, but sometimes in his hat-band. This coin was the one he carried from late 1966 through to the early 1970s.

A Jimi Hendrix cardboard coat hanger, by Saunders Enterprises, with a cut-out slot to hang a pair of trousers, 1967, 17in (43cm) high.
£100–120
$145–175 🔨 Bon

A black and white photograph of Buddy Holly, by Lew Allen, at the Auditorium Theater, Rochester, New York, limited edition, signed and titled by Allen, sold without copyright, 19 January 1958, 11 x 14in (28 x 35.5cm).
£220–250
$320–360 🔨 FO
Lew Allen was the only photographer to document this event.

A copy of the 'Elmore James memorial album' 12in LP, issued by Sue Records, 1965.
£40–50
$60–75 ⊞ TOT

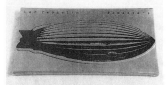

An Elton John silkscreen concert poster, for a concert arranged by Entecom, with Noir as a supporting act, purple and black on a white ground, January 1971, 30 x 20in (76 x 51cm).
£180–220
$260–320 🔨 FO
Entecom was the Entertainment Committee of Southampton University Students Union, and concerts were held in the Old Union Refectory. These posters were produced by the Southampton University Students Union, and designed by John Liverton, then Publicity Officer.

A Led Zeppelin 'Remasters' promotional CD, four tracks, boxed, American, 1990.
£25–30
$35–45 ⊞ TOT

A Manic Street Preachers concert ticket, for a concert at Bournemouth Academy, signed and inscribed, together with a colour photograph taken by the drummer, Sean Moore, 19 October 1992, ticket 2¾ x 3½in (7 x 9cm).
£25–35
$35–50 🔨 Bon(C)

◄ **A Bank of England one pound note signed by Annie Lennox,** 1990s, 2½ x 5½in (6.5 x 13.5cm).
£60–80
$90–115 🔨 Bon

A black leather biker jacket, by T/T Leathers, worn by Freddie Mercury on the promo for 'Crazy Little Thing Called Love' in 1979, and the 'Crazy' European Tour in 1980, with an image of Mercury wearing a similar jacket on stage.
£1,000–1,200
$1,500–1,750 ⚒ FO
This jacket was originally purchased at a Queen Fan Club convention. Many years later the new owner met Mercury in Greece and jokingly asked if he would like to buy the jacket back, to which the response was 'I never buy anything second-hand, my dear!'

A copy of 'Negativeland' 12in LP, issued by Seeland Records, American, 1980.
£40–50
$60–75 ⊞ TOT

An Oasis singles collection '(What's the Story) Morning Glory', in a gold cigarette pack box with black and green lettering, early 1990s, 6in (15cm) high.
£20–25
$30–35 ⚒ SAF

Cross Reference
See Colour Review
(page 246–248)

◄ **An Oasis one-sided 'I am the Walrus' 12in promotional single,** limited edition of 250, mint condition, 1994.
£250–350
$360–500 ⊞ TOT

An Ozzy Osbourne 'Blizzard of Oz' flightcase and Marshall bass amp, the flightcase with white stencilled lettering, containing a Marshall JCM 800 Bass Series amplifier, 1980s, flightcase 58in (147.5cm) wide.
£250–300
$360–440 ⚒ Bon(C)

► **An Elvis Presley lady's handbag mirror,** with facsimile inscription, surrounded by a pale green rim, c1957, 3in (7.5cm) diam.
£40–50
$60–75 ⊞ MURR

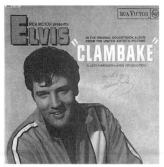

A signed Elvis Presley mono album, from the soundtrack of the film *Clambake*, issued by RCA Victor, inscribed and signed in black ballpoint on the front cover 'My best to you Elvis Presley' 1968.
£400–450
$580–650 ➤ FO

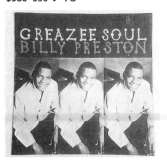

A Billy Preston 'Greazee Soul' 12in mono LP, mint condition, 1969.
£18–22
$27–33 ⊞ TOT

A Cliff Richard concert flyer and booking form, for a gig at City Hall, Sheffield on 14 April 1964, printed in red and yellow, mounted and framed, 11½ x 5½in (29 x 14cm).
£25–35
$35–50 ⊞ BTC

A Las Vegas postcard signed by Elvis Presley, with inscription in red fibre pen 'To Charline, Elvis Presley August 70' on the reverse, 3½ x 11in (9 x 28cm).
£250–300
$360–440 ➤ Bon(C)

A white silk shirt worn by Prince, during his 'Lovesexy' tour and in the tour programme photographs, together with a copy of the programme, 1988.
£400–500
$580–720 ➤ FO

A photograph of the Rolling Stones, taken by the River Thames, signed by Mick Jagger, Brian Jones, Keith Richards, Bill Wyman and Charlie Watts, 1960s, 10 x 8in (25.5 x 20.5cm).
£420–500
$600–720 ➤ VS

An Elvis Presley memorial plate, the rim with blue lettering, red and yellow star motifs and a gilt edge, 1978, 10in (25.5cm) diam.
£15–20
$20–30 ➤ SAF

A black and white promotional photograph of R.E.M., with Michael Stipe's initials and Pete Buck's and Mike Mills' signatures, and 'Hi – Bill Berry' in blue marker, framed and glazed, 1990s, 16 x 14in (40.5 x 35.5cm).
£120–140
$175–200 ➤ FO

A Rolling Stones stereo 12in LP with 3-D cover, 'Their Satanic Majesties Request', issued by Decca, 1967.
£70–80
$100–115 ⊞ TOT

A Sex Pistols 'Holidays in the Sun' poster, promoting the LP issued by Virgin Records, 1977, 28in (71cm) square.
£250–300
$360–440 ⊞ IQ

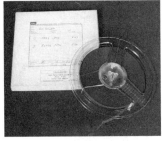

A Rod Stewart recording tape, recorded at the Abbey Road studio, featuring 'Baby Jane' and 'Ready Now', 1983, in original box, 7in (18cm) square.
£20–25
$30–35 ⤻ SAF

A Wurlitzer 1800 jukebox, holds 52 records, in perfect working order, 1956, 56in (142cm) high.
£4,750–5,250
$7,000–7,500 ⊞ MARK

A Sex Pistols 'Pretty Vacant' promotional poster, 1978, 28 x 39in (71 x 99cm).
£350–400
$500–580 ⊞ IQ

Seven Throbbing Gristle cassettes, recorded at live concerts, issued by Industrial Records, 1976–81.
£10–15
$15–20 each ⊞ MVX

A cream plastic part scratch plate signed by Frank Zappa, with a doodle of a man smoking, 7in (18cm) wide.
£120–140
$175–200 ⤻ FO

A Rock-Ola 120 Hi-Fi jukebox, holds 120 records, 1957, 54in (137cm) high.
£2,500–3,000
$3,600–4,400 ⤻ GAZE

A signed colour photograph of Britney Spears, c2000, 10 x 8in (25.5 x 20.5cm).
£60–70
$90–100 ⤻ VS

A 'Velvet Underground & Nico' 12in LP, issued by Verve, the sleeve with original peel-off banana, 1960.
£60–70
$90–100 ⤻ SAF

A Rock-Ola 744 jukebox, holds 100 records, in working order, with keys and records, 1970s, 45in (114.5cm) high.
£400–500
$580–720 ⤻ SAF

Scent Bottles

A Webb cameo glass scent bottle, red glass with fuchsia design in white, and 'Remember the giver' engraved on the silver collar, 1883, 2½in (6.5cm) high.
£600–800
$870–1,150 ⊞ ALiN

A Webb cameo glass scent bottle, dark green glass with poppy and butterfly design in white, marked 'Stakenasa', 1885, 3¼in (8.5cm) high.
£700–900
$1,000–1,300 ⊞ ALiN

A silver-mounted cut-glass scent bottle, Birmingham 1906, 5in (12.5cm) high.
£100–150
$145–220 ⊞ CoHA

A clear and frosted glass scent bottle, decorated with a silhouette of a dancing female nude below a border of roses, with copper mount and stand, c1920, 8in (20.5cm) high.
£55–65
$80–95 ⊞ TWAC

A Blue Lagoon talcum powder bottle, by Dubarry, with Art Deco-style blue frosted glass, original labels, c1930, 6in (15cm) high.
£16–18
£24–27 ⊞ HUX

An Art Nouveau perfume bottle, decorated with moulded flowers, stained black, with matching stopper, French, 5½in (14cm) high.
£300–350
$440–500 ⊞ LBe

▶ **A Joy de Jean Patou plastic display bottle,** black with gold lettering and neck string, red domed top, French, 1950s, 7in (18cm) high.
£85–95
$125–140 ⊞ LBe

An Adorée perfume bottle, by E. Roy, with a frosted glass stopper in the form of a kneeling female nude, French, 1930s, 4in (10cm) high, with original box.
£300–350
$440–500 ⊞ LBe

A Potter & Moore's Mitcham Lavender green glass bottle, with screw top, 1935, 5½in (14cm) high.
£14–17
$21–25 ⊞ HUX

An Elizabeth Arden gift set, each clear glass bottle with a brass top and set with a coloured stone, in a grey pouch and original box, 1950s, 3in (7.5cm) high.
£85–95
$125–140 ⊞ LBe

Science & Technology

A bronze sundial, by Benjamin Scott, the engraved compass, months and hours dissected with indicators to London, Constantinople, Babylon and other place names and a coat-of-arms, 18thC, base 15½in (39.5cm) diam.
£700–800
$1,000–1,200 ➤ EH

A lacquered-brass micrometer, with bevelled glass, for measuring paper, c1850–60, 2½in (6.5cm) diam.
£80–100
$115–145 ⊞ TOM

A brass sextant, by W. F. Cannon, London, in a mahogany case, 19thC, 9¾in (25cm) wide.
£320–370
$450–550 ➤ TRM

▶ **An engine-turned ivory thermometer,** with original glass dome, c1860, 10in (25.5cm) high.
£400–450
$550–650 ⊞ RAY

An Excise Office boxwood and brass barrel dipping rule, by Loftus, London, in five sections, c1870, 50in (127cm) long extended, in original leather case.
£70–80
$100–120 ⊞ TOM

A Victorian dip circle, in a mahogany case, 11in (28cm) high.
£450–500
$650–720 ⊞ ETO
A magnetic needle, mounted in a vertical graduated circle, indicates by its dip the direction of the earth's magnetism and measures the amount of the dip.

▶ **A lacquered-brass carbon arc lamp,** by F. J. Cox, London, on a mahogany base, c1870, 16in (40.5cm) high.
£250–300
$360–440 ⊞ TOM

A hydrometer, by Brown & Brothers, Edinburgh, c1890, 11in (28cm) long, in a wooden case.
£38–42
$50–60 ⊞ FST
This instrument was used to determine the gravity of liquids.

A surveyor's cross, by H. Morin, with original lacquer, c1890, 10in (25.5cm) long, in original wooden box.
£340–380
$500–550 ⊞ ETO

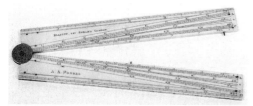

An ivory sector, by Elliot, London, c1900, 6in (15cm) long.
£20–30
$30–45 ⊞ TOM

Two brass three-draw telescopes,
top. c1890–1910, 19in (48.5cm) extended.
£35–45
$50–60
bottom. c1890–1910, 24in (61cm) extended.
£65–75
$90–110 ⊞ HEG

A boxwood cavalry map/paper holder, the reverse with protractor and compass, 1909, 10in (25.5cm) high.
£100–120
$145–175 ⊞ FST

▶ **A brass monocular microscope,** in a fitted mahogany case with accessories, the bronze triform base inscribed 'H.P. Aylward, 164 Oxford Rd., Manchester', c1900, 14in 35.5cm high.
£200–250
$300–350 ↗ WW

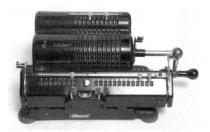

A Schubert calculator, c1920, 11in (28cm) wide.
£200–230
$300–330 ⊞ ETO

▶ **A Lietl binocular microscope,** 1920–30, 14in (35.5cm) high, in a mahogany box with lenses.
£225–250
$320–360 ⊞ HEG

A brass inclinometer, c1910, 4in (10cm) high, in a leather case.
£65–75
$95–115 ⊞ FST
This instrument was used for measuring the intensity of the earth's magnetic force, as shown by the inclination of the magnetic needle.

A compass in a watch case, with chain, 1920.
£35–40
$50–60 ⊞ HO

A specific gravity thermometer, with full set of weights and ivory-mounted scale, 1920s, 7in (18cm) high, in a wooden box.
£55–65
$80–100 ⊞ FST

A wimshorst machine, c1920, 12in (30.5cm) high.
£340–380
$500–550 ⊞ ETO

A Philips terrestrial globe, c1950, 19in (48.5cm) high.
£240–270
$350–400 ⊞ ETO

A Bakelite and brass desk fan, 1940s, 9in (23cm) high.
£55–65
$80–100 ⊞ SPT

A Fowler's long scale chrome slide rule, 1950s, 5in (12.5cm) diam, in leather case.
£40–50
$60–75 ⊞ TOM

▶ **A British Aluminium Co cased advertising barometer,** 1950s, 6in (15cm) diam.
£30–35
$40–50 ⊞ RTW

A Sinclair ZX Spectrum, 128K, with printer and two microdrives, c1980, 12in (30.5cm) wide.
£80–100
$115–145 ⊞ CGX

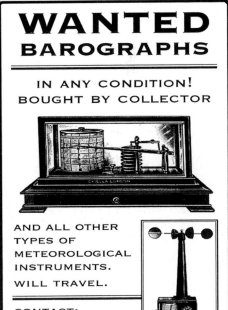

Medical Instruments

A set of ivory-handled scalpels, and twin-bladed tortoiseshell bistoury, c1830, 7in (18cm) long, in a mahogany case.
£225–245
$330–360 ⊞ WAC

An amputation set, by Coxeter, London, including saws, scalpels and hammer, 19thC, 11in (28cm) wide, in a brass-bound mahogany box.
£370–450
$550–650 ⋏ RBB

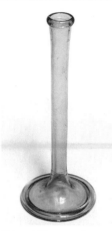

A hand-blown yellow glass stethoscope, c1840, 10in (25.5cm) high.
£165–185
$250–280 ⊞ HO

A pair of cobalt-blue glass chemist's rounds, with red, black and gold-painted labels, 1850–60, 8½in (21.5cm) high.
£170–200
$250–300 ⋏ BBR

▶ **A brass enema set,** by Arnold & Sons, London, c1880, 52in (132cm) long, in a fitted case.
£250–275
$350–400
⊞ FST

◀ **A silver-plated brass ear trumpet,** with all-over leaf engraving, inscribed 'F.C. Rein & Son, Patentees, sole inventors and only makers, 108 Strand, London', 19thC.
£550–600
$800–880 ⋏ RBB

A Zeiss haemacytometer set, early 20thC, in a fitted box, 10in (25.5cm) wide.
£400–450
$580–650 ⊞ ETO
This apparatus was used for counting red and white blood cells.

A nurse's pulse-taking half-minute sand timer, 1910, 4in (10cm) long.
£20–25
$30–40 ⊞ HO

A Cressoline Vapo-Cresolena vaporizer inhaler, early 20thC, 7in (18cm) high.
£40–50
$60–75 ⊞ FST

Further reading

Miller's Collecting Science & Technology, Miller's Publications, 2001

◀ **A manometer,** c1925, 12in (30.5cm) high, in a wooden case.
£125–145
$180–200 ⊞ FST
This apparatus was used to test lung pressure.

Scripophily

An Indiana Coal and Railway Company $500 bond, printed in black and white, green seal, denomination underprint, coupons attached, 1881.
£30–35
$40–50 ⊞ SCR

A Tesoreria Nacional de Puerto Rico 25 pesos bond, authorized by the Provincial Junta, with a vignette of a coat-of-arms, 1813.
£100–120
$145–175 🔧 P

A Geat Republic Gold & Silver Mining Co £50 bond, printed with vignettes of Lincoln, Queen Victoria, mining stamps, eagle and the White House, 1867.
£130–150
$200–220 🔧 P

▶ **A Dock Sud de la Capital 100 pesos certificate,** printed in black with a vignette of a mythical female overlooking ships and a harbour, within a red border, Buenos Aires, 1889.
£55–65
$80–95 ⊞ GKR

A New York Central and Hudson River Railroad Company $1,000 bond, printed in orange and black with a vignette of a speeding loco passing ships in harbour, 1898.
£15–18
$20–25 ⊞ SCR

Miller's is a price GUIDE not a price LIST

A Chemins de fer Ethiopiens bearer share, depicting the king on horseback with camels and followers waiting for a train to pass, printed in brown on a cream ground, Paris, 1899.
£200–225
$300–330 ⊞ SCR

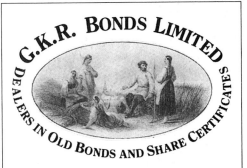

◀ **A Sir James Laing & Sons £10 preference share,** depicting a wooden-hulled ship, printed in pink on a cream ground, 1899.
£60–70
$90–100 ⊞ GKR

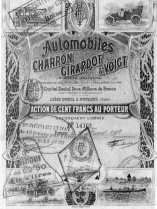

A Canadian Mortgage Association bearer share, with vignettes of farming and city scenes, printed in brown, blue and beige, 1910.
£40–45
$60–70 ⊞ SCR

A Banco de Cartagena bond, depicting part of a Velazquez painting, printed in brown on a white ground, red revenue stamp, c1900.
£30–35
$40–50 ⊞ SCR

An Automobiles Charron Girardot & Voigt 100 franc share certificate, with vignettes of cars and a flying machine, printed in green and yellow, 1902.
£85–95
$125–145 ⊞ SCR

◄ **A Paris-France 500 franc bond,** with a vignette of five ladies by 'Mucha 98', four small hole cancellations, printed in brown on a buff ground, 1927.
£250–300
$350–450 ⊁ P

▶ **A Republic of China Secured Sinking Fund $1,000 bond,** issued by J. P. Morgan, New York, countersigned by the Bank of China, 1937.
£600–650
$870–950 ⊁ P

A Brazil Railway Company $100 share, with a vignette of a train on an iron bridge in a jungle, uncancelled, printed in black and pink on a cream ground, 1911.
£850–950
$1,250–1,350 ⊁ P

An A La Reine d'Angle-terre share certificate, with a vignette of Queen Victoria during a visit to France in the 1840s, printed in pink and turquoise on a cream ground, 1924.
£30–40
$45–60 ⊞ GKR

▶ **An Electricas Reunidas de Zaragoza SA bearer share,** depicting a government building and a map of the area serviced by the company, printed in brown and black, 1968.
£16–18
$22–28 ⊞ SCR

◄ **A Casino des Fleurs de Beaulieu 500 franc share,** with a vignette of a casino overlooking the sea at Nice, with coupons, printed in pink and blue, dated 1929.
£30–35
$45–50 ⊞ GKR

Sewing

A cherrywood, maple and oak tri-leg yarn winder, with square wheel, 1780–1800, 42¾in (108.5cm) high.
£135–155
$200–225 ⊞ EON

A Victorian lady's papier mâché workbox, by Jennens & Bettridge, the black ground decorated with polychrome and gilt with floral arabesques inlaid with mother-of-pearl, the silk-lined interior fitted with small boxes, instruments and mother-of-pearl reels, impressed 'Jennens & Bettridge makers to the Queen', 12in (30.5cm) wide.
£450–500
$650–720 ⚒ HYD

A pair of polished steel scissors, by C. A. Arnold, London, 19thC, 5½in (14cm) long.
£16–18
$22–28 ⊞ WAC

Four mother-of-pearl thread winders, c1850, largest 1¾in (4.5cm) diam.
£20–40
$30–60 each ⊞ VB

◄ **A Continental lace-maker's glass lamp,** 6in (15cm) high.
£145–165
$200–250 ⊞ DHA

A Tunbridge ware pin cushion, c1870, 1in (2.5cm) high.
£80–90
$115–125 ⊞ AMH

A green-painted pine sewing box, the revolving thread holder above a box with a drawer, decorated with a black wavy line, American, 19thC, 6½in (16.5cm) high.
£430–480
$630–700 ⚒ SK(B)

A Mauchline ware needle holder, 1870, 8in (20.5cm) long.
£50–60
$75–90 ⊞ MB

A miniature pair of scissors, from an étui, 19thC, 2in (5cm) long.
£70–80
$100–125 ⊞ HO

A carved ivory sewing clamp, c1880, 5in (12.5cm) long.
£65–85
$100–125 ⊞ VB

A mother-of-pearl and abalone silver thimble case, c1880, 1½in (4cm) long.
£60–70
$90–100 ⊞ VB

A Bradbury & Co treadle sewing machine, for leather boots and shoes, with cast-iron frame and wooden table, c1884, 39in (99cm) high.
£600–640
$870–950 ⊞ WSM

A tape measure, in the shape of an iron, c1890. 2in (5cm) long.
£75–85
$110–125 ⊞ VB

A Celluloid tape measure, in the form of a Lifeboat man, c1900, 2¼in (5.5cm) high.
£90–100
$130–150 ⊞ VB

A tape measure, in the shape of a Highland terrier, c1900, 2in (5cm) high.
£80–100
$115–145 ⊞ VB

A silver thimble, Birmingham 1905, 1in (2.5cm) high.
£25–35
$30–50 ⊞ CoHA

Cross Reference
See Colour Review (page 313)

◄ A Singer 99K sewing machine, with a laminated wood carrying case, 1937, 19in (48.5cm) high.
£75–85
$110–125 ⊞ WSM

A tape measure, in the form of Edward, Prince of Wales, 1920s, 2¼in (5.5cm) high.
£85–95
$125–145 ⊞ VB

Shipping

A set of four handle plates, commemorating the Battle of Trafalgar, each depicting a tomb with a plaque inscribed 'Sacred to Nelson', beneath an anchor and 'Trafalgar', among war trophies, within a Greek key pattern border, handles missing, 1805, 3¼in (8.5cm) wide.
£445–485
$650–700 ⊞ TML

A Sherwood's ship's binnacle lamp, c1870, 11in (28cm) high.
£90–110
$130–160 ⊞ FST

Two cabinet cards, depicting *The Gypsy* shipwreck on the Avon estuary with *Sea King* rescue tug, c1880, 6½ x 4½in (16.5 x 11.5cm).
£20–25
$30–40 each ⊞ J&S

A diorama of a three-masted ship, in a glazed and ebonized case, c1900, 33in (84cm) wide.
£600–700
$870–1,000 🔨 GH

◄ **A Royal Navy mess bucket,** with brass label, c1900, 16in (40.5cm) high.
£40–45
$60–65 ⊞ B&R

A brass ship's bell, inscribed *Fragrant, 1908*, 10in (25.5cm) high.
£300–350
$450–500 ⊞ COB

Sheet music for 'The Ship that will Never Return', by F. V. St Clair, dedicated to the *Titanic* Relief Fund, c1912–13, framed and glazed.
£50–60
$70–90 ⋟ CDC

▶ A watercolour of the *Empress of Ireland,* blue, black, red and cream, in a seashell frame, 1914, 6½in (16.5cm) diam.
£50–60
$70–90 ⊞ RUSS

◀ An RRS *Discovery II* wooden ship's register, displaying a list of 17 ship's officers and crew with 'aboard' and 'ashore' slots, 1929, 17¼in (43.5cm) high.
£850–950
$1,250–1,350 ⊞ TML
The Royal Research Ship *Discovery II* was launched for the Antarctic from St Katharine's Dock in December 1929.

A US Navy theodolite, by W. & L. E. Gurley, Troy, American, 1918, 15in (38cm) high.
£450–500
$650–720 ⊞ BoC

A Royal Navy ship's brass clock, 1929, 8in (20.5cm) diam.
£800–900
$1,200–1,300 ⊞ BoC

▶ A White Star Line silver-plated napkin ring, by Elkington, c1920, 2in (5cm) diam.
£25–30
$30–40 ⊞ CRN

A French Line silver and brass plaque, 1926, 8in (20.5cm) high.
£200–230
$300–330 ⊞ COB

A bronze ship's propeller, by Buntons, Sudbury, 1920s, 14in (35.5cm) diam.
£125–150
$180–220 ⊞ OLA

▶ A model of a sailing dinghy, carved from a single piece of cedar wood, 1930, 8in (20.5cm) long.
£180–200
$250–300 ⊞ BoC

A set of eight Art Deco greetings cards, depicting life on board the great liners, printed in colour, c1920, 8½ x 6in (20.5 x 15cm).
£8–10
$12–15 ⊞ MAP

◀ **A German African Lines timetable**, 1935, 8 x 6in (20.5 x 15cm).
£9–12
$14–18 ⊞ J&S

Cross Reference
See Colour Review (page 315)

A hand-built model boat, *Deglet Nour*, with diagonal planking and water-cooled diesel engine, painted cream and blue, 1940s, 36in (91.5cm) long.
£1,200–1,400
$1,800–2,000 ⊞ BoC

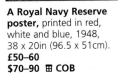

A Royal Navy Reserve poster, printed in red, white and blue, 1948, 38 x 20in (96.5 x 51cm).
£50–60
$70–90 ⊞ COB

An HM Yacht *Britannia* **embroidered blazer badge**, gold, red, green and blue on a black ground, 1990s, 4in (10cm) wide.
£10–15
$15–20 ⊞ COB

Four full colour *QEII* **first day postal covers**, 1969–82, 4 x 7in (10 x 18cm).
£10–15
$15–20 each ⊞ COB

Silver & Metalware
Silver

A Victorian silver and ivory travelling apple corer, Birmingham 1857, 5in (12.5cm) long.
£330–360
$450–500 ⊞ CoHA

▶ **A pair of Victorian silver and steel boot pulls,** by A. L. & S. and M. C., with foxes on the handles, 8in (20.5cm) long.
£600–650
$870–950 ⊞ BEX
These silver pulls were used for riding boots.

A Victorian engraved silver tankard, Exeter 1860, 4in (10cm) high.
£120–150
$175–225 ⚒ SWO

A Victorian silver vinaigrette, by Samson Mordan & Co, in the shape of a hunting horn, London 1889, 4in (10cm) long.
£370–420
$550–630 ⚒ P(L)

A silver three-piece tea service, on four compressed ball feet, teapot Birmingham 1897, cream jug and sugar basin Birmingham 1898, 40oz.
£320–360
$480–550 ⚒ CDC

An engraved silver jam spoon, Sheffield 1895, 5in (12.5cm) long.
£20–25
$30–35 ⊞ HO

A silver pepper pot, 1882, 4in (10cm) high.
£50–55
$70–80 ⊞ HO

Items in the Silver & Metalware section have been arranged in date order within each sub-section.

◀ **A silver box,** embossed with leaf scrolls, the domed lid with gadrooned edge, by W. N., Sheffield 1897, 4in (10cm) long.
£110–130
$150–200 ⚒ GAK

A pair of silver nut dishes, in the shape of leaves, with foliate-pierced and applied edges and cast pierced feet, by G. H., London 1899, 8in (20.5cm) wide, 15oz.
£200–250
$300–350 ⚒ GAK

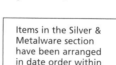

A pair of pierced silver salts, with blue glass liners, Birmingham 1904, 2in (5cm) high.
£200–230
$300–330 ⊞ CoHA

A silver miniature pepper pot, set with red and black Scottish stones, Birmingham 1904, 2in (5cm) high.
£120–150
$175–225 ⊞ HCA

A card marker, with silver base, used for bridge, 1909, 2½in (6.5cm) high.
£140–160
$200–230 ⊞ HCA

A silver miniature pincushion, in the shape of a polar bear, 1909, 1½in (4cm) long.
£700–800
$1,000–1,200 ⊞ HCA

A set of four silver menu holders, by Mappin & Webb, depicting game birds, a gentleman with a shotgun and a gundog, Birmingham 1912–13, 1½in (4cm) high.
£700–775
$1,000–1,200 ⊞ HCA

Further reading

Miller's Silver & Plate Buyer's Guide,
Miller's Publications, 2001

◀ **A silver condiment set,** with blue glass liners, Chester 1930, pepper pot 3½in (9cm) high.
£280–330
$400–475 ⊞ HCA

A five-bar silver toast rack, Birmingham 1943, 4in (10cm) high.
£70–80
$100–120 ⊞ ASAA

A hand-beaten silver sugar bowl, cream jug and spoon, Birmingham 1968, spoon 4in (10cm) long.
£400–450
$580–650 ⊞ CoHA

A prototype textured silver pepper mill, by Stuart Devlin, with a central polished band between two chased textured bands, base stamped 'London 1975', 8in (20.5cm) high.
£500–600
$700–850 ⚒ P(Ba)

Silver Plate

A William IV Old Sheffield plate silver teapot, with a bone handle, c1830, 11in (28cm) long.
£180–220
$250–330 ⊞ ASAA

Miller's is a price GUIDE not a price LIST

A Victorian silver-plated three-bar toast rack, by Elkington & Co, 4in (10cm) high.
£100–120
$145–175 ⊞ CoHA

A silver-plated bread fork, with a mother-of-pearl handle, c1910, 6in (15cm) long.
£18–20
$25–30 ⊞ HO

A set of engraved silver-plated teaspoons, with sugar tongs, c1920, in original box, 14in (35.5cm) wide.
£35–40
$50–60 ⊞ HO

Metalware

A brass and iron skimmer, c1770, 24in (61cm) long.
£200–225
$290–330 ⊞ SEA

A pewter salt, c1800, 4in (10cm) diam.
£50–55
$70–80 ⊞ HO

A painted metal tray, decorated with a mythical hunting scene in green, red, brown and cream, within a floral panelled border, 19thC, 30in (76cm) long.
£450–550
$650–800 ↗ RBB

A branding iron, 'EH', 19thC, 15in (38cm) long.
£15–18
$20–25 ⊞ HCJ

▶ **A Victorian cast-iron free-standing heater,** by F. R. Embassy, 40in (101.5cm) high.
£200–250
$300–350 ⊞ CRN

A copper coffee pot, with swan-neck spout and turned ebony handle, the hinged domed cover with a bell metal acorn finial, mid-19thC, 12¾in (32.5cm) high.
£85–100
$125–145 ↗ WW

A Victorian tin crumb pan, with turned wood handle, painted green with yellow pansies, 14in (35.5cm) long.
£10–12
$15–18 ⊞ VB

A folding novelty pocket knife, the cover decorated with a chessboard motif, French, late 19thC, 1in (2.5cm) diam.
£45–50
$65–75 ⊞ MRW

A brass birdcage, c1880, 61in (155cm) high on stand.
£350–375
$500–550 ⊞ JACK

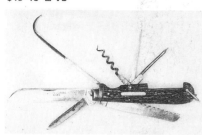

A Victorian clasp knife, by Joseph Rodgers & Sons, comprising 4¼in (11cm) blade, saw blade, 2½in (6.5cm) blade, hoof hook, corkscrew, awl and probe, the two-piece staghorn grip with vacant escutcheon containing tweezers and needle, marked, 5in (12.5cm) long closed.
£240–280
$350–420 ⚒ WAL
The firm of Joseph Rodgers & Sons, Sheffield, was one of the leading producers of multi-bladed knives in the 19th century. In 1822, in order to celebrate their Royal appointment by George IV, Rodgers made a knife with 1822 blades, one for each year in the Christian calendar. For the Great Exhibition in 1851 they manufactured a giant knife with 75 blades and tools. The company's mark was a star and cross.

A brass wine keg spigot, c1900, 8in (20.5cm) long.
£7–10
$10–15 ⊞ FST

Two lead models of polar bears, on a block of soapstone, c1920, 2in (5cm) square.
£25–30
$35–45 ⊞ HAL

Two bronze drink measures, c1920, largest 3in (7.5cm) high.
£55–75
$80–110 ⊞ WAB

Two lead models of cats, one black with a green bow, one ginger with an orange bow, beneath a green umbrella, German, 1920, 3in (7.5cm) high.
£110–140
$160–200 ⊞ HAL

▶ **A chrome tray,** with orange Bakelite ends, 1930s, 15in (38cm) wide.
£55–65
$80–95 ⊞ LBe

A lead model of a cat, possibly by Heyde, German, 1920s, 2in (5cm) high.
£40–50
$60–80 ⊞ HAL

Sixties & Seventies

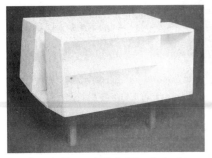

A painted plywood Mark II book donkey, by Ernest Race for Isokon, on hardwood uprights, 1960s, 21in (53.5cm) long.
£150–170
$220–250 ⊞ ORI
In 1931 engineer Jack Pritchard and architect Wells Coates founded Isokon (Isometric Unit Construction), a progressive company that produced plywood furniture for the modernist 'minimum interior'. One of the company's best-known designs was the Penguin Donkey, so-called because it was specifically designed to hold the new paperback books pioneered in Britain by Sir Allen Lane's Penguin publishing imprint (established 1935). After WWII, the Penguin Donkey was remodelled for Isokon by the British designer Ernest Race (1913–64).

A Fornasetti ceramic calendar, 1963, 3¼in (8.5cm) high.
£25–30
$35–45 ⊞ DSG

A Sparklets chrome and black plastic soda syphon, 1960s, 12in (30.5cm) high.
£45–55
$65–80 ⊞ ZOOM

◄ **A Ridgway bowl,** decorated with Barbecue pattern, 1960s, 6¾in (17cm) diam.
£165–185
$240–270 ⊞ HSt

◄ **A Troika vase,** decorated with an abstract pattern in brown, oatmeal and blue, 1970, 8in (20.5cm) high.
£60–80
$90–115 ⋋ P(B)

A Portmeirion coffee pot, decorated with Majic City pattern, 1960s, 12½in (32cm) high.
£45–55
$65–80 ⊞ LEGE

A St Ives Pottery Troika wheel vase, decorated in oatmeal, brown and blue, c1965, 12in (30.5cm) diam.
£300–350
$450–500 ⊞ HUN

A pair of Grundig speakers, 1960s, 36in (91.5cm) high.
£450–500
$650–720 ⊞ HSt

LOCATE THE SOURCE
The source of each illustration in Miller's can be found by checking the code letters below each caption with the Key to Illustrations, pages 444–452.

► **Six Ironstone Pottery Beefeater mugs,** 1960s–70s, 3in (7.5cm) high.
£30–40
$45–60 ⋋ FLD

A Harvey Guzzini plastic picnic set, in the shape of a bowling ball, 1970s, 13in (33cm) diam.
£50–55
$75–80 ⊞ HSt

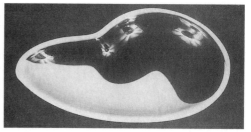

A Hornsea cream and black ashtray, 1970s, 6in (15cm) long.
£2–4
$4–6 ⊞ UNI

A chrome ceiling light, 1970s, 20in (51cm) high.
£200–250
$300–360 ⊞ ZOOM

A pair of red and black plastic chairs, on metal bases, Belgian, 1970s.
£400–450
$580–650 ⊞ HSt

A moulded plastic rock lamp, naturalistically coloured, internally lit, Italian, 1970s, 17in (43cm) diam.
£200–250
$300–360 ↗ TREA

Cross Reference
See Lighting (page 272)

A Westclox chrome and plastic Big Ben clock, with a blue face, 1970s, 7½in (19cm) high.
£45–55
$65–80 ⊞ ZOOM

A Circle Sections B fabric panel, by Alexander Girard, light purple with purple silkscreen design, signed, slightly faded, 1972, 73in (185.5cm) long.
£220–270
$330–400 ↗ TREA

A chrome and orange and white plastic lamp, Italian design, 1970s, 27in (68.5cm) diam.
£175–225
$250–320 ⊞ ZOOM

◀ **A San Marino ceramic plaque,** decorated with brown and black cats, c1970, 15in (38cm) long.
£40–50
$60–75 ⊞ DSG

A freestanding brown plastic ashtray, 1970s, 20½in (52cm) high.
£35–40
$50–60 ⊞ ZOOM

Smoking & Snuff Taking

An ivory snuff mull, the oval disc engraved 'WJ 1753', the lip with crescent-shaped mount engraved 'Isabella Moffatt, So.Shields', 2in (5cm) high.
£250–300
$360–440 ⚒ P(Ed)

A horn and brass snuff mull, c1780, 4in (10cm) long.
£250–300
$360–440 ⊞ HO

A burr-mulberry and ebony-inlaid snuff box, 1790, 3½in (9cm) long.
£130–160
$200–230 ⊞ MB

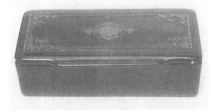

A birchwood tobacco-chopping board, 19thC, 6in (15cm) wide.
£60–75
$100–110 ⊞ NEW

A papier mâché and pewter-inlaid snuff box, 1840, 4in (10cm) long.
£50–60
$75–90 ⊞ MB

An olive green glass snuff jar, with wide neck and rolled flared lip, pontil scar to base, 6¼in (16cm) high.
£100–120
$145–175 ⚒ BBR

▶ **A cedar cigar cabinet,** 19thC, 21in (53.5cm) high.
£200–250
$300–350 ⊞ OTT

A Charles Stewart Parnell silver and gilt cigarette case, by W. W. and F. D., the lid inscribed with the arms of the Askwith family with motto 'Honesta Quam Splendida', the inside also inscribed, 1889, 3¼in (8cm) long, in original Carrington & Co presentation case.
£450–500
$650–720 ⊞ TML
George Ranken Askwith, Baron Askwith (1861–1942) was a barrister, arbitrator and member of many government committees and commissions.

A Great Exhibition clay pipe, by T. Blake, the bowl decorated with a view of the Crystal Palace exhibition buildings, 1851, 7in (18cm) long.
£100–120
$145–175 ⊞ TML

An ebony, ivory and silver pipe tamper, modelled as a truncheon, enclosing metal picker, 19thC, 3in (7.5cm) long.
£150–180
$220–280 ⊞ AEF

A Champagne E. Mercier & Co advertising cigar cutter, 1900, 2in (5cm) long.
£145–165
$200–240 ⊞ EMC

► A Gibson's Burslem hand-painted ashtray, decorated with black cats wearing red ribbons, 1910, 4in (10cm) wide.
£85–95
$125–140
⊞ LBe

A Bollinger advertising cigar cutter, modelled as a champagne bottle, 1900, 2¼in (5.5cm) high.
£85–95
$125–140 ⊞ EMC

A brass lighter, depicting an airship, 1905, 2in (5cm) diam.
£85–95
$125–140 ⊞ SSM

◄ A jade and ebony cigarette holder, 1920s, 6in (15cm) long.
£30–35
$45–50 ⊞ AnS

An Oriental-style brass smoking set, comprising cigarette holder, case and matchbox, 1930s, in a fitted case, 9 x 6in (23 x 15cm).
£40–50
$60–75 ⊞ AnS

► An IJOB metal cigarette-making machine, c1925, 10in (25.5cm) long.
£20–25
$30–35 ⊞ HUX

A brass and aluminium table cigarette lighter, 1940s, 4in (10cm) high.
£16–18
$20–25 ⊞ CRN

► A Bakelite seaside souvenir ashtray, 1940s–50s, 5in (12.5cm) diam.
£10–15
$15–20 ⊞ RTT

◄ A lighter, with crocodile skin cover, 1940s, 4¼in (11cm) high.
£85–95
$125–140 ⊞ LBe

A chrome lift lighter, c1950, 3in (7.5cm) square.
£40–45
$60–65 ⊞ HarC

A brass and copper cigarette lighter, modelled as a lighthouse, 1940s, 8in (20.5cm) high.
£20–25
$30–35 ⊞ HarC

Sport

A leather dog fighting collar, with steel spikes, 18thC, 9in (23cm) long.
£55–65
$80–95 ⊞ SA

A silver-plated trophy, for Charing Cross Hospital athletics, 1897, 14in (35.5cm) high.
£75–85
$110–125 ⊞ SA

A Victorian mahogany revolving billiard cue stand, 44in (112cm) high.
£1,600–2,000
$2,300–3,000 ⚷ RBB

Manual of Croquet, *its appointments and laws; by An Experienced Player,* published by Milner & Sowerby, original printed and decorated wrappers, rubbed and chipped, 1867, 12°.
£130–150
$200–220 ⚷ DW

A silver-plated trophy, for Cambridge University Sports Club 100 yards race, 1891, 8in (20.5cm) high.
£50–55
$70–80 ⊞ SA

A set of four bowling woods, 1900–10, 5in (12.5cm) diam.
£40–50
$60–75 ⊞ WaR

◀ **A set of four badminton rackets,** c1910, 27in (68.5cm) high.
£225–275
$330–400 ⊞ SMW

A 66th University Boat Race rudder, part-painted in Cambridge blue, the Cambridge University crew and 'Lost by 3 Lengths' inscribed in gilt, 1909, 18in (45.5cm) long.
£700–800
$1,000–1,150 ⚷ S

A set of badminton poles and net, 1920s–30s, poles 31in (78.5cm) long.
£60–75
$90–110 ⊞ SPA

◀ **A Stevengraph,** entitled 'The Meet', No. 165, c1910, 5 x 8in (12.5 x 20.5cm).
£100–120
$145–175 ⊞ VINE

A pair of brown and black leather cycling shoes, c1920.
£30–35
$45–50 ⊞ SA

A pair of lady's brown leather cycling boots, 1920.
£90–110
$130–160 ⊞ PSA

▶ **A wood and leather lacrosse stick,** 1920s, 43in (109cm) long.
£30–40
$45–60 ⊞ SPT

A Whiff-Waff table tennis game, comprising vellum battledores, net with attachments and a tube of balls, c1922, in original box 20in (51cm) long.
£50–60
$75–90 ➤ P(NW)

A pair of wooden exercise clubs, 1920s, 18in (45.5cm) high.
£30–35
$45–50 ⊞ SPA

◀ **A pair of brown leather mountaineering boots,** with steel cleats, c1930.
£55–65
$80–95 ⊞ SA

A black and white photograph of Clare College Athletes, 1925, framed and glazed, frame 14 x 16in (35.5 x 40.5cm).
£35–45
$50–65 ⊞ WAB

A pair of men's brown leather running spikes, c1930.
£30–35
$45–50 ⊞ SA

▶ **A wooden rounders bat,** 1940s, 17in (43cm) long.
£35–45
$50–65 ⊞ SMW

A XIVth Olympiad official linen flag, printed in red, black, green, yellow and blue on a white ground, 1948, 47in (119.5cm) long.
£375–425
$560–620 ➤ S

A pair of brown leather chaps, with rawhide fringes, c1930, 40in (101.5cm) long.
£100–125
$145–180 ⊞ SA

An Olympic Games
table lamp, modelled as
the Olympic torch, 1948,
25in (63.5cm) high.
£150–180
$220–260 ⚒ P(NW)

▶ A pair of Jacques &
Co mahogany croquet
mallets, with brass-ended
square sections, c1950,
37in (94cm) long.
£150–175
$220–250 ⊞ SA

A leather, plastic and steel bayonet fencing
mask, 1950s, 15in (38cm) long.
£75–85
$110–125 ⊞ SA

A straw boater, with patent securing
device, c1950, 15in (38cm) diam.
£30–35
$45–50 ⊞ SA

A traditional northern darts
board, without 25 and triples,
c1950, 18in (45.5cm) diam.
£25–30
$35–45 ⊞ SA

A leather medicine ball, 1950s,
14in (35.5cm) diam.
£55–65
$80–95 ⊞ PSA

▶ A Sussex stoolball bat,
c1950, 18in (45.5cm) long.
£10–15
$15–20 ⊞ AL

A J. Salter & Son leather rugby
ball, 1950s.
£55–65
$80–95 ⊞ PSA

An oak, steel and brass discus,
c1950, 7¼in (18.5cm) diam.
£15–20
$20–30 ⊞ WAB

Ted's Idol — Babe Ruth

◀ A 'Life of
Ted Williams'
baseball gum
card, depicting
Babe Ruth, 1959.
£65–75
$95–110 ⊞ HALL

▶ A wooden
hurling stick,
c1960, 36in
(91.5cm) long.
£10–15
$15–20 ⊞ WAB

Cricket

◀ A pair of white leather and leather-covered bamboo skeleton cricket pads, c1880–90, 23in (58.5cm) long.
£140–160
$200–230 ⊞ PEZ

A W. G. Grace Bakelite pipe bowl, embossed 'Centuplico', c1895, 4in (10cm) long.
£100–120
$145–175 ♪ P(Ba)

W. G. Grace, 'W G', Cricketing Reminiscences & Personal Recollections, signed by L. C. H. Palairet, published by Bowden, 1899, 8°.
£140–180
$200–260 ♪ VS

W. G. Grace, one page handwritten letter regarding a match between Worcester Park Beagles and London County, dated 22 May 1900.
£350–400
$500–580 ♪ P(Ba)

The Eleventh Australian Tour 1902, with adverts and portraits, issued by Cricket.
£260–300
$380–440 ♪ VS

◀ A pair of Staffordshire figures of cricketers, decorated in white with orange caps and bats and blue jackets, on oval bases, 20thC, 9¾in (25cm) high.
£200–250
$300–360 ♪ RTo

A Geo. G. Bussey Sports Demon Driver cricket bat, with patent leather grip, c1910, 34in (86.5cm) long.
£90–100
$130–145 ⊞ PEZ

▶ A black and white photograph of the Australian Cricket Team, the mount signed by the team, framed and glazed, 1934, 15 x 20in (38 x 51cm).
£240–280
$350–400 ♪ G(B)

Fishing

A steel eel gleave, c1830, 12in (30.5cm) long.
£50–55
$70–80 ⊞ SA

Three Victorian brass winches, largest 2in (5cm) diam.
£120–135
$170–200 ⊞ SA

◄ **A wooden hoop landing net,** with belt clip and brass end cap, 1880–1900, 37in (94cm) long.
£110–125
$160–180 ⊞ PEZ

A fishing silk, with a black and white print entitled 'The Angler's Companion', 1850, 17in (43cm) square.
£150–175
$220–250 ⊞ SA

► **A Britannia metal exhibitor's pass,** for the Great International Fisheries Exhibition, London, 1883, 2in (5cm) diam.
£50–80
$70–110 ⊞ OTB

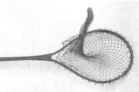

A Nottingham 4in wood and brass spine-back reel c1880.
£50–55
$70–80 ⊞ SPA

An Eaton & Deller 2¾in brass Hercules-style trout fly reel, with nickel-silver pillars and centre screw, maker's logo, c1890.
£120–160
$175–225 ⊞ OTB

► **A Bernard & Son 4½in all brass salmon fly wheel,** with twin-pillared foot and black ebonite handle, c1910.
£60–90
$100–130 ⊞ OTB

A 3½in brass plate wind trout/salmon reel, c1900.
£50–60
$70–90 ⊞ PSA

► **A fly line greaser,** with tortoiseshell cover, felt-lined, 1910–30, 2¾in (7cm) long.
£20–30
$30–45 ⊞ OTB

A black and white photograph of members of a fishermen's club, framed and glazed, c1910, 8 x 10in (20.5 x 25.5cm).
£40–45
$60–65 ⊞ SA

A bottle of Hardy's Odourless Paraffin for Dry Flies, with wood-capped cork stopper, 1920–30, 2½in (6.5cm) high.
£100–120
$145–175 ⊞ OTB

A pair of brown leather and canvas wading and fishing boots, 1920s.
£40–45
$60–65 ⊞ SA

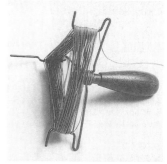

► **A hand-held wood and wire line drier,** 1920s, 4in (10cm) wide.
£20–30
$30–45 ⊞ OTB

A Scarborough 5in mahogany and brass fishing reel, with Slater catch mechanism, stamped 'Eton Son', 1920s.
£45–65
$60–95 ⊞ WAB

A Nottingham 3½in aluminium-backed walnut reel, later catch, c1920.
£40–45
$60–65 ⊞ SA

► **A 7in aluminium and brass big game reel,** c1930.
£65–75
$95–115 ⊞ SA

A Farlow Cairnton Killer nickel-silver priest, the head engraved with maker's name, c1930, 5¼in (13.5cm) long.
£80–100
$115–145 ⊞ OTB

A syringe-style plated brass sliding disgorger,
patented 1928, 1930s, 9in (23cm) long.
£50–60
$75–90 ⊞ OTB

A steel and brass fishing gaff, with mahogany handle
and belt hook, 1930s, 21in (53.5cm) long.
£110–130
$160–190 ⊞ PEZ

*Allcock's Anglers Guide
and Abridged List of
Fishing Tackle,* 1937–38,
7 x 6in (18 x 15cm).
£40–50
$60–75 ⊞ AnS

**A leather-bound full reed
angler's creel,** with offset hole
for catch, original strap, 1930s,
13in (33cm) long.
£100–120
$145–175 ⊞ PEZ

Cross Reference
See Colour Review
(page 319)

A Hardy fly box, in tortoiseshell effect, name
stamped on lid, the interior with fitted chenille
pipe-cleaner bars, 1930s, 6¼in (16cm) wide.
£50–60
$75–100 ⊞ OTB

**A Army & Navy 4⅛in
perfect-style salmon fly
reel,** with rim-mounted
drag adjustment and brass
foot, 1930–40.
£100–120
$145–175 ⊞ PEZ

**A Modern Arms 4in
Company mahogany
and brass star-back sea
reel,** with brass-backed
perforated drum, c1950.
£20–30
$30–45 ⊞ OTB

▶ **A Hardy Perfect 4in
salmon fly reel,** with
circular nickel-silver line
guide, with grey enamel
finish and scroll bordered
straight line name, c1950.
£100–130
$145–190 ⊞ OTB

A fisherman's chrome folding penknife, c1950,
4in (10cm) long.
£40–45
$60–65 ⊞ SA

Football

A Newcastle United £100 share certificate, dated 12 November 1908, 7 x 10in (18 x 25.5cm).
£210–240
$300–350 ⚒ P(NW)

A County Football Match programme, Yorkshire v. Durham, 1876.
£230–260
$330–360 ⚒ DW

An FA Cup Final steward's badge, Bury v. Derby, gold lettering on a blue ground, 1903, 2in (5cm) diam.
£240–280
$350–400 ⚒ P(NW)

▶ **A wooden football supporter's rattle,** 1910, 13in (33cm) long.
£15–18
$20–25 ⊞ DQ

A brown leather football, c1920.
£150–200
$220–300 ⊞ SMW

A pair of brown leather football boots, 1940s.
£65–75
$90–110 ⊞ SPT

An International Match programme, England v. Wales, 13 April 1940, 7 x 6in (18 x 15cm).
£180–220
$275–325 ⚒ P(NW)

A home match programme, Arsenal v. Chelsea, 1 March 1947, fuel emergency edition, 4°.
£160–190
$230–280 ⚒ DW

A pair of brown leather and cane shin pads, 1945. 9in (23cm) long.
£65–75
$90–110 ⊞ Mo

▶ **A match programme,** Manchester United v. Grimsby, 31 August 1946, printed in black, white and red, repaired, 9 x 6in (23 x 15cm).
£150–180
$220–260 ⚒ P(NW)

A *Manchester Evening News* colour souvenir picture of **Manchester United**, signed by the team members, March 1957.
£550–650
$800–950 ⚖ CDC

Three World Cup tickets, for Old Trafford, dated 13, 16 and 20 July 1966, 4in (10cm) square.
£320–360
$450–500 ⚖ P(NW)

▶ **A photograph of Sir Stanley Matthews,** with later autograph, mounted, 1974, 16 x 10in (40.5 x 25.5cm).
£130–150
$200–220 ⊞ SSL

Golf

◀ **A Standard Golf Co Miles aluminium putter,** with hickory shaft, c1910, 36in (91.5cm) long.
£130–150
$200–220 ⊞ PEZ

▶ **A Smith patent anti-shank mashie golf club,** with hickory shaft, c1910, 39in (99cm) long.
£65–75
$90–110 ⊞ PEZ

A rubber core golf ball, decorated with concentric rings to six poles, the centres joined by straight lines, minor damage, early 20thC.
£500–600
$800–950 ⚖ S

▶ **A pewter cigarette box,** with a square mesh golf ball and club on lid, c1930, 6in (15cm) wide.
£140–160
$200–230 ⊞ PEZ

A silver-plated cruet set, with golf clubs surmounted by a golf ball, blue glass liner in salt, c1910, 5in (12.5cm) high.
£90–110
$130–160 ⊞ SA

The Jimmy for Alex Patrick brassie golf club, with hickory shaft and leather grip, c1915, 36in (91.5cm) long.
£80–90
$115–135 ⊞ PEZ

◀ **A pair of Church's lady's golfing shoes,** in brown leather, c1950.
£50–55
$75–80 ⊞ SA

Tennis

Lawn tennis descended from 'Real Tennis', an indoor sport first played in medieval France and known as *Jeu de Paume* (palm game). The ball, which was made from sheepskin, and later from cloth, was first struck with the bare hand, then from the 15th century with a racket. Since the indoor court was bigger than a modern outdoor court, Real Tennis was the preserve of Royalty and the very wealthy. Henry VIII created a court at Hampton Court which is still in use today and in 1789, when Louis XVI locked the Third Estate out of their usual meeting place, the National Assembly of France retired to the King's tennis court at Versailles, where they swore the famous 'Tennis Court Oath', vowing never to disperse until France had a constitution.

It was another revolution, this time a technical one, that facilitated the emergence of lawn tennis the following century. Thanks to the developments in rubber, there was a new type of tennis ball and the invention of the lawn mower ensured you could have a smooth lawn. The man generally credited with inventing lawn tennis is Major Walter Wingfield who, in 1873 published a book of rules for 'Sphairistike or Lawn Tennis' and marketed kits for his new outdoor game. It was an instant success with both sexes, although women's long skirts and large hats meant that they were restricted to serving underarm. In 1875, the All-England Croquet Club at Wimbledon decided to set one of its lawns aside for tennis, and 1877 saw the first Wimbledon Tennis Championship.

An E. Nusser & Co fantail tennis racket, with convex wedge and scored handle, retailed by Harrods, early 20thC, 27in (68.5cm) long.
£55–65
$80–100 ⚲ P(NW)

A mahogany tennis racket press, c1900, 12in (30.5cm) long.
£115–125
$170–180 ⊞ SA

A silver tennis trophy, probably for a British Army competition, inscribed with winners' names, cast with a band of palm leaves supported on three tennis rackets within a laurel wreath, on an ebonized plinth, Indian, c1895, 6½in (16.5cm) high.
£300–400
$440–580 ⚲ S

◄ **A Talmo fish-tail tennis racket,** c1930, 27in (68.5cm) long.
£55–65
$80–100 ⊞ SA
The fish-tail tennis racket was designed to prevent the hand perspiring excessively.

A Spalding Pancho Gonzales autograph tennis racket, 1970s, 27in (68.6cm) long.
£25–30
$35–45 ⊞ SA

► **A box of Dunlop tennis balls,** 1965, 8in (20.5cm) long.
£15–20
$20–30 ⊞ HUX

Stanhopes

Stanhopes are named after Charles, 3rd Earl of Stanhope (1753–1816), British nobleman, statesman and inventor of a range of scientific devices including the Stanhope microscope lens. It was not until the second half of the 19th century, however, and with the development of micro-photography, that the custom emerged of placing a tiny Stanhope lens over a miniature photograph, and containing it in a piece of jewellery or a small souvenir. The man credited with first producing these decorative 'Stanhopes' in 1864, was the Victorian scientist Sir David Brewster, well-known for his optical work.

Queen Victoria herself was an early fan of Stanhope jewellery, and these novelty items soon became a popular craze. Stanhopes appear in many materials, from ivory to wood to minerals, and in every form from needlework tools to writing implements to brooches and charms. The majority contain photographs of favourite tourist attractions, and other subjects include portraits, famous events (such as major exhibitions) and, occasionally, naughty pictures, generally found on smoking implements or other objects likely to appeal to a male rather than female user.

Although Stanhopes were produced well into the 20th century, the golden age was the late Victorian and Edwardian periods. Values depend on material and design.

A Victorian wooden needlecase Stanhope, probably rosewood, 3½in (9cm) long.
£65–75
$90–110 ⊞ VB

A Victorian hoof letter opener Stanhope, 7½in (19cm) long.
£25–35
$30–50 ⊞ VB

A pen Stanhope, with bone handle, 1890–1900, 6in (15cm) long.
£85–95
$125–145 ⊞ MLa

A Victorian bog oak pig Stanhope, showing a view of Horsham, ½in (1.5cm) long.
£40–50
$60–75 ⊞ VB

A Victorian pen Stanhope, with bone handle, 7in (18cm) long.
£30–35
$45–50 ⊞ VB

A silver-plated propelling pencil Stanhope, 1890–1900, 3½in (9cm) long.
£100–120
$145–175 ⊞ MLa

▶ **A bookmark Stanhope,** showing views of Farnham, 1890–1900, 4in (10cm) long.
£100–120
$145–175 ⊞ MLa

A papier mâché spectacle case Stanhope, 1890–1900, 7in (18cm) long.
£180–200
$250–300 ⊞ MLa

Sunglasses & Lorgnettes

Sunglasses were developed in the second half of the 19th century to protect explorers on polar expeditions from snow blindness. In 1930, the Bausch and Lomb optical company (manufacturer of Ray-Bans) produced green-tinted lenses for US airforce pilots and in the ensuing decade, sunglasses took off as a fashion item, reflecting the new craze for sporting holidays and suntans. In 1937, Edwin Land (inventor of the Polaroid Camera) set up the Polaroid Institution in Cambridge, Massachusetts, which produced polarized filters for spectacles and other items ranging from binoculars to military gunsights. In the 1950s, a huge range of extravagant designs were introduced and the post-war period saw 'shades' becoming an essential cool accessory sported by film stars, pop singers and celebrities.

A gold-rimmed lorgnette, with a lacquered case inlaid with mother-of-pearl, c1880, 3in (7.5cm) long.
£50–60
$75–90 ⊞ VB

A pair of men's side-panelled sunglasses, c1920, 6in (15cm) wide, with original case.
£70–80
$100–115 ⊞ MRW

A pair of Mardi Gras sunglasses, the plastic frames applied with fabric flowers, 1950s, 6in (15cm) wide.
£60–80
$90–115 ⊞ SpM

A pair of cat's-eyes sunglasses, the black plastic frames with diamanté trim, 1950s, 6in (15cm) wide.
£38–42
$55–60 ⊞ SpM

A pair of Swank sunglasses, the brown plastic frames with diamanté trim, French, 1950s, 5in (12.5cm) wide.
£35–40
$50–60 ⊞ SpM

A pair of cat's-eyes sunglasses, the blue plastic frames with red trim, 1950s, 6in (15cm) wide.
£30–35
$45–50 ⊞ SpM

▶ **A pair of Henri Guillet plastic sunglasses,** French, 1950s, 6in (15cm) wide.
£40–50
$60–75 ⊞ ZOOM

▶ **A black plastic lorgnette,** with mother-of-pearl and paste stone decoration, 1950–60, 10in (25.5cm) wide.
£60–70
$90–100 ⊞ SBL

A pair of Polaroid sunglasses, with blue plastic frames, c1960, 6in (15cm) wide.
£30–35
$45–50 ⊞ SBL

Teddy Bears & Soft Toys

A straw-filled teddy bear, with original eyes, wearing a black velvet jacket, c1915, 13¾in (35cm) high.
£175–200
$250–290 ⊞ BaN

A white mohair and straw-filled dog-on-wheels, with original eyes, c1920, 11¾in (29cm) high.
£250–300
$360–450 ⊞ BaN

A Chiltern blonde mohair teddy bear, with glass eyes, swivel head and jointed arms and legs, some restitching to pads, c1930, 15in (38cm) high.
£100–150
$145–220 ⚒ Bon(C)

A mohair and straw-filled Felix the Cat, with original boot button eyes, c1930, 19in (48cm) high.
£250–300
$360–440 ⊞ BaN

A Chiltern blonde mohair musical teddy bear, with orange glass eyes and tartan jacket, c1930, 16in (41cm) high.
£250–300
$360–440 ⚒ Bon(C)

► **A black cloth cat,** with mohair face, original red felt jacket and beige velvet trousers, buckled shoes and a cane, c1930, 15in (38cm) high.
£350–450
$500–650 ⊞ BaN

A Chiltern golden mohair teddy bear, with glass eyes, swivel head, jointed arms and legs, slight wear, c1930, 19in (48cm) high, with a framed photograph of it with its original owner.
£280–350
$400–500 ⚒ Bon(C)

> **Cross Reference**
> See Colour Review (page 385)

◄ **A Merrythought blonde mohair teddy bear,** with glass eyes, shaved muzzle, swivel head, jointed arms and legs, c1930, 21in (53cm) tall, with a photograph of the bear with its original owner.
£570–650
$800–950 ⚒ Bon(C)

A Farnell golden mohair teddy bear, with glass eyes, fully jointed body and tan Rexine pads, 1930s, 20in (51cm) high.
£450–550
$650–800 *Bon(C)*

A Berg black cat, with red bow, Austrian, 1930s, 5½in (14cm) high.
£85–95
$125–140 ⊞ **LBe**

A brown mohair teddy bear, possibly Chiltern, with glass eyes, shaved snout, slight wear and pads recovered, c1930, 21in (53.5cm) high, with a child's tapestry-seated wooden chair.
£250–300
$360–440 *Bon*

A Dean's polar bear and cub, with original labels, 1949, 17in (43cm) high.
£400–450
$580–650 ⊞ **DAn**

A soft toy bear, wearing a black hat and green sweater, 1930s–40s, 34in (86.5cm) high.
£60–80
$90–115 *SWO*

l. A Steiff golden artificial silk teddy bear, with brown-backed glass eyes, jointed arms and legs, squeeze voice-box, some repairs, German, c1947, 13½in (34cm) high.
£850–1,000
$1,250–1,500
r. A Steiff brown artificial silk teddy bear, with glass eyes, growler inoperative, German, c1949, 10¼in (26cm) high.
£800–950
$1,200–1,400 *S(S)*

A Steiff spaniel, 'Cockie', with original chest and ear tags, original collar, German, c1960, 4¾in (12cm) high.
£50–60
$75–90 ⊞ **TED**

A golden mohair teddy bear, possibly Chad Valley, with orange glass eyes, swivel head and jointed arms and legs, c1950, 29in (73.5cm) high.
£100–150
$145–220 *Bon(C)*

▶ **A Steiff tabby cat,** with original button and yellow tag in ear, original ribbon and bell, German, 1968–76, 4in (20cm) high.
£50–60
$75–90 ⊞ **TED**

Telephones

A Telefon Fabrik Automatic DO8 telephone, steel and brass with wooden handgrip, Danish, c1908.
£450–500
$650–720 ⊞ OTC

An Ericsson magneto corporation telephone, steel and brass with wooden handgrip, not converted for BT use, Swedish, 1920s.
£300–330
$440–480 ⊞ OTC

A cream Bakelite telephone, 1930s, 6in (15cm) high.
£300–350
$450–500 ⊞ HEG

◀ **A black Bakelite telephone,** converted for BT use, German, 1945–60, 6½in (16.5cm) high.
£80–100
$115–145 ⊞ HEG

A Bell Telephones black Bakelite telephone, with Bakelite and brass bell set No. 64d, converted for BT use, Belgian, 1930s–40s.
£200–240
$280–350 ⊞ OTC

Miller's is a price GUIDE not a price LIST

▶ **A Bakelite wall-mounted telephone,** c1950, 10in (25.5cm) high.
£100–125
$145–180 ⊞ AOY

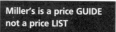

◀ **A black Bakelite telephone,** with bell box, c1950, 7in (18cm) high.
£175–200
$250–280 ⊞ AOY

▶ **A black Bakelite telephone,** with Bell On/Bell Off switches, c1950, 6in (15cm) high.
£125–145
$180–200 ⊞ AOY

A Bell Telephones green telephone, Belgian, 1956–66.
£125–150
$180–220 ⊞ OTC

A black telephone, converted for BT use, French, 1950–60, 5½in (14cm) high.
£40–50
$60–75 ⊞ HEG

A white telephone, converted for BT use, German, c1950s, 6½in (16.5cm) high.
£100–120
$145–175 ⊞ HEG

A copper and brass-finished telephone, with black handset, Belgian, 1956–1966, 5½in (14cm) high.
£85–95
$125–140 ⊞ HEG

A black thermoplastic telephone, American, 1978–80, in original sealed carton.
£80–90
$115–130 ⊞ OTC

A GPO Queen's Silver Jubilee telephone, with type 64d bell set, 1977.
£125–140
$180–200 ⊞ OTC

Textiles & Costume

A needlework panel of the Finding of Moses, worked in coloured wools and chenille on silk, with watercolour detailing, unfinished, early 19thC, 16½in (42cm) wide, in a wooden frame.
£160–200
$230–280 ➤ RTo

A sampler, by Elizabeth Cole, worked on silk, 1839, 13 x 10in (33 x 25.4cm), in a wooden frame.
£780–850
$1,100–1,250 ⊞ HIS

A sampler, worked by Ellan Christian Prosser, Aged 10 Years, 1840, in coloured thread, 13 x 12½in (33 x 32cm).
£120–150
$175–220 ➤ RTo

A sampler, by Mary Henry Macduff, decorated with a verse, flowers, birds, figures and religious artefacts, 1866, 19 x 15¾in (48.5 x 40cm), in a simulated rosewood frame.
£280–340
$400–500 ➤ AG

A collection of patchwork quilt squares, from the Bidwell Family & Friends Album, pieced and/or appliquéd cotton squares in various patterns and colours, most signed in ink by the maker, minor staining, American, c1860, largest 11½in (29cm) square.
£700–800
$1,000–1,150 ➤ SK(B)

A Victorian cotton patchwork quilt, Welsh, 66 x 65in (167.5 x 165cm).
£55–65
$80–95 ⊞ JJ

A narrow loom wool blanket, in orange and black on cream, Welsh, late 19thC, 70in (178cm) wide.
£65–75
$95–110 ⊞ JJ

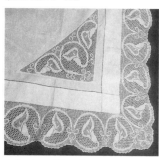

A linen and hand-crocheted lace tablecloth, c1900, 54in (137cm) square.
£80–90
$115–130 ⊞ JuC

◄ **A linen and drawn thread-work tablecloth,** c1910, 51in (129.5cm) square.
£50–60
$75–90 ⊞ JuC

A Battenburg drawn threadwork and linen tablecloth, c1910.
£45–50
$65–75 ⊞ JuC

A linen and hand-crotcheted lace tablecloth, Mary Card design No. 68, 'The Garden Cloth', c1920, 52in (132cm) square.
£90–100
$130–150 ⊞ JuC

An Art Nouveau floral design pink quilt, with lemon-yellow reverse, c1900, 83 x 75in (211 x 190.5cm).
£400–500
$580–720 ⊞ JJ

A silk tea cosy, designed as a pierrot, with hand-painted face, 1920s, 14in (35.5cm) high.
£120–150
$175–220 ⊞ LBe

▶ A fake fur fabric tea cosy, designed as a poodle, with a green bow, 1930s, 13in (33cm) high.
£100–125
$145–180 ⊞ LBe

A black satin underwear case, with a lucky black cat panel, 1930s, 7in (18cm) square.
£20–25
$30–35 ⊞ LBe

A pair of Jolly Golly design curtains, multi-coloured on an orange ground, 1960s–70s, 72 x 48in (183 x 122cm).
£15–18
$20–30 ↗ FLD

▶ A length of Deco Revival-style fabric, with male dancers in blue and green on a white ground, 1970s, 108 x 48in (274.5 x 122cm).
£35–40
$50–60 ⊞ HSt

A yellow and brown fringed wool blanket, Welsh, 1960, 94 x 72in (239 x 183cm).
£35–50
$50–75 ⊞ DE

Costume

Over the past few years, interest in vintage clothing has expanded considerably and become far more mainstream. Selfridges department store in London now includes a vintage section alongside its contemporary designer concessions. Top Shop, at their flagship store in Oxford Street, stocks vintage clothing next to the latest high street fashions. When Julia Roberts wore vintage Valentino to the Oscars ceremony, second-hand clothing became the ultimate in Hollywood glamour and today's fashion magazines continually mix old with new.

The great joy of collecting vintage clothes is the pleasure of wearing them. Some enthusiasts go the whole way, perhaps dressing top-to-toe in 1920s style, complete with make-up and hairstyle to match. Others simply accessorize contemporary outfits with a vintage scarf or handbag, using the past to enhance the present.

Buying clothes from an antique dealer or flea market is an adventure and you never know what you will find. Often people go for a period that suits their figure. Slim and leggy girls might chose 1960s or '20s, while the more curvaceous might try 1950s or even Edwardian. Some pieces (particularly pre-1900) can be too fragile to wear easily, and when buying vintage clothing it is always important to check condition. Clothes should also be tried on. Over the decades, our figures have changed and each generation grows bigger than the last. If you want to collect and wear 1920s shoes, for example, your feet will need to be far smaller than today's average size.

As the following selection shows, there is a huge range of antique clothing to choose from. Compared to their modern day, mass-produced equivalents, pieces are often far better made (if they weren't they wouldn't have lasted so long) and competitively priced (though as with modern fashion, expect to pay more for a good designer label). Finally, if you collect vintage clothing, not only do you have the enjoyment of wearing your collectables but you can virtually guarantee that no-one is going to turn up dressed exactly like you.

A child's cotton piqué coat, with mother-of-pearl buttons, c1900.
£60–65
$90–95 ⊞ JuC

◀ A silk **Masonic apron,** embroidered in silk, chenille, metallic threads and sequins with Masonic symbols and initials 'J.B.' on a white ground, with yellow ribbon on a blue silk border, early 19thC, 18½in (47cm) high, mounted on blue velvet fabric in a giltwood frame.
£450–550
$650–800 🔨 SK(B)

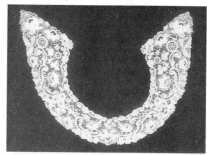

A child's Brussels lace *point de gaze* collar, c1890, 10in (25.5cm) wide.
£45–50
$65–75 ⊞ JuC

A figured brown wool two-piece walking dress, with high neck, emphasized shoulder decoration and bustle back, c1890s.
£130–150
$190–220 ⊞ CCO

◀ An electroplated nickel silver belt, c1900, 26in (66cm) long.
£100–110
$145–160 ⊞ LBe

A taupe wool two-piece suit, the jacket with buttons down the back, 1930.
£40–50
$60–75 ⊞ **DE**

An eau-de-nil silk crêpe evening dress, with hand-painted flower detail, late 1930s.
£160–180
$230–260 ⊞ **LaF**

◄ **A red satin dress,** with a fur collar and self-fabric belt, 1950s.
£30–35
$45–50 ⊞ **HSt**

A Christian Dior black suit, 1950s.
£170–190
$250–275 ⊞ **SBT**

◄ **A pink silk dress and coat,** labelled 'Carnegie London', with self-fabric button loops and covered buttons, 1960.
£35–45
$50–65 ⊞ **DE**

◄ **A Western-style brown satin Occupied Japan souvenir shirt,** with a white panel embroidered with a golden dragon, 1940s–50s.
£150–175
$220–250 ⊞ **SpM**

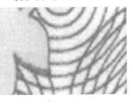

A Crown Prince green gabardine bowling shirt, American, 1950s.
£65–75
$95–75 ⊞ **SpM**

◄ **A Jeannie Brand brown jersey cocktail dress,** 1950.
£25–35
$35–50 ⊞ **DE**

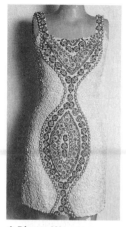

A Dianna Warren cream, blue and gold beaded and sequinned dress, dress shortened, 1960s.
£60–70
$90–100 ⊞ DE

A Cathy McGowan's Boutique purple tricel dress, 1970s.
£45–55
$65–80 ⊞ DE
In 1963, nineteen-year-old Cathy McGowan went from being a secretary earning £10 ($15) a week to star presenter on *Ready Steady Go* – the successful British TV pop programme. Dubbed 'Queen of the Mods', Cathy became a fashion icon for young girls, who imitated her long fringed hairstyle, theatrical makeup and clothes. Various products ranging from dresses to cosmetics were brought out under her name.

A green, black, purple and yellow psychedelic pattern skirt, labelled 'Dori, London', 1970s.
£10–15
$15–20 ⊞ DE

A Diane von Furstenberg red and white cotton jersey shirt dress, 1970s.
£125–145
$180–200 ⊞ SBT

A Biba green and black sequinned jacket, 1970s.
£175–195
$250–280 ⊞ SBT

A Jean Muir dark green wool crêpe two-piece suit, 1970s.
£300–350
$450–500 ⊞ SBT

A safari-style grey jersey suit, with flared trousers, 1970s.
£30–40
$45–60 ⊞ HarC

Cross Reference
See Colour Review (page 387)

A Today's Man short-sleeved cotton shirt, with a blue and green palm tree pattern, American, 1970s.
£20–25
$30–35 ⊞ HSt

A Vivienne Westwood punk jacket, c1976.
£450–500
$650–720 ⊞ IQ
This jacket is from her first shop, Let It Rock.

A Vivienne Westwood green cotton asymmetric shirt, with one sleeve, from the Witches Collection, c1983.
£200–250
$300–360 ⊞ ID

Coat Hangers & Hat Stands

A child's felt-covered golly coat-hanger, 1930s, 12in (30.5cm) wide.
£85–95
$125–140 ⊞ LBe

> **Miller's is a price GUIDE not a price LIST**

A pair of wood and steel coat and hat hooks, French, c1910, 11in (28cm) high.
£70–90
$100–130 each ⊞ RUL

▶ **A brass and wood robe-hanger,** 1930s, 18in (45.5cm) high.
£25–30
$35–45 ⊞ SPT

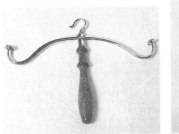

A wooden hatstand, with a hand-painted figure of an Egyptian-style dancing girl, 1920s, 12in (30.5cm) high.
£150–175
$220–250 ⊞ LBe

◀ **A wicker mannequin,** 1950–60, 70in (178cm) high.
£65–75
$95–110 ⊞ NET

Hats

A Breton brown bonnet, with lace trim and taffeta bow, French, 18thC.
£180–200
$260–300 ⊞ JuC

A Victorian velvet and lace bonnet, trimmed with ostrich feathers.
£55–65
$80–95 ⊞ Ech

A Honiton bobbin-lace fall cap, c1860, 24in (61cm) wide.
£40–45
$60–65 ⊞ JuC

An Edwardian black velvet hat.
£85–95
$125–195 ⊞ LBe

A child's straw hat, trimmed with floral-printed ribbon, 1920s.
£80–100
$115–145 ⊞ Ech

A cast-iron flower press, with a wooden handle, c1920, 8¼in (21cm) long.
£100–120
$145–175 ⊞ MSB
These presses were used to mould silk flowers for hats.

◄ **A grey felt Homburg hat,** 1930s.
£20–30
$30–45 ⊞ DE

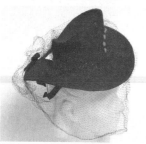

A black straw hat, with silk netting and red grosgrain ribbon trim, 1940s.
£85–95
$125–140 ⊞ LBe

A black felt hat and veil, 1940s.
£30–35
$45–50 ⊞ CCO

A black straw hat, decorated with felt flowers, c1930.
£35–40
$50–60 ⊞ DE

► **A black and white leather hat,** with leather flower decoration, 1960s.
£10–12
$15–18 ⊞ CCO

Shawls & Scarves

► **A Lancashire clogger's wool shawl,** late 19thC, 30 x 125in (76 x 317.5cm).
£55–65
$80–95 ⊞ DE

A red, black and blue paisley shawl, some damage, early 20thC, 66in (167.5cm) square.
£100–150
$145–220 ⊞ JPr

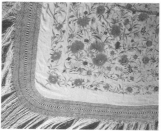

A brown and white printed wool shawl, with magenta border, c1860–70, 60 x 120in (152.5 x 305cm).
£85–95
$125–140 ⊞ DE

◄ **A multicoloured embroidered piano shawl,** Chinese, c1900, 66in (167.5cm) square.
£250–300
$350–450 ⊞ JuC

A red, gold and black scarf, inscribed 'Gay Times at Churchill's Club, 1940s, 35in (89cm) square.
£130–150
$190–220 ⊞ LBe

A Courtier rayon scarf, Nuits de Paris, multicoloured with blue border, 1939–45, 25in (63.5cm) square.
£50–60
$75–90 ⊞ REN

A Festival of Britain synthetic fabric scarf, with multicoloured London Views, 1951, 29in (74cm) square.
£50–60
$75–90 ⊞ REN

A yellow handkerchief, with black poodles, 1950s, 18in (45.5cm) square.
£8–10
$12–15 ⊞ LBe

An Oliver Messel silk scarf, with the Coronation coach, 1953, 35in (89cm) square.
£120–140
$175–200 ⊞ REN

A red, black and yellow Paloma Picasso scarf, 1980s, 34in (86.5cm) square.
£85–95
$125–140 ⊞ LBe

Shoes

▶ **A pair of pattens,** leather and wood mounted on an oval iron ring, c1780–1830.
£150–165
$220–250 ⊞ HO
Pattens were overshoes, worn to protect ordinary shoes from the mud and wet.

◀ **A pair of gentleman's silver shoe buckles,** by R. E., London 1813, 2½in (6.5cm) wide.
£100–120
$145–175 ⚲ PFK

A silver button hook, London 1887, 15in (38cm) long.
£500–550
$720–800 ⊞ SHa

An iron shoe stretcher, c1880, 15in (38cm) long.
£20–25
$30–35 ⊞ FST

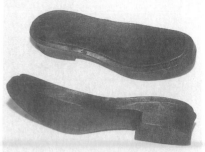

A pair of wood clog bases, French, c1900.
£12–15
$17–20 ⊞ Cot

A pair of lady's black wool and leather ankle boots, by Delta, with button fastening, 1900.
£80–90
$115–130 ⊞ CCO

A pair of brown leather field boots, with trees, 1910.
£125–145
$180–200 ⊞ SPT

A pair of black leather shoes, 1920s.
£30–40
$45–60 ⊞ CCO

A pair of tan leather boots, with trees, 1910.
£85–95
$125–140 ⊞ SPT

A pair of black satin court shoes, with diamanté decoration to heels, 1920s.
£35–40
$50–60 ⊞ CCO

A pair of silver leather evening shoes, labelled 'Dolcis, Made in Budapest', c1930.
£30–35
$45–50 ⊞ CCO

◄ **A pair of child's Utility white buckskin boots,** 1940s.
£25–30
$35–45 ⊞ TT

A pair of white suede peep-toe shoes, by Physical Culture, 1940s.
£35–40
$50–60 ⊞ CCO

A pair of Utility snakeskin shoes,
1940–50.
£85–95
$125–140 ⊞ SpM

A pair of Perspex and plastic shoes,
with a 4in (10cm) heel,
late 1950s–60s.
£55–65
$80–95 ⊞ SpM

A pair of white leather shoes,
by Natale Ferrario, Italian, 1957.
£350–400
$500–580 ⊞ LBe
Rather than being supported
by a heel, these 'heel-less high-
heel shoes' have a metal sole
extension. Perhaps unsurprisingly,
this design was only produced
for a short period of time and
'invisible stiletto' shoes are now
very collectable.

A pair of platform shoes, with
black patent plastic uppers and clear
Perspex bases, 1970.
£50–60
$75–90 ⊞ BEV

**A pair of brown leather platform
boots,** with snakeskin decoration,
1970s.
£70–80
$100–115 ⊞ CCO

▶ **A pair of black suede shoes,**
by Salvatore Ferragamo, 1980s.
£65–75
$95–110 ⊞ SBT

Underwear

▶ **A pair of lady's embroidered
split-leg bloomers,** with lace
trim, c1920.
£35–40
$50–60 ⊞ JuC

**A pair of Mary Quant white
Tiffany Lace tights,** 1960s, original
package 9 x 7in (23 x 18cm).
£12–15
$15–20 ⊞ CCO

A black lace corset, by Lady
Marlene, 1950s, in original box.
£55–65
$80–95 ⊞ LBe

◀ **A pair of nylon Y-Front
underpants,** 1970s.
£4–5
$5–7 ⚒ FLD

Tiles

A set of majolica tiles, decorated in brown, orange and green, Dutch, 17thC, 5in (12.5cm) square.
£270–300
$390–440 ⊞ OLA

A Delft tile, with manganese border, the blue and white hexagonal centre with a horseman in a country landscape, Dutch, 18thC, 5in (12.5cm) square.
£90–100
$130–150 ⊞ JHo

A manganese tile, depicting a man resting on a bench in a country landscape, Dutch, 18thC, 5in (12.5cm) square.
£25–30
$35–45 ⊞ JHo

A Liverpool blue and white tile, depicting Moses and the Tablets, 1760, 5in (12.5cm) square.
£145–165
$200–240 ⊞ JHo

A London blue and white tile, depicting St Paul escaping, 1760, 5in (12.5cm) square.
£100–125
$145–180 ⊞ JHo

An encaustic floor tile, decorated in brown and white, 19thC, 6in (15cm) square.
£8–10
$10–15 ⊞ OLA

A set of 12 William de Morgan tiles, decorated with Persian-style stylized leaves and flowers in turquoise and green, impressed Merton Abbey marks, minor chips, 1880s, 6in (15cm) square.
£2,000–2,500
$2,900–3,600 ⋏ S(S)

Three Minton tiles, Spring, Autumn and Winter, late 19thC, 8in (20.5cm) square.
£90–100
$130–150 each ⊞ OLA

A Quimper tile/pot-stand, decorated with a Breton lady within a brown border, c1943, 8½in (21.5cm) square.
£60–70
$90–100 ⊞ SER

Colour Review

◀ **A Terries mohair teddy bear,** with clear glass eyes, stitched nose, eyes and paws and cloth pads, 1920s, 24in (61cm) high.
£650–750
$1,000–1,100 ⚖ Bon

▶ **A Schuco plush monkey scent bottle,** worn, c1920, 4in (10cm) high.
£100–150
$150–220 ⊞ A&J

A mohair teddy bear, with original boot-button eyes and coat, c1910–15, 12in (30.5cm) high.
£250–300
$350–450 ⊞ TED

▶ **A mohair teddy bear,** with articulated limbs, early 20thC, 20in (51cm) high.
£100–120
$150–180 ⚖ G(L)

◀ **A mohair musical teddy bear,** possibly a glockenspiel bear by Helvetic, with clear glass eyes, pink stitched nose, velvet paw pads, jointed at head, shoulders and hips, concertina musical movement in tummy, Austrian, c1920, 12in (30.5cm) high.
£550–650
$800–950 ⚖ Bon(C)

A Chad Valley mohair teddy bear,
with orange glass eyes, jointed at
head, shoulders and hips, some wear,
paw pads recovered, button in left
ear, c1930, 25in (63.5cm) high.
£1,000–1,200
$1,500–1,750 ⚒ Bon

A plush teddy bear, with glass
eyes, cotton pads and feet, ring-pull
growl mechanism, the body stuffed
with wood wool, some damage,
1940s, 29in (74cm) high.
£40–50
$60–75 ⚒ DN

A Farnell mohair teddy bear,
with orange glass eyes, black
stitched nose, mouth and claws,
leatherette paw pads, jointed at
neck, shoulders and hips, c1940,
19in (48.5cm) high.
£360–420
$500–500 ⚒ Bon(C)

A Steiff cat, 'Suzi', with green bow,
1959–69, 4in (10cm) high.
£50–60
$75–90 ⊞ TED

A Steiff plush dog, 'Waldi', with
glass eyes and stitched nose, the
leather collar with original paper
label, 1960, 17¼in (44cm) long.
£140–170
$200–250 ⚒ DN

A Steiff Pekinese dog, 'Peky', with
original ribbon and chest tag, no
button, 1960s, 3¼in (8.5cm) high.
£30–40
$45–60 ⊞ TED

**A Merrythought Cheeky
acrylic teddy bear,** 1960s,
16in (40.5cm) high.
£300–350
$450–500 ⚒ CAu

A Steiff Peggy penguin,
with chest tag but
no button, c1960,
19½in (49.5cm) high.
£100–150
$150–200 ⊞ TED

A Marietta mohair bear,
by Pamela Adams for
ABC Bears, with hessian
hat, Welsh, 1999,
16in (40.5cm) high.
£120–135
$175–200 ⊞ BOL
This is a one-off
example of this bear.

**A Steiff Toad of Toad
Hall,** limited edition,
1999, 11in (28cm) high.
£125–145
$180–220 ⊞ Ann

A Georgian silk and needlework picture, depicting a muse laying flowers at the tomb of Shakespeare, in *verre églomisé* mount, 12¼ x 9¾in (32.5 x 25cm), in a rosewood frame.
£180–220
$260–320 ⚮ AH

A wool sampler, by Mary Combs, embroidered with a butterfly, birds and trees, 1848, 13 x 14in (33 x 35.5cm).
£550–600
$800–870 ⊞ HIS

A Victorian beaded pot stand, 9in (23cm) square.
£100–120
$150–175 ⊞ CAL

A Hamadan cushion, made from a vintage Turkey carpet, c1910, 14 x 16in (35.5 x 40.5cm).
£40–50
$60–75 ⊞ DNO

A machine-made quilt, with central solid diamond on a Paisley ground, 1920–30, 71 x 58in (180.5 x 147cm).
£50–100
$75–150 ⊞ JJ

A wide-loom double-weave bed cover, Welsh, c1920, 80 x 70in (203 x 178cm).
£50–60
$75–90 ⊞ JJ

A length of fabric, with abstract pattern, 1950s, 60 x 44in (152.5 x 112cm).
£20–25
$30–35 ⊞ FLD

A bathroom curtain, decorated with cosmetic, hairdressing, shaving and washing accessories, 1950s, 50 x 14in (127 x 35.5cm).
£10–12
$15–20 ⊞ FLD

A petit point spectacle case, 1950s, 6in (15cm) high.
£30–35
$45–50 ⊞ LBe

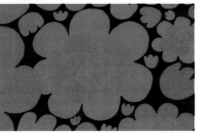

◀ **A length of curtain fabric,** 1970s, 86in (218.5cm) long.
£20–25
$30–35 ⊞ HSt

A silk calèche, supported on cane hoops, 1830s, 15in (38cm) diam.
£250–275
$360–400 ⊞ CCO
A calèche is a collapsible hooped bonnet, designed to protect the face.

A fine wool two-piece dress, with figured velvet satin decoration to skirt and bodice, c1880.
£180–200
$260–200 ⊞ CCO

◄ **A chiffon and devoré tea dress,** 1930s.
£300–350
$450–500 ⊞ HSt

► **A straw hat,** with velvet trim, c1915, 12in (30.5cm) diam.
£85–95
$125–140 ⊞ CCO

A satin hat, with appliqué flowers and rouleau trim, 1920s.
£90–100
$130–150 ⊞ Ech

A straw cloche hat, with ribbon decoration, 1920, 8in (20.5cm) diam.
£50–55
$75–80 ⊞ CCO

◄ **An Andrade silk Hawaiian-style shirt,** made for the Royal Hotel Resort Shop, Honolulu, 1930s–40s, medium size.
£250–285
$360–410 ⊞ SpM

A two-piece printed georgette dress, 1930s.
£80–110
$120–160 ⊞ DE

A WWII Victory scarf, decorated with the national flags of the Allies, 25in (63.5cm) square.
£70–80
$100–115 ⊞ REN

► **A Flame of Time tie,** designed by Salvador Dali for Smoothie Imperial, late 1940s, 13in (33cm) long, in original box.
£250–300
$360–450 ⊞ SpM

An erotic 'girlie' tie, 1950s, 2½in (6.5cm) wide.
£125–150
$180–220 ⊞ SpM

A Victor Jocelyn floral print dress, with matching scarf, late 1950s.
£30–40
$45–60 ⊞ DE

► **A Pucci print shirt,** 1960s.
£435–485
$625–700 ⊞ SBT

A Courrèges suit, 1960s.
£500–550
$720–800 ⊞ SBT

A rayon Hawaiian-style shirt, with scenic print, Japanese, late 1950s.
£125–150
$180–220 ⊞ SpM

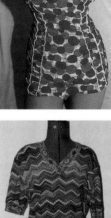

A Missoni two-piece skirt and top, 1970s.
£300–350
$450–500 ⊞ SBT

◄ **A Christian Dior hat,** with silk flowers on a net base, 1964, 12in (30.5cm) diam, in original Harrod's box.
£65–75
$95–110 ⊞ CCO

◄ **A cotton swimsuit,** made by Blue Lake Swimware, with boned cups, elasticized back and original label, 1950s.
£12–15
$18–20 ⊞ DE

A georgette tiered hanky-point evening dress, with psychedelic floral print, 1970.
£30–35
$45–50 ⊞ DE

A Vivienne Westwood Portrait Collection T-shirt-style dress, printed with breasts and Boucher-style print framed with gold and red foil, c1990.
£120–150
$175–220 ⊞ ID

A Louis Feraud velvet and silk jacket, 1970s.
£40–45
$60–65 ⊞ HSt

◄ **A Louis Feraud silk dress,** with diamanté buttons, 1970s, size 14.
£30–35
$45–50 ⊞ HSt

A Victorian mahogany boot jack, 35in (89cm) high.
£140–160
$200–230 ⊞ SPU

► **A pair of lady's knee-high buttoned boots,** leather and patterned wool, c1915, 17in (43cm) high.
£100–120
$150–175 ⊞ CCO

◄ **A pair of gentleman's leather boots,** with wooden trees, 1890, 26in (66cm) high.
£130–150
$190–220 ⊞ MLL

A Taj Mahal silk slipper, with steel heel, 1950s, heel 1½in (4cm) high.
£75–85
$110–125 ⊞ SpM
Gloria Swanson had 250 pairs of these shoes.

A pair of Society Debs platform shoes, by Lester Pincus, unworn, 1940s, heel 5in (12.5cm) high.
£165–185
$240–270 ⊞ SpM

A pair of Mary Quant rubber shoes, with attached knee-high socks, 1960s, 9in (23cm) high.
£400–450
$580–650 ⊞ CCO

A pair of Mary Quant clear rubber boots, with red lining and metal zip, 1960s.
£400–450
$580–650 ⊞ CCO

A pair of Pretty Birds lace-up shoes, in multi-coloured suede, unworn, 1970.
£20–25
$30–35 ⊞ DE

A pair of Biba glitter rubber boots, with original label, early 1970s, 14in (35.5cm) high.
£125–150
$180–220 ⊞ CCO

A pair of Vivienne Westwood boots, with leather uppers and wooden soles, unworn, 1980s.
£175–195
$250–280 ⊞ SBT

A pair of Charles Jourdan strap shoes, 1990s.
£50–60
$75–90 ⊞ SBT

A painted wooden Noah's Ark, with four people and over 100 pairs of animals and birds, sliding side panel replaced, German, late 19thC, 25in (63.5cm) wide.
£1,500–2,000
$2,000–3,000 ⚒ Bon(C)

◄ **A Victorian child's chrome musical box,** plays three tunes, with winding mechanism, 5in (12.5cm) diam.
£50–60
$75–90 ⊞ HO

► **A wood and tinplate model car,** coachbuilt, 1910–20, 18in (45.5cm) long.
£90–100
$130–150 ⊞ MRW

A Pigmyphone toy gramophone, 1920s, 6in (15cm) high.
£70–80
$100–115 ⊞ JUN

A child's bucket with lid, c1925, 7in (18cm) high.
£35–40
$50–60 ⊞ HUX

A Distler tinplate clockwork fire engine, with extending ladder, four seated firemen and Balloon Cord tyres, German, 1920s, 11½in (19cm) long.
£230–280
$330–400 ⚒ Bon(C)

A clockwork 2in gauge tank locomotive, No. 112, with a coal tender and a quantity of track, 1920s, 15in (38cm) long.
£350–380
$500–580 ⚒ G(B)

A clockwork marionette theatre, with steel stage and printed card awning suspended over a swinging platform with Celluloid figures, Japanese, 1930s, 10¼in (26cm) wide, in original box.
£650–700
$900–1,000 ⚒ Bea(E)

► **A Hornby miniature porter's barrow and luggage set,** c1925, in original box, 8in (20.5cm) long.
£100–120
$150–175
⊞ HOB

◄ **A child's tin wind-up gramophone,** 'The Fairy Phone', and book of records, c1930, 10in (25.5cm) long.
£450–500
$650–720
⊞ MCC

Three Hornby 0 gauge accessories, No. 1 Footbridge with lattice sides, No. 1 level crossing, single track, No. 2 Signal Cabin with glued posters, late 1930s.
£85–100
$125–150 ⚘ **DN**

A Hornby 0 gauge No. 2 Special Pullman car, 'Loraine', 1930s, 15in (38cm) long, in original box.
£200–240
$300–350 ⚘ **DN**

A Bassett-Lowke steam-powered destroyer, *Vivacious,* with wooden hull, minor damage, 1934, 39in (99cm) long, in original box, together with a postcard showing the *Vivacious* at sea.
£1,400–1,800
$2,000–2,500 ⚘ **Bon(C)**

A Meccano car, 1930s, 14in (30.5cm) long, in original box.
£375–425
$550–600 ⊞ **JUN**

A Chad Valley clockwork car, c1935, 11¼in (29cm) long.
£180–220
$250–300 ⊞ **HUX**

A child's bucket, decorated with a scene of children playing on the beach, 1930s, 7in (18cm) high.
£35–40
$50–60 ⊞ **HUX**

A tinplate clicker, c1930s, 3in (7.5cm) high.
£15–20
$20–30 ⊞ **MRW**

▶ **A Hornby 0 gauge No. 2E station,** 'Margate', with electric bracket lamps, c1936, in original box.
£320–360
$450–500 ⚘ **DN**

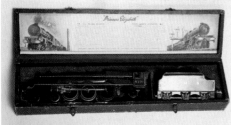

◀ **An engine and tender,** *Princess Elizabeth,* 1938, in original wooden box, 23in (58.5cm) long.
£2,000–2,300
$3,000–3,400 ⊞ **HOB**

▶ **A Britains gnome,** partly painted, c1939, 5½in (14cm) high.
£60–70
$90–100 ⊞ **RUSS**

A Crescent garage set, with metal figures and accessories, incomplete, c1949, 14in (35.5cm) wide.
£450–500
$650–720 ⊞ MRW

A Britains set of eight lead soldiers, No. 2035, 1949–59, 2in (5cm) high, in original box.
£160–180
$230–260 ⊞ UCO

A Hornby No. 50 clockwork goods train set, 1950s, in original box.
£200–220
$300–320 ✗ WAL

An Austin A40 pedal car, 1950s, 39in (99cm) long.
£500–600
$720–870 ✗ HAL

A wooden rocking horse, with horsehair mane and tail, stud eyes, fabric saddle and leather trimming and tack, probably made by J. Collinson & Sons, mid-20thC, 39½in (100cm) high.
£270–320
$400–450 ✗ DN

A Dinky Toys Austin van, No. 471, 1950, 3½in (9cm) long.
£100–125
$150–180 ⊞ UCO

A Lion's Bros Brooklands pedal car, c1952, 39in (99cm) long.
£900–1,000
$1,300–1,500 ⊞ JUN

A tinplate Rocket Racer, Japanese, 1950, 7in 18cm) long.
£100–120
$150–175 ⊞ HUX

◀ **A plywood 56-piece jigsaw puzzle,** c1950s, in original box, 8 x 6in (20.5 x 15cm).
£6–8
$10–15 ⊞ J&J

A TM Space Control toy gun, Japanese, c1950, 4in (10cm) wide.
£60–80
$90–115 ⊞ HUX

A lead figure of Andy Pandy, 1950s, 3in (7.5m) high.
£50–60
$75–90 ⊞ RUSS

A Matchbox commercial vehicle set, comprising No. 5 double-decker bus, No. 11 Esso road tanker, No. 21 long-distance coach, No. 25 Bedford 12cwt van, No. 35 Marshall horse box, No. 40 Bedford 7 ton tipper, No. 47 Trojan Brooke Bond Tea and No. 60 Morris J2 pick-up, late 1950s, boxed.
£300–350
$450–500 ⚹ WAL

A Dinky Toys Guy Flat Truck, No. 512, 1950s, 6in (15cm) long, in original box.
£225–255
$320–350 ⊞ UCO

A clockwork tin model car, French, 1950s.
£225–245
$320–350 ⊞ JUN

An SFA tinplate friction space ship, French, 1950s, 6in (15cm) diam.
£30–35
$40–50 ⊞ HUX

A Matchbox Lesney Foden cement mixer, No. 26, 1950s–60s, 2in (5cm) long, boxed.
£950–1,100
$1,400–1,600 ⚹ VEC

◄ **A Selco plastic musical box,** late 1950s, 11in (29cm) long.
£12–15
$15–20 ⊞ MRW

A Britains set of 12 lead soldiers, No. 2108, Drums and Fifes of the Welsh Guard, 1956, figures 2¼in (5.5cm) high, in original box.
£560–620
$800–870 ⚹ VEC

A Tri-ang Austin Healy 100/6, electric, 1/20 scale, 1950s, 9in (23cm) long, in original box.
£150–180
$220–260 ⊞ UCO

A Modern Toys tinplate Moon Rocket, Japanese, 1950s, 9in (23cm) long.
£180–200
$260–300 ⊞ HUX

A Tri-ang Minic clockwork articulated pantechnicon, with forward-control cab, boxed.
£130–160
$200–230 ⚹ WAL

◀ A Corgi Toys
Mobilgas tanker,
No. 1140, late 1960s,
8in (20.5cm) long, boxed.
£285–325
$400–480 ⊞ UCO

▶ A Corgi Toys Batmobile,
No. 267, 1960s,
6in (15cm) long, boxed.
£350–400
$500–580 ⊞ UCO

A Corgi Toys James Bond 007
Aston Martin DB5, No. 261, late
1960s, 4in (10cm) long, boxed.
£265–300
$380–450 ⊞ UCO

A GEAG tin robot, Japanese, 1970,
9½in (24cm) high, boxed.
£280–300
$400–450 ⊞ HUX

A Corgi Toys Man from UNCLE
'Thrush-Buster', No. 497, early
1970s, 12in (30.5cm) long.
£265–300
$380–450 ⊞ UCO
This model in white would be
worth £800–1,000.

▶ A Corgi Toys James
Bond 007 Toyota GT,
No. 366, from 'You Only
Live Twice', early 1970s,
4in (10cm) long, boxed.
£265–300
$380–450 ⊞ UCO

A Corgi Toys Batboat, No. 107, 2nd series,
early 1970s, 6in (15cm) long, boxed, unopened.
£85–95
$125–145 ⊞ UCO

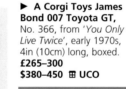

A Smurfs figure of Bully
with umbrella, 1960s–70s,
3in (7.5cm) high.
£10–12
$15–18 ⊞ CMF

◀ A Duncan Fire Wheels
plastic yo-yo, American,
1973, 2¼in (5.5cm) diam.
£10–15
$15–20 ⊞ YO

A Rainbow Arts Turrican computer
game, c1990, 7½in (19cm) high.
£1–2
$2–3 ⊞ CGX

A wooden cream skimmer, c1900, 9½in (24cm) long.
£30–35
$40–50 ⊞ B&R

An inlaid apprentice-piece tray, with folding sides, by A. J. Abreau, Funchal, Madeira, 1850, 18in (45.5cm) long.
£270–300
$400–440 ⊞ MRW

A Tartan ware egg, 1820, 2½in (6.5cm) long.
£60–75
$90–110 ⊞ RdeR

A mahogany, brass and ivory book-holder, c1900, 13in (33cm) high.
£60–70
$90–100 ⊞ HO

◄ **A carved wooden model of a flying fish,** from Pitcairn Island, c1930, 12in (30.5cm) long.
£100–120
$145–175 ⊞ HUM

A burr-mulberry snuff box, 1820, 3½in (9cm) diam.
£80–100
$115–145 ⊞ MB

A cabinet-maker's painted pine tool compactum, with mahogany-lined lid and sliding box with hinged cover above dummy drawers and small drawers, with contemporary and later tools, initialled 'J.B.C.', 19thC, 39in (99cm) wide.
£1,800–2,000
$2,600–3,000 ⋌ HAM

A Mauchline ware bottle holder, 1880s, 4in (10cm) high.
£50–60
$75–90 ⊞ VBo

An Ashanti wood figure, with ornamental coiffure, raised scarification marks to face, neck and back, applied carved pine feet, black varnished patina, Ghanaian, 19thC, 16in (40.5cm) high.
£150–180
$220–260 ⋌ F&C

A Tunbridge ware box for matches, c1900, 4in (10cm) long.
£90–100
$130–145 ⊞ VB

A boxwood container, with fitted glass medicine bottle, c1910, 5in (12.5cm) high.
£60–70
$90–100 ⊞ FST

A brass multi-seal, embossed with the days of the week, 1840–60, 1½in (4cm) diam.
£65–75
$90–110 ⊞ WAC

A Victorian stand-up cut-out birthday card, c1880, 5in (12.5cm) high.
£150–180
$220–260 ⊞ SDP

A set of calling cards, 1930s, 3½ x 2in (9 x 5cm).
£30–35
$45–50 ⊞ LBe

A Tunbridge ware stamp box, by A. Botton, commemorating the Festival of Britain, 1951, 3½in (9cm) long.
£130–150
$200–220 ⊞ VB

A Victorian paper knife Stanhope, the gilt-metal handle modelled as Napoleon, with ivory blade, 4½in (11cm) long.
£55–65
$80–100 ⊞ VB

A Victorian punched paper and appliqué Valentine's card, c1880, 6 x 5in (15 x 12.5cm).
£18–20
$20–30 ⊞ J&S

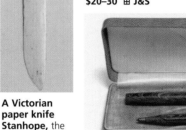

A Waterman's 92½ lady's pen and pencil set, decorated with red and black hard rubber ripple, c1920, 6in (15cm) long, in original treasure chest box.
£90–100
$130–145 ⊞ PPL

A Simplex tinplate typewriter, model No. 250, 1930–40, in original box.
£20–30
$30–45 ➢ BBR

▶ A Parker 51 cocoa and lustraloy fountain pen and liquid lead pencil set, 1950s, 5in (12.5cm) long.
£150–175
$220–250
⊞ PPL

A late Victorian silver-plated pen wipe, 2in (5cm) long.
£25–30
$35–45 ⊞ HO

A pencil sharpener, modelled as a car, cold metal with brass and chrome top, 1930s–50s, 1in (2.5cm) long.
£20–25
$30–40 ⊞ RUSS

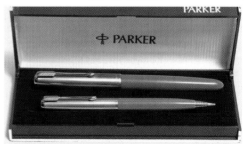

Collectables Under £5

Six boxed valves, 1930–60, largest 7in (18cm) long.
£1–5
$2–7 each ⊞ GM

A paste and glass brooch, 1930s, 1½in (4cm) wide.
£4–5
$6–7 ⊞ STP

A Victorian glass codd bottle, 9in (23cm) high.
£3–4
$5–7 ⊞ BoC

An Arthur Meakin cup and saucer, 1950s–60s, cup 3½in (9cm) high.
£3–4
$5–6 ⋨ FLD

A copy of *Britannia and Eve* magazine, 1946, 12 x 9in (30.5 x 23cm).
£3–5
$5–7 ⊞ MRW

An enamelled metal MS *Dunera* badge, 1950s, 1in (2.5cm) diam.
£4–5
$6–7 ⊞ COB

An illustrated souvenir brochure for Blackpool, late 1950s, 9 x 5in (23 x 12.5cm).
£0.50–1
$1–2 ⊞ MRW

A serviette holder, modelled as a parasol, 1960s, 10in (25.5cm) high.
£4–5
$6–7 ⋨ FLD

A pair of Y-front underpants, 1970s.
£4–5
$6–7 ⋨ FLD

A *Titanic* 3D magnet, Canadian, 1990s, 3in (7.5cm) high.
£3–4
$5–6 ⊞ MAP

▶ **A Wade model of Thumper,** 1956–65, 1¾in (4.5cm) high.
£2–4
$3–6 ⋨ BBR

A pressed aluminium number-plate, reflective paint, Bristol, 1973.
£1–2
$2–3 ⊞ MW

Collectables of the Future

A Vivienne Westwood carrier bag, 2001, 15 x 16in (38 x 40.5cm).
Free ⊞ MM
It is not just designer clothes that are collectable, but also designer carrier bags. Even if you are only buying a pair of socks, always ask for a big bag to take them home in.

An airline sick bag, 2001, 9 x 5in (23 x 12.5cm).
Free ⊞ MM
With airlines all over the world faced with financial crisis, one of the repercussions could be an increase in airline collectables, with the most unlikely items associated with this industry being sought after.

A Martin Rowson pen and watercolour cartoon, 'Britannia's Suitors', signed, 2001, 7½ x 16in (19 x 40.5cm).
£200–250
$300–350 ⊞ POL
Britain has a long tradition of political satire, and this illustration was produced by one of the country's leading cartoonists.

A Harry Potter crew jacket and cap, from the first film *Harry Potter and the Philosopher's Stone*, the black cotton baseball cap with 'Harry Potter' embroidered across the front, the black bomber jacket with fleece-lined collar and embroidered 'stunt world crew' on the left breast and 'Harry Potter The Movie' on the back.
£325–375
$470–560 ↗ FO
Whilst Harry Potter commercial merchandise has been produced in vast quantities, original material from the flm already has a collectable value, and this crew jacket and cap was sold at auction before the film was even released.

An assay mark, commemorating the Golden Jubilee of Queen Elizabeth II, 2002, minimum 1mm wide.
July 2002 marks the Golden Jubilee of Her Majesty Elizabeth II. A voluntary hallmark was created to mark the event, only the 4th Royal commemorative mark in almost 700 years of hallmarking. Applied to gold, silver and platinum articles from 1 January to 31 December 2002, this Golden Jubilee Hallmark adds an interesting feature to an article in precious metal.

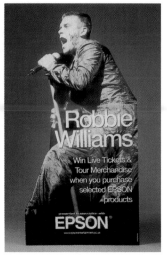

A Robbie Williams autographed standee, by Epson, signed by Robbie Williams, slight creasing, c1999, 71½in (181.5cm) high.
£250–300
$350–450 ↗ S
Ephemera connected with famous popstars can command high prices and the value of this object is enhanced by the fact that it is signed by Robbie.

A Stuart Crystal Aura angled vase, designed by Jasper Conran, 2001, 11in (28cm) high.
£90
$130 ⊞ WED
Fashion designers do not just restrict themselves to clothing and this vase is by Jasper Conran, one of the leading names in British fashion.

Tools

A wooden moulding plane, by J. Rogers, 1734–65, 9¾in (25cm) long.
£20–30
$30–45 ⊞ **WO**

A combination ebony-handled tool, comprising capped screwdriver, with pull-out turn screw revealing tweezers and nipple key, with a pricker at the end of the grip, 1840–50, 5½in (14cm) wide.
£80–100
$115–145 ⊞ **SPA**

A German silver and rosewood smoothing plane, with burr walnut infill, Scottish, c1870, 7in (18cm) long.
£325–375
$470–570 ⊞ **TOM**

A wheelwright's traveller, for measuring cartwheel circumference, c1880, 17in (43cm) high.
£55–65
$80–95 ⊞ **HCJ**

A Continental jeweller's or goldsmith's brass steelyard balance, early 19thC, 4in (10cm) long.
£85–95
$125–140 ⊞ **WO**

A blacksmith-made cart jack, mid-19thC.
£35–40
$50–60 ⊞ **WO**

◀ **A beech plough plane,** by Sims, London, with brass fittings, 19thC, 9in (23cm) long.
£15–30
$20–45 ⊞ **WO**

A barrister's ivory and steel hammer, c1870, 7in (18cm) long.
£55–65
$80–95 ⊞ **HO**

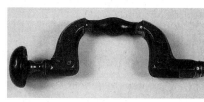

A Marples brass and ebony Ultimatum brace, 19thC, 13in (33cm) long.
£220–280
$320–420 ⊞ **WO**

LOCATE THE SOURCE
The source of each illustration in Miller's can be found by checking the code letters below each caption with the Key to Illustrations, pages 444–452.

A wood and iron adze, c1880, 30in (76cm) high.
£35–45
$50–65 ⊞ **HCJ**

◄ **A mitre shoot,** with wooden threads and multi-adjustment, German, 19thC, 32in (81.5cm) long.
£45–55
$65–80 ⊞ **WO**

A brass Lancashire-pattern shoulder plane, with a shaped mahogany handle, c1900, 9in (23cm) long.
£80–100
$115–145 ⊞ **TOM**

► **A reciprocating drill,** by Goodell-Pratt, patent No. 1895, American, early 20thC.
£28–35
$40–50 ⊞ **WO**

A cabinet-maker's tool chest, the painted exterior enclosing a mahogany interior with oval veneered panel to underside of lid, fitted with a variety of drawers and lidded compartments, early 20thC, 36½in (93cm) wide.
£300–350
$440–500 ⟋ **N**

Three gunmetal violin-maker's planes, by Ed. Preston, c1910, largest 2¼in (5.5cm) long.
£120–150
$175–220 each ⊞ **MRT**

A Stanley 45 plane, with rack of blades, early 20thC, 12in (30.5cm) long.
£65–85
$95–125 ⊞ **WO**

A billhook, by W. Bingham of Shadoxhurst, Kent, 20thC, 16½in (42cm) long.
£18–25
$27–35 ⊞ **WO**

Planes

Planes, used by carpenters for smoothing and moulding wooden surfaces, are among the most collectable woodworking tools. Examples have been found dating back to Roman times and over the centuries innumerable designs have been produced, both in terms of function (shaping different surfaces and objects) and decoration.

A general jobber's steel drill gauge, American, c1930, 6in (15cm) wide.
£15–18
$20–27 ⊞ **FST**

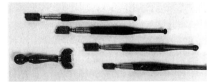

Five wood, brass and steel glass-cutters, c1930, largest 7in (18cm) long.
£8–15
$12–20 each ⊞ **WAB**

A boxwood and brass rope gauge, c1935, 5in (12.5cm) long.
£23–27
$35–40 ⊞ **FST**

A wood and brass travelling knife-grinder, with original paint-work, 1930, 79in (200.5cm) high.
£700–800
$1,000–1,200 ⊞ **MLL**

Toys

An acrobat toy, the two figures joined by mercury-filled bars, on folding stairs, the base with storage drawer, French, c1875, 7in (18cm) wide.
£950–1,100
$1,400–1,600 ↗ SK(B)

▶ **A tinplate clockwork exercising boy,** wearing a striped blue cap, grey sailor suit, red socks and black shoes, early 20thC, 7½in (19cm) high, in original box.
£425–475
$620–700 ↗ Bea(E)

Cross Reference
See Colour Review
(page 391)

A wooden stable, the exterior with brick-effect paper, with two skin-covered horses in full tack, and a tinplate and wood cart, painted blue and red, with wire rails and steering mechanism, 1880s, stable 10¾in (27.5cm) wide.
£150–200
$220–300 ↗ Bon

▶ **A red Tri-ang scooter,** c1900, 32in (81.5cm) high.
£250–300
$360–440 ⊞ STE

◀ **A Dover Toys Mr Jolly articulated wooden toy,** with green hat and painted face, red and black striped socks, 1910, 12in (30.5cm) high, with original box.
£55–65
$80–95 ⊞ J&J

A filigree metal pram, German, 1898, 5in (12.5cm) wide.
£150–200
$220–300 ⊞ PSA

A DRP Junior tin typewriter, with tin cover, German, 1920s, 8in (20.5cm) wide.
£55–65
$80–95 ⊞ JUN

A set of alphabet picture blocks, decorated with chromolithographed letters and pictures of animals and toys, German, c1920, box 15in (38cm) wide.
£450–550
$650–800 ⚲ Bon

Two boxes of Wm Collins coloured magic lantern slides, 'The Pied Piper' and 'Night Before Christmas', from Disney's *Silly Symphony*, c1930, 6in (15cm) wide.
£10–15
$15–20 each ⊞ J&J

A papier mâché model of Bonzo, white on a green base, c1930, 6½in (16.5cm) high.
£45–50
$65–75 ⊞ MRW

▶ **A DRGM clockwork railway porter,** printed tin, pushing an opening trunk on a barrow, c1930, 6in (15cm) wide.
£50–60
$75–90 ⚲ AH

A Tri-ang push-along dog-on-wheels, grey and white, 1930s, 18in (45.5cm) high.
£20–30
$30–45 ⊞ JUN

A tin bucket, decorated with anthropomorphic dogs playing on a beach, c1940, 5½in (14cm) high.
£30–35
$45–50 ⊞ HUX

A brown plastic nodding dog, 1950s–60s, 5in (12.5cm) long.
£15–20
$20–30 ⊞ RUSS

◀ **A wooden lesson board,** the paper roll operated by wind-round mechanism, c1950, 12in (30.5cm) wide.
£30–35
$45–50 ⊞ HO

A 'Riders of the Range' bagatelle game, based on the characters in *Eagle* comic, blue, yellow, red and brown on green, 1950s, 12in (30.5cm) high.
£20–25
$30–35 ⊞ J&J

A bronze-coloured plastic Citroen 2CV car, French, c1960, 6in (15cm) long.
£15–20
$20–30 ⊞ RTT

A Lumar 99 Evening Citizen white plastic competition yo-yo, early 1960s, 2¼in (5.5cm) diam.
£12–15
$17–20 ⊞ YO

A Thomas Damm Troll cow,
with brown mane, Danish, 1960s,
7in (18cm) high.
£25–35
$35–50 ⊞ PLB

A Thomas Damm Troll donkey,
with blonde mane, Danish, 1960s,
3in (7.5cm) high.
£25–35
$35–50 ⊞ PLB

A Peyo Smurf chimney-sweep,
blue with black clothes, 1960s–70s,
2¼in (5.5cm) high.
£10–12
$15–18 ⊞ CMF

A Spectra Star yellow plastic yo-yo,
with a Batman motif, American,
early 1970s, 2½in (5.5cm) diam.
£6–8
$9–12 ⊞ YO

**A Lionel 100th Anniversary train
clock,** the train revolving round the
clock once an hour, with authentic
railroad sounds, and light sensor to
switch off sound at night, American,
1980s, 14in (35.5cm) diam.
£30–35
$45–50 ⋏ LSK

**A Firebird Flying Shark computer
game,** for the Spectrum 48k/128k
computer, 1987, 5½ x 4in
(14 x 10cm) high.
£1–3
$2–5 ⊞ CGX

◄ **A McDonald's Smurf,** blue with
white hat, 1996, 2¼in (5.5cm) high.
£1–3
$2–5 ⊞ CMF

A Flintstones Wilma in car, multi-
coloured, 1993, 3in (7.5cm) high.
£1–2
$2–3 ⊞ CMF
**This was a plastic free gift from
Burger King.**

▶ **A Tom Kuhn Flying Camel
laser-carved rock maple yo-yo,**
American, 1996, 2¼in (5.5cm) diam.
£45–50
$65–75 ⊞ YO

**A Spectra Star glow-in-the-dark
plastic yo-yo,** with *Nightmare
Before Christmas* figure, 1996,
2¼in (5.5cm) diam.
£8–10
$12–15 ⊞ YO

Aeroplanes

A tinplate clockwork passenger monoplane, lithographed with red and black details and RAF roundels, and passengers at windows, German, 1920s, 9in (23cm) long.
£80–120
$115–175 ➤ Bon(C)

A Lehmann tinplate model of a Heinkel HE 111 plane, painted in green, with swastikas to tail, original instruction booklet and box, c1938, 5in (12.5cm) wide.
£475–525
$690–750 ⊞ TOB

▶ **A Meccano single-engined biplane,** with seated pilot, silver finish with RAF roundels and tail markings, 1930s, wingspan 16in (40.5cm).
£70–90
$100–130
➤ WAL

An Arnold tinplate clockwork Douglas DC6B aeroplane, in Scandinavian Airlines livery, 1950s, wingspan 11½in (29cm).
£160–190
$230–275 ➤ VEC

Boats

A Hornby clockwork No. 2 Speedboat, 'Swift', with red hull and cream deck, original key and internal packing, 1930s.
£140–180
$200–260 ➤ VEC

An A-class model yacht, 'Vanity', designed by Marine Models, clinker-built by F. Kemp, with wooden mast and boom, linen sails, brass and metal fixtures and painted wooden stand, with registration certificate, results for 1935, photographs and accessories, 1930–35, mast 9¾in (25cm) high.
£1,500–1,800
$2,150–2,600 ➤ TRM
This yacht was raced under Model Yachting Association rules at Windermere Club.

A Gamages wooden pond yacht, the hull painted blue, c1930, 38in (96.5cm) high.
£300–350
$440–500 ⊞ PEZ

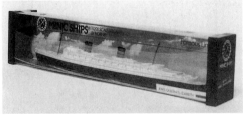

A Hornby Minic Ships diecast model of RMS *Queen Elizabeth,* scale 1:1200, 1972, 12in (30.5cm) long.
£50–55
$75–80 ⊞ FA

Miller's is a price GUIDE not a price LIST

Diecast Vehicles

A diecast car, brown with red cross on door, American, c1910, 4in (10cm) long.
£45–50
$65–75 ⊞ MRW

A Dinky Toys Foden Diesel 8-wheel wagon, No 901, with second-type cab in red and fawn with red hubs, 1954–57, with original box.
£180–220
$260–320 ⚲ P(L)

▶ A Dinky Toys Foden Flat Truck, No. 903, second-type cab in blue, with orange flat-bed and light blue hubs, 1954–56, with original box.
£130–160
$190–230
⚲ P(L)

▶ A Dinky Toys Trojan Esso van, No. 450, red, 1954–57, 3in (7.5cm) long, with original box.
£70–90
$100–130 ⊞ HAL

A Dinky Toys Motorway Police Car, No. 269, 1950s, 4in (10cm) long, with original box.
£100–120
$145–175 ⊞ UCO

▶ A Dinky Toys blue police box, late 1950s, 3in (7.5cm) high.
£30–35
$45–50 ⊞ UCO

A Dinky Toys red Foden Flat Truck, No. 905, with chains, 1950s, 7in (18cm) long, with original box.
£245–275
$350–400 ⊞ UCO

A Corgi Toys Chipperfields Circus crane truck, 1960–68, 8in (20.5cm) long, with original box.
£70–80
$100–115 ⊞ WI

A Primo Renault Tour de France Waterman vehicle, cream with six cast-in blue ink-bottles to each side, red lettering, French, early 1960s, 5in (12.5cm) long, with original box.
£230–260
$330–380 ↗ WAL

▶ A Corgi Toys Chipperfields Circus animal cage, No. 1123, 1960–68, 4in (10cm) long, with original box.
£30–40
$45–60 ⊞ WI

A Dinky Toys AA Patrol Service Minivan, No. 274, early 1960s, 3in (7.5cm) long, with original box.
£130–150
$190–220 ⊞ UCO

▶ A Corgi Toys Superior Ambulance, No. 437, c1965, 5in (12.5cm) long, with original box.
£70–80
$100–115 ⊞ WI

A Dinky Supertoys Autobus Parisien ou Urbain, No. 889, made for the French market, early 1960s, 9in (23cm) long, with original box.
£180–200
$260–300 ⊞ UCO

l. A Corgi Toys Ferrari Berlinetta 250 Le Mans, 1960s, 4in (10cm) long, with original box.
£25–30
$35–50
r. A Corgi Toys Ferrari Berlinetta 250 Le Mans, worn, 1960s, 4in (10cm) long.
£4–6
$6–9 ⊞ HAL

A Dinky Toys Fourgon Peugeot J7 Dépannage Autoroutes, No. 570A, with figures and signs, made for the French market, mid-1960s, original box 10in (25.5cm) long.
£140–170
$200–250 ↗ P(WM)

A Matchbox Series Superfast Mercedes 300SE Coupé, No. 46, in trial colour of orange-yellow with green tinted glass and off-white interior, late 1960s–70s.
£280–320
$400–460 ⚡ VEC

A Corgi Toy Green Hornet, No. 268, early 1970s, 5in (12.5cm) long, with original box.
£325–375
$450–550 ⊞ UCO

A Matchbox Model of Yesteryear 1914 Prince Henry Vauxhall, red with white upholstery, gold wire wheels, 1960–70, 4in (10cm) long, with original box.
£7–9
$10–15 ⊞ HAL

A Corgi Toys James Bond Toyota 2000GT, No. 336, red and black with white interior, 1976, 4in (10cm) long, with original box.
£85–95
$125–140 ⊞ UCO

A Corgi Toys The Monkees Monkeemobile, No. 277, red and white, with figures, 1969–70, 6in (15cm) long, with original box.
£325–375
$500–560 ⊞ UCO

An Airfix Micronauts Neon Orbiter, with figure, 1976, 7¼in (18.5cm) long, with original box.
£15–20
$20–30 ⊞ OW

A Corgi Batman gift set, No. 40, comprising Batmobile, Batboat on trailer and Batcopter, 1977–80, with original box.
£500–550
$700–800 ⚡ WAL

▶ **A Corgi James Bond 007 Secret Service Game,** No. 22, comprising Space Shuttle, Lotus Esprit, Aston Martin, rockets and bandits, 1980–82.
£800–900
$1,200–1,300 ⚡ Bon(C)

Model Soldiers & Figures

A Britains South Australian Lancers Set No. 49, with four Lancers and an Officer with sword on one-eared galloping horses, 1901–19, 3in (7.5cm) high.
£320–360
$450–500 ↗ P(L)

A Britains Pontoon Section of the Royal Engineers Set No. 203a, with four-horse team, light harness with two drivers in khaki service dress, flat wagon, pontoon and roadway section, 1928.
£400–450
$600–650 ↗ VEC

A Britains Zoological Series giraffe, No. 912, minor damage, 1929–41, with original box.
£200–220
$300–330 ↗ S(S)

A Britains motorcycle with sidecar, No. 641, with figures, minor damage, 1932–41.
£450–500
$650–720 ↗ Bon(C)

▶ **A set of white metal figures of Adolf Hitler and two SS guards,** Hitler wearing a tan coat and hat, the guards wearing black SS uniforms, c1938, 2in (5cm) high.
£15–20
$20–30 ⊞ IE

A Britains Togoland Warriors set, in natural colours, 1954–59, 2in (5cm) high, with original box.
£160–180
$230–260 ⊞ UCO

▶ **A Timpo Arctic set,** brown, cream and green, 1946, on original card.
£200–220
$300–330 ↗ WAL

◀ **A set of 10 white metal Royal Marines and mounted officer,** c1960, 2in (5cm) high.
£60–70
$90–100 ⊞ IE

Pedal Cars

A Eureka-style sepia tandem pedal car, probably Spanish, many parts missing, 1920s.
£1,500–2,000
$2,200–3,000 ⊞ CARS

A Tri-ang pedal car, red with white wheels, 1950s–60s.
£90–100
$125–145 ⊞ JUN

A pedal car, red with white trim, 1920s.
£550–650
$800–950 ⊞ JUN

▶ A Tri-ang Austin A40 pedal car, in blue pressed steel with opening bonnet showing dummy engine and spark plugs with leads, battery to power working lights and horn, opening boot and adjustable seat, 1960s, 48in (122cm) long.
£350-420
$500–620 ⊞ CARS

A Tri-ang Overlander pedal car, cream with red wheels, rusty, c1960.
£80–100
$115–145 ⊞ JUN

Robots

▶ A Super Moon Explorer battery-operated plastic robot, with black body and red feet, c1960, 12in (30.5cm) high, with original box.
£75–85
$115–125 ⊞ UCO

A battery-operated tin robot, with plastic fittings, Japanese, 1960s, 11in (28cm) high.
£60–70
$80–100 ⚒ AG

A battery-operated robot, Japanese, 1960s, 12in (30.5cm) high.
£125–150
$180–220 ⊞ HUX

Rocking Horses

A Lines Brothers rocking horse, on a bow rocker, c1880, 30in (76cm) high.
£800–900
$1,150–1,300 ⊞ STE

A child's wooden horse, with original paint decoration, French, 18thC, 26in (66cm) high.
£750–850
$1,100–1,250 ⊞ FCL

A Victorian dapple grey rocking horse, on a green-painted stand, 46½in (118cm) high.
£800–1,000
$1,150–1,500 ⚒ JNic

▶ **A Lines Brothers rocking horse,** restored to original dapple grey colouring, on a trestle and cruciform stand, 1900–10, 55in (140cm) long.
£700–800
$1,000–1,1500 ⚒ HOLL

◀ **A dapple grey rocking horse,** with saddle, reins and stirrups, on a red and black trestle stand, c1890, 38in (96.5cm) high.
£100–125
$145–180 ⊞ GBr

A Collinson rocking horse, with original hair and dapple grey paintwork, on a trestle stand, c1930.
£300–350
$450–500 ⊞ STE

A dapple grey rocking horse, on a trestle stand, early 20thC, 46in (117cm) high.
£550–650
$800–950 ⊞ KA

A painted pine rocking horse, with brass-tacked leather seat, on a trestle stand, early 20thC, 39½in (100.5cm) high.
£500–600
$720–870 ↗ CGC

◄ **A Collinsons rocking horse,** with original hair and leather tack, on a trestle stand, c1940.
£400–500
$580–720 ⊞ STE

► **A Tri-ang Mobo bucking bronco,** on a red metal stand, restored, 1950, 35½in (90cm) high.
£675–750
$980–1,100 ⊞ AQ

Sci-Fi & TV

A Masuda tinplate battery-operated Sonicon Rocket, with attachable radar, and whistle which activates both vehicle and radar, Japanese, 1950s, 11in (28cm) long, in original box.
£330–360
$480–520 ✦ Bon(C)

A battery-operated Star Roto Robot, 1970s, 14in (35.5cm) high, in original box.
£25–30
$35–45 ⊞ PLB

A Thunderbirds Parker porcelain figure, by English Porcelain Classics, 1999, 21in (53.5cm) high, in original box.
£250–300
$350–450 ⊞ UCO

A Daiya Astronaut Rocket Gun, blue and red, Japanese, 1960s, 9in (23cm) wide.
£70–80
$100–115 ⊞ HUX

◀ A Thunderbirds Parker figure, wearing brown jacket and striped trousers, 1966, 12in (30.5cm) high.
£80–90
$115–130 ⊞ UCO
If Parker still had his original chauffeur's hat the price would be doubled.

A Star Wars Millennium Falcon diecast model, c1980, 6½in (16.5cm) long.
£35–40
$50–60 ⊞ CMF

A Dr Who Mechanoid, by Herts Plastic Moulders, green plastic, 1965, 8in (20.5cm) high, in original packaging.
£350–400
$500–650 ⊞ WHO
In 1965, this Mechanoid sold for 4s 11d (just under 25p). Today it is extremely rare to find an unopened example. Smaller versions were produced by Cherilea Toys and these now attract a price range of £75–100 ($110–150).

Cross Reference
See Doctor Who
(page 176)

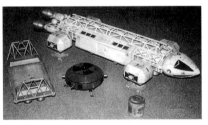

A Space 1999 Eagle Transporter spaceship, original wood, Perspex, metal and plastic studio model, with accessories including Freighter Module, Space Mine and a nuclear waste container, 1975, 22in (56cm) long.
£8,500–9,500
$12,300–13,800 ✦ FO

Five Star Wars plastic figures, c1980, largest 4in (10cm) high.
£4–8
$5–10 each ⊞ HAL

◀ A Star Wars Imperial Cruiser diecast model, with inner ship, c1980, 7½in (19cm) long.
£20–25
$30–35 ⊞ CMF

WALLIS & WALLIS

EST. 1928

WEST STREET AUCTION GALLERIES, LEWES, SUSSEX, ENGLAND BN7 2NJ
TEL: +44 (0)1273 480208 FAX: +44 (0)1273 476562

Britain's Specialist Auctioneers of Diecast Toys, Model Railways, Tin Plate Toys & Models

2002 AUCTION SALES

Sale	97	February 11th	Sale 101 July 15th
Sale	98	March 18th	Sale 102 August 27th
Sale	99	April 29th	Sale 103 October 7th
Sale	100	June 10th	Sale 104 November 18th

A rare mid 1930s Märklin clockwork powered tin plate liner.
Sold for £2,050 in our October 2001 sale.

Catalogues £8.50 incl. postage. Overseas (Airmail) £9.50 inc. postage

"Get to know the real value of your collection"

Our previous catalogues are available at £2.25 each, including postage, complete with prices realised.

TO ENTER ITEMS FOR AUCTION PLEASE ASK FOR ENTRY FORM

email: grb@wallisandwallis.co.uk   web site: http://www.wallisandwallis.co.uk

Tinplate

A tinplate clockwork Citroen coupé, maroon with tan roof, restored, c1925, 15¾in (40cm) long.
£270–300
$400–450 ➢ S(S)

A blue Minic tinplate clockwork Chrysler Air-flow saloon car, some wear, 1930, 5in (12.5cm) long.
£50–60
$75–90 ⊞ HAL

A Tippco tinplate clockwork fire engine, with four firemen, 1930s, 9½in (24cm) long.
£230–275
$330–400 ➢ P(WM)

A Tri-ang Minic clockwork Luton transport van, second series, No. 24M, red and blue, late 1940s, 6in (15cm) long, in original box.
£130–150
$190–220 ➢ WAL

A Tri-ang Minic clockwork transport van, red and green, 85M, minor rusting, 1950s, 5in (12.5cm) long, in original box.
£75–95
$110–150 ➢ WAL

A Tri-ang Minic clockwork articulated mechanical horse and trailer, No. 40M, red cab and dark green trailer with drop-down tailgate, 1950s, 7in (18cm) long, in original box.
£120–140
$175–200 ➢ WAL

Minics

The Minic range was launched by Tri-ang in 1935 and continued until 1963. Similar in size to diecast vehicles, Minics were made from tinplate with a clockwork mechanism (later models were fitted with a 'Push and Go' flywheel drive). Parts were high in quality and well detailed and the finished models were dipped in paint to achieve a high gloss finish. They were also scaled to fit with 0 gauge railway sets, hence their appeal to train collectors today. Minics were made in smaller quantities than their diecast rivals and the paint tended to chip easily, making examples in good condition hard to find. Tri-ang products are marked with a gold-coloured triangle or embossed mark, representing the partnership of the three Lines brothers who founded this offshoot of the family toy business in 1919.

A Mettoy tinplate Indianapolis car, red and yellow, 1950s, 13in (33cm) long.
£285–325
$420–470 ⊞ JUN

◀ **A Tri-ang Minic clockwork mechanical horse and trailer,** No. 73M, red cab and green trailer with two cables, 1950s, 7in (18cm) long, with coloured leaflet and key.
£120–140
$175–200 ➢ VEC

A Marusan tinplate battery-operated Smoky Joe red car and smoking driver, Japanese, 1950s, 10in (25.5cm) long, in original box.
£90–110
$130–160 ➢ Bon(C)
The rubber-headed pipe-smoking driver has an opening by his mouth to allow the smoke to exit.

Trains

A Hornby gauge 0 No. 2 Special Pullman coach, 'Zenobia', brown and cream livery, 1920s, 12in (30.5cm) long.
£100–120
$145–175 ↗ WAL

A Bing gauge 0 clockwork Midland Railway 4–2–2 locomotive, 'Johnson', with six-wheel tender No. 650, maroon livery, German, c1914.
£550–650
$800–950 ↗ P(L)

► **A Bing gauge 1 clockwork 0–4–0 locomotive, '**King Edward VII 1902'. with four-wheel LNWR tender, 1920s, 14in (35.5cm) long.
£140–170
$200–250 ↗ P(WM)

◄ **A Hornby No. 2 Special 4–4–2 tank engine,** green, 1930, 11in (28cm) long.
£125–150
$180–220 ⊞ HOB

An A. & J. van Riemsdyke gauge 00 clockwork 0–6–0T Peckett's No. 1952 locomotive, c1930, 4in (10cm) long, in original tin.
£80–100
$115–145 ↗ P(WM)

A Hornby No. 1 Pullman Coach Corsair, brown and cream livery, 1930, 7in (18cm) long.
£35–40
$50–60 ⊞ HOB

A Hornby gauge 0 No. 1 crane truck, blue, 1935, 6in (15cm) long, in original box.
£50–60
$75–90 ⊞ HOB

◄ A Hornby Great Western truck, with container, c1936, 7in (18cm) long.
£65–75
$95–110 ⊞ HOB

► A electric No. 2E tin train shed, brick and slate-effect, 1936, 20in (51cm) long.
£400–450
$580–650 ⊞ HOB

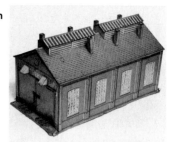

A Bassett-Lowke gauge 0 4–6–2 locomotive, 'Flying Scotsman', No. 4472, with eight-wheel LNER tender, green livery, 1930s.
£700–900
$1,000–1,300 ⚒ P(L)

A Hornby Dublo DL1 gauge 0 clockwork locomotive and tender, 'Sir Nigel Gresley', No. 4498, 1938–41.
£200–250
$290–360 ⚒ P(WM)

A Hornby clockwork Southern A950 locomotive, 1937, 8in (20.5cm) long.
£125–150
$180–220 ⊞ HOB

► A Bassett-Lowke Trix Twin gauge 00 Railway Gift Set, with 4–6–2 'Princess' 6201 locomotive and tender, three coaches and transformer, late 1930s, in original display box.
£600–700
$870–1,000 ⚒ P(WM)

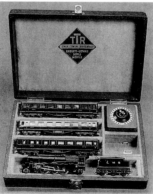

A Hornby 4–4–2T Southern 2091 electric locomotive, late 1930s, in original box.
£350–400
$500–580 ⚒ P(WM)

► An Exley gauge 0 LNER suburban coach, brown livery, c1946, 14in (35.5cm) long, in original box.
£300–350
$450–500 ⊞ HOB

A Hornby train set, c1950, in original box, 18 x 16in (45.5 x 40.5cm).
£300–350
$450–500 ⊞ HOB

◄ A Meccano Esso petrol tank, black, 1949–54, 3½in (9cm) long, in original box.
£45–50
$65–75 ⊞ CWO

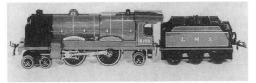

A Hornby No. 2 E320 4–4–2 electric locomotive, 'Royal Scot', No. 6100, with six-wheel LMS tender, red livery, c1950, 14in (35.5cm) long, in original box.
£260–320
$380–450 ✎ AH

A Märklin electric 2–6–6–2 Crocodile goods locomotive, with articulated body, green livery, German, c1960.
£500–550
$720–800 ✎ P(L)

A Hornby Dublo 3250 electric coach, 1962–63, in original box.
£200–240
$290–350 ✎ P(L)

A Wrenn WP100 boxed set, comprising 4–6–0 'Cardiff Castle' locomotive and tender and three Hornby Dublo Pullman coaches, 1968, 8in (20.5cm) long.
£180–210
$260–300 ✎ LSK

A J. & M. Models gauge 1 articulated three-coach rake, teak wood-grain effect, with detailed interiors, 1980s, 45in (114.5cm) long.
£650–700
$950–1,000 ✎ WAL

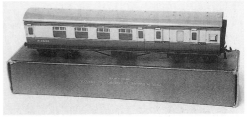

A Hornby Dublo tinplate coach, red and cream livery, 1950s, 8in (20.5cm) long, in original box.
£8–12
$12–18 ⊞ HAL

◄ **A Bassett-Lowke gauge 0 1st Class coach,** No. 3995, red and cream livery, 1950s, 14in (35.5cm) long.
£120–145
$175–200 ✎ WAL

A Micromodels threshing outfit, printed in colour on card, c1960s, 3 x 5in (9 x 12.5cm).
£4–5
$5–7 ⊞ MRW

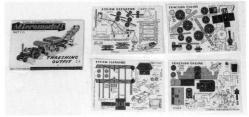

Treen & Wood

A nut and ivory vinaigrette, 19thC, ½in (1.5cm) long.
£80–100
$115–145 ⊞ LBr

A carved wood knitting sheath, c1850, 7in (18cm) long.
£65–75
$100–120 ⊞ WAB

A yew-wood dice shaker,
19thC, 4in (10cm) high.
£25–35
$30–50 ⊞ ALA

A Tartan ware ribbon holder, 1890–1910,
2½in (6.5cm) high.
£70–80
$100–120 ⊞ VBo

A mahogany basque,
carved with birds in a
flowering tree, a huntsman
with a spear and a lion,
monogrammed 'SW', dated
1765, 13½in (34.5cm) long.
£220–250
$320–360 ⚒ DA

A Mauchline ware miniature saucepan, 1870,
1½in (4cm) high.
£60–70
$90–100 ⊞ MB

**A Tunbridge ware
puzzle box,** containing a
seven-piece puzzle, c1870,
2in (5cm) square.
£140–150
$200–220 ⊞ AMH

**A Mauchline ware napkin
ring,** depicting Carisbrooke
Castle, 1890–1910,
2in (5cm) high.
£10–12
$15–18 ⊞ VBo

◀ **A Mauchline ware
larch and sycamore vesta,**
1870, 2½in (6.5cm) high.
£60–70
$90–100 ⊞ MB

A wooden nutcracker,
carved as an old
person's head, c1890,
8in (20.5cm) long.
£80–90
$115–130 ⊞ MLa

A wooden nutcracker,
carved as a dog's head,
with glass eyes, 1920s,
7in (18cm) long.
£65–75
$90–110 ⊞ MLa

Valentines

St Valentine was a Roman martyr, clubbed to death for his support of Christians. It is not known how he became the patron saint of lovers, although the date of Valentine's day, 14 February, has been associated both with the ancient belief that birds traditionally choose their mate on that day and with the Roman Lupercalia – a fertility festival – that took place in mid-February.

Valentine cards became popular in the 19th century thanks to improvements both in printing technology and the postal service. As well as bearing lithographed imagery, cards were embossed, decorated with fabric trimmings and with lace paper, a process said to have been invented by British manufacturer Joseph Addenbrooke in 1834. They came in various styles: flat, 3D, moveable. Some were contained in elaborate presentation boxes and the cosmetics company Rimmel produced scented valentines. Values today depend on imagery, complexity and condition.

A Georgian bone love token, ½in (4cm) long.
£35–40
$50–60 ⊞ VB

◀ **A Victorian forget-me-not card,** blue, green and silver, 1879, 5 x 3½in (12.5 x 9cm).
£18–22
$25–35 ⊞ TAC

An early Victorian hand-painted Valentine card, 10 x 7in (25.5 x 18cm).
£110–130
$145–185 ⊞ WI

A Victorian cut-out Valentine card, c1860, 7 x 5in (18 x 12.5cm).
£40–45
$60–70 ⊞ SDP

◀ **A Victorian die-cut Valentine card,** 8in (20.5cm) square.
£35–40
$50–60 ⊞ WI

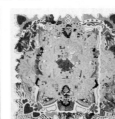

A Victorian punched paper and appliqué Valentine card, green, red and lilac on a white ground, c1880, 6 x 4in (15 x 10cm).
£15–20
$20–30 ⊞ J&S

A Victorian forget-me-not card, blue, red, green and yellow, 1879, 5 x 3½in (12.5 x 9cm).
£18–22
$25–35 ⊞ TAC

▶ **A Victorian moveable pop-up Valentine card,** c1880, 5 x 4in (12.5 x 10cm).
£140–160
$200–230 ⊞ SDP

A pop-up 'Jazz Band' Valentine card, with three cherubs on a bandstand playing musical instruments, framed and glazed, c1925, 11¾ x 9in (30 x 23cm).
£55–65
$80–100 ⋟ RTo

Walking Sticks

A wooden walking stick, with a dog's-head handle, glass eyes and gold collar, c1870, 34in (86.5cm) long.
£280–330
$400–500 ⊞ GBr

A brass self-defence cane, the handle in the form of a medieval head wearing a long cap with curled brim, on a coconut shaft with horn ferrule, c1860, 36½in (92.5cm) long.
£1,300–1,600
$2,000–2,300 ⊞ MGe

An ebonized cane, the pewter handle with four faces, c1860, 36in (89cm) long.
£250–300
$360–440 ⊞ GBr

A mahogany cane, with carved lion handle, c1870, 33in (84cm) long.
£110–130
$160–200 ⊞ GBr

A briar-wood walking stick, with a rabbit's-head handle, plain silver collar, c1880, 36in (89cm) long.
£500–600
$720–870 ⊞ MGe

A malacca cane, the shagreen crook handle with gilt collar, horn ferrule, c1910, 35½in (90cm) long.
£300–350
$450–500 ⊞ MGe

A wooden folk art walking stick, carved as a snake eating a frog on a thorny branch, with ball and hand handle, 19thC, 32in (81.5cm) long.
£110–130
$160–200 ⊞ GBr

A wooden cane, with greyhound handle and silver collar, c1880, 34in (86.5cm) long.
£200–225
$300–330 ⊞ GBr

◀ **A hardwood walking stick,** the ivory handle modelled as a lady's leg wearing a button-sided boot, late 19thC, 36¾in (93.5cm) long.
£750–820
$1,000–1,200 ➹ DMC

An umbrella, with silver swan's-head handle, by Charles William West, London 1914, 34in (86.5cm) long.
£150–180
$220–260 ➹ WW

An Edwardian celluloid dog parasol handle, brown and cream, 3in (7.5cm) high.
£14–16
$20–25 ⊞ VB

Wallpaper

Wallpaper is a subject new to this guide. Modern interest in interior design has stimulated demand both for architectural salvage and vintage décor. There is an established market for fine examples of historic wall coverings: *papiers peints* from the 18th century, original Arts and Crafts designs from the 19th. A strip of William Morris wallpaper from 1892, the floral pattern inscribed with pencilled notes, recently fetched £36,000 ($52,000) at a Glasgow auction. Such items appeal to the academic collector (for example design and architecture historians) and wallpaper fragments often end up being framed like paintings.

This section, however, is devoted to the more humble world of washable vinyl and is dominated by post WWII wallpaper. Such material is bought by those who wish to do up a room in a period style, or by enthusiasts with a specific collectable passion (ie Mabel Lucie Attwell or Thunderbirds).

A set of nine Mabel Lucie Attwell wallpaper cut-outs, by Sanderson, in reds, greens, yellows and blues, c1930, 10in (25.5cm) square.
£150–180
$220–260 ⊞ MEM

A roll of wallpaper, by Crown, printed with landmarks and modes of transport in yellow, green, red and blue, 1960, 20½in (52cm) wide, 17in (43cm) repeat.
£55–65
$80–95 per repeat ⊞ TWI

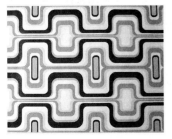

A roll of embossed wallpaper, depicting a historical scene in green, blue, yellow and grey, 1950, 21in (53.5cm) wide.
£30–35
$40–50 ⊞ TWI

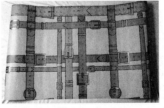

A roll of wallpaper, by Crown, printed in brown and orange on a beige ground, 1960, 20¾in (52.5cm) wide, 21in (53.5cm) repeat.
£55–65
$80–95 per repeat ⊞ TWI

▶ **A roll of *Thunderbirds* wallpaper,** by ITC ENT, blue, yellow and red, 1992, 20½in (52cm) wide, 21in (53.5cm) repeat.
£45–50
$65–75 per repeat ⊞ TWI

◀ **A roll of wallpaper,** black, grey, cream and white, 1970, 21in (53.5cm) wide, 21in (53.5cm) repeat.
£65–75
$100–120 per repeat ⊞ TWI

A roll of wallpaper, printed with a French scene in red, green, yellow and blue on a white ground, 1960, 20½in (52cm) wide, 18in (45.5cm) repeat.
£75–85
$115–125 per repeat ⊞ TWI

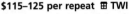

A roll of wallpaper, by Crown, orange, brown, beige and white, 1970, 21in (53.5cm) wide.
£20–25
$30–40 ⊞ TWI

Watches & Clocks

A silver-plated pocket watch, c1895, 40mm diam.
£40–50
$60–75 ⊞ AOH

A Swiss lever half-hunter pocket watch, signed 'H Goodman 17 London Road Twickenham', London import mark and maker's mark 'GB', 1904, 20mm diam.
£250–290
$350–400 ⊞ PT

▶ **A silver pocket watch stand,** Birmingham 1904, 3in (7.5cm) high.
£50–60
$75–90 ⊞ AOH

A Goliath travelling watch, in a silver-fronted leather travelling case, key wind, enamel dial slightly damaged, Birmingham 1908, 5in (12.5cm) high.
£55–65
$80–95 ⚒ GAK

A stainless steel extra flat Universal mechanical pocket watch, with 17 jewel movement, c1930, 40mm diam.
£160–190
$225–275 ⊞ HARP

A Rolex Oyster wristwatch, the steel case with gold bezel, original dial, c1950.
£550–650
$800–1,000 ⊞ HARP

An Omega Constellation stainless steel wristwatch, officially certified chronometer, automatic day date, black dial, c1973.
£350–400
$500–600 ⊞ HARP

A Heuer mechanical stopwatch, c1980.
£80–100
$115–145 ⊞ HARP

A Heuer Regatta automatic wristwatch, with five minute indication on the dial for yacht racing, c1980.
£500–600
$720–870 ⊞ HARP

A Swatch plastic advertising wall-hanging battery-operated wristwatch, red, black and green, 1980s.
£70–80
$100–120 ⚒ BBR

▶ **A Longines silver wristwatch,** 1980s, 9in (23cm) long.
£400–450
$600–650 ⊞ LBe

◀ **A Seiko Chronograph RAF quartz wristwatch,** minor scratching, 1984.
£125–145
$180–220 ⊞ HARP

A KLG Plugs grey glass advertising wall clock, 1930s, 12in (30.5cm) high.
£300–350
$440–500 ⊞ MURR

A Bulle electric mantel clock, 1920s, 10in (25.5cm) high.
£90–110
$130–160 ↗ SWO

An oak mantel clock, in the manner of Gustave Serrurier-Bovy, with brass dial, striking on a gong, c1900, 14in (35.5cm) high.
£600–700
$875–1,000 ↗ S(S)

Miller's is a price GUIDE not a price LIST

▶ **A Westclox Scotland wall clock,** yellow and white, with tin rim, 1960, 7½in (19cm) diam.
£70–80
$100–115 ⊞ Mo

A walnut longcase clock, with anodised dial, on cushion base and shaped square feet, 1930s, 77in (195.5cm) high.
£525–625
$750–900 ↗ DA

A Dartington Glass pyramid clock, 1980s, 3¾in (9.5cm) high.
£8–10
$12–15 ⊞ Law

World War II

A National Service information booklet, issued by HMSO, in red and white, 1939, 9 x 6in (23 x 15cm).
£6–10
$10–15 ⊞ J&S

Sheet music for *Thumbs Up,* in red, black and white, 1940, 12 x 9½in (30.5 x 24cm).
£4–5
$5–7 ⌖ RUSS

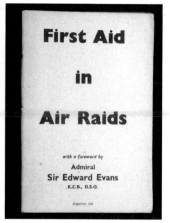

First Aid in Air Raids, with a foreword by Admiral Sir Edward Evans, KCB, DSO, yellow with black lettering, 1941, 7 x 5in (18 x 12.5cm).
£2–3
$5–6 ⊞ HUX

An ARP Home First Aid Case, by Boots Pure Drug Co, black with yellow lettering, 1940s, 12¾in (32.5cm) long.
£25–30
$35–45 ⊞ HUX

A brown RAF autograph book, 1941, 4 x 5in (10 x 12.5cm).
£35–45
$50–65 ⊞ COB

A metal Spitfire badge, 1939–45, 1½in (4cm) long.
£35–40
$50–60 ⊞ REN

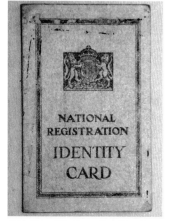

A National Registration Identity Card, 1943, 8¾ x 5½in (22 x 14cm).
£1–2
$2–3 ⊞ HUX

Bristol Evening Post, Victory Day, 1945, 17 x 12in (43 x 30.5cm).
£5–8
$7–10 ⊞ J&S

A commemorative horse brass, 1945, 4in (10cm) diam.
£35–40
$50–60 ⊞ PJo

Writing

An ivory-handled steel ink eraser, 18thC,
6in (15cm) long.
£35–40
$50–60 ⊞ PPL

A Samuel Pemberton hand-engraved silver porte-crayon, with ruler, c1800, 4½in (11.5cm) long.
£125–150
$180–220 ⊞ PPL

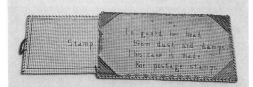

A needlework card for postage stamps, c1860,
2½ x 3½in (6.5 x 9cm).
£20–30
$30–45 ⊞ VB

A silver novelty pencil, in the shape of a rifle, c1880,
4in (10cm) long.
£190–220
$275–325 ⊞ PPL

A Victorian cast-iron and glass inkwell, with pen holder,
5in (12.5cm) wide.
£130–150
$200–220 ⊞ MRW

A golden amber-coloured glass tea kettle inkwell, 2in (5cm) high.
£110–130
$160–200 ⋟ BBR

A bellowing man inkwell, the brown and tan salt-glazed face with quill hole to forehead, garland of grapes and vines to the edge,
3in (7.5cm) high.
£80–90
$115–135 ⋟ BBR

◄ **A Perry & Co glass inkwell,** with blue glass lid, c1890,
2in (5cm) high.
£50–60
$75–90 ⊞ PPL

A brass travelling inkwell, c1890,
2in (5cm) high.
£40–45
$60–65 ⊞ HO

▶ **A Sampson Mordan silver Popular desk pen and pencil set,** marked, c1890, 6½in (16.5cm) long, in original box.
£225–250
$320–360 ⊞ PPL

▶ **A seal/tamper,** with bone handle, 19thC, 1½in (4cm) long.
£15–20
$20–30 ⊞ WAC

◀ **A Victorian cast-iron documents spike,** 6in (15cm) long.
£25–30
$35–45 ⊞ HO

A Sampson Mordan gold carpenter's pencil, in a holder, hallmarked, 1920, 3½in (9cm) long.
£140–160
$200–230 ⊞ PPL

◀ **A brass seal,** with acorn handle, inscribed 'E', 1890–1910, 3in (7.5cm) long.
£28–32
$37–42 ⊞ WAC

An Onoto hard rubber pump-filler fountain pen, black with 18ct gold bands, 1920s, 6in (15cm) long.
£90–100
$130–145 ⊞ PPL

▶ **A Conway Stewart Dinkie red and black mottled fountain pen,** 1926, 3½in (9cm) long.
£60–80
$95–115 ⊞ RUS

A Swan Minor SM2.57 blue, black and gold marble fountain pen, 1920s, 5in (12.5cm) long.
£65–75
$95–110 ⊞ PPL

A Parker Lucky Curve True Blue fountain pen, 1920s, 5in (12.5cm) long.
£90–110
$130–160 ⊞ PPL

A Parker Falcon gold-plated Lattice fountain pen, 1979, 5in (12.5cm) long.
£100–120
$145–175 ⊞ RUS

An Ever-Sharp Skyline pen and pencil, 1940, 5in (12.5cm) long.
£110–130
$160–200 ⊞ AOH

Record Breakers

This section is devoted to objects that have made significant or record breaking prices at auction.

The world's first Christmas card, signed by Henry Cole, 1843, 3 x 5in (7.5 x 12.5cm).
World Record Price
£22,350
$32,400 ⚹ HAld

▶ A FA Cup winner's gold medal, presented to Stanley Matthews in 1953, 2in (5cm) high.
World Record Price
£23,500
$34,000 ⚹ S(O)
Stanley Matthews was one of Britain's most famous and respected football players. When his 1953 FA Cup winner's gold medal came up for auction at Sotheby's it sold for £23,500 setting a new world record for an FA Cup winner's medal. The purchaser was Nick Hancock, TV presenter and Stoke City fan.

A Dunhill-Namiki Giant *maki-e* lacquer fountain pen, decorated with two dragons, signed 'Shogo', 1928–30, 6in (15cm) long.
World Record Price
£183,000
$265,000 ⚹ Bon

▶ A coffin-shaped cobalt-blue glass poison bottle, embossed 'Patent 5658 Poison' within a shield, entwined initials within a circle, c1871, 6½in (16.5cm) high.
World Record Price
£9,750
$14,000 ⚹ BBR
This is perhaps the rarest of all poison bottles. In 1871, G. F. Langford was granted provisional patent protection for a bottle in the shape of a coffin. It appears not to have been a popular design and was soon dropped from production. Only three were known to exist until a bottle digger excavated this example from a Pontefract dump. Sold by bottle specialists BBR, it fetched an auction record of £9,750.

A *Thunderbirds* puppet, Parker, wearing a pin-striped morning suit, white shirt and black bow-tie, 1960s, 20in (51cm) high, in later custom-made storage case.
World Record Price
£38,000
$55,000 ⚹ FO
Parker was Gerry Anderson's favourite *Thunderbirds* character and he appeared in all 32 episodes of the television series. When it came up for auction at Fleetwood Owen's sale of film and TV memorabilia, this original Parker puppet from the series sold for £38,000. F.A.B.!

A Pelham clown string puppet, wearing a red hat and a camouflage suit, 1948–50, 12in (30.5cm) high.
World Record price
£1,350
$2,000 ⚹ DN
Pelham puppets were extremely popular in the 1950s and '60s and many people still have one lurking in the attic. This clown came up for auction at Dreweatt Neate and was sold to a telephone bidder for a record price of £1,350, exceeding the figure paid earlier this year for a prototype tortoise puppet.

Baca

BRITISH ANTIQUES AND COLLECTABLES AWARDS

presented by

In association with

Celebrating the Winners of BACA 2001

The Dorchester Hotel played host to the second of the British Antiques and Collectables Awards on Tuesday 19th June 2001. These Awards are designed to recognize excellence across the Antiques and Collectables industry. This year saw the inclusion of eight new Awards, and it is envisaged that over the following years BACA will rotate its Awards and/or Categories to include all areas of the trade.

How to Vote for 2002

The voting process for the 2002 Awards begins now and will end in March 2002.
For a voting form, please write to BACA or log on to the website:

BACA/Miller's
2-4 Heron Quays
London E14 4JP
www.baca-awards.co.uk

To date, BACA have received an overwhelming response – be it nominations, ideas, support and sponsorship. We would be very interested to hear from you on the subject of new Categories and new Awards for 2002 - but most importantly of course, we want your vote!

PROUDLY SPONSORED BY

The BACA *Winners...*

CATEGORY 1
General Antiques Dealer

LONDON (INSIDE M25)
sponsored by
Windsor House Antiques
28-29 Dover Street, Mayfair, London W1X 3PA

UK (OUTSIDE M25) *sponsored by*
David J. Hansord & Son
6 & 7 Castle Hill, Lincoln,
Lincolnshire LN1 3AA

CATEGORY 2
Specialist Antiques Dealers

FURNITURE
Norman Adams
8-10 Hans Road, Knightsbridge, London SW3 1RX

CERAMICS
Roderick Jellicoe
3a Campden Street, off Kensington Church St,
London W8 7EP

CLOCKS, WATCHES & SCIENTIFIC INSTRUMENTS
Brian & Joy Loomes
Calf Haugh Farmhouse, Pateley Bridge, Harrogate,
N. Yorks HG3 5HW

SILVER & PLATE
Nicholas Shaw Antiques
Great Grooms Antiques Centre, Parbrook,
Billingshurst, West Sussex RH14 9EU

COLLECTABLES
Ropewalk Antiques
Rye, East Sussex TN31 7NA

TOYS & DOLLS
Yesterday's Child
Angel Arcade, 118 Islington High Street,
London N1 8EG

JEWELLERY
N. Bloom & Son
The New Bond St Antiques Centre,
124 New Bond Street, London W1S 1DX

ARMS & ARMOUR
Trident Arms
96-98 Derby Road, Nottingham NG1 5FB

COSTUMES & TEXTILES
Linda Wrigglesworth Ltd
34 Brook Street, London W1K 5DN

ARCHITECTURAL & GARDEN
LASSCO
The London Architectural Salvage
and Supply Co, St Michael's Church,
Mark Street, London EC2 4ER

CATEGORY 3
Auction Houses

LONDON (INSIDE M25)
Phillips
101 New Bond Street, London W1S 1SR

UK (OUTSIDE M25)
Tennants Auctioneers
The Auction Centre, Leyburn,
N. Yorkshire DL8 5SG

CATEGORY 4
Associated Awards

 For a significant
contribution to the
popular appreciation
of Antiques
The BBC Antiques Roadshow

FAIR OF THE YEAR
Olympia Fine Art & Antiques Fair
June 2000, Olympia, London

BEST IN-HOUSE EXHIBITION *sponsored by* Antiques Trade GAZETTE
Pelham Galleries
"East and West:
Masterpieces of Lacquer Furniture",
24-25 Mount Street, London W1Y 5RB

AUCTIONEER OF THE YEAR
Ben Lloyd
Mallams, Bocardo House, St Michael's Street,
Oxford OX1 2DR

BEST ANTIQUES WRITER *sponsored by*
Christopher Wood
Christopher Wood Gallery, 20 Georgian House,
10 Bury Street, London SW1Y 6AA

SERVICES AWARD: BEST FREIGHT CARRIER *sponsored by* CHRISTIE'S
Lockson
29 Broomfield Street, London E14 6BX

MILLER'S CLUB **BEST ANTIQUES TOWN/VILLAGE**
Horncastle, Lincolnshire

Directory of Specialists

If you require a valuation for an item it is advisable to check whether the dealer or specialist will carry out this service, and whether there is a charge. Please mention Miller's when making an enquiry. Having found a specialist who will carry out your valuation, it is best to send a description and photograph of the item to them, together with a stamped addressed envelope for the reply. A valuation by telephone is not possible. Most dealers are only too happy to help you with your enquiry, however, they are very busy people and consideration of the above points would be welcomed.

Berkshire

Collect It!, Unit 11, Weller Drive,
Hogwood Industrial Estate,
Finchampstead RG40 4QZ
Tel: 0118 973 7888
sales@collectit.co.uk www.collectit.co.uk
Magazine for Collectors.

Mostly Boxes, 93 High Street, Eton,
Windsor SL4 6AF
Tel: 01753 858470
Fax: 01753 857212
Antique wooden boxes.

Special Auction Services, The Coach
House, Midgham Park,
Reading RG7 5UG
Tel: 0118 971 2949
Fax: 0118 971 2420
www.invaluable.com/sas/
*Commemoratives, pot lids & Prattware,
Fairings, Goss & Crested, Baxter & Le
Blond prints.*

Cambridgeshire

Antique Amusement Co, Mill Lane,
Swaffham Bulbeck CB5 0NF
Tel/Fax: 01223 813041
www.aamag.co.uk
*Vintage amusement machines also
auctions of amusement machines,
fairground art and other related
collectables.*

Cloisters Antiques, 1A Lynn Road,
Ely CB7 4EG Tel: 01353 668558
info@cloistersantiques.co.uk
www.cloistersantiques.co.uk
*Sewing, writing, heavy horse and
antiquarian books.*

Canada

Waddington's, 111 Bathurst Street,
Toronto, ON M5V 2R1
Tel: 416 504 9100 Fax: 416 504 0033
www.waddingtonsauctions.com
Auctioneers.

When The Hammer Goes Down,
440 Douglas Avenue, Toronto,
ONT M5M 1H4 Tel: 416 787 1700
BIDCALR@home.com
www.bidcalr.com
Auctioneers.

Cheshire

The Antique Garden, Grosvenor
Garden Centre, Wrexham Road,
Belgrave, Chester CH4 9EB
Tel: 01244 629191
Mobile: 07976 539 990
Fax: 01829 733802
info@antique-garden.co.uk

www.antique-garden.co.uk
*Original antique garden tools and
accessories.*

Collector's Corner, PO Box 8,
Congleton CW12 4GD
Tel: 01260 270429
Tel/Fax: 01260 298996
dave.popcorner@ukonline.co.uk
Beatles and pop memorabilia.

Dollectable, 53 Lower Bridge Street,
Chester CH1 1RS
Tel: 01244 344888/679195
Fax: 01244 679469
Antique dolls.

On The Air, The Vintage Technology
Centre, The Highway, Hawarden,
(Nr Chester), Deeside CH5 3DN
Tel/Fax: 01244 530300
www.vintageradio.co.uk
Vintage radios.

Sweetbriar Gallery, Robin Hood Lane,
Helsby WA6 9NH Tel: 01928 723851
Mobile 07860 907532
Tel: 01928 724153
sweetbr@globalnet.co.uk
www.sweetbriar.co.uk
Paperweights.

Charles Tomlinson, Chester
Tel/Fax: 01244 318395
charles.tomlinson@lineone.net
charles.tomlinson@btinternet.com
www.lineone.net/-charles.tomlinson
Scientific instruments.

Cleveland

Vectis Auctions Ltd/Barry Potter
Auctions, Fleck Way, Thornaby,
Stockton-on-Tees TS17 9JZ
Tel: 01642 750616 Fax: 01642 769478
admin@vectis.co.uk
admin@barrypotterauctions.com
www.vectis.co.uk
www.barrypotterauctions.co.uk
Toy auctions.

Cornwall

Gentry Antiques, Little Green, Polperro
PL13 2RF Tel: 01503 272 361
info@cornishwarecollector.co.uk
www.cornishwarecollector.co.uk
*Cornish ware. Also at Gray's Antique
Market Mews, London W1
Tel: 020 7792 1402*

Derbyshire

Bear Hugs Restoration - On Tired Old
Bears, Bev McNab, Long Cottage,
Eggington Road, Etwall DE65 6NB

Tel/Fax: 01283 734147
bevmcnab@talk21.com
www.bear-hugs.co.uk
*Superior restoration on Yesterdays
Bears! Have your Teddy Bear restored
back to life!*

Devon

The Pen and Pencil Lady
Tel: 01647 231619
penpencilady@aol.com
www.penpencilady.com

Dorset

Ancient & Gothic Tel: 01202 431721
Antiquities.

Books Afloat, 66 Park Street, Weymouth
DT4 7DE Tel: 01305 779774
*Books on all subjects, liner and naval
memorabilia, shipping company china,
ships bells, old postcards, models,
paintings.*

The Crow's Nest, 3 Hope Square,
opp. Brewers Quay, Weymouth DT4 8TR
Tel: 01305 786930
peter.ledger3@btopenworld.com
Nautical collectables.

Dalkeith Auctions Ltd, Dalkeith Hall,
Dalkeith Steps, Rear of 81 Old
Christchurch Road, Bournemouth
BH1 1YL Tel: 01202 292905
how@dalkeith-auctions.co.uk
www.dalkeith-auctions.co.uk
*Auctions of postcards, cigarette cards,
ephemera and collectors items.*

Hardy's Collectables, 862 Christchurch
Road, Boscombe, Bournemouth
BH7 6DQ Tel: 07970 613077
www.poolepotteryjohn.com
Poole pottery.

Murrays' Antiques & Collectables
Tel: 01202 309094
*Shipping, motoring, railway, cycling items
always require. Also advertising related
items, eg showcards, enamel signs, tins &
packaging and general quality
collectables. Anything old and interesting.*

Old Button Shop Antiques, Lytchett
Minster, Poole BH16 6JF
Tel: 01202 622169
Buttons & collectables.

Poole Pottery, Sopers Lane, Poole
BH17 7PP Tel: 01202 666200
Fax: 01202 682894
www.poolepottery.com
Poole Pottery.

www.collectorsworld.net, PO Box 4922, Bournemouth BH1 3WD
Mobile 07860 791588
info@collectorsworld.biz
www.collectorsworld.net
www.collectorslondon.com
www.collectorsworld.biz
19th and 20th century watches, clocks, cameras. Toys, Dinky, Corgi and diecast. TV/film related, tinplate cars, boats, planes, robots, dolls and teddy bears. Disneyana, memorabilia. Open 24 hours and on the web.

Essex

Brandler Galleries, 1 Coptfold Road, Brentwood CM14 4BN
Tel: 01277 222269 Fax: 01277 222786
john@brandler-galleries.com
www.brandler-galleries.com

Nick Garner Tel: 07970 206682 or 01245 261863
nickgarner@btinternet.com
www.ngarners.co.uk
Sally Tuffin, Dennis china, Dartington, Highland stoneware, Roger Cockram, Moorcroft, and more. Antiques and collectables. Outlets in Chipping Ongar and Ipswich. Ring for details.

GKR Bonds Ltd, PO Box 1, Kelvedon CO5 9EH Tel: 01376 571711
Fax: 01376 570125
Old bonds and share certificates.

Haddon Rocking Horses Ltd, 5 Telford Road, Clacton on Sea CO15 4LP
Tel: 01255 424745 Fax: 01255 475505
millers@haddonrockinghorses.co.uk
www.haddonrockinghorses.co.uk
Rocking horses.

Megarry's and Forever Summer, Jericho Cottage, The Duckpond Green, Blackmore CM4 0RR
Tel: 01277 821031 or 01277 822170
Antiques, Arts & Crafts. 11am–5pm Wed–Sun closed Mon and Tues. Member Essex Antiques Dealers Association.

The Old Telephone Company, The Old Granary, Battlesbridge Antiques Centre, Nr Wickford SS11 7RF
Tel: 01245 400601
Fax: 01245 401054
gp@theoldtelephone.co.uk
www.theoldtelephone.co.uk
Period telephones.

Gloucestershire

Bread & Roses, Durham House Antique Centre, Sheep Street, Stow on the Wold GL54 1AA Tel: 01451 870404 or 01926 817342
Kitchen antiques 1800–1950s.

Grimes House Antiques, High Street, Moreton-in-Marsh GL56 0AT
Tel/Fax: 01608 651029
grimes_house@cix.co.uk
grimeshouse.co.uk cranberryglass.co.uk

Olliff's Architectural Antiques, 19–21 Lower Redland Road, Redland, Bristol BS6 6TB Tel: 0117 923 9232

Fax: 0117 923 9880
marcus@olliffs.com
www.olliffs.com

Park House Antiques & Toy Museum, Park Street, Stow-on-the-Wold GL54 1AQ Tel: 01451 830159
info@thetoymuseum.co.uk
www.thetoymuseum.co.uk
Come and see one of the best private collections of old toys in the country. Admission £2, OAPs £1.50. Summer 10am–1pm, 2–5pm. Winter 11am–1pm, 2–4pm. Closed Tues and all May. Please ring to confirm if travelling long distance. We buy old toys and teddy bears.

Specialised Postcard Auctions, 25 Gloucester Street, Cirencester GL7 2DJ
Tel: 01285 659057 Fax: 01285 652047
Sales of early postcards and ephemera.

Telephone Lines Ltd, 304 High Street, Cheltenham GL50 3JF
Tel: 01242 583699 Fax: 01242 690033
Telephonelines.freeserve.co.uk
www.telephonelines.net
Antique telephones.

Hampshire

Classic Amusements Tel: 01425 472164
pennyslot@aol.com
www.classicamusements.net

Cobwebs, 78–80 Old Northam Road, Southampton SO14 0PB
Tel/Fax: 023 8022 7458
www.cobwebs.uk.com
Ocean liner memorabilia. Also naval and aviation items.

Goss & Crested China Centre & Museum, incorporating Milestone Publications, 62 Murray Road, Horndean PO8 9JL Tel: (023) 9259 7440
Fax: (023) 9259 1975
info@gosschinaclub.demon.co.uk
www.gosscrestedchina.co.uk
Goss & Crested china.

The Old Toy Shop, PO Box 4389, Ringwood BH24 1YN
Tel: 01425 470180
djwells@btinternet.com
www.TheOldToyShop.com
Clockwork, steam & electric vintage toys & memorabilia and figures.

Romsey Medal Centre, PO Box 169, Romsey SO51 6XU
Tel: 01794 324488 Fax: 01794 324411
post@romseymedals.co.uk
www.romseymedals.co.uk
Orders, decorations & medals.

Solent Railwayana Auctions
Tel: 01489 584633
Railway relics and model railway items. Also Railwayana auctions.

Hertfordshire

Brown & Merry, Tring Market Auctions, Brook Street, Tring HP23 5EF
Tel: 01442 826446 Fax: 01442 890927
sales@tringmarketauctions.co.uk
www.tringmarketauctions.co.uk

Forget-Me-Knot Antiques, Over the Moon, 27 High Street, St Albans AL3 4EH Tel: 01727 848907
Tel/Fax: 01923 261172
Jewellery.

Isle of Wight

Nostalgia Toy Museum, High Street, Godshill, Ventnor PO38 3HZ
Tel: 01983 730055 Fax: 01983 821296
Diecast toys specialist and museum.

Kent

20th Century Marks, 12 Market Square, Westerham TN16 1AW
Tel: 01959 562221
Mobile 07831 778992
Fax: 01959 569385
lambarda@btconnect.com
www.20thcenturymarks.co.uk
Original 20th century design.

Chris Baker Gramophones, All Our Yesterdays, 3 Cattle Market, Sandwich CT13 9AE Tel: 01304 614756
cbgramophones@aol.com
Specialist dealer in gramophones and phonographs.

Beatcity, P O Box 229, Chatham ME5 8WA Tel/Fax: 01634 200444
Mobile: 07770 650890
Darrenhanks@beatcity.co.uk
www.beatcity.co.uk
Beatles and rock & roll memorabilia.

Candlestick & Bakelite, PO Box 308, Orpington BR5 1TB
Tel: 020 8467 3743/3799
candlestick.bakelite@tesco.net
www.candlestickandbakelite.co.uk
Telephones.

Dragonlee Collectables
Tel: 01622 729502
Noritake.

Paul Haskell Tel: 01634 891796
Mobile: 07774 781160
www.antiqueslotmachines.inuk.com
Old mechanical slot machines.

Stuart Heggie, 14 The Borough, Northgate, Canterbury CT1 2DR
Tel/Fax: 01227 470422
Vintage cameras, optical toys and photographic images.

J & M Collectables Tel: 01580 891657
jandmcollectables@tinyonline.co.uk
Postcards, Crested china, Osborne (Ivorex) plaques and small collectables including Doulton, Wade, etc.

Lambert & Foster, 102 High Street, Tenterden TN30 6HT
Tel: 01580 762083 Fax: 01580 764317
lf@tenterden14.freeserve.co.uk
www.lambertandfoster.co.uk
Antique auction rooms.

Barbara Ann Newman, London House Antiques, 4 Market Square, Westerham TN16 1AW Tel: 01959 564479
Antique dolls, Teddy bears and collectables.

The Old Tackle Box, PO Box 55, High Street, Cranbrook TN17 3ZU
Tel & Fax 01580 713979
tackle.box@virgin.net
Old fishing tackle.

Pretty Bizarre, 170 High Street, Deal CT14 6BQ Tel: 07973 794537
1920s–1970s ceramics and collectables.

The Neville Pundole Gallery, 8A & 9 The Friars, Canterbury CT1 2AS
Tel: 01227 453471
www.pundole.co.uk
Moorcroft and contemporary pottery and glass.

Stevenson Brothers, Bethersden, Ashford, Kent TN26 3AP Tel: 01233 820363 / 07000 Dobbin Fax: 01233 820580
sales@stevensonbros.com
www.stevensonbros.com
Makers and restorers of rocking horses.

Wenderton Antiques
Tel: 01227 720295 (by appt only)
Kitchenware.

Woodville Antiques, The Street, Hamstreet, Ashford TN26 2HG
Tel: 01233 732981
woodvilleantiques@netscapeonline.co.uk
Tools.

Lancashire

Decades, 20 Lord St West, Blackburn BB2 1JX Tel: 01254 693320
Original Victorian to 1970s clothing, accessories, jewellery, decorative textiles, and more.

Jazz Art Deco.com Tel: 07721 032277
jazzartdeco@btinternet.com
www.jazzartdeco.com
Art Deco.

Tracks, PO Box 117, Chorley PR6 0UU
Tel: 01257 269726 Fax: 01257 231340
sales@tracks.co.uk
Beatles and pop memorabilia.

Leicestershire

Pooks Transport Bookshop, Fowke Street, Rothley LE7 7PJ
Tel: 0116 237 6222 Fax: 0116 237 6491
pooks.motorbooks@virgin.net
Motoring books and automobilia.

Lincolnshire

Cleethorpes Collectables, 34 Alexander Road, Cleethorpes DN35 8LF
Tel: 01472 291952
www.cleethorpescollectables.co.uk
Dealers in modern fine arts to antiques.

Junktion, The Old Railway Station, New Bolingbroke, Boston PE22 7LB
Tel: 01205 480068/480087
Advertising and packaging, automobilia, slot machines, pedal cars, etc.

Skip & Janie Smithson
Tel/Fax: 01754 810265
Mobile: 07831 399180
Kitchenware.

London

Angling Auctions, P O Box 2095, W12 8RU Tel: 020 8749 4175
Mobile: 07785 281349
Fax: 020 8743 4855
neil@anglingauctions.demon.co.uk
Angling auctions.

The Antique Dealer, 115 Shaftesbury Avenue, WC2H 8AD
Tel: 020 7420 6684
Fax: 020 7420 6685
info@theantiquedealer.co.uk

Banana Dance Ltd, 16 The Mall, Camden Passage, 359 Upper St, Islington N1 0PD Tel: 020 8699 7728
Mobile: 07976 296987
jonathan@bananadance.com
www.bananadance.com
Decorative Arts of the 1920s and the 1930s. Also at Northcote Road Antiques Market, Unit 20, 155A Northcote Road, Battersea, SW11

Beverley, 30 Church Street/Alfie's Antique Market, Marylebone NW8 8EP
Tel/Fax: 020 7262 1576
Mobile: 07776 136003
Art Deco furniture, glass, figures, metalware and pottery.

Biblion, Grays Antique Market, 1–7 Davies Mews, Mayfair W1Y 2LP
Tel: 020 7629 1374
info@biblion.co.uk
www.biblion.com
Antiquarian books, maps & prints.

Bloomsbury Book Auctions, 3 & 4 Hardwick Street, Off Rosebery Avenue, EC1R 4RY Tel: 020 7833 2636/7 or 020 7636 1945
Fax: 020 7833 3954
info@bloomsbury-book-auct-.com
www.bloomsbury-book-auct.com
Book auctions.

Bonhams, 101 New Bond Street, W1S 1SR Tel: 020 7629 6602/7468 8233
www.bonhams.com
Auctioneer.

Christie's South Kensington Ltd, 85 Old Brompton Road, SW7 3LD
Tel: 020 7581 7611 info@christies.com
www.christies.com
Auctioneers.

The Collector, Tom Power, 4 Queens Parade Close, Friern Barnet N11 3FY
Tel: 020 8361 7787/020 8361 4143
collector@globalnet.co.uk
Contemporary collectables including Royal Doulton, Beswick, Pendelfin, Worcester, Lladro, Border Fine Art, Wade, Wedgwood, Coalport, Bossons, Lilliput Lane, David Winter, etc.

Comic Book Postal Auctions Ltd, 40–42 Osnaburgh Street, NW1 3ND
Tel: 020 7424 0007
Fax: 020 7424 0008
comicbook@compuserve.com
www.compalcomics.com
Comic book auctions.

Dix-Noonan-Webb, 1 Old Bond Street, W1S 4PB Tel: 020 7499 5022
Fax: 020 7499 5023
auctions@dnw.co.uk
www.dnw.co.uk
Auctioneers and valuers of Orders, decorations and medals, coins, tokens and banknotes.

eBay International AG, Unit 6, Dukes Gate, Acton Lane, Chiswick W4
Tel: 020 7384 6717
Fax: 020 7384 9728
ebay.co.uk

Michael German Antiques Ltd, 38B Kensington Church Street, W8 4BX
Tel: 020 7937 2771
www.antiquecanes.com
Walking canes, arms and armour.

Gooday Gallery, 14 Richmond Hill, Richmond TW10 6QX
Tel: 020 8940 8652
Mobile: 077101 24540
goodaygallery@aol.com
Arts & Crafts, Art Deco, Art Nouveau, Tribal, 1950s and 60s.

Harlequin House Puppets & Masks, 3 Kensington Mall, W8 4EB
Tel: 020 7221 8629
Best collection of Pelham puppets, also antique rod puppets from Polka Theatre Wimbledon, old ventriloquist dummies, Czech puppets, Punch & Judy. Open Tues, Fri and Sat 11am–5.30pm.

Adrian Harrington, 64a Kensington Church Street, W8 4DB
Tel: 020 7937 1465
Fax: 020 7368 0912
rare@harringtonbooks.co.uk
www.harringtonbooks.co.uk
Antiquarian books, prints and maps.

David Huxtable Tel: 07710 132200
david@huxtablesoldadv.demon.co.uk
Old advertising collectables. Also now at Portobello Road on Sats, Basement Stall 11/12, 288 Westbourne Grove W11

Charles Jeffreys Posters & Graphics, 12 Octavia Street, SW11 3DN
Tel: 020 7978 7976
Mobile: 07836 546150
Fax: 020 7978 6315
charlie@cjposters.com
www.cjposters.com
Specialising in selling original, rare and collectable posters from the birth of modernism through bauhaus to the 60s and 70s pop art and psychedelic culture including contemporary posters.

Francis Joseph Publications, 5 Southbrook Mews, SE12 8LG
Tel: 020 8318 9580
office@francisjoseph.com
Books on 20thC ceramics and glass.

Timothy Millett Ltd, Historic Medals and Works of Art, PO Box 20851, SE22 0YN Tel: 020 8693 1111
Mobile: 07778 637 898
tim@timothymillett.demon.co.uk

Murray Cards (International) Ltd,
51 Watford Way, Hendon Central,
NW4 3JH Tel: 020 8202 5688
Fax: 020 8203 7878
murraycards@ukbusiness.com
www.murraycards.com/
Cigarette & trade cards.

Colin Narbeth & Son Ltd, 20 Cecil
Court, Leicester Square, WC2N 4HE
Tel: 020 7379 6975

Onslow's, The Depot, 2 Michael Road,
SW6 2AD Tel: 020 7371 0505
*19th and 20th century posters,
railwayana, motoring, aviation, Titanic
and ocean liner collectors items. Sales
held twice a year, usually April
and October.*

Stevie Pearce, Stand G144, Alfies
Antique Market, 13–25 Church Street,
Marylebone NW8 8DT
Tel: 020 7723 2526/5754
Fax: 020 7724 5404
Stevie@steviepearce.co.uk
www.SteviePearce.co.uk
*Antique costume jewellery and fashion
items 1900–1970.*

Rumours, 10 The Mall, Upper Street,
Camden Passage, Islington N1 0PD
Tel/Fax: 01582 873561
Mobiles 07836 277274/07831 103748
Rumdec@aol.com
Moorcroft pottery.

Totem Records, 168 Stoke Newington,
Church Street, N16 0JL
Tel: 020 7275 0234
Fax: 020 7275 0111
sales@totemrecords.com
www.totemrecords.com
*Secondhand records, tapes, CDs
bought, sold and exchanged.*

Twinkled, Units 28/29, Village Market,
Stockwell Street, Greenwich SE10
Tel: 0208 4880930/07940 471574
Fax: 020 7207 8596
info@twinkled.net
www.twinkled.net
*Sat & Sun only. Also at High St
Antiques Centre, 39 High St, Hastings
Old Town, East Sussex TN34
01424 460068 (closed Weds).*

Unique Collections, 52 Greenwich
Church Street, SE10 9BL
Tel: 020 8305 0867 Fax: 020 8853 1066
glen@uniquecollections.co.uk
www.uniquecollections.co.uk
Old toys bought and sold.

Nigel Williams Rare Books, 22 & 25 Cecil
Court, WC2N 4HE Tel: 020 7836 7757
*Books. First editions, illustrated,
childrens and detective.*

Wimbledon Sewing Machine Co Ltd
and The London Sewing Machine
Museum, 292–312 Balham High Road,
Upper Tooting, SW17 7AA
Tel: 020 8767 4724 Fax: 020 8767 4726
wimbledonsewingmachinecoltd@btinternet.com
www.sewantique.com

*Antique sewing machines bought
and sold. Collection of antique
sewing machines.*

Yesterday Child, Angel Arcade,
118 Islington High Street, N1 8EG
Tel: 020 7354 1601
Tel/Fax: 01908 583403
Antique dolls and dolls house miniatures.

Middlesex

Hobday Toys Tel: 01895 636737
Fax: 01895 621042
wendyhobday@freenet.co.uk
Tinplate toys, trains and dolls houses.

John Ives, 5 Normanhurst Drive,
Twickenham TW1 1NA
Tel: 020 8892 6265 Fax: 020 8744 3944
jives@btconnect.com
*Reference books on antiques
and collecting.*

Norfolk

Roger Bradbury Antiques, Church Street,
Coltishall NR12 7DJ Tel: 01603 737444
Fax: 01603 737018
*Chinese blue and white porcelain
circa 1690–1820.*

Cat Pottery, 1 Grammar School Road,
North Walsham NR28 9JH
Tel: 01692 402962
Winstanley cats.

Northamptonshire

The Old Brigade, 10A Harborough Road,
Kingsthorpe, Northampton NN2 7AZ
Tel: 01604 719389 Fax: 01604 712489
theoldbrigade@easynet.co.uk
www.theoldbrigade.co.uk
Military antiques.

Nottinghamshire

T. Vennett-Smith, 11 Nottingham Road,
Gotham NG11 0HE Tel: 0115 983 0541
Fax: 0115 983 0114
info@vennett-smith.com
www.vennett-smith.com
*Ephemera and sporting
memorabilia auctions.*

Oxfordshire

Dauphin Museum Services, PO Box 602,
Oxford OX44 9LU Tel: 01865 343542
sales@Dauphin.co.uk
www.Dauphin.co.uk
Mount-making and conservation.

Michael Jackson Antiques, The Quiet
Woman Antiques Centre, Southcombe,
Chipping Norton OX7 5QH
Tel: 01608 646262
Mobile: 07831 402238
mjcig@cards.fsnet.co.uk
www.our-web-site.com/cigarette-cards
Cigarette cards.

Otter Antiques, 20 High Street,
Wallingford OX10 0BP
Tel: 01491 825544
www.antique-boxes.com
*Sale and restoration of antique wooden
boxes, always over 100 in stock.*

Alvin Ross Tel: 01865 772409
vintage.games@virgin.net
Pelham puppets.

Stone Gallery, 93 The High Street,
Burford OX18 4QA
Tel: 01993 823302
mail@stonegallery.co.uk
www.stonegallery.co.uk
*Specialist dealers in antique and
modern paperweights, gold and silver
designer jewellery and enamel boxes.*

Teddy Bears of Witney, 99 High Street,
Witney OX8 6LY
Tel: 01993 702616
Teddy bears.

Pembrokeshire

Arch House Collectables, St George
Street, Tenby SA70 7JB
Tel: 01834 843246
archhouse@onetel.net.uk
Pen Delfins.

Republic of Ireland

Michelina & George Stacpoole, Main
Street, Adare, Co Limerick
Tel: 00 353 6139 6409
stacpool@iol.ie
Pottery, ceramics, silver and prints.

Scotland

Bow Well Antiques, 103 West Bow,
Edinburgh EH1 2JP
Tel: 0131 225 3335
Specialists in all things Scottish.

Courtyard Antiques,
108A Causewayside, Edinburgh EH9 1PU
Tel: 0131 662 9008

Edinburgh Coin Shop, 11 West
Crosscauseway, Edinburgh EH8 9JW
Tel: 0131 668 2928/667 9095
Fax: 0131 668 2926
Coins, medals, militaria and stamps.

Shropshire

Decorative Antiques, 47 Church Street,
Bishop's Castle SY9 5AD
Tel/Fax: 01588 638851
enquiries@decorative-antiques.co.uk
www.decorative-antiques.co.uk
*Decorative objects of the 19th
and 20thC.*

Mullock & Madeley, The Old Shippon,
Wall-under-Heywood, Nr Church
Stretton SY6 7DS
Tel: 01694 771771
Fax: 01694 771772
auctions@mullockmadeley.co.uk
www.mullockmadeley.co.uk
Sporting auctions.

Somerset

Bath Antiques Online, Bartlett Street
Antiques Centre, Bartlett Street,
Bath BA1 2QZ
Tel: 01225 311061
Tel/Fax: 0117 939 1333
info@bathantiquesonline.com
www.BathAntiquesOnline.com

Bookbasket.co.uk, 30A Monmouth Street, Bath BA1 2AN
Tel: 01225 484877 Fax: 01225 334619
www.bookbasket.co.uk
Specialising in books on antiques and collectable subjects at discount prices.

Lynda Brine, Assembly Antiques, 5–8 Saville Row, Bath BA1 2QP
Tel: 01225 448488
lyndabrine@yahoo.co.uk
www.scentbottlesandsmalls.co.uk
Perfume bottles.

Cottage Collectibles, Pennard House, East Pennard, Shepton Mallet BA4 6TP
Tel: 01749 860731
Sheila@cottagecollectibles.co.uk
www.cottagecollectibles.co.uk
Open Mon–Sat 9.30–5.30pm and by appointment. English and Continental country antiques and kitchenalia.

Julia Craig, Bartlett Street Antiques Centre, 5–10 Bartlett Street, Bath BA1 2QZ Tel: 01225 448202/310457
Mobile: 07771 786846
Textiles.

Richard Dennis Publications, The Old Chapel, Shepton Beauchamp, Ilminster TA19 0LE Tel: 01460 240044
Fax: 01460 242009
richarddennispublications.com
www.richarddennispublications.com
Publisher.

Philip Knighton, 11 North Street, Wellington TA21 8LX
Tel: 01823 661618
gramman@msn.com
Wireless, gramophones and all valve equipment.

The London Cigarette Card Co Ltd, Sutton Road, Somerton TA11 6QP
Tel: 01458 273452 Fax: 01458 273515
cards@londoncigcard.co.uk
www.londoncigcard.co.uk
Cigarette and trade cards.

Joanna Proops Antique Textiles & Lighting, 34 Belvedere, Lansdown Hill, Bath BA1 5HR Tel: 01225 310795
Antique textiles and vast selection of chandeliers and wall lights.

Richard Twort Tel/Fax: 01934 641900
Mobile: 077 11 939789
Barographs and all types of meteorological instruments.

Staffordshire

Peggy Davies Ceramics, Freepost Mid 16669, Stoke-on-Trent ST4 1BJ
Tel: 01782 848002 Fax: 01782 747651
rhys@kevinfrancis.co.uk
www.kevinfrancis.co.uk
Ceramics-Limited edition Toby jugs and figures.

Keystones, PO Box 387, Stafford ST16 3FG Tel/Fax: 01785 256648
gkey@keystones.demon.co.uk
www.keystones.co.uk
Denby pottery.

Gordon Litherland, 25 Stapenhill Road, Burton on Trent DE15 9AE
Tel: 01283 567213
Fax: 01283 517142
pubjugs@aol.com
Bottles, breweriana and pub jugs, advertising ephemera and commemoratives.

The Potteries Antique Centre, 271 Waterloo Road, Cobridge, Stoke on Trent ST6 3NR
Tel: 01782 201455
Fax: 01782 201518
www.potteriesantiquecentre.com
Collectable ceramics.

Trevor Russell Vintage fountain pens, PO Box 1258, Uttoxeter ST14 8XL
gtantiques@onetel.net.uk
Buying, selling and repairing fountain pens.

Suffolk

Jamie Cross, PO Box 73, Newmarket CB8 8RY jamiecross@aol.com
www.thirdreichmedals.com
We buy and sell, value for probate and insurance British, German and foreign war medals, badges and decorations.

W. L. Hoad, 9 St. Peter's Road, Kirkley, Lowestoft NR33 0LH
Tel/Fax: 01502 587758
William@whoad.fsnet.co.uk
www.cigarettecardsplus.com
Cigarette cards.

Surrey

David Aldous-Cook, PO Box 413, Sutton SM3 8SZ Tel/Fax: 020 8642 4842
Reference books on antiques and collectables.

British Notes, PO Box 257, Sutton SM3 9WW Tel/Fax: 020 8641 3224
pamwestbritnotes@compuserve.com
www.west-banknotes.co.uk
Banking collectables.

Childhood Memories Tel: 01252 793704
Fax: 01252 793704
maureen@childhood-memories.co.uk
www.childhood-memories.co.uk
Antique Teddies, dolls and miniatures.

Julian Eade Tel: 01491 575059
Mobile: 07973 542971
Doulton Lambeth stoneware and signed Burslem wares.

Howard Hope, 19 Weston Park, Thames Ditton KT7 0HW Tel: 020 8398 7130
Fax: 020 8398 7630
phonoking@virgin.net
www.gramophones.uk.com
Specialising for 30 years in gramophones, phonographs, anything related to the history of recorded sound and other mechanical/musical items. Dealing by correspondence only, please no visits - call first. Colour pictures of any item in stock can be sent on request by email. Exporting worldwide. Shipping quotations given for any machine.

East Sussex

Tony Horsley Tel: 01273 550770
Fax: 01273 550855
Candle extinguishers, Royal Worcester and other porcelain.

Ann Lingard, Ropewalk Antiques, Rye TN31 7NA Tel: 01797 223486
Fax: 01797 224700
ann-lingard@ropewalkantiques.freeserve.co.uk
Antique pine furniture and kitchenware.

Mad about Mabel, P O Box 900, Lewes BN7 1TF Tel: 01273 477246
All Mabel Lucie Attwell creations from bathroom plaques to original artwork. Bi-annual mail order available.

Twinkled, High St Antiques Centre, 39 High Street, Hastings TN34
Tel: 01424 460068
info@twinkled.net www.twinkled.net
Closed Weds. Also at Greenwich Sat & Sun, see entry under London.

Wallis & Wallis, West Street Auction Galleries, Lewes BN7 2NJ
Tel: 01273 480208
Fax: 01273 476562
auctions@wallisandwallis.co.uk
www.wallisandwallis.co.uk
Specialist auctioneers of militaria, arms, armour, coins and medals. Also die-cast and tinplate toys, Teddy bears, dolls, model railways, toy soldiers and models.

West Sussex

Limited Editions, 2 Tarrant Street, Arundel BN18 9DG
Tel: 01903 883950
Fax: 01903 883518
limited@editions-shop.freeserve.co.uk
www.limitededitionsshop.co.uk
Ceramics including Kevin Francis, David Winter, Lilliput Lane, J. P. Editions, Moorcroft, Royal Doulton, Pendelfin, Belleek, Lladro, etc.

USA

Antique European Linens, Emil & Pandora Balthazar, PO Box 789, Gulf Breeze, FL 32562-0789, 14 North Palafox St, Pensacola, FL 32501
Tel: 850 432 4777
Textiles, inc pillows and duvets.

Dragonflies Antiques and Decorating Center, Frank & Cathy Sykes, 24 Center Street, Wolfeboro, New Hampshire 03894 Tel: 603 569 0000

M. Finkel & Daughter, 936 Pine Street, Philadelphia, Pennsylvania 19107-6128
Tel: 215 627 7797
mailbox@finkelantiques.com
www.finkelantiques.com
Antique samplers and needlework.

Randy Inman Auctions, PO Box 726, Waterville, Maine 04903
Tel: 207 872 6900 Fax: 207 872 6966
inman@inmanauctions.com
www.inmanauctions.com
Auctioneer specialising in advertsing, coin-op, gambling devices, automata,

soda pop, coca cola, breweriana, robots and space toys, C.I. and tin toys, Disneyana, mechanical music, mechanical and still banks, quality antiques.

Sloan's, 4920 Wyaconda Road, N. Bethesda, MD 20852
Tel: 301 468 4911/800 649 5066
www.sloansauction.com
Auctioneers and appraisers.

Treadway Gallery, Inc., 2029 Madison Road, Cincinnati, OH 45208
Tel: 513 321 6742
www.treadwaygallery.com
20th century art.

Triple "L" Sports Antiques, PO Box 281, Wintrop, ME 04364
Tel/Fax: 207 377 5787
lllsport@ctel.net
Winchester collectibles, fishing, hunting, baseball, football, golf, tennis, memorabilia and advertising.

Wales

A.P.E.S. Rocking Horses, Ty Gwyn, Llannefydd, Denbigh LL16 5HB
Tel/Fax: 01745 540365
macphersons@apes-rocking-horses.co.uk
Rocking horses.

The Emporium, 112 St Teilo St, Pontarddulais, Nr Swansea SA4 1QH
Tel: 01792 885185
Brass & cast iron.

Michael James Tel: 01874 665487
Mobile: 07970 619737
Railway lamp specialist.

Jen Jones, Pontbrendu, Llanybydder, Ceredigion SA40 9UJ
Tel: 01570 480610
Quilt expert dealing mainly in Welsh quilts and blankets. Between 200 and 300 quilts in stock with a comparable number of blankets. Looking to buy as well as sell.

Warwickshire

Chinasearch, PO Box 1202, Kenilworth CV8 2WW
Tel: 01926 512402
Fax: 01926 859311
helen@chinasearch.uk.com or jackie@chinasearch.com
www.chinasearch.uk.com
Discontinued dinner, tea and collectable ware bought and sold.

Chris James Medals & Militaria, Warwick Antiques Centre, 22–24 High Street, Warwick CV34 4AP
Tel: 01926 495704/07710 274452
www.medalsandmilitaria.com
British, German, Japanese and USSR medals, swords, militaria and aviation items. For sale and purchased. 'The International', The National Motorcycle Museum, Birmingham. The U.K's largest militaria fair - 2002 dates (all Sundays) 24th Feb, 16th June, 15th Sept, 1st Dec and 23rd Feb 2003. 10am–3.30pm. A.M.&S.E., PO Box 194, Warwick. Tel: 01926 497340

Tango Art Deco & Antiques, 46 Brook Street, Warwick CV34 4BL
Tel: 01926 496999/0121 704 4969
info@tango-artdeco.co.uk
www.tango-artdeco.co.uk
Large Art Deco specialist shop. Open Thur–Sat 10am–5pm.

West Midlands

Antiques Magazine, H.P. Publishing, HP Publishing, 2 Hampton Court Road, Harborne, Birmingham B17 9AE
Tel: 0121 681 8000
Fax: 0121 681 8005
subscriptions@antiquesbulletin.com
www.antiquesbulletin.com
Weekly guide to buying and selling antiques.

Wiltshire

Dominic Winter Book Auctions, The Old School, Maxwell Street, Swindon SN1 5DR
Tel: 01793 611340
Fax: 01793 491727
info@dominicwinter.co.uk
www.dominicwinter.co.uk
Auctions of antiquarian and general printed books & maps, sports books and memorabilia, art reference & pictures, photography & ephemera (including toys, games and other collectables).

Worcestershire

BBM Jewellery & Coins (W. V. Crook), 8–9 Lion Street, Kidderminster DY10 1PT Tel: 01562 744118
Fax: 01562 825954
wiliamvcrook@aol.com
Antique jewellery and coins.

John Neale, 11A Davenport Drive, The Willows, Bromsgrove B60 2DW
Tel/Fax: 01527 871000
Vintage trains & toys.

Yorkshire

Antique & Collectors' Centre, 35 St Nicholas Cliff, Scarborough YO11 2ES
Tel: 01723 365221
sales@collectors.demon.co.uk
www.collectors.demon.co.uk
International dealers in stamps, postcards, silver, gold, medals, cigarette cards and many more collectables.

BBR, Elsecar Heritage Centre, Wath Road, Elsecar, Barnsley S74 8HJ
Tel: 01226 745156
sales@bbrauctions.co.uk
www.onlinebbr.com
Advertising, breweriana, pot lids, bottles, Cornishware, Doulton and Beswick, etc.

Briar's C20th Decorative Arts, Skipton Antiques & Collectors Centre, The Old Foundry, Cavendish Street, Skipton BD23 2AB
Tel: 01756 798641
Art Deco ceramics and furniture, specialising in Charlotte Rhead pottery.

The Camera House, Oakworth Hall, Colne Road (B6143), Oakworth, Keighley BD22 7HZ
Tel: 01535 642333
colin@the-camera-house.co.uk
Online catalogue: www.the-camera-house.co.uk
Cameras & photographic equipment from 1850. Cash purchases, part exchanges, sales and repairs. National and International mail order a speciality. Valuations for probate & insurance. Online catalogue. Please ring or email before visiting. Prop. C Cox.

Country Collector, 11–12 Birdgate, Pickering YO18 7AL
Tel: 01751 477481
Art Deco ceramics, blue and white, pottery and porcelain.

The Crested China Co, The Station House, Driffield YO25 7PY
Tel: 01377 257042
dt@thecrestedchinacompany.com
www.thecrestedchinacompany.com
Goss and Crested china.

Echoes, 650a Halifax Road, Eastwood, Todmorden OL14 6DW
Tel: 01706 817505
Antique costume, textiles including linen, lace and jewellery.

Gerard Haley, Hippins Farm, Black Shawhead, Nr Hebden Bridge HX7 7JG
Tel: 01422 842484
Toy soldiers.

John & Simon Haley, 89 Northgate, Halifax HX1 1XF
Tel: 01422 822148/360434
toysandbanks@aol.com
Old toys and money boxes.

Harpers Jewellers Ltd, 2/6 Minster Gates, York YO1 7HL
Tel: 01904 632634
harpersjewellers@btinternet.com
www.vintage-watches.co.uk
Vintage and modern wrist and pocket watches. Sothebys.com associate dealer.

Linen & Lace, Shirley Tomlinson, Halifax Antiques Centre, Queens Road/Gibbet Street, Halifax HX1 4LR
Tel: 01484 540492/01422 366657
Antique linen, textiles, period costume and accessories.

Sheffield Railwayana Auctions, 43 Little Norton Lane, Sheffield S8 8GA
Tel/Fax: 0114 274 5085
ian@sheffrail.freeserve.co.uk
www.sheffieldrailwayana.co.uk
Railwayana, posters and models auctions.

The Troika Man
Tel: 01535 667294
thetroikaman@aol.com
www.troikapottery.org
Troika pottery.

Directory of Collectors' Clubs

With new Collectors' Clubs emerging every day this directory is by no means complete. If you wish to be included in next year's directory or if you have a change of address or telephone number, please inform us by 1 November 2002.

Age of Jazz Ceramic Circle (Linking Art Deco Websites) Fantasque House, Tennis Drive, The Park, Nottingham NG7 1AE www.ageofjazz.com

American Spoon Collectors Bill Boyd, 7408 Englewood Lane, Raytown, MO 64133-6913, U.S.A. Tel: 011 816 356 742

Association of Bottled Beer Collectors 127 Victoria Park Road, Tunstall, Stoke-on-Trent, Staffordshire ST6 6DY Tel: 01782 821459 michael.peterson@ntlworld.com www.abbc.org

Association of Comic Enthusiasts: (ACE)! L'Hopiteau, St Martin du Fouilloux 79420, France Tel: 00 33 5 49 70 21 14 user218763@aol.com www.collectorfair.com/clubs/aca/index.html

Autograph Club (A.C.O.G.B) of Great Britain SAE to Mr R. Gregson, 47 Web Crescent, Dawley, Telford, Shropshire TF4 3DS acogbnews@netscapeonline.co.uk www.acogb.com

Avon Magpies Club Mrs W. A. Fowler, 36 Castle View Road, Portchester, Fareham, Hampshire PO16 9LA Tel: 023 92 642393 wendy@avonmagpies.fsnet.co.uk

Badge Collectors' Circle c/o Frank Setchfield, 57 Middleton Place, Loughborough, Leicestershire LE11 2BY Tel: 01509 569270 f.setchfield@ntlworld.com www.thebadge.co.uk

Belleek Collectors' Group UK The Hon Chairman Mr Jan Golaszewski, 5 Waterhall Avenue, Chingford, London E4 6NB

The James Bond Collectors' Club PO Box 1570, Christchurch, Dorset BH23 4XS Tel: 0870 4423007 (Mon–Fri 9am–6pm) Solo@enterprise.net

British Art Medal Society Philip Attwood, c/o Dept of Coins and Medals, The British Museum, London WC1B 3DG Tel: 020 7323 8260 pattwood@thebritishmuseum.ac.uk www.bams.org.uk/

The British Beermat Collectors' Society Hon Sec, 69 Dunnington Avenue, Kidderminster, Worcestershire DY10 2YT www.britishbeermats.org.uk

British Compact Collectors' Society, SAE to: PO Box 131, Woking, Surrey GU21 9YR

British Novelty Salt & Pepper Collectors' Club Ray Dodd (Secretary), Coleshill, Clayton Road, Mold, Flintshire CH7 1SX

British Numismatic Society c/o Warburg Institute, Woburn Square, London WC1H 0AB

British Watch & Clock Collectors' Association Tony Woolven, 5 Cathedral Lane, Truro, Cornwall TR1 2QS Tel: 01872 264010 tonybwcca@cs.com www.timecap.co.uk

Bunnykins Collectors' Club 6 Beckett Way, Lewes, East Sussex BN7 2EB Tel: 01273 479056 bunnykins.collectorsclub@btinternet.com

The Buttonhook Society (US contact) c/o Priscilla Stoffel, White Marsh, Box 287, MD 21162-0287, U.S.A. Tel: 410 256 5541 info@thebuttonhooksociety.com www.thebuttonhooksociety.com

Cambridge Paperweight Circle PO Box 941, Comberton, Cambridge PDO CB3 7GQ Tel: +44 (0)20 8337 7077 www.adc-ltd.demon.co.uk/paperweights

Carlton Ware Collectors' Club 5 Southbrook Mews, London SE12 8LG Tel: 020 8318 9580

The Carnival Glass Society (UK) Limited PO Box 14, Hayes, Middlesex UB3 5NU cgs.sec@btinternet.com www.members.aol.com/uk.cgs

The Cartophilic Society of Great Britain Ltd Membership secretary Alan Stevens, 63 Ferndale Road, Church Crookham, Fleet, Hampshire GU52 6LN Tel: 01252 621586 www.csgb.co.uk

Cat Collectables 297 Alcester Road, Hollywood, Birmingham, West Midlands B47 5HJ Tel: 01564 826277 cat.collectables@btinternet.com

Chintz Club of America PO Box 6126, Folsom CA 95763, U.S.A.

Cigarette Case Collectors' Club 19 Woodhurst North, Raymead Road, Maidenhead, Berkshire SL6 8PH Tel: 01628 781800 colin.grey1@virgin.net

The City of London Phonograph and Gramophone Society Colin Loffler Membership Secretary, 13 Tennyson Drive, Newport Pagnall MK16 8PH

Clarice Cliff Collectors' Club Fantasque House, Tennis Drive, The Park, Nottingham NG7 1AE www.clariceclliff.com

The Coleco Collectors' Club Ann Wilhite, 610 W 17th Freemont NE 68025, U.S.A.

The Comic Journal c/o Bryon Whitworth, l'Hopiteau, St Martin du Fouilloux 79420, France Tel: 00 33 5 49 70 21 14 user218763@aol.com www.collectorfair.com/clubs/aca/index.html

Commemorative Collectors' Society c/o Steven Jackson, Lumless House, Gainsborough Road, Winthorpe, Newark, Nottinghamshire NG24 2NR Tel: 01636 671377

Corgi Collector Club c/o Corgi Classics Ltd, Meridian East, Meridian Business Park, Leicester LE3 2RL Tel: 0870 607 1204 jenny@collectorsclubs.org.uk www.corgi.co.uk

Cornish Collectors' Club PO Box 58, Buxton, Derbyshire SK17 0FH Tel: 01298 687070 cornish@btconnect.com

The Costume Society St Paul's House, Warwick Lane, London EC4P 4BN www.costumesociety.org.uk

Cricket Memorabilia Society Steve Cashmore, 4 Stoke Park Court, Stoke Road, Bishop's Cleeve, Cheltenham, Gloucestershire GL52 8US cms87@btinternet.com www.cms.cricket.org

Danesby Collectors' Club Fantasque House, Tennis Drive, The Park, Nottingham NG7 1AE www.danesby.co.uk

Devon Pottery Collectors' Group Mrs Joyce Stonelake, 19 St Margarets Avenue, Torquay, Devon TQ1 4LW Tel: 01803 327277 Virginia Brisco@care4free.net

Embroiderers' Guild Janet Jardine, Apartment 41, Hampton Court Palace, East Molesey, Surrey KT8 9AU Tel: 020 8943 1229 administrator@embroderersguild.com www.embroiderersguild.com

ETB Radford Collectors' Club Wendy Wright, 27 Forest Mead, Denmead, Waterlooville, Hampshire PO7 6UN Tel: 02392 267483/01275 871359 www.radfordcollect.com

The European Honeypot Collectors' Society John Doyle, The Honeypot, 18 Victoria Road, Chislehurst, Kent BR7 6DF Tel/Fax: 020 8467 2053 johnhoneypot@hotmail.com www.geocities.com/tehcsuk

Fan Circle International Sec: Mrs Joan Milligan, 'Cronk-y-Voddy', Rectory Road, Coltishall, Norwich NR12 7HF

Festival of Britain Society c/o Martin Packer, 41 Lyall Gardens, Birmingham, West Midlands B45 9YW Tel: 0121 453 8245 martin@packer34.freeserve.co.uk www.packer34.freeserve.co.uk

Fieldings Crown Devon Collectors' Club PO Box 74, Corbridge, Northumberland NE45 5YP Tel: 07802 513784 www.fieldingscrowndevclub.com

The Flag Institute 44 Middleton Road, Acomb, York YO24 3AS

Florence Membership Society Liza Burgon Society Secretary, Florence (UK) Ltd, 41 Evelyn Street, Beeston, Nottingham NG9 2EU Tel: 0115 9229902 FlorenceSociety@aol.com www.florence-sculptures.it

Friends of Blue Ceramic Society T. Sheppard, 45a Church Road, Bexley Heath, Kent DA7 4DD www.fob.org.uk

Friends of Broadfield House Glass Museum Broadfield House Glass Museum, Compton Drive, Kingswinford, West Midlands DY6 9NS Tel: 01384 812745

The Furniture History Society c/o Dr. Brian Austen, 1 Mercedes Cottages, St. John's Road, Haywards Heath, West Sussex RH16 4EH Tel: 01444 413845

Goss Collectors' Club Mrs Schofield, Derbyshire Tel: 0115 930 0441

Goss & Crested China Club & Museum incorporating Milestone Publications 62 Murray Road, Horndean, Hampshire PO8 9JL Tel: (023) 9259 7440 info@gosschinaclub.demon.co.uk www.gosscrestedchina.co.uk

The Hagen-Renaker Collectors' Club Jenny Palmer, 3651 Polish Line Road, Cheboygan, Michigan 49721, U.S.A.

Jonathan Harris Studio Glass Ltd Woodland House, 24 Peregrine Way, Apley Castle, Telford, Shropshire TF1 6TH Tel: 01952 246381/588441 jonathan@jhstudioglass.com www.jhstudioglass.com

The Hornby Railway Collectors' Association 2 Ravensmore Road, Sherwood, Nottingham NG5 2AH

Hornsea Pottery Collectors' and Research Society c/o Val and Terry Healey, 32 Hill View Road, Chelmsford, Essex CM1 7RX Membership@hornseacollector.co.uk www.hornseacollector.co.uk

Hugglets Teddy Bear Club PO Box 290, Brighton, East Sussex BN2 1DR Tel: 01273 697974 info@hugglets.co.uk www.hugglets.co.uk

International Correspondence of Corkscrew Addicts Don MacLean, 4201 Sunflower Drive, Mississauga, Ontario L5L 2L4, Canada

The International Gnome Club Liz Spea, 22841 Kings Ct, Hayward CA 94541-4326, U.S.A.

International Golliwog Collector Club PO Box 612, Woodstock, New York 12498, U.S.A.

International Perfume Bottle Association Details from Lynda Brine, Assembly Antique Centre, 5-8 Saville Row, Bath, Somerset BA1 2QP Tel: 01225 448488

Just Golly! Collectors' Club SAE to Mrs A. K. Morris, 9 Wilmar Way, Seal, Sevenoaks, Kent TN15 0DN Tel: 01732 762379 quinntheeskimo@btinternet.com www.gollycorner.co.uk

King George VI Collectors' Society (Philately) 98 Albany, Manor Road, Bournemouth, Dorset BH1 3EW

Lock Collectors' Club Mr Richard Phillips, 'Merlewood', The Loan, West Linton, Peebleshire EH46 7HE Tel: 01968 661039 rphillips52@btinternet.com

The Maling Collectors' Society PO Box 1762, North Shields NE30 4YJ info@maling-pottery.org.uk www.maling-pottery.org.uk

Manor Ware Club c/o 66 Shirburn Road, Upton, Torquay, Devon TQ1 4HR

The Matchbox Toys International Collectors' Association Kevin McGimpsey, PO Box 120, Deeside, Flintshire CH5 3HE Tel: 01244 539414 kevin@matchboxclub.com www.matchboxclub.com

Memories UK Mabel Lucie Attwell Club Abbey Antiques, 63 Great Whyte, Ramsey, Nr Huntingdon, Cambridgeshire PE26 1HL Tel: 01487 814753

Merrythought International Collectors' Club Ironbridge, Telford, Shropshire TF8 7NJ Tel: 01952 433116 contact@merrythought.co.uk

Milk Bottle News Paul Luke, 60 Rose Valley Crescent, Stanford-le-Hope, Essex SS17 8EF Tel: 01375 679527 www.milkbottlenews.org.uk

Moorcroft Collectors' Club W. Moorcroft PLC, Sandbach Road, Burslem, Stoke-on-Trent, Staffordshire ST6 2DQ Tel: 01782 820510 club@moorcroft.com www.moorcroft.com

Muffin the Mule Collectors' Club 12 Woodland Close, Woodford Green, Essex IG8 0QH Tel/Fax: 020 8504 4943 ra@hasler.fsnet.co.uk www.Muffin-the-Mule.com

Keith Murray Collectors' Club (Patron Constance Murray) Fantasque House, Tennis Drive, The Park, Nottingham NG7 1AE www.keithmurray.co.uk

Musical Box Society of Great Britain PO Box 299, Waterbeach, Cambridgeshire CB4 8DT mbsgb@kreedman.globalnet.co.uk www.mbsgb.org.uk

Observers Pocket Series Collectors' Society (OPSCS) Alan Sledger Secretary, 10 Villiers Road, Kenilworth, Warwickshire CV8 2JB Tel: 01926 857047

The Official Betty Boop Fan Club Bobbie West, 10550 Western Avenue 133, Stanton CA 90680-6909, U.S.A. Tel: 00 714 816 0717

Old Bottle Club of Great Britain Alan Blakeman, c/o BBR, Elsecar Heritage Centre, Nr Barnsley, Yorkshire S74 8HJ Tel: 01226 745156 sales@bbrauctions.co.uk onlinebbr.com

The Old Hall (Stainless Steel Tableware) Club Nigel Wiggin, Sandford House, Levedale, Stafford ST18 9AH Tel: 01785 780376 oht@gnwiggin.freeserve.co.uk www.oldhallclub.co.uk

Ophthalmic Antiques International Collectors' Club 3 Moor Park Road, Northwood, Middlesex HA6 2DL

Orders and Medals Research Society PO Box 1904, Southam CV47 2ZX Tel: 01295 690009 petedeehelmore@talk21.com www.omrs.org.uk

The Oriental Ceramic Society The Secretary, 30b Torrington Square, London WC1E 7JL Tel: 020 7636 7985 ocs-london@beeb.net

Pedal Car Collectors' Club (P.C.C.C.) Secretary A. P. Gayler, 4/4a Chapel Terrace Mews, Kemp Town, Brighton, East Sussex BN2 1HU Tel: 01273 601960 www.brmmbrmm.com/pedalcars

Pen Delfin Family Circle Nancy Falkenham, 1250 Terwillegar Avenue, Oshawa, Ontario L1J 7A5, Canada Tel: 0101 416 723 9940

The Family Circle of Pen Delfin Susan Beard, 230 Spring Street N.W., 1248, Atlanta, Georgia 30303, U.S.A. Freephone US only 1-800 872 4876

The Pewter Society Llananant Farm, Penallt, Monmouth NP25 4AP secretary@pewtersociety.org www.pewtersociety.org

Photographic Collectors' Club of Great Britain Membership Office P.C.C.G.B., 5 Buntingford Road, Puckeridge, Ware, Hertfordshire SG11 1RT Tel: 01920 821611 www.pccgb.org

Pilkington's Lancastrian Pottery Society Wendy Stock, Sullom Side, Barnacre, Garstang, Preston, Lancashire PR3 1GH Tel: 01995 603427 Barry@pilkpotsoc.freeserve.co.uk www.pilkpotsoc.freeserve.co.uk

Poole Pottery Collectors' Club Poole Pottery Limited, Sopers Lane, Poole, Dorset BH17 7PP Tel: 01202 666200/670333 www.poolepottery.co.uk

The Postcard Club of Great Britain c/o Mrs D Brennan, 34 Harper House, St James's Crescent, London SW9 7LW Tel: 020 7771 9404

The Pot Lid Circle Collins House, 32/38 Station Road, Gerrards Cross, Buckinghamshire SL9 8EL Tel: 01487 773194/01753 279001

Potteries of Rye Society Membership Secretary Barry Buckton, 2 Redyear Cottages, Kennington Road, Ashford, Kent TN24 0TF Tel: 01233 647898 barry.buckton@tesco.net

Royal Doulton International Collectors' Club Royal Doulton, Sir Henry Doulton House, Forge Lane, Stoke-on-Trent, Staffordshire ST1 5NN Tel: 01782 404040 www.icc@royal-doulton.com

Rugby Memorabilia Society PO Box 1093, Thornbury, Bristol BS35 1DA Tel: 01454 884077 (Evenings) rms@cadnoinc.globalnet.co.uk www.rugby-memorabilia.co.uk

The Russian Doll Collectors' Club Gardener's Cottage, Hatchlands, East Clandon, Surrey GU4 7RT Tel: 01483 222789 graham@russiandolls.co.uk www.russiandolls.co.uk

Scientific Instrument Society Wg Cdr G. Bennett (Executive Officer), 31 High Street, Stanford in the Vale, Faringdon, Oxfordshire SN7 8LH Tel: 01367 710223 www.sis.org.uk

Silhouette Collectors' Club c/o Diana Joll, Flat 5, 13 Brunswick Square, Hove, East Sussex BN3 1EH Tel: 01273 735760

The Silver Spoon Club of Great Britain c/o Terry & Mary Haines, Glenleigh Park, Sticker, St Austell, Cornwall PL26 7JD Tel/Fax: 01726 65269 enquiries@silver-spoon.com

Snuff Bottle Society Michael Kaynes, 1 Tollard Court, West Hill Road, Bournemouth, Dorset BH2 5EH Tel/Fax: 01202 292867 mikekaynes@snuffbottles.madasafish.com

Society of Tobacco Jar Collectors (USA) 19 Woodhurst North, Raymead Road, Maidenhead, Berkshire SL6 8PH Tel: 01628 781800 colin.grey1@virgin.net

The Soviet Collectors' Club PO Box 56, Saltburn by the Sea TS12 1YD Tel: 01287 623667

St Clere Carlton Ware PO Box 161, Sevenoaks, Kent TN15 6GA Tel: 01474 853630 stclere@aol.com www.stclere.co.uk

Susie Cooper Collectors' Club Panorama House, 18 Oakley Mews, Aycliffe Village, Co. Durham DL5 6JP www.susiecooper.co.uk

The SylvaC Collectors' Circle 174 Portsmouth Road, Horndean, Waterlooville, Hampshire PO8 9HP Tel: 023 9259 1725 www.sylvacclub.com

Telecommunications Heritage Group PO Box 561, South Croydon, Surrey CR2 6YL Tel: 020 8407 2129 www.thg.org.uk

The Thimble Society c/o Bridget McConnel, Geoffrey Van Arcade, 107 Portobello Road, London W11 2QB Open Sat antiques@thimblesociety.co.uk www.thimblesociety.co.uk

The Tool and Trades History Society Jane Rees Chairman & Membership Secretary, Barrow Mead Cottage, Rush Hill, Bath, Somerset BA2 2QP

Torquay Pottery Collectors' Society Membership Secretary, c/o Torre Abbey, The Kings Drive, Torquay, Devon TQ2 5JX Tel: 01274 611478 scandymag@aol.com www.torquaypottery.com

Totally Teapots The Novelty Teapot Collectors' Club Vince McDonald, Euxton, Chorley, Lancashire PR7 6EY Tel/Fax: 01257 450366 www.totallyteapots.com

Train Collectors' Society James Day Membership Secretary, PO Box 20340, London NW11 6ZE Tel/Fax: 020 8209 1589 tcsinformation@btinternet.com www.traincollectors.org.uk

Tremar Collectors' Club Jim Castle, 11 Brockley Mews, Brockley, London SE4 2DJ Tel: 020 7252 9879 tremarcollectors@hotmail.com

The Victorian Military Society PO Box 5837, Newbury, Berkshire RG14 3FJ

The Vintage Model Yacht Group Trevor Smith, 1A Station Avenue, Epsom, Surrey KT19 9UD Tel: 020 8393 1100

The Wade Watch Carole Murdoch & Valerie Moody, 8199 Pierson Ct, Arvada CO 80005, U.S.A. Tel: (303) 421 9655

Kathie Winkle Collectors 'Club SAE to Mrs Nadin-Leath, Greenacres, Calbourne Road, Carisbrooke, Isle of Wight PO30 5AP

The Writing Equipment Society c/o Mr John S. Daniels, 33 Glanville Road, Hadleigh, Ipswich, Suffolk IP7 5SQ www.wesoc.co.uk

Directory of Markets & Centres

Cheshire

Davenham Antique Centre, 461 London Road, Davenham, Northwich CW9 8NA Shop Tel: 01606 44350 Fax: 01606 782317 maxwells@connectfree.co.uk www.antiques-atlas.com/davenham

Derbyshire

Alfreton Antique Centre, 11 King Street, Alfreton DE55 7AF Tel: 01773 520781 www.alfretonantiques.supanet.com
30 dealers on 2 floors. Antiques, collectables, furniture, books, militaria, postcards, silverware. Open 7 days Mon–Sat 10am–4.30pm, Sun 11am–4.30pm.

Chappells Antiques Centre, King Street, Bakewell DE45 1DZ Tel: 01629 812496 ask@chappellsantiquescentre.com www.chappellsantiquescentre.com
Over 30 dealers inc BADA & LAPADA members. Quality period furniture, ceramics, silver, plate, metals, treen, clocks, barometers, books, pictures, maps, prints, textiles, kitchenalia, lighting, furnishing accessories, scientific, pharmaceutical and sporting antiques from the 17th–20thC. Open Mon–Sat 10am–5pm, Sun 11am–5pm. Closed Christmas Day, Boxing Day, New Year's Day.

Heanor Antique Centre, Ilkeston Road, Heanor DE75 7AE Tel: 01773 531181 sales@heanor.co.uk
Open 7 days. 10.30am–4.30pm. 70+ dealers.

Matlock Antiques, Collectables & Riverside Café, 7 Dale Road, Matlock DE4 3LT Tel: 01629 760808 Proprietor W. Shirley. www.matlock-antiques-collectable.cwc.net
Over 70 dealers.

Devon

Quay Centre, Topsham, Nr Exeter EX3 0JA Tel: 01392 874006 www.antiquesontopshamquay.co.uk
80 dealers on 3 floors. Antiques, collectables and traditional furnishings. Ample parking. Open 7 days, 10am–5pm.

Gloucestershire

Durham House Antiques Centre, Sheep Street, Stow-on-the-Wold GL54 1AA Tel: 01451 870404
30+ dealers. Town and country furniture, metalware, books, ceramics, kitchenalia, silver, jewellery, sewing ephemera and samplers. Mon–Sat 10am–5pm, Sun 11am–5pm. Stow-on-the-Wold, Cotswold home to over 40 antique shops, galleries and bookshops.

Gloucester Antiques Centre, The Historic Docks, 1 Severn Road, Gloucester GL1 2LE Tel: 01452 529716 www.antiques.center.com
Open Mon–Sat 10am–5pm, Sun 1pm–5pm

Hampshire

Lymington Antiques Centre, 76 High Street, Lymington SO41 9AL Tel: 01590 670934 *30 dealers. Open Mon–Fri 10am–5pm, Sat 9am–5pm. Clocks, watches, silver, glass, jewellery, toys & dolls, books, furniture, textiles.*

Herefordshire

The Hay Antique Market, 6 Market Street, Hay-on-Wye HR3 5AF Tel: 01497 820175
Open 6 days 10am–5pm, Sun 11am–5pm. 17 separate units on 2 floors selling pine, country and period furniture. Rural and rustic items. China, glass, jewellery, linen and period clothes. Pictures, lighting, brass and collectables.

Mulberry's Antiques & Vintage Costume, Hereford HR1 2NH Tel: 01432 350101 mulberrysantiques@hotmail.com
A wide range of antiques and collectables on 2 floors - furniture, fine china, porcelain, silver, jewellery, textiles, pre-1930s clothing and accessories, objets d'art, prints, oils and watercolours. Trade Welcome.

Humberside

Hull Antique Centre, Anderson Wharf, Wincolmlee, Hull HU2 8AH Tel: 01482 609958 www.@thehullantiquecentre.com
Open Mon–Fri 9am–5pm, Sat & Sun 10am–4pm

Kent

Castle Antiques, 1 London Road (opposite Library), Westerham TN16 1BB Tel: 01959 562492
Open Mon–Sat 10am–5pm . Phone for Sunday times. 4 rooms of antiques, small furniture, collectables, rural bygones, costume, tools, glass, books, linens, jewellery, kitsch, retro-clothing. Services: advice, valuations, theatre props, house clearance, talks on antiques.

Malthouse Arcade, High Street, Hythe CT21 5BW Tel: 01303 260103

Lancashire

GB Antiques Centre, Lancaster Leisure Park, (the former Hornsea Pottery), Wyresdale Road, Lancaster LA1 3LA Tel: 01524 844734 *140 dealers in 40,000 sq ft of space. Porcelain, pottery, Art Deco, glass, books, linen, mahogany, oak and pine furniture. Open 7 days 10am–5pm.*

The Antique & Decorative Design Centre, 56 Garstang Road, Preston PR1 1NA Tel: 01772 882078 Fax: 01772 252842 Paul@antiquecentre.fsnet.co.uk antique_centre@antiqueweb.co.uk www.antiqueweb.co.uk/centre/ Paulallisonantiques.co.uk
Open 7 days a week 10am–5pm. 25,000 sq.ft. of quality antiques, objets d'art, clocks, pine, silverware, porcelain, upholstery, French furniture for the home & garden.

Kingsmill Antique Centre, Queen Street, Harle Syke, Burnley BB10 2HX Tel: 01282 431953 Fax: 01282 839470

Leicestershire

Oxford Street Antiques Centre, 16-26 Oxford Street, Leicester LE1 5XU Tel: 0116 255 3006
30,000 sq.ft. on 4 floors. Extensive range of Victorian, Edwardian and later furniture etc. Open Mon–Fri 10am–5.30pm, Sat 10am–5pm, Sun 2–5pm.

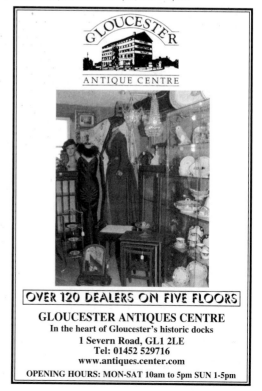

Lincolnshire

Cleethorpes Collectables, 34 Alexander Road, Cleethorpes DN35 8LF Tel: 01472 291952

St Martins Antiques Centre, 23a High Street, St Martins, Stamford PE9 2LF Tel: 01780 481158 peter@st-martins-antiques.co.uk www.st-martins-antiques.co.uk

London

Alfie's Antique Market, 13–25 Church Street NW8 8DT Tel: 020 7723 6066 post@eAlfies.com www.eAlfies.com

Covent Garden Antique Market, Jubilee Market Hall, Covent Garden WC2 Tel: 020 7240 7405 *Every Monday*

Grays Antique Market, 1–7 Davies Mews W1K 5AB Tel: 020 7629 7034 grays@clara.net www.graysantiques.com

Northcote Road Antique Market, 155a Northcote Road, Battersea SW11 6QB Tel: 020 7228 6850 *Open 7 days. 30 dealers offering a wide variety of antiques & collectables.*

Palmers Green Antiques Centre, 472 Green Lanes, Palmers Green N13 5PA Tel: 020 8350 0878 Mobile: 0785 506 7544 *Over 40 dealers. Specialising in furniture, jewellery, clocks, pictures, porcelain, china, glass, silver & plate, metalware, kitchenalia and lighting, etc. Open 6 days a week, closed Tues. Weekdays & Sats 10am–5.30pm, Sun 11am–5pm, open Bank Holidays. Removals & house clearances, probate valuations undertaken, quality antiques and collectables sold on commission basis.*

Norfolk

Tombland Antique Centre, Augustine Steward House, 14 Tombland, Norwich NR3 1HF Tel: 01603 619129 or 761906 *Open Mon–Sat 10am–5pm.*

Northamptonshire

The Brackley Antique Cellar, Drayman's Walk, Brackley NN13 6BE Tel: 01280 841841

Situated under the Co-op supermarket. Open 7 days 10am–5pm. Very large range of antiques and collectables. 30,000 sq.ft. of showroom with up to 100 dealers.

Nottinghamshire

Newark Antiques Centre, Regent House, Lombard Street, Newark NG24 1XP Tel: 01636 605504

Oxfordshire

Antiques on High, 85 High Street, Oxford OX1 4BG Tel: 01865 251075 *Open 7 days a week 10am–5pm. Sundays & Bank Holidays 11am–5pm. 35 dealers with a wide range of quality stock.*

Jackdaw Antiques Centres Ltd, 5 Reading Road, Henley-on-Thames RG9 0AS Tel: 01491 572289 sales@jackdaw-antiques.co.uk www.jackdaw-antiques.co.uk *Approx 1,000 sq ft of collectables (modern & discontinued), furniture, books, specialist areas, Carlton Ware, Doulton, Beswick.*

Lamb Arcade Antiques Centre, High Street, Wallingford OX10 0BS Tel: 01491 835166 *Open 10am–5pm daily, Sat till 5.30pm, Bank Holidays 11am–5pm. Furniture, silver, porcelain, glass, books, boxes, crafts, rugs, jewellery, lace and linens, pictures, tin toys, motoring and aviation memorabilia, antique stringed instruments, sports and fishing items, decorative and ornamental items.*

Shropshire

Stretton Antiques Market, Sandford Avenue, Church Stretton SY6 6BH Tel: 01694 723718 *60 dealers under one roof.*

Somerset

Bartlett Street Antique Centre, 5–10 Bartlett Street, Bath BA1 2QZ Tel: 01225 466689 info@antiques-centre.co.uk www.antiques-centre.co.uk

Staffordshire

Rugeley Antique Centre, 161 Main Road, Brereton, Nr Rugeley WS15 1DX Tel: 01889 577166 info@rugeleyantiquecentre.co.uk www.rugeleyantiquecentre.co.uk *Open Mon–Sat 9am–5pm, Sun & Bank Holidays 12 noon–4.30pm.*

Tutbury Mill Antiques Centre, Tutbury Mill Mews, Tutbury DE13 9LU Tel: 01283 520074 www.antiquesplus.co.uk *Open Mon–Sat 10am–5pm, Sun 12 noon–5pm*

Surrey

Maltings Monthly Market, Bridge Square, Farnham GU9 7QR General tel: 01252 726234 Mkt Organiser Tel: 01252 717434 FarnMalt@aol.com www.farnhammaltings.com *9.30am–4pm first Sat of the month.*

East Sussex

High Street Antiques, 39 High Street, Hastings TN34 3ER Tel: 01424 460068

West Sussex

Roundabout Antiques Centre, 7 Commercial Square, Haywards Heath RH16 7DW Shop Tel: 01444 417654 *Several specialist dealers with good quality extensive stock. Open Tues–Sat 10am–5pm. Specialising in musical instruments - ring Angie 01273 835926.*

Tyne & Wear

The Antique Centre, 2nd floor, 142 Northumberland St, Newcastle-upon-Tyne NE1 7DQ Tel: 0191 232 9832 timeout-antiques@btinternet.co.uk www.timeout-antiques.co.uk *Mon–Sat 10am–5pm.*

Wales

Offa's Dyke Antique Centre, 4 High Street, Knighton, Powys LD7 1AT Tel: 01547 520145

The Works Antiques Centre, Station Road, Llandeilo, Carmarthenshire SA19 6NH Tel: 01558 823964 *Closed Mon. 5,000sq ft. 49 dealers. Ample parking. Free tea & coffee.*

Warwickshire

Barn Antiques Centre, Station Road, Long Marston, Nr Stratford-upon-Avon CV37 8RB Tel: 01789 721399 *One of the largest traditional Antique Centres in the Midlands. Now over 13,000 sq ft. Open 7 days 10am–5pm. Antique furniture, antique pine, linen and lace, old fireplaces and surrounds, collectables, pictures and prints, silver, china, ceramics and objet d'art.*

Dunchurch Antiques Centre, 16a Daventry Road, Dunchurch (Nr Rugby) Tel: 01788 522450 *Open 7 days 10am–5pm. 11 dealers specialising in furniture, china, glass, books, postcards, stamps, clocks, toys, trains.*

Stratford Antiques Centre, 59-60 Ely Street, Stratford-upon-Avon CV37 6LN Tel: 01789 204180

West Midlands

Birmingham Antique Centre, 1407 Pershore Road, Stirchley, Birmingham B30 2JR Tel: 0121 459 4587 Fax: 0121 689 6566 *Open 7 days.*

Worcestershire

Worcester Antiques Centre, Unit 15, Reindeer Court, Mealcheapen Street, Worcester WR1 4DS Tel: 01905 610680 *Open Mon–Sun 10am–5pm, Mon–Sat 10am–5pm (Dec). Porcelain, silver, jewellery, Art Nouveau, Arts & Crafts, leather.*

Yorkshire

Cavendish Antique & Collectors Centre, 44 Stonegate, York YO1 8AS Tel: 01904 621666 sales@yorkantiquescentre.co.uk www.yorkantiquescentre.co.uk *Open 7 days 9am–6pm. Over 50 dealers on 3 floors.*

Stonegate Antiques Centre, 41 Stonegate, York YO1 8AW Tel: 01904 613888 sales@yorkantiquescentre.co.uk www.yorkantiquescentre.co.uk *Open 7 days 9am–6pm. Over 110 dealers on 2 floors.*

York Antiques Centre, 1a Lendal, York YO1 8AA Tel: 01904 641445 *15 dealers. General antiques. Open Mon–Sat 10am–5pm*

USA

Antique Village, North of Richmond, Virginia, on Historic US 301, 4 miles North of I-295 Tel: 804 746 8914 *Mon, Tues, Thurs, Fri 10am–5pm, Sat 10am–6pm, Sun 12 noon–6pm, Closed Wed. 50 dealers specialising in Art Pottery, country & primitives, Civil War artifacts, paper memorabilia, African art, toys, advertising, occupied Japan, tobacco tins, glassware, china, holiday collectibles, jewellery, postcards.*

Antiques at Colony Mill Marketplace, 222 West Street, Keene, New Hampshire 03431 Tel: (603) 358 6343 www.antiques.colonymill.com *Open Mon–Sat 10am–9pm, Sun 11am–6pm. Over 200 booths. Period to country furniture, paintings & prints, Art Pottery, glass, china, silver, jewellery, toys, dolls, quilts, etc.*

The Coffman's Antiques Markets, at Jennifer House Commons, Stockbridge Road, Route 7, PO Box 592, Great Barrington, MA 01230 Tel: (413) 528 9282/(413) 528 9602 www.coffmansantiques.com

Michiana Antique Mall, 2423 S. 11th Street, Niles, Michigan 49120 michianaantiquemall@compuserve.com www.michianaantiquemall.com *Open 7 days a week 10am–6pm.*

Quechee Gorge Antiques & Collectibles Center, Located in Quechee Gorge Village Tel: 1 800 438 5565 *450 dealers. Open all year, 7 days a week. Depression glass, ephemera, tools, toys, collectibles, Deco, primitives, prints, silver and fine china.*

Showcase Antique Center, PO Box 1122, Sturbridge, MA 01566 Tel: 508 347 7190 www.showcaseantiques.com *Open Mon, Wed, Thurs 10am–5pm, Fri, Sat 10am–5pm, Sun 12 noon–5pm, closed Tues. 170 dealers.*

Key to Illustrations

Each illustration and descriptive caption is accompanied by a letter code. By referring to the following list of Auctioneers (denoted by *) and Dealers (•), the source of any item may be immediately determined. Inclusion in this edition in no way constitutes or implies a contract or binding offer on the part of any of our contributors to supply or sell the goods illustrated, or similar articles, at the prices stated. Advertisers in this year's directory are denoted by (†).

If you require a valuation for an item, it is advisable to check whether the dealer or specialist will carry out this service and if there is a charge. Please mention Miller's when making an enquiry. Having found a specialist who will carry out your valuation it is best to send a photograph and description of the item to the specialist together with a stamped addressed envelope for the reply. A valuation by telephone is not possible. Most dealers are only too happy to help you with your enquiry; however, they are very busy people and consideration of the above points would be welcomed.

A&H • Architectural & Historical Salvage, Spa Street, Ossett, Wakefield, Yorkshire WF5 0HJ Tel: 01924 262831

A&J • A & J Collectables, Bartlett Street Antique Centre, 10 Bartlett Street, Bath, Somerset BA1 2QZ Tel: 01225 466689

AEF • A & E Foster Tel: 01494 562024

AEL • Argyll Etkin Ltd, 1–9 Hills Place, Oxford Circus, London W1R 1AG Tel: 020 7437 7800 argyll.etkin@btconnect.com

AG * Anderson & Garland (Auctioneers), Marlborough House, Marlborough Crescent, Newcastle-upon-Tyne, Tyne & Wear NE1 4EE Tel: 0191 232 6278

AH * Andrew Hartley, Victoria Hall Salerooms, Little Lane, Ilkley, Yorkshire LS29 8EA Tel: 01943 816363

AHa •† Adrian Harrington, 64a Kensington Church Street, London W8 4DB Tel: 020 7937 1465 rare@harringtonbooks.co.uk www.harringtonbooks.co.uk

AHJ •† Arch House Collectables, St George Street, Tenby, Pembrokeshire SA70 7JB Tel: 01834 843246 archhouse@onetel.net.uk

AL •† Ann Lingard, Ropewalk Antiques, Rye, East Sussex TN31 7NA Tel: 01797 223486 ann-lingard@ropewalkantiques.freeserve.co.uk

ALA • Alexander Antiques, Post House, Small Dole, Henfield, West Sussex BN5 9XE Tel: 01273 493121

ALiN • Lineham, Andrew Fine Glass, The Mall, Camden Passage, London N1 8ED Tel: 020 7704 0195 andrew@andrewlineham.co.uk www.andrewlineham.co.uk

AM • Alison Massey, MBO 32/33 Grays Antiques, 1–7 Davies Mews, London W1K 5AB Tel: 020 7629 7034

AMC • Amelie Caswell Tel: 0117 9077960

AMH • Amherst Antiques, Monomark House, 27 Old Gloucester Street, London WC1N 3XX Tel/Fax: 01892 725552 Mobile: 07850 350212 amherstantiques@monomark.co.uk

AMR • Amron Antiques Tel: 01782 566895

ANA * Anthemion Auctions, 2 Llandough Trading Park, Penarth Road, Cardiff Wales CF11 8RR Tel: 029 2071 2608

AND * Anderson's Auction Rooms Ltd, Unit 7, Prince Regent Business Park, Prince Regent Road, Castereagh, Belfast, Northern Ireland BT5 6QR Tel: 028 9040 1888

ANG •† Ancient & Gothic Tel: 01202 431721

Ann • Annie's Dolls & Teddies Tel: 01424 882437 anniestoys@btinternet.com www.anniestoys.com

AnS • The Antique Shop, 30 Henley Street, Stratford upon Avon, Warwickshire CV37 6QW Tel: 01789 292485

AOH • Antiques on High, 85 High Street, Oxford OX1 4BG Tel: 01865 251075

AOT • Annie's Old Things, PO Box 6, Camphill, Queensland 4152, Australia Tel: 0061412353099 annie@fan.net.au

AOY • All Our Yesterdays, 3 Cattle Market, Sandwich, Kent CT13 9AE Tel: 01304 614756 chrisbaker@uk.packardbell.org

APC • Antique Photographic Company Ltd Tel: 01949 842192 alpaco@lineone.net www.thesaurus.co.uk/cook

AQ • Antiquated, 10 New Street, Petworth, West Sussex GU28 0AS Tel: 01798 344011

ARB • Arbour Antiques Ltd, Poet's Arbour, Sheep Street, Stratford-on-Avon, Warwickshire CV37 6EF Tel: 01789 293453

ARo •† Alvin Ross Tel: 01865 772409 vintage.games@virgin.net

ASA • A. S. Antiques, 26 Broad Street, Pendleton, Salford, Greater Manchester M6 5BY Tel: 0161 737 5938

ASAA • ASA Antiques, 5–10 Bartlett Street, Bath, Somerset BA1 2QZ Tel: 01225 421037/312781

ASB * Andrew Spencer Bottomley, The Coach House, Thongs Bridge, Holmfirth, Yorkshire HD7 2TT Tel: 01484 685234 andrewbottomley@compuserve.com

ASH • Ashburton Marbles, Great Hall, North Street, Ashburton, Devon TQ13 7QD Tel: 01364 653189

ATH • Apple Tree House Tel: 01694 722953

AU • Auto Suggestion Tel: 01428 722933

AVT • Alexander von Tutschek Tel: 01225 465532

B&R •† Bread & Roses, Durham House Antique Centre, Sheep Street, Stow on the Wold, Gloucestershire GL54 1AA Tel: 01451 870404 or 01926 817342

BAJ • Beaulieu Autojumble, Beaulieu, Hampshire

BaN •† Barbara Ann Newman, London House Antiques, 4 Market Square, Westerham, Kent TN16 1AW Tel: 01959 564479

BAO •† Bath Antiques Online, Bartlett Street Antiques Centre, Bartlett Street, Bath, Somerset BA1 2QZ Tel: 01225 311061 info@bathantiquesonline.com www.BathAntiquesOnline.com

BAY • George Bayntun, Manvers Street, Bath, Somerset BA1 1JW Tel: 01225 466000 EBayntun@aol.com

BBA *† Bloomsbury Book Auctions, 3 & 4 Hardwick Street, Off Rosebery Avenue, London EC1R 4RY Tel: 020 7833 2636/7 or 020 7636 1945

info@bloomsbury-book-auct-.com
www.bloomsbury-book-auct.com

BBR *† BBR, Elsecar Heritage Centre, Wath Road, Elsecar, Barnsley, Yorkshire S74 8HJ
Tel: 01226 745156
sales@bbrauctions.co.uk
www.onlinebbr.com

BD • Banana Dance Ltd, 16 The Mall, Camden Passage, 359 Upper St, Islington, London N1 0PD
Tel: 020 8699 7728 Mobile: 07976 296987
jonathan@bananadance.com
www.bananadance.com

BDA • Briar's C20th Decorative Arts, Skipton Antiques & Collectors Centre, The Old Foundry, Cavendish Street, Skipton, Yorkshire BD23 2AB Tel: 01756 798641

Bea(E) * Bearnes, St Edmund's Court, Okehampton Street, Exeter, Devon EX4 1DU
Tel: 01392 422800

BEV •† Beverley, 30 Church Street/Alfie's Antique Market, Marylebone, London NW8 8EP
Tel: 020 7262 1576 Mobile: 07776136003

BEX • Daniel Bexfield Antiques, 26 Burlington Arcade, London W1V 9AD Tel: 020 7491 1720

BIB •† Biblion, Grays Antique Market, 1–7 Davies Mews, Mayfair, London W1Y 2LP
Tel: 020 7629 1374 info@biblion.co.uk
www.biblion.com

BiR • Bill Robson Tel: 01434 270206

BKS * Bonhams, Montpelier Street, Knightsbridge, London SW7 1HH Tel: 020 7393 3900
www.bonhams.com

BLH * Ambrose, Ambrose House, Old Station Road, Loughton, Essex IG10 4PE Tel: 020 8502 3951

BLM • Bill Little Motorcycles, Oak Farm, Braydon, Swindon, Wiltshire SN5 0AG
Tel: 01666 860577

BND • Brian Barnfield, Bourbon Hanby Antiques Centre, 151 Sydney Street, Chelsea, London SW3 6NT Tel: 020 7565 0002

BoC • Bounty Antiques Centre, 76 Fore Street, Topsham, Devon EX3 0HQ Tel: 01392 875007
Mobile: 07939 526504

Bon * Bonhams, Montpelier Street, Knightsbridge, London SW7 1HH Tel: 020 7393 3900
www.bonhams.com

Bon(C) * Bonhams, 65–69 Lots Road, Chelsea, London SW10 0RN Tel: 020 7393 3900
www.bonhams.com

BONA • Bonapartes, 13 George Street, Bath, Somerset BA1 2EN Tel: 01225 423873

BRG •† Brandler Galleries, 1 Coptfold Road, Brentwood, Essex CM14 4BM Tel: 01277 222269

BRT • Britannia, Grays Antique Market, Stand 101, 58 Davies Street, London W1Y 1AR
Tel: 020 7629 6772

BRU • Brunel Antiques, Bartlett Street Antiques Centre, Bath, Somerset BA1 2QZ
Tel: 0117 968 1734

BSA • Bartlett Street Antique Centre, 5/10 Bartlett Street, Bath, Somerset BA1 2QZ
Tel: 01225 466689
info@antiques-centre.co.uk
www.antiques-centre.co.uk

BSa • Ben Satterthwaite Tel: 07811 128689

BTC •† Beatcity, P O Box 229, Chatham, Kent ME5 8WA Tel/Fax: 01634 200444
Mobile: 07770 650890
Darrenhanks@beatcity.co.uk
www.beatcity.co.uk

BUR • House of Burleigh Tel: 01664 454570
HousBurl@aol.com

BWA • Bow Well Antiques, 103 West Bow, Edinburgh, Scotland EH1 2JP
Tel: 0131 225 3335

C&R • Catchpole & Rye, Saracen's Dairy, Pluckley, Ashford, Kent TN27 0SA Tel: 01233 840457

CAL • Cedar Antiques Ltd, High Street, Hartley Wintney, Hampshire RG27 8NY
Tel: 01252 843252

CAm • Classic Amusements Tel: 01425 472164
pennyslot@aol.com
www.classicamusements.net

CARS • C.A.R.S. (Classic Automobilia & Regalia Specialists), 4–4a Chapel Terrace Mews, Kemp Town, Brighton, East Sussex BN2 1HU
Tel: 01273 60 1960

CAu * Cotswold Auction Company, Chapel Walk Saleroom, Chapel Walk, Cheltenham, Gloucestershire GL50 3DS Tel: 01242 256363

CB • Christine Bridge Antiques, 78 Castelnau, London SW13 9EX Tel: 07000 445277

CBGR •† Chris Baker Gramophones, All Our Yesterdays, 3 Cattle Market, Sandwich, Kent CT13 9AE
Tel: 01304 614756 or 614756
cbgramophones@aol.com

CBP *† Comic Book Postal Auctions Ltd, 40–42 Osnaburgh Street, London NW1 3ND
Tel: 020 7424 0007
comicbook@compuserve.com
www.compalcomics.com

CCB • C. Bowdell, PO Box 65, Grantham, Lincolnshire NG31 6QR Tel: 01476 563206

CCC •† The Crested China Co, The Station House, Driffield, Yorkshire YO25 7PY
Tel: 01377 257042
dt@thecrestedchinacompany.com
www.thecrestedchinacompany.com

CCO • Collectable Costume Tel: 07980 623926

CDC * Capes Dunn & Co, The Auction Galleries, 38 Charles Street, Off Princess Street, Greater Manchester M1 7DB Tel: 0161 273 6060/1911

CGC * Cheffins, 2 Clifton Road, Cambridge CB2 4BW
Tel: 01223 213343 www.chefins.co.uk

CGX • Computer & Games Exchange, 65 Notting Hill Gate Road, London W11 3JS
Tel: 020 7221 1123

CHA • Chislehurst Antiques, 7 Royal Parade, Chislehurst, Kent BR7 6NR Tel: 020 8467 1530

CJP • Charles Jeffreys Posters & Graphics, 12 Octavia Street, London SW11 3DN Tel: 020 7978 7976
Mobile: 07836 546150
charlie@cjposters.com
www.cjposters.com

CMF • Childhood Memories Tel: 01252 793704
maureen@childhood-memories.co.uk
www.childhood-memories.co.uk

CMS * Calcutt Maclean Standen, The Estate Office, Stone Street, Cranbrook, Kent TN17 3HD
Tel: 01580 713828

CoA • Country Antiques (Wales), Castle Mill, Kidwelly, Carms, Wales SA17 4UU
Tel: 01554 890534

COB •† Cobwebs, 78–80 Old Northam Road, Southampton, Hampshire SO14 0PB
Tel/Fax: 023 8022 7458
www.cobwebs.uk.com

CoCo • Country Collector, 11–12 Birdgate, Pickering, Yorkshire YO18 7AL Tel: 01751 477481

CoHA • Corner House Antiques and Ffoxe Antiques By appointment Tel: 01367 252007
jdhis007@btopenworld

CORD • Corder Collectible Radios
paul@pcorder.freeserve.co.uk

Cot • Cottage Collectibles, Pennard House, East Pennard, Shepton Mallet, Somerset BA4 6TP Tel: 01749 860731 sheila@cottagecollectibles.co.uk www.cottagecollectibles.co.uk

CrF • Crowdfree Antiques, Fairview, The Street, Stanton, Suffolk IP31 2DQ Tel: 0870 444 0791 info@crowdfree.com

CRIS • Cristobal, 26 Church Street, London NW8 8EP Tel: 020 7724 7230 Mobile: 07956 388194

CRN •† The Crow's Nest, 3 Hope Square, opp. Brewers Quay, Weymouth, Dorset DT4 8TR Tel: 01305 786930

CS • Christopher Sykes, The Old Parsonage, Woburn, Milton Keynes, Bedfordshire MK17 9QM Tel: 01525 290259 www.sykes-corkscrews.co.uk

CTO •† Collector's Corner, PO Box 8, Congleton, Cheshire CW12 4GD Tel: 01260 270429 dave.popcorner@ukonline.co.uk

CWO • www.collectorsworld.net, PO Box 4922, Bournemouth, Dorset BH1 3WD Mobile: 078 60 791588 info@collectorsworld.biz www.collectorsworld.net www.collectorslondon.com www.collectorsworld.biz

CYA • Courtyard Antiques, 108A Causewayside, Edinburgh, Scotland EH9 1PU Tel: 0131 662 9008

DA * Dee, Atkinson & Harrison, The Exchange Saleroom, Driffield, Yorkshire YO25 7LD Tel: 01377 253151 www.dee-atkinson-harrison.co.uk

DAD • Decorative Arts @ Doune, Stand 26, Scottish Antique and Arts Centre, By Doune, Stirling, Scotland FK16 6HD Tel: 01786 461 439 Mobile: 07778 475 974 gordonfoster@excite.co.uk fionamacsporran@btinternet.com

DAn • Doll Antiques Tel: 0121 449 0637

DBo • Dorothy Bowler, Ely Street Antique Centre, Stratford-on-Avon, Warwickshire CV37 6LN Tel: 01789 204180

DCA • Devon County Antique Fairs, The Glebe House, Nymet Tracey, Crediton, Devon EX17 6DB Tel: 01363 82571

DD * David Duggleby, The Vine St Salerooms, Scarborough, Yorkshire YO11 1XN Tel: 01723 507111 www.davidduggleby.com

DE •† Decades, 20 Lord St West, Blackburn, Lancashire BB2 1JX Tel: 01254 693320

DEC •† Decorative Antiques, 47 Church Street, Bishop's Castle, Shropshire SY9 5AD Tel: 01588 638851 enquiries@decorative-antiques.co.uk www.decorative-antiques.co.uk

DFA • Delvin Farm Antiques, Gormonston, Co Meath, Republic of Ireland Tel: 00 353 1 841 2285 info@delvinfarmpine.com john@delvinfarmpine.com www.delvinfarmpine.com

DgC • Dragonlee Collectables Tel: 01622 729502

DHA • Durham House Antiques Centre, Sheep Street, Stow-on-the-Wold, Gloucestershire GL54 1AA Tel: 01451 870404

DHAR • Dave Hardman Antiques, West Street, Witheridge, Devon EX16 8AA Tel: 01884860273 Mobile: 0797 973 7126 hardmanantiques@talk21.com

DID • Didier Antiques, 58–60 Kensington Church Street, London W8 4DB Tel: 020 7938 2537/07836 232634

DLP • The Dunlop Collection, P.O. Box 6269, Statesville NC 28687, U.S.A. Tel: (704) 871 2626 or Toll Free Telephone (800) 227 1996

DMC * Diamond Mills & Co, 117 Hamilton Road, Felixstowe, Suffolk IP11 7BL Tel: 01394 282281

DMG • DMG Fairs, PO Box 100, Newark, Nottinghamshire NG24 1DJ

DN * Dreweatt Neate, Donnington Priory, Donnington, Newbury, Berkshire RG14 2JE Tel: 01635 553553

DNo/ DNO • Desmond & Amanda North, The Orchard, 186 Hale Street, East Peckham, Kent TN12 5JB Tel: 01622 871353

DNW *† Dix-Noonan-Webb, 1 Old Bond Street, London W1S 4PB Tel: 020 7499 5022 auctions@dnw.co.uk www.dnw.co.uk

DOL •† Dollectable, 53 Lower Bridge Street, Chester CH1 1RS Tel: 01244 344888/679195

DOR • Dorset Reclamation, Cow Drove, Bere Regis, Wareham, Dorset BH20 7JZ Tel: 01929 472200 info@dorsetrec.u-net.com www.dorset-reclamation.co.uk

DP • No 7 Antiques, 7 High Street, Dulverton, Somerset TA22 9HB Tel: 01398 324457

DPO • Doug Poultney, 219 Lynmouth Ave, Morden, Surrey SM4 4RX Tel: 020 8330 3472

DQ • Dolphin Quay Antique Centre, Queen Street, Emsworth, Hampshire PO10 7BU Tel: 01243 379994 www.antiquesbulletin.com/dolphinquay

Dri • Drivepast Automobilia Tel: 01452 790672

DRJ • The Motorhouse, DS & RG Johnson, Thorton Hall, Thorton, Buckinghamshire MK17 0HB Tel: 01280 812280

DSG • Delf Stream Gallery, 14 New Street, Sandwich, Kent CT13 9AB Tel: 01304 617684 www.delfstreamgallery.com

DW *† Dominic Winter Book Auctions, The Old School, Maxwell Street, Swindon, Wiltshire SN1 5DR Tel: 01793 611340 info@dominicwinter.co.uk www.dominicwinter.co.uk

E * Ewbank, Burnt Common Auction Room, London Road, Send, Woking, Surrey GU23 7LN Tel: 01483 223101 www.ewbankauctions.co.uk

Ech •† Echoes, 650a Halifax Road, Eastwood, Todmorden, Yorkshire OL14 6DW Tel: 01706 817505

EH * Edgar Horn Fine Art Auctioneers, 46–50 South Street, Eastbourne, East Sussex BN21 4XB Tel: 01323 410419 www.edgarhorns.com

EMC • Sue Emerson & Bill Chapman, Bourbon Hanby Antiques Centre, Shop No 18, 151 Sydney Street, Chelsea, London SW3 6NT Tel: 020 7351 1807

EMP • The Emporium Antique Centre Too, 24 High Street, Lewes, East Sussex BN7 2 LU Tel: 01273 477979

EON • Eugene O'Neill Antique Gallery, Echo Bridge Mall, 381 Elliot Street, Newtown Upper Falls MA 02164, U.S.A. Tel: (617) 965 5965

ERC • Zenith Antiques (Elizabeth Coupe), Hemswell Antiques Centre, Caenby Corner Estate, Hemswell Cliff, Gainsborough, Lincolnshire DN21 5TJ Tel: 01427 668389

ES • Ernest R Sampson, 33 West End, Redruth, Cornwall TR15 2SA Tel: 01209 212536

ET • Early Technology, 84 West Bow, Edinburgh, Scotland EH1 2HH Tel: 0131 226 1132

ETO • Eric Tombs, 62a West Street, Dorking, Surrey RH4 1BS Tel: 01306 743661

EV • Marlene Evans, Headrow Antiques Centre, Headrow Centre, Leeds, Yorkshire Tel: 0113 245 5344. Also at Red House Antiques Centre, Duncombe Place, York Tel: 01904 637000

EXC • Excalibur Antiques, Taunton Antique Centre, 27–29 Silver Street, Taunton, Somerset TA1 3DH Tel: 01823 289327

F&C * Finan & Co, The Square, Mere, Wiltshire BA12 6DJ Tel: 01747 861411

FA • Fagin's, Old Whiteways Cider Factory, Hele, Exeter, Devon EX5 4PW Tel: 01392 882062

Fai • Fair Finds Antiques, Rait Village Antiques Centre, Rait, Perthshire, Scotland PH2 7RT Tel: 01821 670379

FCL • French Country Living, Rue de Remparts & 21 rue de L'Eglise, 06250 Mougins, France Tel: 00 33 4 93 75 53 03 F.C.L.com@wanadoo.fr

FL • Falling Leaves Antiques, Mailing address only: 79 Valley Road, Westport CT 06880, U.S.A. fl@TIAS.com www.tias.com

FLD • Flying Duck, 320/322 Creek Road, Greenwich, London SE10 9SW Tel: 020 8858 1964 Mobile: 07831 273303

FMa • Francesca Martire, Stand F131–137, Alfie's Antique Market, 13–25 Church Street, London NW8 0RH Tel: 020 7724 4802

FO * Fleetwood Owen, 25 Ivor Place, London NW1 6HR Tel: 0207 563 5400

FST • Curiosities and Collectables, Gloucester Antiques Centre, he Historic Docks, 1 Severn Road, Gloucester GL1 2LE Tel: 01452 529716

G(B) * Gorringes Auction Galleries, Terminus Road, Bexhill-on-Sea, East Sussex TN39 3LR Tel: 01424 212994 bexhill@gorringes.co.uk www.gorringes.co.uk

G(L) * Gorringes inc Julian Dawson, 15 North Street, Lewes, East Sussex BN7 2PD Tel: 01273 472503 auctions@gorringes.co.uk www.gorringes.co.uk

G&CC •† Goss & Crested China Centre & Museum incorporating Milestone Publications, 62 Murray Road, Horndean, Hampshire PO8 9JL Tel: (023) 9259 7440 info@gosschinaclub.demon.co.uk www.gosscrestedchina.co.uk

GAA • Gabrian Antiques Tel: 01923 859675 gabrian.antiques@virgin.net

GaB • Garden Brocante Tel: 0118 9461905

GAC •† Gloucester Antiques Centre, The Historic Docks, 1 Severn Road, Gloucester GL1 2LE Tel: 01452 529716 www.antiques.center.com

GAD • Decodence Tel: 07831 326326 gad@decodence.demon.co.uk

GAK * Aylsham Salerooms, 8 Market Place, Aylsham, Norfolk NR11 6EH Tel: 01263 733195

GAZE * Thomas Wm Gaze & Son, Diss Auction Rooms, Roydon Road, Diss, Norfolk IP22 3LN Tel: 01379 650306 www.twgaze.com

GBr • Geoffrey Breeze Antiques, 6 George Street, Bath, Somerset BA1 2EH Tel: 01225 466499

GeN •† Gentry Antiques, Little Green, Polperro, Cornwall PL13 2RF Tel: 01503 272 361/020 7792 1402 info@cornishwarecollector.co.uk www.cornishwarecollector.co.uk

GH * Gardiner Houlgate, The Bath Auction Rooms, 9 Leafield Way, Corsham, Nr Bath, Somerset SN13 9SW Tel: 01225 812912 gardiner-houlgate.co.uk www.invaluable.com/gardiner-houlgate

GKR •† G.K.R. Bonds Ltd, PO Box 1, Kelvedon, Essex CO5 9EH Tel: 01376 571711

GLa • Glassdrumman Antiques, 7 Union Square, The Pantiles, Tunbridge Wells, Kent TN4 8HE Tel: 01892 538615

Gle * Glendinings & Co, 101 New Bond Street, London W1Y 9LG Tel: 020 7493 2445

GM •† Philip Knighton, 11 North Street, Wellington, Somerset TA21 8LX Tel: 01823 661618 gramman@msn.com

GRa •† Grays Antique Market, 1–7 Davies Mews, London W1K 5AB Tel: 020 7629 7034 grays@clara.net www.graysantiques.com

GRI •† Grimes House Antiques, High Street, Moreton-in-Marsh, Gloucestershire GL56 0AT Tel/Fax: 01608 651029 grimes_house@cix.co.uk www.grimeshouse.co.uk www.cranberryglass.co.uk

GRo • Geoffrey Robinson, GO77–78 (Ground floor), Alfies Antique Market, 13–25 Church Street, Marylebone, London NW8 8DT Tel: 020 7723 0449

GV • Garth Vincent, The Old Manor House, Allington, Nr Grantham, Lincolnshire NG32 2DH Tel: 01400 281358

GWR • Gwen Riley, Stand 12, Bourbon Hanby Antique Centre, 151 Sydney Street, Chelsea, London SW3 6NT Tel: 020 7352 2106

HaG • Harington Glass, 2–3 Queen Street, Bath, Somerset BA1 1HE Tel: 01225 482179

HAK •† Paul Haskell Tel: 01634 891796 Mobile: 07774 781160 www.antiqueslotmachines.inuk.com

HAL •† John & Simon Haley, 89 Northgate, Halifax, Yorkshire HX1 1XF Tel: 01422 822148/360434 toysandbanks@aol.com

HALB • Halbzwolf, Eschstrabe 21b, 32257 bunde, Germany Tel: 00 49 05223 52 58

HAld * Henry Aldridge & Son, Unit 1, Bath Road Business Centre, Devizes, Wiltshire SN10 1XA Tel: 01380 729199

HALL • Hall's Nostalgia, 389 Chatham Street, Lynn MA 01902, U.S.A. Tel: 001 781 595 7757 playball@hallsnostalgia.com www.hallsnostalgia.com

HAM * Hamptons International, 93 High Street, Godalming, Surrey GU7 1AL Tel: 01483 423567 fineart@hamptons-int.com www.hamptons.co.uk

HaR • Mr A. Harris Tel: 020 8906 8151 Mobile: 079 56 146083

HarC •† Hardy's Collectables, 862 Christchurch Road, Boscombe, Bournemouth, Dorset BH7 6DQ Tel: 07970 613077 www.poolepotteryjohn.com

HARP •† Harpers Jewellers Ltd, 2/6 Minster Gates, York YO1 7HL Tel: 01904 632634 harpersjewellers@btinternet.com www.vintage-watches.co.uk

HBr • www.horsebrass.co.uk, Diane Wilkinson, Cuddington Lane, Cuddington, Northwich, Cheshire CW8 2SY Tel/Fax: 44 (0) 1606 882555 brasses@horsebrass.co.uk www.horsebrass.co.uk/

HCA • Hilltop Cottage Antiques, 101 Portobello Road, London W11 Tel: 01451 844362 Mobile: 0777 365 8082 noswadp@AOL.com

HCJ • High Class Junk

HEG •† Stuart Heggie, 14 The Borough, Northgate, Canterbury, Kent CT1 2DR Tel: 01227 470422

HEL • Helios Gallery, 292 Westbourne Grove, London W11 2PS Tel: 077 11 955 997 heliosgallery@btinternet.com www.heliosgallery.cpm

HIS • Erna Hiscock & John Shepherd, Chelsea Galleries, 69 Portobello Road, London W11 Tel: 01233 661407 Mobile: 0771 562 7273

HO • Houghton Antiques, Houghton, Cambridgeshire Tel: 01480 461887 Mobile: 07803 716842

HOB •† Hobday Toys Tel: 01895 636737 wendyhobday@freenet.co.uk

HOLL * Holloways (RICS), 49 Parsons Street, Banbury, Oxfordshire OX16 5PF Tel: 01295 817777 enquiries@hollowaysauctioneers.co.uk www.hollowaysauctioneers.co.uk

HON • Honan's Antiques, Crowe Street, Gort, County Galway, Republic of Ireland Tel: 00 353 91 31407

HOP •† The Antique Garden, Grosvenor Garden Centre, Wrexham Road, Belgrave, Chester CH4 9EB Tel: 01244 629191 Mobile: 07976 539 990 info@antique-garden.co.uk www.antique-garden.co.uk

HSt • High Street Antiques, 39 High Street, Hastings, East Sussex TN34 3ER Tel: 01424 460068

HT • Heather's Treasures Tel: 01202 624018

HUM • Humbleyard Fine Art, Unit 32 Admiral Vernon Arcade, Portobello Road, London W11 2DY Tel: 01362 637793

HUN • Huntercombe Manor Barn, Henley-on-Thames, Oxfordshire RG9 5RY Tel: 01491 641349 wclegg@thecountryseat.com www.thecountryseat.com

HUX •† David Huxtable, Sats at Portobello Road, Basement Stall 11/12, 288 Westbourne Grove, London W11 Tel: 07710 132200 david@huxtablesoldadv.demon.co.uk

HYD * Hy Duke & Son, Dorchester Fine Art Salerooms, Dorchester, Dorset DT1 1QS Tel: 01305 265080

I&M • I & M Collectables Tel: 01942 205688 Mobile: 07768551801 kben@tinyworld.co.uk

ID • Identity, 100 Basement Flat, Finsborough Road, London SW10 9ED Tel: 020 7244 9509

IE • Imperial Echoes, The Antique Centre, 59–60 Ely Street, Stratford-upon-Avon, Warwickshire CV37 6LN Tel: 01789 204180

IQ • Cloud Cuckooland, 12 Fore Street, Mevagissey, Cornwall PL26 6UQ Tel: 01726 842364 inkquest@dial.pipex.com www.inkquest.dial.pipex.com/

IS • Ian Sharp Antiques, 23 Front Street, Tynemouth, Tyne & Wear NE30 4DX Tel: 0191 296 0656

IW • Islwyn Watkins, Offa's Dyke Antique Centre, 4 High Street, Knighton, Powys, Wales LD7 1AT Tel: 01547 520145

J&J • J & J 's, Paragon Antiquities Antiques & Collectors Market, 3 Bladud Buildings, The Paragon, Bath, Somerset BA1 5LS Tel: 01225 463715

J&S • J.R & S.J Symes of Bristol Tel: 0117 9501074

JACK •† Michael Jackson Antiques, The Quiet Woman Antiques Centre, Southcombe, Chipping Norton, Oxfordshire OX7 5QH Tel: 01608 646262 Mobile: 07831 402238 mjcig@cards.fsnet.co.uk www.our-web-site.com/cigarette-cards

JAK • Clive & Lynne Jackson Tel: 01242 254375 Mobile: 0410 239351

JBB • Jessie's Button Box, Great Western Antique Centre, Bartlett Street, Bath, Somerset BA1 5DY Tel: 0117 929 9065

JBL • Judi Bland Tel: 01276 857576

JE •† Julian Eade Tel: 01491 575059 Mobile: 07973 542971

JEB • Jenni Barke, Scottish Antique and Arts Centre, Carse of Cambus, Doune, Perthshire, Scotland FK16 6HD Tel: 01786 841203

JEZ • Jezebel, 14 Prince Albert Street, Brighton, East Sussex BN1 1HE Tel: 01273 206091

JHa • Jeanette Hayhurst Fine Glass, 32a Kensington Church Street, London W8 4HA Tel: 020 7938 1539

JHo • Jonathan Horne, 66 Kensington Church Street, London W8 4BY Tel: 020 7221 5658

JJ • Jen Jones, Pontbrendu, LLanybydder, Ceredigion, Wales SA40 9UJ Tel: 01570 480610

JM * Maxwells of Wilmslow, 133A Woodford Road, Woodford, Cheshire SK7 1QD Tel/Fax: 0161 439 5182

JMC • J & M Collectables Tel: 01580 891657 jandmcollectables@tinyonline.co.uk

JMW • JMW Gallery, 144 Lincoln Street, Boston MA02111, U.S.A. Tel: 001 617 338 9097 www.jmwgallery.com

JNic * John Nicholson, The Auction Rooms, Longfield, Midhurst Road, Fernhurst, Surrey GU27 3HA Tel: 01428 653727

JOL • Kaizen International Ltd, 88 The High Street, Rochester, Kent ME1 1JT Tel: 01634 814132

JP • Janice Paull, Beehive House, 125 Warwick Road, Kenilworth, Warwickshire CV8 1HY Tel: 01926 855253

JPr •† Joanna Proops Antique Textiles & Lighting, 34 Belvedere, Lansdown Hill, Bath, Somerset BA1 5HR Tel: 01225 310795

JU • Jukebox Showroom, 9 Park Parade, Gunnersbury Avenue, London W3 9BD Tel: 020 8992 8482/3

JuC • Julia Craig, Bartlett Street Antiques Centre, 5–10 Bartlett Street, Bath, Somerset BA1 2QZ Tel: 01225 448202/310457 Mobile: 07771 786846

JUN •† Junktion, The Old Railway Station, New Bolingbroke, Boston, Lincolnshire PE22 7LB Tel: 01205 480068/480087 Mobile: 07836 345491

JW • Julian Wood, Exeter Antique Lighting, Cellar 15, The Quay, Exeter, Devon EX2 4AY Tel: 01392 490848

KA • Kingston Antiques Centre, 29–31 London Road, Kingston-upon-Thames, Surrey KT2 6ND Tel: 020 8549 2004/3839 enquiries@kingstonantiquescentre.co.uk www.kingstonantiquescentre.co.uk

KES •† Keystones, PO Box 387, Stafford ST16 3FG Tel: 01785 256648 gkey@keystones.demon.co.uk www.keystones.co.uk

KNI * Knight's, Cuckoo Cottage, Town Green, Alby, Norwich, Norfolk NR11 7HE Tel: 01263 768488

L&E * Locke & England, 18 Guy Street, Leamington Spa, Warwickshire CV32 4RT Tel: 01926 889100 www.auctions-online.com/locke

LaF • La Femme Tel: 0117 950 4983 jewels@joancorder.freeserve.co.uk

Law • Malcolm Law Collectables, Greenways Garden Centre, Bethersden, Kent Mobile: 0777 3211603

LBe • Linda Bee Art Deco, Stand L18–21, Grays Antique Market, 1–7 Davies Mews, London W1Y 1AR Tel: 020 7629 5921

LCC •† The London Cigarette Card Co Ltd, Sutton Road, Somerton, Somerset TA11 6QP Tel: 01458 273452 cards@londoncigcard.co.uk www.londoncigcard.co.uk

LDC • L & D Collins Tel: 020 7584 0712

LeB • Le Boudoir Collectables, Bartlett Street Antique Centre, Bath, Somerset BA1 2QZ Tel: 01225 311061 www.bathantiquesonline.com

LEGE • Legend Tel: 0117 926 4637

LF *† Lambert & Foster, 77 Commercial Road, Paddock Wood, Kent TN12 6DR Tel: 01892 832325

LIB • Libra Antiques Tel: 01580 860569

LSK * Lacy Scott and Knight, Fine Art Department, The Auction Centre, 10 Risbygate Street, Bury St Edmunds, Suffolk IP33 3AA Tel: 01284 763531

Ma • Marie Antiques, Stand G136–138, Alfie's Antique Market, 13–25 Church Street, London NW8 8DT Tel: 020 7706 3727 marie136@globalnet.co.uk www.marieantiques.co.uk

MAP • Marine Art Posters, 71 Harbour Way, Merchants Landing, Victoria Dock, Port of Hull, Yorkshire HU9 1PL 01482 321173

MAr • Mint Arcade, 71 The Mint, Rye, East Sussex TN31 7EW Tel: 01797 225952

MARK •† 20th Century Marks, 12 Market Square, Westerham, Kent TN16 1AW Tel: 01959 562221 Mobile: 07831 778992 lambarda@btconnect.com www.20thcenturymarks.co.uk

MB •† Mostly Boxes, 93 High Street, Eton, Windsor, Berkshire SL4 6AF Tel: 01753 858470

MCC • M.C. Chapman Antiques, Bell Hill, Finedon, Northamptonshire NN9 5NB Tel: 01933 681260

MD • Much Ado About Deco, The Antiques Centre, 59–60 Ely Street, Stratford-upon-Avon, Warwickshire CV37 6LN Tel: 01789 204180

MED * Medway Auctions, Fagins, 23 High Street, Rochester, Kent ME1 1LN Tel: 01634 847444

MEM •† Memories UK, Mabel Lucie Attwell Club, Abbey Antiques, 63 Great Whyte, Ramsey, Nr Huntingdon, Cambridgeshire PE26 1HL Tel: 01487 814753

MFB • Manor Farm Barn Antiques Tel: 01296 658941 Mobile: 07720 286607 mfbn@btinternet.com www.btwebworld.com/mfbantiques

MGC • Midlands Goss & Commemoratives, The Old Cornmarket Antiques Centre, 70 Market Place, Warwick CV34 4SO Tel: 01926 419119

MGe • Michael German Antiques Ltd, 38B Kensington Church Street, London W8 4BX Tel: 020 7937 2771 www.antiquecanes.com

MI • Mitofsky's, 101 Terenure Road East, Dublin 6, Republic of Ireland Tel: 00 353 1 492 0033 info@mitofskyartdeco.com www.mitofskyartdeco.com

Mit * Mitchells, Fairfield House, Station Road, Cockermouth, Cumbria CA13 9PY Tel: 01900 827800

ML • Memory Lane, Bartlett Street Antiques Centre, 5/10 Bartlett Street, Bath, Somerset BA1 2QZ Tel: 01225 466689

MLa • Marion Langham Tel: 020 7730 1002 mlangham@globalnet.co.uk ladymarion@btinternet.com

MLL • Millers Antiques Ltd, Netherbrook House, 86 Christchurch Road, Ringwood, Hampshire BH24 1DR Tel: 01425 472062 mail@millers-antiques.co.uk www.millers-antiques.co.uk

MLu • Michael Lucas Antiques, Admiral Vernon Antiques Arcade, Portobello Road, London W11 Tel: 020 8650 1107 Mobile: 07850 388288

Mo • Mr Moore

MRT • Mark Rees Tools Tel: 01225 837031

MRW • Malcolm Welch Antiques, Wild Jebbett, Pudding Bag Lane, Thurlaston, Nr. Rugby, Warwickshire CV23 9JZ Tel: 01788 810 616

MSB • Marilynn and Sheila Brass, PO Box 380503, Cambridge MA 02238-0503, U.S.A. Tel: 617 491 6064

MUR •† Murray Cards (International) Ltd, 51 Watford Way, Hendon Central, London NW4 3JH Tel: 020 8202 5688 murraycards@ukbusiness.com www.murraycards.com

MURR • Murrays' Antiques & Collectables Tel: 01202 309094

MVX • Music & Video Exchange, 1st Floor, 38 Notting Hill Gate, London W11 3HX Tel: 020 7243 8574

MW • Malcolm Wells Tel: Miller's 01580 766411

N * Neales, 192–194 Mansfield Road, Nottingham NG1 3HU Tel: 0115 962 4141

NET • Nettlebed Antique Merchants, 1 High Street, Nettlebed, Henley on Thames, Oxfordshire RG9 5DA Tel: 01491 642062

NEW • Newsum Antiques, 2 High Street, Winchcombe, Gloucestershire GL54 5HT Tel: 01242 603446/07968 196668

NP • The Neville Pundole Gallery, 8A & 9 The Friars, Canterbury, Kent CT1 2AS Tel: 01227 453471 www.pundole.co.uk

OCAC • Old Cornmarket Antiques Centre, 70 Market Place, Warwick CV34 4SO Tel: 01926 419119

OCB • The Old Children's Bookshelf, 175 Canongate, Edinburgh, Scotland EH8 8BN Tel: 0131 558 3411

OD • Islwyn Watkins, Offa's Dyke Antique Centre, 4 High Street, Knighton, Powys, Wales LD7 1AT Tel: 01547 520145

OLA • Olliff's Architectural Antiques, 19–21 Lower Redland Road, Redland, Bristol, Gloucestershire BS6 6TB Tel: 0117 923 9232 marcus@olliffs.comwww.olliffs.com

OND • Ondines, 14 The Mall, Camden Passage, London N1 Tel: 01865 882465

ONS * Onslow's, The Depot, 2 Michael Road, London SW6 2AD Tel: 020 7371 0505 Mobile: 078 31 473 400

OO • Pieter Oosthuizen, Unit 4 Bourbon Hanby Antiques Centre, 151 Sydney Street, London SW3 6NT Tel: 020 7460 3078

OPB • Olde Port Bookshop, 18 State Street, Newburyport, Massachusetts 01950, USA Tel: 001 978 462 0100 Oldeport@ttlc.net

ORI • Origin 101, Gateway Arcade, Islington High Street, London N1 Tel: 07769 686146/07747 758852 David@origin101.co.uk www.naturalmodern.com www.origin101.co.uk

OTA •† On The Air, The Vintage Technology Centre, The Highway, Hawarden, (Nr Chester), Deeside, Cheshire CH5 3DN Tel/Fax: 01244 530300 www.vintageradio.co.uk

OTB •† The Old Tackle Box, PO Box 55, High Street, Cranbrook, Kent TN17 3ZU Tel/Fax 01580 713979 tackle.box@virgin.net

OTC •† The Old Telephone Company, The Old Granary, Battlesbridge Antiques Centre, Nr Wickford, Essex SS11 7RF Tel: 01245 400601 gp@theoldtelephone.co.uk www.theoldtelephone.co.uk

OTT • Otter Antiques, 20 High Street, Wallingford, Oxfordshire OX10 0BP Tel: 01491 825544 www.antique-boxes.com

OVE • Chuck Overs

OW • Off World, Unit 20, Romford Shopping Halls, Market Place, Romford, Essex RM1 3AT Tel: 01708 765633

P *† Bonhams, 101 New Bond Street, London W1S 1SR Tel: 020 7629 6602/7468 8233 www.bonhams.com

P(B) * Bonhams, 1 Old King Street, Bath, Somerset BA1 2JT Tel: 01225 310609

P(Ba) * Bonhams, 10 Salem Road, Bayswater, London W2 4DL Tel: 020 7229 9090

P(Ed) * Bonhams, 65 George Street, Edinburgh, Scotland EH2 2JL Tel: 0131 225 2266

P(L) * Bonhams, Hepper House, 17a East Parade, Leeds, Yorkshire LS1 2BH Tel: 0113 244 8011

P(NW) * Bonhams, New House, 150 Christleton Road, Chester CH3 5TD Tel: 01244 313936

P(WM) * Bonhams, The Old House, Station Road, Knowle, Solihull, West Midlands B93 0HT Tel: 01564 776151

PAC •† The Potteries Antique Centre, 271 Waterloo Road, Cobridge, Stoke on Trent, Staffordshire ST6 3NR Tel: 01782 201455 www.potteriesantiquecentre.com

PAR • Park House Antiques & Toy Museum, Park Street, Stow-on-the-Wold, Gloucestershire GL54 1AQ Tel: 01451 830159 info@thetoymuseum.co.uk www.thetoymuseum.co.uk

PC Private Collection

PEZ • Alan Pezaro, 62a West Street, Dorking, Surrey RH4 1BS Tel: 01306 743661

PFK * Penrith Farmers' & Kidd's plc, Skirsgill Salerooms, Penrith, Cumbria CA11 0DN Tel: 01768 890781

PGA • Paul Gibbs Antiques, 25 Castle Street, Conway, Gwynedd, Wales LL32 8AY Tel: 01492 593429/596533

PJo • Paul Jones, The Quiet Woman Antiques Centre, Southcombe, Chipping Norton, Oxfordshire OX7 5QH Tel: 01608 646262

PLB • Planet Bazaar, 149 Drummond Street, London NW1 2PB Tel: 0207 387 8326 Mobile: 07956 326301 maureen@planetbazaar.demon.co.uk www.planetbazaar.co.uk

POL • Book Shop, 8 Artillery Row, London SW1 Tel: 020 7828 0010

Pott *† Potteries Specialist Auctions, 271 Waterloo Road, Cobridge, Stoke on Trent, Staffordshire ST6 3HR Tel: 01782 286622

PPH • Period Picnic Hampers Tel: 0115 937 2934

PPL • The Pen and Pencil Lady Tel: 01647 231619 penpencilady@aol.com www.penpencilady.com

PSA • Pantiles Spa Antiques, 4, 5, 6 Union House, The Pantiles, Tunbridge Wells, Kent TN4 8HE Tel: 01892 541377

PT • Pieces of Time, (1–7 Davies Mews), 26 South Molton Lane, London W1Y 2LP Tel: 020 7629 2422

Q&C • Q&C Militaria, 22 Suffolk Road, Cheltenham, Gloucestershire GL50 2AQ Tel/Fax: 01242 519815 Mobile: 07778 613977 john@qc-militaria.freeserve.co.uk www.qcmilitaria.com

QW • Quiet Woman Antiques Centre, Southcombe, Chipping Norton, Oxfordshire OX7 5QH Tel: 01608 646262

Rac • Field, Staff & Woods, 93 High Street, Rochester, Kent ME1 1LX Tel: 01634 846144

RAR * Romsey Auction Rooms, 86 The Hundred, Romsey, Hampshire SO51 8BX Tel: 01794 513331

RAY • Derek & Tina Rayment Antiques, Orchard House, Barton Road, Barton, Nr Farndon, Cheshire SY14 7HT Tel: 01829 270429

RBA • Roger Bradbury Antiques, Church Street, Coltishall, Norfolk NR12 7DJ Tel: 01603 737444

RBB * Brightwells Ltd, Fine Art Salerooms, Ryelands Road, Leominster, Herefordshire HR6 8NZ Tel: 01568 611122

RCo • Royal Commemorative China Tel: 020 8863 0625 royalcommemorative@hotmail.com

RdeR • Rogers de Rin, 76 Royal Hospital Road, London SW3 4HN Tel: 020 7352 9007

RDG • Richard Dennis Gallery, 144 Kensington Church Street, London W8 4BN Tel: 020 7727 2061

RdV • Sudbury Antiques, Roger de Ville Tel: 01889 564311 Mobile: 07798 793857

RECL • Minchinhampton Architectural Salvage Co, Cirencester Road, Chalford, Stroud, Gloucestershire GL6 8PE Tel: 01285 760886 masco@catbrain.com www.catbrain.com

REG • Regatta Antiques, Antiques Centre, 151 Sydney Street, Chelsea, London SW3 6NT Tel: 020 7460 0054

REN • Paul & Karen Rennie, 13 Rugby Street, London WC1N 3QT Tel: 020 7405 0220 www.rennart.co.uk

RFA * Rowley Fine Art, The Old Bishop's Palace, Little Downham, Ely, Cambridgeshire CB6 2TD Tel: 01353 699177 mail@rowleyfineart.com www.rowleyfineart.com

RIA • Riverside Antiques, 60 Ely Street, Stratford-upon-Avon, Warwickshire Tel: 01789 262090

RMC •† Romsey Medal Centre, PO Box 169, Romsey, Hampshire SO51 6XU Tel: 01794 324488 post@romseymedals.co.uk www.romseymedals.co.uk

RTo * Rupert Toovey & Co Ltd, Star Road, Partridge Green, West Sussex RH13 8RJ Tel: 01403 711744

RTT • Rin Tin Tin, 34 North Road, Brighton, East Sussex BN1 1YB Tel: 01273 672424/733689

RTW •† Richard Twort Tel/Fax: 01934 641900 Mobile: 077 11 939789

RUL • Rules Antiques, 62 St Leonards Road, Windsor, Berkshire SL4 3BY Tel: 01753 833210/01491 642062

RUS • Trevor Russell Vintage Fountain Pens, PO Box 1258, Uttoxeter, Staffordshire ST14 8XL gtantiques@onetel.net.uk

RUSK • Ruskin Decorative Arts, 5 Talbot Court, Stow-on-the-Wold, Cheltenham, Gloucestershire GL54 1DP Tel: 01451 832254

RUSS • Russells Tel: 023 8061 6664

RWA • Ray Walker Antiques, Burton Arcade, 296 Westbourne Grove, London W11 2PS Tel: 020 8464 7981 rw.antiques@btinternet.com

S * Sotheby's, 34–35 New Bond Street, London W1A 2AA Tel: 020 7293 5000/0207 2935205 www.sothebys.com

S(NY) * Sotheby's, 1334 York Avenue, New York NY 10021, U.S.A. Tel: 00 1 212 606 7000

S(O) * Sotheby's Olympia, Hammersmith Road, London W14 8UX Tel: 020 7293 5000

S(S) * Sotheby's Sussex, Summers Place, Billingshurst, West Sussex RH14 9AD Tel: 01403 833500

SA • Sporting Antiques, St Ives, Cambridgeshire Tel: 01480 463891 john.lambden@virgin.net

SAF * Saffron Walden Auctions, 1 Market Street, Saffron Walden, Essex CB10 1JB Tel: 01799 513281

Sama • Samax, Bartlett Street Antiques Centre, 5–10 Bartlett Street, Bath, Somerset BA1 2QZ Tel: 01225 466689

SAS *† Special Auction Services, The Coach House, Midgham Park, Reading, Berkshire RG7 5UG Tel: 0118 971 2949 www.invaluable.com/sas/

SBL • Twentieth Century Style Tel: 01822 614831

SBT • Steinberg & Tolkien, Vintage & Designer Clothing, 193 Kings Road, London SW3 5EB Tel: 020 7376 3660

SCM • Scarabond & The Moon, Scottish Antique and Arts Centre, Carse of Cambus, Doune, Perthshire, Scotland FK16 6HD Tel: 01786 841203

SCR • Herzog, Hollender Phillips & Company, The Scripophily Shop, PO Box 14376, London NW6 1ZD Tel/Fax: 020 7433 3577 hollender@dial.pipex.com Currency.dealers-on-line.com/ScripophilyShop

SDP • Stage Door Prints, 9 Cecil Court, London WC2N 4EZ Tel: 020 7240 1683

SEA • Mark Seabrook Antiques, 9 West End, West Haddon, Northamptonshire NN6 7AY Tel: 01788 510772

SEE • Liz Seeber Old Cookery, Food & Wine Books, The Old Vicarage, 3 College Road, Brighton, East Sussex BN2 1JA Tel: 01273 684949 seeber.books@virgin.net www.lizseeberbooks.co.uk

SER • Serendipity, 125 High Street, Deal, Kent CT14 6BQ Tel: 01304 369165/01304 366536 dipityantiques@aol.com

SEY • Mike Seymour, The Directors Cut, The Antiques Centre, Ely Street, Stratford-upon-Avon, Warwickshire CV37 6LN Tel: 07931 345784 mike@seymour.gsbusiness.co.uk

SHA • Shambles, 22 North Street, Ashburton, Devon TQ13 7QD Tel: 01364 653848

SK * Skinner Inc, The Heritage On The Garden, 63 Park Plaza, Boston MA 02116, U.S.A. Tel: 001 617 350 5400

SK(B) * Skinner Inc, 357 Main Street, Bolton MA 01740, U.S.A. Tel: 001 978 779 6241

SLL • Sylvanna LLewelyn Antiques, Unit 5, Bourbon-Hanby Antiques Centre, 151 Sydney Street, Chelsea, London SW3 6NT Tel: 020 7598 1278

SMI •† Skip & Janie Smithson Tel/Fax: 01754 810265 Mobile: 07831 399180

SMW • Sporting Memorabilia of Warwick, 13 Market Place, Warwick CV34 4FS Tel: 01926 410600 sales@sportantiques.com www.sportsantiques.com

SOL *† Solent Railwayana Auctions Tel: 01489 584633

Som • Somervale Antiques, 6 Radstock Road, Midsomer Norton, Bath, Somerset BA3 2AJ Tel/Fax: 01761 412686 Mobile: 07885 088022 ronthomas@somervaleantiquesglass.co.uk www.somervaleantiquesglass.co.uk

SPA • Sporting Antiques, 10 Union Square, The Pantiles, Tunbridge Wells, Kent TN4 8HE Tel: 01892 522661

SpM • Sparkle Moore, The Girl Can't Help It!/Cad Van Swankster, G100 & G116 Ground Floor, Alfies Antique Market, 13–25 Church Street, Marylebone, London NW8 8DT Tel: 020 7724 8984 Office: 0208 809 3923 sparkle.moore@virgin.net www.grays.clara.net

SPT • Sporting Times Gone By, Warehouse (Clubhouse) Tel: 01903 885656 Mobile: 07976 942059 www.sportingtimes.co.uk

SPU • Spurrier-Smith Antiques, 28, 30, 39 Church Street, Ashbourne, Derbyshire DE6 1AJ Tel: 01335 343669/342198

SRA *† Sheffield Railwayana Auctions, 43 Little Norton Lane, Sheffield, Yorkshire S8 8GA Tel: 0114 274 5085 ian@sheffrail.freeserve.co.uk www.sheffieldrailwayana.co.uk

SSL • Star Signings Ltd, Unit E16/E17 Grays in the Mews, 1–7 Davies Mews, London W1K 5AB Tel: 020 7491 1010 Mobile: 07973 840625

SSM • Sue Scott Motoring Memorabilia Tel: 01525 372757

StC • St Clere Carlton Ware, P O Box 161, Sevenoaks, Kent TN15 6GA Tel: 01474 853630 stclere@aol.com www.stclere.co.uk

STE •† Stevenson Brothers, The Workshop, Ashford Road, Bethersden, Ashford, Kent TN26 3AP Tel: 01233 820363 sales@stevensonbros.com www.stevensonbros.com

STP •† Stevie Pearce, Stand G144, Alfies Antique Market, 13–25 Church Street, Marylebone, London NW8 8DT Tel: 020 7723 2526/5754 Stevie@steviepearce.co.uk www.SteviePearce.co.uk

SWB •† Sweetbriar Gallery, Robin Hood Lane, Helsby, Cheshire WA6 9NH Tel: 01928 723851 Mobile: 07860 907532 sweetbr@globalnet.co.uk www.sweetbriar.co.uk

SWO * G E Sworder & Sons, 14 Cambridge Road, Stansted Mountfitchet, Essex CM24 8BZ Tel: 01279 817778 www.sworder.co.uk

T&D • & Dolls, 367 Fore Street, Edmonton, London N9 0NR Tel: 020 8807 3301

TAC • Tenterden Antiques Centre, 66–66A High Street, Tenterden, Kent TN30 6AU Tel: 01580 765655/765885

TB • Millicent Safro, Tender Buttons, 143 E.62nd Street, New York NY10021, U.S.A. Tel: (212) 758 7004 Fax: (212) 319 8474 Author of BUTTONS

TBoy • Toy Boy, G64–65 Alfies Antique Market, 13–25 Church Street, Marylebone, London NW8 8DT Tel: 020 7723 5613

TCG • 20th Century Glass, Kensington Church Street Antique Centre, 58–60 Kensington Church Street, London W8 4DB Tel: 020 7938 1137 Tel/Fax: 020 7729 9875 Mobile: 07971 859848

TED •† Teddy Bears of Witney, 99 High Street, Witney, Oxfordshire OX8 6LY Tel: 01993 702616

TEN * Tennants, The Auction Centre, Harmby Road, Leyburn, Yorkshire DL8 5SG Tel: 01969 623780

TF * Tayler & Fletcher, London House, High Street, Bourton-on-the-Water, Cheltenham, Gloucestershire GL54 2AP Tel: 01451 821666 www.tayler-and-fletcher.co.uk

TMA *† Brown & Merry, Tring Market Auctions, Brook Street, Tring, Hertfordshire HP23 5EF Tel: 01442 826446 sales@tringmarketauctions.co.uk www.tringmarketauctions.co.uk

TMa • Tin Man, St Ives, Cambridgeshire Tel: 01480 463891 john.lambden@virgin.net

TMi • T. J. Millard Antiques, Bartlett Street Antiques Centre, Bath, Somerset Tel: 01225 469785

TML • Timothy Millett Ltd, Historic Medals and Works of Art, PO Box 20851, London SE22 0YN Tel: 020 8693 1111 Mobile: 07778 637 898 tim@timothymillett.demon.co.uk

TOB •† The Old Brigade, 10A Harborough Road, Kingsthorpe, Northampton NN2 7AZ Tel: 01604 719389 theoldbrigade@easynet.co.uk www.theoldbrigade.co.uk

TOM•† Charles Tomlinson Tel/Fax: 01244 318395 charles.tomlinson@lineone.net charles.tomlinson@btinternet.com www.lineone.net/-charles.tomlinson

TOT •† Totem, 168 Stoke Newington, Church Street, London N16 0JL Tel: 020 7275 0234 sales@totemrecords.com www.totemrecords.com

TPC • Pine Cellars, 39 Jewry Street, Winchester, Hampshire SO23 8RY Tel: 01962 777546/867014

TRA • Tramps, Tuxford Hall, Lincoln Road, Tuxford, Newark, Nottinghamshire NG22 0HR Tel: 01777 872 543 info@trampsuk.com

TREA * Treadway Gallery, Inc., 2029 Madison Road, Cincinnati, Ohio 45208, U.S.A. Tel: 001 513 321 6742 www.treadwaygallery.com

TRM * Thomson, Roddick & Medcalf, 60 Whitesands, Dumfries, Scotland DG1 2RS Tel: 01387 255366

TRO •† The Troika Man Tel: 01535 667294 thetroikaman@aol.com www.troikapottery.org

TT • Treasures in Textiles Tel: 01244 328968

TUN • Tunbridge Wells Antiques, 12 Union Square, The Pantiles, Tunbridge Wells, Kent TN4 8HE Tel: 01892 533708

TWAC • Talbot Walk Antiques Centre, The Talbot Hotel, High Street, Ripley, Surrey GU23 6BB Tel: 01483 211724

TWI •† Twinkled, Units 28/29, Village Market, Stockwell Street, Greenwich, London SE10 Tel: 0208 4880930/07940471574 info@twinkled.net www.twinkled.net Also at: High St Antiques Centre, 39 High Street, Hastings, East Sussex TN34 Tel: 01424 460068 info@twinkled.net www.twinkled.net

TWr • Tim Wright Antiques, Richmond Chambers, 147 Bath Street, Glasgow G2 4SQ Tel: 0141 221 0364

TYL * John Taylors, 14–18 Cornmarket Chambers, Louth, Lincolnshire LN11 9PY Tel: 01507 603648

UCO •† Unique Collections, 52 Greenwich Church Street, London SE10 9BL Tel: 020 8305 0867 glen@uniquecollections.co.uk www.uniquecollections.co.uk

UNI • No longer trading

UTP • Utility Plus, 66 High Street, West Ham, Pevensey, East Sussex BN24 5LP Tel: 01323 762316 07850 130723

V&S • No longer trading

VB • Variety Box Tel: 01892 531868

VBo • Vernon BowdenTel: 01202 763806

VCL • Vintage Cameras Ltd, 256 Kirkdale, Sydenham, London SE26 4NL Tel: 020 8778 5416 info@vintagecameras.co.uk www.vintagecameras.co.uk

VEC *† Vectis Auctions Ltd/Barry Potter Auctions, Fleck Way, Thornaby, Stockton-on-Tees, Cleveland TS17 9JZ Tel: 01642 750616 admin@vectis.co.uk admin@barrypotterauctions.com www.vectis.co.uk www.barrypotterauctions.co.uk

VINE • Vine Antiques Tel: 01235 812708

VP • VintagePostcards.com, 60–C Skiff Street, Suite 116, Hamden CT 06517, U.S.A. Tel: 001 203 248 6621 quality@VintagePostcards.com www.VintagePostcards.com

VS *† T. Vennett-Smith, 11 Nottingham Road, Gotham, Nottinghamshire NG11 0HE Tel: 0115 983 0541 info@vennett-smith.com www.vennett-smith.com

VSP * Van Sabben Poster Auctions, PO Box 2065, 1620 EB Hoorn, Netherlands Tel: 31 229 268203 uboersma@sabbenposterauctions.nl www.vsabbenposterauctions.nl

WAB • John Lambden Tel: 01480 463891 john.lambden@virgin.net

WAC • Worcester Antiques Centre, Unit 15, Reindeer Court, Mealcheapen Street, Worcester WR1 4DF Tel: 01905 610680

WAL *† Wallis & Wallis, West Street Auction Galleries, Lewes, East Sussex BN7 2NJ Tel: 01273 480208 auctions@wallisandwallis.co.uk www.wallisandwallis.co.uk

WaR • Wot a Racket, 250 Shepherds Lane, Dartford, Kent DA1 2PN Tel/Fax: 01322 220619 wot-a-racket@talk21.com

WBH * Walker, Barnett & Hill, Cosford Auction Rooms, Long Lane, Cosford, Shropshire TF11 8PJ Tel: 01902 375555

WCa • Wendy Carmichael, S126–129 Alfies Antique Market, 13–25 Church Street, London NW8 8DT Tel: 020 7723 6066

WD * Weller & Dufty Ltd, 141 Bromsgrove Street, Birmingham, West Midlands B5 6RQ Tel: 0121 692 1414 wellerdufty@freewire.co.uk www.welleranddufty.co.uk

WED • Wedgewood, Barlaston, Stoke on Trent, Staffordshire ST12 9ES Tel: 0800 317 412

WHO • The Who Shop International Ltd, 4 Station Parade, High Street North, East Ham, London E6 1JD Tel: 020 8471 2356 Mobile: 07977 430948 whoshop@hilly.com www.the.whoshop.com

WI • David Winstone, Bartlett Street Antique Centre, 5–10 Bartlett Street, Bath, Somerset BA1 2QZ Tel: 01225 466689 Mobile: 07979 506415 winstampok@netscapeonline.co.uk

WilP * W&H Peacock, 26 Newnham Street, Bedford, MK40 3JR Tel: 01234 266366

WO • Woodville Antiques, The Street, Hamstreet, Ashford, Kent TN26 2HG Tel: 01233 732981 woodvilleantiques@netscapeonline.co.uk

WP •† British Notes, PO Box 257, Sutton, Surrey SM3 9WW Tel: 020 8641 3224 pamwestbritnotes@compuserve.com www.west-banknotes.co.uk

WRe • Walcot Reclamations, 108 Walcot Street, Bath, Somerset BA1 5BG Tel: 01225 444404

WSA • West Street Antiques, 63 West Street, Dorking, Surrey RH4 1BS Tel: 01306 883487

WSM •† Wimbledon Sewing Machine Co Ltd and The London Sewing Machine Museum, 292–312 Balham High Road, Upper Tooting, London SW17 7AA Tel: 020 8767 4724 wimbledonsewingmachinecoltd@btinternet.com www.sewantique.com

WW * Woolley & Wallis, 51–61 Castle Street, Salisbury, Wiltshire SP1 3SU Tel: 01722 424500/01722 411854

YEST • Yesterday's, V.O.F. Yesterday's, Maaseikerweg 202, 6006 AD Weert, The Netherlands Tel: 0475 531207

YO • Martin Burton, 201 Hull Road, York YO10 3JY Tel: 01904 415347 yoyomonster@jugglers.net

YR • Yorkshire Relics of Haworth, 11 Main Street, Haworth, Yorkshire BD22 8DA Tel: 01535 642218 Mobile: 07971 701278

ZOOM • Zoom, Arch 65 Cambridge Grove, Hammersmith, London W6 Tel: 07000 9666 2001 Mobile: 07958 372975 eddiesandham@hotmail.com www.retrozoom.com

Index to Advertisers

David Aldous-Cook 49
Alfies . . . .*front end paper*
Ancient & Gothic 23
Angling Auctions 363
Antique Amusement Co .20
The Antique Garden 213
Antiques Magazine 89
A.P.E.S. Rocking Horses 412
Arch House Collectables 126
Baca Awards 30
Chris Baker Gramophones 325
Bath Antiques Online 393
BBR Auctions .58, 103, 115
Beatcity 331
Beverley 150
Biblion 50
Bloomsbury Book Auctions 55
Bonhams 104
Bookbasket.co.uk 79
Roger Bradbury Antiques 149
Brandler Galleries 186
Bread & Roses 267
British Notes 295
Brown & Merry 137
Candlestick & Bakelite 373
Cat Pottery 87
Cavendish Antiques & Collectors Centre 443
Chinasearch 123
Christie's South Kensington . . . .*back cover*
Classic Amusements 21
Cleethorpes Collectables 152
Cobwebs 349
Collect It! . . . .*back end paper*
The Collector 91, 143
Collector's Corner 329
Comic Book Postal Auctions Ltd 159
Corgi Collector Club 409
The Crested China Company 110
The Crow's Nest 347
Dalkeith Auctions 308
Peggy Davies Ceramics . . . .*front end paper*
Decades 377
Decorative Antiques 136
Richard Dennis Publications 32
Dix Noonan Webb 277
Dollectable 181
Julian Eade 146
eBay 247
Echoes 379
Edinburgh Coin Shop .276
Forget-Me-Knot Antiques 251
Gentry Antiques 116
G.K.R. Bonds Ltd 343
Gloucester Antiques Centre 441
Gordon 'ole Bottle Man 11, 59, 63
The Goss Collectors' Club 111
The Goss and Crested China Club 109
Grays Antique Market . . . .*back end paper*
Grimes House Antiques 195
Haddon Rocking Horses 412
G. M. Haley 410
John & Simon Haley 289, 407
Hardy's Collectables 129
Harpers Jewellers 425
Adrian Harrington 51

Paul Haskell 22
Heanor Antiques Centre 439
Stuart Heggie 85
W. L. Hoad 157
Hobdays Toys 417
Tony Horsley Antiques 151
Huxtable's 15
John Ives 53
Michael Jackson 155
Michael James 326
Jazz Art Deco.com 28
Francis Joseph Publications 73, 145
Junktion .13, 22, 38, 411
Keystones 101
Phillip Knighton 323
Lambert & Foster 117
Limited Editions 147
Linen & Lace 375
Ann Lingard 261
The London Cigarette Card Company Ltd 158
The London Sewing Machine Museum 345
Memories U.K 33
Miller's Publications 122
Mostly Boxes 61
Mullock & Madeley 362
Murray Cards 156
John Neale 419
Barbara Ann Newman 179
Northcote Road Antiques Market 442
Nostalgia Toy Museum 403
The Old Brigade 281
The Old Tackle Box 364
The Old Telephone Company 373
On The Air 321
Stevie Pearce 253
Pooks Transport Bookshop 39
Poole Pottery Collectors Club 128
Potteries Antique Centre 135
Pretty Bizarre 95
Joanna Proops 381
Romsey Medal Centre 279
Alvin Ross 312
Rumours 124
Sheffield Railwayana Auctions 327
Skip & Janie Smithson 271
Solent Railwayana 328
Special Auction Services 107
Specialised Postcard Auctions 307
Stevenson Brothers 413
Sweetbriar Gallery 199, 227
Teddy Bears of Witney 385
Telephone Lines Ltd 372
Tombland Antiques Centre 442
Charles Tomlinson 339
Totem Records 335
Tracks 2, 330, 333
The Troika Man 141
20th Century Marks 315
Richard Twort 341
Unique Collections 408
Vectis Auctions Ltd 395
T. Vennett-Smith 201, 361
Wallis & Wallis 283, 415
Dominic Winter 37
Yesterday Child 178

Index

Italic page numbers denote colour pages; **bold** numbers refer to information and pointer boxes

A

A&BC Gum *190*
Abonne 16
Abreau, A.J. *397*
ABS *239*
Adams, C. & Son 284
Adams, Pamela *386*
Adams, Richard 54
Adams, Truda 128
Adams & Co 302, 303
advertising & packaging 9–16, *65–6*
　advertisement & showcards 12, *66, 69, 70,* 228
　breweriana 62–4, *76*
　enamel signs 13–14, 228
　mirrors *66, 76,* 81, 228
　smoking *317*
　tins 15–16, 33, *65–6*
adzes 401
Aero 10
aeronautica 17–19, *67*
　balloons & airships 18–19, *67*
　toy aeroplanes 406
Aesop 54
aide-memoires 29
air guns 284
Airfix 409
airships 18–19
Alba Cigarettes *317*
albums, photograph 297–8
ale mullers 269
Alexandra 109
All-Blacks 47
Alldays & Onions 43, 44
Allwyn 22
Alt, Beck & Gottschalk 179
amber jewellery 260
American Locomotive Works 287
amethyst glass *194*, 275
Amplion 325
amputation sets 342
amusement & slot machines 20–2
Anderson, Hans 54
andirons 27
Andrade *388*
animal figures 87, *399*
　Beswick *78*, 90
　Burmantofts 93
　Crown Devon 99
　Denby 101
　egg cups 106
　Goss & crested china 112
　majolica 119
　metalware 353
　Mosaic *149*
　owls *238*, 294
　Pendelfins 126

Radford 132
Royal Copenhagen 133
Royal Doulton 102, 103
Shelley 135
Staffordshire 137, 138
SylvaC 140, *152*
Wade 142
Wemyss 144
Winstanley *152*
annuals 159–60, *186, 314*
antiquities 23–4
Antler 231
Anton, O. *242*
anvils 43
apple corers 350
apple peeling machines 269
apple racks 270
arc lamps 339
Arcadian 109
architectural salvage 25–7
　door stops & boot scrapers 26
　heating 26–7
Ardath 157
Arden, Elizabeth 338
Ardente 323
Army & Navy 364
Arnold 406
Arnold, C.A. 345
ARS Edition 154
Art Deco 28
　buttons 83
　ceramics 28
　clocks 28
　compacts *188*
　furniture 28
　glass *194*
　greetings cards 348
　jewellery 28, *233,* 251–3, 259, 260
　lighting 28, 273
　taps 42
　watches 28
Art Nouveau 29, *68*
　buttons 83
　corkscrews 168
　furniture 30
　glass 29, *194,* 216
　jewellery 29, *68, 233,* 260
　lighting 29, 272
　metalware 29, *68*
　scent bottles 338
　textiles 375
Arteluce 273
Artemide *239*
Arts & Crafts 30, *68,* 293
Ashanti figures *397*
Ashtead Pottery 304
ashtrays 357
　aeronautica 19
　Bakelite 299, 357
　breweriana 62
　Butlin's 81

Fifties 206
　glass *198,* 218
　railwayana 327
　Sixties & Seventies 355
　Troika 141
asparagus cradles 127
assay marks *400*
Attwell, Mabel Lucie 31–3, 69, 308, 423
Ault *78*
Austin *393*
Austrian jewellery 255
autographs 34–7
　autograph books 426
　black history & memorabilia 48
　collectables of the future *400*
　crime 175
　Doctor Who 176, 177
　politics 304
　sport *319*
Automatic Amusement Co 20
Automatic Sports Co 20
automobilia 38–9
Avon *320*
Aynsley 166, *241*

B

Babycham *76*
Baccarat 220, 227
badges *399*
　advertising 10
　aeronautica 17
　automobilia 38
　blazer 349
　Butlin's 81
　commemorative *187, 277*
　emergency services 288
　Mabel Lucie Attwell 33
　military 280–1
　politics *240, 241,* 303
　railwayana 327
　rock & pop *248*
　shipping *314*
　Sixties & Seventies *316*
　sport *319, 320,* 365
　World War II 426
badminton 358
bagatelle games 404
bags
　airline sick bags *400*
　carrier bags *400*
　handbags & luggage *200,* 230–1, *238*
Bainbridge *243*
Bajazzo 22
Bakelite
　ashtrays 299, 357
　calendars 300
　cigarette holders 299
　coffee grinders 299
　money boxes *239*

pipe racks 299
telephones 372
Tiemaster 299
tobacco jars 299
vesta cases 299
balloons & airships 18–19, *67*
balls 360
　croquet *319*
　football 365
　golf 366
　rugby 360
　tennis 367
Banania 48, *71*
Bang, Arne 139
bangles *234,* 251
Bank of England 295, 296, 334
banknotes 295–6, 334
Banks, Iain 49
Barbie dolls 182, *316*
bargeware *78,* 88
Barker, Cicely Mary 54, *74*
Barker, Samuel & Son 92
Barker Bros 96
Barlow, Hannah 102
barometers 228, 341
Barovier *197*
Barrie, J.M. 31
barrister's hammers 401
Barrois, Madame 179
baseball *319,* 360
basins 41, 42
baskets
　ceramic 95, 131
　garden & farm collectables 213
　linen 267
　wicker 267
Bassano *78*
Bassett-Lowke *392,* 418, 419
bathrooms 40–2
Battenburg drawn threadwork 375
Baxter, Geoffrey *198,* 220, *315, 316*
beadwork
　handbags *200,* 230
　pot stands *387*
beakers
　ceramic 94, 165, 265
　commemorative 161, 165
　plastic 161, 300
　silver 30
bears 370–1, *385–6*
The Beatles 34, *246,* 329–31
bed covers *387*
bed sheets 32
beer glasses 225
Beetall 267
Beeton, Isabella 56
Bell Telephones 372–3

Bellarmine 58
bells
   glass *194*, 221
   ship's 348
belts 376
Bénédictine *76*
Benson 272, 274
Bentley of London 285
Benton, C.P. *243*
Berg 371
Berg, Elis 218
Bergman, Franz *238*
Bernières, Louis de *72*
Berning, Otto & Co 84
Beswick
   animals *78*, 90
   breweriana 64, *76*
   vases 206
Beveridge, William 304
Biba 378, *390*
Bibles 57
bicycles 43–4, *70*
bidets 40
Biene & Davis 230
billhooks 402
billiards 358
Bimini 83
Bing 417
Bingham, W. 402
bird scarers 213
birdcages 353
Bird's *66*
Birn Bros *74*
birthday cards *398*
biscuit barrels
   Carlton Ware 94
   chintz ware 96
   glass *194*
   T.G. Green 114, 116,
147
   wood 271
biscuit rollers 271
biscuit tins 15, 33, *65*, *69*,
228, *240*, *314*
bisque dolls 179–80, *189*
black basalt 143
black history & memorabilia
45–8, *71*
Blackmore, James 229
Blackmore, R.D. *72*
Blake, T. 356
blankets 374, 375
blazer badges 349
bloomers 383
blue & white ceramics *78*,
91–2
Blue Lake Swimware *389*
blunderbusses 284
Blyton, Enid 54
B.N.D. *189*
BOAC 17
boats, toy *392*, 406
bobbins, lacemaker's *313*
Boda *197*
bog oak 258
Bohemian glass *196*, 226
Bois Durci 258
Bollinger 357
bonbon dishes 112
bonds, scripophily 343–4
Bo'ness *78*, 127
bonnets 379, *388*

Bonzo *78*
book donkeys 354
book-holders *397*
bookends 126
bookmarks 368
books 49–57, *72–4*, 294
   annuals 159–60, *186*
   black memorabilia 46,
47
   children's books 54–6
   cookbooks 56–7
   crime 174, 175
   Mabel Lucie Attwell
31–3, *69*
   politics *241*, 301, 304,
306
   prayer books & Bibles 57
   sport *318*, 358, 361,
364
boot jacks *390*
boot pulls 350
boot scrapers 26
Booths 92, 117
boots 382, 383, *390*
   cycling 359
   fishing 363
   football 365
   mountaineering 359
Boots 59, 171
bottle jacks 269
bottle stoppers 64, *76*
bottles 58–9, *75*
   automobilia 39
   collectables under £5
399
   commemorative *240*
   Guinness 229
   poison bottles 59, *75*,
429
   scent bottles 28, 338
Bougie Du Siècle *67*
Bourjois 171
Bourne 249, 250
Bovey Tracey *78*
Bovril 10
bowling 358
bowls
   blue & white 92
   ceramic *78*, *80*, 94,
96–8, 101, 118–21, 125,
128, 135, 136, 139, 143,
144, 330, 354
   glass *194*, *196*, *197*,
217, 218, 220, 223
   kitchenware 263
   plastic *239*
   wooden 204, 264
boxes 60–1
   Art Nouveau *68*
   ceramic 94, 98, 99
   cigarette boxes 99, *317*,
366
   commemorative ware
161, 162
   jet 257
   kitchenware 270
   papier-mâché 345, 356
   plastic *239*
   sewing boxes *313*, 345
   silver 350
   snuff boxes 60, 356, *397*
   Tunbridge ware *397*, *398*

   wooden 161
boxing *320*
bracelets *234*, 251, 254,
256–8
braces 401
Bradbury & Co 346
Bradbury Cycles 44
branding irons 352
Brannam, C.H. 117
Brannam, Charles *78*
Braque, Georges 49
brass
   Art Nouveau 29, 30
   Arts & Crafts 30
   boxes 162
   buttons 82, 83
   candlesticks 274
   corkscrews 169
   horse brasses 232, 426
   kettles 266
   kitchenware 264, 267,
269
   taps 40, 41
Brasso 13
breadboards *235*, 271
breakfast cups 119
breakfast sets 95
Brent-Dyer, Elinor M. *74*
Brent Leigh 127
Bretby 117, *238*, 263
Breton bonnets 379
Breuer, Otto *198*, 220
breweriana 62–4, *76*
   Guinness 228–9
Brigden, Alison *152*
Briggs, David *146*
Bristol glass *187*
Bristol Longline 206
Britains *392–4*, 410
Britannic Aeroplane 17
British Aluminium Co 341
British American Novelty
Co 21
British Lion *244*, 311
British National Doll Co
181
Britten, Benjamin 49
Brocks *236*
Brontë Yorkshire Liqueurs
62
bronze
   figures 46
   medals 276
   plaques *67*
brooches 23, *233*, *234*,
252–4
   antiquities 23, 24
   Art Nouveau 29
   Arts & Crafts *68*
   Christmas 154, *185*
   collectables under £5
399
   jet 256–8
Brooke Bond 158
Brooklands 38
Brown & Brothers 340
Brownfield & Son 117
Browning, Elizabeth Barrett
49
Brunhoff, Jean de *74*
brushes 171, *188*
Brussels lace 376

Bryan's Magic Machines
22
Buchan, John 49
Buchanan's Black & White
Whisky 62, 63
buckets 265
   child's *391*, 404
   fire 285, 286
   mess buckets 347
   milk 265
buckles 332, 381
Buckley pottery 105
buglets 43
buildings, ceramic 103,
109, 111, 174
Bulle 425
Bulwark Cut Plug Tobacco
16
Buntons 348
bureaux *68*
Burgess & Leigh *240*
Burgoyne *245*
Burleigh Ware *79*, 93
Burmantofts *78*, 93
Burrows Engineering 44
Bursley Ware 132
Bush 323, 324
busts
   Art Deco 28
   ceramic 108–10
   politics *241*, 302, 303,
305
Butler, Frank *146*
Butler & Wilson 255
Butlin's 81
butter boxes 264, 265
butter dishes 95, 96, 265
butter prints 264
Butterton, Mary *146*
button-hooks *77*, 381
buttons *77*, 82–3
Buzzini, Chris 227

C
cabinets 30
cachepots *148*
Cadbury's 16
cafetières 115, 261, 262
Cain, James M. *72*
Caithness *199*, 227
cake decorations 153, 262
cake stands 123
Calcott Bros *70*
calculators 208, 340
calèches *388*
calendars
   ceramic 354
   erotica 202
   Mabel Lucie Attwell 31,
33
   perpetual 300
   rock & pop 331
Caley crackers 154
Caley Double Fruit *66*
calling cards *198*, *398*
cameo boxes 94
cameo glass 338
cameos 254, 257
cameras 84–6, *239*
Camp Coffee *66*
Campanian antiquities 24
Campbell, Alice *146*

can openers 269
Canadian Club Whisky 63
candelabra, glass 221
candle moulds 274
candlesticks *236*, 274
  ceramic 94, 124, 134
  glass 48, *196*, *197*, 219, 222
cane ware 106
canes, walking 422
Cannon, W.F. 339
Capo Nord 220
carafes 64
carbide lamps 275
card games 47
card holders *71*
card markers 351
Cardew, Michael 139
cards
  birthday cards *398*
  cabinet cards 347
  calling cards *190*, *398*
  Christmas cards 153, *185*, 429
  cigarette cards 19, 155–8, 176, *187*, *190*
  greetings cards 348
  playing cards *193*, 209, 228, *314*
  showcards 12, *66*, *70*, 228
  trade cards 155, 158, *318*
  Valentines *398*, 421
  see also postcards
Carlton Ware 19, *79*, 94–5, 109–10, 228
Carnation Milk 12
Carnegie, Hattie *234*
Carnival glass *194*, 220, *240*
carrier bags *400*
Carroll, Lewis 55
cars
  automobilia 38–9
  bumper stickers *240*
  number-plates **39**, 39, *399*
  pedal cars *393*, 411
  plastic 404
  tinplate *391*, 416
  diecast *393*–6, 407–9
cart jacks 401
cart wheels 212
Carter, Stabler & Adams 128
cartes de visite 297, 303
Cartlidge, George 29
cartoons *241*, 304, *400*
Cassandre, A.M. *243*, 310
cast iron see iron
Castiglioni 274
Cathy McGowan Boutique 378
cattle drinkers 212
Cauldon *236*
CDs 332
celluloid
  buttons 83
  dolls *69*
ceramics *78*–80, 87–144, *146*–52

advertising 9
aeronautica 17, 18, 19, *67*
animals *78*, 87, 90, 93, *149*
antiquities 23–4
architectural salvage 25
Art Nouveau 29, *68*
bargeware *78*, 88
Beswick *78*, 90
black memorabilia 46, 47
blue & white *78*, 91–2
bottles 58
Burleigh Ware *79*, 93
Burmantofts *78*, 93
buttons 82, 83
Carlton Ware *79*, 94–5
Charlotte Rhead 132–3
chintz ware **96**, 96, *148*, *150*
Clarice Cliff *80*, 97
commemorative 162–4, 166, *187*, *240*–1, 288, 301–6
Copeland 98
Crown Devon *80*, 99
Crown Ducal 99
cups, saucers & mugs 100
Denby 101, *146*
Doulton 102–4, *146*
earthenware, stoneware & country pottery 105
egg cups 106
fairings 107
Fifties *191*, 206
figures 108, *147*
Goss & crested china 109–12
Gouda 112
jugs 117
kitchenware 262–3
lustre ware 118, 119–20, 143, 162
Mabel Lucie Attwell 31–3, *69*
majolica 119, *148*
Maling 119–20, *148*
Mason's Ironstone 120
Meakin 121–2
Midwinter 123, *148*
Moorcroft 124, *148*
Noritake 125, *149*
Pendelfins 126
plates & dishes 127
politics *240*–1, 301–6
Poole Pottery 128
pot lids & Prattware 129–30, *149*
Quimper 131, *150*
Radford 132, *150*
Rosenthal 133
Royal Copenhagen 133–4, *150*
Royal Winton 134, *150*
Ruskin 134
Shelley 135, *150*–1
Shorter 136
Sixties & Seventies *316*, 354
Staffordshire 137–8, *151*

studio pottery *80*, 139
Susie Cooper *80*, 98, *147*–8
SylvaC 140, *152*
T.G. Green 113–16, *147*–8, 162, 164, 166
Troika 141, *152*
Wade 142
Wedgwood 143
Wemyss 144, *152*
Worcester 144, *152*
  see also bowls; plates etc
Chad Valley
  dolls 178
  games *193*, 209, 210
  teddy bears 371, *386*
  toys *392*
chairs
  Fifties *191*, 205
  garden furniture 214, *316*
  Sixties & Seventies 355
chambersticks 135, 136, *236*, 274
Champagne E. Mercier & Co 357
Champagne glasses 224, 225
chandeliers 273
Chanel 251
chaps 359
character jugs 93, 103, 105, 136, *146*, *185*, *241*, *246*
Charbonnel & Walker 166
chargers 30, *68*, *79*, *80*, 139, 141
chatelaine pins *233*
cheese dishes 96
cheese moulds 265
chemist's rounds 342
cheque books 201
Chéret, Jules *242*
Chermayeff, Serge 322
cheroot holders *70*, 299
Cherry Blossom 9
chess sets 177, 209
Chesterfield cigarettes *185*
chests 230
  military 280
  tool chests *397*, 402
children
  books 54–6
  clothes 376
Chiltern 370, 371
chimney pots 25
Chinese
  fans 203
  jewellery *233*
chintz ware **96**, 96, *148*, *150*
Chippendale glass 222–3
Chocolat Lanvin 10
chocolate boxes 33, 166, *187*
chocolate moulds 268
chokers 258, 260
choppers 263
Christie, Agatha 49
Christmas 153–4, *185*
Christmas cards 153, *185*, 429

chromolithograph scraps *190*, 201
Church's 366
churns 265
cigar cabinets 356
cigar cases *317*
cigar cutters 169, 357
cigarette boxes 99, *317*, 366
cigarette cards 19, 155–8, 176, *187*, *190*
cigarette cases *188*, 356
cigarette holders 299, *317*, 357
cigarette lighters *317*, 357
cigarette-making machines 357
cigarette packets 9
cigarette tins 66
cisterns 40, 42
claret labels 62
Clark, S.C.J. 263
Clarke, Derek *80*
Clark's Night Lights *236*
Clarkson, Derek 139
Clarnico 16, *67*
clasp knives 353
clay pipes 356
Claymore Whisky *76*
Claypits Ewenny 105
Cliff, Clarice *80*, 97, 136
Clinch & Co 64
clocks 425
  Art Deco 28
  Art Nouveau 30
  Guinness 229
  militaria *237*
  owls 293, 294
  ship's 348
  Sixties & Seventies 355
  toy 405
clockwork toys *391*, *394*, 403, 404
clog bases 382
clogs, ceramic 131
clothes 376–8, *388*–9
collectables of the future *400*
  film & TV 207, 208
  rock & pop *246*, *248*, 335, 336
  sport *320*
  underwear 383, *399*
clubs, golf 366
coal scuttles 27, 30, 280
Coalbrookdale 27, 214
Coalport 127
coat hangers 379
coats 377
Coca-Cola 11, 39
cocktail shakers *198*
cocktail sticks 48
Cocteau, Jean 49
Codd bottles *75*, *399*
coffee cups *79*, *80*, 97, 123, *147*, *148*
coffee grinders *235*, 270, 299
coffee pots 118, 123, 143, *150*, 352, 354
coffee sets 115, 206
colanders 262, 300

Colark Ship Model Builders 288
collars, lace 376
collectables of the future 400
collectables under £5 399
Colledge, Albert 101
Colledge, Glyn 101, 146
Collins, Wm 404
Collinsons 413
Colman's Mustard 15
Colonial 322
Columbia 324, 325
Combex 48
combs 161
comics 159–60, 186
commemorative ware 161–6, 187
 ceramics 102, 240–1, 288, 301–6
 exhibitions 161
 horse brasses 232, 426
 jewellery 252
 medals 276–7
 military 162–3
 royalty 163–6
compacts 172–3, 187, 188, 315
compasses 341
comports 125, 164
compotes 216, 222
Compton Pottery 108
computer games 396, 405
computers 341
condiment sets 125, 263, 306, 351
Conran, Jasper 400
Conran, Terence 123
consommé dishes 98
Continental
 compacts 172
 figures 108
 tools 401
Conway Stewart 428
cookbooks 56–7
cool boxes 200
Cooper, Susie 80, 98, 147
Cooperative Wholesale Society (C.W.S.) 10, 65, 322
Copeland 98, 162, 164, 268
Copeland & Garrett 106
Copeland Spode 92
copper
 Art Nouveau 29, 68
 Arts & Crafts 30, 68
 buttons 82
 kettles 235, 266
 kitchenware 261, 268, 269
coral jewellery 233
corbels 25
Corgi Toys 396, 408, 409
cork presses 62
corkscrews 167–9
Cornish Ware 113–16, 148
Coro 254
Coronation Ale 59
Coronet cameras 84
Coronet Ware 110

Correia 227
corsets 383
cosmetics & hairdressing 170–3, 188
 compacts 172–3, 187, 188, 315
 shaving 173
Cosmos 321
costume see clothes
Coty 171
country pottery 105
Courage Brewery 259
Courrèges 389
Courtier 381
Coventry Eagle Bicycles 70
Cox, F.J. 339
Coxeter 342
crackers, Christmas 154, 185
Cradock 74
cranberry glass 194, 221
Crapper, Thomas & Co 42
Crawford's Biscuits 11
cream cans 264
cream jugs 114, 133, 197, 221, 351
creamware 118, 187
creels 364
Crescent 393
Cressoline 342
crested china 109–12
crime 174–5
croquet 319, 358, 360
Crown 206, 423
Crown Derby 99
Crown Devon 80, 99
Crown Ducal 99, 132–3, 165
crucifixes 257
cruet sets 99, 114, 115, 239, 366
crumb pans 353
cufflinks 233, 259
Cunard 314
Cunard White Star 314
cups & saucers 100
 Clarice Cliff 97
 coffee cups 79, 80, 97, 123, 147, 148
 Maling 119
 Meakin 121, 122, 399
 Midwinter 123
 Moorcroft 124
 moustache cups 173
 plastic 330
 Quimper 131
 Shelley 151
 studio pottery 139
 T.G. Green 115
curtains 375, 387
Curtis, Honor 141
Cusden, Leonard 242
cushions 387
custard cups 143
Cuticura 171
cycling 359
Cyclops 44
Czechoslovakian
 firefighting 287
 glass 197
 jewellery 233

D
daguerreotypes 285
dairying 264–5
Daiya 414
Dali, Salvador 388
Damm, Thomas 405
Danish jewellery 234
Dansette 325
Dansk 204
Dartington Glass 425
darts boards 360
Davenport 106
Davesn, Pierre 273
Davidson, George 196, 222–3
Davis, J. 46
Davis, Lindsey 50
Davy, Arthur 14
de Morgan, William 384
Dean's 371
Deans Rag Book Co 71
decanters 194, 197, 221, 223
Dedham Pottery 92
deed boxes 61
Delft tiles 384
Delta 382
Denby 101, 146, 249, 250
Dennis's Pig Powders 65
DEP 179, 180
Derbyshire 100
desk lamps 236, 273, 274
dessert dishes 120
Detmold, Edward 54
Deva Dassy 172
Devlin, Stuart 351
Dexter, Colin 50
diamanté jewellery 253–5, 260
Diana Cargo 100
Diase 47
dice 209
dice shakers 420
Dickens, Charles 50, 72
Dicker's Dorset Sausages 12
diecast vehicles 393–6, 407–9
Dinky Toys 393–5, 407–8
dinner services 101, 123
Dior, Christian 254, 255, 260, 377, 389
dioramas 347
discuses 360
dishes
 ceramic 79, 96, 110–12, 120, 125, 127, 131–3, 135, 148, 191
 glass 216, 217
 kitchenware 262
 silver 350
Disney, Walt 55, 77, 142
Distler 391
Dixon, James & Sons 30
Doctor Who 176–7, 193, 395, 414
document spikes 428
dogs, ceramic 87, 90, 99, 102, 103
Dolby, I.E.A. 50
Dolcis 382
dolls 178–84, 189

bisque 179–80, 189
 black memorabilia 46, 48, 71
 dolls' houses & dolls' house furniture 183–4, 189
 Father Christmas 153
 Mabel Lucie Attwell 69
 pincushion 313
 plastic 181–3, 189
 rock & pop 330
 Sixties & Seventies 316
dolly tubs 25
Don Pottery 78
Donyatt 105
doors 25
doorstops 26, 99
Doulton
 buildings 103
 fairy lights 236
 figures 104
 foot warmers 250
 jugs 102, 103, 164
 lavatory seats 41
 pilgrim flasks 146
 teapots 102
 vases 102, 103
 see also Royal Doulton
Dover Toys 403
Doyle, Sir Arthur Conan 50, 72
Dragsted, Aage 219
drawn threadwork 375
Dresser, Dr Christopher 78
dresses 376–8, 388, 389
dressing table sets 149, 171
DRGM 404
drill gauges 402
drills 402
drinking glasses 224–5
drinks mats 305
drinks trolleys 316
DRP 403
Dubarry 338
dumps 199, 226–7
Duncan Fire Wheels 396
Duncan Mirylees 184
Dunhill-Namiki 429
Dunlop 367
Dunlop, Sybil 254
Dunville's Whisky 62
Durex 11
Dutch lighting 275

E
Eagle 44, 262
ear trumpets 342
earrings 234, 255, 256, 258
earthenware 105
 bowls 136
 buttons 83
 plates 153
Eastman Kodak 84
Edbar International Corp 239
edged weapons 282
Edgington, John 232
Edison Bell 12
egg boxes 10, 262
egg cups 92, 93, 106,

113, 135
egg racks 271
egg separators 115, 263
egg timers *314*
Egyptian antiquities 23
EKCO 11, *245*, 322
Elkasley, Tom 309
Elkington & Co 352
Ellgreave Pottery 105
Elliot 340
Elliott Bros *237*
Elmas *66*
Elme 219
emergency services
  firefighting 285–8
  police 288
EMI *245*
Emor *245*
Empire Apparatus 287
Empire Ware 117
enamel
  Art Nouveau 29
  buttons *77*
  Fifties *191*, 204
  kitchenware *235*, 266
  signs 13–14, 43, *65, 66,*
228, 328
encaustic tiles 384
English Porcelain Classics
414
epaulettes 258
ephemera, 201, *190*
Ericsson 372
erotica 202
Etronic 323
Etruscan antiquities 23
Evans 172
evening dresses 377, *389*
Ever Ready 44
Ever-Sharp 428
Excelsior 41
exhibitions,
commemorative ware 161
Exley 418
Expo 84

F

Facente, Bebe 220
faïence
  baskets 131
  jardinières *78*
  pilgrim flasks *146*
  stick stands 93
  vases 93, 133, *150*
fairings 107
fairylights *236*, 275
fans *190*, 203
  advertising 10, *76, 317*
  electric 341
Farlow Cairnton 363
farm collectables *see*
garden & farm collectables
Farnell 371, *386*
Farrow & Jackson 167
Faulks, Sebastian 50
fencing 360
Fenton *194*
Feraud, Louis *389*
Ferd Mülhens 171
Ferragamo, Salvatore 383
Ferrario, Natale 383
Ferriera, Anna Castelli *316*

Ferro & Lazzarini 227
Fielding *68*
Fifties *191*, 204–6
  furniture *191*, 205
  pottery & porcelain *191,*
206
figures
  advertising 62, 63, *65,*
71, 76
  breweriana 63, 64
  bronze 46
  ceramic *70, 78,* 108,
147
  Christmas 154
  commemorative 164
  fairings 107
  glass 196, 217, 219
  Goldscheider *147*
  Hummel *148*
  model soldiers & figures
393, 394, 410
  Osbornes 292
  Pendelfins 126
  politics 302
  Royal Copenhagen
133–4
  Royal Doulton 103–4
  Royal Worcester *152*
  sport *318*
  Staffordshire 137–8,
151, 174, 302, 361
  wood *397*
  Worcester 144
  see also animal figures
film & TV *192,* 207–8
  posters *244, 248,*
310–11, 331
finials 214
fire dogs 26
fire surrounds 27
firearms *237,* 284
Firebird 405
firefighting 285–8
first aid cases 426
fish dishes 131
fish slices 269
Five Cents 10
flags 359
flasks
  ceramic 58, *75*
  pilgrim flasks *146*
  Reform flasks 302
  spirit flasks 163
Fleming, Ian 50–1, *72*
Flos 274
flour shakers 114
flower blocks 222
flower holders 99
flower pots 105
flower presses 380
fly-traps 261
foot warmers 249–50
Foreign 106
forks 24, 271, 352
Fornasetti, Piero *191,* 354
Forrester, Thomas & Son
117
fountain pens *398,* 428,
429
foxhunting 358
Fraipont, G. *242*
frames, photograph 298

Francis, Kevin 108, *241*
Fraser, Eric 10
Fray, J. 277
French
  aeronautica *67*
  bicycles *70*
  toys 403
French jet 256–8
French Line 348
fruit bowls 121
Fry's 14, 15, *65*
Fullers Earth 16
furniture
  Art Deco 28
  Art Nouveau 30
  Arts & Crafts 30, *68*
  dolls' house 183–4
  Fifties *191,* 205
  garden 214
  Sixties & Seventies *316*
Fürstenberg 87
Furstenberg, Diane von
378
future collectables *400*
Fyffes 10

G

gaffs, fishing 364
galette turners 270
Gallaher Cigarettes 12,
155, 157
Gamages 406
games 47, *193,* 209–11
  jigsaws 211, *393, 395*
Games, Abram *243*
Gamy *67*
garden & farm collectables
212–15
  furniture 214
  sculpture & ornaments
214–15
  traps 215
gas lamps 272
Gas Light & Coke Co 10
Gaspari, Lucciano 219
Gaudy Welsh 100
gauges 402
Gaymer's Cyder 64
GEAG *396*
GEC 323
Gecophone 321
German
  advertising 10
  bicycles *70*
  breweriana *76*
  clocks 294
  emergency services 286,
288
  jewellery 259
  tools 401
  toys 403
Ghyczy, Peter *316*
Gibson, H.P. & Sons 210
Gibson's 357
Gillette, Mrs F.L. 57
gin glasses 224
ginger beer bottles 59, *75*
ginger jars 120
Girard, Alexander 355
Gitanes *76*
glass *194–9,* 216–27
  antiquities 24

Art Deco, *194*
Art Nouveau 29, *194,*
216
  bottles 58–9, *75, 399,*
429
  Butlin's 81
  buttons 82, 83
  candlesticks 48
  Carnival glass *194,* 220,
240
  commemorative ware
161, *187*
  cranberry glass *194,* 221
  Davidson & Chippendale
glass *196,* 222–3
  decanters *194, 197,*
221, 223
  drinking glasses 224–5
  dumps & paperweights
199, 226–7
  figures 196
  inkwells 427
  jugs 207
  nightlights 275
  paperweights 294
  scent bottles 338
  Sixties & Seventies *315,*
316
  tumblers 202
  see also bowls; vases *etc*
Glasse, Hannah 57
globes 341
glove boxes 61
gnomes 214–15, 228, *241*
goblets *196*
Goebels 108
gold
  assay marks *400*
  jewellery 29, 252, 254,
258–60
Goldscheider *68,* 108, *147*
Goliath 424
Gollies 48, *71*
Goodall Lamb & Heighway
30
Goodall's 209
Goodell-Pratt 402
Goodwin & Co 284
Goss 109–12
Goss, W.H. 164
Gottschalk, Moritz 184
Gouda Zuid-Holland 112
Gould, Elizabeth 293
Gould, John 293, 294
Goya Films 310
GPO 373
Grace, W.G. 361
Grafton 112, *147*
Grafton, Sue 51
Grahame, Kenneth 55
grain measures 271
gramophone needle tins
47, *67*
gramophone needles 12
gramophones *245,* 324–5
  children's *391*
graters *235,* 270
grates 27
Gray-Stan 217
Gray's Pottery *147*
Gredington, Arthur 90
Green, James 127

Green, T.G. 113–16, **114**, 147–8, 162, 164, 166, 263
Greene, Graham 51, 72
Greener, Henry 225
greetings cards 71, 348
Greig 242
Grundig 354
Guerlain 170
Guillet, Henri 369
Guinness 228–9
guitars 246
Gurley, W. & L.E. 348

H

Hachiya, Michihiko 51
Hagler, Stanley 234
Hai Karate 173
hairdressing 170, 188
Haley 288
Hallam, Arthur 206
Hallenberg, Gotlieb Geibler 169
hallmarks 400
Hall's Wine 76
Hamadan cushions 387
Hamilton bottles 75
hammers, barrister's 401
hampers 231
Hancock & Sons 29, 148
handbags & luggage 200, 230–1, 238
handkerchiefs 69, 202, 381
Handy 249
Handysides 58
Hansen, Fritz 205
Hardy 364
Hargreaves, Roger 250
Harmony 200
Harris Bacon 12
Harrod's 230
Harvey Guzzini 355
Harvino 154
Haskell, Miriam 234, 255, 258
Hasselblad 84
hat boxes 230
hat pins 255
hat stands 379
hats 285, 360, 379–80, 388, 389
heaters 352
Heathkit 324
heating 26–7
Hebert Leupin 317
Heeley, James & Sons 167, 168
helmet plates 280
helmets 280, 281, 286–8
Helvetic 385
Hemingway, Ernest 51
Hendrix, Jimi 246, 334
Henschel, William 150
Henshall, Rev Samuel 167
Herts Plastic Moulders 414
Heubach Koppelsdorf 180
Heuer 320, 424
Hey, G. 112
Heyde 353
Hickson, Joan 55
Higham, J. 43
Hill, Janet McKenzie 57

Hill, Reg 192
Hills 154
Him, Lewitt 309
Hite, Shere 72
HMV 245, 324, 325
Hoelund, Eric 197
Hollinshead & Kirkham 117
Holmegaard 139, 198, 218–20, 225
Homepride 263
Honiton lace 379
hoof picks 167
Hooper Automatic Co 21
horn
    buttons 82
    jewellery 256
    snuff mulls 356
Hornby 391–2, 406, 417–19
Hornby, Nick 51
Horner, Charles 68, 255
Hornsea 355
hors d'oeuvres dishes 93
horse brasses 232, 426
horses, rocking 393, 412–13
hot water bottles 249–50
housework 267
Hovay Betoia 205
Hovells 185
Hudson's Soap 9, 13
Hugnet, Georges 52
Humber 43
Hummel 108, 148, 154
Huntley & Palmer 15, 33, 66, 127, 228
hurling sticks 360
hydrometers 340

I

ice buckets 204, 219
ice-cream moulds 268
Iceberg Cigarettes 9
ICI 12
Ideal Standard 27
Iittala Glass 223
IJOB 357
IM Pointmaster 325
Imperial Glass Co 194
inclinometers 340
Ingram's 9
ink erasers 427
inkstands 194
inkwells 44, 119, 294, 427
iron
    architectural salvage 26
    breweriana 62
    garden furniture 214
    heating 26–7
    kettles 266
    money boxes 289
irons 267
ironstone 120
Ironstone Pottery 316, 354
Isle of Wight Pottery 139
Isokon **354**, 354
ITC ENT 423
ivory
    buttons 77, 83
    fans 203

J

J. & M. Models 419
Jack-in-the-Pulpit vases 194, 216
jackets 378, 389
Jacobs, Carl 205
Jacobsen, Arne 205
Jacques & Co 360
Jaeger le Coultre 85
jam pots 33, 68, 97
Jaques, L. & Son 209
jardinières
    Clarice Cliff 97
    copper 29
    Doulton 102
    faïence 78
    Wemyss 144
jars 105, 120
    storage jars 116, 148, 152, 204, 206, 235, 263
jasper ware 106
jelly moulds 268
Jennens & Bettridge 345
Jennings 22
Jensen, Georg 253
Jerome, Jerome K. 52
jet jewellery 256–8
jewellery 233–4, 251–60
    Art Nouveau 29, 68
    Arts & Crafts 30, 68
    bracelets 234, 251, 254, 256–8
    brooches 29, 68, 233, 234, 252–4, 256–8, 399
    cameos 254, 257
    earrings 234, 255, 256, 258
    hat pins 255
    jet 256–8
    jewellery sets 258
    men's accessories 233, 259
    necklaces 30, 233, 234, 239, 257, 260
    pendants 68, 233, 258, 260
    pins 154, 185
    rings 315
jigsaw puzzles 81, 211, 393, 395
Joachim 251
Jobling 217
Jocelyn, Victor 389
Johnnie Walker 62
Jones, A.E. 274
Jones, George 119
Joseff of Hollywood 233
jotters 32
Jourdan, Charles 390
Jover & Son 237
jugs
    breweriana 62–4, 76
    caricature jugs 304
    ceramic 78–80, 92–5, 98, 102, 103, 105, 109, 113–15, 117–22, 131–3, 147, 150, 151, 238
    character jugs 103, 105, 136, 146, 185, 241, 246
    commemorative 162–4, 166, 302, 304
    glass 194, 197, 218, 221

musical 80, 99
silver 351
stoneware 301
Toby jugs 78, 154, 306
juice sets 239
jukeboxes 248, 337
Jumeau 189

K

Kandya 205
Katzhütte 28
KB 323
Kemp, F. 406
kendo masks 318
Kendrick 235
Kent, James 96, 148
Kent's 262
Kestner 179
kettles 68, 235, 266
Kewpie dolls 189
key rings 39, 48
Kigu 173
King Sol 250
Kinnerton's 33
Kirchner, Raphael 307
Kirker Greer & Co 76
kitchenware 235, 261–71
    ceramics 262–3
    choppers 263
    dairying 264–5
    enamel bins & tins 235, 266
    kettles 235, 266
    laundry & housework 267
    moulds 235, 268
    utensils 235, 269–70
    wood 235, 270–1
Kitchiner, William 57
Kitson, A. 305
Kiwi Boot Polish 9
KLG Plugs 425
knife-grinders 402
knitting sheaths 420
knives
    antiquities 24
    clasp knives 353
    kitchenware 271
    paper knives 9, 398
    penknives 169, 364
    pocket knives 353
Koch, Karl 309
Kodak 84–5
Kolster Brander 245
Koppel, Henning 253
Kosta 218
Kramer 251
Krenchel, Herbert 191
Kudelski 325
Kuhn, Tom 405

L

La Rue, Thomas de 47
lace
    caps 379
    collars 376
    fans 203
lace-maker's bobbins 313
lace-maker's lamps 345
lacrosse 359
ladles 269

Lagerbielke, Erika *198*
Laird, G. *68*
Lalique 217, 226
Lambert & Butler 155
lamps *see* lighting
Lancashire Insurance
Company 9
Lane, Kenneth Jay *234*
Lanes, Selma G. *74*
lanterns 272, 275, 286
Latvian firefighting 287
laundry & housework 267
lavatory bowls 40–2
Lawleys 250
Lawson, William 63
Leach, Bernard 139, *148*
Leach, Michael 139
lead figures 154
League of American
Wheelmen 43
Lear, Edward 52, 294
Lefèvre-Utile *65*
Legras 29
Lehmann 406
Leica 85
Leigh, Mabel 136
Leitz, Ernst 85
lemon squeezers 270
Lenci 178
lesson boards 404
letter openers 368
Lever's Toilet Soaps 9
Lewis, Ann 141
Liberty & Co *77, 78*
Lichtenstein, Roy 310
Liebig 158
Lietl 340
lighters *188*, 229, *317*,
357
lighting *197, 236*, 272–5,
360
    Art Deco 28
    Art Nouveau 29
    Christmas tree *185*
    lace-maker's lamps 345
    lanterns 272, 275, 286
    nightlights & fairylights
    236, 238, 275
    oil lamps 272, 293
    railwayana 326, 327
    shipping 347
    Sixties & Seventies 355
    see also candlesticks
Limoges *189*
linen baskets 267
linen tablecloths 374–5
Lines Brothers 412, 413
Lionel 405
Lion's Bros *393*
liqueur glasses 224, 225
lithographs *67*, 293
Little Fivewin 21
Liverpool 384
Lloyd Loom 267
lockets 256
Loftus 339
London Airport 17
London Anti-Slavery
Convention 46
Long John Whisky *76*
longcase clocks 425
Longchamps *148*

Longines 424
Longpark 166
Longton 153
lorgnettes 369
Lorraine 273
loudspeakers 354
love tokens 421
loving cups *187*, 303
Lucas 275
luggage 230–1
Lumar 404
lustre ware 118, 119–20,
143, *148*, 162
lustres, glass 221
Lutken, Per *198*, 218–20,
219
Lyons' Tea *71*
Lyons Toffees *66*

M
Macallan 64
McDonald's *405*
Mace, John *243*
maces 280
McVitie & Price 15
magazines 291, *314, 399*
    erotica 202
    Fifties *191*
    film & TV *192*, 207
    garden & farm
    collectables 213
magic lanterns 84, 404
magnets *399*
Maiori 220
Maison Lyons 16
majolica 119, *148*, 384
Maling 118, 119–20, *148*
mangles 267
manicure sets 170
mannequins 379
manometers 342
mantel clocks 425
manuscripts, black history
& memorabilia 45
Mappin & Webb 171, 351
marbles *193*, 209
marcasite jewellery 252
Marcella *65*
Mardi Gras 369
Margrave Brothers *76*
Marietta *386*
Marine Models 406
Märklin 419
marmalade pots *148*
Marples 401
Marseille, Armand 179,
180
Marston, Thompson &
Evershed 12
Marusan 416
Maryland Stella *317*
Masonic aprons 376
Mason's Ironstone 120
Massier, Delphine 119
Massier, Jerome 87
Masuda 414
Matador 262
Matania, Fortunino *243*
match books 202, *237*
Matchbox toys *394, 395*,
409
matchholders 107

matchstrikers 9, 107, *317*
Mattel 178, 182–3
Mauchline ware 61, 298,
345, *397*, 420
Maws 249
Max, Peter *244*
Max Jentsch & Meerz 21
May, J. & J. *187*
Maydew *188*
Mayer, Mitchell 255, 260
Mayer, T.J. & J. 129
Mayhew, Henry 52
Mazda *236*
Mdina 219
Meakin 121–2, *240, 399*
Meanie Toys 306
Measham Ware *78*
measures 271, 353
measuring jugs 115
meat dishes *78*, 92
Mecca Cigarettes *319*
Meccano *392*, 406, 418
Mechanical Trading Co 20
medals 276–8
    bicycle *70*
    black memorabilia 46
    commemorative 276–7
    firefighting 287
    military 278
    politics 301, 303
    sport *318*, 429
medical instruments 342
medicine spoons 169
meerschaum pipes *317*
men's accessories *233*,
259
menu holders 351
menus 165
Merrythought 48, 370,
386
Messel, Oliver 381
metalware 352–3
    Art Nouveau 29, 30
    Arts & Crafts 30, *68*
Mettoy 416
micrometers 339
Micromodels 419
microscopes 340
Midas of Miami 231
Midland Bank 289
Midwinter 123, *148*
militaria & emergency
services *237*, 280–8
    badges, plates &
    uniforms 280–1
    commemorative ware
    162–3
    edged weapons 282
    firearms *237*, 284
    firefighting 285–8
    medals 278
    police 288
milk churns 265
milk jugs 92, 93, 117,
132, *150*
Milkmaid Condensed Milk
14
Miller, Herman 205
Mills, Arthur G. *243*
Milne, A.A. 52, 56
Milton Bradley Co *193*
Mini-Match 22

Minic *394*, **416**, 416
Minolta 85
Minton
    chargers *68*
    egg cups 106
    figures 302
    jugs 117
    majolica 119
    tiles 384
    trios 100
Minton, John *243*
mirrors
    advertising 66, *76*, 81,
    228
    Arts & Crafts 30
    hand mirrors *188*, 335
Mirsch Company 310
Missoni *389*
Mr Therm 10
Mitchell, John 184
Mobo 44
Mocha ware *147*, 166
models
    aeronautica 17, 19
    buildings 103, 109, 111,
    174
    film & TV *192*, 208
    Goss & crested china
    109–12
    shipping 347–9
    wooden *397*
    see also animal figures;
    figures
Modern Arms Company
364
Modern Toys *394*
Monart *196*, 217
money, paper 295–6, 334
money boxes *71*, 88, *237*,
239, 289
Montjoye 29
Moorcroft 124, *148*
Moore & Co 118
Morin, H. 340
Morris, Rev F.O. 52
Morris, Tony 128
Morris, William 52
Morrison Ingham & Co 41
Mosanic *149*
Moser 223
Mougin Frères 28
moulds, kitchenware *235*,
268
mountaineering 359
mouse mats 306
moustache cups 173
muff warmers 249
muffin dishes 96
mugs
    black memorabilia 46
    ceramic 32, 91, 97, 100,
    113, 114, *146*, 206, 354
    commemorative ware
    163–6, *187*
    glass 81
    plastic 330
    politics *240*, 305
Muir, Jean 378
Murano glass
    bowls 217
    candlesticks 48
    figures 219

paperweights 227
vases 197, 198, 218
Muratti, B., Sons & Co 15
Murphy 322, 323
Murray, Keith 143
music
musical boxes 391, 394
musical jugs 80, 99
rock & pop 246–8,
329–37
sheet music 348, 426
Mycenaean antiquities 23

N

Nabloes 112
Nadeau, J.A. 13
Nairn 316
nameplates, railwayana
326–8
Nanking Cargo 149
napkin rings 348, 420
National 325
necklaces 30, 233, 234,
239, 257, 260
needle holders 313, 345,
368
needlework 374, 387
Negri 47
Negronoir 71
Nestor Fausta Luxe 66
Newcastle 118
newspaper racks 191
newspapers 290–1
commemorative 164–6
crime 174
politics 304–5
World War II 426
see also magazines
nightlights 236, 238, 275
Nistri, Enzo 310
Nixey, W.C. 267
Noah's Arks 391
Noilly Prat 64
Noke, Charles 103
Nolon 250
Norene 255
Noritake 125, 149
Northwood Glass Co 220
number plates 39, 39, 399
nursery ware 31–2, 127,
151
Nusser, E. & Co 367
nutcrackers 420
nutmeg graters 270
Nuutajarvi, Oiva Toikka
218
Nuutajarvi Notsjo 217
Nyman, Gunnel 217

O

O'Brian, Patrick 52
Ocean Cadre 245
Oertle, Hans 242
Ogden's 19
oil flasks 223
oil lamps 272, 293
Oiles, Edvin 219
Old Bill 127
Old Fulham Pottery 250
Old Grand Special Scotch
Whisky 63

Old Hall 33
Old Taylor Bourbon
Whiskey 63
Omega 424
O'Neill, Rose 180
Onions, Judith 115
Onoto 428
opaline glass 194
Orange Maid 14
Orrefors 198, 218
Osbornes 292
Ovaltine 9, 12
owls 238, 293–4
Oxo 14, 166
oyster-servers 119

P

packaging see advertising
& packaging
Packard 38
Paillard 85
paisley shawls 380
Palitoy 182
Palmqvist, Sven 218
Panton, Verner 191
paper, watermarks 161
paper knives 9, 398
paper money 295–6, 334
paperweights
ceramic 87
glass 199, 226–7, 294
papier mâché
boxes 345, 356
busts 305
figures 65
models 404
spectacle cases 368
paraffin cookers 262
paraffin stoves 27
Paragon 206
Parian
busts 110, 302, 303
jugs 117
Park, W.S. & Son 170
Parker 398, 428
Parker Brothers 193
Pascal 16
paste jars 130
pastille burners 137
pastry cutters 261
patchwork quilts 374
Patou, Jean 338
pattens 381
Paysandu Ox Tongues 66
pearl jewellery 234
Pearline 275
pearlware 18, 91
Pears, Charles 309
Pears, Iain 52
Pear's Soap 102, 173
Pearson's 149
pedal cars 393, 411
Pedigree 182
Peek Frean 33
Pegrams 65
Pelham 312, 429
Pemberton, Samuel 427
pen stands 239
pen wipes 398
pencil sharpeners 398
pencils 368, 398, 427, 428
pendants 68, 233, 258, 260

Pen Delfins 126
penknives 169, 364
penny licks 216
pens 368, 398, 427, 428,
429
pepper pots 115, 293,
350, 351
Pepsodent 66
Pernod 64
Perrier Water 10
Perry & Co 427
pestles 270
Peter Pan 324
Peters, Ellis 52
petrol pumps 38
Petrolux 27
pewter inkwells 44
Peynet, Raymond 133
Peyo 405
Philadelphia Chewing Gum
Corporation 158
Philco 322
Philips 245, 321, 323
Phillips, Godfrey 156
Philips globes 341
phonograph cylinders 245
photograph frames 29,
298
photography 297–8
albums 297–8
autographs 34–7
black memorabilia 46,
48
cameras 84–6
commemorative 187
firefighting 285, 286
politics 241, 305
railwayana 326
rock & pop 329, 332,
334, 336, 337
sport 320, 359, 361,
363, 366
Physical Culture 382
Picasso, Paloma 381
pickle dishes 91
picnic hampers 231
picnic sets 355
Pigmiphone 391
Pigot & Co 53
pilgrim flasks 146
Pilkington's Royal
Lancastrian 118
Pillsbury Dough Boy 11
Pilod, Jean 309
Pimlott, Ben 241
pin dishes 131, 164
pincushions 313, 345, 351
pipe racks 299
pipe tampers 356
pipes 317, 356, 361
pistols 237, 284
Pittsburgh Electrical
Specialities Co 19
planes 401, **402**, 402
plant stands 30
planters 136
plaques
aeronautica 67
brass 25
breweriana 64
ceramic 118, 125, 126,
133, 141, 355

commemorative 163
Osbornes 292
politics 240
Plastacrush 236, 274
plastic 239, 299–300
buttons 77, 83
dolls 181–3, 189
plates
aeronautica 18, 19, 67
blue & white 91, 92
ceramic 78, 80, 97, 101,
113, 114, 119–24, 127,
128, 131, 134, 143, 144,
148, 150, 152, 153, 294,
316
commemorative ware
162, 163, 166, 187,
240–1, 301, 303, 305, 306
glass 218, 220
Mabel Lucie Attwell 31,
32
platters, ceramic 91, 92
Player, John & Sons 156–8
playing cards 46, 193,
209, 228, 314
Pleydell-Bouverie, Katherine
139
Plichta 144
plique-a-jour enamel 29
poison bottles 59, 75, 429
Polaroid 85, 369
police 288
politics 240–1, 301–6
Polyflex 181
pond yachts 406
Poole Pottery 19, 67, 128,
294
pop music 246–8, 329–37
porcelain
animals 87
buttons 77
commemorative ware
165
Rosenthal 133
port glasses 224
Portmeirion 354
Poschmeyer 68
postal covers, first day 349
postcards 307–8, 314
aeronautica 18, 19
bicycles 44
black memorabilia 47,
48
commemorative 161
Mabel Lucie Attwell 33
militaria 237
posters 242–4, 309–11
bicycles 70
erotica 202
film posters 192, 244,
248, 310–11, 331
militaria 237
politics 241, 305, 306
railwayana 326, 328
rock & pop 248, 331,
334, 337
shipping 349
Sixties & Seventies 315
'wanted' posters 174,
175
posy bowls 140
posy vases 38, 221

pot lids 129–30, *149*, 161, 162
pot stands 26, 384, *387*
Potter & Moore 338
pottery *see* ceramics
Poulsen, Louis & Co *236*
powder bowls 221
powder compacts *187, 315*
powder horns 284
Powell, Barnaby *197*
Powell, James & Sons *197, 198*, 220, 225, *315, 316*
Power, E.J. 322
Powolny, Michael 216
Practo *66*
prams 403
Pratchett, Terry 53
Pratt, F. & R. 129, 130
Prattware 129–30, 137, *149*
prayer books 57
preserve pots 144, *152*, 222
Presley, Elvis *248*, 335–6
Prestige *235*
Preston, Ed. 402
Primo 408
prints
  aeronautica *67*
  chromolithograph scraps *190*, 201
  owls 293
  sport *318*
  Tretchikoff prints 311
programmes
  commemorative 164–6, *187*
  rock & pop 330, 331
  sport *318*–20, 365
  theatre *71*, *190*, 202
propelling pencils 368
propellors 348
Protector Lamp & Lighting Co 275
Pucci *200*, 231, *389*
pudding basins 154, 262
puddings, Christmas 154, *185*
puppets 294, 312, 429
Puritan Soles 11
purses *200*, 230
Pye *245*, 322
Pyrita 263

Q
Quadrant 44
Quant, Mary *315*, 383, *390*
quilts 374, 375, *387*
Quimper 131, *150*, 384
Quine, R.H. 59
Quistgaard, Jens *191*, 204

R
Race, Ernest 354
rackets
  badminton 358
  tennis 367
Rackham, Arthur 54
Radford 132, *150*

radiators 27
Radio Acoustics Products 323
radios *245*, 321–4
railwayana 326–8
Rainbow Arts *396*
Raisor Star 173
Raleigh *70*
Rambler 323
ranges, kitchen 262
Rank Organisation *244*, 310
Rankin, Ian 53
Rapitan 11
rattles, football 365
Ravenscroft of London 282
Ravilious, Eric 143, *187*
Rawlings, Marjorie Kinnan 57
razors 173, 228
Read, Herbert 53
Read, Piers Paul 175
record breakers 429
records
  commemorative 161
  rock & pop *246, 248*, 330, 332, 334–7
reels, fishing *319*, 362–4
Reform flasks 302
Reichenbach, Carl George von *68*
Remington *66*
reticules *68*
RFC 17
Rhead, Charlotte 132–3, 165
Rhodian Cigarettes *317*
Rhum Georgetta 48
ribbon holders 420
Ricard Anisette 64
Richards, Frank 56
Ridgway 354
Riemsdyke, A. & J. 417
rings *315*
Roberts, Michael & Co *237*
Roberts radios 324
Robertson's 47, *71*
robots, toy 411
rock & pop *246*–8, 329–37
Rock-Ola 337
rocking horses *393*, 412–13
Rodgers, Gladys 118
Rodgers, Joseph & Sons 353
Rogers Pottery 105
Rolex 424
rollers, garden 212
rolling pins *187*, 270–1
Rolls-Caydon 321
Rolls-Royce 38
Roman antiquities 24
Rookwood *150*
rope gauges 402
Rosebud 181
Rosenthal 133
Ross Valve Mfg. Co 287
rounders bats 359
Roussel, Leo 17
Rowling, J.K. *74*

Rowntree's 14, 15, 165, *185*, *187*
Rowson, Martin *241*, *400*
Roy, E. 338
Royal Barum Ware 117
Royal Brierley 218
Royal Copenhagen 133–4, *150*
Royal Crown Derby 87, 306
Royal Doulton 102–4, 165
  animals 102, 103, *238*
  breweriana 62, 64
  figures 103, 104, *241*
  jardinières 102
  jugs 19, 102, 103
  lavatories 42
  mugs 165
  plates 18
  soap dishes 102
  steins *70*
  vases 102, 103
  see also Doulton
Royal Dux 108
Royal Winton 96, 134, *150*
Royal Worcester 144, *152*, 166
royalty, commemorative ware 163–6
Royle's 9
Ruberoid *66*
rugby 360
rummers 225
Ruskin Pottery 83, 118, 134
Russell, R.D. 322
Russell Hobbs 143
Ruston Power 14
Rye Pottery 206, *238*

S
Saarinen, Eero 205
Sabino 226
Sadler 67
St Ives Pottery 354
St Louis *199*, 227
salad servers 99
salt-glazed stoneware
  bottles 58
  flasks 58, 302
  mugs 100
salt shakers 114
Salter, J. & Son 360
salts 351, 352
Samian antiquities 24
samplers 374, *387*
Samson Mordan & Co 350, 427, 428
San Marino 355
Sanatogen *65*
sand timers 342
Sandeman 63
Sanderson 86, 423
Sannon, W.F. *314*
Sarfatti, Gino 273
Satsuma *77*
saucepans 261
saucers *see* cups and saucers
Savignac, Raymond 309
Savoie pottery 105

scales 261, 264
scalpels 342
scarves 380–1, *388*
scent bottles 28, *196*, 338
Schiaparelli *234*, 251
Schmidt, Conrad W. 9
Schubert 340
Schuco *238*, *385*
Schweinberger, Emma Gismondi *239*
sci-fi toys *393*, 395, 414
science & technology 339–42
  medical instruments 342
scissors 345, 346
sconces 273, 274
scooters 403
Scott, Anthony 118
Scott, Benjamin 339
Scott, Sir Walter *72*
Scottish jewellery 252
scrap albums *190*, 201
scripophily 343–4
sculpture, garden 214–15
seals *398*, 428
Seddon Diesel 38
Seeburg *248*
Seguso *315*
Seguso Viro 220
Seiko 424
Selco *394*
Serruvier-Bovy, Gustave 425
serviette holders *399*
Sèvres 106
sewing *313*, 345–6
sewing machines *313*, 346
sextants *314*, 339
SFA *394*
S.F.B.J. 180, *189*
Shafer, L.A. *242*
Shakers 212
Shakespeare, William 53
Shamrock Whiskey *76*
Shanks & Co 40, 42
Sharp's 16
shaving 173
shawls 380–1
sheet music 348, 426
Shelley 32, 100, 135, *150*–1
sherry glasses 224, 225
shin pads 365
shipping *314*, 347–9
shirts 377, *378*, *388*, *389*
Shoenau & Hoffmeister 180
shoes 359, 366, 381–3, *390*
  shoe stretchers 382
  shoe warmers 250
Shorter, Colin 136
Shorter & Son 136
showcards 12, *66*, *70*, 228
sick bags *400*
signs
  enamel 13–14, 43, *65*, *66*, 228
  railwayana 328
Silber Fleming 184
silver 350–1
  antiquities 24

Art Nouveau 29, *68*
Arts & Crafts 30, *68*
buckles 381
button hooks 381
buttons *77*, 82, 83
claret labels 62
compacts 172
corkscrews 167, 168
jewellery 29, 30, *68*, 251, 252–4, 258–60
medals 276, 277
photograph frames 298
silver plate 348, 352
thimbles 346
watches 424
Silvertone 322, 324
Simon & Halbig 46, *71*, 153, 180, 184, *189*
Simplex *398*
Sims 401
Sinclair 341
Singer 346
Sirota, Benny 141
Sitzendorf *188*
Sixties & Seventies *315–16*, 354–5
skillets 261
skimmers 264, 352, *397*
skirts 378
skyphos *238*, 293
slippers *390*
slipware 105, 139, 262
slot machines 20–2
Smith, Adam 301
Smith's 15
Smith's Pinewood Cigarettes 155
smoking & snuff taking *317*, 356–7
Smurfs *396*, 405
snuff boxes 60, 356, *397*
soap *246*
soap dishes 41, 42, 69, 102
Société Générale d'automatique 20
Society Debs *390*
soda syphons 354
soft toys 370–1, *385–6*
soldiers, model *393*, *394*, 410
Solère, Ferdinand 274
solitaire boards *193*
solitaire sets 131
Sony 324
Southwick Union Pottery 118
Sowerby 216
spades 212
Spalting 367
Sparklets 354
specimen vases *194*
spectacle cases 368, *387*
Spectra Star 405
Sphinx *71*, 154
spigots 353
spill vases 137, 138, *151*, 293
spirit flasks 163
Spode 106
spongeware 92
spoons

children's *69*
medicine spoons 169
silver 350–2
silver-plated 154
sport *318–20*, 358–67
cricket *320*, 361
fishing *319*, 362–4
football *318–19*, 365–6
golf *319*, 366
medals *318*, 429
tennis 367
Sposato, John *244*
sprayers, garden 212
Staffordshire 137–8, *151*
animals 137, 138
buildings 174
egg cups 106
figures 137–8, *151*, 174, 302, 361
jugs *151*
lavatory bowls 41
meat platters *78*
mugs 91
oil lamps 272
pastille burners 137
pot lids 162
spill vases 137, 138, *151*
watchholders 138
stamp boxes 60, 61, *398*
Standard Plastic Products 330
Stanhopes 368, *398*
Stanley 402
Stanley, Henry M. 53
Star Wars 414
Staunton 209
steel buttons *77*
steelyard balances 401
Steiff 294, 371, *386*
Stein, Lea *68*
Steinfeldt Blasberg *313*
steins 43, *70*, 76
stethoscopes 342
Stevengraphs 43, 358
Stevens, Thomas 43
Stewart-Hill, A. *242*
stick stands 93
Stock Sons & Taylor 40
Stolckwerk *65*
Stombelt 217
stone
architectural salvage 25
garden ornaments 214–15
stoneware 105
bottles 59
commemorative ware 163, 164
jardinières 102
jugs 98, 102, 105, 301
pots 139
teapots 139
vases *78*, 139
see also salt-glazed stoneware
stoolball 360
stools *191*, 205
stoops 138
stopwatches *320*, 424
storage jars 116, *148*, *152*, 204, 206, *235*, 263
Stormer, Emily E. 102

Stourbridge 221
Stratton 173
string holders *69*, 206
Stromberg 218, 219
Stuart Crystal *400*
Stuben 217
studio pottery *80*, 139
sucriers 98
sugar bowls *69*, 88, 114, 133, 221, 223, 351
sugar cutters 269
sugar jars 262
sugar shakers *80*, 94, 96, *148*
suitcases 231
suits 377, 378, *389*
Sunderland 118
sundials 339
sunglasses *191*, *239*, 369
supper sets 92
Sutcliffe, Stuart 329
Swan 112, 428
Swan Vestas 14
Swank 369
Swansea 163–4
Swatch 424
sweet tins 15, 16, 81, *192*
Swift *70*
Swift, Jonathan 56
swimsuits *389*
Swiss watches 17, 424
swords 282
SylvaC 140, *152*, *185*
syringes, garden 212

T
table lamps *236*, 273, 360
table tennis 359
tablecloths 374–5
tables *191*, 205
Taddy & Co 155, *190*
Tait, Jessie 123
Taiyo *395*
Taj Mahal slippers *390*
Tala 262
talcum powder 171
Talmo 367
tandems 44
tankards
glass 225
ceramic 91, 303
silver 350
tantaluses 223
tape measures 11, 346
tape recorders *245*, 325
taps 40, 41, 42
Tarot tea reading cups 100
Tartan ware 61, 289, *397*, 420
Tasco 86
Tassie, James 301
tea bowls 100, *149*
tea caddies 60, *79*
tea cosies 375
tea services
ceramic *69*, 123, 125, 229
silver 350
Teacher's Scotch Whisky 63
teapots
bargeware 88

ceramic *67*, *78*, 94–6, 98, 101, 113–15, 119, 123, 134, 139, *148*, 305
silver plate 352
teaspoons 352
technology *see* science & technology
teddy bears & soft toys 370–1, *385–6*
Telefon Fabrik 372
telephones 372–3
telescopes 340
television *192*, 207–8
terracotta jugs 166
Terries *385*
Terry, Ellen 53
Tessina 86
textiles & costume 374–83, *387–90*
coat hangers & hat stands 379
costume 376–8, *388–9*
hats 285, 360, 379–80, *388*, *389*
shawls & scarves 380–1, *388*
shoes 381–3, *390*
underwear 383, *399*
Thanet 44
Thatcher, Margaret *241*, 306
theatre programmes *71*, 190, 202
theodolites 348
thermometers 48, 207, 265, 339
Thibaud Gibbs & Co 173
thimble cases *313*, 346
thimbles 346
Thomasch 108
Thorssen, Nils *150*
thread winders 345
Thunderbirds *395*, 414, 423, 429
tie pins 259
ties *315*, *388*
tights 383
tiles 384
Timpo 410
tinplate toys *392*, *393*, 406, 416
tins
advertising & packaging 15–16, *65–6*
biscuit tins 15, 33, *65*, *69*, 228, *240*, *314*
black memorabilia 47, *71*
Christmas 154, *185*
commemorative ware 165, 166, *187*
kitchenware *235*, 266
sweet tins 15, 16, 81, *192*
Tippco 416
tipstaffs 288
Tivoli 22
toast racks 351, 352
toasting forks 269
tobacco jars 299
tobacco tins 15
Toby jugs *78*, 154, 306

Today's Man 378
tool chests 397, 402
tools 401–2
Toorop, Jan Th. 309
toothbrush holders 32, 42, 92
toothbrushes 47
Topps Bubblegum 158, 190
torchère stands 71
Torsiene, B.B. 235
towel rails 42
toys 391–6, 403–19
  aeroplanes 406
  boats 392, 406
  diecast vehicles 393–6, 407–9
  Doctor Who 177
  model soldiers & figures 393, 394, 410
  pedal cars 393, 411
  robots 411
  rocking horses 393, 412–13
  sci-fi & TV 393, 395, 414
  teddy bears & soft toys 370–1, 385–6
  tinplate 392, 393, 406, 416
  trains 392, 393, 417–19
trade cards 155–8, 318
trains, toy 392, 393, 417–19
traps 215, 261
trays
  breweriana 62
  ceramic 95
  Mabel Lucie Attwell 32
  metal 352, 353
  tin 229
  wooden 204, 397
treen 397, 420
Trend Decor 316
Tretchikoff prints 311
Tri-ang 189, 394, 403, 404, 411, 413, **416**, 416
Triboulot, Nicholas 220
tricycles 44
Trifari 154, 234, 238, 253
trios 98, 100, 114, 121, 125, 132, 135, 147
Troika 141, 152, 354
trolleys 316
trophies 39, 43, 358, 367
troughs, stone 215
trugs 213
truncheons 288
trunks 230
TSB 289
Tudor antiquities 24
Tuffin, Sally 152
tumblers
  glass 202, 224
  plastic 239
Tunbridge ware
  boxes 60, 61, 397, 398, 420
  jewellery 252
  pincushions 313, 345
Tupperware 235, 239, 300
tureens 121

TV dinner plates, 148
TV toys 393, 395, 414
20th Century-Fox 310–11
Twyfords 42
tygs 162, 165
Tyndall, Robert 74
typewriters 398
  toy 403
Typhoo Tea 156

U
Ude, Louis Eustache 57
umbrella stands 239
umbrellas 422
underwear 383, 399
uniforms 281
Unite, George 62
United Airlines 17
United Artists 244, 310, 311
Universal 244, 310
Universal Camera Corporation 86
Upton, Bertha 46
Upton, Florence 46
urns, ceramic 166
utensils, kitchenware 235, 269–70
Utility shoes 382, 383

V
Val St Lambert 218
Valentines 398, 421
Valentines & Sons 31–3
valves, wireless 321, 399
Van der Beek, Harmsen 54
Vanderbilt, Gloria 260
vanity cases 231
vaporizer inhalers 342
Vasart 197
vaseline glass 216
vases
  Art Nouveau 29
  ceramic 78, 80, 93–9, 101–3, 113, 118, 120, 124, 128, 131–6, 139, 141, 143, 146, 148–51, 185, 191, 206, 354
  glass 194, 196–8, 216–22, 315, 400
  plastic 300
Vauxhall glass 257
vegetable racks 262
vehicle excise licences 38
vehicles, diecast 393–6, 407–9
Venetian glass 196, 217, 234
Venini 220
Ventnor Ceramics 306
Versace, Gianni 220
vesta cases 17, 299, 420
videos 306
Villemot, Bernard 244
vinaigrettes 350, 420
vinegar bottles 206
Vinolia 173
Vitascope 28
Vodaphone 320
Vulcan 287
vulcanite 258

W
Waddington's 209, 211, 228
Wade 142
Wadeheath 142
Wain, Louis 56
Walker's Universal Mixture 59
walking sticks 422
wall lights 28
wall masks 68
wall plates 127
wall vases 144
wallets 330
Wallis Gimson 240
wallpaper 316, 423
Walsh, J.H. 57
Walters, Minette 72
warming dishes 32
warming stands 26
Warner, P.F. 53
Warren, Dianna 378
wash bags 171
washbowls 117
watch chains 259
watch fobs 18
watch stands 258
watches 17, 28, 229, 424
watchholders 138
water barrels 280
water fountains 40
water jugs 78
watercolours 348
watering cans 212
Waterman 398
watermarks 161
Watkin, Mr 90
Watney's Ale 64
Watson, W. & Sons 86
Webb, Sidney & Beatrice 304
Webb, Thomas 225, 338
Wedgwood 143
  bowls 143
  breweriana 62
  egg cups 106
  electrically-heated pots 143
  mugs 187
  paperweights 294
  plates 143
  vases 143
weighing machines 261
Weiss 185, 233, 258
Wellings, Norah 48
Wemyss 144, 152
West, Charles William 422
Westclox 355, 425
Westwood 163
Westwood, Vivienne 378, 389, 400
wheelwright's travellers 401
Whiff-Whaff 359
whisks 269
whisky dispensers 76
whisky measurers 64
whistles 327
Whitby jet 256–7
White Star Line 65, 314
Whitefriars
  lamp bases 197

paperweights 227
  vases 198, 220, 315, 316
  wine glasses 225
White's, R. 13
Whiteway's Cydrax 12
Whiting & Davis 231
wicker
  bags 200, 230
  baskets 267
wig powderers 170
Wil-Wat 112
Wilde, Oscar 72
Wilkinson, Norman 309
Wilkinson's 80
William & Son 169
Willow Art 112
Wills, W.D. & H.O. 156, 157, 190
wimshorst machines 341
Winchcombe 139
windmills 215
wine antiques
  bottles 58
  corkscrews 167–9
  glasses 224–5
  wine keg spigots 353
Winstanley 87, 152
Winton & Grimwades 250
Wirkkala, Tapio 218, 223
WMF 29, 44
wood
  architectural salvage 25
  bowls 204
  boxes 60
  buttons 77, 82
  kitchenware 235, 264, 270–1
  treen 397, 420
Worcester 144, 152
World Cup Willie 16
World War II 426
Wrenn 419
Wright, William Frederick 169
Wrigley's Chewing Gum 11
wristwatches 424
writing 398, 427–8
wrought iron see iron
Wurlitzer 337
Wyon, T. 276

Y
Yardley 171, 173, 188
yarn winders 345
Yelland Pottery 139
yokes 264
yoyos 396, 404, 405
Ysart, Paul 227

Z
Zegler, Athur 310
Zeiss 85–6, 342
Zieman, Hugo 57
Zippo 11
Zorki 86
Zsolnay 238
Zulu Lulu 48